Managing Inflation and Supply Chain Disruptions in the Global Economy

Ulas Akkucuk
Uşak University, Turkey

IGI Global
PUBLISHER of TIMELY KNOWLEDGE

A volume in the Advances in Logistics, Operations, and Management Science (ALOMS) Book Series

Published in the United States of America by
IGI Global
Business Science Reference (an imprint of IGI Global)
701 E. Chocolate Avenue
Hershey PA, USA 17033
Tel: 717-533-8845
Fax: 717-533-8661
E-mail: cust@igi-global.com
Web site: http://www.igi-global.com

Library of Congress Cataloging-in-Publication Data

Names: Akkucuk, Ulas, 1975- editor.
Title: Managing inflation and supply chain disruptions in the global economy / Ulas Akkucuk, editor.
Description: Hershey, PA : Business Science Reference, [2023] | Includes bibliographical references and index. | Summary: "This book deals scientifically with this post pandemic phenomenon of rising prices and supply chain disruptions that are expected to become a permanent issue that will affect all countries, and highlights way for the business community to deal with it"-- Provided by publisher.
Identifiers: LCCN 2022020095 (print) | LCCN 2022020096 (ebook) | ISBN 9781668458761 (hardcover) | ISBN 9781668458778 (paperback) | ISBN 9781668458785 (ebook)
Subjects: LCSH: Industrial management--Effect of inflation on. | Inflation (Finance) | Business logistics.
Classification: LCC HD49.5 .M36 2022 (print) | LCC HD49.5 (ebook) | DDC 658.15--dc23/eng/20220427
LC record available at https://lccn.loc.gov/2022020095
LC ebook record available at https://lccn.loc.gov/2022020096

This book is published in the IGI Global book series Advances in Logistics, Operations, and Management Science (ALOMS) (ISSN: 2327-350X; eISSN: 2327-3518)

British Cataloguing in Publication Data
A Cataloguing in Publication record for this book is available from the British Library.

For electronic access to this publication, please contact: eresources@igi-global.com.

Advances in Logistics, Operations, and Management Science (ALOMS) Book Series

John Wang
Montclair State University, USA

ISSN:2327-350X
EISSN:2327-3518

Mission

Operations research and management science continue to influence business processes, administration, and management information systems, particularly in covering the application methods for decision-making processes. New case studies and applications on management science, operations management, social sciences, and other behavioral sciences have been incorporated into business and organizations real-world objectives.

The **Advances in Logistics, Operations, and Management Science** (ALOMS) Book Series provides a collection of reference publications on the current trends, applications, theories, and practices in the management science field. Providing relevant and current research, this series and its individual publications would be useful for academics, researchers, scholars, and practitioners interested in improving decision making models and business functions.

Coverage

- Organizational Behavior
- Finance
- Production Management
- Decision analysis and decision support
- Political Science
- Networks
- Information Management
- Services management
- Risk Management
- Operations Management

IGI Global is currently accepting manuscripts for publication within this series. To submit a proposal for a volume in this series, please contact our Acquisition Editors at Acquisitions@igi-global.com or visit: http://www.igi-global.com/publish/.

The Advances in Logistics, Operations, and Management Science (ALOMS) Book Series (ISSN 2327-350X) is published by IGI Global, 701 E. Chocolate Avenue, Hershey, PA 17033-1240, USA, www.igi-global.com. This series is composed of titles available for purchase individually; each title is edited to be contextually exclusive from any other title within the series. For pricing and ordering information please visit http://www.igi-global.com/book-series/advances-logistics-operations-management-science/37170. Postmaster: Send all address changes to above address.

Titles in this Series

For a list of additional titles in this series, please visit: http://www.igi-global.com/book-series/advances-logistics-operations-management-science/37170

Considerations and Characteristics of the Millennial Leader in Today's Global Society
Tymon M. Graham (TMGraham Consulting, LLC, USA)
Business Science Reference • © 2023 • 300pp • H/C (ISBN: 9781668447116) • US $240.00

Moving From R&D Development to Production and Sales in Start-Up Companies Emerging Research and Opportunities
Amiram Porath (APC, Israel)
Business Science Reference • © 2022 • 300pp • H/C (ISBN: 9781799856856) • US $215.00

Advancing Interpersonal Emotion Regulation and Social Regulation
Donta S. Harper (Argosy University, USA)
Information Science Reference • © 2022 • 384pp • H/C (ISBN: 9781668424780) • US $215.00

Handbook of Research on Activating Middle Executives' Agency to Lead and Manage During Times of Crisis
Ann-Marie Wilmot (The University of the West Indies, Mona, Jamaica) and Canute Sylvester Thompson (The University of the West Indies, Mona, Jamaica)
Business Science Reference • © 2022 • 415pp • H/C (ISBN: 9781668443316) • US $325.00

Business Models to Promote Technology, Culture, and Leadership in Post-COVID-19 Organizations
Joseph Robert Heinzman (Western Governors University, USA) Debbie S. Judge (Western Governors University, USA) Vincent Franklin (Western Governors University, USA) and Jim A. McCleskey (Western Governors University, USA & Houston Community College System, USA)
Business Science Reference • © 2022 • 300pp • H/C (ISBN: 9781668443583) • US $250.00

Global Risk and Contingency Management Research in Times of Crisis
Narasimha Rao Vajjhala (University of New York Tirana, Tirana, Albania) and Kenneth David Strang (W3-Research, USA & RMIT University, Australia)
Business Science Reference • © 2022 • 356pp • H/C (ISBN: 9781668452790) • US $270.00

Applied Guide for Event Study Research in Supply Chain Management
Lincoln C. Wood (University of Otago, New Zealand & Curtin University, Australia)
Information Science Reference • © 2022 • 261pp • H/C (ISBN: 9781799889694) • US $215.00

IGI Global
PUBLISHER of TIMELY KNOWLEDGE

701 East Chocolate Avenue, Hershey, PA 17033, USA
Tel: 717-533-8845 x100 • Fax: 717-533-8661
E-Mail: cust@igi-global.com • www.igi-global.com

Table of Contents

Preface xvi

Chapter 1
In Search of a Remedy for Disruptions: Assessing the Effects of Inflationary Pressures on Supply Chains During the COVID-19 Era 1
Elad Harison, Shenkar College of Engineering and Design, Israel

Chapter 2
Inflation and COVID-19 Supply Chain Disruption 10
Oindrila Chakraborty, J. D. Birla Institute, India

Chapter 3
Inflation and the Stock Market: Money Illusion in Borsa Istanbul 24
Cenk C. Karahan, Boğaziçi University, Turkey
Han N. Özsöylev, Özyeğin University, Turkey

Chapter 4
Spillover of COVID-19: Impact on the Global Economy 41
Peterson K. Ozili, Independent Researcher, UK
Thankom Arun, Essex University, UK

Chapter 5
Relocation Strategy of Global Supply Chain and Value Chain Under Deglobalization 62
José G. Vargas-Hernández, Posgraduate and Research Department, Tecnológico Mario Molina Unidad Zapopan, Mexico

Chapter 6
Human Resource Management Effects Functioning on Balanced Scorecard: Jordanian Public Joint-Stock Companies 81
Biljana Stojan Ilic, Megatrend University of Belgrade, Serbia
Safwan Al Salaimeh, Aqaba University of Technology, Jordan
Slavica S. Andjelic, Modern Business School of Belgrade, Serbia
Gordana P. Djukic, Faculty of Economics, The University of Belgrade, Serbia

Chapter 7
Importance of Leadership in Managing Post-Pandemic Crises 104
Yasin Galip Gencer, Yalova University, Turkey
Sema Nur Batirlik, Yalova University, Turkey

Chapter 8
Multi-National Companies and Their Progress in Turkey 123
Yasin Galip Gencer, Yalova University, Turkey
Sema Nur Batirlik, Yalova University, Turkey

Chapter 9
Supply Chain Disruptions and the Effects on Price Stability: An Intercountry Analysis 132
Oya Ekici, İstanbul University, Turkey

Chapter 10
Sustainability Model for Solid Waste Management to Support the Global Economy 151
Sami Gören, Umm Al-Qura University, Saudi Arabia

Chapter 11
Identifying Key Issues to Handle the Inflation Problem in the Healthcare Industry Caused by Energy Prices: An Evaluation With Decision-Making Models 162
Serkan Eti, İstanbul Medipol University, Turkey
Hasan Dinçer, İstanbul Medipol University, Turkey
Yaşar Gökalp, İstanbul Medipol University, Turkey
Serhat Yüksel, İstanbul Medipol University, Turkey
Dilan Kararoğlu, İstanbul Medipol University, Turkey

Chapter 12
Green Transformation in Logistics Within the Scope of the European Green Deal 179
Mehri Banu Erdem, Kahramanmaraş Sütçü İmam University, Turkey
Nuri Özgür Doğan, Nevşehir Hacı Bektaş Veli University, Turkey

Chapter 13
COVID-19 Pandemic-Related Supply Chain Disruptions and Impacts on the Global Economy 199
Yeliz Demirkıran, Yaşar University, Turkey

Chapter 14
Can Renewable Energy Investments Be a Solution to the Energy-Sourced High Inflation Problem? 220
Hasan Dinçer, İstanbul Medipol University, Turkey
Serhat Yüksel, İstanbul Medipol University, Turkey
Çağatay Çağlayan, İstanbul Medipol University, Turkey
Duygu Yavuz, İstanbul Medipol University, Turkey
Dilan Kararoğlu, İstanbul Medipol University, Turkey

Chapter 15
Breaking Supply Chains and Inflationist Impact in the COVID-19 Process: The Example of Turkey 239
Meltem Duğru, Trakya Üniversitesi Uzunköprü Uygulamali Bilimler Yüksekokulu, Turkey

Chapter 16
Will BRENT Reach the $300 Mark? 257
Ulas Akkucuk, Usak University, Turkey

Chapter 17
Automotive Industry Challenges: Crises, Disruptions, and Taxes 268
Ulas Akkucuk, Usak University, Turkey

Chapter 18
Internal Audit, Internal Control Systems in Finance Industry in the Changing Business Environment, Evidence From Turkey as an Emerging Economy: Banking Applications, Internal Systems 281
Fatih Kayhan, Kırklareli University, Turkey

Chapter 19
Blockchain in International Trade Documents Management Using NAHP Technique: Case of Kapikule and Istanbul Border Customs 293
Kenan Güler, ATEZ Software Technologies, Turkey
Esengul Salihoglu, Sivas Cumhuriyet University, Turkey
Emre Ozturk, ATEZ Software Technologies, Turkey
Osman Pala, Karamanoglu Mehmetbey University, Turkey

Compilation of References 311

About the Contributors 350

Index 355

Detailed Table of Contents

Preface xvi

Chapter 1
In Search of a Remedy for Disruptions: Assessing the Effects of Inflationary Pressures on Supply Chains During the COVID-19 Era.. 1
Elad Harison, Shenkar College of Engineering and Design, Israel

This chapter assesses the effects of worldwide supply chain disruptions, focusing on the role of the U.S. monetary policy as a catalyst that contributed to the shift of consumer demand from its pre-COVID-19 equilibrium. It analyses how stimulus payments and quantitative easing facilitated labour shortages in supply chain operations and how the growing demand increased the magnitude of shortages, followed by a bullwhip effect in orders from retailers. The study argues that the economic equilibrium between supply and demand for goods that has been greatly affected by the outbreak of COVID-19 has also been affected by substantial monetary changes that have further increased the scope of supply chain disruptions due to their inflationary effects.

Chapter 2
Inflation and COVID-19 Supply Chain Disruption 10
Oindrila Chakraborty, J. D. Birla Institute, India

The distressful situation in the global economy is caused by the unforeseen peril introduced by the COVID-29 pandemic, including the rising inflation and its trajectory over the interruption of supply chain management and therefore encouraging all sorts of novel disruptions to maintain market equilibrium. The disruptive innovation in the supply chain management was inflicted due to the disparity of demand and supply in a few industries as a result if intermittent production and consumption and created a temporary bottleneck in the otherwise seamless supply chain management. Pandemic-driven containment forced people to accumulate savings and invest in alternative sources of incomes. This chapter explores the pandemic-caused economic bottlenecks.

Chapter 3
Inflation and the Stock Market: Money Illusion in Borsa Istanbul 24
Cenk C. Karahan, Boğaziçi University, Turkey
Han N. Özsöylev, Özyeğin University, Turkey

The stock market suffers from money illusion, discounting real cash flows at nominal discount rates. Subsequent research has also shown that the cross-section of stock returns is impacted differently by inflation. This cross-sectional variance across risky and safe stocks makes one of the most puzzling anomalies, risk (beta) anomaly, stronger in inflationary periods. This chapter tests the hypothesis that higher inflation leads to stronger mispricing of risk in stock market due to money illusion effect in Turkey, one of the emerging countries afflicted with perennial high inflation. The results show that although money illusion and mispricing were not visibly present in hyper-inflationary period in 1990s, the anomalous pricing of risky securities was remarkably high in inflationary periods over the last two decades, with a distinct mispricing due to the inflationary pressure that commenced with the COVID-19 pandemic. These varying results across the vastly different inflation regimes can be explained by rational inattention and impact of past experience of inflation on investment behavior.

Chapter 4
Spillover of COVID-19: Impact on the Global Economy 41
Peterson K. Ozili, Independent Researcher, UK
Thankom Arun, Essex University, UK

How did a health crisis translate to an economic crisis? Why did the spread of the coronavirus bring the global economy to its knees? The answer lies in two methods by which coronavirus stifled economic activities. First, the spread of the virus encouraged social distancing which led to the shutdown of financial markets, corporate offices, businesses and events. Second, the exponential rate at which the virus was spreading, and the heightened uncertainty about how bad the situation could get, led to flight to safety in consumption and investment among consumers, investors and international trade partners. We focus on the period from the start of 2020 through March when the coronavirus began spreading into other countries and markets. We draw on real-world observations in assessing the restrictive measures, monetary policy measures, fiscal policy measures and the public health measures that were adopted during the period. We empirically examine the impact of social distancing policies on economic activities and stock market indices. We also empirically the effect of COVID infection cases and COVID deaths on macroeconomic performance during the 2020 to 2021 period. The findings reveal that the increasing number of lockdown days, monetary policy decisions and international travel restrictions severely affected the level of economic activities and the closing, opening, lowest and highest stock price of major stock market indices. We also find that the rising number of COVID cases and rising death cases led to a significant increase in global inflation rate, global unemployment rate, and global energy commodity index.

Chapter 5
Relocation Strategy of Global Supply Chain and Value Chain Under Deglobalization 62
José G. Vargas-Hernández, Posgraduate and Research Department, Tecnológico Mario Molina Unidad Zapopan, Mexico

This chapter aims to critically analyze the implications that the national protectionist policies have on the global supply and value chains and the relocation of production. The analysis is based on the assumptions that the global economy is facing the possibility of decoupling of many trade connections, and this trend favors deglobalization processes that have long been promoted by populism, nationalism, and economic protectionism. It is concluded that global supply, production, and value chains, although being economically efficient, are no longer any more secure under national protectionist policies, and therefore, the relocation of production processes is mainly due to the increase in the level of income and wages of the developing countries that are the destination, and which reduce the advantages to relocate.

Chapter 6
Human Resource Management Effects Functioning on Balanced Scorecard: Jordanian Public Joint-Stock Companies 81
Biljana Stojan Ilic, Megatrend University of Belgrade, Serbia
Safwan Al Salaimeh, Aqaba University of Technology, Jordan
Slavica S. Andjelic, Modern Business School of Belgrade, Serbia
Gordana P. Djukic, Faculty of Economics, The University of Belgrade, Serbia

The "speed" of modern business—as well as changes in the environment—have led administrative organizations on the path of additional challenges. These organizations tirelessly strive for the realization of advanced systems, adapting their business to modern ideas and trends and gaining market advantage. In this way, organizations become modern and contemporary in their understandings of internal functioning. The study presented by the authors in the chapter aimed to determine the impact of human resource management (HRM) functions on the balanced scorecard in Jordanian public joint-stock companies. In the research, adequate statistical and descriptive methods were used. The results of the study recommend the creation of an organizational culture that promotes the optimal and effective use of HRM functions in the organizational environment.

Chapter 7
Importance of Leadership in Managing Post-Pandemic Crises 104
Yasin Galip Gencer, Yalova University, Turkey
Sema Nur Batirlik, Yalova University, Turkey

The concept of leadership, which is the subject of many academic studies, is accepted as a phenomenon which is also emphasized in social sciences. With globalization and rapid and continuous development in the field of communication technologies, it has caused radical changes in many subjects from economy to politics, from organizational structures to management approach. In this study, firstly, the definition of the concept of leadership was made. Then, the scale studies in the literature related to the subject of leadership are included. Leadership theories, postmodern leadership types, and common leadership types are explained. With the research, the concept of leadership, which still does not have a clear definition in the literature and is changing day by day, has been extensively studied. The aim of the study is to contribute to the academic literature about the concept of leadership. Moreover, the study also aims to clarify the increasing importance of leadership in managing post-pandemic crises.

Chapter 8
Multi-National Companies and Their Progress in Turkey 123
Yasin Galip Gencer, Yalova University, Turkey
Sema Nur Batirlik, Yalova University, Turkey

Although multinational companies are both a cause and a result of economic globalization, it is also a driving force that enables economic globalization to expand its sphere of influence around the world. Today, international relations require not only states but also the existence of non-state actors to be taken into account. Multinational companies have increased both their numbers and activities with globalization. The increasing role of multinational companies has begun to be limited not only to economic activities. They can take on a function of shaping the policies of underdeveloped nation states. In this study, the definition, characteristics, and historical development of multinational companies are explained. Then, the organizational structure of these companies is mentioned. The place of multinational companies in the world and in Turkey is explained and the study is concluded. The concept of a multinational company has been examined with the research. The aim of the study is to explain the concept of multinational companies in a broad perspective.

Chapter 9
Supply Chain Disruptions and the Effects on Price Stability: An Intercountry Analysis 132
Oya Ekici, İstanbul University, Turkey

The widespread impact of price instability issues in the world has originated in global financial problems for more than three decades, and the effect of wars on the price changes remained mostly local or regional. But today, the impact of price instabilities rooted in supply chain bottlenecks is broader and more persistent in nature. With this changing price instability structure, analyzing the interdependence in production among the countries and exploring their effect on countries' inflation levels has become crucial. With this motivation, the chapter examines these relations by the BVAR model. The interdependence of countries' own purchasing managers' index, representing the supply chain disruptions, and their impulse on the producer price index, representing the inflation, are captured by the BVARs. The chapter focuses on the cases of a group of specific economies and chooses three countries: Germany, the United States, and Turkey. The findings remark that these countries' inflation levels are associated with their major trading partners' supply chain disruptions.

Chapter 10
Sustainability Model for Solid Waste Management to Support the Global Economy 151
Sami Gören, Umm Al-Qura University, Saudi Arabia

Extravagancy is the key point of inflation. We consume more than necessary; we generate waste without any responsibility. Expanded consumption and depletion of resources are becoming more serious than ever. As the world population and standard of living are increasing, the amount of solid waste is also increasing. Not only the quantity but also the types of the wastes increase and become difficult to recycle due to composite wastes. With the aim of preserving the environment, this chapter will introduce the sustainability model to support the global economy. Waste management and recycling technologies, which effectively turn waste into resources, will be a great tool, especially in rapidly developing nations. The following should be a Motto in life: "the practice of treasuring and using all things as long as possible." While economies continue to grow, this motto spirit restrained the generation of waste and motivated the development of technology for reuse, recycling, and effective use through heat recovery for energy.

Chapter 11
Identifying Key Issues to Handle the Inflation Problem in the Healthcare Industry Caused by Energy Prices: An Evaluation With Decision-Making Models 162
Serkan Eti, İstanbul Medipol University, Turkey
Hasan Dinçer, İstanbul Medipol University, Turkey
Yaşar Gökalp, İstanbul Medipol University, Turkey
Serhat Yüksel, İstanbul Medipol University, Turkey
Dilan Kararoğlu, İstanbul Medipol University, Turkey

This study investigated how energy inflation in the health sector can be controlled. In this context, research has been carried out using both the AHP and the DEMATEL methods. A comprehensive literature review was carried out, and four different criteria were determined. In order to determine which of these criteria is more important, an analysis was carried out using these two different methods. According to the results obtained, it has been determined that the use of renewable energy is the most important factor in eliminating the inflation caused by energy prices in the health sector. Because the best criterion is the same for both the results of AHP and DEMATEL, this situation gives information about the coherency and reliability of the study. Hence, appropriate strategies can be provided based on these results to minimize the inflation problem in the healthcare industry. The findings indicate that it would be appropriate for hospitals to give importance to the use of renewable energy. In this way, hospitals will be able to produce the energy they need themselves.

Chapter 12
Green Transformation in Logistics Within the Scope of the European Green Deal........................... 179
Mehri Banu Erdem, Kahramanmaraş Sütçü İmam University, Turkey
Nuri Özgür Doğan, Nevşehir Hacı Bektaş Veli University, Turkey

Problems such as global warming, climate change, and depletion of resources have arisen due to the increase in consumption around the world, the use of resources as if they are endless, and the creation of environmental pollution. This put the future of all living things in danger. For this reason, the European Union took action and led the world in this regard by issuing the European Green Deal in December 2019. The European Green Deal directly or indirectly concerns the entire sector. Therefore, businesses should integrate their activities with greening through planning and R&D studies in this regard. At this point, one of the most affected industries is logistics. Sustainable logistics is part of the European Green Deal. In this chapter, the issue of sustainable logistics has been evaluated within the scope of the European Green Deal.

Chapter 13
COVID-19 Pandemic-Related Supply Chain Disruptions and Impacts on the Global Economy 199
Yeliz Demirkıran, Yaşar University, Turkey

Humanity and the business world have had a very challenging period in the last two years due to unprecedented disease outbreaks. In December 2019, a novel infectious respiratory disease was found in Wuhan, Hubei Province, China. This disease affected almost all industries and all countries, regardless of developed or developing. The pandemic caused supply chain disruptions around the globe. In this study, the author presented the supply chain disruptions in detail caused by the COVID-19 pandemic, which is a specific type of disruption factor, and showed their global economic impacts. Country- and industry-specific cases and examples are examined. In addition, the measures that have been taken by the government authorities to alleviate the global economic impact of the pandemic are discussed.

Chapter 14
Can Renewable Energy Investments Be a Solution to the Energy-Sourced High Inflation Problem? 220
Hasan Dinçer, İstanbul Medipol University, Turkey
Serhat Yüksel, İstanbul Medipol University, Turkey
Çağatay Çağlayan, İstanbul Medipol University, Turkey
Duygu Yavuz, İstanbul Medipol University, Turkey
Dilan Kararoğlu, İstanbul Medipol University, Turkey

The aim of this study is to examine the relationship between renewable energy and inflation. Within this framework, Turkey is taken into consideration. In this context, the data regarding inflation rate and renewable energy usage for the years between 1990 and 2020 is examined. This data is obtained from the website of the World Bank. Engle Granger cointegration analysis is considered to examine the relationship between these factors. The findings demonstrate that there is a long-term relationship between the variables. In other words, it is understood that renewable energy usage affects inflation for Turkey in the long term. Therefore, it would be appropriate for countries to prioritize renewable energy investments. In this way, countries will be able to produce their own energy, and their dependence on foreign energy will decrease. Thus, they will not be affected much by the increases in energy prices. In this context, investments should be made primarily in renewable energy technologies.

Chapter 15
Breaking Supply Chains and Inflationist Impact in the COVID-19 Process: The Example of Turkey 239
Meltem Duğru, Trakya Üniversitesi Uzunköprü Uygulamali Bilimler Yüksekokulu, Turkey

The COVID-19 pandemic started as a process full of uncertainties, and the first case was detected in Turkey in March 2020. The panic process that started after that date has had negative effects on the economy in the following periods. While the effects have reflections on foreign trade due to the fact that it is a global process, the change in consumption and demand patterns in the country has changed all the balances. Thus, it is important to address the changes in almost every aspect of our lives and to examine them during the crisis period. Breaking the supply chains in the changing balances and to understand the importance of the supply chains accordingly are the subjects of this study. This study investigated how Turkey spent the COVID-19 process due to its economic structure and geopolitical location and, in addition, how it managed its supply chains. As a result of the research, it was concluded that if the deficits in the supply chains can be evaluated, the crisis process can be turned into an opportunity.

Chapter 16
Will BRENT Reach the $300 Mark? 257
Ulas Akkucuk, Usak University, Turkey

Petrol crises have crippled the economies of the developed nations may times in modern history. Still, fossil fuels are an important source of transportation, and price changes deeply affect the social and economic wellbeing of the citizens. While research on alternative fuels is on the rise and there are many incentives, the reliance on fossil fuels is not diminished. Lately, as a result of the conflict in Ukraine, petrol prices went up again. This chapter will shed light on the past crises and will try to examine how much further petrol prices can go. Also, the relationship between energy prices and subjective wellbeing will be illustrated with examples from the literature. The chapter will also offer some suggestions for a sustainable green world.

Chapter 17
Automotive Industry Challenges: Crises, Disruptions, and Taxes 268
Ulas Akkucuk, Usak University, Turkey

The automotive sector is one of the important sectors in both the developed world and the developing countries. For developing countries, this industry is a course of income coming from export models. For the developed nations, the automotive sector can create quality jobs and offer after-sales and service job opportunities as well. The automotive industry was challenged during the COVID-19 pandemic as shortages for some parts halted production in different parts of the world. Also, sales of automobiles increased in some parts due to commuters avoiding mass transit in fear of the pandemic. Tax collection is also another issue associated with this industry. In some countries, heavy taxes are levied on the vehicles with some possible drawbacks. This chapter will talk about the causes and remedies for the disruptions in the supply chain. The issue of taxation will also be discussed offering some possible solutions. Green energy and public transportation will be offered as remedies to the problems of the industry and the more general problem of global warming.

Chapter 18
Internal Audit, Internal Control Systems in Finance Industry in the Changing Business Environment, Evidence From Turkey as an Emerging Economy: Banking Applications, Internal Systems 281
Fatih Kayhan, Kırklareli University, Turkey

The purpose of this chapter is to review internal audit and internal control functions in the banking industry by taking into account the international COSO framework. The financial industry is regarded as one of the key elements of a stable economy. It is a well-known fact that financial institutions in general—banks in particular (public or private, foreign or local)—need to have a sound internal system to implement the high principle of 'maker-checker-supervisor-auditor'. The study examines the application of internal systems in the Turkish banking industry primarily and covers not only the theory, application, and legislative sides, but also organizational structure and development of audit and control activity in the banking sector.

Chapter 19
Blockchain in International Trade Documents Management Using NAHP Technique: Case of Kapikule and Istanbul Border Customs 293
Kenan Güler, ATEZ Software Technologies, Turkey
Esengul Salihoglu, Sivas Cumhuriyet University, Turkey
Emre Ozturk, ATEZ Software Technologies, Turkey
Osman Pala, Karamanoglu Mehmetbey University, Turkey

This study aims to explore the potential of blockchain technology in digitalization of documents used in foreign trade processes and to embody the advantages it can bring to customs clearance processes. The work is in two stages. In the first stage, the authors examined the document flow between the parties in customs clearance processes through three different digitalization scenarios using blockchain technology. They have come to the conclusion that rapid adaptation to innovations based on blockchain technology in the field of document management in international trade customs clearance processes is advantageous. In the second stage, they analyzed the priorities of the rational decision-making process with the NAHP method. The main challenges facing the transition to new technology are the need to train staff for new systems, the need to develop and improve new internal processes, the time spent reaching agreements with trading partners in the transition period, and the alignment of technological developments with legislation.

Compilation of References 311

About the Contributors 350

Index 355

Preface

During the post pandemic days inflation has turned out to be a major problem for all of the countries of the developed world. The problem has been exacerbated in developing nations such as Turkey and Argentina which had problems even before the pandemic. Energy prices have increases and with the increase in transportation costs it has somehow been difficult for many retailers to stock up the shelves as they did before the pandemic. It is well understood by many that the rising prices and supply chain disruptions will not be temporary and will be a permanent phenomena to be dealt with future executives. This book will try to uncover the many ways businesses can deal with this new phenomenon.

Managing Inflation and Supply Chain Disruptions in the Global Economy is an essential reference source that discusses the incorporation of sustainability in various facets of business management. Featuring research on topics such as disruptive logistics, production planning, and renewable energy sources, this book is ideally designed for researchers, practitioners, students, managers, policymakers, academicians, economists, scholars, and educators seeking coverage on sustainable practices in supply chains to ensure a cleaner environment.

The many academic areas covered in this publication include:

- Inflation
- COVID-19
- Supply Chain Disruption
- Sustainable operations
- Green procurement
- Carbon emissions
- Green transportation
- Smart cities
- Retail Management
- Container Trade
- Digital Transformation
- Disruptive Logistics
- E-Commerce
- Green Supply Chains
- Life Cycle Costing
- Multi-Criteria Decision Making
- Health Care
- Renewable Energy Sources

I am very happy to finalize the tenth book project I realized with IGI Global. I gave the first book proposal to IGI Global in the summer of 2013. This first book was finalized towards fall 2014 and published as hard copy in January 2015. This publication included 28 contributions. It has been nearly seven years since the release. Later it also enjoyed Web of Science indexation. Sustainable development over the years has enjoyed ever more attention in the academic community. As a result I decided to pursue other book projects with similar titles. This last book contains 19 valuable contributions from eminent authors from different countries. The countries include Turkey, India, Israel, Jordan, Mexico, Saudi Arabia, and Republic of Serbia.

Chapter 1 starts the discussion with an excellent analytical paper entitled "In Search of a Remedy for Disruptions". This chapter assesses the effects of worldwide supply chain disruptions, focusing on the role of the U.S. monetary policy as a catalyst that contributed to the shift of consumer demand from its pre-COVID-19 equilibrium. It analyses how stimulus payments and quantitative easing facilitated labour shortages in supply chain operations and how the growing demand increased the magnitude of shortages, followed by a bullwhip effect in orders from retailers. The study argues that the economic equilibrium between supply and demand for goods that has been greatly affected by the outbreak of COVID-19 has also been affected by substantial monetary changes that have further increased the scope of supply chain disruptions due to their inflationary effects.

Chapter 2 is about "Inflation and COVID-19 Supply Chain Disruption". The distressful situation in the global economy, caused by the unforeseen peril introduced by COVID driven pandemic in every walk of lives including the rising inflation and its trajectory over the interruption of supply chain management and therefore encouraging all sorts of novel disruption to maintain market equilibrium. The disruptive innovation in the supply chain management was inflicted due to the disparity of demand and supply in a few industries as a result if intermittent production and consumption and created a temporary bottleneck in the otherwise seamless supply chain management. Pandemic driven containment forced people to accumulate savings and investing in alternative sources of incomes; foisting off artificial inflation surreptitiously with the jeopardy of closing every physical formats of business to customer sector, needless to mention the retail sector to reduce social interaction and to stop spread of the extremely contagious disease. Though this book chapter, the target audience would get a fair idea about the pandemic inflected economical bottlenecks.

Chapter 3 investigates "Inflation and Stock Market: Money Illusion in Borsa Isanbul". The stock market suffers from money illusion, discounting real cash flows at nominal discount rates. Subsequent research has also shown that the cross-section of stock returns is impacted differently by inflation. This cross-sectional variance across risky and safe stocks makes one of the most puzzling anomalies, risk (beta) anomaly, stronger in inflationary periods. This chapter tests the hypothesis that higher inflation leads to stronger mispricing of risk in stock market due to money illusion effect in Turkey, one of the emerging countries afflicted with perennial high inflation. The results show that although money illusion and mispricing is not visibly present in hyper-inflationary period in 1990's, the anomalous pricing of risky securities are remarkably high in inflationary periods over the last two decades, with a distinct mispricing due to the inflationary pressure that commences with COVID pandemic. These varying results across the vastly different inflation regimes can be explained by rational inattention and impact of past experience of inflation on investment behavior.

Chapter 4 is a discussion on "Spillover of COVID-19 Impact on the Global Economy". We empirically test the effect of COVID infection cases and COVID deaths on macroeconomic performance during the 2020 to 2021 period. The findings reveal that the increasing number of lockdown days, monetary policy decisions and international travel restrictions severely affected the level of economic activities and the closing, opening, lowest and highest stock price of major stock market indices. We also find that the rising number of COVID cases and rising death cases led to a significant increase in global inflation rate, global unemployment rate, and global energy commodity index.

Chapter 5 focuses on "Relocation Strategy of Global Supply Chain and Value Chain Under Deglobalization". This paper aims to critically analyze the implications that the national protectionist policies have on the global supply and value chains and the relocation of production. The analysis is based on the assumptions that the global economy is facing the possibility of decoupling of many trade connections and this trend favors deglobalization processes have long been promoted by populism, nationalism, and economic protectionism. It is concluded that global supply, production, and value chains although being economically efficient, are no longer any more secure under national protectionist policies and therefore, the relocation of production processes is mainly due to the increase in the level of income and wages of the developing countries that are the destination, and which reduce the advantages to relocate.

Chapter 6 is another look at the "Importance of Human Resource Management Effects Functioning on Balanced Scorecard: Jordanian Public Joint-Stock Companies". The "speed" of modern business - as well as changes in the environment - have led administrative organizations on the path of additional challenges. These organizations tirelessly strive for the realization of advanced systems, adapting their business to modern ideas and trends, and gaining market advantage. In this way, organizations become modern and contemporary in their understandings of internal functioning. The study presented by the authors in the chapters aimed to determine the impact of human resource management (HRM) functions on the balanced scorecard in Jordanian public joint-stock companies. In the research adequate statistical and descriptive methods were used. The results of the study recommend the creation of an organizational culture that promotes the optimal and effective use of HRM functions in the organizational environment.

Chapter 7 examines "Importance of Leadership in Managing Post-Pandemic Crises". The concept of leadership, which is the subject of many academic studies, is accepted as a phenomenon which is also emphasized in social sciences. With globalization, rapid and continuous development in the field of communication technologies; It has caused radical changes in many subjects from economy to politics, from organizational structures to management approach. In this study, firstly, the definition of the concept of leadership was made. Then, the scale studies in the literature related to the subject of leadership are included. In the following chapters, leadership theories, postmodern leadership types and common leadership types are explained. With the research, the concept of leadership, which still does not have a clear definition in the literature and is changing day by day, has been extensively studied. The aim of the study is to contribute to the academic literature about the concept of leadership. Moreover, the study also aims to clarify the increasing importance of leadership in managing post pandemic crises.

Chapter 8 focuses on "Multinational Companies and Their Progress in Turkey". Although multinational companies are both a cause and a result of economic globalization; it is also a driving force that enables economic globalization to expand its sphere of influence around the world. Today, international relations require not only states but also the existence of non-state actors to be taken into account. Multinational companies have increased both their numbers and activities with globalization. The increasing role of multinational companies has begun to be limited not only to economic activities. They can take on a function of shaping the policies of underdeveloped nation states. In this study, the definition, characteristics and historical development of multinational companies are explained. Then, the organizational structure of these companies is mentioned. In other chapters, the place of multinational companies in the world and in Turkey is explained and the study is concluded. The concept of multinational company has been examined with the research. The aim of the study is to explain the concept of multinational companies in a broad perspective.

Chapter 9 illustrates "Supply Chain Disruptions and the Effects on Price Stability: An Intercountry Analysis". The widespread impact of price instability issues in the world has originated in global financial problems for more than three decades, and the effect of wars on the price changes remained mostly limited to local - or regional. But today, the impact of price instabilities rooted in supply chain bottlenecks is broader and has persistent nature. With this changing price instabilities structure, analyzing the interdependence in production among the countries and exploring their effect on countries' inflation levels become crucial. With this motivation, the chapter examines these relations by the BVAR model. The interdependence of countries' own Purchasing Managers' Index, representing the supply chain disruptions, and their impulse on the Producer Price Index, representing the inflation, are captured by the BVARs. The chapter focuses on the cases of a group of specific economies and chooses three countries: Germany, the United States, and Turkey. The findings remark that these countries' inflation levels are associated with their major trading partners' supply chain disruptions.

Chapter 10 is "Sustainability Model for Solid Waste Management to Support the Global Economy". Extravagancy is the key point of inflation. We consume more than necessary; we generate waste without any responsibility. Expanded consumption and depletion of resources are becoming more serious than ever. As the world population and standard of living are increasing, the amount of solid waste is also increasing. Not only the quantity but also the types of the wastes increase and become difficult to recycle due to composite wastes. With the aim of preserving the environment, this chapter will introduce the sustainability model to support the global economy. Waste management and recycling technologies, which effectively turn waste into resources will be a great tool, especially in rapidly developing nations. The following proword should be motto in life: "the practice of treasuring and using all things as long as possible." While economies continue to grow, this motto spirit restrained the generation of waste and motivated the development of technology for reuse, recycling and effective use through heat recovery for energy.

Chapter 11 provides examples on "Identifying Key Issues to Handle Inflation Problem in the Healthcare Industry Caused by Energy Prices: An Evaluation With Decision-Making Models". In this study, it was investigated how energy inflation in the health sector can be controlled. In this context, research has been carried out using both the AHP and the DEMATEL method. A comprehensive literature review was carried out and 4 different criteria were determined. In order to determine which of these criteria is more important, an analysis was carried out using these two different methods. According to the results obtained, it has been determined that the use of renewable energy is the most important factor in eliminating the inflation caused by energy prices in the health sector. Because the best criterion is the same for both the results of AHP and DEMATEL, this situation gives information about the coherency and reliability of the study. Hence, appropriate strategies can be provided based on these results to minimize inflation problem in healthcare industry. The findings indicate that it would be appropriate for hospitals to give importance to the use of renewable energy. In this way, hospitals will be able to produce the energy they need themselves.

Chapter 12 performs an analysis of "Green Transformation in Logistics Within the Scope of the European Green Deal". Problems such as global warming, climate change and depletion of resources have arisen due to the increase in consumption around the world, the use of resources as if they are endless, and the creation of environmental pollution. This put the future of all living things in danger. For this reason, the European Union took action and led the world in this regard by issuing the European Green

Deal in December 2019. The European Green Deal directly or indirectly concerns the entire sector. Therefore, businesses should integrate their activities with greening through planning and R&D studies in this regard. At this point, one of the most affected industry is the logistics. Sustainable logistics is part of the European Green Deal. In this section, the issue of sustainable logistics has been evaluated within the scope of the European Green Deal.

Chapter 13 explores the "COVID-19 Pandemic-Related Supply Chain Disruptions and Impacts on the Global Economy". Humanity and the business world have had a very challenging period in the last 2 years due to unprecedented disease outbreaks. In December 2019, a novel infectious respiratory disease was found in Wuhan, Hubei Province, China. This disease affected almost all industries and all countries, regardless of developed or developing. The pandemic caused supply chain disruptions around the globe. In this study, we presented the supply chain disruptions in detail caused by the COVID-19 pandemic, which is a specific type of disruption factor, and show their global economic impacts. Country and industry-specific cases and examples are examined. In addition, we discussed the preventions that have been taken by the government authorities to alleviate the global economic impacts of the pandemic.

Chapter 14 answers the question, "Can Renewable Energy Investments Be a Solution to the Energy-Sourced High Inflation Problem?" The aim of this study is to examine the relationship between renewable energy and inflation. Within this framework, Turkey is taken into consideration. In this context, the data regarding inflation rate and renewable energy usage for the years between 1990 and 2020 is examined. This data is obtained from the website of World Bank. Engle Granger cointegration analysis is considered to examine the relationship between these factors. The findings demonstrate that there is a long-term relationship between the variables. In other words, it is understood that renewable energy usage affects the inflation for Turkey in the long term. Therefore, it would be appropriate for countries to prioritize renewable energy investments. In this way, countries will be able to produce their own energy and their dependence on foreign energy will decrease. Thus, they will not be affected much by the increases in energy prices. In this context, investments should be made primarily in renewable energy technologies.

Chapter 15 is on "Breaking Supply Chains and Inflationist Impact in the COVID-19 Process: The Example of Turkey". The COVID-19 epidemic has started as a process full of uncertainties and the first case was detected in Turkey in March 2020. The panic process that started after this date has been negative effects on the economy in the following periods. While the effects have reflections on foreign trade due to the fact that it is a global process, on the other hand, the change in consumption and demand patterns in the country has changed all the balances. Thus, it is important to address the changes in almost every aspect of our lives and to examine them during the crisis period. Breaking the supply chains in the changing balances and to understand the importance of the supply chains accordingly are the subject of this study. In this study, it was investigated how Turkey spent the COVID-19 process due to its economic structure and geopolitical location, and in addition, how it managed its supply chains. As a result of the research, it was concluded that if the deficits in the supply chains can be evaluated, the crisis process can be turned into an opportunity.

Chapter 16 is on the rising petrol prices. Chapter 17 is about "Automotive Industry Challenges: Crises, Disruptions, and Taxes". Chapters 18 and 19 are about internal audit and block chain technologies. I hope the readers will benefit from reading this work.

Ulaş Akküçük
Uşak University, Turkey
July 2022

Chapter 1
In Search of a Remedy for Disruptions:
Assessing the Effects of Inflationary Pressures on Supply Chains During the COVID-19 Era

Elad Harison
Shenkar College of Engineering and Design, Israel

ABSTRACT

This chapter assesses the effects of worldwide supply chain disruptions, focusing on the role of the U.S. monetary policy as a catalyst that contributed to the shift of consumer demand from its pre-COVID-19 equilibrium. It analyses how stimulus payments and quantitative easing facilitated labour shortages in supply chain operations and how the growing demand increased the magnitude of shortages, followed by a bullwhip effect in orders from retailers. The study argues that the economic equilibrium between supply and demand for goods that has been greatly affected by the outbreak of COVID-19 has also been affected by substantial monetary changes that have further increased the scope of supply chain disruptions due to their inflationary effects.

1. INTRODUCTION

COVID-19 was, and still is, a life changing event that affected nearly every aspect of the global economy, including the demand and the supply of services and goods in every sector of the economy. Lockdowns and quarantines worldwide, notably in China—the world's leading production hub—affected the supply of labour, raw materials, and finished products, causing significant disruptions in manufacturing, shipping, and transportation of goods. Additionally, stimulus payments issued by the government to selected groups of citizens, companies whose income and revenues were negatively affected by the pandemic, or to all citizens, as evidenced in the U.S., caused major changes in consumer behaviour. This fostered

DOI: 10.4018/978-1-6684-5876-1.ch001

Figure 1. (a) Unemployment rate; seasonally adjusted, (b) Nonfarm payroll employment; seasonally adjusted (U.S. Bureau of Labor Statistics, 2022).

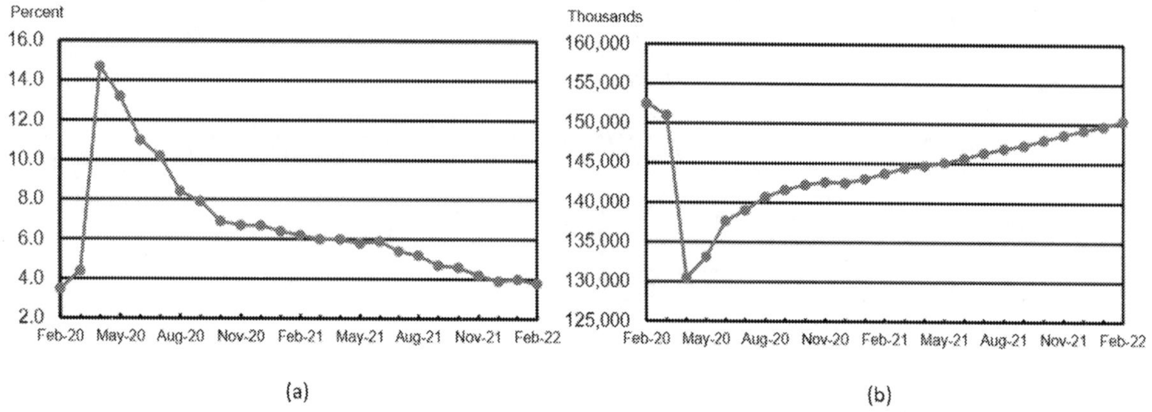

growth in the demand for consumer goods, which facilitated additional demand for raw materials and production facilities when these resources were at their lowest supply and inventory levels.

Some of these effects are indeed attributed to labour shortages resulting from long periods of lockdowns in many countries worldwide (see Table 1), which led to a reduction in production capacities in many economy sectors. Here, the economic equilibrium between supply and demand for goods has also been greatly affected by these major events. Before COVID-19, demand was influenced largely by factors such as population growth, economic growth, market trends, and changes in consumer behaviour and preferences. However, monetary policies implemented by governments worldwide (and particularly the quantitative easing and the stimulus created by the U.S. Federal Reserve) caused major shifts in demand for goods, services, and raw materials, impacting an already fragile global economy.

Since the global outbreak of COVID-19 in March 2020, the changes in infection rates and the appearance of new variants in the population, as well as the development and distribution of new vaccines and methods for treating patients, have dictated the market dynamics in terms of the availability of resources, such as labour, production, and shipping facilities. Consumer behaviour was also affected in terms of the propensity of consumers to purchase new services and goods, changes in their personal income, and the level of their risk aversion to engaging in the purchase of costly products as well as day-to-day goods. Here, purchasing behaviour was influenced by the availability of goods, which was volatile in nature due to supply chain disruptions.

Global supply chains need to function in a complete coherence resulting in an uninterrupted flow of goods throughout all the parts that construct them as intra- and inter-linked chains. However, when a single part of the supply chain suffers from a shortage of resources necessary to carry out its functions or bottlenecks, such as labour shortages (Fig. 1a and b), disruptions begin to appear in all other parts of the supply chain, affecting its functioning and the balance of received and issued goods. For example, in October 2021, a shortage of 80,000 truck drivers in the U.S. was reported (ATA, 2021). Other disruptions in supply chains were present in maritime shipping operations, where shortages in available shipping containers existed throughout 2020-2021. Additionally, backlogs of ships awaiting off-loading in major ports worldwide for long periods created additional disruptions in supply chains due to scheduling changes of cargo ships and shipments (Notteboom et al., 2021).

Table 1. Total number of days under lockdown between March 2020-October 2021 by country (based on national media and government sources).

Country	Total number of days under lockdown
Argentina	63-245
Australia (different regions)	52-263
Austria	118
Azerbaijan	152
Bangladesh	169
Belgium	119
Bulgaria	169
Canada (different regions)	65-123
Colombia	97
Croatia	39
Czech Republic	201
Denmark	99
Estonia	31
Finland	20
Germany (different regions)	43-298
Greece	181
Hungary	13
India (different regions)	10-62
Iran	47
Iraq	20
Ireland (different regions)	14-227
Israel	72
Italy (different regions)	93-129
Kuwait	21
Malaysia	187
Mexico	70-114
Netherlands	220
New Zealand	73-185
Nigeria	13
Oman	49
Philippines (different regions)	49-62
Poland	85
Portugal	73
Romania	48
Russia (different regions)	33-50
Saudi Arabia (different regions)	84-104
Singapore	158
South Africa	80
Spain	56
Sri Lanka	137
Switzerland	83
Thailand	67
Turkey (different regions)	4-18
Ukraine	38
United Arab Emirates	22
United Kingdom (different regions)	21-213
United States (different regions)	26-110
Venezuela	57
Vietnam (different regions)	21-57

The sources of disruptions in maritime supply chains (MSCs) that account for approximately two thirds of the freight transported to the EU (EC, 2019) were as follows:

- Lockdowns and reduced production capacity by manufacturers (due to lack of workers or predicted decline in demand for raw materials) resulted in reduced shipments from plants to distributors and large consumers.
- Similarly, lockdowns prohibited full-scale plant operations, particularly those that could not store bulks of assembly parts and raw materials. Though these shipments were paid for in advance, producers were asked not to deliver them to their clients until production was restored to its former scale.
- The reduction in commercial activities and operations at the beginning of the global pandemic (March 2020) resulted in the suspension of investments in new supply chain facilities or in expanding existing establishments, such as warehouses, production lines, and vessels. This phenomenon led to lower availability of means of transportation, production, and storage in 2021-2022, whilst, at the same time, logistics companies struggled to catch up with the increasing demand for their services.
- Disruptions in parts of the supply chain (for example, due to labour shortages or implementation of COVID safety measures) caused further, and often more severe, disruptions in the succeeding streamline of operations that depend on them.
(Mańkowska et al., 2021)

Some of the anecdotal evidence, in particular since the beginning of 2022, indicate that supply chain disruptions have picked up throughout and after the major COVID-19 outbreak that affected both the production, distribution, shipping and transportation sectors, resulting in product shortages amongst U.S. retailers (CNN, 2022; Washington Post, 2022; Daily Mail, 2022). However, while product and grocery shortages are largely attributed to labour shortages, the massive growth of demand during the pandemic has largely been overlooked. Labour shortages can be attributed to major changes in the job market and decreasing propensity of employees to return to work (Groshen, 2020; Marcén and Morales, 2021), while demand growth is connected to the distribution of stimulus by the U.S. government (as well as by other governments worldwide).

2. THE POST-COVID MONETARY SIDE-EFFECTS: A PARADIGM SHIFT IN THE DEMAND FOR GOODS

Supply chain disruptions are largely attributed to changes in supply and demand of goods and the difficulty in mitigating the differences between peak periods in demand and lower supply. These phenomena result from lower industrial activity due to the implementation of lockdowns and social distancing throughout COVID-19. Nonetheless, while assessing the ongoing fractions of the flow of materials and goods through national and international supply chains, one wonders whether other essential processes within the under-currents of the global economy that have taken place during the pandemic have significantly contributed, or have even facilitated, the long-term shifts that have caused the disruptions in supply chains, as we have experienced since the COVID-19 outbreak.

Figure 2. The U.S. money supply (M1)

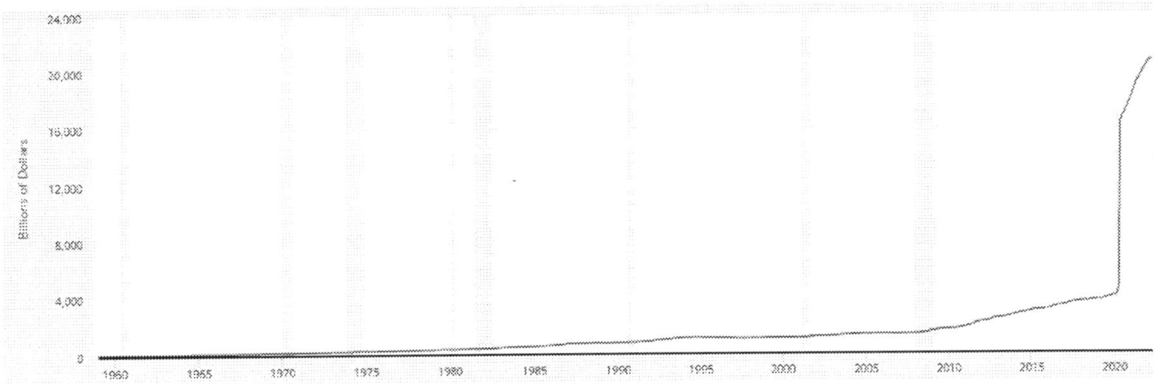

The focal points of discussion and research that explores supply chain disruptions refer to the lack of resources, such as the availability of logistics professionals, lack of investments in new infrastructure, and lack of essential means of transportation and storage (such as the shipping container crisis of 2020-2021). However, this study addresses the less explored challenges that supply chain operations experience due to the excess demand developed following the elevated levels of liquidity in the U.S. market in this period.

Since the outbreak of COVID-19 in March 2020, the U.S. government has issued a series of stimulus payments to every U.S. citizen. In many cases, stimulus payments were necessary to assist citizens who lost their jobs or experienced a substantial reduction in their personal income and financial means due to the pandemic and implemented social distancing measures. Nonetheless, payments were indiscriminately distributed throughout the economy, including to well-to-do citizens, hence initiating consumption growth. The distribution of funds was supported by the expansion of the monetary base of the U.S. dollar by the Federal Reserve. U.S. dollars were generated and transferred to the government to support this operation in return for bonds issued by the U.S. Treasury to the Federal Reserve. Additionally, new monetary funds were distributed to the market through purchases of corporate bonds and mortgage-backed securities (MBS) by the Federal Reserve to support the stability of the economy and to provide liquidity to firms.

Between March and June 2020, the U.S. money supply increased by almost 300%, from 4.2 to 16.5 billion dollars. During the same period, the U.S. monetary aggregate (M2, which includes the M1 as well as savings deposits and small-denomination time deposits) increased by approx. 17% from 15.5 to 18.1 billion dollars (see Fig. 2 and 3).

Nonetheless, the monetary expansion, i.e. the Federal Reserve's COVID quantitative easing, of 2020-2021, created excess liquidity as a result of artificially increasing the disposable income of consumers, resulting in exponential growth in demand for goods when production and transportation facilities have not fully recovered and have not returned to their full operational scales.

In this respect, the distribution of stimulus funds has caused two major shifts from the market equilibrium: first, supply chains were already functioning at partial capacity due to labour shortages and safety restrictions, lowering supply levels at any point of the curve. Second, the demand has been elevated by the provision of additional funds to consumers, thus shifting the demand curve from its pre-COVID equilibrium. Consequently, the tectonic shifts in both supply and demand—and the resulting changes in consumer price elasticities virtually for any product—expanded the supply gap. This gap has already

Figure 3. The U.S. monetary aggregate (M2) (Board of Governors of the Federal Reserve System, 2022).

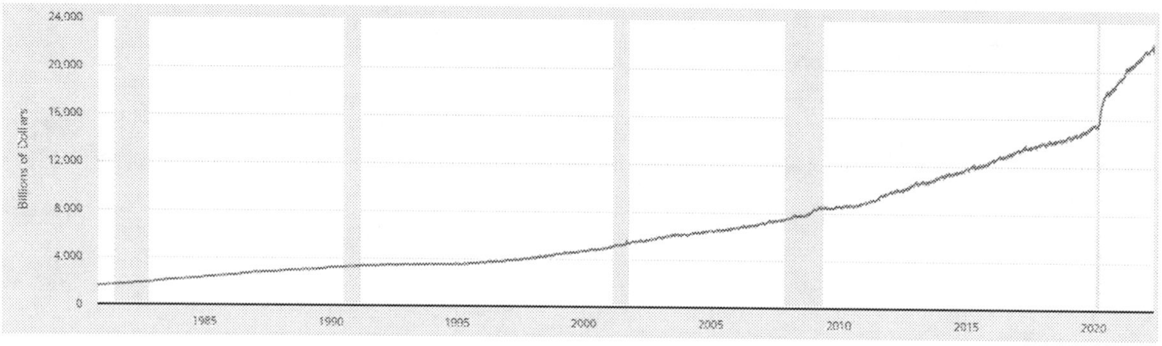

developed since the COVID outbreak, and affects the balance between the required level of goods needed for purchase by consumers and inventory levels, resulting in product shortages and unfulfilled demand.

In turn, the growing demand for goods has led to two additional major effects on the global economy: first, the reduction in production capacities and transportation facilities. Additionally, supply shortages of goods has created a growing demand for raw materials and commodities, necessary for production, resulting in further price increases for consumer goods. Second, commodity prices have substantially increased, sparking an ongoing increase in consumption due to consumer expectations about inflation, inflation rates as reflected in the growth in consumer price index (CPI) (see Fig. 4), and the foreseen interest rate hikes by the Federal Reserve. The interest rate hikes are expected to negatively affect the future borrowing costs of consumers.

3. MONETARY POLICY AND THE BULLWHIP EFFECT

The provision of monetary funds to consumers and the stimulation of additional disposable funds led to excessive economic activity in the U.S. market that has generated ongoing disruptions since the COVID-19 outbreak. These market dynamics have caused inflationary pressures due to the major gap between supply and demand and the abundance of funds in the hands of consumers, affecting the value of money and, consequently, the prices of goods.

Figure 4. U.S. Consumer Price Index (CPI) (Board of Governors of the Federal Reserve System, 2022).

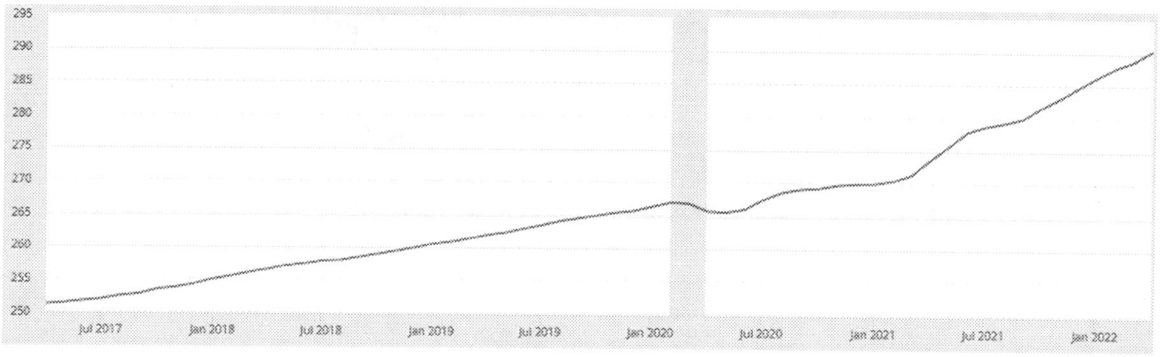

Earlier signs of expected price increases for goods, and the attempts of producers and retailers to mitigate their impact on consumer demand, appeared with the widespread adoption of "shrinkflation" practices. These practices involve supplying smaller packaged products using the same former pricing, aiming to preserve the propensity of consumers to purchase these goods at the same pre-inflation pricing.

Shrinkflation helps to preserve demand by sustaining the price levels of goods as before, while downsizing the products. From a theoretical standpoint, it seems that consumers should be indifferent whether prices increase or shrinkflation practices are applied. However, Kim's (2022) study on the effects of shrinkflation in the Korean milk market reports that had this practice not been applied, the demand for milk could decrease by 34%. In particular, shrinkflation is largely applied in the U.S. in the food and hospitality sectors (Portland Press Herald, 2022), though other examples can be found in different consumption goods (Saleh et al., 2018).

In order to ease the increase in prices of virtually every commodity and goods and the rate of inflation, the Federal Reserve has decided to change its monetary policy from quantitative easing (Q.E.) to quantitative tightening (Q.T.), hence lowering the excess of liquidity in the market (and, consequently, increasing the value and the purchasing power of the U.S. dollar, while lowering price). In March 2022, the Federal Reserve approved a series of interest rate increases, putting greater pressure on households and companies and, hence, lowering the volume of consumption and debt.

The policy measures applied by the Federal Reserve have led to a decrease in consumer demand. As Altomonte et al. (2012) noted, post the financial crisis of 2008 and the global recession that followed, "amplified fluctuations of trade with respect to GDP could be associated to the so-called 'bullwhip effect'… that is, a magnification of the initial demand shock along the supply chain due to an adjustment of production and stocks to new expectations." Indeed, retailers observing the growth in consumer demand increased the magnitude of orders of consumer goods at the beginning of 2022. However, unstable production schedules and supply lead time of goods, and the decrease in demand since the second quarter of 2022, led to increases in retailers' inventory. This can be attributed to economic recovery programs being discontinued by the government, larger orders and higher levels of unsold goods. For example, in April 2022, Walmart reported that its inventory was 56.5 billion dollars (26% increase from last year). Target's inventory was 15.1 billion dollars (43% increase from last year).

The bullwhip effect that led to rising inventory levels of retailers signifies a current shift from the elevated demand curve of consumers to lower demand levels, due to the increase in interest rates and the quantitative tightening initiated by the Federal Reserve, hence resulting in a different sort of supply chain disruptions—excess inventory and unsold products.

4. CONCLUSION

The worldwide COVID-19 outbreak, and the implemented social distancing and medical safety measures created major changes in every aspect of our lives, including in the labour market, personal consumption, and the management of supply chains aimed at fulfilling any level of consumer demand. The disruptions resulted in shortages of different products, from chips to baby formulas. This is expected to proceed through the next year.

While assessing the reasons that underlie the ongoing imbalance in supply chain operations, we can identify multiple processes that each affected the global system in its own manner but, when combined, they created a negative synergy that led to the current state of supply chains worldwide and, in particular, in the U.S.

First, the distribution of stimulus payments and the quantitative easing that took place by the U.S. government, and the increase in money supply to support these operations, elevated the demand of consumers virtually for any type of goods. This increased not only the demand for final goods but also the demand for raw materials.

Second, the stimulus payments distributed to every U.S. citizen negatively impacted the American labour market by lowering the propensity of employees to return to their former workplaces, particularly low-paying jobs. Consequently, labour shortages are present throughout the U.S. economy, but are significant in logistics and supply chain operations, such as transportation, warehouse management, production, and port operations. This lack of professionals amplifies the scope of disruptions.

Third, the safety measures and the worldwide lockdowns reduced the supply and the imports from countries that specialise in the production of physical goods (notably China) to the world's largest consumption-based economy, hence confronting the growing demand in the U.S. market with a restricted supply of goods.

Fourth, the growing gap between the level of demand and the supply of goods created inflationary pressures, resulting in a bullwhip effect, where retailers have increased their orders to address the growth in demand and prevent further shortages in goods.

The complexity of the current state of the global supply chains has been multiplied by the change in supply and demand and the shift from the former equilibrium between producers, supply chain operators, and consumers during the COVID-19 outbreak and the period that followed it. However, the return to the previous conditions pre-COVID-19 that balanced the economy is a subject to debate regarding the policy decisions taken by the U.S. Federal Reserve, including interest changes and quantitative tightening that target the large demand at a high social and economic costs.

Therefore, the COVID-19 and post-COVID-19 era exemplified the complex relations between monetary policy, public health guidelines, and the performance of global supply chains. The outbreak of the pandemic—an event of unparalleled magnitude in modern history—emphasised how fragile and easily affected our global, inter-connected markets and operations are, and how the reliance on imported goods, in particular when the money supply is affected by policy makers to mitigate short-term issues, may have a greater impact on the economy as a whole in the long-term.

REFERENCES

Altomonte, C., di Mauro, F., Ottaviano, G., Rungi, A., & Vicard, V. (2012). *Global value chains during the great trade collapse: a bullwhip effect?* ECB Working Paper, No. 1412. European Central Bank (ECB).

American Trucking Associations. (2021, Oct. 25). *Driver Shortage Update 2021*. https://www.trucking.org/sites/default/files/2021-10/ATA%20Driver%20Shortage%20Report%202021%20Executive%20Summary.FINAL_.pdf

Board of Governors of the Federal Reserve System. (2022, May 1). *Economic Research*. Federal Bank of St. Louis. https://research.stlouisfed.org/

CNN. (2022, Jan. 13). *Here's why grocery stores are struggling to stock their empty shelves.* https://edition.cnn.com/2022/01/11/business-food/grocery-store-shelves-empty/index.html

European Commission (2019). *Performance of freight transport (tkm): Statistical pocketbook 2019.* Directorate General for Mobility and Transport (DG MOVE).

Groshen, E. L. (2020). COVID-19's impact on the U.S. labor market as of September 2020. *Business Economics (Cleveland, Ohio)*, *55*(4), 213–228. doi:10.105711369-020-00193-1 PMID:33204039

Kiml. K. (2022, February 26) Consumers' Preference for Downsizing Over the Package Price Increase. doi:10.2139/ssrn.4044401

Mail, D. (2022, Jan. 11). *'It's like a Soviet store during 1981': Grocery stores across the US have empty shelves as supply chain crisis and COVID combine to make basics like milk, bread, meat, canned soups and cleaning products hard to find.* https://www.dailymail.co.uk/news/article-10392001/Empty-shelves-grocery-stores-US.html

Mańkowska, M., Pluciński, M., Kotowska, I., & Filina-Dawidowicz, L. (2021). Seaports during the COVID-19 Pandemic: The Terminal Operators' Tactical Responses to Disruptions in Maritime Supply Chains. *Energies*, *14*(14), 4339–4360. doi:10.3390/en14144339

Marcén, M., & Morales, M. (2021). The intensity of COVID-19 non-pharmaceutical interventions and labor market outcomes in the public sector. *Journal of Regional Science*, *61*(4), 775–798. doi:10.1111/jors.12535 PMID:34230691

Notteboom, T., Pallis, T., & Rodrigue, J. P. (2021). Disruptions and resilience in global container shipping and ports: The COVID-19 pandemic versus the 2008–2009 financial crisis. *Maritime Economics & Logistics*, *23*(2), 179–210. doi:10.105741278-020-00180-5

Portland Press Herald. (2022, May 15). *Fewer nuggets, smaller salads: Shrinkflation hits U.S. restaurants.* https://www.pressherald.com/2022/05/15/fewer-nuggets-smaller-salads-shrinkflation-hits-u-s-restaurants/

Saleh, R. M., Ramzani, S. R., & Phung, S. P. (2018). Shrinkflation from consumer's perspective: An exploratory study using crystal products in Egypt. *Eurasian Journal of Analytical Chemistry*, *13*(6).

U.S. Bureau of Labor Statistics. (2022, June 3). *The Employment Situation - February 2022.* https://www.bls.gov/news.release/pdf/empsit.pdf

Washington Post. (2022, Jan. 19). *Why Are U.S. Grocery Shelves Out of Everything Again?* https://www.washingtonpost.com/business/why-are-us-grocery-shelves-out-of-everything-again/2022/01/18/1afc0028-784b-11ec-9dce-7313579de434_story.html

Chapter 2
Inflation and COVID-19 Supply Chain Disruption

Oindrila Chakraborty
J. D. Birla Institute, India

ABSTRACT

The distressful situation in the global economy is caused by the unforeseen peril introduced by the COVID-29 pandemic, including the rising inflation and its trajectory over the interruption of supply chain management and therefore encouraging all sorts of novel disruptions to maintain market equilibrium. The disruptive innovation in the supply chain management was inflicted due to the disparity of demand and supply in a few industries as a result if intermittent production and consumption and created a temporary bottleneck in the otherwise seamless supply chain management. Pandemic-driven containment forced people to accumulate savings and invest in alternative sources of incomes. This chapter explores the pandemic-caused economic bottlenecks.

INTRODUCTION

The unexampled encounters and aftershocks, summoned by the novel corona virus disease 2019 (COVID 19) and the following robust pandemic, inflicted by it, has adduced a havoc disturbance to the entire gamut of normal activities in the lives of most individuals across nations. The darkest side of the disease is the sudden and pathetic blow of negative events, those followed one after the other, without giving a chance to the people to adjust to this level of adversity. As a consequence, it has created a significant and spasmodic chaos in the psychological, behavioural, social and economic facets of life, jeopardising the balance of the Gaia Paradigm of the planet. As the part of such disturbances, the devastating impact of overall Inflation with its obvious impression on the economy has to be undeniable and obvious along with many other domains across the border, as an aftermath. The reasons have been manifolded. One of such reasons is the house bound condition for most of the individuals without any voluntary socialising, barring a few into the emergency services. Thus, the nature of the expenditure pattern, which was solemnly dependent on the lavish and extravagant social lifestyles, was drastically hampered and dropped below the average for the last few decades. It clearly reflected on the gradual increase of Inflation rate, to strike

DOI: 10.4018/978-1-6684-5876-1.ch002

a balance and to save the economy from an obvious descending condition. It is more explainable through the norms of intermittent Lockdowns and its impact on the social behaviour. Such erratic and unsure series of events made many individuals completely insecure with the fear of unemployability, pay cut, unnecessary transfer and many of the negative apprehensive scenarios. It was reflected and aggravated through the Government imposed social distancing norms, making people more mentally vulnerable and pushed them to find a psychological recluse through more of individual savings. Hence suddenly there was a decline in consumer expenditure with an unusual increase in individual savings, especially, due to lack of travelling and outdoor recreational cost (Dunn, Hood, and Driessen 2020). During this pandemic period, people have been more inclined towards buying necessary household items rather than engaging into impulse and fad buying.

The disruption of Supply Chain has been another detrimental outcome of the pandemic. On one side, it diminished the production by the sudden shut down of the manufacturing plants and on the other hand, the consumption pattern got curtailed due to less of outside visits and lack of spending due to aforementioned causes. The only aberration has been information technology and the related industry, flourishing with the advent of the stochastic employment and thereafter strengthening the online aka digitised dependence in every field of business transactions like medical, service, recreation, academia and most visibly in retail industry (Kwan and Mertens 2020).

Background of COVID-19-Driven Pandemic

The December 31st 2019 was the darkest day of recent history, as on the day China Health Authority alarmed the World Health Organization (WHO) to be vigilant of a new disease, spreading uncontrollably in and beyond the borders. By that time various cases of pneumonia of unknown origin started getting reported in Wuhan City in Hubei Province in central China. The cases started getting reported since December 8th, 2019 apparently in several neighbourhood hospitals and clinics, near to local Hunan Seafood Wholesale Market (an age old wet market, mainly meant for animal produce)though all patients were not from that exact location (Xinhuanet News Report, 2019). The Wuhan city has been always a transportation hub with an extremely large population dwelling there, therefore the chances of spread of infection was severe, followed by the predicted course of action. On 7th January, 2019, the novel coronavirus, which was initially abbreviated as 2019-nCoV by world Health organisation, was confirmed and collected from the throat swab sample of a patient for the first time in the same year beyond border (Yin, 2019). The pathogen was renamed as severe acute respiratory syndrome coronavirus 2 (SARS-CoV-2) by the Coronavirus Study Group (de Wit et al., 2016) and the disease was renamed again as coronavirus disease 2019 (COVID-19) by the World Health Organisation. Till the time of 30th January, 2019, 7736 confirmed cases and 12,167 suspected cases had been already identified in China and 82 confirmed cases had been identified in eighteen other countries (Yin,2019). On the same day, WHO alerted the SARS-CoV-2 outbreak as a Public Health Emergencyof International Concern (PHEIC) (Yin,2019).

As per the declaration of the National Health Commission of China on 4th February, 2019, the mortality rate in China was 2.1% (NHS press conference,2020) and that of other countries was 0.2% (World Health Organization,2020). Amongst the cases of hospitalization, the mortality rate was much higher and ranged between 11% and 15% (Huang et al,2020), (Chen et al., 2020). COVID-19 was already known as moderately infectious disease with an extremely high mortality rate. The information available in public domain and plethora of available literatures were giving a clear indication of the severity of the disease.

As already indicated, COVID 19 driven pandemic first took its the uncontrollable turn in Wuhan, China around December, 2019 and later spread across all countries with its severity in every aspect, arresting the normal flow of life. Every country was warned to make their public aware of the protective care to sustain the pandemic, as gesture of precaution. The protective care was inclusive of social distancing norms along with all sorts of cleaning protocols like washing of hands, wearing face-shields/ masks and any other surfaces, frequently in use. It also included prohibition for social gathering to stop the spread of the dangerous disease (Sintema, 2020).

As already discussed in the introductory phase, the social distancing norm affected the social behaviour gravely and so was the buying pattern. Along that because of interrupted opening of plants and retail outlets, it became difficult to maintain a steady demand and Supply ratio in agriculture, food and retail industry. Based on such disturbing scenario, it became obvious not to have a seamless supplies everywhere and hence the subject becomes of crucial significance for further discussion.

MAIN RESEARCH FOCUS

The main aim of the research paper is to cross examine the COVID 19 inflicted disturbances ineconomies and thereafter the inflation created by such disturbances through contemporary literature review. The author tries to investigate the situation in different fields through secondary data and to find out the probable solution proposed for it.

Impact of Covid on Global Economy

COVID-19, as already discussed, was initiated in Wuhan, China and had been propagated in more than hundred countries all over the world, infecting more than one million population (Sohrabi *et al.*, 2020). It became not only a global health threat, but also apparently a quintessential factor to disrupt the global economy. As predicted by the experts COVID-19 would diminish the global GDP growth by one-half a percentage in the financial year 2020 (from 2.9% to 2.4%) and will continue to damage further. In the contemporary global village, where any significant incident in any part of the world will have consequences across the world, economy is no exception (Bobdey, 2020). Chinese government, had to shut down the key production units, in order to curb the diffusion of the lethal Corona virus. As a result of this sudden decision of shut down of the global manufacturing centre-China, it eventually accelerated the disruption in the global supply chain across different sectors with diverse multiplicity from pharmaceutical sectors to the automobile sectors. The disruption of supply chain in pharmaceutical industry in China had affected rest of the other countries during this exigency, where the prices of critical medicines were hiked due to dearth of raw material supplies from China. Not only medicines, the criticality of disruption manifested in almost every industry. Since the Chinese manufacturing hub had halted the production of almost everything except the emergency supplies, in their production units, the prices of raw materials like metals decreased universally leading to significant stagnation in various metal producing economies (Maffioli, 2020).

Echoing China, other countries also followed the same covid protocols by restricting public gatherings and shutting down schools, colleges, institutions, organisations, large social gatherings, events, and other community activities. Maximum other countries got the manifestation of primary infections from travellers coming from pandemic areas and hence took the decision of cancelling all flight operations in international fields and sealed the borders. People also started to consider less of travels due to the fear of infection, leading to huge flight cancellations. That caused a profuse financial loss for most of the aviation companies. Consequently it led to reduction in oil demand and subsequently in the oil price, which led to the biggest decline in oil prices in the global market ever since the Gulf war. The expeditious decline in oil prices, along the blanket reduction in global industrial manufacturing everywhere, subsequently introduced a brisk fall in the global stock markets with a steep fall of 20% within a short tenure. Hence the more economic performance had been hindered, fluctuating the standards of financial sustainability, especially for developing countries. Further studies are required to fathom the extension of economic distress and more investigations are to be conducted by global policymakers to restrain the economic fallout.

COVID INFLICTED INFLATION

Inflation could be categorised into Covid Sensitive aka Inflicted Inflation and Covid insensitive Inflation. The price inflation before pandemic and at the very beginning of pandemic was not induced by covid and hence termed as covid insensitive inflation, while due to the lock down phase the kind of disruptive economy resulted in the enormous price rise is termed as covid sensitive price inflation. This chapter will be dealing with only covid sensitive inflation. During Covid inflicted pandemic even the parameters and tracking of data have been changed from conventional methods and parameters. The tracking has been done almost immediately due to more advanced devices and technologies like mobile data, web search, digital transaction record etc. (Baker et al., 2020; Carvalho et al., 2020; Cicala, 2020; Kuchler et al., 2020), though it has been always observed as the constraints for all the econometricians across the world, keeping in mind the dilemma of forecasting the inflation (Marsilli, 2017). Because of the precautionary restrictive practices, COVID inflicted pandemic has forced several governments to impose several unusual means, with explicit and implicit impact on domestic consumption patterns, thus, affecting overall Consumer Price Index, as a measure of Inflation, negatively (Jaworski,2021).

Agriculture Related Supply Chain Risks and COVID-19

Agricultural Supply chains are defined as 'the set of activities included in a "farm to fork" progression, including activities such as farming (i.e. cultivation of land for crop production), processing/production, testing, packaging, warehousing, transportation, distribution and marketing' (Tsolakis et al. 2014). Agricultural supply chain comprises of all the activities of physical production, operations and logistics especially physical distribution of the products through a highly competitive channel members based system to meet the needs of end customers for post purchase satisfaction (Chandrasekaran and Raghuram 2014). The stake holding members of agricultural supply chain consists of members like food acquisition partners, processing unit, manufacturing plants, distributing houses and related third party & fourth party logistics, agents, food service organisations, hospitality & food retailers (Sgarbossa and Russo 2017). Different terms have been used to such as food supply chain to especially emphasize the food relating supply chain ignoring the procurement part (Zirham and Palomba 2016). Some other terms like agriculture value chain (Brewin 2016), post-harvest supply chain (Mvumi, Matsikira, and Mutambara, 2016), fruit supply chain (Glowacz and Rees, 2016), agri-business supply chain (Bhagat and Dhar,2011), perishable produce supply chain fresh produce supply chain (Glowacz and Rees, 2016) and horticulture supply chain (Mahajan et al. 2014) are also used to highlight specialised domains under the same umbrella. The agricultural supply chains consist of three vital domains like farming & agriculture yields, processing & storage, and physical distribution of the products. Agricultural Supply chains are affected by drastic disruptions caused by complicated operational bottlenecks like produce seasonality, varied production buffer times, lack of standardisation of quantity & quality, trade & inventory storage restrictions, and lack of transparency in tracking mechanism. These pitfalls reflect into extreme disruptions of agro based economy (van der Vorst, Beulens, and van Beek 2000; Dong, 2006), thus, examining such agro based food related supply chain difficulties should throw deeper lights into agro-food organisations to tackle disruptive risks in better way, smoothening the seamless performance. COVID 19 is no exception to this rule. It resulted in all sorts of restrictions and errors due to dearth of manual labour and random technical dependence with limited and less trained manpower (Sharma et al, 2020). The recognised risks not only dampened the productivity of the agricultural economy and Supply Chain but also crumbled agricultural supply chain performance. The ceaseless pandemic has a drastic effect on food security and has unfavourably impacted community health and its incomes diversity (Deaton and Deaton 2020). The novel pandemic scenario has generated momentous and erratic supply - demand consequences as a sheer challenge in front of the supply chain management (Gray,2020). Other cardinal mentionable risks invited by the pandemic are transportation challenges during national lockdowns, international border sealing, farm-financial instability, and migrant labour-management problems (Ker, 2020).

Almost all developing countries have been strongly relying on agro-economy through agricultural imports and agricultural supply chain and any disturbance in that system could bring a devastating impact on the total economy by disrupting the natural market condition and thereby crashing the economy; inflation to balance such sluggish economy may be another instrument to strike on (Sharma et al, 2020).

Food and Agriculture Organisation has already highlighted and confirmed that COVID19 has impacted perilously the agricultural supply chain, with global concern for food security (Siche, 2020). The effect of keeping people away from socialising has brutally spoiled economic conditions of most of the countries especially the agricultural domain (Barichello, 2020).

Travel bans resulted in direct impact on food consumption pattern due to sudden shut down of Entertainment and Hospitality industry(most either being completely shut down as per COVID protocol or having lean& essential activities at the most to run the show during slack time)and in turn affected Agricultural supply chain management in a critical manner, with low supply and erratic demands (Sharma et al, 2020). Since Agricultural Supply chain is primarily run by labour-intensive sectors like animal(fisheries, meat products)diaries and high- yield crops, the impact of pandemic driven lockdown is taking a heavy toll on the labour economy due to restrictive policies, especially the migrating labourers are completely jobless and shaken up by restrictive movements and nation wide curfews; hence losing their ability to contribute into the supply chain. COVID-19 has been Consequentially knocking down on global food dependence by affecting the related import and export business. With the intensive labour market problems, horticultural yields, which contribute a quintessential part of the fresh food related supply chain business, have endured a heavy loss. Most of the shipping ports across the world were swarming with reefer containers that could not be moved because of trade restrictions. Thus, the there were bound to distract to less significant ports without any evident business opportunities, culminating in considerable revenue losses for the supply-chain and logistics providers, despite having every contemporary and befitting tools (Hey,2020).Globally all supply chain management related business houses, embarked on a new journey in dealing with COVID-19 with an unprecedented track record and experience. They are exploring the darkest phase with an exigency based expedition. In these trying times, there is a requirement to probe with insightful exploration of the alternate solution through applied research based on agricultural supply chains which are in process. Ker (2020) and Hobbs (2020) have examined such difficult scenarios in the literature reviews and have aimed on the COVID-19 inflicted agricultural risks and its feasible theoretical solutions to deal with it. Miscellaneous strategies like exploration of more befitting industry 4.0 technologies, supply chain integration and collaboration(collaborative planning, forecasting and replenishment-CPFR)and shared responsibilities are recognised for more sustainable future to stop this peril.

Food Related Supply Chain Management and COVID19

Food related supply chain is basically another bifurcation of Agricultural supply chain and should be considered as another specialized horizon under agro-marketing domain. The only difference is it illuminate the impact of COVID related disruptions more in hospitality industry and associated domain like retails to capture the food-service based sectors rather than food-manufacturing sectors and related transferability and logistic issues.

Akter (2020) observed an aculeate amplification of food prices at the onset of pandemic as a result of simultaneous and acuminated price hike in multiple cross economies, correlating with house-bound and hoarding behaviours of apparently afraid and insecure consumers; generated out of unpredictable, sudden and exigency based restrictive policy change of governments across countries. According to the author, restrictions favored at least 1% hike in price index, reflecting in the overall direct inflation rate across all economies.

Ebrahimy et al (2020) documented more evidences, relating to increase in food price during pandemic, with little evidence of inflation, while using holistic approach and indices. They also accentuated the prototypical contributory role of animal produce like meat, dairy and preserved products (canned foods) in the price inflation at the outset of the pandemic, as a part of already mentioned conspicuous hoarding behaviour and panic buying, during March 2020.During the same period, it has also been documented to completely vacate retail counters and shelves due to impulsive buying and stock piling activities of consumers, making the price collector unable to record price for business sake(Jaworski,2021), the price collector had to log for similar products to check price, rather than recording these from barren outlets. The disappearance of products were mostly ranked as per pricing pattern i.e. comparatively economic products were retailed before the expensive ones, unless the brands were extremely significant. Jaravel and O'Connell (2020) recorded a decline in sale for about 8% of distinguished products making it available on shelves at the onset of the pandemic in the UK, it incident is popularly known as "lack of matching" problem, reducing coherence of the inflation time series, and overestimation of factual inflation. As per Diewert and Fox (2020) web scraping could have been a solution to the food inflation, since using same brand every time and hoarding that brand led to emptied retail counters, an alternate choice of brand can reduce hoarding of item and therefore inflation. The covid inflicted pandemic introduced a contiguous and corporeal hike in inflation uncertainty. Armantier et al. (2020) emphasized a steep polarization in inflation related beliefs, with a considerable number of respondents primarily believing at the onset of pandemic that it will trigger a high inflation, and the other set of respondents believing otherwise i.e. to result in low inflation leading to deflation due to restrictive policies and stay in home condition. Indeed, Kumar et al. (2015) believed to consider this high-inflation uncertainty to be of paramount importance in the set of metrics indicating un-anchored inflation type of expectations. Also the transition of online shopping behaviour led to capturing of real-time data through Web scraping overwriting the need for data mining of records from traditional retails (Jaworski,2021).

It has been well documented by several researchers that the stakeholders on retail, and distribution side of the food supply chain have been impacted adversely by sudden demand-side hike (panic buying, hoarding), supply shortages, and transportation issues without any hobnobbing and parity amongst supply chain members (Hailu 2020) resulting in almost collapsing conditions, which injected more panic buying in the consumers, making it almost a never-ending vicious cycle.

Issues, Controversies and Problems

There have been couple of issues in the supply chain disruptions and its projection in the economy.

The estimate of the financial statements during this phase of transition had not been realistic, as database of physical distribution channel was not giving the real-time holistic scenario for the entire economy and hence a disparity between the actual decline in economy with its inflationary effect and projected amount of inflation became extremely evident without capturing the true element and was bound to be a topic of discussion for the economists and financial experts (Derevyankina and Yankovskaya, 2020). The business transactions of online platforms were many a times overlooked creating an unstable projection trajectory. Though COVID-19 has brutally wedged every country in the global economy and has caused several supply chain disruptions globally in true sense, but the gap projected by statistical figures was actually that robust or not was the question in hand (Ivanov 2020; Choi 2020; Govindan, Mina, and Alavi 2020).

Another issue was, the increasing complication of supply chains in almost every sector of businesses with uncertain supplies of raw materials and labour problems. The reasons, at the beginning of pandemic were difficult to figure out. Later on, it became evident with the obvious causes like lack of resources, especially the manpower . The reason of lack of resources visibly could extenuate the problem of disruptive supplies but ultimately it is not impossible to improve the performance of the firm in terms of better supply and customer satisfaction, in case handled with utter sincerity (Brandon-Jones et al, 2014).

The erratic demands related to restricted consumption patterns and the intermittent shutting down of Manufacturing units also surfaced as a problem scenario, as scarcity of items on the retail shelves increased the price of certain goods, indulged by the hoarding behaviours of customers. This price hike also reflected as an raising sign for commodity market and in turn was reflective of multiplier effect in the economy.

Another issue could have been the power dilemma between Government and business tycoons. Government imposed restrictive policies forced business giant to move towards more of philanthropic activities as a positive brand building exercise for them. This in turn, has been proved to be the blessing in disguise and could be projected as the only positive sign of the pandemic.

Novel Initiatives and Disruptive Innovations in Supply Chain Management: The Contemporary Trend to Resolve Issues in Dysfunctional Supplies during Turbulent Times

COVID-19 is hugely impacted by fear of uncertainty in every walks of life (Platje et al., 2020; van Dam and Webbink, 2020).

The basic challenge of sustainable development and to resolve issues of erratic supplies during COVID-19 period had been simultaneous occurrence of several other disastrous situations apart from COVID itself, like violent hurricanes, severe weather change, which resulted in innumerable number of deaths and an almost breakdown of socio-economic development, with a difficult projection of Sustainable developmental goals with no long term assured outcomes(Mirza, 2003; Stott, 2016).It was also aggravated with difficulties like the collapse of production facilities in many places (Chowdhury, 2017).

COVID 19 has opened up a new horizon altogether. Since it has redefined and gone for a paradigm shift in terms of the power negotiation between government and corporate entities. The manipulative intense competition amongst the corporate houses has gone for a toss, compromising the supply chain due to government directives, especially for Corporate giants. They were earlier controlling the power games by forcefully keeping their brands over insignificant others, in distribution channels, especially, in retail outlets. In turn, the business houses started with more corporate social responsibilities and sustainable developments for brand building exercise, so that a pull works for their brands over the usual push mechanism, which dominated the market for years(Hörisch et al., 2019). The corporate giants also had been keen to develop more new concepts and innovations to settle the unsettled market and to regain their market share(Hummel and Hörisch, 2020). There have been several suggestions from academia and industry captains. Like Markard and Rosenbloom (2020), advised and insisted on low carbon Innovations to prevent further pandemic inflicted economic disruption. Kemp et al. (2020) noticed decreased transaction of commercial ðshing and marine trafðc to lessen disturbance of marine lives in order to increase uninterrupted supplies later on and also to increase the tourism to have indirect impact on more efficient supply chain management in future times (Naidoo and Fisher, 2020; Kemp et al., 2020). Goffman (2020) argued in favour of reduced environmental crisis and in turn better stability in demand-supply equilibrium post pandemic. To decrease costs, augmentation of supply chain efficiency and to quick respond to customer demands, supply chains have broadened worldwide chain partners with more dependence on online transformation and collaborative efforts of local third party delivery systems and logistic partners as the disruptive innovations to sustain from sudden pandemic induced insecurity and unexpected shocks (Sharifi and Ismail, 2006; Yang and Yang, 2010).

Probable Solutions, Recommendations and Discussion

There has been no one solution fits all scenario. On the one hand, opening of new production facilities and lean management of the companies(most of the companies are working with 50%-80% man power) enabled the corporate houses to regain and compensate for their losses. On the other hand, Corporate Social Responsibilities of the companies helped them to regain the faith of the lost customers during the trying times. The digital transformation also helped the business houses to gain flawless access to the doorstep of households, irrespective of the movement facilities of the customers, during lock down or otherwise. The disruption of Supply chain could also be handled with digital transformation more efficiently. Supply chain integration (CPFR) and tie up with third party and fourth party logistics providers (3PLs and 4PLs) could have been more prudential in this aspect. The transportation problem has been taken care of my withdrawal of lock down and simultaneous communication of the unintended delay to the consumers. Consumers are generally empathetic towards unintentional problems and limited resources due to covid related exigencies and protocols.

Web scraping could be a useful solution for data mining related disparity to solve the gap between real-time data and conventional book entries, for financial statements.

Another probable positive outcome of the slack period of pandemic is the temporary break in the service sectors like hospitality and aviation industry. It gave the companies a chance to strategic redesign and to rebuild their service blue print. Many companies had been constantly being vigilant with their overall maintenance and service feedback over this time.

The best part of the strategic redesign had been the goals for sustainable development and the betterment of society. Pandemic has given a new vision to the business world to see the world with 'one-ness' without myopic short-sighted, self centric business motives.

CONCLUSION

There have been several endeavours to deal with seamless supplies, despite tremendous disturbances during the turbulence of COVID-19 induced pandemic. Starting from strategists to academic stalwarts researchers to corporate head honchos, everyone tried to reduce the uncertainty driven undulating demand and Supply and ultimately to flatten the curve.

As already discussed, several strategic redefining like supply chain integration to digital transformation had been taken place to deal with the difficult time. They are the key success stories to handle the capacious and eccentric path of supply chain management aka fluctuations during this pandemic era. The lean management along with the help of technological advancement like automation and analytics (Warehouse Management System- WMS, Vendor Management System/ Vendor Management Inventory-VMS,Entrepreneurship Resource Planning- ERP, Just in Time production- JIT, Retailer-Supplier Partnership-RSP, Best of breed approaches in IT etc.) and robotics also accentuated the achievement of the goal.While web scraping helped in smoothening theirregularities in financial data recording. The best outcome is of course enlightenment of myopic business organisations to think beyond their egotistical perspective and to work towards sustainable goals for long run.

FUTURE RESEARCH DIRECTION

The research has been primarily based on secondary data and hence does not delve into the criticality of all the sectors, except Food, Pharmaceuticals, Aviation, Retail and Hospitality industry. Therefore it leaves behind an abundance of opportunity to fathom the reasons of supply chain mis-management, disruption and fluctuations and thereby upheavals in economic conditions in the market place.

REFERENCES

Akter, S. (2020). The impact of COVID-19 related 'stay-at-home' restrictions on food prices in Europe:findings from a preliminary analysis. *Food Security*, *12*(4), 719–725. doi:10.100712571-020-01082-3 PMID:32837638

Armantier, O., Kos¸ar, G., Pomerantz, R., Skandalis, D., Smith, K.T., Topa, G., & Van der Klaauw, W. (2020). *How Economic Crises Affect Inflation Beliefs: Evidence From the COVID-19 Pandemic*. Federal Reserve Bank of New York Staff Report 949.

Baker, S. R., Farrokhnia, R., Meyer, S., Pagel, M., & Yannelis, C. (2020). *How does household spending respond to an epidemic? Consumption during the 2020 COVID-19 pandemic*. NBER Working Papers 26949. National Bureau of Economic Research.

Barichello, R. (2020). *The COVID-19 Pandemic: Anticipating its Effects on Canada's Agricultural Trade. Canadian Journal of Agricultural Economics/Revue CanadienneD'agroeconomie*. doi:10.1111/cjag.12244

Bhagat, D., & Dhar, U. R. (2011). Agriculture Supply Chain Management: A Review. *IUP Journal of Supply Chain Management*, *8*(3), 7–25.

Bobdey, S., & Ray, S. (2020). Going viral–Covid-19 Impact Assessment: A Perspective beyond Clinical Practice. *Journal of Marine Medical Society*, *22*(1), 9–12. doi:10.4103/jmms.jmms_12_20

Brandon-Jones, E., Brian, S. C., Autry, W., & Kenneth, P. J. (2014). A Contingent Resource-Based Perspective Of Supply Chain Resilience And Robustness. *The Journal of Supply Chain Management*, 54–75.

Brandon-Jones, E., Squire, B., & Van Rossenberg, Y. G. T. (2014). The impact of supply base complexity on disruptions and performance: The moderating effects of slack and visibility. *International Journal of Production Research*, *53*(22), 6903–6918. doi:10.1080/00207543.2014.986296

Carvalho, V.M., Hansen, S., Ortiz, A., Ramon Garcıa, J., Rodrigo, T., Rodriguez Mora, S. & Ruiz, J. (2020). *Tracking the COVID-19 Crisis with High-Resolution Transaction Data (DP14642)*. CEPR Discussion Papers.

Chandrasekaran, N., & Raghuram, G. (2014). *Agribusiness Supply Chain Management*. CRC Press.

Chen, N., Zhou, M., Dong, X., Qu J., Gong, F., & Han, Y. (2020). Epidemiological and Clinical Characteristics of 99 Cases of 2019 Novel Coronavirus Pneumonia in Wuhan, China: A Descriptive Study. *Lancet*.

Choi, T. M. (2020). Innovative "Bring-Service-Near-Your-Home Operations Under Corona-Virus (COVID-19/SARS-CoV-2) Outbreak: Can Logistics Become the Messiah?" *Transportation Research Part E: Logistics and Transportation Review*.

Choi, T. Y., & Krause, D. R. (2006). The supply base and its complexity:Implications for transaction costs, risks, responsiveness, and innovation. *Journal of Operations Management*, *24*(5), 637–652. doi:10.1016/j.jom.2005.07.002

Chowdhury, R. (2017). The rana plaza disaster and the complicit behavior of elite NGOs. *Organization*, *24*(6), 938–949. doi:10.1177/1350508417699023

Cicala, S. (2020). *Early economic impacts of COVID-19 in Europe: a view from the grid*. Working Paper, University of Chicago.

de Wit, E., van Doremalen, N., Falzarano, D., & Munster, V. J. (2016). SARS and MERS: Recent insights into emerging coronaviruses. *Nature Reviews. Microbiology*, *14*(8), 523–534. doi:10.1038/nrmicro.2016.81 PMID:27344959

Deaton & Deaton. (2020). Food Security and Canada's Agricultural System Challenged by COVID-19. *Canadian Journal of Agricultural Economics/Revue canadienned'agroeconomie, 68*(2), 143–149. doi:10.1111/cjag.v68.2

Derevyankina, E. S., & Yankovskaya, D. G. (2020). The impact of Covid-19 on supply chain management and global economy development. *International Journal of Supply Chain Management, 9*(4), 765–774.

Diewert, W. E., & Fox, K. J. (2020). *Measuring real consumption and CPI bias under lockdown conditions*. NBER Working Papers 27144, National Bureau of Economic Research.

Ebrahimy, E., Igan, D., & Peria, S. M. (2020). *The Impact of COVID-19 on Inflation: Potential Drivers and Dynamics*. International Monetary Fund.

Glowacz, M., & Rees, D. (2016). Using Jasmonates and Salicylates to Reduce Losses Within the Fruit Supply Chain. *European Food Research and Technology, 242*(2), 143–156. doi:10.100700217-015-2527-6

Goffman, E. (2020). In the wake of COVID-19, is glocalization our sustainability future? *Sustainability: Science, Practice, and Policy, 16*(1), 48–52.

Govindan, K., Mina, H., & Alavi, B. (2020). A Decision Support System for Demand Management in Healthcare Supply Chains Considering the Epidemic Outbreaks: A Case Study of Coronavirus Disease 2019 (COVID-19). *Transportation Research Part E, Logistics and Transportation Review, 138*, 101967. doi:10.1016/j.tre.2020.101967 PMID:32382249

Gray, R. S. (2020). *Agriculture, Transportation, and the COVID-19 Crisis*. Canadian Journal of Agricultural Economics/Revue CanadienneD'agroeconomie. doi:10.1111/cjag.12235

Hailu, G. (2020). Economic Thoughts on COVID-19 for Canadian Food Processors. *Canadian Journal of Agricultural Economics/Revue canadienned'agroeconomie, 68*(2), 163–169.

Hey, J. (2020). Coronavirus: Measuring the Market Impact. *Fruitnet*. www.fruitnet.com/asiafruit/article/181021/coronavirus-measuring-the-market-impact

Hobbs, J. E. (2020). Food Supply Chains During the COVID-19 Pandemic. *Canadian Journal of Agricultural Economics/Revue canadienned'agroeconomie, 68*(2), 171–176. doi:10.1111/cjag.v68.2

Hörisch, J., Wulfsberg, I., & Schaltegger, S. (2019). The iñuence of feedback and awareness of consequences on the development of corporate sustainability action over time. *Business Strategy and the Environment, 29*(2), 638–650. doi:10.1002/bse.2394

Huang, C., Wang, Y., Li, X., Ren, L., Zhao, J., & Hu, Y. (2020). *Clinical Features of Patients Infected with 2019 Novel Coronavirus in Wuhan*. Lancet. doi:10.1016/S0140-6736(20)30183-5

Hummel, P., & Hörisch, J. (2020). The hidden power of language: How 'value creation accounting' iñuences decisions on expenditures, cost reductions and staff costs, *Sustainability Accounting. Management and Policy Journal, 11*(1), 187–206. doi:10.1108/SAMPJ-04-2018-0111

Ivanov, D.Implications for STEM education. (2020). Predicting the Impacts of Epidemic Outbreaks on Global Supply Chains: A Simulation-Based Analysis on the Coronavirus Outbreak (COVID-19/SARS-CoV-2) Case. *Transportation Research Part E, Logistics and Transportation Review*, *136*, 101922. doi:10.1016/j.tre.2020.101922 PMID:32288597

Jaravel, X., & O'Connell, M. (2020). *Inflation Spike and Falling Product Variety during the Great Lockdown*. CEPR Discussion Papers No. 14880.

Jaworski, K. (2021). Measuring food inflation during the COVID-19 pandemic in real time using online data: A case study of Poland. *British Food Journal*, *123*(13), 260–280. doi:10.1108/BFJ-06-2020-0532

Kemp, P. S., Froese, R., & Pauly, D. (2020). COVID-19 provides an opportunity to advance a sustainable UK ðsheries policy in a post-Brexit brave new world. *Marine Policy*, *120*, 104–114. doi:10.1016/j.marpol.2020.104114 PMID:32834407

Ker, N. (2020). Experience Versus Expectation: Farmers' Perceptions of Smart Farming Technologies for Cropping Systems Across Europe. *Precision Agriculture*, *21*(1), 34–50. doi:10.100711119-019-09651-z

Kuchler, T., Russel, D., & Stroebel, J. (2020). *The geographic spread of COVID-19 correlates with structure of social networks as measured by Facebook*. NBER Working Papers 26990, National Bureau of Economic Research.

Kumar, S., Afrouzi, H., Coibion, O., & Gorodnichenko, Y. (2015). Inflation targeting does not anchor inflation expectations: Evidence from firms in New Zealand. *Management*, *24*(5), 637–652.

Kwan, S. H., & Mertens, T. M. (2020). Market assessment of COVID–19. *FRBSF Economic Lett.*, *2020*(14), 1–5.

Leal Filho, W., Brandli, L. L., Lange Salvia, A., Rayman-Bacchus, L., & Platje, J. (2020). COVID-19 and the UN sustainable development goals: Threat to solidarity or an opportunity? *Sustainability*, *12*(13), 5343. doi:10.3390u12135343

Maffioli, E. M. (2020). How is the World Responding to the 2019 Coronavirus Disease Compared with the 2014 West African Ebola Epidemic? The Importance of China as A Player in the Global Economy. *The American Journal of Tropical Medicine and Hygiene*, *102*(5), 924–925. doi:10.4269/ajtmh.20-0135 PMID:32162604

Mahajan, Caleb, Singh, Watkins, & Geyer. (2014). Post-harvest Treatments of Fresh Produce. *Philosophical Transactions of the Royal Society A: Mathematical, Physical and Engineering Sciences*, *372*.

Markard, J., & Rosenbloom, D. (2020). A tale of two crises: COVID-19 and climate. *Sustainability: Science, Practice, and Policy*, *16*(1), 53–60.

McKibbin, W. J., & Fernando, R. (2020). The global Macroeconomic Impacts of COVID-19: Seven Scenarios [Working Papers]. Canberra, AU: CAMA, The Australian National University.

Mirza, M. M. Q. (2003). Climate change and extreme weather events: Can developing countries adapt? *Climate Policy*, *3*(3), 233–248. doi:10.3763/cpol.2003.0330

Mvumi, B., Matsikira, L. T., & Mutambara, J. (2016). The Banana Post-Harvest Value Chain Analysis in Zimbabwe. *British Food Journal, 118*(2), 272–285. doi:10.1108/BFJ-08-2014-0293

Naidoo, R., & Fisher, B. (2020). Reset sustainable development goals for a pandemic world. *Nature, 583*(7815), 198–201. doi:10.1038/d41586-020-01999-x PMID:32632244

NHS Press Conference. (2020, Feb. 4). *National Health Commission (NHC) of the People's Republic of China*. http://www.nhc.gov.cn/xcs/xwbd/202002/235990d202056cfcb202043f202004a202070d2020 07f209703b202113c202000.shtml

Platje, J., Harvey, J., & Rayman-Bacchus, L. (2020). COVID-19 – reñections on the surprise of both an expected and unexpected event. *The Central European Review of Economics and Management, 4*(1), 149–162. doi:10.29015/cerem.874

Sgarbossa, F., & Russo, I. (2017). A Proactive Model in Sustainable Food Supply Chain: Insight From a Case Study. *International Journal of Production Economics, 183*, 596–606. doi:10.1016/j.ijpe.2016.07.022

Sharifi, H., Ismail, H. S., & Reid, I. (2006). Achieving agility in supply chain through simultaneous 'design of' and 'design for' supply chain. *Journal of Manufacturing Technology Management, 17*(8), 1078–1098. doi:10.1108/17410380610707393

Sharma, R., Shishodia, A., Kamble, S., Gunasekaran, A., & Belhadi, A. (2020). Agriculture supply chain risks and COVID-19: Mitigation strategies and implications for the practitioners. *International Journal of logistics Research and Application*, 1-27. doi:10.1080/13675567.2020.1830049

Siche, R. (2020). What is the Impact of COVID-19 Disease on Agriculture? *Scientia Agropecuaria, 11*(1), 3–6. doi:10.17268ci.agropecu.2020.01.00

Sintema, E. J. (2020). *Effect of COVID-19 on the performance of grade 12 students*. Academic Press.

Sohrabi, C., Alsafi, Z., & O'Neill, N. (2020). World Health Organization Declares Global Emergency: A Review of the 2019 Novel Coronavirus (COVID19). *International Journal of Surgery, 76*, 71–76. doi:10.1016/j.ijsu.2020.02.034

Stott, P. (2016). How climate change affects extreme weather events. *Science, 352*(6293), 1517–1518. doi:10.1126cience.aaf7271 PMID:27339968

Tsolakis, N. K., Keramydas, C. A., Toka, A. K., Aidonis, D. A., & Iakovou, E. T. (2014). Agrifood Supply Chain Management: A Comprehensive Hierarchical Decision making Framework and a Critical Taxonomy. *Biosystems Engineering, 120*, 47–64. doi:10.1016/j.biosystemseng.2013.10.014

van Dam, Y. K., & Webbink, J. F. (2020). Reñecting on reñections on COVID-19. *The Central European Review of Economics and Management, 4*(2), 7–19. doi:10.29015/cerem.876

van der Vorst, J. G., Beulens, A. J., & van Beek, P. (2000). Modelling and Simulating Multi-Echelon Food Systems. *European Journal of Operational Research, 122*(2), 354–366. doi:10.1016/S0377-2217(99)00238-6

World Health Organization. (2020). *WHO: Coronavirus disease 2019 (COVID-19) situation report – 23.* https://www.who.int/docs/default-source/coronaviruse/situation-reports/20200212-sitrep-20200223-ncov.pdf?sfvrsn=20200241e20200219fb20200278_20200212

Xinhuanet News Report. (2020). http://www.xinhuanet.com/english/2020-01/09/c_138690570.htm

Yang, B., & Yang, Y. (2010). Postponement in supply chain risk management: A complexity Perspective. *International Journal of Production Research*, *8*(7), 1901–1912. doi:10.1080/00207540902791850

Yin, Y., & Wonderlink, R. G. (2019). MERS, SARS and other coronaviruses as causes of pneumonia. *Respiratory*, *23*, 130–137. PMID:29052924

Zumla, A., Chan, J. F., Azhar, E. I., Hui, D. S., & Yuen, K. Y. (2016). Coronaviruses–Drug Discovery and Therapeutic Options. *NationalReviews Drug Discovery*, *15*(5), 327–347. doi:10.1038/nrd.2015.37 PMID:26868298

Chapter 3
Inflation and the Stock Market:
Money Illusion in Borsa Istanbul

Cenk C. Karahan
https://orcid.org/0000-0002-2686-6959
Boğaziçi University, Turkey

Han N. Özsöylev
Özyeğin University, Turkey

ABSTRACT

The stock market suffers from money illusion, discounting real cash flows at nominal discount rates. Subsequent research has also shown that the cross-section of stock returns is impacted differently by inflation. This cross-sectional variance across risky and safe stocks makes one of the most puzzling anomalies, risk (beta) anomaly, stronger in inflationary periods. This chapter tests the hypothesis that higher inflation leads to stronger mispricing of risk in stock market due to money illusion effect in Turkey, one of the emerging countries afflicted with perennial high inflation. The results show that although money illusion and mispricing were not visibly present in hyper-inflationary period in 1990s, the anomalous pricing of risky securities was remarkably high in inflationary periods over the last two decades, with a distinct mispricing due to the inflationary pressure that commenced with the COVID-19 pandemic. These varying results across the vastly different inflation regimes can be explained by rational inattention and impact of past experience of inflation on investment behavior.

INTRODUCTION

Inflation is on the increase around the world following the COVID-19 pandemic, with food and energy prices reaching record highs. This has led to a lively discussion in the financial press on the impact of high inflation on asset prices,[1] whether the current spike is transitory or longer lasting,[2] and how investors can protect their wealth against rising prices, in particular, by shifting their investments into stocks.[3] The economic literature provides conflicting hypotheses on how stock prices would react to inflation. On the one hand, according to *the hedging hypothesis*, stock prices would rise in response to higher

DOI: 10.4018/978-1-6684-5876-1.ch003

inflation since stocks are real assets and therefore offer a hedge against the impact of inflation in eroding real returns (e.g., see Fama and Schwert 1977, Fama 1981, Boudoukh and Richardson 1993, Bekaert and Wang 2010). On the other hand, according to *the money illusion hypothesis*, stock prices would fall when expected inflation increases as investors discount real cash flows with nominal discount rates and thus undervalue stocks in times of high inflation (e.g., see Modigliani and Cohn 1979, Ritter and Warr 2002, Cohen et al. 2005). Given these competing hypotheses, the connection between inflation and stocks is an empirical question.

Several studies on the U.S. stock market have reported empirical evidence consistent with the money illusion hypothesis (e.g., Ritter and Warr 2002, Campbell and Vuolteenaho 2004, Cohen et al. 2005). In particular, Cohen et al. (2005) theoretically show that, in a stock market suffering from money illusion, the security market line is flatter (steeper) than the one predicted by CAPM (with no money illusion) when the expected inflation is high (low). In accordance with this theoretical observation, the authors find that the empirical security market line of U.S. stocks is flatter relative to the CAPM prediction in times of high inflation and steeper in times of low inflation. It follows that during inflationary periods money illusion can provide a theoretical justification for the well-established beta anomaly, the empirical finding that high beta stocks have lower risk-adjusted returns than low beta stocks.

It is somewhat incredulous that stock market investors, with trillions of dollars at stake, would suffer from money illusion and mistake nominal discount rates for the real ones. However, if inflation is not usually a salient concern for investors, then they may not react to inflation because of rational inattention, that is, they may choose not to process information about inflation as absorbing all available information is either infeasible or prohibitively costly (e.g., see Mankiw and Reis 2002, Sims 2003, Katz et al. 2017). Also, recent empirical evidence shows that the inflation experienced personally affects individuals' inflation expectations as well as their willingness to invest in the stock market (Malmendier and Nagel 2016, D'Acunto et al. 2021). Since inflation in the U.S. was tamed in the early 1980s and has been low since then until the outbreak of the COVID-19 pandemic, U.S. investors may have become relatively insensitive to inflation in their portfolio allocation decisions. What if inflation varied significantly over time, and at times proved to be costly to ignore? Would the stock market still suffer from money illusion then?

To answer this question, Turkish stock market Borsa Istanbul is used as a testing ground in this chapter. Turkey is an emerging country afflicted with perennial high inflation and with a large and internationally connected stock market (among the largest 20 stock markets in terms of market capitalization for the last couple of decades). The country experienced a hyperinflationary period from 1980s to 2000s, inflation was brought to single digits by 2004 and stayed relatively low until recently. The inflation once again reached double digits in recent years: it was 16.2% in March 2021. Average inflation in the OECD area, which Turkey is part of, was 2.4% in the same month.

With a dataset spanning the period from January 1989 to March 2021, it is documented that Turkish stock prices exhibit behavior consistent with the money illusion hypothesis. In particular, the slope of the Turkish security market line (SML) is significantly and negatively related to inflation. When periods with different inflationary regimes are investigated separately, this chapter documents a more nuanced picture: the impact of inflation on the SML is insignificant during the hyperinflationary period from January 1992 to December 2002 whereas the SML is flatter than the one predicted by CAPM for the period between January 2003 and March 2021 during which inflation was relatively tame. However, the observation for the latter period is mostly due to inflation's impact on the intercept of the SML rather than its slope – the impact on the slope is statistically insignificant. When the COVID period (January 2020 to March 2021) with a new high inflationary regime is looked into separately, stronger support for the money illusion hypothesis is found: the SML during this period is flatter compared to the broader timespan of January 2003 to March 2021 and the negative relationship between inflation and the slope of the SML is both statistically and economically strongly significant.

The findings from the Turkish stock market are broadly consistent with the idea that mispricing across stocks due to money illusion is partly due to rational inattention and impact of past experience of inflation on investment behavior: During the hyperinflationary period of 1992-2002, Turkish investors have already been experiencing very high levels of inflation since 1980s and they likely knew ignoring inflation would be very costly thus paid attention to it. During the same period, inflation had no significant impact on the SML and therefore there was no cross-sectional mispricing among stocks driven by money illusion. On the other hand, during 2003-2021 when inflation was relatively tame compared to the past but still high compared to other countries, we see money illusion creeping in. The negative and strongly significant relationship between inflation and the slope of the SML observed during the COVID period lends support to the idea that Turkish investors may have been ignoring inflation due to it being relatively tame and stable prior to the outbreak of the pandemic and that the high inflation regime following the pandemic manifested itself in stronger mispricing across stocks induced by money illusion.

Background

Since Irving Fisher devoted a book to the subject (Fisher, 1928), it has been widely recognized that people may suffer from money illusion in the sense of mistakenly considering an increase in the nominal value due to inflation to be an increase in the real purchasing power. In their survey study, Shafir, Diamond, and Tversky (1997) find that money illusion is a widespread phenomenon in the United States. In an experimental study, Fehr and Tyran (2008) show that presence of money-illusioned agents can have important effects on aggregate outcomes.

Money illusion leads to mispricing in financial markets and the Modigliani and Cohn (1979) hypothesis is arguably the most popular explanation of such mispricing: investors discount real cash flows with nominal discount rates which, in turn, causes stocks to be undervalued when expected inflation is high and overvalued when expected inflation is low. Many early empirical studies find a negative relation between inflation and real stock returns (e.g., Bodie 1976, Jaffe and Mandelker 1976, Nelson and Schwert 1977, and Fama and Schwert 1977).

More recent studies have focused on possible mispricing induced by money illusion in stock markets:[4] Ritter and Warr (2002) find that the bull market starting in 1982 was partly due to the stock market being undervalued, caused by money illusion. Campbell and Vuolteenaho (2004) show that the price-dividend ratio of the aggregate stock market index is negatively related to expected inflation, consistent with the money illusion hypothesis. Chen, Lung, and Wang (2009) find that even though money illusion can explain the level of mispricing in the stock market, it does not explain the volatility of mispricing. While these studies focus on the implication of money illusion hypothesis for the pricing of the aggregate stock market relative to the Treasury bills, Cohen et al. (2005) show that the hypothesis also has implications for the pricing of risky stocks relative to safe stocks: the empirical security market line of U.S. stocks is flatter relative to the one predicted by CAPM in times of high inflation and steeper in times of low inflation.

In this chapter, we apply the empirical methodology of Cohen et al. (2005) to the Turkish stock market to investigate whether there is any cross-sectional mispricing induced by money illusion among Turkish stocks. However, going beyond Cohen et al. (2005) and the existing literature, we also examine whether investors' rational inattention to and past experiences of inflation may affect the degree of mispricing across stocks driven by money illusion. The Turkish stock market provides an ideal testing ground for this hypothesis since the country has experienced significantly different inflation regimes in the last few decades. Our findings are broadly consistent with the posited hypothesis, thus contribute to the extant literature on the money illusion hypothesis (see the aforementioned studies), the burgeoning literature on rational inattention (e.g., Mankiw and Reis 2002, Sims 2003, Katz et al. 2017), and the new yet impactful literature on the relationship between past experiences of inflation and investment behavior (e.g., Malmendier and Nagel 2016, D'Acunto et al. 2021).[5]

DATA AND METHODOLOGY

This part of the chapter describes and documents the properties of the data used. Furthermore, the methodology used in the empirical analyses is outlined.

The authors retrieve the adjusted stock prices and market capitalizations for all stocks available at the moment using the most extensive and trustworthy data set for the Turkish stock market from Finnet.[6] The monthly data dates back to January 1989 and ends in March 2021. The final prices of delisted corporations are manually updated by assigning a price of zero if the cause is liquidation and the proper last trade price if the reason is merger, acquisition, or voluntary delisting.[7] The funds, real estate trusts and ETFs are dropped from consideration. The final data set comprises of monthly returns denominated in Turkish liras on 552 individual equities traded at Borsa Istanbul for over 32 years. The market return is calculated as the average value-weighted return of all eligible stocks.

The risk-free rate is calculated as the 1-month US Treasury Bill rate plus local inflation minus US inflation. This proxy is used as risk-free rate to compensate for the fact that Turkish government bond rates are not always risk-free, and they often outperform stock market returns for extended periods, resulting in a negative equity premium. This estimate is a good choice since it proxies an overseas investor's risk-free return in Turkey that is parity adjusted or hedged. Monthly US risk-free rates are retrieved from Prof. Ken French's website[8], which is compiled based on return data from Ibbotson Associates. The monthly Consumer Price Index (CPI) data for Turkey and the US are compiled by OECD and retrieved from Federal Reserve Bank of St. Louis website.[9]

The main methodology examines if lagged inflation values have an impact on slope and intercept of Security Market Line (SML) based on Capital Asset Pricing Model (CAPM) (Sharpe, 1960; Lintner, 1975). In order to reach a reasonable estimate of beta and return relationship, classical approach is to group individual assets into portfolios that offer cross-sectional spread in market betas. The most widely used way of constructing such portfolios is to estimate individual stock betas in a time series regression and group them into portfolios based on lagged estimates of stock level betas. This study uses a time series regression of 36-month rolling windows with a minimum of 12 months of observations to estimate stock level betas. The stocks are then classified into portfolios for 375 months between 1990m1 to 2021m3.

The main results are based on 10 beta-sorted test portfolios, with results for 20 test portfolios presented as a robustness test. Since the earlier years in the data has relatively low number of stocks, testing the model with a cross-section of 10 test portfolios seems a reasonable choice to avoid disproportionately small number of stocks in portfolios. Before proceeding with cross-sectional tests, one has to retrieve post-formation betas for the test portfolios. The portfolio betas are once again estimated via a time-series regression of 36-month rolling windows with a minimum of 24-month data input, yielding test portfolios with beta estimates for 351 months between 1992m1 to 2021m3.

The time series CAPM regression utilized for beta estimates is

$$R_{i,t} - r_{f,t} = \alpha_{j,t} + \beta_i \left(R_{m,t} - r_{f,t} \right) + \varepsilon_{i,t} \tag{1}$$

where $R_{i,t}$ is the return for stock or portfolio i, $r_{f,t}$ is the risk-free return, $R_{m,t}$ is the market return and $\varepsilon i_{,t}$ is the error term for stock or portfolio i. The regression yields a beta estimate that can be used in cross sectional regressions to estimate SML and test the validity of CAPM, following the standard methodology by Fama and MacBeth (1973). Specifically, for each cross section, we regress the monthly excess return on each of the 10 beta-sorted test portfolios j on a constant and the portfolios' trailing-window postformation beta.

$$R_j - r_f = \gamma + \beta_j \lambda + \xi_j \tag{2}$$

The equation above is the test of Security Market Line (SML) and coefficients of the regression are in fact excess returns themselves. The outputs of 351 cross sectional regressions provide intercept and slope estimates. As long as the trailing postformation betas are reasonably reliable forecasts of future betas, the intercept portfolio return will be the excess return on a zero-beta stock portfolio and the slope portfolio return will be the excess return on a unit-beta portfolio, i.e. equity risk premium. As such, this study defines these time series as $^3 = r^e_{intercept}$ and $\lambda = r^e_{slope}$, two key return series spanning 351 months between 1992m1 and 2021m3. These two portfolios' return series with constant betas of 0 and 1 are used in time series regressions in the next stage to test inflation impact. The tests follow

$$r^e_{\text{intercept},t} = a_1 + b_1 \left(R_{m,t} - r_{f,t} \right) + c_1 \pi_{t-1} + u_{1,t}, \tag{3}$$

$$r^e_{slope,t} = a_2 + b_2 \left(R_{m,t} - r_{f,t} \right) + c_2 \pi_{t-1} + u_{2,t}, \tag{4}$$

where π_{t-1} is the trailing month's inflation. The intercept and slope portfolio's excess returns are regressed on a constant, the contemporaneous market excess return, and lagged inflation. This regression tests follow the specification by Cohen et al. (2005), the seminal paper testing the Modigliani and Cohn's (1979) hypothesis. The inflation series is demeaned and exponentially smoothed following the methodology of the existing literature. The coefficients of the regressions (3) and (4) would allow testing the hypotheses that inflation impacts the abnormal returns (intercept) and price of risk (slope) in the market.

EMPIRICAL FINDINGS

Real vs. Nominal Returns

Before proceeding to the results of regression tests, this subsection shows the broader impact of inflation on stock returns in Turkey, an emerging market with long periods of high inflation. In order to visualize the nominal returns vs. the inflation adjusted real returns, Figure 1 tracks the cumulative value of 1 lira invested in a weighted average portfolio of Borsa İstanbul stocks at the beginning of 1992. The nominal value of the lira invested soars to 12611 liras with a geometric average return of 2.73% per month. However, when inflation is taken into consideration, the geometric average return drops to 0.49% per month accumulating around 5.73 liras over 351 months until 2021m3. This dramatic lack of performance in real terms hurts the investors' appetite for stock market, especially for the much-desired long-term investors.

Test Portfolios, Slope and Intercept

Table 1 presents summary statistics for the 10 beta-sorted test portfolios that are the basis of our reported tests. The beta values are the average of the postformation betas for 351 months in our sample. The average betas range from 0.659 to 1.215, although monthly values of beta estimates show a larger variation and range. The risk measured by standard deviation also shows a steady rise from low beta portfolios to high beta portfolios. The risk-adjusted returns measured by Sharpe ratio, on the other hand, do not display any discernible trend. The detailed look into risk-return relationship through an asset pricing model and differentiating between dynamics of subperiods would allow us to document any existing pattern.

Table 2 presents the summary statistics of the key variables and outputs of slope and intercept of Security Market Line, as estimated via the cross-sectional regression in Equation (2). Arithmetic averages of returns, somewhat higher than the geometric average, imply robust market returns. However, if one considers the intercept, which is the excess return of unit-beta portfolio, i.e., the equity risk premium, it is a relatively low 0.60%. This results in a flat SML on average. The wide range and variability of the slope and intercept also demonstrate the changing dynamics and the risk pricing of the market.

The variation in inflation, slope and intercept become more evident in Figure 2. The inflation levels are visibly high until early 2000s. The slope and intercept show greater variation in 1990s and early 2000s. The inflation is relatively under control for the time period since 2003. This moderation period includes the global financial crisis and some local macroeconomic turbulence, yet the relative stability continues uninterrupted up until the last couple of years. There is a visible spike in inflation and more variability in slope and intercept since 2020, which coincides with the COVID pandemic and its economic repercussions. The most enduring effect of the pandemic on the world economy would be inflation. That is a direct result of disruptions in product and money flow and monetary policies in countering those effects.

Changing Inflation and CAPM

The main argument of this chapter is that inflation impacts the slope of SML negatively. The flatter slope implies that equity risk premium in the market is lower than expected, hence the market is not valuing the risk properly. Secondary effect tested is that the inflation would have a positive impact on the intercept, leading to abnormal returns on zero or low beta portfolios. These two results together would document a beta anomaly that is stronger due to higher inflation.

Figure 1. Cumulative nominal and real returns of 1 Lira invested at the beginning of 1992. Nominal return averages to 2.73% per month, while the real return is 0.49% per month Source: The monthly CPI data for Turkey [TURCPIALLMINMEI] is compiled by OECD and retrieved from FRED, Federal Reserve Bank of St. Louis website https://fred.stlouisfed.org. Stock market data is retrieved from Finnet.

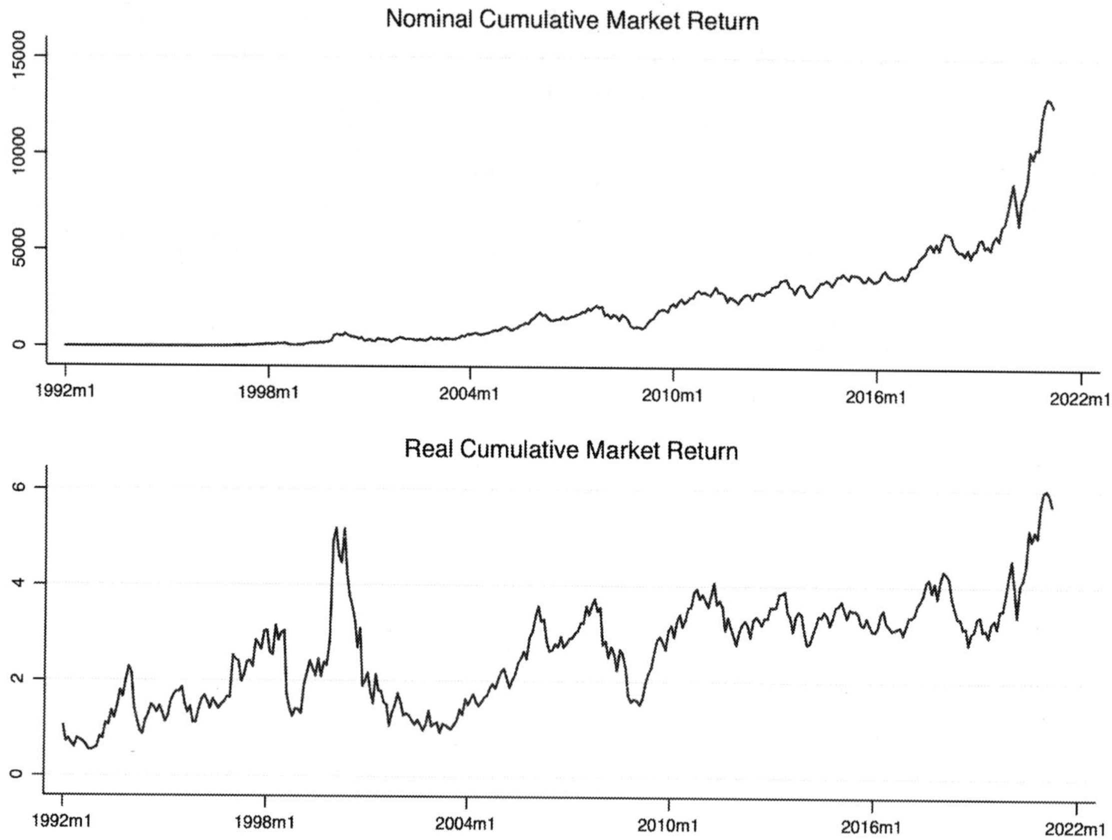

Table 1. Return statistics for 10 Beta-sorted portfolios

Beta-Sorted Portfolios	Beta	Portfolio Return	Excess Return	Standard Deviation	Monthly Sharpe Ratio
1	0.659	0.034	0.011	0.116	0.094
2	0.795	0.031	0.008	0.116	0.072
3	0.783	0.034	0.011	0.129	0.089
4	0.869	0.039	0.016	0.138	0.117
5	0.937	0.035	0.012	0.134	0.090
6	0.960	0.033	0.010	0.134	0.076
7	0.971	0.037	0.015	0.138	0.107
8	1.084	0.041	0.018	0.149	0.119
9	1.130	0.038	0.015	0.155	0.099
10	1.215	0.043	0.020	0.162	0.123

Table 2. Summary statistics of key variables

	N	Mean	Std. Dev.	min	p25	Median	p75	max
Market Return	351	0.035	0.127	-0.393	-0.039	0.025	0.09	0.81
Risk-free Return	351	0.022	0.026	-0.013	0.004	0.013	0.037	0.235
Excess Return	351	0.012	0.124	-0.441	-0.055	0.006	0.07	0.762
Inflation	351	0.022	0.025	-0.014	0.005	0.013	0.034	0.234
Slope	351	0.008	0.158	-0.538	-0.077	-0.004	0.078	0.719
Intercept	351	0.006	0.144	-0.548	-0.056	0.003	0.064	0.664

The main tests of the above hypotheses are conducted through regressions (3) and (4). Table 3 reports the results for the entire sample of 351 months. The results show the negative impact of inflation on slope, which is statistically significant. However, it has a negative impact on intercept as well. The results imply that SML is flatter but the low beta securities do not necessarily have higher abnormal returns. Pricing of risk is impacted by inflation on average. However, we cannot conclusively say beta anomaly becomes stronger in inflationary periods. The results are robust to the number of test portfolios, as the findings for 10 and 20 test portfolios are essentially the same.

In order to document the dynamic nature of the relationship between inflation and stock market, the sample period is classified into quartiles based on the level of inflation. The statistics of financial conditions are summarized in Table 4. The level of inflation differential across quartiles is almost 10-fold, as the Turkey has been through hyperinflation during the sample period.

The differences in the performance of CAPM SML in different inflationary periods are visualized in Figure 3. The theoretical SLM is the line that goes through (0,0) and (1, Average excess return for the period) on the graph that maps the beta of a portfolio with its excess return. Empirical SML is the line fitted to the excess returns and betas of the 10 test portfolios. The first quartile with low inflation period surprisingly shows an inverted SML line, in contrast with our expectations. This implies that beta anomaly is stronger for the lowest inflationary period. For other quartiles, the results are in line with the money illusion hypothesis. Second quartile with a moderate inflation level does not show beta anomaly as the empirical SML coincides with the theoretical one. As inflation goes up in the third quartile, the beta anomaly becomes stronger. The fourth quartile also has a flatter SML, albeit weaker than the third quartile.

Subperiods and COVID Pandemic

The results based on the inflation quartiles are somewhat inconsistent with the money illusion hypothesis and the findings in the US market. However, one has to note that Turkey's macroeconomic conditions and stock market are vastly different from a developed country like the US. This emerging market has been through a hyperinflationary period for more than a decade. Furthermore, Borsa İstanbul is a relatively young and underdeveloped market with its peculiar dynamics. The results make it clear that further analysis is needed. This subsection divides the time period into three to test the hypothesis across different eras.

The decade of 1990's until 2002 is marked with political instability, economic turbulence and heightened market volatility for Turkey. Therefore, the dynamics of the period may differ from the later more stable years. Table 5 reports the results of test for the 132 months covering this particularly vola-

Figure 2. Monthly inflation in Turkey along with slope and intercept variables documented through cross-sectional regressions Source: The monthly CPI data for Turkey [TURCPIALLMINMEI] is compiled by OECD and retrieved from FRED, Federal Reserve Bank of St. Louis website https://fred.stlouisfed.org

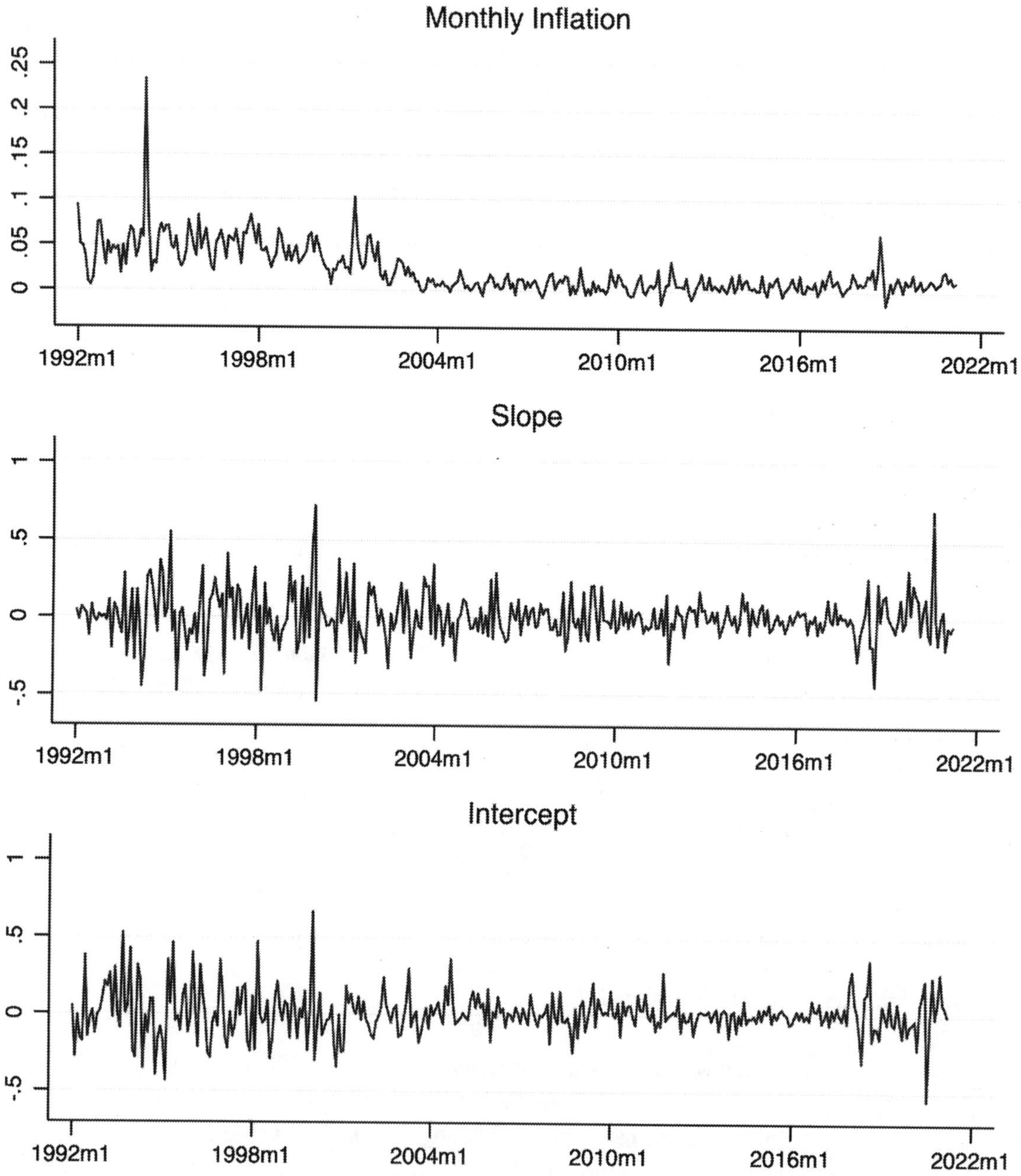

tile period. The results show inflation's impact on slope and intercept to be statistically insignificant. Money illusion hypothesizes that inflation would have an outsized impact especially in high inflation

Table 3. Regression results for the entire sample period, 351 months covering 1992m1 to 2021m3

	N=10 Beta Sorted Portfolios		N=20 Beta Sorted Portfolios	
VARIABLES	**Intercept**	**Slope**	**Intercept**	**Slope**
Constant (a_1, a_2)	-0.021*** (0.004)	-0.022*** (0.004)	-0.022*** (0.004)	-0.021*** (0.004)
$R_M - r_f$ (b_1, b_2)	0.329*** (0.092)	0.644*** (0.092)	0.450*** (0.092)	0.515*** (0.089)
Lagged Inflation (c_1, c_2)	-1.372*** (0.210)	-0.712*** (0.244)	-1.313*** (0.257)	-0.777*** (0.205)
Observations	351	351	351	351
R-squared	0.109	0.261	0.220	0.269
Robust standard errors in parentheses. *** p<0.01, ** p<0.05, * p<0.1				

periods. Turkey's results in this period show that the theory does not hold either due to hyperinflation or excessive noise in the data.

Turkey had macroeconomic stability since 2003, which is also evident in the inflation levels in Figure 2. Since the last two decades had relatively different dynamics, it warrants a separate look. Table 6 reports the results of money illusion tests in this period. Flatter SML is slightly evident from negative slope coefficients for lagged inflation, yet they are statistically insignificant.

The final analysis is for the COVID pandemic period, as this period is marked with global inflationary pressures. The start of the period is taken as the beginning of 2020 as the first quarantines began in China impacting the global supply chains. The period ends with our sample in 2021m3. The results documented in Table 7 show a very strong and significant impact of inflation on slope and intercept. The slope is flattened with a rising intercept, indicating a particularly strong beta anomaly.

The visual representations of SML in Figure 4 show the beta anomaly across these three periods. High inflation period, with a staggering average monthly inflation of 4.51%, shows no discernible beta anomaly. This period is highly volatile and the stock market is relatively new. The results are not in line with the theories built in developed markets and they may not follow most theoretical expectations. The second period since 2003 with an average monthly inflation of 0.80% shows a slightly flat slope implying a weak beta anomaly. This result is in line with the money illusion theory as low-inflation would yield weaker anomalous pricing. The COVID pandemic period has a relatively high inflation of 1.16% per month. The SML shows a flatter slope, hence a stronger beta anomaly. This latter period of heightened inflation eventually shows money illusion effect for Turkey. The results of the last two decades, a

Table 4. Return and inflation statistics for quartile subperiods divided based on inflation level

Inflation Quintiles	Market Return	Ave. Portfolio Return	Risk-free Return	Inflation
1	0.010	0.014	0.007	0.006
2	0.023	0.023	0.006	0.009
3	0.026	0.027	0.027	0.028
4	0.083	0.085	0.052	0.052

Figure 3. Empirical relation between excess returns and betas presented via Security Market Line (SML) in different inflationary periods

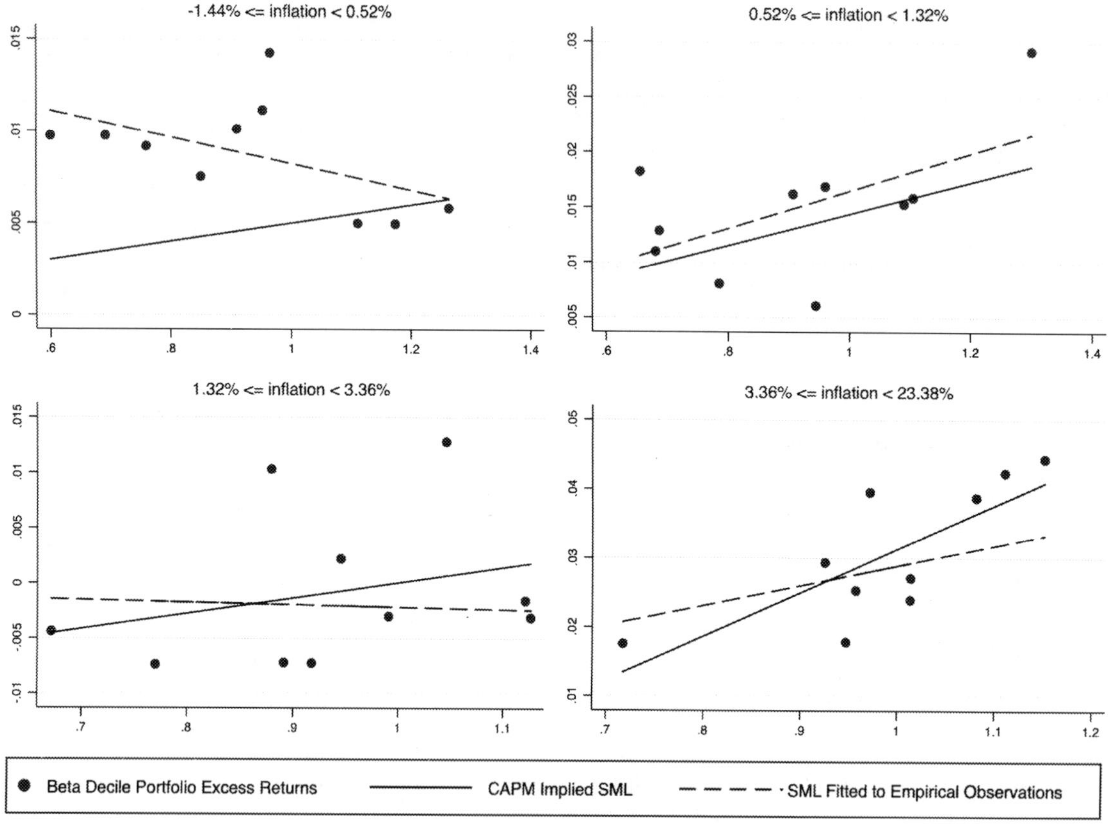

Table 5. Regression results for the hyper-inflationary period, 132 months covering 1992m1 to 2002m12

	N=10 Beta Sorted Portfolios		N=20 Beta Sorted Portfolios	
VARIABLES	Intercept	Slope	Intercept	Slope
Constant (a_1, a_2)	0.005 (0.045)	-0.051 (0.046)	-0.020 (0.026)	-0.026 (0.025)
$R_M - r_f$ (b_1, b_2)	0.392*** (0.115)	0.574*** (0.111)	0.493*** (0.115)	0.465*** (0.111)
Lagged Inflation (c_1, c_2)	-2.371 (1.706)	0.381 (1.798)	-1.390 (0.934)	-0.582 (0.924)
Observations	132	132	132	132
R-squared	0.135	0.249	0.247	0.251
Robust standard errors in parentheses. *** p<0.01, ** p<0.05, * p<0.1				

Table 6. Regression results for the recent decades marked with lower inflation, 219 months covering 2003m1 to 2021m3

	N=10 Beta Sorted Portfolios		N=20 Beta Sorted Portfolios	
VARIABLES	**Intercept**	**Slope**	**Intercept**	**Slope**
Constant (a_1, a_2)	-0.042* (0.022)	-0.001 (0.022)	-0.036* (0.018)	-0.009 (0.017)
$R_M - r_f$ (b_1, b_2)	0.142* (0.074)	0.855*** (0.076)	0.309*** (0.067)	0.675*** (0.066)
Lagged Inflation (c_1, c_2)	2.796* (1.543)	-0.728 (1.543)	2.374* (1.317)	-0.125 (1.214)
Observations	219	219	219	219
R-squared	0.022	0.293	0.085	0.297
Robust standard errors in parentheses. *** p<0.01, ** p<0.05, * p<0.1				

long period with relatively tame inflation and recent surge in prices due to COVID pandemic, prove the theory of money illusion in Turkey.

CONCLUSION

This chapter reviewed the theoretical and empirical literature on inflation's impact on stock market with an angle specifically on pricing of risk. High inflation leads stock market participants to have a distorted view on value of money, aptly named money illusion, resulting in mispricing of risky securities. This mispricing manifests itself in a flatter Security Market Line (SML). The implication is that risky (high beta) securities do not generate enough risk adjusted returns, whereas less risky (low beta) securities

Table 7. Regression results for the recent pandemic period with inflationary pressures, 15 months covering 2020m1 to 2021m3

	N=10 Beta Sorted Portfolios		N=20 Beta Sorted Portfolios	
VARIABLES	**Intercept**	**Slope**	**Intercept**	**Slope**
Constant (a_1, a_2)	0.262*** (0.092)	-0.303*** (0.083)	0.247*** (0.071)	-0.277*** (0.060)
$R_M - r_f$ (b_1, b_2)	0.111 (0.288)	0.898*** (0.278)	0.565*** (0.131)	0.392*** (0.108)
Lagged Inflation (c_1, c_2)	21.181*** (7.562)	-23.391*** (6.809)	18.996*** (5.814)	-20.491*** (4.851)
Observations	15	15	15	15
R-squared	0.033	0.232	0.177	0.212
Robust standard errors in parentheses. *** p<0.01, ** p<0.05, * p<0.1				

Figure 4. Empirical relation between excess returns and betas presented through Security Market Line (SML) in different subperiods

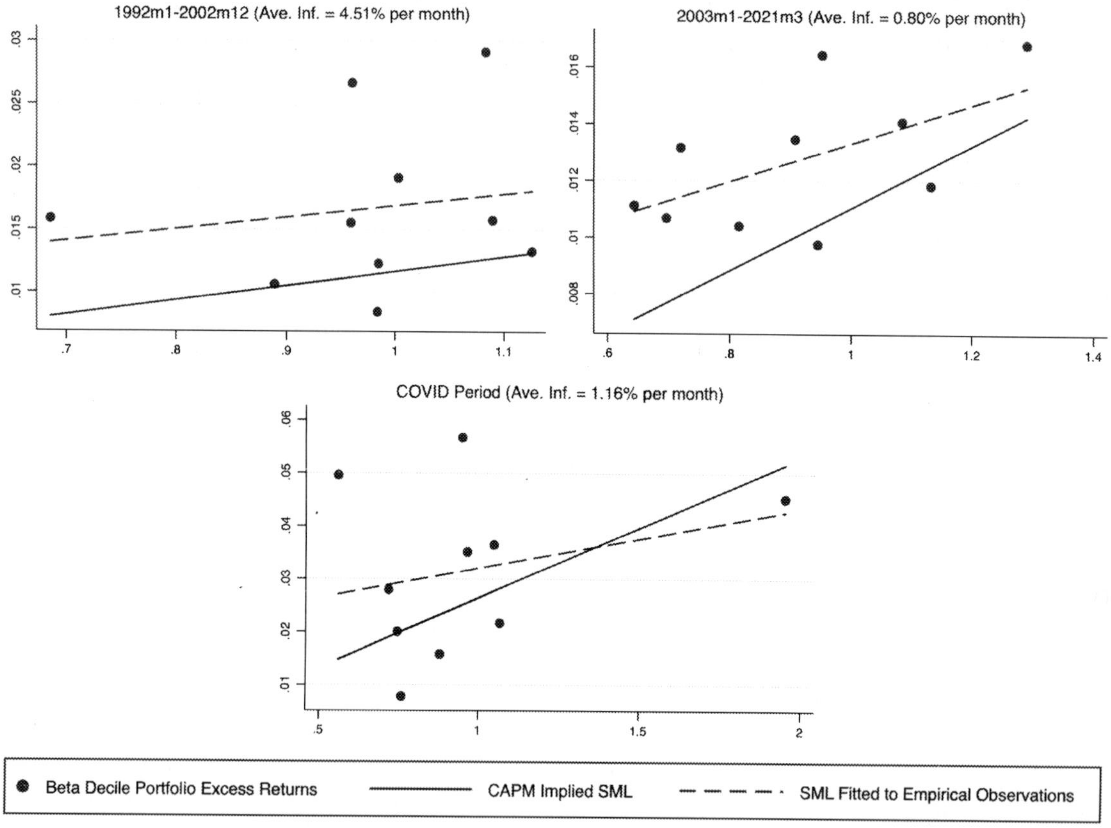

generate positive abnormal returns. This anomalous observation in violation of the conventional risk-return paradigm is called beta anomaly and it is expected to get stronger in inflationary periods.

The theory is empirically tested by regressing slope and intercept of SML with lagged inflation values. Empirical portion of the chapter tests money illusion in Turkey, one of the major emerging countries with perennially high inflation. The explanatory power of inflation on SML slope is significant and negative, proving the existence of money illusion in a broader sense over the 351 months of sample period. However, negative impact on intercept along with inconsistent results across the four quartiles of inflation regimes, necessitates a closer look.

When the hyperinflationary period of 1992-2002 is studied separately, the impact of inflation on SML becomes insignificant. This period in Turkey is marked with high inflation and volatile markets. Furthermore, Borsa İstanbul stock market can be considered in its infancy after being established in 1986. 1990's followed by a local financial crisis in 2001 defines a period where the investor base never lived through a low inflation period to have a point of reference. However, Turkey had a relatively tame inflation for years after 2003. This latter period, when tested separately, shows a flatter SML, albeit due to an impact on intercept rather than slope.

As prices are surging across the world since the advent of COVID pandemic in early 2020, Turkey is not immune to inflationary pressures. These global headwinds together with the local macroeconomic turbulence caused an increase in inflation in the country. After years of relatively stable prices, high inflationary period proves a suitable test case for money illusion. Regression results and visual demonstration of SML show that slope is indeed significantly flatter over the pandemic months with higher intercept.

The results of empirical tests show that money illusion is alive and well in Turkey. Inflation does impact price of risk causing a stronger beta anomaly. However, one should note that impact of high inflation becomes visible only relative to a period of stable prices. The long period of hyperinflation in the early years of Borsa İstanbul is not a viable test case. However, recent pandemic with its inflationary pressures following relatively stable years does eventually show a stronger beta anomaly. Turkish stock market data are largely consistent with the hypothesis that mispricing across stocks owing to money illusion is partially attributable to rational inattention and the influence of prior inflation experience on investment behavior. Turkish investors living through hyperinflationary period presumably realized that ignoring inflation would be highly costly, so they paid attention to it between 1992 and 2002. During the same time span, inflation had no effect on the SML, hence there was no cross-sectional mispricing among equities caused by money illusion. On the other hand, we find money illusion seeping in throughout the period 2003-2021, when inflation was relatively low compared to the past but remained high compared to other nations. The negative and highly significant relationship between inflation and the slope of the SML observed during the COVID period lends support to the idea that Turkish investors may have ignored inflation because it was relatively tame and stable prior to the outbreak of the pandemic. The implication for the astute investors is that if stability in macroeconomic conditions are on the horizon, relatively risky securities shall become attractive investment opportunities.

REFERENCES

Acker, D., & Duck, N. W. (2013). Inflation illusion and the US dividend yield: Some further evidence. *Journal of International Money and Finance*, *33*, 235–254. doi:10.1016/j.jimonfin.2012.11.018

Asness, C. (2000). Stocks versus bonds: Explaining the equity risk premium. *Financial Analysts Journal*, *56*(2), 96–113. doi:10.2469/faj.v56.n2.2347

Asness, C. (2003). Fight the Fed model: The relationship between future returns and stock and bond market yields. *Journal of Portfolio Management*, *30*(1), 11–24. doi:10.3905/jpm.2003.319916

Basak, S., & Yan, H. (2010). Equilibrium asset prices and investor behaviour in the presence of money illusion. *The Review of Economic Studies*, *77*(3), 914–936. doi:10.1111/j.1467-937X.2009.00596.x

Bekaert, G., & Engstrom, E. (2010). Inflation and the stock market: Understanding the Fed model. *Journal of Monetary Economics*, *57*(3), 278–294. doi:10.1016/j.jmoneco.2010.02.004

Bekaert, G., & Wang, X. (2010). Inflation risk and the inflation risk premium. *Economic Policy*, *25*(64), 755–806. doi:10.1111/j.1468-0327.2010.00253.x

Bodie, Z. (1976). Common stocks as a hedge against inflation. *The Journal of Finance*, *31*(2), 459–470. doi:10.1111/j.1540-6261.1976.tb01899.x

Boudoukh, J., & Richardson, M. (1993). Stock returns and inflation: A long-horizon perspective. *The American Economic Review*, *83*, 1346–1355.

Brunnermeier, M. K., & Julliard, C. (2008). Money illusion and housing frenzies. *Review of Financial Studies*, *21*(1), 135–180. doi:10.1093/rfs/hhm043

Campbell, J. Y., & Vuolteenaho, T. (2004). Inflation illusion and stock prices. *The American Economic Review*, *94*(2), 19–23. doi:10.1257/0002828041301533

Chen, C. R., Lung, P. P., & Wang, F. A. (2009). Stock market mispricing: Money illusion or resale option? *Journal of Financial and Quantitative Analysis*, *44*(5), 1125–1147. doi:10.1017/S0022109009990238

Cohen, R. B., Polk, C., & Vuolteenaho, T. (2005). Money illusion in the stock market: The Modigliani-Cohn hypothesis. *The Quarterly Journal of Economics*, *120*(2), 639–668. doi:10.1162/0033553053970133

D'Acunto, F., Malmendier, U., Ospina, J., & Weber, M. (2021). Exposure to grocery prices and inflation expectations. *Journal of Political Economy*, *129*(5), 1615–1639. doi:10.1086/713192

Fama, E. F. (1981). Stock returns, real activity, inflation, and money. *The American Economic Review*, *71*, 545–565.

Fama, E. F., & MacBeth, J. D. (1973). Risk, return, and equilibrium: Empirical tests. *Journal of Political Economy*, *81*(3), 607–636. doi:10.1086/260061

Fama, E. F., & Schwert, G. W. (1977). Asset returns and inflation. *Journal of Financial Economics*, *5*(2), 115–146. doi:10.1016/0304-405X(77)90014-9

Fehr, E., & Tyran, J.-R. (2008). Limited rationality and strategic interaction: The impact of the strategic environment on nominal inertia. *Econometrica*, *76*(2), 353–394. doi:10.1111/j.1468-0262.2008.00836.x

Fisher, I. (1928). *The Money Illusion*. Adelphi Company.

Jaffe, J. F., & Mandelker, G. (1976). The Fisher effect for risky assets: An empirical investigation. *The Journal of Finance*, *31*(2), 447–458. doi:10.2307/2326616

Katz, M., Lustig, H., & Larsen, L. (2017). Are stocks real assets? Sticky discount rates in stock markets. *Review of Financial Studies*, *30*(2), 539–587. doi:10.1093/rfs/hhw072

Lee, B. S. (2010). Stock returns and inflation revisited: An evaluation of the inflation illusion hypothesis. *Journal of Banking & Finance*, *34*(6), 1257–1273. doi:10.1016/j.jbankfin.2009.11.023

Lintner, J. (1975). The valuation of risk assets and the selection of risky investments in stock portfolios and capital budgets. In *Stochastic Optimization Models in Finance* (pp. 131–155). Academic Press. doi:10.1016/B978-0-12-780850-5.50018-6

Malmendier, U., & Nagel, S. (2016). Learning from inflation experiences. *The Quarterly Journal of Economics*, *131*(1), 53–87. doi:10.1093/qje/qjv037

Mankiw, N. G., & Reis, R. (2002). Sticky information versus sticky prices: A proposal to replace the new Keynesian Phillips curve. *The Quarterly Journal of Economics*, *117*(4), 1295–1328. doi:10.1162/003355302320935034

Modigliani, F., & Cohn, R. A. (1979). Inflation, rational valuation and the market. *Financial Analysts Journal, 35*(2), 24–44. doi:10.2469/faj.v35.n2.24

Nelson, C. R., & Schwert, W. (1977). Short-term interest rates as predictors of inflation: On testing the hypothesis that the real rate of interest is constant. *The American Economic Review, 67*, 478–486.

Ritter, J. R., & Warr, R. S. (2002). The decline of inflation and the Bull Market of 1982-1999. *Journal of Financial and Quantitative Analysis, 37*(1), 29–61. doi:10.2307/3594994

Shafir, E., Diamond, P. A., & Tversky, A. (1997). On Money Illusion. *The Quarterly Journal of Economics, 112*(2), 341–374. doi:10.1162/003355397555208

Sharpe, S. A. (2002). Re-examining stock valuation and inflation: The implications of analysts' earnings forecasts. *The Review of Economics and Statistics, 84*(4), 632–648. doi:10.1162/003465302760556468

Sharpe, W. F. (1964). Capital asset prices: A theory of market equilibrium under conditions of risk. *The Journal of Finance, 19*(3), 425–442.

Sims, C. A. (2003). Implications of rational inattention. *Journal of Monetary Economics, 50*(3), 665–690. doi:10.1016/S0304-3932(03)00029-1

Wei, C. (2010). Inflation and stock prices: No illusion. *Journal of Money, Credit and Banking, 42*(2-3), 325–345. doi:10.1111/j.1538-4616.2009.00289.x

KEY TERMS AND DEFINITIONS

Beta (Risk) Anomaly: Empirical observation that high beta (risk) securities underperform low beta (risk) securities on a risk-adjusted basis, which is a violation of conventional financial theory that dictates higher risk should be accompanied by higher return.

Capital Asset Pricing Model (CAPM): A theoretical model that ties required expected return of an asset to its undiversifiable market risk.

Equity Risk Premium: A measure of excess return that investing in the stock market is expected to provide over a risk-free rate. It is the compensation that investors seek for taking on the relatively higher risk of equity investing.

Nominal Return: Measure of return before taking inflation into consideration.

Rational Inattention: The idea that economic decision makers cannot absorb all available information but can choose which pieces of information to process.

Real Return: Measure of return that is adjusted by rate of inflation, hence loss of purchasing power. Real return would be reached by subtracting inflation from nominal return.

Security Market Line (SML): Graphical representation of CAPM that shows differing levels of market risk (beta) for assets on x-axis mapped against the expected return of the corresponding asset on y-axis.

Sharpe Ratio: A measure of risk-adjusted return that describes how much excess return you receive for the volatility of holding a riskier asset.

ENDNOTES

1 See, for example, "Inflation poses a duration problem for investors", *Financial Times*, 16 June 2021; "Inflation could mean value stocks' time to shine", *Wall Street Journal,* 26 October 2021; "Flight to 'safe haven' funds runs its own risk", *Financial Times,* 7 March 2022.

2 "Inflation is coming. How much, for how long?", *New York Times*, 6 June 2021.

3 See "Best investments to beat inflation", Forbes, 28 December 2021 and "Stocks as inflation hedge is new catch-all narrative for market rally", Bloomberg, 22 March 2022.

4 There is a wide literature investigating the implications of money illusion for financial markets (including but also going beyond stocks): a non-exhaustive list includes Asness (2000, 2003), Sharpe (2002), Brunnermeier and Julliard (2008), Basak and Yan (2010), Lee (2010), Bekaert and Engstrom (2010), Wei (2010), and Acker and Duck (2013).

5 A brief description of the latter two literatures can be found in the Introduction.

6 We thank Finnet, the leading data vendor to the Turkish financial industry, for graciously granting us access to their extensive database.

7 We thank Ali Nezih Akyol in helping us verify the data on delisted firms with his meticulously hand-collected delisting announcements.

8 Monthly US risk-free rates are retrieved from Ken French's website, https://mba.tuck.dartmouth.edu/pages/faculty/ken.french/data_library.html

9 The monthly CPI data for Turkey [TURCPIALLMINMEI] and the US [CPALTT01USM657N] are compiled by OECD and retrieved from FRED, Federal Reserve Bank of St. Louis website, https://fred.stlouisfed.org.

Chapter 4
Spillover of COVID-19: Impact on the Global Economy

Peterson K. Ozili
Independent Researcher, UK

Thankom Arun
Essex University, UK

ABSTRACT

How did a health crisis translate to an economic crisis? Why did the spread of the coronavirus bring the global economy to its knees? The answer lies in two methods by which coronavirus stifled economic activities. First, the spread of the virus encouraged social distancing which led to the shutdown of financial markets, corporate offices, businesses and events. Second, the exponential rate at which the virus was spreading, and the heightened uncertainty about how bad the situation could get, led to flight to safety in consumption and investment among consumers, investors and international trade partners. We focus on the period from the start of 2020 through March when the coronavirus began spreading into other countries and markets. We draw on real-world observations in assessing the restrictive measures, monetary policy measures, fiscal policy measures and the public health measures that were adopted during the period. We empirically examine the impact of social distancing policies on economic activities and stock market indices. We also empirically the effect of COVID infection cases and COVID deaths on macroeconomic performance during the 2020 to 2021 period. The findings reveal that the increasing number of lockdown days, monetary policy decisions and international travel restrictions severely affected the level of economic activities and the closing, opening, lowest and highest stock price of major stock market indices. We also find that the rising number of COVID cases and rising death cases led to a significant increase in global inflation rate, global unemployment rate, and global energy commodity index.

1. INTRODUCTION

This paper explores the spillover effect of COVID-19 on the global economy. In 2019, there was anxiety about the impact of a US-China trade war, the US presidential elections and Brexit on the World

DOI: 10.4018/978-1-6684-5876-1.ch004

Economy. On account of these, the IMF had predicted moderated global growth of 3.4 percent. COVID emerged in late 2019, and was declared a pandemic in January 2020. COVID-19 – the disease caused by SARS-CoV-2 – metamorphosed into the Delta variant in 2021, the omicron variant in 2021 and the Deltacron variant in 2022. The emergence of COVID-19 unexpectedly changed global outlook. Due to fear and uncertainty, and to rational assessment that firms' profits are likely to be lower due to the impact of COVID-19, global stock markets erased about US$6 trillion in wealth in one week from 24th to 28th of February of 2020. The S&P 500 index lost over $5 trillion in value in the same week in the US while the S&P 500's largest 10 companies experienced a combined loss of over $1.4 trillion (Reuters, 2020), although some of these were recovered in the subsequent week. Some of the loss in value was due to rational assessment by investors that firms' profits would decline due to the impact of the coronavirus.

The International Air Transportation Association (IATA) stated that the air travel industry would lose US$113 billion if the COVID-19 outbreak was not quickly contained (IATA, 2020). The IMF downgraded its growth projection for the global economy as the COVID-19 outbreak threw its earlier projection into serious doubt. The tourism industry was affected as the travel opportunities for Chinese tourists, who usually spend billions annually, were severely curtailed. There were increased flight cancellations, cancelled hotel bookings and cancelled local and international events worth over $200billion. The flow of goods through global supply chains vastly reduced significantly given that China was the world's largest manufacturer and exporter, and the Chinese government ordered the closure of major factories in the country. Countries like Iran, Italy and France issued stay-at-home nationwide policies to control the spread of the virus, which had already caused multiple deaths and was putting pressure on the national public healthcare infrastructure. Such stay-at-home policies planted the seeds of recession in developed countries, and there was a general consensus among economists that the coronavirus pandemic would plunged the world into a global recession (Financial Times, 2020). The International Monetary Fund in March stated that it expected a global recession that would be at least as bad as the 2007-8 global financial crisis followed by a recovery in 2021. (Georgieva, 2020).

The literature on the cause of recessions is vast (see Jagannathan et al, 2013; Stiglitz, 2010; Gaiotti, 2013; Bezemer, 2011; Mian and Sufi, 2010; Bentolila et al, 2018; Bagliano and Morana, 2012). But the cause of the 2020 global recession was novel in modern history. The coronavirus triggered a new type of recession that was different from the past triggers of a recession. For instance, the Asian debt crisis of 1997 was caused by the collapse of the Thai baht in July 1997, which created panic that caused a region-wide financial crisis and economic recession in Asia (Radelet and Sachs, 1998). The 2008 global financial crisis, which translated to a recession, was caused by loose monetary policy which created a bubble, followed by subprime mortgages, weak regulatory structures, and high leverage in the banking sector (Allen and Carletti, 2010). The 2016 recession in Nigeria was caused by the fall in the price of crude oil, balance of payment deficit, adoption of a fixed-float exchange rate regime, an increase in the pump price of petrol, activities of pipeline vandals and infrastructure weaknesses. The 2010 recession in Greece was caused by the after-effect of the global financial crisis, structural weaknesses in the Greek economy, and lack of monetary policy flexibility as a member of the Eurozone (Rady, 2012).

In this paper, we show how the coronavirus outbreak led to spillovers into major sectors of the global economy, and how fast policy response by several governments either triggered and prolonged the recession while trying to save the lives of citizens. We also investigate the effect of social distancing policies on the level of economic activities and stock index prices.

The discussion in this paper contributes to the financial crisis and pandemic literature (Allen and Carletti, 2010; Jagannathan et al, 2013; Mian and Sufi, 2010; Stiglitz, 2010; Ozili, 2020a). This paper contributes to the literature by showing that non-financial factors and/or non-economic factors can trigger both a financial and economic meltdown in unprecedented ways. The implication for financial stability is that future stress testing of the resilience of the financial system should take into account human health factors as an important element in their stress testing exercises.

The rest of the paper is structured in the following way. Section 2 shows a representation of the spread of COVID-19 in some countries and regions. Section 3 discusses the global spillovers. Section 4 shows the various fast policy responses adopted in several countries during the pandemic. Section 5 highlight some of the issues of the fast policy actions taken during the 2020 pandemic. Section 6 presents the empirical analysis. Section 7 concludes.

2. SPREAD OF COVID-19

Table 1 reports the real-time data on the spread of the coronavirus (or COVID-19) based on data obtained from Worldometer. The data shows that the United States had the highest number of confirmed cases, confirmed deaths and total recovery from COVID, infected individuals, followed by India, Brazil, France, the United Kingdom and Germany as at 17rd of March 2022. The statistics is reported in Table 1.

Data from the World Health Organisation in table 2 showed that the COVID pandemic affected each region differently as at 17th March 2022. For example, the European region had the largest spread of COVID, amounting to 41% of total confirmed cases and 31% of total deaths due to COVID. The Americas had the second largest spread of COVID, amounting to 32% of total confirmed cases and 45% of total deaths due to COVID. The eastern Mediterranean region and the African region recorded the lowest number of confirmed cases while the Western Pacific region and the African region recorded the lowest number of total deaths. The African region had the lowest spread of COVID, amounting to 2% of total confirmed cases and 3% of total deaths due to COVID.

3. GLOBAL SPILLOVER

Initially, the perception was that the COVID-19 pandemic would be localized in China only. It later spread across the world through the movement of people. The economic pain became severe as people were asked to stay at home. The effect of the pandemic became was felt in various sectors of the economy with travel bans affecting the aviation industry, sporting event cancellations affecting the sports industry, the prohibition of mass gatherings affecting the events and entertainment industries (Horowit, 2020; Elliot, 2020).

There are parallels between the COVID-19 crisis and the events of 2007-2008: as in 2020, many people in the earlier recession assumed the impacts would largely be localized (in that case based on an assumption that the subprime mortgage crisis would be a relatively minor problem affecting only the US, but ultimately affecting the global financial system) (Elliot, 2020). The sudden economic disruption caused by COVID-19 is not only destructive but also has spillover implications because it created demand and supply shocks in almost every area of human endeavor (El-Erian, 2020; Ozili, 2020b).

Table 1. Top 20 countries COVID-19 statistics as at 17th March 2022

	Country	Confirmed cases (Total)	Confirmed Deaths (Total)	Recovered (Total)
	World	464,655,799	6,082,998	396,971,917
1	USA	81,289,602	994,739	56,631,117
2	India	43,001,477	516,162	42,454,546
3	Brazil	29,478,039	656,003	28,063,760
4	France	23,758,447	140,613	22,394,358
5	UK	19,911,115	163,248	18,473,970
6	Germany	17,843,545	126,248	14,142,500
7	Russia	17,484,257	363,039	15,934,645
8	Turkey	14,623,028	96,853	14,245,809
9	Italy	13,563,466	157,314	12,351,985
10	Spain	11,260,040	101,416	10,502,784
11	Argentina	8,985,836	127,334	8,791,259
12	Netherlands	7,327,235	21,736	5,767,747
13	Iran	7,135,719	139,387	6,805,081
14	Vietnam	6,820,458	41,607	3,547,488
15	Colombia	6,078,487	139,361	6,805,081
16	Indonesia	5,939,082	153,212	5,523,393
17	Japan	5,911,813	26,600	5,344,759
18	Poland	5,863,414	113,980	4,912,654
19	Mexico	5,619,780	321,619	4,912,654
20	Malaysia	3,900,433	34,099	3,567,003
Source: Worldometer. Note that there may be unconfirmed cases which were never reported to the public health authorities.				

Table 2. WHO Regional Situation Report in Numbers as of 17th March 2022

Region	Confirmed cases	Total Deaths
World	460,280,168	6,050,018
European region	189,964,699	1,910,254
Region of the Americas	149,185,071	2,663,778
Eastern Mediterranean	21,466,737	338,737
Western Pacific Region	34,575,245	196,313
South East Asia	56,686,444	770,289
African region	8,501,208	170,634
Source: Situation by region report of the World Health Organisation		

3.1. Spillover to the Travel Industry

The coronavirus outbreak led the governments of many countries to impose restrictions on non-essential travel to countries affected by COVID-19, indefinitely suspending tourism travel, work visas and immigrant visas. Some countries placed a complete travel ban on all forms of inward or outward travel, shutting down all airports in the country. At the height of the coronavirus pandemic, most airplanes flew almost empty due to mass passenger cancellations. The travel restrictions imposed by governments subsequently led to the reduction in the demand for all forms of travel which forced some airlines to temporarily suspend operations such as Air Baltic, LOT Polish Airlines, La Compagnie, and Scandinavian Airlines. Such travel restrictions cost the tourism industry alone a loss of over $200 billion globally, excluding other loss of revenue for tourism travel, and were forecast to cost the aviation industry a total loss of $113billion according to IATA. In 2020 alone, the pandemic triggered a 75% decline in international tourist arrivals compared with the same period in 2019. The airlines that were affected sought bailout support from the government. US airlines sought a $50bn bailout fund for the US Airline industry alone. The GTBA reported that the business travel sector would lose $820 billion in revenue due to the coronavirus pandemic.

3.2. Spillover to the Hospitality Industry

Restaurant businesses have been affected during the pandemic mainly through the government-announced 'stay-at-home policy' and 'social distancing' movement restriction imposed by the government in many countries. This led to rapid shutdowns in cities and states to control the spread of the coronavirus, which threw many restaurants and hotels across the country into sudden shock. Hotels across the world witnessed booking cancellations worth billions of dollars, and the hotel industry sought a $150bn bailout (IATA, 2020). Restaurant executives laid off staff as they shut down their businesses temporarily. Many customers stayed at home, preferring to eat cooked meals at home. Some restaurant executives criticized the government for imposing the stay-at-home and social distancing policy which destroyed many small restaurants and pub businesses in small cities. They argued that governments' announcement of stay-at home policies or social distancing policies was an indirect way of telling people not to come to the pubs, hotels and restaurants, which was a way of silently destroying the hospitality industry during the pandemic (Bristol, 2020). Multiple hotels in the US, UK and in some European counties announced the temporary suspension of normal operations which puts the estimated loss of jobs to 24.3 million globally, and 3.9 million in the US alone due to the decline in hotel occupancy during the pandemic period. The economic impact of the pandemic on the hotel industry was more severe than the 9/11 and 2008 recessions combined.

3.3. Spillover to the Sports Industry

The sports industry was severely affected during the 2020 coronavirus outbreak. The pandemic led to the cancellation of many sporting events. In the football segment, major European football leagues in England and Scotland announced the immediate suspension of football matches for 6 weeks until 30th April. The Turkish super league was the last major European league to suspend its matches. In Formula One, the Monaco Grand Prix was cancelled. The Tokyo Summer Olympic and Paralympic games were postponed. In the hockey segment, the 2020 hockey games in England was postponed. England's FIH

Pro League games scheduled for 2nd to 3rd and 16th to 17th May were postponed. In rugby games, the Pro14 final scheduled for 20th June at the Cardiff City Stadium was cancelled. The major league rugby (MLR) was cancelled for the remainder of the 2020 season. In the baseball segment, all major baseball league season games were called off in Mexico and Puerto Rico. The Motorsport game in Portugal was postponed after the Portuguese government declared a state of emergency and suspended all sporting events in the country. In the snooker segment, the World snooker championship to be held in Sheffield from 18th April to 4th May, was postponed. In the swimming segment, the 2020 European Aquatics Championship scheduled for 11th to 24th in Hungary was postponed until August. In the golf segment, the LPGA tour was rescheduled for 10th to 13th September 2020. The resulting loss in revenue to the sponsors and organizers of the cancelled games ran into billions of dollars. Sporting events resumed in many countries in 2021 and 2022. But there were partial restrictions on the amount of participants in sport venues and the compulsory wearing of face masks at sport events.

3.4. Spillover to Oil-Dependent Countries

3.4.1. The Oil Price War: A Contributing Factor

Early in 2020, the price of oil fell due to the oil price war between Russia and Saudi Arabia. The coronavirus pandemic worsened the situation through the reduction in the demand for oil. The imposed travel restrictions during the pandemic, which led to a reduction in the movement of people and goods, resulted in a fall in demand for aviation fuel, coal and other energy products, which subsequently led to a fall in oil price due to low demand. The coronavirus crisis also affected a wide range of energy markets such as the coal, gas and renewable energy markets, but its impact on oil markets was more severe because it stopped the movement of people and goods, which led to a drastic decline in the demand for transport fuels. When Saudi Arabia later supplied excess oil to the world, the market was flooded with too much oil, exceeding demand during the COVID-19 pandemic, and subsequently leading to a fall in oil price.

3.4.2. Loss of Oil Revenue to Oil-Dependent Countries

The effect of the pandemic on oil-dependent countries was severe. The global decline in oil price combined with the low demand for oil products in the international market led to a significant shortfall in oil revenue to oil-dependent countries, which increased current account deficits and worsened the balance of payment position of many oil-dependent countries such as Venezuela, Angola and Nigeria. These countries also faced increasing pressure on their foreign exchange reserves, which subsequently led to the devaluation of local currencies against the dollar. Countries like Kenya, Nigeria and South Africa experienced a reduction in the price of petrol in the local gas stations. National budgets were also affected. The sustained decline in global oil price due to the COVID-19 pandemic meant that the current national budget became outdated for most oil-dependent countries, and had to be revised because it did not reflect the current economic reality since the budget was priced at a higher oil price from 2019. Consequently, the national budget of some oil-dependent countries ran into massive deficits which forced some countries to either (i) seek foreign loan from the IMF, World Bank and other lenders to fund their budget deficits, or (ii) create a new budget that was priced using the current low oil price in the global market.

3.5. Spillover to Import-Dependent Countries

Many import-dependent countries were severely affected during the early stages of the coronavirus pandemic. Many countries imported their essential commodities from major exporting countries like China, India and Japan, and depend largely on these countries for the consumption of essential commodities. The reduction in goods flowing through the global supply chain, and substantial reliance on China for imported goods, led to shortages of supplies to import-dependent countries as China shut down many of its export factories. This led to increases in the price of the remaining stock of imported supplies already in import-dependent country, which also triggered inflationary pressures on the price of basic commodities despite the general low demand for imports due to the coronavirus pandemic. It was difficult to find alternative imports after China's shut-down because many countries had partially or fully closed their borders which stifled international trade at the time.

3.6. Spillover to the Financial Sector: Banks and Fintech

In 2020, the macroeconomic slowdown led to a rise in nonperforming loans in the banking sector by 250 basis points. Private sector banks had the highest exposure to credit risk during the outbreak. Nonperforming loans arose from loans issued to small and medium scale enterprises (SMEs), airlines, hotels, tour operators, restaurants, retail, construction and real estate businesses. During the pandemic, there was a general decline in the volume of bank transactions, a decline in card payments and a fall in the use of ATM cash machines worldwide. This led to fewer fees collected by banks which negatively affected banks' profit. Fintech businesses were also affected. Some Fintech businesses witnessed very low patronage by consumers leading to loss of revenue and profits, which negatively affected the equity investment of venture capitalists that funded existing and new Fintech firms. This made many venture capitalists begin to hoard new equity which led to the drying up of financing for some Fintech businesses. On the other hand, the lockdowns due to the coronavirus outbreak resulted in higher demand for some sorts of online services such as online shopping.

3.7. Spillover to Financial Markets

During the 2020 coronavirus outbreak, the most visible outcome of the COVID-19 crisis on financial markets was the effect on the global stock market. Global stock markets lost $6 trillion in value over six days from 23 to 28 February in 2020, according to S&P Dow Jones Indices. Between February 20 and March 19, the S&P 500 index fell by 28% (from 3,373 to 2,409), the FTSE 250 index fell by 41.3% (from 21,866 to 12,830), and the Nikkei fell by 29% (from 23,479 to 16,552). In the same period, large international banks witnessed a plunge in their share price, for example, Citigroup's share price fell by 49% (from US$78.22 to US$39.64), JP Morgan Chase's share price fell by 38% (from US$137.49 to US$85.30), and Barclays' share price fell by 52% (from £181.32 to £86.45). Although the oil price war, in which Russia and Saudi Arabia were driving down oil price by increasing oil production, played a role in the fall in stock markets indices, the subsequent fall in stock market indices in March was mainly due to investors' flight to safety during the coronavirus pandemic.

3.8. Spillover to the Event Industry

Prior to 2020, the event sector contributed significantly to the economy. In 2018, for instance, business events hosted more than 1.5 billion participants across more than 180 countries (Oxford Economics). The events industry generated more than $1.07 trillion of direct spending, representing spending to plan business events, produce business events, business events-related travel, and direct spending by exhibitors. The industry also created 10.3 million direct jobs globally and generated $621.4 billion of direct GDP.

During the 2020 coronavirus outbreak, the events industry was hit financially by a large number of cancellations — exhibitions, live music shows, conference, weddings, parties, corporate events, brand launches, trade shows, and more. Several big events were cancelled, for instance, the E3 and SXSW tech events were cancelled which led to direct losses beyond $1 billion. Informa delayed or cancelled events worth £400m over coronavirus pandemic. The 2020 Met Gala was postponed indefinitely. In the US, many big event management companies that were hit financially by the coronavirus outbreak appealed for federal aid from the U.S. government. The event ticketing segment of the industry was also affected. One of the biggest global ticketing and events company 'Eventbrite' announced that the COVID-19 outbreak materially affected its business outlook for 2020. The effect of the increasing cancellation on Eventbrite was so bad that the company had to withdraw its previously published 'positive outlook' for the first quarter of 2020. The effect of the outbreak on global live events was worsened by the social distancing policy imposed by several governments.

3.9. Spillover to the Entertainment Industry

The pandemic affected movie production, theatres and other entertainment activities. The global film industry incurred a $5 billion loss during the 2020 coronavirus outbreak. Several Hollywood movie productions were postponed indefinitely which meant goodbye to theatre and cinema. The International Alliance of Theatrical Stage Employees (IATSE) reported that an estimated 120,000 below-the-line entertainment industry jobs were lost due to the coronavirus pandemic, most of which were theatrical stage employees. The pandemic shutdown resulted in the loss of 120,000 jobs held by its 150,000 members, and the IATSE advocated that the entertainment industry should be included in the planned federal stimulus (or bailout) package. In Italy, the COVID-19 outbreak severely affected the entertainment industry which incurred losses estimated to run into the millions of euros per week: from February 23 to March 1, 2020. There were estimated losses of 7.3million euros in the film screening sector, 7.2million euros in the theater segment, 4.1million euros in the live music segment, 2.5 million euros in the dance activities segment and 1.8 million euros in the exhibition segment. In the UK, an estimated 50,000 industry freelancers were expected to lose their jobs as a result of the COVID-19 pandemic according to BECTU (Broadcasting, Entertainment, Communications and Theatre Union). Collectively, unemployment levels in the entertainment industry rose to unprecedented highs, and yet there were doubts as to whether the entertainment industry would receive part of the planned federal stimulus package as many lawmakers argued that the entertainment industry was not a main driver of the economy, and some argued that the entertainment industry does not contribute much to economic activities compared to the financial and manufacturing sectors.

Although the entertainment activities revived in 2021 and 2022, the performance of the entertainment industry did not reach its pre-COVID level due to slow economic recovery. Box office data shows that the number of tickets sold were 221,762,724 and 498,162,785 tickets in 2020 and 2021 respectively compared to 1,314,169,169 and 1,225,910,803 tickets in 2018 and 2019 respectively. This showed that the number of movie theaters goers reduced by approximately 83% during the COVID period compared to the pre-COVID period. Also, total box office revenue was $2,033,566,047 and $4,568,154,099 in 2020 and 2021 respectively compared to $11,972,083,658 and $11,229,345,558 in 2018 and 2019 respectively. This showed that the revenue generated from film declined by approximately 83.1% during the COVID period compared to the pre-COVID period.

3.10. Spillover to the Health Sector

The impact of COVID-19 on the health sector was severe in 2020 compared to 2021 and 2022. In 2020, many countries witnessed high demand for public health services. Public hospitals were overwhelmed with high demand for healthcare but the majority of the testing equipment were in private hospitals. China temporarily closed all hospitals in the central city of Wuhan, the epicenter of a coronavirus outbreak. Iran's hospitals struggled to cope with the coronavirus outbreak. In Spain, the Spanish government nationalized all private hospitals and healthcare providers as the virus was spreading very rapidly. Singapore had sufficient healthcare facilities and workers to cope with the growing number of COVID-19 patients, and private hospitals were inviting and accepting foreign COVID-19 patients. The Ministry of Health (MOH) in Singapore subsequently advised all doctors in public and private hospitals, and private specialist clinics, to immediately stop accepting new foreign patients who do not live in Singapore.

The coronavirus outbreak also affected the pharmaceutical supply chain. Drug makers around the world relied heavily on ingredients made in Chinese factories. About 60% of the world's active pharmaceutical ingredients (API) were made in China before the coronavirus outbreak, and the coronavirus outbreak caused severe supply problems as China shutdown majority of its factories including factories that produce drugs. Many pharmaceutical companies did not store up substantial amounts of APIs prior to the coronavirus outbreak, and as a result, some essential drugs were in short supply. The pharmaceutical companies that had stored up a substantial amount of APIs in their warehouse refused to sell them for fear of running out of supplies while others were willing to sell only at a very high price. The overreliance on Chinese API manufacturers posed the biggest risk to the global pharmaceutical industry and the COVID-19 outbreak amplified the risk even further.

Health insurers were also affected during the 2020 coronavirus outbreak. Many health insurers in the US could not cope with the insurance payments to hospitals and the insurers sought to be included in the planned federal relief stimulus package as the health sector's economic outlook was negative. The S&P 500 Managed Health Care index fell to 7% in February indicating that investors felt the health care sector would be severely hit. Moody's rating agency downgraded the nonprofit and public healthcare sector's outlook from stable to negative because of the continued spread of the coronavirus disease (COVID-19). Moody's reported that the health sector was likely to see fewer cash flow in 2020 compared to 2019 and falling revenue due to the cancellation of elective surgeries. The ratings agency also stated that even if the coronavirus outbreak could be contained, nonprofit healthcare companies were already facing rising expenses and widespread uncertainty. Also, investment bankers that invested heavily in health care pressured health care companies and medical supply firms to consider ways through which they can profit from the crisis by increasing prices. The effect of the outbreak on the health sector was the increase in the number of deaths due to the short supply of drugs, lack of vaccine to cure the patients, insufficient number of hospital beds and insufficient isolation centers to cater for the rising number of COVID-19 cases.

In mid-2021, COVID vaccines were developed by major pharmaceutical companies and ready to be distributed to many countries after approval by the World Health Organisation. Rich countries purchased about 78% of the total vaccines available in the world at the time, leaving only 22% for poorer countries. This led to COVID-19 vaccine inequality as richer countries were at an advantage than poorer countries. Although some rich countries agreed to donated some vaccines to poorer countries, it did not help to reduce to the COVID-19 vaccine inequality between rich and poor countries. Some of the vaccines that were distributed to poor countries and to developing countries were nearing their expiry date at the time the vaccines reached those countries.

3.11. Spillover to the Education Sector

The impact of the pandemic on the education sector was remarkable in several ways. The coronavirus disrupted the $600 billion higher education industry. At the early stages of the pandemic in 2020, educators and students around the world felt the ripple effect of the coronavirus as colleges and universities were instructed to shut down after the coronavirus was declared a public health emergency in many countries. There were school closures of some kind in 44 countries on four continents, including Africa, with hundreds of millions of students around the world facing disruptions. The outbreak had a more severe consequence on schools that did not have an online learning platform. Moody's, a credit rating agency, downgraded the U.S. higher education outlook from 'stable' to 'negative', because 30% of the colleges and universities in the US already had a weak operating performance, and it was difficult for these colleges and universities to adapt with the financial and academic changes required to cope with the coronavirus outbreak. Also, UNESCO reported that the COVID-19 outbreak disrupted the education of at least 290.5 million students worldwide. Public schools in the US were closed, Australia shut down some schools, while countries like Israel, Nigeria, Egypt, Italy, France, and Spain shut down all schools, and this created some form of unemployment for teachers. Northern Ireland's government suspended all examinations in its colleges and universities. Multiple U.S. based universities that ran a study abroad program overseas instructed students to return home from Italy, France and Spain as the coronavirus outbreak became severe in those countries. On the positive side, there were suggestions that the coronavirus outbreak increased the importance of online education and distance learning, but the reality was that only a small percentage of the world's education is taught online. For instance, in the US alone, about 2.4 million undergraduates which is equivalent to 15% of the total undergraduate students in the US studied entirely online in the fall of 2019, according to Eduventures. This showed that, even before the outbreak, the use of online education was already low, and it was unlikely that the outbreak would lead to a radical shift from classroom education to online education. Only few schools had the capacity to arrange a distance learning program for their students. Finally, countries like Canada, UK and US combined lost billions in education revenue as foreign students either quit their studies or had to return home, while other foreign students looked elsewhere for quick education when the travel restrictions prevented them from studying in Canada, UK and US during the outbreak.

Data obtained from UNESCO revealed that by the end of 2021, the global impact of the COVID pandemic was significant. The COVID pandemic affected over 10.5million learners in the world, which represented 0.7% of total enrolled learners, and there were only one country-wide learning closures by the end of 2021. In the first quarter of 2022, the total number of affected learners rose to 43.5million, which represented 2.8% of total enrolled learners, and there were 6 country-wide closures. This numbers show that the impact of COVID on global learning was significant and increased from 2020 to 2022.

4. FAST POLICY RESPONSE TO COVID IN 2020

4.1. General policy response

The policy measures introduced by policy makers around the world to cope with the coronavirus-induced global recession can be divided into four categories: (i) monetary measures, (ii) fiscal measures, (iii) public health measures, and (iv) human control measures. \

4.2. Policy Response to COVID Pandemic by Developing CEEMEA Countries in 2020

Some policy response (and measures) taken by Central and Eastern Europe, Middle East and Africa (CEEMEA) countries as of March 24 in 2020 are shown in table 4.

4.3. Fiscal Policy Measures during the COVID Pandemic in 2020

Fiscal policy measures were also announced in many countries to mitigate the negative economic impact of COVID-19, as shown in table 5.

4.4. Monetary Policy Measures to the COVID Pandemic in 2020

Some expansionary monetary measures were adopted by many central banks to stimulate the economy through interest rate adjustments, as shown in table 6 and 7.

Money supply measures were also adopted by many central banks through bond purchases programs or as direct coronavirus relief funds. Table 7 below shows the total central bank spending by some central banks to stimulate the economy.

5. FAST POLICY RESPONSE: ISSUES

5.1. A difficult decision

Policy makers in government, including central banks were faced with two major decisions, which is to: 'save the people before saving the economy', or 'save the economy before saving the people'. One choice had to be made because it was difficult to achieve both at the same time. You cannot save the people and the economy at the same time, because to save the people (who are also economic agents) during the COVID outbreak you have to tell them to stay at home in order to control the spread of coronavirus which means economic activities will have to stop or reduce significantly, which will trigger an economic slowdown or recession. Policy makers in many countries felt it was better to save the people before saving the economy, and as a result, many countries plunged into a recession.

Table 3. Some fast policy response during the 2020 COVID pandemic

	Type	Fast policy response adopted by policy makers	Countries
1	Monetary policy measures	(i) Granting regulatory forbearance to banks, (ii) granting principal or interest moratorium to debtors affected by COVID-19	Ireland, China, Nigeria and Italy
		Central bank provision of liquidity to financial (bond and equity) markets	China and US
		Central bank purchase of bonds and securities that were plunging in value rapidly	Australia, EU and Canada
		Lowering interest rate by Central banks	Turkey, US, New Zealand, Japan and UK, Nigeria, South Korea and Canada
		Sustained flow of credit to banks, SMSEs, public health sector, individuals and essential businesses	Australia, Nigeria, US and UK
2	Fiscal measures	Government approving a large federal stimulus package for sectors and industries most affected by the COVID-19 pandemic	UK, US, Australia and Nigeria
		Provision of income support for individuals	Australia, US, UK and India
		Social welfare payments to support each household	Australia, US
3	Public health measure	Public quarantine	India, US, UK and almost every country
		Border quarantine	Poland, Vietnam, India, UK, US, Pakistan, Australia and Colombia
		Issuing a stay-at-home policy	Italy, Iran, Nigeria and UK
		Social distancing policy	South Africa, US, UK, UAE, Singapore, Nigeria, Japan, China, India, Germany, Pakistan, Australia, South Korea and Israel
4	Human control measures	Temporary release of prisoners from overcrowded prisons	Iran and US
		Shut-down of air, land and sea borders	Taiwan, India, Mexico, US., Germany, Serbia and Nigeria
		Shutdown of schools	UK, Spain, Italy, South Africa, Nigeria and US
		Using the military to enforce a coronavirus stay-at-home lockdown	Malaysia, Italy, US, Israel, South Africa and Spain
		Travel ban	EU, US, Argentina, Austria, Australia, Bolivia, Cambodia, Canada, China, Cape Verde, Cambodia, Colombia, Croatia, Denmark, Egypt, Germany, Greece and Haiti
		Visa denial and suspension	South Africa, Canada, Singapore, China, Nigeria, Ghana, Kenya, Bolivia and Brazil

5.2. Contradictory or Conflicting Policy Response

During the 2020 coronavirus pandemic, many of the fast policy responses were insufficient even though the policies were formulated with good intentions. Monetary policy, for instance, helped to calm financial markets but it did not stop the recession. Central banks responded to the coronavirus outbreak by changing monetary policy variables such as lowering interest rates and increasing money (or credit) supply to crucial sectors of the economy. But monetary policy alone could not induce demand when there was a

Table 4. Policy Measures to Combat Spread of Coronavirus in Central and Eastern Europe, Middle East and African Countries in 2020

	Foreign travel restrictions	Internal travel restrictions	State of emergency declared	Limiting mass gathering	Closing down of schools	Restricting shops & restaurants	Remarks
Czech	✓		✓	✓	✓	✓	(i) Closure of shops and restaurants to reopen on March 25
Hungary	✓		✓	✓	✓		(i) State of emergency declared, indefinitely.
Poland	✓		✓	✓	✓	✓	(i) Shops have limited working hours, (ii) restaurants and entertainment venues closed until March 28
Romania	✓		✓	✓	✓	✓	(i) Decision announced days after the new government was voted in on March 16
Russia	✓			✓	✓		(i) Restricted flights from and to high risk areas, (ii) schools closed for 3 weeks
Ukraine	✓	✓		✓	✓	✓	(i) All air travel suspended, (ii) shop and/or local transport closure varies by region or city
Egypt	✓			✓	✓		(i) Partial suspension of mass gatherings - does not ban religious gatherings, but places some limitations on the number of people in mass gatherings
Israel	✓	✓		✓	✓	✓	(i) Emergency measures to be enforced by the police, (ii) 80% of employees to stay at home.
Lebanon	✓	✓		✓	✓	✓	-
Saudi Arabia	✓	✓		✓	✓	✓	-
Turkey	✓	✓		✓	✓	✓	(i) Curfew imposed on citizens 65 years old or older, (ii) around 10,000 people arriving from abroad under quarantine
Ghana	✓			✓	✓		
Kenya	✓			✓	✓		
Nigeria	✓			✓	✓		(i) Closed all kinds of school, (ii) partial shutdown of offices.
South Africa	✓			✓	✓	✓	(i) State of national disaster declared, (ii) 21-day lockdown announced on March 23
India	✓	✓		✓	✓	✓	Announced a 21-day nationwide lockdown

Source: Goldman Sachs Global Investment Research (exhibit 4)

Table 5. Fiscal Policy Measures to Combat Spread of Coronavirus in 2020

Countries	Total Increase in Direct Spending	% of GDP	Fiscal Support via Loans and Loan Guarantees	% of GDP	Remarks
US	USD $484bn	2.4	USD2.3tn	9.3	Measures announced
UK	GBP 350bn	11.8	GBP330bn	10.7	Measures announced
Canada	C$ 107bn	6.2	-	-	Measures announced
Czech	CZK 100bn	1.8	CZK900bn	15.9	Measures announced
Poland	ZL 212bn	9	ZL700mn	0.1	-
Romania	RON 9bn	0.9	EUR 400mn	0.2	-
Russia	RUB 1.4tn	0.3	-	-	Measures announced
Egypt	EGP 50bn	0.8	EGP50bn	0.8	-
Israel	ILS 2.8bn	0.4	-	-	
Saudi Arabia	SR 120 billion	3.9	-	-	-
Turkey	100 billion LIRA	185	-	-	Increased credit, lower taxes and deferred payments
Nigeria	NGN3.5tn	2.3	$6.9bn	7.5	Measured announced
India	₹1.7 lakh crore	967	$1 billion	0.04	World bank loan

Source: Media reports and Central Banks' press release

general flight to safety among consumers and investors – not many people were buying anything or making new investments. It became clear to many economists that monetary policy is not a vaccine, it cannot cure a recession. The expansionary monetary policies adopted in many countries during the outbreak encouraged economic activities but economic agents were unable to engage in economic activities because governments had imposed social distancing restrictions amid fear of contacting the coronavirus during the outbreak. The central bankers were 'expecting' particular outcomes and wanted to shift the needle in that direction as much as they could, but in reality their best efforts wouldn't achieve all that much.

5.3. Using Broad Fiscal Expenditure and Sector Priority

Some countries used a federal fiscal stimulus (or bail-out) package to mitigate the effect of COVID-19 on the economy during the outbreak. Choosing which sectors will receive part of the stimulus package and which sectors will not receive the stimulus package became a political issue in some countries like the UK and US as it stirred up debates as to whether the government considered the entertainment sector, hospitality sector and the circular economy to be less important and insignificant to the economy and ineligible to receive some funding from the federal stimulus package compared to the banking sector, the manufacturing, education, pharmaceutical and the aviation sectors which were considered to be

Table 6. Monetary Policy Measures Announced to Mitigate the Negative Economic Impact of COVID-19 in 2020 in Central & Eastern Europe, Middle East and African countries

Countries	Monetary policy rate			New asset purchases	Credit and liquidity facilities	Additional
	As of January 1	Current rate	End of 2nd Quarter			
Czech	2.00	1.75	1.00	Government bonds	Increased FX swap stock	-
Hungary	0.90	0.90	0.90	-	-	Grace period for loans extended to firms under FGS scheme
Poland	1.50	1.00	0.50	Government bonds	-	Decreased reserve requirement and increased interest rate
Romania	2.50	2.00	1.50	Government bonds	-	-
Russia	6.25	6.00	6.00	FX sales	-	-
Ukraine	13.50	10.00	8.50	FX Sales	-	-
Egypt	12.25	9.25	9.25	-	-	Measures discussed to reduce loan burden on firms and households
Israel	0.25	0.25	0.10	Government bonds		-
Saudi Arabia	2.25	1.00	-	-	-	-
Turkey	12.00	9.75	-	-	-	Wide range of measures such as new credit facilities, reduced reserve requirements, etc.
Ghana	16.00	14.50	14.50	-	-	Reduced primary reserve requirement and other ratios to release liquidity
Kenya	8.50	7.25	-	-	-	Reduced cash reserve ratio, extensive loan restructuring
Nigeria	13.50	13.50	-	-	-	Measures towards moving away from multiple FX regimes, reduced intervention rate, reducing federal interest rate.
India	5.15	4.4	-		3.74 lakh crore liquidity injected	Reduced CRR to 3%. Three-month moratorium on term loans outstanding. Total liquidity injection 3.4% of GDP
South Africa	6.50	5.25	4.75	-	-	-

Source: Goldman Sachs Global Investment Research (exhibit 6). GS refers to Goldman Sachs.

significant contributors to the economy. Some members of excluded sectors protested because they felt that the government did not consider their industry as significant contributors to the economy.

5.4. Fast Policy Destroyed some Segment of the Hospitality Industry Very Fast

Policies such as the ‘stay-at-home policy’ and the ‘social distancing policy’ severely damaged the income of restaurants, pub, shops and hotels in many locations, in some cases, led to the shutdown of these businesses. The policies negatively affected many businesses in the hospitality industry in ways that were not anticipated, and the government failed to take responsibility for the failure of small and large businesses that did not survive the coronavirus outbreak due to the government-imposed social

Table 7. Central bank spending in 2020

S/N	Central Bank	Amount	Covid-19 Policy response
1	Reserve bank of India	\$50 billion	India adopted a 'whatever it takes' policy which suggest an uncapped amount of spending
2	Central bank of Russia	300-billion ruble (\$4 billion)	Anti-coronavirus crisis fund
3	Bank of Canada	C\$1.0 billion (US\$703 million)	Purchase of government bonds, beginning with purchase of C\$5 billion per week
4	ECB	€750bn (£637bn) (\$796.2billion)	Emergency fund for bond purchase program for EU member countries
5	Bank of England	£ 200 billion pounds (\$248 billion)	Multiple rounds of quantitative easing.
6	Federal reserve	more than \$3 trillion	Asset purchase exceeding US\$3 trillion
7	People Bank of China	500billion yuan (\$79 billion)	To rescue a virus-weakened economy
8	Reserve Bank of South Africa	-	Fiscal authorities take responsibility for economic recovery from COVID, not the central bank
9	Bank of France	45 billion euros (\$48.9billion)	Country allocation from the ECB rescue fund
10	Central bank of Italy	25 billion euros (\$27.2billion)	Country allocation from the ECB rescue fund
11	Reserve bank of Australia	A\$90 billion (\$56 billion)	Coronavirus support fund
12	Central bank of Brazil	1.2 trillion real (\$231 billion)	Financial support was provided to counter the effects of COVID-19
	Total	\$4.541 trillion	

distancing and lockdown restrictions. It was either the social distancing policy was implemented too early, or the policy was taken to the extreme by citizens and travelers who were afraid to patronize such businesses for fear of contracting the COVID-19 disease.

6. EMPIRICAL ANALYSIS: IMPACT OF SOCIAL DISTANCING POLICIES

6.1. Effect of Social Distancing on Economic Activities

In this section, we conducted multiple analyses. In the first analysis, we examine whether social distancing policies affected economic activities. We collected one-month data from the 23rd of March to 23rd April, 2020. We focused on this narrow sample period as it allows us to capture the direct and immediate impact of social distancing policies on stock market performance and the level of general economic/business activities at the peak of the coronavirus crisis in March and April of 2020. We then collect data from stock markets in four continents: North America, Africa, Asia and Europe. We extract stock market information on the closing price, (CP), lowest price (LP) and highest price (HP) from the leading stock market indicators in the four continents: the FTSE 500 index (UK), SP 500 (US), the Nikkei 225 (Japan) and the SA Top 40 index (South Africa). In the estimations, we take the natural logarithm of each price data to reduce the observed skewness in the stock price data distribution. Also, we collected data on Purchasing Managers' Index (PMI) for Japan, UK, US and South Africa for the month of March and April. The PMI is an index of the prevailing direction of economic trends in the manufacturing and service sectors. It is derived from monthly surveys of private sector companies. The PMI is used as a proxy for the level of general economic/business activities (EC). For the explanatory variables, we use three variables to capture social distancing policies: the number of lockdown days (SDL), restriction in internal movement (RIM), and international travel restrictions (IR). We also control for monetary policy decision (MP), size of fiscal policy spending (FP) and the number of COVID-19 confirmed cases (CC) reported in the four countries. We take the natural logarithm of the FP and CC variable observations to reduce the observed skewness in the FC and CC data distribution. Data for the RIM, IR, MP, FP and CC variables were collected from the 'Oxford COVID-19 Government Response Tracker (OxCGRT) database'. OxCGRT is a database that monitor governments' policy response during the outbreak. The SDL variable was calibrated in the following way: the first day of lockdown is assigned a value '1', the second day of lockdown is assigned a value '2', the fifth day of lockdown is assigned a value '5' and so on. Finally, the data gives us a panel data.

The model is a multivariate model, estimated using a least square regression, shown below.

$$ECi,t = c + SDLi,t + RIMi,t + IRi,t + MPi,t + FPi,t\,CCi,t + ei,t \tag{1}$$

$$SMi,t = c + SDLi,t + RIMi,t + IRi,t + MPi,t + FPi,t + CCi,t + ei,t \tag{2}$$

Where,

EC = level of general economic activities
SM = the log vector of stock market variables: CP, ΔCP, LP and HP
i = country
t = business day of the week

The results are reported in table 8. The SDL coefficient is negative and significant in column 1, 2, 3, 4 and 5. This indicates that the number of lockdown days significantly affected the closing, opening, lowest and highest stock prices and the level of general economic activities (EC). The RIM coefficient is positive and significantly related to EC and the stock price variables. This indicates that the imposed restriction on internal movement had a positive effect on the level of economic activities and the closing, opening, lowest and highest stock price. The IR coefficient is negatively related to EC and all the stock price variables in columns (1) to (5). This indicates that the international travel restriction imposed during the coronavirus pandemic had a significant and negative effect on the level of economic activities as well as stock prices. The MP coefficient is negatively related to EC and the stock price variables in columns (1) to (5). This indicates that monetary policy decisions had a significant and negative effect on the level of economic activities and for the closing, opening, lowest and highest stock prices. The FP coefficient is positive and significant in all estimations, and indicates that the size of fiscal policy spending had a positive impact on stock prices and the level of economic activities. The CC coefficient is negative and insignificant, which indicates that the number of confirmed cases did not have a significant effect on the level of economic activities.

Table 8. Impact of social distancing policy on stock markets and general business activities

	(1)	(2)	(3)	(4)	(5)
	Closing Price (CP)	Opening price (OP)	Lowest Price (LP)	Highest Price (HP)	EC
SDL	-0.113*** (-4.87)	-0.112*** (-4.85)	-0.112*** (-4.87)	-0.112*** (-4.91)	-0.588*** (-3.20)
RIM	1.369* (1.90)	1.388* (1.95)	1.325* (1.86)	1.430** (2.02)	30.356*** (5.36)
IR	-0.580*** (-4.99)	-0.579*** (-5.05)	-0.587*** (-5.10)	-0.571*** (-4.99)	2.706*** (2.95)
MP	-1.107*** (-6.10)	-1.113*** (-6.22)	-1.096*** (-6.12)	-1.125*** (-6.32)	-11.517*** (-8.07)
FP	0.0003*** (40.67)	0.0003*** (41.2)	0.0003*** (41.07)	0.0003*** (41.44)	0.001*** (21.68)
CC	0.685*** (4.37)	0.680*** (4.39)	0.691*** (4.45)	0.674*** (4.37)	-1.467 (-1.19)
R^2	83.47	83.87	83.96	83.84	61.47
Adjusted R^2	82.29	82.72	82.71	82.68	58.71
Observation	76	76	76	76	76

SDL = number of lockdown days. RIM = restriction on internal movement. IR = international travel restrictions. MP = monetary policy rates. FP = natural logarithm of fiscal policy spending. CC = natural logarithm of the number of confirmed cases. EC = level of general business/economic activities. CP = natural logarithm of closing stock price for each stock index. LP = natural logarithm of lowest stock price for each stock index. HP = natural logarithm of highest stock price for each stock index. OP = natural logarithm of opening stock price for each stock index. ***, **, * represent statistical significance at the 1%, 5% and 10% level. T-statistic are reported in parenthesis

6.2. Effect of COVID Cases and Deaths on Global Macroeconomic Variables

Next, we analyzed the effect of rising COVID cases and COVID deaths on some macroeconomic indicators. We collected data for 'global energy commodity price index', 'world GDP growth', 'global inflation rate' and 'global unemployment rate' from the world bank database. Data for COVID confirmed cases and COVID deaths were collected from the World Health Organisation (WHO) database.

The data was collected for the year 2020 to 2021 and the data is annual in its trend. The data was estimated used ordinary least square regression. The results are reported in table 9 and 10 below. The result in table x shows that the COVID cases are positively related to the global inflation rate, global unemployment rate, and global energy commodity index. The result implies that the rising number of COVID cases led to a significant rise in global energy commodity price, a rise in global inflation and a rise in global unemployment rate.

Similarly, the result in table y shows that the COVID deaths are positively related to the global inflation rate, global unemployment rate, and global energy commodity index. The result implies that the rising number of COVID deaths led to a significant rise in global energy commodity price, a rise in global inflation and a rise in global unemployment rate.

The implication of the findings reported in section 5.1 is that fiscal policy spending appears to be more effective in mitigating the effect of the COVID-19 pandemic than monetary policy decisions particularly because the adoption of accommodative monetary policies by many central banks can exacerbate

Table 9. Effects of COVID cases on global macroeconomic variables

	Global energy commodity price index	World GDP growth	Global inflation rate	Global unemployment rate
	Coefficient (p-values)	**Coefficient (p-values)**	**Coefficient (p-values)**	**Coefficient (p-values)**
Total confirmed cases	3.289* (0.082)	0.065 (0.28)	0.202* (0.83)	0.350** (0.02)
*, ** denotes significance at the 10% level and 5% level respectively				

inflationary pressures that could worsen macroeconomic stability in the short term. Meanwhile, the implication of the findings reported in section 5.2 is that the rising COVID infections and death cases led to rising global inflation rate, rising unemployment rate and rising energy prices

7. CONCLUSION

In this paper, we analyzed the coronavirus outbreak and the spillover to the global economy which triggered the global recession in 2020. In the paper, we noted that policy makers in many countries were under pressure to respond to the coronavirus outbreak. As a result, many governments made fast policy decisions that had far-reaching positive and negative effects on their respective economy. Social distancing policies and lockdown restrictions were imposed in many countries, and there have been arguments that social distancing policies can trigger a recession.

In the paper, we empirically estimated the effect of social distancing on stock markets. We also investigated the effect of COVID cases and deaths on macroeconomic performance. The results (in section 5) showed that a 30-day social distancing policy or lockdown restriction negatively affected the economy through a reduction in the level of general economic activities and through its negative effect on stock prices. The result also showed that the rising COVID infection cases and COVID deaths led to a rise in global inflation rate, unemployment rate and energy prices.

These results reflect that dilemma that countries faced during the crisis. Lawmakers in many countries supported an extended social distancing policy, damning the consequences of social distancing on the economy. The recession that followed, which many countries experienced, was a reflection of the difficult choice that policy makers had to make in choosing whether to save the economy before saving the people or to save the people before saving the economy; many countries chose the latter. There were

Table 10. Effect of COVID deaths on global macroeconomic variables

	Global energy commodity price index	World GDP growth	Global inflation rate	Global unemployment rate
	Coefficient (p-values)	**Coefficient (p-values)**	**Coefficient (p-values)**	
Total deaths	4.161* (0.083)	0.081 (0.83)	0.256* (0.85)	0.443** (0.02)
*, ** denotes significance at the 10% level and 5% level respectively				

criticisms that the policies were too fast, premature or insufficient, and that the policies contradicted one another in some areas, for instance, the accommodative monetary policy encouraged economic agents to engage in economic activities while the lockdowns and social-distancing (stay-at-home) policy prevented economic activities from taking place.

Although the negative effects, as shown in the results, are noteworthy, there is also a need to not waste this crisis because it creates an opportunity to introduce important reforms in the global health sector. On the bright side, the coronavirus-induced public health crisis created an opportunity for many governments to make lasting reforms in the public health sector. Some countries, like the UK and Spain, repaired their public health care system during their crisis. Other countries fixed the existing shortcomings in public infrastructure such as transportation systems, the disease detection systems in public hospitals, and preparing for the transition to online education. Some governments also used the crisis as an opportunity to fix the economic system and the financial system.

Our study has some limitations. The main limitation of this research paper is the short period of analysis due to limited dataset. The short dataset is because the COVID pandemic is ongoing at the time of writing. A longer study period may capture the socioeconomic consequences of government policies during the coronavirus crisis. Also, as future events unfold, there could be spillovers to other sectors that we did not analyse in this study. Future studies on spillovers could be extended to two directions. First, future studies can examine the impact on government policy on the informal economy. Second, it would be important to explore how banks and financial institutions react to economic policy developments during the coronavirus crisis.

REFERENCES

Allen, F., & Carletti, E. (2010). An overview of the crisis: Causes, consequences, and solutions. *International Review of Finance*, *10*(1), 1–26. doi:10.1111/j.1468-2443.2009.01103.x

Bagliano, F. C., & Morana, C. (2012). The Great Recession: US dynamics and spillovers to the world economy. *Journal of Banking & Finance*, *36*(1), 1–13. doi:10.1016/j.jbankfin.2011.06.002

Bentolila, S., Jansen, M., & Jiménez, G. (2018). When credit dries up: Job losses in the great recession. *Journal of the European Economic Association*, *16*(3), 650–695. doi:10.1093/jeea/jvx021

Bezemer, D. J. (2011). The credit crisis and recession as a paradigm test. *Journal of Economic Issues*, *45*(1), 1–18. doi:10.2753/JEI0021-3624450101

Bristol. (2020). *The government threw us under the bus': How Bristol food businesses are working to survive coronavirus.* Bristol Cable Media.

El-Erian, M. (2020). *The Coming Coronavirus Recession and the Uncharted Territory Beyond*. Foreign Affairs, Media Report. Available at: https://www.foreignaffairs.com/articles/2020-03-17/coming-coronavirus-recession

Financial Times. (2020). *Global recession already here, say top economists.* Available at: https://www.ft.com/content/be732afe-6526-11ea-a6cd-df28cc3c6a68

Gaiotti, E. (2013). Credit availability and investment: Lessons from the great recession. *European Economic Review, 59*, 212–227. doi:10.1016/j.euroecorev.2012.12.007

Georgieva, K. (2020). *IMF Managing Director Kristalina Georgieva's Statement Following a G20 Ministerial Call on the Coronavirus Emergency*. IMF Press statement. Available at: https://www.imf.org/en/News/Articles/2020/03/23/pr2098-imf-managing-director-statement-following-a-g20-ministerial-call-on-the-coronavirus-emergency

Horowit, J. (2020). *The global coronavirus recession is beginning.* CNN. Media Report. Available at: https://edition.cnn.com/2020/03/16/economy/global-recession-coronavirus/index.html

IATA. (2020). *Potential for revenue losses of $113bn due to COVID-19 crisis.* IATA.

Jagannathan, R., Kapoor, M., & Schaumburg, E. (2013). Causes of the great recession of 2007–2009: The financial crisis was the symptom not the disease. *Journal of Financial Intermediation, 22*(1), 4–29. doi:10.1016/j.jfi.2012.06.002

Larry Elliot, L. (2020). Prepare for the coronavirus global recession. *The Guardian*. Available at: https://www.theguardian.com/business/2020/mar/15/prepare-for-the-coronavirus-global-recession

Mian, A., & Sufi, A. (2010). The great recession: Lessons from microeconomic data. *The American Economic Review, 100*(2), 51–56. doi:10.1257/aer.100.2.51

Ozili, P. (2020b). COVID-19 in Africa: Socio-economic impact, policy response and opportunities. *The International Journal of Sociology and Social Policy*. Advance online publication. doi:10.1108/IJSSP-05-2020-0171

OziliP. K. (2020a). 100 Quotes from the Global Financial Crisis: Lessons for the future. *Available at* SSRN 3500921. doi:10.1108/978-1-80043-095-220201014

Radelet, S., & Sachs, J. (1998). *The onset of the East Asian financial crisis (No. w6680)*. National Bureau of Economic Research. doi:10.3386/w6680

Rady, D. A. M. (2012). Greece debt crisis: Causes, implications and policy options. *Academy of Accounting and Financial Studies Journal, 16*, 87.

Reuters. (2020). *Coronavirus, oil collapse erase $5 trillion from U.S. stocks*. Author.

Stiglitz, J. E. (2010). *Interpreting the Causes of the Great Recession of 2008. Financial system and macroeconomic resilience: revisited.* Bank for International Settlements.

Chapter 5
Relocation Strategy of Global Supply Chain and Value Chain Under Deglobalization

José G. Vargas-Hernández
https://orcid.org/0000-0003-0938-4197
Posgraduate and Research Department, Tecnológico Mario Molina Unidad Zapopan, Mexico

ABSTRACT

This chapter aims to critically analyze the implications that the national protectionist policies have on the global supply and value chains and the relocation of production. The analysis is based on the assumptions that the global economy is facing the possibility of decoupling of many trade connections, and this trend favors deglobalization processes that have long been promoted by populism, nationalism, and economic protectionism. It is concluded that global supply, production, and value chains, although being economically efficient, are no longer any more secure under national protectionist policies, and therefore, the relocation of production processes is mainly due to the increase in the level of income and wages of the developing countries that are the destination, and which reduce the advantages to relocate.

INTRODUCTION

This chapter discusses the relocation of the global supply chain. Due to globalization, supply chains behave globally. Materials and products have been transferred and manufacturing facilities have been allocated globally. On the other, deglobalization has occurred many times. It is almost impossible for a company to control globalization and deglobalization trend. However, companies construct supply chains and change their structure globally according to internal and external factors.

The processes of economic globalization are in difficulties, showing a contraction in international trade flows in 2019, which are aggravated by the responses that companies have given to the health emergency. The outbreak of the coronavirus pandemic has immediate negative effects with a considerable impact on global trade, investment, and financial flows. Coronavirus is changing the way the world does business for bad or good. Business corporations and companies are being forced to rethink their

DOI: 10.4018/978-1-6684-5876-1.ch005

global value, production, and logistics chains, shaped to maximize efficiency and profits. Resilience, recovery, and adaptation are becoming relevant in the world economy (Javorcik, 2020).

This analysis shows expansive periods of free trade alternate with other periods in which protectionist measures and the relocation of production are part of a process that is called deglobalization and is characterized by a reduction in export growth that is compensated with increased consumption of the domestic market to defend national interests. Some developed economies have trade imbalances with negative effects on less developed countries.

The current environment of economic, social, political and health instability has intensified the increase in the economic costs of transaction and coordination of the subsidiaries of multinational companies located in other international host territories, making relocation processes unviable, for which they have initiated processes of repression or de-globalization to return its production to the countries of origin. This situation has meant stagnation, and in some cases, a reversal in business strategy to deepen the globalization processes of companies (Meyer and Peng, 2016).

The level of economic integration in globalization processes is well advanced, as it has been shown that when production in some provinces of China is paralyzed, the supply of inputs to other companies from other nations has affected, a situation of vulnerability that has motivated deglobalization as a response that makes relocation more profitable with the repatriation of factories (Zhu et al., 2020).

This paper first makes a critical analysis of the national protectionist policies and its implications on the global supply and value chains and how these two factors determine the strategy of the relocation of production. Finally, a discussion is offered on these issues.

BACKGROUND

National Protectionism Policy

Protectionism has returned, and it will be having to think about it if it is wanted to reap all the benefits and implement this reasoned "deglobalization" that it called for and that now seems inevitable (Sapir, 2016). The term deglobalization was coined by Sapir (2011) to refer to the protectionism of countries that have a similar level of development and economic growth limited by the commercial and financial dimensions of globalization than through outsourcing and relocation processes of large companies, groups of production centers. Deglobalization processes are characterized by the recovery of the sovereignty of nations, reduction of their interdependence, implementation of automatic and protectionist policies to reduce economic and commercial relations.

In a protectionist policy, countries increase restrictions on the free flow of trade, finance, and people, reinforcing their national borders and are oriented towards deglobalization processes that threaten the internationalization of higher education, for example, which remains confined, although it is already advised to deepen the advancement of online education through platforms that reach all places, including the most remote places in the world (James, 2018). The concern about these changes is the depth in which they must occur to save and overcome the advances of globalization, so it can be considered that the advances will be different and different as it had been advancing before, although it is necessary that competition be promoted while cooperative and collaborative relationships are fostered.

Deglobalization is an inverse process to globalization that is manifested by the protectionist and regulatory economic and trade policies of the nation-states as well as the trade wars that are carried out between the great economic and commercial powers. To protect national production, domestic markets increase tariff barriers with the intensification of trade wars between western and eastern markets. What the health crisis has done is accelerate the process.

The international competition on economic systems in the world economy is reduced to economic structures and enterprises mechanisms of macroeconomic players supported by the strengthened functions of the state to stabilize macroeconomics, protect intellectual property rights, to ensure legality and enforcement of contracts, infrastructure provision, and other microeconomic policies to establish incentives and mechanisms for corporate governance, stimulating research and development, investments in human development. Protectionist, nationalist, and populist policies can be functional or dysfunctional depending on their correct design and implementation.

Some of the phenomena that disappointed the scope of the globalization economy were job insecurity and flexibility due to stagnant wages and rising unemployment. The far right has channeled discontent to promote protectionist measures. These situations have given rise to deglobalization processes through the implementation of protectionist economic policies. A greater presence of the State is necessary in the face of the challenges of economic growth, greater economic and social equality, social inclusion, environmental sustainability, protection of biodiversity and conservation of socio-ecosystems, the energetic and climate crisis, etc.

History of National Protectionism Policy

During the winter war era from 1914 to 1945, from the outbreak of World War I until the end of World War II, globalization processes were in retreat from the first time, after a period of increased economic integration from 1870 until 1914 (Broadberry and Harrison, 2005). After the First World War, protectionism and nationalism were on the rise as international institutions and organizations weakened, but the economic depression deepened. After the year 1918, with the rise of nationalism, international organizations were weakened, an economic depression arose that drove national states to protective economic models.

The abandonment of global economic integration is an option for nation-states framed by a Keynesian scheme through the implementation of protectionist trade measures and maintaining democracy. These methods favored the economic growth of some developed countries that later embraced economic globalization (Rodrik, 2000 and 2007; Steinberg, 2007, p. 45). The countries that remained with borders closed to trade through protectionist and nationalist measures were imposed asymmetric trade conditions, as was the case with the colonies. When these nations achieved their independence, they could already take off in their economic and social development.

After the Second World War, a system of international governance institutions was established with the programs of the Marshall Plan, the Bretton Woods institutions, the United Nations (UN), and the General Agreement on Customs Tariffs (GATT) (Reinalda, 2009). During this period of globalization, retreatment and economic dislocation led to reduced integration, the Great Depression and protectionism as the solution. After World War II, and until the 1980s, new global institutions for economic cooperation were created and developed to promote economic integration and enable national economies to be opened to foreign markets (Spero and Hart, 1997). In 1989 the slow food movement was created to protect the consumption of local products, cultures, traditions, and gastronomic customs perceived as healthier and safer (Petrini, 2001). The movement aims to create awareness of decisions for food consumption and its origin.

During the international financial crisis of 2008 and 2009, the leaders of the most advanced economies managed adequately to avoid the trend of protectionist economic nationalism. The national state recovers functions that were taken from it and, together with international institutions, assumes responsibilities to protect national economies and societies. In 2017, China promoted globalization as a mechanism for economic integration, generating wealth and multilateral cooperation, while the United States promoted trade protectionism (Liu et al., 2018). Protectionist trade policies used as an instrument for multilateral and bilateral negotiations do not always result in benefits for the country that promotes them, as has been recently demonstrated in the case of the United States, which has encountered strong resistance from the trend of economic globalization processes.

Modern National Protectionism Policy in North America

In 2018, many North American companies announced the relocation and transfer of their production plants back to the national territory. In 2019, the Kearney index detected a strategic trend in company production towards a greater weight of the "made in America" content of manufacturing production (Doh et al., 2021). In part, this was achieved by the warning that if they wanted to receive the protection of the American legal system, they should return the jobs. European countries grant aid through anti-crisis plans to their companies that disengage from tax havens.

Following North American policy, France encourages the repatriation of its companies, while Japan favors its companies that return from China with incentives. Nation-states have difficulty regulating the financialization that dominates the real economy and offshore strategies, as well as putting limits on the power of monopolies in the digital economy (Rasiah et al., 2010).

The unilateral discourses practiced by some powers attempt to control the world agenda of globalization processes through neo-protectionist mechanisms under the world economy revolving around a multipolarity. Geo-economics and geopolitical analyzes show a transition of leadership from the global economy to China. Now the United States plays the option of a more protectionist economy that drastically affects the economies that are more dependent on global trade. However, the slowdown in economic globalization began long before the pandemic, which has contributed to accelerating it by declining national economies.

The goal of the new United States government was to eliminate the trade deficit through the implementation of protectionist and nationalist fiscal policies, and started a trade war against its trading partners, but above all with China, its main competitor, but which had repercussions worldwide, because it drastically reduced world trade. The elimination of the deficit simply to date, has not been achieved, but also worsened and deepened. The coronavirus health crisis imposed a truce on the trade war that paralyzed the negotiations of trade relations. However, the largest producer of medical supplies is in China (Qin, 2020). With the health crisis, countries want to maintain their own economic activities and be in proximity through protectionism. Consistent with this, multinational companies plan to repatriate in reshoring part of their international production.

The world economy faced threats in its globalization process long before the 2020 health crisis, such as the growing challenge of trade wars and the protectionism of the economies of different national states with the implementation of a tariff war. The health crisis is the result of negative externalities of an interconnected world in globalization processes that are perceived to be linked to physical security in identity and economic spheres, whose responsibility to protect against risks has fallen more on the nation-state rather than on the international community.

Economic Deglobalization Trend

The health crisis caused by the pandemic has accelerated the protectionist tendencies and the populist and nationalist policies of the nations and has caused tensions and trade wars in the face of the fall in international trade flows and foreign direct investment. The health crisis has accelerated and deepened this trend of economic deglobalization through protectionist actions, reduction of multilateral treaties, etc., with economic consequences that are legible, but uncertain and unpredictable (Didea and Ilie, 2020).

The protectionist tensions that lead to a trade war constitute a reconsideration in the opposite direction to the progress of trade liberalization. This situation that arises unilaterally resists the continued opening of markets and international economies to position itself as a closed economy, erodes economic, commercial, and political relations with its partners. In other words, the country that was the greatest promoter of economic globalization processes is now the greatest opponent of deepening economic, commercial, and financial relations.

The liberalization of regulations of local financial markets that protected the host countries from foreign investments allows MNES to have access to local natural resources and get actively involved in local markets. Because of this deregulation, the global FDI flows had increased regularly until 2000 and since then it had been falling until it reached a peak in 2007 (World Bank, 2016).

Now local governments have tried to implement different initiatives with protectionist measures against global markets since 2008, as ways to recover the economic growth of their economies, resulting in limitations to international trade. All these initiatives are strengthened to weaken the processes of economic globalization and cry out for deglobalization (Irwin, 2020). After the subprime crisis, citizens demand to governments for protection of their own interests against the globalization interest through the redesign and implementation of more protective economic and financial liberalization policies.

The processes of economic globalization are being pressured by isolationist positions that seek to deepen the self-sufficiency of national states to protect local interests over global interests. These changes in perspective have implications and effects on the harmonious development of people. The national state recovers relevant functions in this process of deglobalization for the financial rescue in the face of the economic debacle of important economic actors and agents, such as multinational companies and financial institutions (Napolitano, 2011). The new scheme is configured with less market and more state with a geopolitical reconfiguration of national borders evidenced in return to nationalist protectionism and more controls on cross-border financial transactions.

Factors such as technology-based automation, protectionist practices in national economies, rapid shipments, and deliveries, among many other factors, contribute to the acceleration of the processes of slowing down or reversing globalization. Rather, the concern is diverted towards how profound these changes that are already occurring will be, but above all in the way they are going to be managed. These trends are driven by rising wages in countries that previously offered low labor cost advantages, as well as protectionism in local economies.

The restrictive and protectionist economic policy measures that materialize in the deglobalization processes are, among the most common, the increase in tariff rates, the establishment of phytosanitary measures, cross-border labor restrictions, limitations on foreign investment, control of movements immigration, trade wars, etc. (Gaillard, 2020). As part of protectionist measures, importers raise their tariff barriers in response to the trade war.

Nation-states are receding, driven by protectionist trends due to falling global trade and investment flows driven by the health crisis. With the health crisis of the pandemic, the nation-states enact protectionist, deglobalizing economic policy measures that reduce and retract the advance of globalization processes, such as, for example, the closure of the border to commercial exchange activities and nationalist control of migratory movements of the population. Nation-states adopt nationalist, populist, and protective economic policies to recover their regulatory functions and fields of action in a gradual process of control of globalizing dynamics.

Trade protectionism is the relevant element of deglobalization for protecting the losers of globalization, assuring gains through imposing high rates of industrial and trade protection and imposing manufacturing tariffs (Findlay and O'Rourke, 2008, p. 401). Trade protectionism is a relevant action implemented in this deglobalization process. Deglobalization processes have repercussions that damage the economies that promote protectionist economic policies. The lack of leadership in the globalization processes makes it easier for each nation to reverse or at least slow down progress by adopting more protectionist measures.

National markets and economies are now less dependent on international markets and rely on the regulations of national economies to protect themselves. To exploit the advantages offered by the new environment, an emerging strategy has emerged that supports the resurgence of protection measures for national markets. The deglobalization of economic integration processes moves the center of gravity back from the market to the sustainable local market through a commercial policy and the use of fiscal, tariff, and quota mechanisms to protect the national production of transnational companies (IMCO, 2020). The uniformity and standardization of commercial regulations threaten regional and local development where the asymmetric is normal for self-protection.

Therefore, the protectionist attempt of an economy has a negative impact on national companies in such a way that the protectionist measures taken unilaterally by a country, and damages the competitiveness of its companies and, therefore, its own economy. It is the same multinational companies that promote the relocation of production, distribution, and consumption processes. Countries now attempt to relocate the production of goods within or near their national borders for the benefit of integrated regions through tariff protection measures.

The deglobalization process is supported by the promotion of protectionist measures and is characterized by export flows, investments, migratory movements, and technological innovation that are reduced or diminished, are reflected in political and economic decisions to orient themselves to domestic demand with measures with tariffs, cross-border restrictions and limitations on investment and foreign labor (Shavshukov and Zhuravleva, 2020).

Greater attention to domestic demand leads governments to reduce the growth of exports through direct or indirect protectionist measures. Countries alone are unlikely to oppose globalization given the omnipotence of global financial markets, so the alternative is to recur to the risks of trade wars more focused on national protectionism. National governments grant tax incentives that benefit protectionism and populism for the repatriation of manufacturing plants and investments. Manufacturing employment is likely to decline while most forms of services employments are likely to be heavily protected from internationalization, therefore avoiding anti-globalization backlashes focus more on improving the quality and provision.

The same powers that before spread the gospel of open market and free trade are the same that now predicate protectionism and support deglobalization markets. It has been said that the global economic and financial elites pursue the creation of a world government by centralizing order and power by protecting from enemies through a surveillance system based on traceability (Vanham, 2019)

Cultural globalization and an increase of human interactions have been the result of the economic, financial, and trade exchanges, contributing to the different values, traditions, customs, habits, etc., are being shared among local communities and other communities in such a way that it is homogenizing a world's culture. Local culture requires protection to maintain its uniqueness at a community level, environmental and development social movements and activists need the support of the nation-state to defend society to defend and protect society from the destructive capacities of economic globalization and global market to exploit the human and natural resources.

MAIN FOCUS

The entire global economic structure is reeling from the health crisis of the pandemic. Governments of Nation-states and corporations are assessing the global market as a growing source of disruption of global value, production, and logistics chains, as well as the source of risk and competitive disadvantages. Local governments are retracting global policies of economic integration and are increasing the protectionist policies for the repatriation of manufacturers (Abdal and Ferreira, 2021). However, other national economies have already developed capabilities to become resilient, recovering, restructuring, and enhancing the new institutional governance emerging from the pandemic.

Global Supply and Value Chain

Trade openness, economics, financial and commercial liberalization, information, and communication technology innovations facilitated the special and operational expansion of transnational and multinational corporations which in turn, contributed to altering the exchange of resources flows and supply chains between intra and inter firm as well as to a global power redistribution. Economic globalization processes accelerated the flow of goods through global supply chains and global trade (Kano et al., 2020).

The development of ICTs and the emergence of the Internet accelerated the processes of globalization with world communication in real time and, with financial digitization and the logistical development of supply and value chains, accelerated the scope of a global economy. Technological and scientific advances have intensified with economic globalization with the monopolistic emergence of digital companies that control the financialization of processes around global supply and value chains where BRICS countries have become the managers of changes in global competitiveness (Barykin et al., 2021).

The value chains as well as the supply chains of the companies in a global economy scenario are distributed throughout the world. Multinational and transnational corporations have established networks of supply chains, subcontractors, and logistics around the world. The networking-based global economy is formed by chains developed by a large group of shadow enterprises that are connected for economic activities across the boundaries of countries and makes meaningless the concept of distance and national borders.

In a competitive global market, the costs of the entire chain of supply, production, and consumption spread worldwide should be the lowest (Bello, 2013). However, globalization is based on the economies of scale and scope due to the location of production where is most efficient is over, while the concern is for the fragility of supply-chain diversification because their processes rely on each other to add their value.

The global production and distribution chains show the fragility of the high dependence on the processes of economic globalization to provide products and inputs to the economies that require them to continue their manufacturing processes. This failure in global production chains has exposed the weaknesses of national security and national industry, arguments that support protectionist positions, such as measures to guarantee supply in national markets. The national security policy acquires greater force by pressing for reversions in global production chains encouraged by supply decisions in local markets.

Starting in the 1990s, global production and value chains grew steadily. Since 2007, with the outbreak of the economic and financial crisis, the indicators of globalization processes show a trend of decrease in global production and supply chains due to a drop in demand from international markets and not so much to the structural changes. Since the financial crisis of 2008-2009, world trade has failed to maintain the level of world GDP due to the emergence of protectionist policies (WTO, 2021). Global economic, financial, health, and contingency crises such as natural disasters have a domino effect that has a greater impact on global production and value chains (FAO, 2021). An example is the tsunami in Japan in 2011 that affected global automobile production chains.

These stagnations in economic globalization processes have negative effects on the global economy due to the relocation of the production chain, although the reorientation may have some positive effects for certain national territories where some phases of this production chain can be carried out to take advantage of low labor costs. Reversing or slowing down the processes of economic globalization will mean changes in the practices and activities of multinational and transnational companies.

Fragmentation of Global Supply Chain

In 2019 there is a high fragmentation of global supply chains, which is deepened by the 2020 health crisis. The ruptures of global supply chains produce a dislocation of production that produces in response to the withdrawal of companies located abroad for The Coronavirus has paralyzed the growth of global trade, which contributes to more than 60% of the domestic product world gross (Ellyat, 2021). This situation has been called deglobalization, aggravated by the health crisis, which has made interconnections more difficult for commercial practices between different countries.

The current scenario of the health crisis has affected the complex global supply and value chains of intermediate goods without being able to stop their fragmentation. This has shown that global supply chains are very vulnerable and complicated for companies to immediately redesign and redirect, which has accelerated de-globalization processes.

The critical situation of the health crisis has forced the space of global logistics and supply chains to be reduced to be replaced by shorter chains in such a way that the localities for the supply of raw materials and production of inputs or parts of a product must be shorter than the places where the final product is assembled (Shih, 2020). The health crisis has highlighted the limitations of global logistics and supply chains in sectors such as electronics, automotive, aeronautical, medical equipment, pharmaceutical products, textile industry, etc. The health crisis has broken global production chains.

The inability of the globalization processes to find a way out of the relocation of the production and supply chains, as well as the inability of the national industry in many countries to produce the required sanitary material, has complicated the economic scenario. The health crisis has exposed the dysfunctionality of global and multinational supply chains, placing excessively dependent companies at vulnerability (Baldwin and di Mauro, 2020). The health crisis has affected the global production chains of countries that are prone to international trade, although it is contradictory that it depends on corporate companies that originally relocated their production processes.

The dependence on imports of inputs for national production through supply chains, has been affected by the health crisis, so many nation-states have accelerated the processes of deglobalization by strengthening the production of inputs and operations in local spaces. Deglobalization processes imply having greater controls over commercial, financial, migration, travel flows, etc., which gives rise to retreats in the global supply and production chains.

Protecting and stimulating national food supply chains can help reduce the impact caused by the health crisis of the pandemic. Global supply and value chains have proven to be inoperative amid the health crisis (Bardt et al., 2021). Multinational corporations transferred their production operations to places where costs were lower, achieving supply through long global supply chains, which were suddenly interrupted during the Covid-19 health crisis, with serious threats to paralyze the production of certain essential products such as ago-food.

Relocation of Production and Supply Chain

Deglobalization processes attempt to unlink local production from global supply chains to reorient production towards the internal market supported by movements in favor of food self-sufficiency and sovereignty based on domestic industrial and agricultural production, undertaken by economic policies and progressive commercials and not by right-wing nationalist governments that only serve the interests of the dominant ethnic and cultural group and displace minorities and immigrants.

With the emergence of the health crisis of the pandemic, countries have had to reconsider their supply chains and value of strategic production activities, as in the case of food production. For this reason, strategic production industries are a priority for national development, which is why they are maintained and strengthened with actions such as the development of local, flexible, and fast supply chains of value chains (Boiral et al., 2021).

Globalization undergoes profound changes with the crisis of the coronavirus pandemic and will not be as we knew it before in the modes of production, distribution, and consumption and in the global production, supply, and value chains. The dynamics of contemporary globalization processes have registered a strong interruption that calls into question the entire international economic system, disrupts global supply and value chains, as well as a slowdown in all economic sectors.

The continuity of the processes of economic globalization requires leading the mitigation of the negative impacts in the production and supply chains in the global economy based on the location in places where costs are lower. The priorities of the production, distribution, and consumption systems are changing their priorities through the location of supply chains as secure as possible rather than as economically as possible as was achieved during globalization (Ibn-Mohammed et al., 2021). The economic efficiencies of globalization processes are being highly questioned with the dysfunctionality of global supply chains that lead to more protectionist economic and fiscal policies.

Deglobalization process

Deglobalization is a period of slowdown and decline in international economic, commercial, financial, and people flows intensified by the coronavirus that has made companies rethink the risks of global supply chains that occur in remote locations. The economic phenomenon of deglobalization of the world economy is a period marked by a decline in commercial and financial flows, intensified by the coronavirus pandemic that has caused a rethinking of the risks of the global chain of supplies that come from geographically remote locations. Disruption of the supply chains of local companies dependent on a global system generates economic losses.

With the interruption of global production and supply chains, and due to perceived risks, production and consumption turn to alternative sources of inputs, goods, and services from local suppliers, passing the acquisition cost to second term Economic deglobalization. Witt (2019) considers the strategic policies that affect the political sustainability of multinational companies, the dynamic organizations of value chain specializations and the national context in which these decisions about strategies, structures, and behaviors are made. The breakdown of global supply chains has direct consequences on the profitability of many of these multinational companies.

The main cause that has given rise to the deglobalization processes, the slowdown in the growth of the global economy, the regression of global supply and value chains, and the increase in protectionism of local economies against multilateral processes, is the reduction of the concerns about external dependence on essential supplies (Abdal and Ferreira, 2021). The regression of global supply and value logistics chains go into regression processes for different causes, such as protectionism, wage increases, and the level of income reduce the advantages of countries that were the destination of relocations. If production is less delocalized, flows in global supply and value chains are reduced, along with the investments that accompany them.

The interruption of global supply chains and, therefore, of value is a consequence of the trade wars started by countries with deficiencies in commercial and financial exchanges. The Sino-US trade war is the landmark event for furthering the tendency of deglobalization with the disruption of the global supply chain and declining global trade flows in value and volume.

The trade wars coupled with the risks of the coronavirus have caused the blockage of global supply chains and international supplies. They have been shortening their global supply and value chains for several years now, because of trade wars, through the relocation of their plants, production processes, and the manufacture of their own components that came from distant locations and through the diversification of the origin of inputs and products. Companies around the world rethink their internationalization decisions as a reaction to dependence on global supply chains that distribute the production of products with the relocation of their plants and their production processes (Nandi et al., 2021). This situation has shown the vulnerability of companies due to their excessive dependence on these chains.

Effect of deglobalization

Deglobalization manifests itself in changes in production systems based on the locations where production is most efficient, leading to many logistical mismatches in supply chains and value in trade connections. The creation of alternative supply chains modifies the rules of globalization processes. For the United States, the intensity of globalization shows vulnerabilities, such as in situations where national economies depend on a single country for the supply of goods, which leads to the blockage of supply chains (Nandi et al., 2021).

Global supply chains are more complex in the production, distribution, and consumption of products that have had to be interrupted or reduced due to the lack of provision of essential components. Globalization is transformed to be different than it was before the pandemic and it is possible that the modes of production, distribution, and consumption are transformed due to changes in the global value, provision, and supply chains.

Destructuring the networks in which currently major strategic activities are included in supply chains, production, management, and distribution on a global scale are organized and interconnected in real time on a sophisticated information and communication system. Companies are moving away from just-in-time production systems to more secure supply chains. The reduction of global supply and value chains negatively affects commercial, financial, investment and people flow. The deglobalization processes are pressing the global production, provision, and value chains to change in organizational forms subject to local decisions.

Multinational companies are already reconsidering their logistics processes for the transport of goods that include socio-ecosystem concerns to try to shorten geographic distances and links in their global supply chains through the use and development of new technologies that reduce the costs and risks of production, increase quality, and respond more quickly to market demand. Multinational companies reconfigure global value chains to strengthen themselves in the face of shocks.

National economies are bounded together in globalization through the supply chains to achieve manufacturing efficiency and better prices in international trade. The flow of international business activities is retracted as global supply and supply chains are reconfigured, prioritizing production over economic efficiency. Business organizations are assessing the location of global supply chains relocating their production elsewhere, which is a globalization trend of natural churn and premises (Paul and Dhir, 2021). International trade replicates its operations while reconfiguring its supply chains sacrificing economic efficiencies in exchange for greater security in the provision of its inputs. International trade is territorially withdrawn to the nation through the reconfiguration of its production chains and supply, leading to importers raising tariff barriers.

Populist and nationalist nation-states have taken up this message, supported by political parties and social organizations to promote actions to deglobalize the economy that attempt to dismantle globalization through withdrawals of global value chains, repatriation of investments, and strategic relocation of Business.

Global supply chains are relocated, which implies the reorganization of production, distribution, and commercialization activities, reinforced with government policies, especially in sectors considered of national security. Returning plants to the country of origin can be more expensive, but in the current conditions of interrupted global supply chains, it turns out to be more productive and competitive due to savings in logistics risks, transportation, tariffs, etc. The reduction of dependence on the provision of supplies from other geographically distant locations through global chains of manufactured inputs has led to relocation or reshoring trends. Not only are the production sites relocated close to the markets, but also innovation, design, logistics, distribution, marketing activities, etc.

New technologies advance innovations in automation, robotization, artificial intelligence, internet of things, etc., which tend to replace the more routine and cheap labor, which implies that global supply and value chains reduce their importance with localized and robotic production.

The deglobalization trend converted into regional trade agreements allows economies to be fully integrated and to take advantage of regional and local value chains. From the crisis that economic globalization is going through, companies that have fewer global supply chains, more regional and therefore shorter with respect to assembly or marketing lines, will emerge strengthened, not necessarily from lower cost suppliers and with minimal inventory levels, which confirms deglobalization. The interruptions of the global supply chains forced people and companies to look for alternative local or regional sources of supply, even though they were more expensive.

The less advanced economies have seen their global value chains reduced with premature processes of deindustrialization, lower economic growth, a commodity boom that has given rise to the Dutch disease phenomenon, non-redistributive and regressive fiscal reforms with an increase in income levels of poverty and inequality. Countries are backtracking in their globalization advances and trying to avoid the continuity of outsourced production chains to maintain strategic production activities internally or as regionally as possible, with more flexible and faster local value chains.

The blockade of global supply chains represents the opportunity for Mexico to be the beneficiary due to its proximity to the North American market, as has been the case in the automotive, electronics, and aeronautical sectors. Without the supplies produced in Mexico by these industrial sectors, the manufacturing of finished products is interrupted. Deglobalization and the T-MEC favor the rapid integration of the sectors of the electrical, automotive, medical equipment, aeronautical, pharmaceutical, aeronautical industries, etc., to the supply chains of North American companies. Complementation among the member countries of the T-MEC facilitates regional integration processes and solves the problem of supply and logistics chains.

Risk assessment focuses on disturbances in production processes mainly due to supply chains of inputs that come from geographically distant locations, or other phenomena such as natural disasters, wars, etc. One of the risks that are run with deglobalization is derived from geopolitical and geoeconomics uncertainty and its impact on investments with repercussions on production levels for global supply chains, exports, and market volatility. Companies have reacted to the perception of risks through a strategy of geographic diversification of sources of supply and production that can affect global trade as production is relocated in the country itself.

The inability of the globalization processes to find a way out of the relocation of the production and supply chains, as well as the inability of the national industry in many countries to produce the required sanitary material, has complicated the economic scenario.

SOLUTIONS AND RECOMMENDATIONS

In a free market system under the invisible hand, companies continue to track the location of their production, distribution, and consumption systems through offshoring or relocation decisions that mean benefits and cost efficiency. Tensions and trade wars accelerated the de-globalization processes under the premise of relocating the production and supply of resources from sources as close as possible, which confirms the trend towards open regionalism.

The processes of economic and financial de-globalization propose that local economies should be reoriented in short circuits towards production for local consumption, avoiding the relocation of companies that generate competition because they look for places where labor costs are lower, production standards and ecological are less restrictive, etc. On the other hand, foreign direct investment movements facilitate the relocation of production systems in global factories, taking advantage of the advantages offered by other national economies in cheap labor, more direct transport systems, the privatization of public companies, etc. The relocation of production is manifested in the flows of direct foreign investment (Grunwald and Flamm, 1985).

The relocation of production processes is mainly due to the increase in the level of income and wages of the developing countries that are the destination, which reduces the advantages to relocating. Delocalized production of companies motivated by lower production costs is returning to a closer place through relocation or reshoring processes. Discontent over the growing impoverishment of the working middle classes in the most developed countries, the precariousness of employment and labor benefits, and the loss of employment due to the relocation and flight of companies to locations where labor costs are lower. The advantages for relocating production, distribution, and consumption systems have been reduced due to an increase in the income and living standards of workers in the countries that were the destination of these relocations.

There are several reasons that are making the processes of economic globalization dysfunctional to the growth and development of some countries, such as the loss of their political and economic sovereignty, growth in unemployment due to the relocation of production, and the increase in automated systems and robotization, which also reduces relocations.

Companies have reacted to the perception of risks through a strategy of geographic diversification of sources of supply and production that can affect global trade as production is relocated in the country itself. Extraterritoriality characterizes economic globalization (Palomares, 2006, p. 30) because of the capacity that transnational companies must relocate production with geographic fragmentation. In such a way, this trend of regional proximity of production occurs, pointing to the relocation of production processes in countries that belong to the same economic region. The processes of regionalization of production are a trend in proximity to consumer markets that ensures the supply of resources, goods, and services in places to consumer markets to respond quickly and flexibly to demand through customization or product customization.

With globalization, companies become more dependent on the places from which the inputs and products necessary for production are provided, so national states are now offering incentives to their companies to return operations that they had relocated to other countries. The continuity of the processes of economic globalization currently marks a break in the breakdown of international economic relations that, although it attempts to relocate production, the competition for the attraction of talent, technology, and more advanced production capacity.

Relocation as a strategy of deglobalization processes has as immediate consequences the increase in labor costs due to differentials between nations, but also to the health crisis, with a tendency to reduce economic inequality. Another trend that accelerates because of relocation is robotization, which in times of pandemic is positive because it reduces the risks of contagion by eliminating or reducing face-to-face contacts. Another trend is the increase and consolidation of teleworking, with many implications for people's movements and the market for office space, parking lots, etc.

The increase in e-commerce is a trend that increases more with relocation and the health crisis of the pandemic. Pandemics have shown the risks that the globalized economy has under the logic of relocation of production to take advantage of lower costs that are then marketed in other regions of the world without establishing the pertinent health controls.

FUTURE RESEARCH DIRECTIONS

Deglobalization processes and their implications on global supply chains remain a topic for future research, which can be presented in scenarios of their future development. A first scenario is one of the soft changes that do not modify the structures of international institutions but that focus on regulating distortions to free trade, as well as the conditions imposed on developing countries. The deconstruction of globalization processes, known as deglobalization, must be for a better reconstruction that truly integrates humanity through economic, political, and social change, and does not disintegrate. This change requires weakening the hegemony of the system of globalizing institutional powers, delegitimizing its ideology and its rules.

On the implications of digital technologies in supply chain values, international governance needs the potential transformation of information and communication technologies for the research and analysis of big data. The integration of the process of economic globalization requires the use of digital technologies for the world government function through the institutionalization, market, and global redistribution functions. The design and implementation of economic policies to promote the positive effects of the digital and political dimensions and eliminate the negative ones of economic globalization processes, enhance global governance and economic integration.

Another important issue to study in the future is the relocation of companies to places of production and local consumption. It is supported by protectionist regulations, recovery of customs fees on imported goods and services, control of capital transfers, levies on financial transactions.

Another topic to be considered for future research is the current deglobalization processes that show a clear subordination of emerging and less developed countries to powerful international financial interests, international organizations, and multinational companies. The construction of alternative integration processes requires national initiatives under a scheme different from the capitalist financial and transnational capital, not only at the economic and commercial level, which is supported by self-organization and self-management to satisfy social needs. These alternative processes of deglobalization have multiple economic, social, environmental, political, sociocultural, gender dimensions, etc. For the deglobalization alternatives to deepen their changes, they must acquire the character of anti-capitalism.

An analysis should be conducted on the difficulties for the processes of economic globalization to be completely reversed, after necessary adjustments that have slowed down progress to overcome the health crisis and the crisis of neoliberal financial capitalism. The construction of alternative integration processes requires national initiatives under a scheme different from the capitalist financial and transnational capital, not only at the economic and commercial level, which is supported by self-organization and self-management to satisfy social needs. These alternative processes of deglobalization have multiple economic, social, environmental, political, sociocultural, gender dimensions, etc.

CONCLUSION

The post-pandemic world economy tends to be less globalized as it is rejected by national governments and populations to protect their national economies. The processes of economic globalization are deepening instead of a gradual process of deglobalization, under the argument of the principle of sovereignty with economic policies and measures that show a tendency towards a nationalist, protectionist, and populist retreat. The actions of national states and international organizations promoting globalization processes such as regional integration treaties for free trade tend to weaken the sovereignty of the states. This is somewhat paradoxical in its contradictory processes due to its origin of globalized localisms that have contributed to strengthening hierarchies and inequalities both between nations and between individuals. It creates victims who lack the protection of the state subject to their localities or force the state to abandon them.

The world order that has prevailed since the Second World War has been considered under the conception of linear processes of irreversible economic globalization and has undergone structural changes in the last ten years that require reconfiguration. This reconfiguration has been called a deglobalization stage and corresponds to a regression of global integration processes in the form of retractions in world trade and international financial investments carried out through nationalist, populist, and protectionist policies.

The movement of trade protectionism as a retreat from the processes of economic globalization with the renegotiation of trade agreements and trade wars was initiated by the United States. The trade war declared by the United States against China tries to weaken its strategic position in economic growth, cooperation, trade, finance, etc. The phenomenon of deglobalization is a popular political cause motivated by protectionist and reindustrializing economic forces.

The nation-states face great challenges to guarantee the protection of the minimum welfare of the citizens. Another consequence of the reversal of the global integration of production processes is the increase in costs and, therefore, consumer prices, which results in a drop in welfare. From an ethical perspective, deglobalization processes should give higher priority to values over interests, cooperative relationships over the competition, and community welfare over efficiency. From this same perspective, real economic thinking strengthens the values of social solidarity, justice, equity, and community to subordinate the action of the market.

Local economies must exercise fiscal and economic policy mechanisms for the protection of their own production, distribution, and consumption systems, as well as their socio-ecosystems from the subsidized importation of large transnational corporations that establish subsidized and artificial prices. A viable alternative as a sample is the emergence of large self-centered spaces that are constituted as poles of economic, political, social, cultural, and civilization power.

The new nationalist and protectionist sentiments that drive the decisions of the n countries have a high impact on migrant workers who seek better economic conditions and greater well-being for their families. Nation-states can prevent the flight of endogenous technological talent to other economies by creating institutional and instrumental frameworks for the establishment and protection of competitive advantages through reindustrialization processes.

REFERENCES

Abdal, A., & Ferreira, D. M. (2021). Deglobalization, Globalization, and the Pandemic: Current Impasses of the Capitalist World-Economy. *Journal of World-systems Research*, *27*(1), 202–230. doi:10.5195/jwsr.2021.1028

Baldwin, R., & di Mauro, B. W. (Eds.). (2020). *Economics in the time of COVID-19*. CEPR Press.

Bardt, H., Ezell, S., Flores, T., González, N., Hattingh, C., Randolph, S., & Bandini, C. (2021). *Global Value Chains After the COVID-19 Crisis*. Global Trade and Innovation Policy Alliance.

Barykin, S. E., Kapustina, I. V., Korchagina, E. V., Sergeev, S. M., Yadykin, V. K., Abdimomynova, A., & Stepanova, D. (2021). Digital Logistics Platforms in the BRICS Countries: Comparative Analysis and Development Prospects. *Sustainability*, *13*(20), 11228. doi:10.3390u132011228

Bello, W. (2013). *Capitalism's Last Stand? Deglobalization in the Age of Austerity*. Zed Books. doi:10.5040/9781350218895

Boiral, O., Brotherton, M.-C., Rivaud, L., & Guillaumie, L. (2021). Organizations' Management of the COVID-19 Pandemic: A Scoping Review of Business Articles. *Sustainability*, *2021*(13), 3993. doi:10.3390u13073993

Broadberry, S., & Harrison, M. (2005). *The economics of World War I*. Cambridge University Press. doi:10.1017/CBO9780511497339

Didea, L., & Ilie, D. M (2020). The State of Emergency and the Economic Repercussions. A New "Avalanche" of Insolvencies. *J.L. & Admin. Sci.*, *89*(13).

Doh, J., Budhwar, P., & Wood, G. (2021). Long-term energy transitions and international business: Concepts, theory, methods, and a research agenda. *Journal of International Business Studies*, *52*(5), 951–970. doi:10.105741267-021-00405-6 PMID:33716348

Ellyat, H. (2021). *Supply chain chaos is already hitting global growth. And it's about to get worse*. CNBC.

FAO. (2021). *The impact of disasters and crises on agriculture and food security*. Food and Agriculture Organization of United Nations.

Findlay, R., & O'Rourke, K. (2008). *Power and Plenty: Trade, War, and the World Economy in the Second Millennium*. Princeton University Press.

Gaillard, N. (2020). *Country Risk. Subtitle The Bane of Foreign Investors*. Springer., doi:10.1007/978-3-030-45788-4

Grunwald, J., & Flamm, K. (1985). *The global factory: Foreign assembly in international trade*. Brookings Institution.

Ibn-Mohammed, T., Mustapha, K. B., Godsell, J., Adamu, Z., Babatunde, K. A., Akintade, D. D., Acquaye, A., Fujii, H., Ndiaye, M. M., Yamoah, F. A., & Koh, S. C. L. (2021). *A critical analysis of the impacts of COVID-19 on the global economy and ecosystems and opportunities for circular economy strategies*. https://www.sciencedirect.com/science/article/pii/S0921344920304869 doi:10.1016/j.resconrec.2020.105169

IMCO. (2020). *Deglobalization. Implications for investors*. Oxford Economics.

Irwin, D. A. (2020). *The pandemic adds momentum to the deglobalization trend*. Peterson Institute for International Economics.

James, H. (2018). Deglobalization: The Rise of Disembedded Unilateralism. *Annual Review of Financial Economics*, *10*(1), 219–237. doi:10.1146/annurev-financial-110217-022625

Javorcik, B. (2020). Coronavirus will Change the Way the World Does Business for Good Businesses will be Forced to Rethink their Global Value Chains. *Financial Times*.

Kano, L., Tsang, E. W. K., & Yeung, H. (2020). Wc. (2020). Global value chains: A review of the multi-disciplinary literature. *Journal of International Business Studies*, *51*(4), 577–622. doi:10.105741267-020-00304-2

Liu, W., Dunford, M., & Gao, B. A. (2018). Discursive construction of the Belt and Road Initiative: From neo-liberal to inclusive globalization. *Journal of Geographical Sciences*, *28*(9), 1199–1214. doi:10.100711442-018-1520-y

Meyer, K., & Peng, M. (2016). Theoretical foundations of emerging economy business research. *Journal of International Business Studies*, *47*(1), 3–22. doi:10.1057/jibs.2015.34

Nandi, S., Sarkis, J., Hervani, A. A., & Helms, M. M. (2021). Redesigning Supply Chains using Blockchain-Enabled Circular Economy and COVID-19 Experiences. *Sustainable Production and Consumption*. https://www.sciencedirect.com/science/article/pii/S2352550920313592 doi:10.1016/j.spc.2020.10.019

Napolitano, G. (2011, April). The two ways of global governance after the financial crisis: Multilateralism versus cooperation among governments. *International Journal of Constitutional Law*, *9*(2), 310–339. doi:10.1093/icon/mor038

Palomares, G. (2006). *Relaciones internacionales en el siglo XXI*. Tecnos.

Paul, J., & Dhir, S. (Eds.). (2021). *Globalization, Deglobalization, and New Paradigms in Business*. Palgrave Macmillan. doi:10.1007/978-3-030-81584-4

Petrini, C. (2001). *Slow food, the case for taste*. Columbia University Press.

Qin, J. Y. (2020). *WTO Reform: Multilateral Control over Unilateral Retaliation – Lessons from the US-China Trade War*. Wayne State University Law School Research Paper No. 2020-73. doi:10.2139/ssrn.3654510

Rasiah, R., Gammeltoft, P., & Jiang, Y. (2010). Home government policies for outward FDI from emerging economies: Lessons from Asia. *International Journal of Emerging Markets*, *5*(3/4), 333–357. doi:10.1108/17468801011058415

Reinalda, B. (2009). *Routledge History of International Organizations: From 1815 to the Present Day*. Routledge. doi:10.4324/9780203876572

Rodrik, D. (2000). How far will international economic integration go? *Journal of Economic Perspective*, *14*(1), 177-186.

Rodrik, D. (2007). *One Economics Many Recipes, Globalization, Institutions and Economic Growth*. Princeton University Press. doi:10.1515/9781400829354

Sapir, J. (2011). *La demondialisation*. Seuil.

Sapir, J. (2016). Jacques Sapir: Donald Trump, président de la démondialisation? *Le Figaro*. https://www.lefigaro.fr/vox/monde/2016/11/10/31002-20161110ARTFIG00233-jacques-sapir-donald-trump-president-de-la-demondialisation.php

Shavshukov, V. M., & Zhuravleva, N. A. (2020). Global Economy: New Risks and Leadership Problems. *Int. J. Financial Stud.*, *8*(1), 7. doi:10.3390/ijfs8010007

Shih, W. C. (2020). Global supply chain in a post-pandemic world. *Harvard Business Review*, (September-October), 2020.

Spero, J. E., & Hart, J. A. (1997). *The Politics of International Economic Relations*. Routledge. doi:10.4324/9781315006154

Steinberg, F. (2005). *Cooperación y Conflicto en el Sistema Comercial Multilateral: La Organización Mundial de Comercio como Institución de Gobernanza Económica Global* (Tesis Doctoral). Departamento de Análisis Económico: Teoría Económica e Historia Económica de la Facultada de Ciencias Económicas y Empresariales de la Universidad Autónoma de Madrid, España.

Vanham, P. (2019). *A brief history of globalization*. World Economic Forum.

Witt, M. A. (2019). De-globalization: Theories, predictions, and opportunities for international business research. *Journal of International Business Studies*, *50*(7), 1053–1077. doi:10.105741267-019-00219-7

World Bank. (2016). *World Bank Data*. http://data.worldbank.org/?display=default

WTO. (2021). *World trade report 2021. Economic resilience and trade*. World Trade Organization.

Zhu, G., Chou, M. C., & Tsai, C. W. (2020). Lessons Learned from the COVID-19 Pandemic Exposing the Shortcomings of Current Supply Chain Operations: A Long-Term Prescriptive Offering. *Sustainability*, *2020*(12), 5858. doi:10.3390u12145858

ADDITIONAL READING

Ivanov, D., & Dolgui, A. (2020). Viability of intertwined supply networks: Extending the supply chain resilience angles towards survivability. A position paper motivated by COVID-19 outbreak. *International Journal of Production Research*, *58*(10), 2904–2915. doi:10.1080/00207543.2020.1750727

Kano, L., Tsang, E. W. K., & Yeung, H. (2020). Global value chains: A review of the multi-disciplinary literature. *Journal of International Business Studies*, *51*(4), 577–622. doi:10.105741267-020-00304-2

Kot, S., Haque, U. A., & Baloch, A. (2020). Supply chain management in smes: Global perspective. *Montenegrin J. Econ*, *16*(1), 87–104. doi:10.14254/1800-5845/2020.16-1.6

Min, S., Zhang, X., & Li, G. (2020). A snapshot of food supply chain in Wuhan under the COVID-19 pandemic. *China Agricultural Economic Review*, *12*(4), 689–704. doi:10.1108/CAER-04-2020-0056

Nagao, T., Ijuin, H., Yamada, T., Nagasawa, K., & Zhou, L. (2022). COVID-19 Disruption Strategy for Redesigning Global Supply Chain Network across TPP Countries. *Logistics*, *6*(1), 2. doi:10.3390/logistics6010002

Pla-Barber, J., Villar, C., & Narula, R. (2021). Governance of global value chains after the Covid-19 pandemic: A new wave of regionalization? *BRQ Business Research Quarterly*, *24*(3), 204–213. doi:10.1177/23409444211020761

KEY TERMS AND DEFINITIONS

Deglobalization: The slow-down or reverse of globalization. A political project opposed to neoliberal globalization. In the first definition, the term describes how global flows of trade, investment, and migration can decline.

Global Supply Chain: A set of activities, facilities, and means of distribution throughout the world necessary to carry out the entire sales process of a product. This is from the search for raw materials, their subsequent transformation, and their transportation and delivery to the final consumer anywhere in the world.

Production Chain: A system made up of people and companies related to each other by a succession of production operations.

Protectionism: A commercial policy established by a government that aims to protect the national industry against foreign competition with the application of tariffs or any other type of import restriction.

Relocation of Production: The international displacement of a production structure.

Value Chains: A theoretical model that graphs and allows to describe the activities of an organization to generate value to the end customer and to it.

Chapter 6
Human Resource Management Effects Functioning on Balanced Scorecard:
Jordanian Public Joint-Stock Companies

Biljana Stojan Ilic
https://orcid.org/0000-0001-6137-8478
Megatrend University of Belgrade, Serbia

Safwan Al Salaimeh
https://orcid.org/0000-0002-8474-3471
Aqaba University of Technology, Jordan

Slavica S. Andjelic
Modern Business School of Belgrade, Serbia

Gordana P. Djukic
https://orcid.org/0000-0001-5419-0725
Faculty of Economics, The University of Belgrade, Serbia

ABSTRACT

The "speed" of modern business—as well as changes in the environment—have led administrative organizations on the path of additional challenges. These organizations tirelessly strive for the realization of advanced systems, adapting their business to modern ideas and trends and gaining market advantage. In this way, organizations become modern and contemporary in their understandings of internal functioning. The study presented by the authors in the chapter aimed to determine the impact of human resource management (HRM) functions on the balanced scorecard in Jordanian public joint-stock companies. In the research, adequate statistical and descriptive methods were used. The results of the study recommend the creation of an organizational culture that promotes the optimal and effective use of HRM functions in the organizational environment.

DOI: 10.4018/978-1-6684-5876-1.ch006

INTRODUCTION

Business organizations are permanently trying to achieve success, and maintain their success and survival - this makes them constantly seek to develop, improve and amend their strategies. In that manner, they develop new products, but also use innovative tools and means. HRM functions are characterized by liaison with the organization's management, as it oversees the organization's relationships with all employees in different departments(Wirtzet al, 2008). The administrations of modern organizations seek some benefit from the knowledge and sciences that researchers constantly create and develop (Al-Khashali, 2009). These efforts lead to new opportunities, continuous progress, and development. The departments concerned with human resources planning have made continuous efforts, to secure the capabilities, and draw up plans responsive to the needs of improving the balanced scorecard to achieve a competitive advantage in quality, responsiveness, cost, customer satisfaction, and critical process performance measures (Al Safou, 2009). The success of organizations in performing their tasks and functions effectively in an integrated manner depends to a large extent on the effective use of these resources (HRM) - because it is an important factor on which the future strategy of the organization depends, seeking to achieve the desired balanced scorecard (Kefi & Kalika, 2009). The organization should provide and meet the needs of other (organizational) departments - which contribute to the creation of appropriate, trained, qualified and well-motivated human resources. This is achieved through training and education policy programs, which are determined by the human resources department. Based on the development and improvement of capabilities within the organization, each organizational unit can achieve strategic goals, both individual and general. In this way, the results can be improved and business can be balanced (Al-Atwi, 2010).

The concept of institutional performance is linked to a system (7-S, s) related to the pillars of the Balanced Scorecard, which includes the existence of Shared-Values, Strategy, Structure, and Management Style commensurate with the company's vision, business systems, and human cadres (staff) -continuous development of the skills needed to perform the company's tasks (Bankeret al, 2009). Because of the importance of the HRM functions of the balanced scorecard, the functions of human resources management have become of special importance at the practical level, intending to correct and monitor the processes of change and development within the various organizations. This importance is visible through the efforts made by Jordanian companies to pay attention to human resources.

BACKGROUND

Theoretical Framework and Previous Studies

The biggest challenge facing organizations today is their ability to transform from isolation, closure, secrecy, and rigidity. They must become open and interactive organizations, that believe in renewal and seek change -following up on new developments and discoveries of modern methods and techniques. They must be adaptive to circumstances and changes. The change in the international and local environment, which included various lifestyles, activities, and sectors, necessitated the modern organizations that believe in the importance of performance excellence, keeping pace with technological development to serve their customers and develop their employees, without which they will neither survive nor grow (Al-Karkhi, 2009)(Ilic& Salaimeh, 2022).

According to many authors - modern and successful organizations are those that collect, manage and use information to ensure the achievement of set goals. Human resource planning is sometimes linked and equated with human capital - including the ability to employ capable staff - depending on the level of their skills, qualifications and decision-making abilities (Al-Karkhi, 2009: 172)(Ilic et al, 2022). Kotler (2000) focuses on improving the functions of HRM and the balanced scorecard aiming to invest the expertise and experience of the organization and monitoring the information resulting from these experiences - reviewing it from time to time to use it in solving the problems within a framework of support and assistance (Kotler, 2000:40). All of that comes from the leadership of the organization in particular and the organizational culture in general. According to Flemming, the ability of any system to survive and maintain its integrity requires that the level of knowledge resulting from it be at least equal to the level of change in the environment. Moreover, because the organization is an open system affected by their surrounding, the change in the organization must match the change in the environment (Flemming, 2017). Valmohammadi & Ahmadi(2015) indicates that the balanced scorecard is the integrated system for the product of the organization's business in light of interaction with the elements of internal and external environment. It includes the performance of individuals in their organizational unit, the performance of organizational units within the framework of the organization's general policies, and the performance of the institution in the context of the economic and social environment and culture (Valmohammadi, & Ahmadi, 2015). Because of the essential goals that the process can achieve, it is given special attention by the HRM department in contemporary organizations. To be successful, HRM introduces important advantages represented by raising the employee morale, making them aware of justice, pushing them to assume responsibility, and providing the objective basis for human resource management activities such as recruitment, training, and similar techniques (Way et al, 2015). Strategic performance is seen as a comprehensive concept and an integrated multi-faceted system. According to this view, the balanced scorecard is on several levels that are almost the individual level (employee performance, human resources, human capital, thought capital); partial functional level (management, values) - the performance of organizational units within the framework of public policies; at the macro level - the performance of the institution is in the context of the economic, social, and cultural environment(Reiche et al, 2019).

The functions of HRM and the balanced scorecard are seen as two inputs to improve performance, productivity, and the pursuit of advanced competitive positions. Organizations must adopt many mechanisms that can enhance the requirements for improving the balanced scorecard, and this stems from the fact that the balanced scorecard is a process. It comes more formally and thoughtfully than accidentally. Therefore, it has become necessary to train managers (and employees) to create mechanisms and systems that support and enhance the balanced scorecard in various fields of business so that departments can keep pace with global and local changes to continue, succeed, develop, survive and excel in performance. Accordingly, improving the functions of HRM and the balanced scorecard is a necessity for administrative development to raise performance levels by developing the skills and capabilities of employees and members of the administrative bodies in the organization. Developing their skills and capabilities requires an effective organization dominated by team spirit, innovation, initiative, and competition. In that way, every individual feels that the organization is his property. This feeling drives employees to expend all their energies and efforts to give all they have for the sake of the excellence and success of the organization.

PREVIOUS STUDIES

Arab and European Studies

The results of the desk survey of literature and previous studies indicated that there are no studies, as far as the researcher knows, directly investigating the effect of human resource management functions in improving the balanced scorecard in Jordanian public joint-stock companies. Therefore, this study tried to employ what was mentioned in previous studies as much as possible, and wherever that was possible to achieve its goals.

Arab Studies

A study of Al-Rashidi "The Impact of the Effectiveness of Applying Human Resources Management Functions on Institutional Performance from the Viewpoint of Employees in Saudi Ministries in the Riyadh Region" aimed to demonstrate the effect of the effectiveness of applying human resource management functions on institutional performance from the point of view of employees in ministries In Saudi Arabia in the Riyadh region (Al-Rashidi, 2009). To achieve the purpose of the study, a questionnaire was developed to measure HRM functions and institutional performance. The study population consisted of 650 employees working in human resources departments in 18 Saudi ministries. The study reached a set of results:

- The effectiveness of implementing the functions of human resources management in the Saudi ministries in the Riyadh region from the respondents' point of view is moderate.
- The level of institutional performance of Saudi ministries in the Riyadh region from the point of view of workers in human resources from the viewpoint of the respondents is average.
- The existence of a statistically significant effect of the effectiveness of applying the functions of human resources management (recruiting and appointing employees, evaluating employee performance, and planning human resources) on the institutional performance of the Saudi ministries in the Riyadh region.

A study of Al-Safou, "Elements of an Operations Strategy and its Impact on the Balanced Scorecard" aimed to determine the effect of the elements of the operations strategy in the areas of the balanced scorecard (Al-Safou, 2009). The study sample included 70 managers from the General Company for Medicines and Medical Supplies in Nineveh. The study concluded that there is a significant correlation between the elements of the operations strategy and the areas of the Balanced Scorecard at the level of the General Company for Medicines and Medical Supplies.

According the Al-Enezi study, author try to identify the impact of some HRM functions on achieving organizational excellence in Saudi Customs. To achieve the study objectives, a questionnaire was developed for data collection - the study population consisted of 631 respondents, the Statistical Package for Social Sciences (SPSS.16) was used, and the study reached a set of results, the most prominent of which are(Al-Enezi, 2010):

- The employees of the Saudi Customs Authority have perceptions of human resources management jobs came to a high degree.

- The existence of an impact of human resource management functions on organizational excellence, and that the functions of human resources management explain an amount (63.3%) of the variance in organizational excellence.
- There are statistically significant differences at a significant level in the respondents' perceptions of HRM functions due to variables (age, educational qualification, and experience).

A study of Al-Atwi, titled "The Impact of Complexity of Work Procedures on Institutional Performance" aimed at identifying the impact of complex work procedures on institutional performance in the Ministry of Justice in the Tabuk region in the Kingdom of Saudi Arabia(Al-Atwi, 2010). The study population consisted of 371 respondents. The most prominent results of the studywere:

- The Ministry of Justice employees 'perceptions of the level of institutional performance was high.
- The existence of an impact of the complexity of work procedures on the institutional performance, and the dimensions of the complexity of work procedures explain an amount 51.8% of the variance in institutional performance.
- There are statistically significant differences in the respondents' perceptions of institutional performance due to variables (age, educational qualification, and experience).

European Studies

According to Banker and colleagues, the study "The Balanced Scorecard: Judgmental Effects of Performance Measures Linked to Strategy" was building a new framework to analyze changes in the balanced scorecard in a selected sample of companies in the American industrial sector (Banker et al, 2004). The proposed framework of the study showed that the profitability index represented by the return on investment is the clearest indicator in determining the changes occurring in the balanced scorecard of the United States companies studied. A study by Kefi and Kalika "The effect of strategic alignment on the balanced scorecard in International European Companies" aimed to show the effect of strategic alignment on the balanced scorecard in European international companies - to demonstrate whether the alignment between information technology strategies, information systems strategies and competitive business strategies related to the balanced scorecard (Kefi, & Kalika, 2005). A sample of the study was taken from 505 international companies whose center was in the European Community. The study concluded that there is an urgent need for more practical studies to clarify the linkages between the harmonization of information technology, information systems, competitive business strategies, and institutional performance, as the success of the harmonization of information systems and competitive business strategies will lead to achieving sustainable competitive advantage.

According to Boating, the study titled "The role of human resource management information systems in human resource management strategies"aimed to investigate the role of HRM information systems in human resource management strategies (Boating, 2007). The study was based on a theoretical basis and the study identified the employees' point of view. HRM specialists in different organizations have the effect of HRM information systems on strategic human resources tasks and employees roles. The results of the study showed that HRM professionals believe that there is no role for HRM information systems in strategic human resources tasks, but they perceive it as an empowerment technique. The study also showed that heads of human resources departments in large organizations believe that there is a role for HRM information systems in supporting human resource strategies.

Wirtz and colleaguesconducted the study of HRM for service excellence and cost efficiency in Singapore Airlines(Wirtzet al, 2008). The study aimed to review the reality of administrative practices that enable the company to achieve excellence in services in an effective manner. The study relied on the method of a personal interview with senior managers of Singapore Airlines, and the results of the study showed that human resource management practices in Singapore Airlines involve strict selection in recruitment, training, and retraining processes, empowering frontline employees to control the quality of services and motivating employees.

Soltani and his colleagues conducted the study "Contrast between human resource management and total quality management in performance management: some evidence" (Soltaniet al, 2009). The study aimed to compare the two approaches of HRM and total quality management (TQM) for performance development. To provide information about the status of performance evaluation a survey was conducted in the United Kingdom (UK) organizations - focusing on the effectiveness of TQM programs. The results of the study showed that TQM is the essential basis for performance evaluation - there is a direct relationship between the application of TQM and the effectiveness of performance, and the effectiveness of TQM programs depends on the level of employee satisfaction, their morale, and organizational culture (Soltani et al, 2003). Achieving the requirements for the success of quality programs requires rethinking the methods of performance evaluation used in the organization.

MAIN RESEARCH FOCUS

Nature of the relationship between HRM Functions and Balanced Scorecard

The problem of the study in the chapter titled „HRM Effects Functioning on Balanced Scorecard - Jordanian Public Joint-Stock Companies" is concentrated in the lack of awareness of the nature of the relationship between the HRM functions and the balanced scorecard in the Jordanian public shareholding companies, which would shackle them and affect their effectiveness and performance. Especially since the companies strive to achieve maximum levels of performance, in addition to developing their jobs according to the requirements of the internal and external business environment (such as forecasting the supply and demand of human resources), setting strategic goals, planning career paths, providing the organization with a stock of competencies -increasing the ability to know the current and expected performance. If the Human Resources Department succeeds in performing this roles, it will have a great impact on the balanced scorecard of the company, so this study comes in an attempt to answer the following question: How to achieve balanced performance in the Jordanian public shareholding companies? The Research importance and objectives of the study can be clarified by highlighting the following points:

- The fact that this study is one of the few studies - to the best of the researcher's knowledge - that linked the functions of human resources management to the variable dependent on the Balanced Scorecard.
- Since this concept is relatively new in the Arab administrative environment in general and in Jordan in particular, subjecting this concept to practical study gives it clear importance within the scientific framework of advanced management methods in acquiring knowledge and skills and using them to improve the level of the balanced scorecard.

- This study can contribute to enriching the Arab library with a modern topic that may gain the interest of researchers and practitioners. This research is considered a starting point for other studies to achieve the desired balanced scorecard through effective human resource planning. In addition to presenting a modern metric that reveals the level of the balanced scorecard of the companies under study, which gives this study distinct practical importance in making use of this measure by applying it to other organizations to identify the level of their strategic performance.

The main research objectives are:

- Identify the functions of human resources management and their impact on improving the balanced scorecard in the Jordanian public shareholding companies. Moreover, to identify the extent of the human resource management functions and the level of the balanced scorecard in the Jordanian public joint-stock companies.
- Present a set of recommendations that help in improving the balanced scorecard in Jordanian public shareholding companies by raising the level of effectiveness of human resources.

The descriptive approach in the study was based on the theoretical dimensions of the HRM functions and the balanced scorecard in the Jordanian public joint-stock companies, through conducting a desk survey, and to build the theoretical framework - reviewing the previous studies. The study relied on using a questionnaire to collect data from the study population to answer the study questions and test its hypotheses.The study society consisted of the Jordanian public shareholding companies listed in the Amman Financial Market, which numbered (243) companies registered at the end of 2019. They are distributed as follows: (104) in the financial sector, (52) in the services sector, (87) in the industrial sector, according to the authority's division of economic sectors. The number of managers in these companies reached (972).A stratified random sample was drawn from (50) companies from different sectors, which constitutes about (20%) of the total companies, distributed in proportion and proportionally consistent with the ratio of the number of companies in the sector to the total number of companies.

Financial, (12) the services sector, (17) the industrial sector, and a simple random sample was drawn from the community of managers, at the rate of 50%, as the number of sample members reached 486 employees. The number of 456 questionnaires were retrieved with a rate of (91.4%), and (13) questionnaires were excluded because they were not valid for analysis. Thus, 443 questionnaires were subjected to analysis, constituting (91.2%) of the study sample, and 45.6% of the study population, which is an acceptable percentage for scientific research purposes according to Safwan and Mohamed (Safwan, Mohamed, 2014) (Safwan, 2007).

THE PRESENTATION

Characteristics of the Study Sample

Table 1 shows that the majority of the sample members were males - their percentage constituted 84%, while the percentage of females was 16% of the total sample members.

As for the educational qualification variable of the study sample, it was found that 63.9% of those who obtained a bachelor's degree, compared to 14.2% of holders of intermediate and general secondary

Table 1. Distribution of study sample individuals according to personal and job variables

Variables	Classes	Numbers	Percent
Qualification	High school or less	29	6.5%
	Intermediate diploma	63	14.2%
	Bachelor of	283	63.9%
	Postgraduate	68	15.3%
Experience	5 years or less	65	14.7%
	6-10 years	116	26.2%
	11-15 years old	178	40.2%
	16 years and over	84	19%
Age	25 years or less	62	14.0%
	26-35 years old	123	27.8%
	36-45 years old	178	40.2%
	46-50 years old	50	11.3%
	51 years and over	30	6.8%
Sex	Male	372	84%
	female	71	16%

Source: Authors' research

diplomas, and finally the percentage of individuals who had general secondary qualifications or less came in the last place (6.5%). This is an indication of the high percentage of undergraduate degree holders working in extractive companies. Concerning experience, individuals who had experience of 11-15 years accounted 40.2%, which was the highest percentage. Moreover, that 26.2% of the study sample had an experience of 6-10 years, and 19% of the study sample had 16 years or more experience, and finally, the percentage of individuals with less than 5 years of experience came in last place (14.7%). This percentage indicates that employees in the extractive companies feel job security, and achieve their needs and desires, which contributed to their remaining in their business centers. Concerning the age variable, the age group of 36-45 years occupied the highest percentage (40.2%), followed by the age group of 26-35 years, with 27.8% of the study sample, which is a logical result. The age group of 25 years or less was about 14%, while the percentage of respondents within the age group 51 years and over reached 6.8%.

The study tool was developed based on the literature, previous studies - on the consulting with experts and specialists. It consists of three parts: the first part was included the necessary demographic information about the respondent, which are educational qualification, experience, gender, and age; the second part was consisted of 22 paragraphs that measure the independent variable and the functions of HRM. This part was also designed based on a studies of Al-Enezi and Al-Rashidi (Al-Enezi, 2010; Al-Rashidi, 2009). That studies included four sub-measures to measure the functions of HRM, in other words: employee recruitment and appointment, training and development, wages and incentives, and performance evaluation; the third part was consisted of 16 paragraphs that measured the dependent variable in the Balanced Scorecard. This part was also designed based on a study of Al-Safou (Al-Safou, 2009). It was included three sub-measures to measure the balanced scorecard, represented in: financial and operating

Table 2. The value of the reliability coefficient for the internal consistency of the instrument as a whole and each dimension of the study

	Dimension	The sequence of paragraphs	Stability coefficient	
			Test-Retest	Alpha
1	Attracting and hiring employees	1-4	0.88	0.78
a	Wages and incentives	5-10	0.86	0.90
P	Training and development	11-16	0.87	0.89
4	Performance evaluation	17-22	0.86	0.86
1-4	HRM functions	1-27	0,91	0.90
1	Financial performance		0.88	0.85
2	Operating performance	23-27	0.92	0.85
1-5	Balanced Scorecard	28-32	**0.92**	**0.85**

Source: Authors' research

performances. All the measures of responses to the scale paragraphs were formed on the five Likert scales and they: - always apply - often apply - sometimes apply - rarely apply - they do not apply at all.

The questionnaire was presented to several referees, including specialized professors and experienced members of faculty in Jordanian universities. To verify the validity of the paragraphs of the questionnaire, their remarks were taken, some paragraphs were reformulated, and the required amendments were made accurately to achieve a balance between the contents of the questionnaire and the paragraphs. Moreover, the questionnaire was presented to a test sample of (30) employees from outside the study sample to identify the degree of response to the validity of the study tool, and they expressed their desire to interact. The stability of the tool was confirmed by the test-retest method by distributing it to an exploratory sample consisting of 25 respondents from outside the study sample, with a difference of two weeks between the two applications, where the stability parameter was extracted, for the tool in its final, total form, and each dimension from the study. The results were as shown in table 2. After data was entered using the statistical package of social sciences (SPSS. V.16), the authors of the chapter applied the following statistical data processing:

- Descriptive statistic measures describe the characteristics of the study sample in percentages,
- Multiple Regression Analysis to test the validity of the study model and the effect of the independent variable on the dependent variable.
- Stepwise Multiple Regression Analysis to test the entry of the independent variables into the dependent variable prediction equation.
- The Variance Inflation Factory test and the Tolerance test ensure that there is no high correlation (Multicollinearity) between the independent variables.
- Skewness test, to ensure that the data follow a normal distribution.
- Cronbach's alpha for internal consistency to verify the stability of the study instrument.

Three hypotheses were defined in the research to achieve the desired results. The *first hypothesis* was: „There is no statistical significance at the level of significance (a<0.05) for the human resource management functions (employee recruitment and appointment, wages and incentives, training and development, performance evaluation) in the balanced scorecard with its dimensions (financial performance, operational performance) in the Jordanian public shareholding companies". The *second hypothesis* was: "There is no statistical significance at the level of significance (a<0.05) for human resource management functions (employee recruitment and appointment, wages, and incentives, training and development, performance evaluation) in financial performance as one of the dimensions of the balanced scorecard". The *third hypothesis* was: "There is no statistical significance at the level of significance (a<0.05) for human resource management functions (employee recruitment and appointment, wages and incentives, training and development, performance evaluation) in operational performance as one of the dimensions of the balanced scorecard". To distinguish between variables, the factors of independent and dependent variables were described in the chapter. The independent variable presents HRM, wages and incentives, training and development, and performance evaluation.

Human Resource Management - the administration that believes that the individuals working in the various levels or activities of the company are the most important resources and it must work to provide them with all means that enable them to carry out their work in their interest and to monitor constantly to ensure their success (Safwan et al, 2012). HRM functions consist of a set of coordinated and integrated functions to direct the use of available resources to achieve organizational goals (Djukic & Ilic, 2020). Moreover, definitions of HRM functions according to the current study can be seen in attracting and appointing employees. This process is concerned with searching for workers in the labor market and filtering them through recruitment applications, selection, and personal interviews to place the right individual in the right place (Al-Hiasat, 2005) (Soltani et al, 2009). This dimension is measured through the paragraphs of the questionnaire (numbers 1-4).

Wages and incentives - are concerned with determining the value and the relative importance of each task (job), determining wages, and determining the wage levels for the jobs. The job is also concerned with proper management of the wage system so that compensation is guaranteed for the different values and bodies of different jobs. It is also concerned with granting fair compensation for distinguished performance, and workers can be motivated for their collective performance, so individual and group incentives appear, and there are incentives for the performance of the company as a whole (Al-Hiyasat, 2005: 34). This dimension is measured through the paragraphs of the questionnaire (numbers 5-10). Training and development - the organization carries out training activities to raise the efficiency of individuals, their knowledge and skills, and direct their attitudes towards specific activities. The organization must determine the needs of the subordinates for training, use appropriate methods, and evaluate the effectiveness of the training (Vointece, 2008). This dimension is measured through the paragraphs of the questionnaire (numbers 11-16). Performance evaluation: Almost every organization is concerned with evaluating the performance of its employees and this is done through certain methods and often divides the direct heads to identify the general competence of workers and to identify aspects of development in performance, as well as working to identify negative deviations to address them immediately and positive deviations to strengthen and develop it (Al-Zoubi, 2009: 23). This dimension is measured through the paragraphs of the questionnaire with the numbers 17-22. The dependent variable represents the balanced scorecard, which consists of Financial performance and Operational Performance. The balanced scorecard includes measures that help evaluate the organization's ability to link its present with its future and the extent of its response to material and human resources - using them in a way that makes it capable of achieving its goals (Djukic & Ilic, 2020). Financial performance refers to the follow-up of compliance with the financial laws and legislations stipulated in the organization and the disclosure of important and substantial financial reports related to its business (Sels et al, 2002). This dimension is measured through

Figure 1. The hypothetical study model
Source: Authors' research

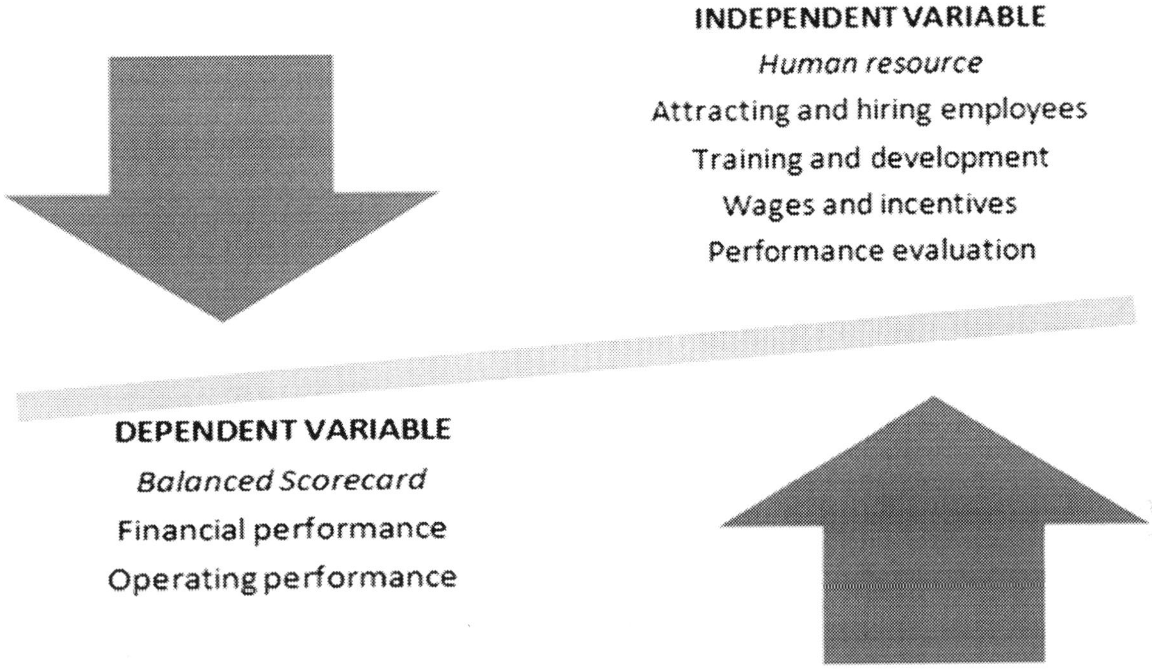

the paragraphs of the questionnaire (numbers 23-27).Operational Performance expresses the broad concept of performance through its interest in the performance of operational and financing operations (Al-Safou, 2009). This dimension is measured through the paragraphs of the questionnaire (numbers 28-32). Figure 1 shows the study model of Independent and dependent variables.

THE RESULTS

Descriptive analysis of all study variables was conducted according to the responses of the study sample members to the paragraphs contained in the questionnaire, where the arithmetic averages and standard deviations were calculated. There were arranged in descending order according to their relative importance based on the value of the arithmetic mean, taking into account the scale used in the study. If the arithmetic means have the value greater than 3.5, then the level of the study sample's estimate is high, but if the arithmetic means the value is 2.5 - 3.49, then the level of the arithmetic mean is medium. If the arithmetic mean is 2.49, then it is low. What is the availability of HRM tasks in Jordanian public joint-stock companies? Table 3 shows that the averages of the respondents' perceptions of HRM tasks - jobs in Jordanian public joint-stock companies came at a high degree.

The overall average of the respondents 'perceptions of HRM jobs in Jordanian public joint-stock companies was 3.56 with a standard deviation (0.55). Training and development ranked first, with an arithmetic average of 3.68, followed by the performance appraisal dimension (3.58), and the third-place came in the dimension of recruiting and appointing employees, with an arithmetic average of 3.55, while the fourth and final dimension of wages have a mean of 3.42. This result is explained by the Jordanian

Table 3. Arithmetic means and standard deviations of the respondents' perceptions of HRM

The sequence of paragraphs	Human resource management functions	SMA	standard deviation	Rank	Level about the arithmetic mean
1-4	Attracting and hiring employees	3.55	0.58	3	High
5-10	Wages and incentives	3.42	0.61	4	Average
11-16	training and development	3.68	0.54	1	High
17-22	Performance evaluation	3.58	0.58	2	High
1-22	Overall average	3.56	0.55	-	High

Source: Authors' research

public shareholding companies possessing a clear vision for future planning of human resources. That vision according employees needs, the changes that are expected to occur in the supply and demand of human resources. It is also expecting that Jordanian public shareholding companies have achieved the success in creating efficient and flexible means of communication among their employees, and various administrative levels. What is the level of the Balanced Scorecard in the Jordanian public joint-stock companies? Table 4 shows that the averages of the Balanced Scorecard level in the Jordanian public joint-stock companies came with a high degree, with the overall average being 3.67.

Table 4. The arithmetic means and standard deviations of the Balanced Scorecard level

Sequence of paragraphs	Balanced Scorecard	SMA	Standard deviation	Rank	Arithmetic mean
23-27	Financial performance	3.68	0.55	1	High
28-32	Operating performance	3.65	0.56	2	High
23-32	Overall average	3.67	0.52	-	High

Source: Authors' research

Standard deviation (0.52), and the financial performance dimension ranked first, with an arithmetic average of 3.68. The operational performance dimension came in last place, with an arithmetic average of 3.65. This reflects the tendency of the Jordanian public shareholding companies to pay attention to the performance by drawing a common strategic vision, working in a team spirit, participating, and building the internal operating system.

Before applying the regression analysis to test the study hypotheses, some tests were performed to ensure that the data fit the assumptions of the regression analysis. Regarding the assumption that there is no high correlation between the independent variables "Multi-Collinearity", the researcher conducted the coefficient of inflation of variance, called "Variance Inflation Factor" (VIF). It was also used the permissible variance test – "Tolerance" for each of the independent variables. Table 5 indicates that if the VIF for the variable exceeds 10 and the value of the permissible variance is less than 0.05 - it can

Table 5. Test of variance gain, permissible variance, and torsion modulus

Variables	Tolerance	Variation evaluation factor (VIF)	Skewness
Attracting and hiring employees	0.313	1.404	0.370
Wages and incentives	0.464	2.156	0.210
training and development	0.561	1.314	0.266
Performance evaluation	0.463	2.263	0.327

Source: Authors' research

be said that this variable has a high correlation with other independent variables and thus will lead to a problem in regression analysis. This rule was relied upon to test the "Multicollinearity" correlation between independent variables.

As table 5 indicates, regarding the value of the VIF, and the tolerance factor for each variable, it can be noted that the value of the VIF for all variables was less than 10 and ranges from 1.314 - 2.263. The tolerance value for all variables was higher than 0.05 and ranges between 0.313 - 0.561. Therefore, it can be said that there is no real problem related to the existence of a high correlation between the independent variables. To investigate the assumption of a normal distribution of the data, it was based on calculating the value of the skewness coefficient of the variables. The value of the skew coefficient for all the variables (table 5) of the study was less than 1 and therefore it can be said that there is the normal distribution of the data. Table 6 shows the validity of the model for testing the study hypotheses.

Table 6. Results of the analysis of variance for regression to ensure the validity of the model

Dependent variable	Degrees of freedom	Determination coefficient R2	The computed F value	Indication level of F
balanced Scorecard	(4,438)	0.657	118.49 *	0.000
Financial performance	(4,438)	0.424	45.55 *	0.000
Operating performance	(4,438)	0.505	62.97 *	0.000

* Statistically significant at (a<0.05) level
Source: Authors' research

Table 6 shows the high value of computed over its tabular value (F) at the level of significance ($a<0.05$) and degrees of freedom (4, 438).The functions of human resources management, explain 65.7% of the variance in the dimension of balanced scorecard. It is also showen that the level of the variance in the dimension of financial performance is 42.4%. Human resources management functions in dimension of operating performance as the table shows was 50.5%. Further directions of research in the study concern the calculation of the value of Human resources management in the interpretation of the dimensions of strategic performance.The multiple linear regression model is based on the assumption that there is a linear relationship between a dependent variable Yi and several independent variables - X1, X2, ... XK and a random bound Ui - expresses this relationship concerning (i) of the observations and k of the independent variables. The relationship between the mentioned factors is shown by formula 1 (Shawabkah et al, 2022) (Al Salaimeh et al, 2015).

Table 7. Results of multiple regression analysis - testing the effect of the dimensions of HRM functions on the balanced scorecard in Jordanian public joint-stock companies

Dimensions of human resource management functions	B	Standard error	Beta	The computed t value	The significance level of t
Attracting and hiring employees	0.216	0.045	0.2015	4.816 *	0.000
Wages and incentives	0.351	0.041	0.350	7.665 *	0.000
training and development	0.151	0.044	0.153	3.434 *	0.001
Performance evaluation	0.210	0.041	0.237	5.176	0.000

* Statistically significant at (α £ 0.01) level
Source: Authors' research

$$Yi = B0 + B1Xi1 + B2Xi2 + \ldots + BKXik + Ui \quad (1)$$

In the further research, the hypotheses were tested in the following ways. The first hypothesis was: There is no statistically significant effect at the level of significance (a<0.05) for HRM functions (recruitment and appointment of employees, wages and incentives, training and development, performance evaluation) in the balanced scorecard with its dimensions (financial performance, operational performance) in joint-stock companies Jordanian public. Table 7 presents the results of multiple regression analysis, testing the effect of the dimensions of HRM functions in Jordanian public joint-stock companies. It is evident from the statistical results in table 7, and from the (t) test values that the following sub-variables: employee recruitment and appointment, wages, and incentives, training, and development, and performance evaluation are the most influential variables for the dimensions of HRM functions in the balanced scorecard of the Jordanian public joint-stock companies. The balance in the Jordanian public shareholding companies, where the calculated values f (t) are (7.665, 4.816, 3.434, and 5.176), respectively (as significant values at the level α£0.01). From the above, it requires the following: Rejecting the null hypothesis, which states that: There is no statistically significant effect at a level of significance (α<= 0.05) for the functions of human resources management in its dimensions.

Performing a "Stepwise Multiple Regression" analysis to determine the importance of each independent variable separately in contributing to the mathematical model, which represents the effect of the dimensions of human resources management functions in the balanced scorecard in Jordanian public joint-stock companies, is as shown in table 8. The order of entry of the independent variables into the regression equation, the wages and incentives variable ranked first and explained an amount (50.7%) of the variance in the dependent variable, and the income of the performance evaluation variable was explained with the wages and incentives variable (60.3%) of the variance in the dependent variable. Follow the employee recruitment and appointment variable, as it was explained with the previous variables (64.6%) of the variance in the dependent variable. Finally the training and development variable entered, as is explained with the previous variables an amount of (65.7%) of the variance in the balanced scorecard in the Jordanian public joint-stock companies as a dependent variable. The second hypothesis was: There

Table 8. "Stepwise Multiple Regression" analysis to predict the balanced scorecard through the dimensions of HRM functions

The order of entry of the independent elements into the prediction equation	R2 value	The computed t value	A significance level of t *
Wages and incentives	The coefficient of determination	9.307 *	0.000
Performance evaluation	0.507	6.548 *	0.000
Attracting and hiring employees	0.603	5.680 *	0.000
Training and development	0.646	3.371 *	0.000

* Statistically significant at (α £ 0.01)
Source: Authors' research

is no statistically significant effect at the level of significance (α<0.05) of human resources management functions (employee recruitment and appointment, wages, and incentives, training and development, performance evaluation) on financial performance as one of the dimensions of the balanced scorecard.

It is evident from the statistical results contained in table 9, concerning the test (t) values that the following sub-variables: employee recruitment and appointment, wages, and incentives, training, and development, performance evaluation, are the most influential variables for HRM functions on financial performance.

As A dimension of the balanced scorecard dimensions in the Jordanian public joint-stock companies, where the calculated values (t) reached (3.687, 4.038, 3.163, and 3.860) respectively, significant values (level of significance α £ 0.01). Based on the above, it follows: Rejecting the null hypothesis, which states that: "There is no statistically significant effect (level of significance α £ 0.05) for the functions of HRM in its dimensions (employee recruitment and appointment, wages, and incentives, training and development, performance evaluation) on financial performance as a dimension of the balanced scorecard in Jordanian public joint-stock companies".

Table 9. Results of multiple regression analysis to test the effect of the dimensions of HRM functions on financial performance

Dimensions of human resource management functions	B	Standard error	Beta	The computed t value	The significance level of t
Attracting and hiring employees	0.227	0.062	0.218	3.678*	0.000
Wages and incentives	0.73	0.068	0.286	4.038 *	0.000
training and development	0.104	0.032	0.134	3.163 *	0.002
Performance evaluation	0.42	0.062	0.226	3.860 *	0.000

* Statistically significant at (α £ 0.01) level
Source: Authors' research

Performing a Stepwise Multiple Regression analysis to determine the importance of each independent variable separately in contributing to the mathematical model, which represents the effect of the dimensions of human resources management functions on financial performance as a dimension of the balanced scorecard dimensions in Jordanian public joint-stock companies, is shown in the table 10.

The table 10 represents the order of the independent variables into the regression equation: the wages and incentives variable ranked first and explained an amount (31.1%) of the variance in the dependent variable; the performance evaluation variable entered as it was explained with the wages and incentives variable (36.7%); a third entered the employee recruitment and appointment variable, as it was explained with the previous variables (40.1%) of the variance in the dependent variable. Finally, the training and development variable was the last one, where it explained with the previous variables an amount (41.3%) of the variance in financial performance.

So, the third hypothesis was: There is no statistically significant effect at the level of significance (α £ 0.05) for human resources management functions (employee recruitment and appointment, wages and incentives, training and development, performance evaluation) on operational performance as one of the Balanced Scorecard dimensions.

Table 10. "Stepwise Multiple Regression" analysis to predict financial performance through the dimensions of HRM functions

The order of entry of the independent elements into the prediction equation	The R2 value of the coefficient of determination	The computed t value	A significance level of t *
Wages and incentives	0.311	7.002 *	0.000
Performance evaluation	0.367	5.784	0.000
Attracting and hiring employees	0.401	4.932 *	0.000
training and development	0.413	2.767*	0.006

* Statistically significant at (α £ 0.01) level
Source: Authors' research

It is evident from the statistical results contained in table 11, and from following up on the values of the (t) test that the sub-variables related (employee recruitment and appointment, wages, and incentives, training, and development, performance evaluation) are the most influential variables for the functions of HRM on operational performance as a dimension.

One of the dimensions of the balanced scorecard in the Jordanian public joint-stock companies, where the calculated values of (t) reached (4.112, 6.606, 2.905, and 3.499), respectively, significant values (at the level of significance α £ 0.01).

Based on the above, it follows: Rejecting the null hypothesis: „There is no statistically significant effect at the level of significance α £ 0.05) for HRM functions (employee recruitment and appointment, wages, and incentives, training, and development, performance evaluation) on operational performance as one Dimension of the Balanced Scorecard.

Performing a "Stepwise Multiple Regression" analysis to determine the importance of each independent variable separately in contributing to the mathematical model, which represents the effect of human

Table 11. Multiple regression analysis - test the impact of HRM functions dimensions on operational performance

Dimensions of human resource management functions	B	Standard error	Beta	The computed t value	The significance level of t
Attracting and hiring employees	0.24	0.060	0.221	4.112 *	0.000
Wages and incentives	0.36	0.055	0.363	6.606	0.000
training and development	0.062	0.021	0.101	2.905 *	0.004
Performance evaluation	0.179	0.056	0.192	3.499 *	0.001

* Statistically significant at (α£0.01) level
Source: Authors' research

resources management functions on operational performance as a dimension of the balanced scorecard dimensions in Jordanian public joint-stock companies, is shown in table 12.

The order of the independent variables into the regression equation are: the wages and incentives variable occupied the first place and explained an amount (42.3%) of the variance in the dependent variable; the income of the employee recruitment variable was explained with wages and incentives (48.6%) of the variance. In the dependent variable, a third entered the performance evaluation variable, explained with the previous variables (40.1%) the variance in the dependent variable. Finally the last was the training and development variable, where it explained with the previous two variables (50.2%) of the variance in operational performance as a dependent variable.

Table 12. "Stepwise Multiple Regression" analysis to predict operating performance through the dimensions of HRM functions

The order of entry of the independent elements into the prediction equation	The R2 value of the coefficient of determination	The computed t value	t*
Wages and incentives	0.423	9.909 *	0
Attracting and hiring employees	0.486	6.768*	0
Performance evaluation	0.496	5.352 *	0
training and development	0.502	4.606 *	0

* Statistically significant at (α£0.01) level
Source: Authors' research

The results indicated that human resource management functions account for 65.7% of the total variance in the balanced card dimension (more than half). Financial performance has a performance of 42%, while human resource management functions have a value of 50.5%, where the operational performance of HRM is most valued.

ISSUES, CONTROVERSIES, PROBLEMS

Based on the conducted study the result is explained by the Jordanian public shareholding companies are that they have a clear vision for future planning of human resources (according to their needs). Jordanian public shareholding companies are expected the changes that can be occured in the supply and demand of human resources. These companies have achieved the expected success in creating efficient means of communication, flexibility among the employees, at various administrative levels. The obtained research results are in accordance with the research results from the studies of the mentioned authors in the background of this chapter (Al-Atwi, 2010) (Al-Enezi, 2010) (Al-Rashidi, 2009) (Soltani et al, 2009) (Kefi, & Kalika, 2005) (Al-Hiasat, 2005). The results indicated that the sub-variables: employee recruitment and appointment, wages and incentives, training and development, performance evaluation, are the most influential variables for the dimensions of HRM functions in the balanced scorecard in the Jordanian public joint-stock companies. The wage and incentives variable ranked first - an amount (50.7%) of the total variance in the functions of HRM. Follow the income of the performance evaluation variable, as it was explained with the wages and incentives variable (60.3%) of the variance in the dependent variable; and the income of the employee recruitment and appointment variable, as it was explained with the previous variables (64.6%) from the variance in the dependent variable. Finally, the training and development variable entered, as is explained with the previous variables an amount (65.7%) of the variance in the balanced scorecard in the Jordanian public joint-stock companies as a dependent variable. All above can be also explained by the fact that employees in Jordanian public joint-stock companies possess distinct mental capabilities and creative capabilities that help to overcome the obstacles they face without complaining, and encourage others to actively participate in achieving the organizational goals . But, the HRM functions in these companies must be based on a comprehensive database of human resources, which can make them more efficient in providing the decision-of top management. So, these companies must have the necessary information to formulate policies and to develop strategies. However, the problem is to develop an incentive system based on data that provides accurate information about the "best" employees motivation in Jordanian joint stock companies. This information should include activities to encourage and reward human resources in all organizations in Jordan. In that way, social justice and prevention of migration of efficient human resources would be achieved. So, the basic problem in Jordan's organizations is to create loyal employees, those who will experience the organization as their home and employees in the organization as their closest associates. Regardless of all previous studies, as well as the research presented in this chapter, there are controversial facts that regardless of the and efforts to create quality human resources, it is still necessary to invest more in motivational factors of Jordanian organizations.

SOLUTIONS AND RECOMMENDATIONS

The results of the study can be interpreted that Jordanian public joint-stock companies face renewed and changing challenges that require senior management to adopt policies and strategies that adapt to these challenges. To achieve their goals it is necessary for organizations to introduce the "successful style" in HRM. Because of the rapid changes in the business environment, higher management must allow freedom for employees at various administrative levels. Top management have to make appropriate decisions without referring to the higher management except in necessary cases. But in the case of critical business situations top management have to create a capable organization for efficiently and effectively providing of services and products (to clients). Effective human resource management is one of the catalytic influences for achieving financial performance. Effective management contributes to better interaction and easier communication between individuals and employees, forming cooperation and harmony between employees and higher management levels. Recommendation for successful business can be the HRM should provide an opportunity for growth, development and fulfillment of employees' aspirations, as well as to facilitate the way of doing business, by creating an excellent organizational climate. Every decision must be made in a way to make benefits of the individuals potential and abilities. To pursue the interests of both the company and the individual, HRM must be aware of the fact that employees need to build consensus on the vision and mission as well as on the values and goals that the company strives to achieve. Recruitment and appointment of employees, wages and incentives, training and development, performance evaluation, are the variables of the functions of human resources management that affect operational performance of the balanced scorecard dimensions in Jordanian public joint-stock companies. The variable of wages (earnings) and incentives took the first place and was explained as a variable on which the performance of employees depends. However, achieving good business performance depends largely on the manner and attitude of the organization towards its employees. It is therefore essential that the availability of human resource management functions contribute to improving operational performance and the ability for employees - to learn in a way that the leader has the role of coach and mentor by providing appropriate incentives, training and development programs, tolerance and guilt avoidance, as well as the presence of a high level of integration between different business tasks and departments. In other words, a strong focus must be based on the authority, competence and experience of responsible managers.

Operational performance must be an important source and solution of empowerment for employees in Jordanian companies to perform their duties, make decisions and solve problems within their specific responsibilities. The "availability" of the human resources management function contributes to the achievement of mutual trust between managers and employees in the organization, which means that employees feel their value and raise business ethic. The "availability" of the human resources management function contributes that employees raise their "working" morale.

FUTURE RESEARCH DIRECTIONS

Future directions of research can be characterized in the following sentences. It is necessary to explore the optimal and effective use of human resources to achieve the set goals and implement a "common" vision in Jordanian organizations. It is necessary to identify problems that lead to conflicts of interest - work on providing tangible results (which can be measured) and on the ways to achieve desired results. It is also very important for Jordanian organizations to investigate and implement adequate changes to some regulations and instructions that concentrate power in the hands of senior management. It must be explore the ways - enabling lower levels of the organization (operational levels) to participate in administrative and executive decision-making. Scientifically research training is needed for Jordanian organizations, and then it can be established appropriate training programs in organizations to empower and encourage employees.

Examine the activation of teamwork by creating formal and informal business teams of management. It is very important to work on connecting employment policy with companies and future needs for their new staff. It is necessary for organizations to focus on the system of selection of general managers, adopting objective criteria based on competencies and merits. It must be determined what merits are needed to "put" one of the employees in the position of general manager. It is also necessary to improve the skills of employees in Jordanian organizations by creating a database and information systems that can provide companies with the necessary and timely information, to formulate a clear strategy for improving the level of a balanced scorecard. For Jordanian organizations it is vary important to work on the development and improvement of the business environment. "Updating" the data, in a way that would enable information to be transmitted, and to connect organizations with the information network. There is a need to examine ways that would help organizations in Jordan to use information to improve their performance, which would also have a positive impact on the quality of services and products they provide to clients and customers.

CONCLUSION

From the above, it can be concluded that the availability of human resource management functions (often) improves the business performance of employees and provokes their positive reaction - not only in the application of procedures but also in the "development" of lower administrative leaders. In this way, employees feel that they are important to the organization and that they are its effective elements. This feeling encourages employees to express opinions and suggestions of important organizational issues. All this together strengthens the commitment to ethical - personal engagement of employees in performing their business tasks. The values of individuals are becoming the values of organization, positively influencing employees to make more efforts for achieving the goals of the companies. In light of the results of the study, a "set" of recommendations indicate the importance of "bringing" human resources closer to the dimension of the management function, so that employees understand how important their contribution is for improving balanced scorecards in Jordanian public companies. Therefore, Jordanian public joint stock companies should focus on improving the balanced scorecards, enabling their human resources to be involved in making organizational management decisions.

ACKNOWLEDGMENT

This research received no specific grant from any funding agency in the public, commercial, or not-for-profit sectors.

REFERENCES

Al-Atwi, J. (2010). *The Impact of Complexity of Work Procedures on Institutional Performance An Empirical Study on Employees of the Ministry of Justice in Tabuk Region in the Kingdom of Saudi Arabia* [Master Thesis]. Mu'tah University, Jordan.

Al-Enezi, F. (2010). *The Impact of Human Resource Management Functions on Achieving Organizational Excellence in Saudi Customs* [Master Thesis]. Yarmouk University.

Al-Hiasat, K. M. (2005). *The Efficiency and Effectiveness of the Strategy of Human Resources Management and Institutional Performance in Jordanian Press Institutions* [Ph.D. Thesis]. Amman Arab University.

Al-Karkhi, M. (2009). *Strategic Planning, an applied theoretical presentation.* Dar Al-Manahij for Publishing and Distribution, Jordan.

Al-Khashali, S. J. (2009). Knowledge Management and its Impact on Organizational Performance: A Field Study in Jordanian Industrial Companies. *Arab Journal of Management, 29*(1), 84–109.

Al-Rashidi, K. M. (2009). *The Effect of Effective Application of Human Resources Management Functions on Institutional Performance from the Viewpoint of Employees in Saudi Ministries in the Riyadh Region* [Master Thesis]. Mutah University, Karak.

Al-Safou, R. D. A. (2009). *Elements of Operations Strategy and Their Impact on the Balanced Scorecard* [Master Thesis]. University of Mosul, Iraq.

Al Salaimeh, S., Saraireh, Z., Hammad, J., & Rawashdeh, A. (2015). Design a Model of Language Identification Tool. *International Journal of Information & Computation Technology, 5*(1), 11–18.

Al-Zoubi, M. A. (2009). *The Impact of Participatory Leadership on Improving the Performance of Human Resources in Kuwaiti Industry Companies.* University of Jordan.

Banker, R. D., Chang, H., & Pizzini, M. J. (2004). The Balanced Scorecard: Judgemental Effects of Performance Measures Linked to Strategy. *The Accounting Review, 79*(1), 1–23. doi:10.2308/accr.2004.79.1.1

Banker, R. D., Chang, H. H., & Majundar, S. K. (2009). Framework for Analyzing Changes in Strategic Performance. *Strategic Management Journal, 17*(9), 23–36.

Boating, A.A.A. (2007). *The Role of Human Resource Information Systems (HRIS) in Strategic Human Resource Management (SHRM)* [Master's thesis]. Swedish School of Economics and Business Administration.

Djukic, G. & Ilic, B. (2020). Sustainable development, social protection and responsibility. *Sürdürülebilir kalkınma, sosyal koruma ve sorumluluk, 2*(1), 83-91.

Flemming, P. L. (2017). Building a Climate of Change with a link through Transformational Leadership and Corporate Culture: A Management key to a Global Environment. *International Journal of Business and Social Research, 7*(1), 44–55.

Ilic, B., Djukic, G., & Nikolic, M. (2022). Rural tourism of Eastern Serbia: Human resources management and motivation. *Economy of Agriculture, 69*(1), 241-255. doi:10.5937/ekoPolj2201241I

Ilic, B. S., & Salaimeh, S. A. (2022). Management of telecommunication operator services in Serbia–Case study Eastern Serbia. *WSEAS Transactions on Business and Economics, 19*(1), 977–984.

Kefi, H., & Kalika, M. (2005). Survey of Strategic Alignment Impacts on Organizational Performancein International European Companies. *Proceeding of the 38th Hawaii International Conference on System Sciences*, 1-10.

Kotler, P. (2000). *Marketing Management.* Prentice Hall.

Reiche, B. S., Lee, Y. T., & Allen, D. G. (2019). Actors, structure, and processes: A review and conceptualization of global work integrating IB and HRM research. *Journal of Management*, *45*(2), 359–38.

Safwan, A.S. (2007). The Optimal Management of Informational Servicing Logistic Systems. *Leonardo Journal of Sciences*, *10*(1).

Safwan, A. S., & Mohammad, B. Y. (2014). Functional structure of special computerized information system. *Journal of Environmental Science, Computer Science and Engineering & Technology*, *4*(1), 1–12.

Safwan, A. S., Zafer, M., Avramenko, V. P., & Shtangee, S. V. (2012). Optimal Resource Allocation Under Bad Compatibility of Functional Limitations. *International Journal of Computer Science and Technology*, *3*(1).

Sels, L., Winne, S., Maes, J., Delmotte, J., Faems, D., & Forrier, A. (2002). *How HRM affects corporate financial performance: Evidence from Belgian SMEs*. Katholieke Universiteit Leuven.

Shawabkah, A. M., Kadir, M. R. B. A., Nori, W., & Hassan, H. B. (2022). Validating the Framework of the Accounting Information Systems Components and Firm Performance: A Conceptual Study. *Wseas Transactions On Business And Economics*, *19*, 985–999.

Soltani, E., Meer, R., & Williams, T. M. (2009). A Contrast of HRM and TQM Approaches to Performance Management: Some Evidence. *British Journal of Management*, *16*(3), 48–59.

Soltani, E., Van der Meer, R., Gennard, J., & Williams, T. (2003). A TQM Approach to HR Performance Evaluation Criteria. *European Management Journal*, *21*, 323–337. doi:10.1016/S0263-2373(03)00052-5

Valmohammadi, C., & Ahmadi, M. (2015). The impact of knowledge management practices on organizational performance: A balanced scorecard approach. *Journal of Enterprise Information Management*, *28*(1), 131–159.

Vointece, S. K. (2008). *Learning Embedded in Organization's Culture Influences Organizational Performance*. University of New Mexico.

Way, S. A., Tracey, J. B., Fay, C. H., Wright, P. M., Snell, S. A., Chang, S., & Gong, Y. (2015). Validation of a multidimensional HR flexibility measure. *Journal of Management*, *41*(4), 1098–1131.

Wirtz, J., Heracleous, L., & Pangarkar, N. (2008). Managing human resources for service excellence and cost effectiveness at Singapore Airlines. *Managing Service Quality*, *18*(1), 4–19.

ADDITIONAL READING

Chowdhury, P., & Shumon, R. (2020). Minimizing the Gap between Expectation and Ability: Strategies for SMEs to Implement Social Sustainability Practices. *Sustainability*, *12*(6408), 6408. Advance online publication. doi:10.3390u12166408

de Miranda Castro, M. V., de Araújo, M. L., Ribeiro, A. M., Demo, G., & Meneses, P. P. M. (2020). *Implementation of strategic human resource management practices: a review of the national scientific production and new research paths*. Revista de Gestão.

Kainzbauer, A., & Rungruang, P. (2019). Science mapping the knowledge base on sustainable human resource management, 1982–2019. *Sustainability, 11*(14), 3938. doi:10.3390u11143938

Mayson, S., & Barrett, R. (2006). The 'science' and 'practice' of HRM in small firms. *Human Resource Management Review, 16*(4), 447–455. doi:10.1016/j.hrmr.2006.08.002

Santana, M., & Lopez-Cabrales, A. (2019). Sustainable development and human resource management: A science mapping approach. *Corporate Social Responsibility and Environmental Management, 26*(6), 1171–1183. doi:10.1002/csr.1765

KEY TERMS AND DEFINITIONS

Balanced Scorecard: Represents the way that organizations align their economic and human resources with environmental business factors in a manner of sustainable business processes.

Financial Performance: EVERY company should have a system for managing economic performance and goals – developed and formalized set of measures for adoption, and control of achieved goals. Every business can be viewed as economic a unit that employs resources to ensure a return on investment.

Human Resources Management: Human resources are an essential part of every collective. Human Resource Management is related to the successful management of knowledge, abilities, skills and competencies, which are key factors for successful business.

Management Innovation: A word Innovation is derived from the Latin word *innovare*, meaning something new. Refers to all types and forms of innovation, i.e., innovation processes and techniques which contribute to the successful operation of the organization by improving business processes.

Public Joint-Stock Company: A type of company which capital is divided into a certain number of shares - in equal amounts. Belongs to the group of legal entities that are responsible for the obligations exclusively with their assets.

Stepwise Multiple Regression: Represents an iterative construction of a regression model in terms of—step by step—a method that examines the choice of independent variables to the final model. This includes adding or removing potential variables sequentially and testing statistical significance after each iteration.

Variance Inflation Factor (VIF): Is represented as a measure of the amount of multicollinearity in a set of multiple regression variants, the ratio of total model variance to model variance that includes only one independent variable.

Chapter 7
Importance of Leadership in Managing Post-Pandemic Crises

Yasin Galip Gencer
https://orcid.org/0000-0003-2133-351X
Yalova University, Turkey

Sema Nur Batirlik
Yalova University, Turkey

ABSTRACT

The concept of leadership, which is the subject of many academic studies, is accepted as a phenomenon which is also emphasized in social sciences. With globalization and rapid and continuous development in the field of communication technologies, it has caused radical changes in many subjects from economy to politics, from organizational structures to management approach. In this study, firstly, the definition of the concept of leadership was made. Then, the scale studies in the literature related to the subject of leadership are included. Leadership theories, postmodern leadership types, and common leadership types are explained. With the research, the concept of leadership, which still does not have a clear definition in the literature and is changing day by day, has been extensively studied. The aim of the study is to contribute to the academic literature about the concept of leadership. Moreover, the study also aims to clarify the increasing importance of leadership in managing post-pandemic crises.

INTRODUCTION

Although leadership has maintained its importance throughout history, it has changed according to the leader need of the period. This concept, which found its place in the state administration before the industrial revolution, started to be discussed in the field of business management after the industrial revolution and became the subject of academic studies with the 20th century. So much so that only in the 20th century, more than 5000 studies were carried out and more than 350 definitions of leadership and leader were put forward (Erçetin, 2000). Although many definitions have been made up to now, a clear definition has not been developed yet (Bass, 1990).

DOI: 10.4018/978-1-6684-5876-1.ch007

When the historical process is examined, in many periods; It is seen that different leadership theories and types, which are affected by cultural differences according to the situation, time and conditions, have emerged.

When leadership theories are examined in the historical process, it is seen that different leadership approaches have emerged depending on the period. Prior to the 1940s, the leadership approach based on innate characteristics left its place to the view that it is a trait that can be learned after the 1940s. This change is going on over the decades and is also effected by the pandemic crises.

1.1. Leadership Concept and Definition

There are many definitions in domestic and foreign studies on the concept of leadership, which has a complex nature. Leadership is difficult to define; It is about having a multidisciplinary aspect and finding differences in the dimension of perception. This situation leads to the emergence of new approaches and definitions about leadership. Leadership definitions are listed in chronological order in the table below.

Table 1. Definitions of Leadership

Author	Year	Leadership Definitions
Stogdil	1948	Leadership; It is defined as the act of influencing the efforts and efforts of an organized group in order to set a goal and achieve this goal.
Prentice	1961	Leadership; is to be successful in the goal of directing human resources.
Rauch and Behling	1984	Leadership; It is the process of influencing the activities of an organized group to achieve a predetermined goal.
Tosun	1987	Leadership is the relationship between individuals (group) gathered around a common goal and a person (leader) who determines their behavior.
Zaleznik	1992	Leadership is the ability to influence the thoughts and actions of individuals.
Jaques and Clement	1994	Leadership; It is the process where an individual sets a specific goal for one or more people and ensures that they act in accordance with these goals in a fully committed manner. It is the process by which an individual sets a specific goal for one or more people and enables them to act in a fully committed manner in accordance with these goals.
Goleman	1998	Leadership; It is the ability to act with a particular group for its current purpose and to channel that group towards the goal, rather than establishing authority over the group.
Zel	2001	Leadership consists of the ability to unite the members of a group in line with certain goals and to influence and mobilize them for the realization of these goals, and the sum of the skills, knowledge and personality traits used in this direction.
Aytürk	2007	Leadership is the ability to persuade individuals with the goal of change and improvement.
Hartog and Koopman	2009	Leadership is a socialized influencing process in which group members are directed to a common goal through that group's leader.
Robbins and Judge	2013	Leadership in definitions that deal with the power of leaders to influence people; It is the ability to influence the existing group in order to willingly make the target group do the behaviors that are believed to be done in order to achieve the goals.

Different definitions have been made throughout the historical process regarding the concept of leadership, which has been discussed by many scientists. This definition, whose history is as old as humanity, was discussed by various researchers in the first quarter of the 20th century; but although many thinkers added their own interpretations, a common definition could not be found (Bass, 1990). The fact that societies are in a constant development and change has differentiated the direction, scope and content of this concept.

These changes have led to the emergence of new leadership styles, and others have been added to the existing leadership types in the literature. Businesses have to cope with constantly changing environments, (Batirlik et al, 2022). There is no clear role for leadership in the concept of history, which means the science of space and time. However, this concept continues to be valid and effective with the effect of change.

1.2. Leadership Theories

Although the validity of the theories created to define leadership, to determine its characteristics and to place the concept of leadership on a scientific level decreases day by day, learning what these theories are in the light of science has an important place in the current study.

1.2.1. Properties Theory

The trait theory is discussed under the name of the theory of having certain traits. This understanding is a theory that argues that the leader has innate abilities and that he acquires his abilities as soon as he is born. Thomas Carlyle, who wrote the stories of leaders with the Great Men's School theory; he tried to explain the theory of features with reference to effective speech, effective use of intelligence, perception ability, decision-making competence, athletic body (Çelik 2016). Over time, instead of this argument, the view that people can acquire leadership qualities through learning and experience has become widespread, and these views have led to the emergence of new approaches (Can, Azizoğlu and Aydın 2011). If we look at the general idea about this theory, it is possible to evaluate the innate characteristics of the leader in terms of dominating the society and the environment.

The most influential leader of 2020 was chosen from the health sector. The reason for this is the Covid-19 epidemic, which spread to the world in 2020 and greatly affected people's lives. The person who was selected as the most effective leader in 2020 was put in the first place by the popular TIME Magazine (Time 2020). When evaluated in terms of the theory of characteristics, it is possible to say that this person takes the first place due to his stance against the new type of virus, while the view that this can be acquired through learning and experience, along with an innate quality, is logical. The reason for the loss of effectiveness of the trait theory is that people have quick access to information in terms of gain and the excess of experience options, with the effect of globalization.

1.2.2. Behavioral Leadership Theory

This theory puts the behavior of the leader rather than the characteristics of the leader on the basis of explaining the leadership process. The idea that criteria such as the leader's communication with the team, the way of making decisions, and the method of resolving the conflict are important issues that increase the effectiveness of the leaders has been emphasized and explained within the framework of the leader's behaviors. Blake and Mouton (1964) and Likert (1976) produced scientific and universal models for these theories that examine actual behaviors. In addition, Ohio University Research Bureau

Table 2. Likert Model Management Types

Leadership Variable	Exploitative Autocratic	Protector Autocratic	Participant	Democratic
Subordinate Trust	Never trusts subordinate.	Servant and master relationship	Partially reliable.	Fully trusts.
Freedom perceived by subordinates	Never feels free.	She/he doesn't feel too free.	She/he feels quite free	She/he feels completely free.
Relationship of superior with subordinates	She/he is rarely consulted.	Sometimes she/he asks for opinions.	She/he generally gets the idea.	She/he always gets ideas.

Source: Kocel, 2013

(1945) explained this theory with their own studies (Can, Azizoğlu and Aydın 2011). With the model put forward by Blake and Mouton, five different leadership characters emerge. These types are:

- **Weak Leadership**
  It shows the lowest level of dedication in doing the necessary work in order to stay in the organizations.
- **City Club Leadership**
  Leader; thoughtful, giving importance to comfort, he cares about bilateral relations, while his interest in production is at a low level.
- **Task leadership**
  Leader; while using his authority to increase productivity, his level of relationship with individuals is low.
- **Middle way leadership**
  It is leadership with a conciliatory personality. The personality and many other traits affect leadership styles (Gencer, 2019)
- **Teamwork leadership**
  It is a leadership style where mutual trust and respect are at the highest level and everyone is connected to each other. High efficiency is obtained in this type of leadership.

Likert (1976), who determined the most important element of an organization as human and capital, worked on the effective use of people and capital. In addition, with the survey studies he conducted in different sectors, he divided the leaders and characteristics of businesses and organizations into four types (Bulut and Minister, 2004):

As can be seen in the table, Likert considered four management styles in his model. According to his thesis, the democratic, participatory form of government appears to be a good theory of leadership. When the relations between the superior and the subordinate are examined, participatory management that trusts the subordinate and consults him will maximize the relationship between the leader and the subordinate, and will also strengthen the subordinate's commitment to the job.

Ohio University Research Bureau (1945) determined that the main elements in leadership behavior are directing subordinates to purpose. They argued that leadership also has two basic dimensions. The first of these is activating the structure, while the other is understanding. (Can, Azizoğlu and Aydın, 2011). In the title of activating the structure, what the leader does to fulfill his duty is taken into account.

These movements are organizing, planning, executing and controlling on behalf of the work to be done. Understanding, on the other hand, reflects the respect and trust that exists between the subordinate and the leader. It is possible to adopt behaviors that meet the needs of the group, do good to them, spare time and listen, exchange ideas with team members, protect justice in the team, and act according to this understanding model (Aydın, 2020).

Conclusions to be drawn from the Ohio model (Can, Azizoğlu and Aydın, 2011):

- If team members expect a leader who will provide less authority, the leader's activating the existing structure will be met with backlash.
- If there is time pressure, the leader who shows understanding behavior will not be successful and complaints will increase.
- If the subordinate's relationship with the superior is not intense, the administration will be of the authoritarian leadership type.
- If the members of the group are in a continuous relationship, they will expect high and superior understanding from the leader.

1.2.3. Situational Leadership

It consists of the fact that leadership is neither an inherited trait that is to come, nor is it an acquired character, systematized by Hersey and Blanchard; Behavioral Ohio State Leadership Theory is combined with Reddin's 3D theory (Aydın, 2020: 83). Robert House and Martin Evans (1970), who developed the Ohio State Leadership theory, provided the situational perspective. These two names have taken the model of way and purpose. The word situational in leadership was used for the first time by Fiedler (1967) (Güler, 2007). Businesses are effected by environmental changes everytime (Yaman et al, 2021). One of these environmental effects is Covid-19 pandemy and it has changed the know-how and habits of the organizations (Gencer, 2017). Pandemy with the crises it brought updates to the leadership styles in the business world.

1.2.3.1. *Purpose-Path Theory*

With this idea based on the word motivation, two factors affecting the behavior of the person were determined. The first of these is the belief and expectation that a person can reach certain results as a result of a certain behavior; the second one is expensive for the results to be reached (Koçel, 2013). The meaning of expectancy theory in terms of leadership is that people can gain morale and motivation in two ways. These; It is the level of the leader's ability to influence expectations and the value given to the result (Can, Azizoğlu, & Aydın, 2011).

According to the theory, the degree of influencing expectations was determined as the way, and the degree of influencing the value given to the result was determined as the goal. There are two main points in the theory of path and purpose. The first of these is to determine the purpose. If the purpose is determined, it will be possible to determine which behaviors deserve the reward. The other is to increase the rewards to be given on the way to the goal (Aydın, 2020).

While the leader determines the path to the goal, his behavior is also effective. Criteria such as the motivation of the employees, the satisfaction of the workers and their performance are shaped by the behavior of the leader. In this model, it is possible to consider four types of leader behavior (Can, Azizoğlu, & Aydın, 2011). These; It is listed as commanding/authoritarian, supportive, participatory

Table 3. Basic Types of Reddin

RELATED	**INTEGRATED**
DISCONNECTED	**COMMITTED**

Source: Can, Azizoğlu ve Aydın, Organizasyon ve Yönetim, 2011

and success-seeking/success-oriented leader behavior (Koçel, 2013). There is no general consensus on whether this model is successful or not. The reason is that there is not enough study in the literature.

1.2.3.2. *Reddin's 3D Theory*

Reddin (1970) classified leadership styles according to the table below:

The disconnected leader is weak in human relations and task dimensions. This leader, who lives by the rules, constantly tries to show corrective behaviors; He does business with written orders and is at a low level in terms of social relations. This type of leaders prefer to avoid conflicts (Ömürgönülşen & Sevim, 2005).

The relevant type of leadership describes the high-level group relationship and the low-level task relationship. This type of leader, who has a conciliatory identity in disagreements, also exhibits a guiding management approach (Ömürgönülşen & Sevim, 2005). Dedicated leader type has high task power and weak human relations. This type of leader, who adopts the authority of the team members, punishes the mistake and covers up the disagreements. The integrated leader type, on the other hand, is high in human relations and mission. It is developed in terms of social relations, while ensuring its administration by sharing common communication and responsibility in terms of duty; it learns from mistakes and produces solutions by going deeper into problems (Ömürgönülşen & Sevim, 2005).

Although Reddin (1970) adopted four basic approaches in the two-dimensional plane, he later assumed that they could not be effective in every place and time. Thus, he added the third window, effectiveness, to its two dimensions. Effectiveness indicates the degree of achievement of the task given by the leader to the subordinate (Can, Azizoğlu, & Aydın, 2011).

Putting the basic leadership behaviors in the center, Reddin separated the leaders who fit the situation as high-effective leaders and the leaders who do not comply as ineffective leaders. low-level leaders; separating them as abandoning leader, missionary leader, conciliatory leader and authoritarian leader; high-level leaders; categorized as bureaucratic leader, developer leader, executive leader and benevolent leader. He considered the degree of effectiveness of leaders by situation, not by behavior. (Aydın, 2020: 90).

1.2.3.3. *Fiedler's Contingency Model*

According to Fiedler (1967), there is no valid and suitable leadership style for all situations (Can, Azizoğlu, & Aydın, 2011). According to Fiedler's theory, there are many forms of leadership in which a person can be effective. This theory emphasizes the individual's being a leader in the group, as well as the development of good and positive relations with talent as well as personal characteristics (Güler, 2007). Factors that will determine the leadership of the person; leader-subordinate relations are listed as the task structure and the authority given by the leader's office.

As a result of these factors, there are eight different situations that come before the leader. These situations differ in terms of whether they are in favor of the leader or not (Can, Azizoğlu, & Aydın, 2011).

Table 4. Fiedler's Leadership Types

Leader Subordinate Relations	Well	Well	Well	Well	Bad	Bad	Bad	Bad
Task Structure	Too Determined		Uncertain		Clearly Determined		Uncertain	
Leader's Authority	More	Little	More	Little	More	Little	More	Little

Source: Can, Azizoğlu & Aydın, 2011

As can be seen in the table below, which is prepared with the leader-subordinate relations, the structure of the task and the authority given by the leader's office, respectively; The leader is most effective in the first case and the lowest in the eighth case.

Leader's effectiveness; It depends on reasons such as the favorable conditions, the suitability of the task, the effect of the authority on the group members, whether the problems and solutions are clear, whether he can get along with his subordinates, and the relationship of trust he has established with his subordinates (Can et al, 2011).

1.3. Leadership Scales

Yurtkoru (2001) explained the success and mainstay of the century we live in in terms of organizations as leading the transformation. He defined people who can define change, impose prudence, and lead the members of the organization to change within the framework of the visions set forth as a transformational leader. Considering the scarcity of studies investigating the relationship between change and transformational leadership in the current period, he conducted research. In the first place, he established a change model, arranged a measurement tool for this model, and formed the change questionnaire from five scales.

Since there is no exemplary model in terms of practice in Turkey, he first translated the questionnaire and then made factor and reliability analyzes. Seven separate companies were analyzed in the study. The aim of this study is to develop the model he designed and to examine the effect of this model on leadership styles. According to the results of the research, it was determined that transformative leadership increased the use of change tools; On the other hand, it was also stated that rewarding is an effective aspect in terms of the change process. In the study, a significant difference was found between superiors and subordinates in terms of understanding. It has been stated that this scale can be used to measure the resistance of employees in organizations to change and to compare the perceptions of separate groups within the organization. In addition, this scale is thought to be a study that administrators of different leadership styles will benefit from in educational evaluations.

Taş and Çetiner (2011) revealed the situation and attitudes of secondary school principals and teachers regarding the transformational leadership style with their research. In the research, a scientific study was conducted by taking the opinions of 167 teachers and the researched data were collected in the scale. In addition to determining the level of implementation of the behaviors of secondary school principals within the scope of transformational leadership, with the study; It was aimed to reveal different purposes. It was also aimed to measure the effect of teachers' different gender, branch, experience and working time with the principal in this research.

According to the research, it was determined that transformational leadership could not be realized at a high level within the framework of school principals. While the researchers noted gender as an important factor, they observed that women viewed transformational leadership more positively than men. It has been stated that the transformational leadership, which remains at a low level in terms of school principals, can be increased with in-house training. According to the results of this study, which is limited to the province of Burdur, they also stated that with the training programs of the relevant ministry, the transformational leadership at the lower level can be increased to a higher level. As a result of the data analysis, t-Test, ANOVA, correlation and mean were calculated and according to the research findings, the behaviors and attitudes of the transformational leadership of the principals were realized at a moderate level.

Akan, Yıldırım and Yalçın (2014) examined the structure of the concept of administration from the past to the present and investigated how the concept of manager was replaced by the concept of leadership with changing periods. Based on the leadership that comes to the fore in current management approaches, they stated that a successful organizational structure is based on the behavior and attitudes of the leader. Within the scope of the study, an item pool was created and a preliminary application was made to 100 teachers.

In the study, different leadership style scales were analyzed and it was aimed to develop a scale with high reliability, suitable for use and validity. To measure the leadership style of school administrators, they developed a scale according to teachers' perceptions and conducted a validity and reliability test with the participation of 499 teachers. They tested the structural validity by applying confirmatory and exploratory analysis as factor analysis.

The reliability study was measured by Spearman Brown, Cronbach Alpha and Test-Retest and the reliability coefficients were calculated. It is thought that this scale, which is a new step for equivalent scales, will come to an intermediate position for future studies. The aspect that distinguishes this scale, which is understandable in terms of language and economical in terms of application, is its ease. Duran, Boz, Behdioğlu, and Aktı (2020) researched the origin of the word conscience and stated the concept of leadership as socially changing, differentiating in its internal structure, experiencing a transformation in its meaning. They deduced that with the change of social necessity, individuals with dissimilar goals became more difficult to gather around a leader, the concept of time gained importance, the importance of moral values began to decrease, and authority and wealth were misused around materialist thinking. In this context, they explained that conscientious leadership came into play and determined that the basic point was the characteristics of the conscientious leader. They identified the type of leadership that protects and empowers those around them, is sensitive to society, has a sense of duty, does not have a low awareness threshold, and integrates moral values with themselves, as a conscientious leader, and they carried out the study around this leadership type.

As a result of various research studies, they considered conscience within the framework of the definition and evaluated it in terms of leadership. In order to measure reliability and validity, exploratory and confirmatory factor analysis was performed with a sample of 1041 people. This scale is a valid, national and local scale tool, as it is made for lecturers, students and organizational members of different population characteristics. Duran, Boz, Behdioğlu, and Aktı (2020) researched the origin of the word conscience and stated the concept of leadership as socially changing, differentiating in its internal structure, experiencing a transformation in its meaning. They deduced that with the change of social necessity, individuals with dissimilar goals became more difficult to gather around a leader, the concept of time gained importance, the importance of moral values began to decrease, and authority and wealth were misused around materialist thinking. In this context, they explained that conscientious leadership came into play and determined that the basic point was the characteristics of the conscientious leader.

They identified the type of leadership that protects and empowers those around them, is sensitive to society, has a sense of duty, does not have a low awareness threshold, and integrates moral values with themselves, as a conscientious leader, and they carried out the study around this leadership type.

1.4. Postmodern Leadership Types

The concept of postmodern has been a word that came into our lives after the Second World War. This concept, which emerged with the end of the second world war, when the universe was dragged into a bipolar stage, came into use with the beginning of the softening period. The word postmodern, which means criticizing modernism and adding questioning to modernism, refers to post-modernism. The globalization process has enabled the emergence of new approaches to human behavior and organizational management. The concept that has an important share among them is the term postmodern leadership. The foundation of this concept, which emerged in order to respond to the needs of the period, was laid in the 1970s (Guven, 2016)

1.4.1. Interactionist Leadership

Interactionist leadership; traditionally discussed with the definition of leadership. In this type of leadership, the leader shows the people in the organization what to do and how. In the understanding of transactional leadership, in an organization conditioned to the same goals, there is a work-based approach between the people who will achieve the goals and the person leading the organization, and these behavioral relationships are handled in four different situations (Koçel, 2013).

The first situation is subject to a certain condition. If the efforts of the employees and the performance they achieve are equal, the leader provides more support and resources to the members of this group. The second situation is when the leader intervenes and directs the actions of those who perform the work. In this type of behavior, the leader determines what the work is to be done and directs the members according to the situation. In the third case, the leader is a little more passive.

However, when there is a problem with the performance of the job, it intervenes and intervenes. The fourth situation is called laissez faire (let them do it). It is the type of leadership that leaves people's goals, workload and standards to themselves and acts with an attitude unrelated to work (Koçel, 2013). In transactional leadership, which includes a traditional structure, there is an exchange relationship between the superior and the following subordinate.

According to Bass (1990), in this type of leadership, the contingency of the rewards for effort and effort is at the forefront, and there are team members who avoid taking on a task (Can, Azizoğlu, & Aydın, 2011). In this approach, which is based on an individual view of the universe, people seek to provide personal benefits. The ethics of this situation is also accepted by scientists as a deficient aspect. The ethical legitimacy of transactional leadership means that the reward or punishment provided to anyone is equally distributed to the others (Taslak, 2008).

There is a typical system between the leader and the employees. While the person who works well, progresses towards the goal and does not interrupt his work wins an award, those who do the opposite face punishment. Bass (1990) divided the interactionist leadership into three groups (Ay and Keleş, 2017). These; active and passive exception, conditional reward, management and full freedom.

In active and passive exceptions, the leader does not directly intervene in the event, but becomes involved in the event that the problem grows. In conditional rewarding, the leader rewards the employees for achieving the determined goals. This award is the motivation of the employees and the method of promise is in question. In complete freedom, the leader does not take ideas from anyone, nor does he give any ideas to anyone. The leader, who does not follow the performance of the employees, does not take action when a problem arises. The validity of this type of leadership is possible with the existence of self-managing organizational charts. This type becomes valid if subordinates use the mechanism presented to them for decision making (Ay and Keleş, 2017).

1.4.2. Transformational Leadership

Transformational leadership is a type of leadership that enables adaptation to the conditions in a continuous and indefinite change environment. It can also be defined as attributing a new vision to the group represented by the leader. Transformational leader gives importance to teamwork and wants communication to be high. It sees the employees in the organization as the most important link of the resource. Using the word innovation, this leader ensures that employees are involved in new ideas and goals. They expect initiative from them (Tokmak, 2020).

Transformational leadership is the type of leadership that is not afraid to take responsibility. It aims to gain the respect and trust of its employees, and tries to develop intelligence, reason and problem-solving skills by explaining its big goals correctly. The leader, who takes care of his subordinates one by one, offers them continuous counseling. While these leaders describe themselves as change agents, they are known to have a broad view, trying to learn throughout life (Can, Azizoğlu, & Aydın, 2011). It can be stated that there are four types in this type of leadership that is devoted to its work, just like the interactional leadership type (Koçel, 2013).

The first type of behavior is to gain the respect of subordinates by setting high motivation and moral standards through the leader's work style. Thus, the loyalty of the employees to the leader will increase. The second type of behavior is emotional motivation.

It is a matter that the leader expresses his goals and ideals according to his values and the desire of the employees to follow the leader will strengthen their commitment to him. The third type of behavior is to bring different perspectives to the existing structure, to bring new ideas and to win them by addressing the group members intellectually. It also invites its employees to intellectualism and encourages them. The business style affects the leadership style (Gencer & Akkucuk, 2018). The last type of behavior is the type of behavior in which the leader consults with his subordinates, follows their development with interest and relevance, and helps his employees (Koçel, 2013).

1.4.3. Moral Leadership

According to the moral leadership type, in order to ensure the relative equality in the organization and balance the scales of justice, the leaders need to convince their employees fairly within the framework of ethics and logic (İşcan and Sayın, 2010). The settlement principle of the idea of justice in the organization consists of these criteria. The moral vision of the person adopted by the members as a leader not only increases the trust among the employees, but also ensures that the work is carried out easily.

Moral leadership and trust in the leader are inseparable parts that complement each other (Yanik and Naktiyok, 2017). If an employee who trusts his leader believes that the justice system is established as a condition of loyalty to the organization, it will be possible to increase his commitment to his job. The fairness of the leader and the trust of the employee is a correlation that progresses in direct proportion.

1.4.4. Visionary Leadership

Turkish definition of the word Vision According to the definition of the unit, which was nationalized under the name of Culture, Language and History Institution; It means appearance, ideal and prudence. In the type of visionary leadership, where ideas and actions come together, the leader must have the ability to create visions that will influence and activate their employees and transfer them to them (Ersan, 2020). The first step to creating a vision is to find the idea. Transmitting the idea into action and communicating it to the employees within the organization is the most essential point of visionary leadership.

Considering today's conditions, the leader, who can renew himself in terms of thought, convinces the members of the organization by putting his ideas into action, and it also helps the employees to adopt himself. A leader who is able to foresee the future means that if he conveys this situation to all units of the organization, he has taken the power and provides the opportunity to carry out a joint work with those who follow him. Visionary leadership is a work of persuasion and the correct and timely understanding of the process with those who do the work is the result of this persuasion (Çelik, 1997).

1.4.5. Crisis Leadership

When the concept of crisis is considered in terms of the organization; It is possible to describe this term as the name given to events and situations that are difficult to predict, disrupt ordinary business, and affect the direction of a certain and established organization. The leader of the organization determines the transformational reaction against the unusual situation.

Leaders who can control the crisis process by managing, exerting influence, strategic thinking and communicating, and positively influencing and directing the shareholders of the organization are included in this type. It is the type of leadership that is tried to get rid of the crisis period with the lowest damage and the highest benefit (Canöz & Öndoğan, 2015).

1.4.6. Learning Leadership

In today's era where information is easily accessible, the leader has to learn the necessary information for the progress of the organization and its impact on the organization. In the type of learning leadership, the leader must build the learning organizational culture and obtain and transfer knowledge as a requirement of the period. Schein (2004), who stated that the leaders will have to continuously improve their learning abilities in the future, determined the following as the main issues (Aydın, 2020):

- Perception
- Motivation,
- Emotional power,
- Openness to difference,
- Systematic thinking.

Accessing, processing and using information is explained as an absolute necessity for the leader. The learning leader develops the capabilities of the members while maintaining his own learning phase.

1.4.7. Symbiotic Leadership

The word symbiotic means coexistence in Greek. Expanding markets and the division of markets, the intensification of technological developments, the intensification of competition conditions have brought together the need for leaders who can benefit innovation and change in organizations. Symbiotic leadership; means creating new, different and creative working conditions (Köksal, 2011: 63). Studying symbiotic leadership, Edwards referred to many points for this leadership (Edwards, 1992: 28). These:

- The joint success of executives and those doing the work is equated with serving customer needs.
- The managers give importance to the opinions of the employees.
- The employees of the organization give importance to the ideas of the administrators and take their thoughts into consideration.
- Both managers and those doing the work know that they will be rewarded fairly for their contribution.
- Managers who make performance appraisals also coach employees for their careers.
- Those who participate in innovative team work are rewarded for their personal contributions.

Leaders must form a symbiotic bond with their employees to foster innovation. Within the framework of this bond, the members of the organization are aware that they will be rewarded equally and they trust their leaders because they believe that fair administration will be achieved. Success or failure will affect the entire organization. It is important for innovative leaders to establish symbiotic bonds so that the organization does not fail.

1.5. Common Types of Leadership

1.5.1. Charismatic Leadership

Charismatic leadership, which is among the contemporary leadership theories, is an important phenomenon for society. When the domestic and foreign literature is examined, it is seen that many definitions are made for the concept of charismatic leadership. Charismatic leaders are people who lead the society, are an important source of power for their followers and add value to them, and also enable their followers to think positively and realize the important points for their lives (Gül & Çöl, 2003).

Charismatic leaders who lead the society create an effective field of attraction through their existing personal characteristics and attitudes. One of the important points in this field of attraction is the leader's self-confidence (Aksit, 2008). In this regard, the self-confidence of the charismatic leader causes a very high sense of loyalty on his followers. On the other hand, when charismatic leaders are considered together with their characteristics, it is seen that some of them raise the society they are in to higher levels and some of them take it to lower levels.

According to Weber (1947), charismatic leadership; It is the personality of extraordinary ability, the existence of an extraordinary situation, the ability to make radical solutions to extraordinary situations, and the ability to make employees believe that they have extraordinary and great power (Ray, 2011). The charismatic leader is the type of leader who is successful during a crisis. While Roosevelt was an example of a charismatic leader who prepared the United States, of which he was President, from the 1929 Depression and prepared for the Last World War, Hitler is another charismatic leader who helped his state, which was defeated in the First World War, to become stronger by adding a new vision (Kardam, 2006).

1.5.2. Autocratic Leadership

In autocratic leadership, which is a frequently encountered leadership style, the authority to manage and decide belongs only to the leader. While the issue of quick and effective decision making is the positive side of this type, the leader's selfish behavior expresses its negative side. As a result of not giving the right to speak to the group members, it may be possible to decrease the motivation of the employees (Bakan and Büyükbeşe, 2010: 75).

The effect of autocratic leadership moves in a positive or negative direction according to the character structure of the governed, work order, and resistance to adaptation. In addition, he is a type of leader who creates an expectation about how and when the necessary work will be done. In this type of leadership, the leader rarely considers the advice of his employees against his thoughts and decisions.

Autocratic leadership refers to absolute dominance over the members of the organization. While there are advantages and disadvantages in this type of leadership, like every leadership, there are those who do not approve of this type of leadership by comparing it to dictatorship, and it is thought to be beneficial for the employees of the organization. These benefits depend on the members in the organization and the characteristics of the members.

1.5.3. Democratic Leadership

The word democracy is a concept derived from the Greek words demos and kratos, which means the rule of the people, and when considered from another perspective, it means polyphony. Democratic leadership is a type that includes employees in the decision-making process, guides and ensures their participation. It is also called participatory leadership because it involves employees in the decision-making process (Aydın, 2020). The participatory leadership type, which is implemented in the administrative structures of the developed first-class countries, carries the efficiency of the societies and the organization to the highest level. In this respect, it is also known as an appropriate type of management (Bakan and Büyükbeşe, 2010). It is possible to list participatory leadership in summary and item form (Güney, 1999). These are listed as follows:

- Organization members feel comfortable and free in all matters.
- The participatory leader acts objectively in all matters.
- The sharing of responsibilities and division of work belong to the members.
- The participatory leader trusts the employees in all matters.
- The participant leader informs the members of the organization about the issue before the debate. This information consists of general information.
- The policy of the organization and the plan of its progress are determined as a result of the members' encouragement to debate.

Participatory leadership includes the characteristics of team leadership in Blake and Mouton's model (Wallace & Sailagyi, 1982) and participative management type in Likert's Theory (Güney, 1999).

1.5.4. Ethical Leadership

The relationship between the concept of ethics and leadership has been discussed for a long time and intensive studies are carried out on it (Bircan & Yeşiltaş, 2012). This leadership type, which deals with morally right and wrong, good and bad, is an applied style that puts right, bad, good and wrong on the basis (Bolat & Seymen, 2003; Tuna, Bircan & Yeşiltaş, 2012).

Ethical leadership is the type of leader who investigates the goals of the people in the organization both in the organization and in their private life and the attitudes they have acquired to achieve this goal, and defines the employees and their behaviors as right, wrong, good and bad (Bolat & Seymen, 2003). According to research and definitions based on ethical values, an ethical leader should exhibit a two-way communication (Bass & Steidlmeier, 1999; Yeşiltaş, Çeken, & Sormaz, 2012). Although this type of leadership has emerged due to the extraordinary situations experienced recently, in the work called Kutadgu Bilig, which means happy information and handled by Yusuf Has Hacib in the 11th century, the ethical values that a leader should have are listed as follows (Yılmaz, 2005; Aykanat & Yıldırım, 2012):

- Being honest
- Demonstrate fair management
- To be brave
- Have good habıts
- Not to be cruel
- Give a prize
- To apply the laws correctly and appropriately
- Patience

The applicability of ethical leadership depends on the creation of a suitable environment for the leader and team members to have similar value judgments and to adopt the basic principles (Erdoğan, 2002; Tayfur, Beytekin, & Yalçınkaya, 2013).

This type of leader tries to balance his own skills with existing value judgments while using his power over team members based on morale. In ethical leadership, rather than paying attention to the characteristics of the team members, it accepts the personal differences, beliefs and ethical values of the employees (Aykanat & Yıldırım, 2012).

1.5.5. Servant Leadership

The concept of servant leadership, which emerged by consciously combining the concepts of leadership and serving (Spears, 2010), was used for the first time in the study of Robert K. Greenleaf in 1970. According to the research, it was stated that this type of leadership emerged with the feeling of serving and then turned into a conscious desire to lead.

Stone (2003) stated in his study that the servant leader focuses on his followers. According to this type of leader, the people who make up these organizations are more important than the organizations. In addition, the leader accompanies his employees in line with ethical principles. There are three values in organizations that host such leaders. These; In the public context, it is listed as the obligation to earn high income, the obligation to satisfy customers and the obligation to create a motivated workforce. When the study in the literature is examined, it is seen that the type of servant leadership is handled in six main dimensions and consists of twenty-six sub-dimensions (Sendjaya et al., 2008: 406). Behaviors related to the dimensions described; transformative influence, relationship of trust, supreme spirituality, authentic self, moral responsibility and voluntaryobedience.

CONCLUSION

At the end of the 20th century, there have been many developments that show that the understanding of management has changed in many areas. The new world faces the businesses by many crises(Akkucuk & Gencer, 2017). Intense competition environment that emerged with globalization, technological developments, cultural differences; This has necessitated a paradigm shift in the organizations' perspectives on management. The pandemies have always influenced the business operations (Gencer & Akkuck, 2017). Leadership styles and the traits of leaders are also affected by the pandemic world. Online meetings and working at home are some of examples fort he changes coming with epidemic diseases. Leadership styles explained in this study are all under the rain of changes resulted by Covid-19 disease.

In order for the changing organizational structures to reach their goals in the 21st century, people with leadership qualities were needed. At this point, leaders have become one of the important tools to achieve sustainable competitive advantage. Moreover, the organizations have to face with post pandemic situations. As all environmental inputs, the epidemic disease also have to be taken into account when the strategic plans are determined. Not only the organizations but also the people working in the business life have to pay attention in the post pandemic life. Leadership styles are also updated and influenced by the epidemic diseases.

In this study, firstly, the concept and definition of leadership is mentioned. In the following sections, leadership scales, leadership theories, postmodern leadership types and common leadership types are explained. In the present study, leadership has been tried to be explained conceptually and theoretically. As a result of the research, it is aimed to explain leadership and leadership types and to shed light on the studies in the field of social sciences.

REFERENCES

Akan, D., Yıldırım, İ., & Yalçın, S. (2014). Okul Müdürleri Liderlik Stili Ölçeğinin Geliştirilmesi (OMLSÖ). *Electronic Journal of Social Sciences, 13*(51).

Akkucuk, U., & Gencer, Y. G. (2017, April). EFQM Model and Sustainability of Organizations. *International Conference on Advances in Management Engineering and Information Technology.*

Akşit, H. (2008). *Yönetim ve Yöneticilik.* Kum Saati Yayınları.

Ay, F.A., & Keleş, K. (2017). Etkileşimci ve Dönüşümcü Liderlik Tarzlarının İşten Ayrılma Niyeti Ve İş Performansı Üzerinde Etkisi. *Gümüşhane Üniversitesi Sağlık Bilimleri Dergisi, 6*(4), 193–203.

Aydın, Ö. (2020). *Liderlik Kuramları Açısından PKK Terör Örgütünde Liderlik ve Abdullah Öcalan*. Gazi Üniversitesi Sosyal Bilimler Enstitüsü Siyaset Bilimi Ve Kamu Yönetimi Anabilim Dalı, Yayınlanmamış Doktora Tezi.

Aykanat, Z., & Yıldırım, A. (2012). Etik Liderlik Ve Örgütsel Adalet İlişkisi: Teorik Ve Uygulamalı Bir Araştırma. *Fırat Üniversitesi Sosyal Bilimler Dergisi*, 260-274.

Aytürk, N. (2007). *Yönetim Sanatı. 5.* Baskı, Nobel Yayınları.

Bakan, İ., & Büyükbeşe, T. (2010). Liderlik "Türleri" ve "Güç Kaynaklarına "İlişkin Mevcut- Gelecek Durum Karşılaştırması. *Karamanoğlu Mehmetbey Üniversitesi Sosyal ve Ekonomik Araştırmalar Dergisi, 2010*(2), 73–84.

Bass, B. M. (1990). From transactional to transformational leadership: Learning to share the vision. *Organizational Dynamics, 18*(3), 19–31. doi:10.1016/0090-2616(90)90061-S

Bass, B. M. (1990). *Bass & Stogdill's Handbook of Leadership, Theory, Research, and Managerial Applications, 3.* The Free Press.

Bass, B. M., & Steidlmeier, P. (1999). Ethics, Character And Authentic Transformational Leadership Behavior. *The Leadership Quarterly, 10*(2), 181–217. doi:10.1016/S1048-9843(99)00016-8

Batırlık, S. N., Gencer, Y. G., & Akkucuk, U. (2022). Global Virtual Team Leadership Scale (GVTLS) Development in Multinational Companies. *Sustainability, 14*(2), 1038. doi:10.3390u14021038

Blake, R., & Mouton, J. (1964). The Managerial Grid. The Key To Leadership Excellence. Gulf Publishing Co.

Bolat, T., & Ve Seymen, O. A. (2003). Örgütlerde İş Etiği Ve Kariyer Yönetimi İlişkisi: Normatif Etik Boyutuyla Bir Değerlendirme. *Yönetim Dergisi: İstanbul Üniversitesi İşletme Fakültesi İşletme İktisadı Enstitüsü, 14*(45), 3-19.

Boz, D., Aktı, Ü., Duran, C., & Behdioğlu, S. (2020). Vicdani Liderlik Ölçeği. *Dumlupinar University Journal Of Social Science/Dumlupinar Üniversitesi Soysyal Bilimler Dergisi*, (66).

Bulut, H., & Meydan, C. H. (2018). Liderlik Tarzlarının Çalışanların Ses Verme Davranışına Etkisi: Kamuda Bir Araştırma. *Ankara Üniversitesi Sbf Dergisi*, 223-244.

Can, H. Y., Azizoğlu, Ö. A., & Aydın, E. M. (2011). *Organizasyon ve Yönetim*. Siyasal Kitabevi.

Canöz, K., & Öndoğan, A. (2015). Kriz yönetiminde dönüşümcü liderin rolü. *Gümüşhane Üniversitesi İletişim Fakültesi Elektronik Dergisi, 3*(1), 36–61.

Çelik, H. (2016). *Demokratik liderlik ve örgütsel güven ilişkisi: Balıkesir merkez ilçeleri örneği*. Academic Press.

Çelik, V. (1997). Eğitim yönetiminde vizyoner liderlik. *Kuram ve Uygulamada Eğitim Yönetimi, 12*(12), 465–474.

Edwards, M. R. (1992). Symbiotic leadership: A creative partnership for managing organizational effectiveness. *Business Horizons, 35*(3), 28–34. doi:10.1016/0007-6813(92)90066-I

Erçetin, Ş. (2000). *Lider Sarmalında Vizyon, 2.* Baskı, Nobel Yayın Dağıtım.

Erdoğan, İ. (2002). *Eğitimde Değişim Yönetimi*. Pegem Yayıncılık.

Ersan, E. (2020). Vizyoner Liderlik Özellikleriyle Mustafa Necati Bey. *Uluslararası Liderlik Çalışmaları Dergisi: Kuram ve Uygulama, 3*(1), 58-64.

Gencer, Y. G. (2017). Structural Design of an E-Commerce Business: Yemeksepeti.com Example From Turkey. *The China Business Review, 16*(7), 327–336.

Gencer, Y. G. (2019). The Necessity of Sustainability in Operations Management in Terms of Various Sectors. In *Ethical and Sustainable Supply Chain Management in a Global Context* (pp. 77–85). IGI Global. doi:10.4018/978-1-5225-8970-9.ch005

Gencer, Y. G., & Akkucuk, U. (2017). Measuring quality in automobile aftersales: AutoSERVQUAL Scale. *Amfiteatru Economic, 19*(44), 110.

Gençer, Y. G., & Akküçük, U. (2018). The Preference of Turkish Consumers on Converged Products: The Smartphone Example. *İstanbul Gelişim Üniversitesi Sosyal Bilimler Dergisi, 5*(1), 221-230.

Goleman, D. (1998). *Working with emotional intelligence*. Bantam.

Gül, H., & Çöl, G. (2003). Atıf Teorisinde Belirtilen Karizmatik Lider Özelliklerinin Üçlü Örgütsel Bağlılık Modeliyle İlişkileri Üzerine Bir Araştırma. *Atatürk Üniversitesi İktisadi Ve İdari Bilimler Fakültesi Dergisi, 3*, 4.

Güler, S. (2007). *Fiedler'in Lpc Ölçeği İle Lise Yöneticilerinin Liderlik Tiplerinin Belirlenmesi*. Yayınlanmış Yüksek Lisans Tezi, Yeditepe Üniversitesi Sosyal Bilimler Enstitüsü.

Güney, S. (1999). *Davranış Bilimleri Açısından Atatürk'ün Liderliği*. Ocak Yayınları.

Güven, S. (2016). Postmodern Dönemde Siyasal Alanın Yapısal Dönüşümü ve Postmodern Siyasi Liderlik. *Akdeniz Üniversitesi İletişim Fakültesi Dergisi*, (25), 294–318.

Hair, J. F. Jr., Black, W.C., Babin, B.J., Anderson, R.E., & Tatham, R.L. (2005). Multivariate Data Analysis (6th ed.). Pearson

Hartog, D. N., & Koopman, P. L. (2009). Örgütlerde Liderlik. *Endüstri, İş ve Örgüt Psikolojisi, 2*, 195–219.

İşcan. (2010). *Ömer Faruk, ve Ufuk Sayın*. Örgütsel Adalet, İş Tatmini ve Örgütsel Güven Arasındaki İlişki. Atatürk Üniversitesi İktisadi Ve İdari Bilimler Dergisi.

Jaques, E., & Clement, S.D (1994). Executive Leadership: A Practical Guide to Managing Complexity. Carson-Hall & Co. Publishers.

Köksal, O. (2011). *Organizasyonel Etkinliği Sağlamanın Yeni Yolu: Simbiyotik Liderlik*. Academic Press.

Kuscu, M., & Arslan, H. (2016). Virtual Leadership At Distance Education Teams. *Turkish Online Journal of Distance Education, 17*(3).

Likert, R., & Likert, J. G. (1976). *New Ways of Managing Conflict*. McGraw-Hill.

Naktiyok, A. (2006). *E-Liderlik: E-Liderlik Özelliklerinin İncelenmesine Yönelik Bir Araştırma*. Academic Press.

Rauch, C. F., & Behling, O. (1984). Functionalism: Basis for an Alternate Approach to the Study of Leadership. In J. G. Hunt, D. Hosking, C. Schriesheim, & R. Stewart (Eds.), *Leaders and Managers: International Perspectives on Managerial Behavior and Leadership* (pp. 45–62). Pergamon. doi:10.1016/B978-0-08-030943-9.50012-7

Ray, S., & Ray, I. A. (2011). An insight into the vision of charismatic leadership: Evidence from recent administrative change in West Bengal province of India. *European Journal of Business and Management, 3*(9), 55–67.

Robbins, S. P., & Judge, T. A. (2013). Örgütsel Davranış. Ankara: Nobel.

Sendjaya, S., Sarros, J. C., & Santora, J. C. (2008). Defining and measuring servant leadership behaviour in organizations. *Journal of Management Studies, 45*(2), 402–424. doi:10.1111/j.1467-6486.2007.00761.x

Spears, L. C. (2010). Character and servant leadership: Ten characteristics of effective, caring leaders. *The Journal of Virtues & Leadership, 1*(1), 25–30.

Stogdill, R. M., & Shartle, C. L. (1948). Methods for determining patterns of leadership behavior in relation to organization structure and objectives. *The Journal of Applied Psychology, 32*(3), 286–291. doi:10.1037/h0057264 PMID:18867065

Stone, C. M. (2003). *A study of the relationship between principals' leadership behaviors and the school culture as perceived by the teachers*. The University of Mississippi.

Taş, A., & Çetiner, A. (2011). Ortaöğretim Okulu Müdürlerinin Dönüşümcü Liderlik Davranışlarını Gerçekleştirme Durumlarına İlişkin Öğretmen Görüşleri. *Journal of Turkish Educational Sciences, 9*(2), 369,392.

Taslak, S. (2008). Göreve İlişkin Çalışmalarda Etkileşimci ve Dönüşümcü Liderlik Üzerine Etiksel Bir Değerlendirme. *Erciyes Üniversitesi İ.İ.B.F. Dergisi*, 121-144.

Tayfur, M., Beytekin, O. F., & Yalçınkaya, M. (2013). İlköğretim Okul Yöneticilerinin Etik Liderlik Özellikleri İle Okullardaki Örgütsel Güven Düzeyinin İncelenmesi (İzmir İl Örneği). *Dicle Üniversitesi Ziya Gökalp Eğitim Fakültesi Dergisi*, 84-106.

Tokmak, M. (2020). Dönüştürücü ve Etkileşimci Liderlik Tarzı İle Negatif İnovasyon Algısı Arasındaki İlişkiye Yönelik Bir Araştırma. *Kahramanmaraş Sütçü İmam Üniversitesi Sosyal Bilimler Dergisi*, 441-464.

Tosun, K. (1987). *İşletme Yönetimi: Genel Esaslar*. İstanbul: İ. Ü. İşletme Fakültesi Yayınları, no:186.

Tuna, M., Bircan, H., & Yeşiltaş, M. (2012). Etik Liderlik Ölçeğinin Geçerlilik ve Güvenilirlik Çalışması: Antalya Örneği. *Atatürk Üniversitesi İktisadi Ve İdari Bilimler Dergisi,* 143-155.

Wallace, M. J., & Szilagyi, A. D. (1982). *Managing behavior in organizations*. Pearson Scott Foresman.

Yaman, S., Demir, B., Batırlık, S. N., & Zeren, F. (2021). Lojistik Sektörü ve Ekonomik Büyüme Arasındaki İlişkinin İncelemesi: G20 Ülkeleri Üzerine Bir Araştırma. *The Journal of International Scientific Researches, 6*(1), 1–9.

Yeşiltaş, M., Çeken, H., & Sormaz, Ü. (2012). Etik Liderlik Ve Örgütsel Adaletin Örgütsel Sapma Davranışları Üzerindeki Etkisi. *Muğla Üniversitesi Sosyal Bilimler Enstitüsü Dergisi*, 18-39.

Yılmaz, E. (2005). *'Etik Liderlik' Öğretmenin Dünyası. Odunpazarı Belediyesi Yayınları Eğitim Dizisi-3*. Mikro Yayıncılık.

Yurtkoru, E. S. (2001). *The role of leadership in the organizational change process*. Yayımlanmamış Doktora Tezi. Marmara Üniversitesi Sosyal Bilimler Enstitüsü. İstanbul Yüksek Lisans Tezi, Balıkesir Üniversitesi Sosyal Bilimler Enstitüsü.

Zaleznik, A. (1992). Managers and Leaders: Are Thet Different? *Harvard Business Review*, (March-April), 126–135.

Zel, U. (2001). *Kişilik ve Liderlik*. Seçkin Yayıncılık.

Chapter 8
Multi-National Companies and Their Progress in Turkey

Yasin Galip Gencer
Yalova University, Turkey

Sema Nur Batirlik
Yalova University, Turkey

ABSTRACT

Although multinational companies are both a cause and a result of economic globalization, it is also a driving force that enables economic globalization to expand its sphere of influence around the world. Today, international relations require not only states but also the existence of non-state actors to be taken into account. Multinational companies have increased both their numbers and activities with globalization. The increasing role of multinational companies has begun to be limited not only to economic activities. They can take on a function of shaping the policies of underdeveloped nation states. In this study, the definition, characteristics, and historical development of multinational companies are explained. Then, the organizational structure of these companies is mentioned. The place of multinational companies in the world and in Turkey is explained and the study is concluded. The concept of a multinational company has been examined with the research. The aim of the study is to explain the concept of multinational companies in a broad perspective.

INTRODUCTION

Multinational companies are seen as one of the important actors of the globalization process. The first examples of multinational companies, which are active in more than one country and can be defined as companies that make investments in countries where they operate outside of their home country, began to be seen in the 19th century.

The emergence of multinational companies in the modern sense took place after the 1929 World Economic Depression. There are many factors in the emergence of such companies (Batirlik et al, 2022).

DOI: 10.4018/978-1-6684-5876-1.ch008

These factors are technical knowledge superiority, economies of scale, low transportation costs, the desire to benefit from economic opportunities, and the desire to compete on a world scale. In addition, due to reasons such as the narrowness of the domestic market of the companies in the country of origin, legal regulations, and ease of access to raw materials, which can be considered external to the companies, national companies choose to become multinational companies.

On the one hand, multinational companies create positive results such as increasing the quality of life and growth rates around the world, increasing the national income of the countries, reducing the production costs with the revival of the local markets in the countries, and positively affecting the balance of payments especially in the countries with current account deficit. Considering the number and investments of multinational companies in the world, it is possible to say that there has been a rapid increase throughout the 20th century.

Definition and Characteristics of Multinational Corporations

Multinational companies have become a frequently used structure with the intensification of globalization and the increase in technological developments. However, they are structures that do not have a clear definition in the academic literature and cannot be fully agreed upon. The fact that the concept cannot be placed in a clear definition is due to the heterogeneity of such companies (Kaymakçı, 2013). Although a definite definition cannot be made, the common features of these companies are; They are listed as operating in more than one country, having central controls for all parts of the company, and these departments following interrelated policies, and being organizations that control small company units in other countries (Tokol, 2001). Multinational corporations are organizations that have branches, companies and partners from the central government(Gencer, 2016).

The way these companies operate is determined by the centre. Branches and small company structures in different places also act in harmony with the center (Yavuz and Sivrikaya, 2009). While the sale of the products and services produced starts and ends within the same organization, the distribution and marketing of the goods is carried out by the organizations affiliated to these companies (Işık, 2005). Multinational companies, which have become important structures in the developing and changing world, have an important mission in economic activities.

The reason why these companies are constantly expanding and increasing their power is; This is due to the fact that they spread production, consumption and dominant capital among countries (Yahşi, 2007). The increase in technological developments has allowed the multinational company structures to increase. These company types, which reduced communication and distribution costs, divided the production process into parts with technological development, and thus, the spread of the company type to the world was realized by ensuring that every process is realized in the possible region. In addition, they have started to become stronger on a world basis and have become competitive with states, not companies (Altan, 2013).

Especially in the last 350-400 years, in the ever-evolving world structure, companies have also kept up with the changes and pioneered the systems that are trying to be placed (Taşçıer, 2018). While the implementation of liberal policies introduced the word privatization, corporate structures belonging to individuals and institutions also gained importance. While the concept of a multinational company emerged in the world structure, where the basic needs of the person, such as shelter, clothing and food, are intertwined with other sectors; a company settled in the center preferred to expand to other countries and to produce, distribute and market in accordance with the region where it has the opportunity(Gencer

& Akkucuk, 2016). By establishing a supply chain suitable for the demographic structure of each region, a policy compatible with these regions has been ensured.

Historical Development of Multinational Companies

Multinational companies are company structures that develop over a long period of time. The first stage of these developments was taken by the states that wanted to reach the resources of other countries. The first multinational company in world history was founded in 1602 as the Dutch East India Company. In the light of the developments from the beginning of the 19th century to the last quarter, companies and firms bought other organizations and created a new market. While this developing company type creates oligopoly structures, in general terms; There are three types of large oligopoly structure that includes continuity, mobile oligopolies for production, and oligopolies for inventions and innovations (Çam, 2011). It is stated that multinational companies gained importance in today's history after the Second World War. The reason for this situation is the positive developments that started to be experienced in international relations after the first half of the 20th century (Gencer, 2018). States that rely on reason and attach importance to technology in the field of public administration, entered into a new restructuring after the war, and with the spread of privatization, companies have directed companies to integrate with the world. Thus, the companies that expanded their fields of activity spread to the world by increasing their numbers (Kaya and Aydemir, 2011).

After the Second World War, the countries' choice of ways to solve their problems had a positive effect on the production sector and enabled the multinational companies to multiply. With the loss of importance of the drawn geographical borders, the number of these company types has increased. Organizations such as the United Nations, the International Monetary Fund and the World Bank, which were established at the end of the war, prepared draft laws and legal texts for multinational companies. With the legal regulations, the economic demands of the companies located in the center were put into practice. Thus, multinational companies have become comparable to states.

Organizational Structure of Multinational Companies

While businesses have evolved into a multinational company structure, there have been differences in the organizational structure (Batirlik & Gencer, 2021). It is an important issue for companies that have started to operate in other countries and opened up to different markets to respond to innovations and design their policies accordingly. When starting a business in a different country, the entry stages can be listed as follows; foreign purchase and sale activity, stock investments, license agreement, branching and opening a joint business.

Businesses that take on a multinational structure take this process in four stages. The first stage is to engage in import activities without making much changes in product management. In the second stage, the administration makes a license agreement with a small amount of change and ensures the transfer of information related to the developing technology. While the third stage is to establish the necessary factories for the investments to be made, sufficient skills should be developed for this stage. In the last stage, significant increases in different investments and non-state resources constitute a significant amount of total assets. (Özalp, 1984).

Organizational structures of multinational companies have some characteristics. These can be listed as follows; (Bayram, 2015):

- Formalize
- Specialization
- Centralization

The use of the defined systems and structures in the decision phase, communication and control phase is called formalization (Alpkan, 2006). The use of formalization varies from country to country. Individuals in the country and people doing the work can approach the formal structure in a positive or negative context (Alpkan, 2006). This formal structure is divided into two as objective and subjective. Objective formalization is defined in the context of different factors such as the number of data given to the members of the organization, organizational charts, organizational instructions, written notifications. Subjective formation, on the other hand, is measured by the values that are not clear, that are out of formal use, that come from the culture that settled down to do the job.

The concept of specialization is the involvement of organizational members in defined and specific jobs. Characteristically, specialization is when employees perform tasks that are appropriate and compatible with them. While specialization is divided into two, like formalization, the first is horizontal specialization and the second is vertical specialization (Yeloğlu, 2008). Horizontal specialization means the fulfillment of the duties assigned to the members of the organization within the determined limits. The member working in this type of specialization adds experience to himself in certain fields. Vertical specialization is a type in which all organizational members are collectively responsible for their performance (Özgür and Zanbak, 2019). The concept of central administration is a system in which decisions that are meaningful for the organization are made by the higher authority. The importance of the central administration varies according to the environmental conditions of the foreign country it enters and the goals of the organization (Taşçıer, 2018).

The enterprise, which has a multinational structure, enters different markets through imports in the first stage. It also chooses the way of importing through a different enterprise. The company, whose import volume is growing, can also establish its own unit for direct imports. The member responsible for the import unit, which he/she assigns from himself/herself, reports to the marketing department. While the increase in imports and sales can lead to the opening of new branches, these branches are shaped according to the business presidency and the central administration, which regulates the policies in different nations (Bayram, 2015). As it can be understood, the organizational structure of multinational companies varies according to the market the company enters, the employees of the organization, and the cultures of people in different countries. Just as each organization may have a different structure, all organizations struggle with similar structures and variability. To adapt to the changing technology conditions, to wait for the organization of other countries and the products they produce and serve, or to produce in accordance with them; Reducing costs through branching can be counted as the factors that enable multinational companies to spread around the world.

Multinational Companies in the World

The spread of modern technology in the world has led to diversification of investments. The efficient use of technology, especially in places in the developing country category, has helped the multinational company structure to become more effective. Technology is one of the most important factors that enable the development of multinational organizations, accelerate their spread and increase their production.

Businesses, which have been using the benefits of technology for years, have managed to expand their business volumes, production capacities and spread areas around the world by becoming multinational.

Multinational companies have become even more effective today, especially after the end of the hot wars, when economic wars took their place. In this period, when competition turned into production and consumption culture increased through marketing and advertising, the existence of multinational organizations was important; A new era has begun in which countries compete with each other and with companies (Akkucuk & Gencer, 2017). With the acceleration of the globalization process and the effect of globalization on the world, multinational companies have become one of the main actors of this period. The spread of multinational companies and the spread of globalization affected each other in parallel, and mutual interaction accelerated this development. It is a generally accepted fact that the concept of globalization cannot be defined separately from multinational companies. The American political scientist Samuel Huntington (2004) also refers to the phenomenon of globalization with this transformative process; individuals, parliaments, companies, non-governmental organizations and other entities. Huntington's globalization; It expresses the increase in international communications, the growth of global organizations and the increase in investments, the proliferation of multinational structures that produce, and the intensification of the presence of international organizations (Huntington, 2004). Multinational organizations, which came to the forefront with the increase of globalization, expanded their fields of activity and found the opportunity to develop their capital. The results of the Great Place to Work Institute's 2020 survey of the world's largest multinational companies also informs us about the situation before Covid-19. While more than ten thousand companies were included in the research conducted in 92 countries, ten million two hundred thousand people were represented. The research criteria were made according to the dimensions of reliability, fair management, respect and team. When this research process is examined, it is seen that the focus is on issues that employees attach importance to spiritually. With this research, it was possible to see the effects of issues such as fair management, trust and respect, which are the elements of democratic, participatory leadership type, on multinational company employees.

The Place of Multinational Companies in Turkey

Multinational companies determine their investments in different regions according to the political, economic, cultural and moral aspects of that country. These factors are the points chosen and considered for profit maximization (Kaymakçı, 2013). While the impact of technology on developed countries is a significant issue for multinational companies, developing countries such as Turkey have limited development and growth potential in the economic context due to the limited progress in technology. In addition to these, the problems encountered in terms of development have pushed Turkey into the background on the way to multinational corporations(Gencer & Akkucuk, 2017).

One of the ways for Turkey, which faces problems in terms of capital, to solve this problem is to eliminate the financial problem by attracting foreign investors. It is important to attract investors directly or indirectly to the country with external financing resources. Located in an interesting region due to its geographical location, rich in underground resources and located in a pass connecting the continents, Turkey has not been able to fully reflect these values to the world.

It is possible to examine Turkey's relations with foreign investors by dividing them into periods. These; It is expressed as two periods before and after the transition to multi-party system, one period after 1980 and another period after 2000 (Kaymakçı, 2013).

1923-1950 Period

As a country that has just emerged from the war, Turkey has laid the foundations of the new economy system with the Economics congresses it has organized (Kayıran and Saygın, 2019). Turkey, which outsources industrial goods and started to produce agricultural products on its own, has turned to industrialization in return for this (Kayıran and Saygın, 2019). As a legal basis, the Law on Encouragement of Industry, enacted in 1927, together with the Securities Exchange Law No. 1447.

The administrators, who did not want to be exposed to external pressure economically, acted sensitively about foreign investors. Despite the economic decisions taken, the planning made and the congresses held; The entry of foreign investors into the country could not reach the expected level due to reasons such as the 1929 Depression, which is called Black Thursday, and affecting the world, the outbreak of the Second World War, and the debts remaining from the State-i Âliye have to be paid (Buluş and Kabaklarlı, 2010).

Among the reasons for Turkey's failure to attract foreign investors to the country are its overprotective policies and the fact that the newly established regime has not settled (Kaymakçı, 2013). Therefore, in the period between 1923 and 1950, foreign investors, who were seen as a source of foreign financing in terms of multinationality, remained hesitant to enter the country(Yaman et al, 2021).

1950-1980 Period

A new era has started in Turkey with those who left the party they were in with a quartet and established a new party and came to power with the 1950 elections (Tuna, 2015). It is seen that more liberal policies have started to be followed since the 1950s. In this new period, which was tried to be placed on a liberal basis, laws were enacted in order to encourage privatization and foreign investments. However, the fact that these laws cause problems in practice and the bureaucracy does not allow foreign investors within the framework of the law, hindered the entry from other countries in terms of trust.

Problems such as the overthrow of the government by a coup, the start of the import substitution policy in the economy, and the inadequacy of the prepared development plans in practice affected the investors negatively in the period between 1950 and 1980 as well. The embargo decisions implemented due to the Cyprus Peace Operation caused the existing investors in the country to shift to other countries. Despite the existence of unfavorable conditions, 325 billion dollars of foreign financing has been inflowed to the country between this period (Kaymakçı, 2013).

1980-2000 Period

Experiencing an economic crisis with the embargo decisions, Turkey entered a new era in economic terms with the 24 January Decisions. These decisions, called stabilization measures, can be listed as follows (Öztürk, Nas and İçöz, 2008):

- Turkey will be redesigned within the framework of free market economy conditions as an economic solution.
- Tight monetary policy will be implemented to prevent inflation from rising.
- Base prices in agricultural products, State Economic Enterprise fees and fuel prices will be adjusted so as not to increase inflation.

- Interest rates will be increased and competition will be realized.
- A floating exchange rate will be adopted and liberal policies will be applied for the inflow of foreign resources.
- The existing government will consult with the International Monetary Fund in terms of economic measures.

When the stabilization measures taken are examined, the enactment of liberal policies, the transition to a free market economy and the adjustment of prices are among the remarkable decisions. Despite the two coups and unstable changes in the government in this period, foreign investors entered the country more than in previous periods. Reasons such as the end of the Cold War and the need for a leading country in the Middle East are also effective here.

Period After 2000

This period started with a law for direct foreign investors. It is a law enacted to encourage foreign investors to enter the country, to protect the rights of foreigners and to inform foreigners by establishing an approval mechanism within the framework of permits in accordance with international standards. In the first half of the period from this period to the present, the entry of multinational companies into the country has become more evident. In the last year of the first half of this period, the capital inflow of foreign investors increased to 9 billion dollars (Kaymakçı, 2013).

When multinational companies are divided into periods and their place in Turkey is examined, it is seen that draft laws encouraging foreign investors are prepared. When the world's globalization process accelerates, companies that choose to expand to different countries and the states that support companies have focused on political, legal and economic criteria. In addition, issues such as demographic structure, social culture awareness, access to new markets were also effective. Political crises, economic turmoil, erratic legal norms, technological advances that have been slow to develop since the establishment of the Republic, have caused Turkey to not be able to determine its place in the globalization phenomenon and foreign resources to not fully enter the country.

Multinational companies, which opened up to the world with long-term gains, abstained from their investments as they could not clearly see the suitable peaceful environment in Turkey. Despite all the negative developments, the geographical conditions, the consumption culture of the people, the location on the transit route, and the fact that it is rich in underground resources are the points that allow foreign investors to enter Turkey and attract them. To gain the trust of multinational companies that want to invest in the country; It can be realized by promising them that they will make long-term gains, encouraging them to invest, and creating constructive mechanisms against economic crises.

CONCLUSION

Multinational companies that emerged as a result of globalization have contributed significantly to this process thanks to their worldwide production activities and division of labor. Changes in the transportation sector as a natural result of the advances in information and communication technologies have helped multinational companies to expand their markets and to produce in different sectors within a single company. The role of the paradigm shift in the economic policies implemented in the significant increase in the number of multinational companies from the time the first modern multinational companies emerged to the present day is very important.

The "neo-liberal" economic policies that were tried to be implemented worldwide after the 1980s provided these companies with the necessary infrastructure support for the global expansion of multinational companies and their investments. Thanks to the policies implemented, countries had to reduce customs duties on the one hand, contrary to global protectionist policies, while seeing the private sector and foreign capital as an important part of their economic development, on the other hand, reducing the role of the state on the market; It has facilitated the entry of multinational companies and foreign capital into countries in different ways.

In this study, firstly, the definition, characteristics and historical development of the concept of multinational company are explained. Afterwards, the organizational structure of these companies is defined under the headings of formalization, specialization and centralization. Finally, the titles of multinational companies in the world and in Turkey are examined in detail. It is thought that the descriptive and explanatory research will contribute to the literature. It is envisaged that more comprehensive studies can be carried out by using quantitative methods in future studies.

REFERENCES

Akkucuk, U., & Gencer, Y. G. (2017, April). EFQM Model and Sustainability of Organizations. *International Conference on Advances in Management Engineering and Information Technology.*

Alpkan, L. (2006). Stratejik Planlama Süreci Bileşenlerinin Firma Performansına Etkileri. *Kocaeli Üniversitesi Sosyal Bilimler Enstitüsü Dergisi,* 21-47.

Altan, M. (2013). *Uluslararası Ekonomi Politik.* Anadolu Üniversitesi Yayınları.

Batırlık, S. N., & Gencer, Y. G. (2021). Sanal Takımlar Üzerine Literatür Taraması. *Social Sciences Studies Journal, 80*(7), 1156–1163. doi:10.26449ssj.3128

Batırlık, S. N., Gencer, Y. G., & Akkucuk, U. (2022). Global Virtual Team Leadership Scale (GVTLS) Development in Multinational Companies. *Sustainability, 14*(2), 1038. doi:10.3390u14021038

Bayram, E. (2015). Çok Uluslu İşletmelerde Örgütsel Yapıya Dair Farklılıklar ve Çok Uluslu İşletmelerin Türkiye'deki Yönetim Yapıları. Yüksek Lisans Tezi, Eskişehir: Anadolu Üniversitesi Sosyal Bilimler Enstitüsü.

Buluş, A., & Kabaklarlı, E. (2010). 1929 Ekonomik Buhranı İle Son Dönem Global Krizin Karşılaştırılması. *Sosyal Ekonomik Araştırmalar Dergisi, 10*(19), 1–22.

Çam, E. (2011). Çok Uluslu Şirketler ve Gelişen Ülkeler. *İstanbul Üniversitesi İktisat Fakültesi Mecmuası, 45*(1-4).

Gençer, Y. G. (2018). Measuring value along the supply chain: A study on white goods sector. *Elektronik Sosyal Bilimler Dergisi, 17*(66), 688–703.

Gencer, Y. G. (2016). Mystery of recycling: Glass and aluminum examples. In *Handbook of research on waste management techniques for sustainability* (pp. 172–191). IGI Global. doi:10.4018/978-1-4666-9723-2.ch009

Gencer, Y. G., & Akkucuk, U. (2016). Reverse logistics: Automobile recalls and other conditions. In *Handbook of research on waste management techniques for sustainability* (pp. 125–154). IGI Global. doi:10.4018/978-1-4666-9723-2.ch007

Gencer, Y. G., & Akkucuk, U. (2017). Measuring quality in automobile aftersales: AutoSERVQUAL Scale. *Amfiteatru Economic*, *19*(44), 110.

Kaya, M., & Cahit, A. (2011). Küreselleşmenin Tarihsel Gelişimi. *Dicle Üniversitesi İktisadi ve İdari Bilimler Fakültesi Dergisi*, 14-36.

Kayıran, M., & Saygın, S. (2019). İzmir İktisat Kongresi. *Eskişehir Osmangazi Üniversitesi Türk Dünyası Uygulama ve Araştırma Merkezi Yakın Tarih Dergisi*, 27-70.

Kaymakçı, O. (2013). Küresel Ekonomide Çok Uluslu Şirketler Ve Türkiye'deki Yansımaları. *Manisa Celal Bayar Üniversitesi Sosyal Bilimler Dergisi*, 224-249.

Özalp, İ. (1984). *Çok Uluslu İşletmelerin Yönetimi*. Anadolu Üniversitesi Basımevi.

Özgür, R. Ö., & Zanbak, M. (2019). Dış Ticarette Uzmanlaşma: Türkiye'de Endüstrilere Yönelik Bazı Tespitler. *İnsan E Toplum Bilim Araştırmaları Dergisi,* 1411-1436.

Öztürk, Ş., Nas, F., & İçöz, E. (2008). 24th January Decisions Neo-Liberal Policies and Agriculture Of Turkey. *Pau J Soc Sci Ins, 1*(2), 15-32.

Taşçıer, A. M. (2018). Neoliberalizmde Merkezileşme- Yerelleşme Gerilimi: İl Özel İdareleri, Yikob Örnekleri ve Yerelde Merkezileşme. *Gazi Üniversitesi Sosyal Bilimler Dergisi,* 650-662.

Tokol, A. (2001). Çok Uluslu Şirketler ve Endüstri ilişkilerine Etkileri. *Endsütri İlişkileri ve İnsan Kaynakları Dergisi, 3*(2).

Tuna, I. (2015). Verilişinin 70.Yılında Demokratikleşme Belgesi Olarak Türk Siyasal Hayatında Dörtlü Takrir. *Çağdaş Türkiye Tarihi Araştırmaları Dergisi*, 203-219.

Yahşi, F. (2007). *Küreselleşme ve İstihdam*. Yüksek Lisans Tezi, Çukurova Üniversitesi Sosyal Bilimler Enstitüsü.

Yaman, S., Demir, B., Batirlik, S. N., & Zeren, F. (2021). Lojistik Sektörü ve Ekonomik Büyüme Arasındaki İlişkinin İncelemesi: G20 Ülkeleri Üzerine Bir Araştırma. *The Journal of International Scientific Researches*, *6*(1), 1–9.

Yavuz, C., & Sivrif, D. (2009). Küreselleşmenin aktörlerinden çokuluslu şirketler ve yönetişim. Küresel Diyalog Konferansı Uluslararası Davraz Kongresi. Isparta, 1217-1236.

Yeloğlu, H. O. (2008). Örgütlerde Yapısal-Stratejik Konfigürasyonlar: Koşulbağımlılık Kuramı, Konfigürasyon Yaklaşımı Bağlamında Örgüt Yapıları Üzerine Önermeler. *Eskişehir Osmangazi Üniversitesi İibf Dergisi*, 155-170.

Chapter 9
Supply Chain Disruptions and the Effects on Price Stability: An Intercountry Analysis

Oya Ekici
İstanbul University, Turkey

ABSTRACT

The widespread impact of price instability issues in the world has originated in global financial problems for more than three decades, and the effect of wars on the price changes remained mostly local or regional. But today, the impact of price instabilities rooted in supply chain bottlenecks is broader and more persistent in nature. With this changing price instability structure, analyzing the interdependence in production among the countries and exploring their effect on countries' inflation levels has become crucial. With this motivation, the chapter examines these relations by the BVAR model. The interdependence of countries' own purchasing managers' index, representing the supply chain disruptions, and their impulse on the producer price index, representing the inflation, are captured by the BVARs. The chapter focuses on the cases of a group of specific economies and chooses three countries: Germany, the United States, and Turkey. The findings remark that these countries' inflation levels are associated with their major trading partners' supply chain disruptions.

INTRODUCTION

Various reasons such as a pandemic, political crisis, disasters, economic crisis, or war may result in supply chain disruptions. Recently, the most significant supply chain bottlenecks in the world have been experienced during the Covid 19 pandemic. Since the beginning of the early phase of the outbreak, the lockdown and short-time working order have disrupted both the production and distribution stages of supply chains. These unexpected developments in the business world restructured the planned jobs, commitments, and even priorities. The experiences increased the costs soon afterward and ultimately led to price surges in the markets of almost all countries. The countries ran into inflation issues with the incidents extended over pandemic time. However, the outcomes of the price instabilities or inflation did

DOI: 10.4018/978-1-6684-5876-1.ch009

not influence the economies in the same way across the countries, as their economic resilience levels are not the same. Clearly, in a global world, the same singular developments lived by the trade partners have led to similar economic consequences hardly these consequences have not been as crucial as in other countries' economies.

For the activities in the global trade, the countries rely necessarily on other countries' production processes. Many European manufacturers are dependent on China and other Asian countries for some crucial goods and semifinal goods. In March 2020, for instance, 60% of the German mechanical industry was disrupted because of the shutdowns in Italy and China (Van Der Putten, 2020). Likewise, in North America, U.S. production contributes to manufacturing in Canada and Mexico, and the lockdowns in the U.S. restricted the trade between the U.S. and these Latin countries (Baldwin and Tomiura, 2020). The disruptive effect of the pandemic did not stay regional since the countries such as Germany, the U.S., China, Japan, and Korea are dominant for all countries' final goods markets (Van Der Putten, 2020).

In terms of the macroeconomy, the severe consequences of the supply disruptions can be traced back to the principal indicators like the growth, employment, or exchange rate. Its impact on price stability is closely related to all these macroeconomic indicators. That is why price stability is one of the keys outcomes that need to be analyzed to grasp the economic impact of the disruptions. Modern supply chains are highly uncertain, and the supply chain processes are very complicated by their nature (Datta, P.P. and Christopher, 2011). On top of that, detecting and analyzing the effect on the prices, which have micro and macro dynamics, get more complicated. From this aspect, it gains prominence to explore the countries' data of the most interconnected partners in trading simultaneously.

In the literature, the relationship between retail prices and the developments in the retail supply chain is investigated by Ballantyne and Langcake (2016), and they found more significant evidence compared with the model built by the exchange rate. Majan and Tomar (2020) examine the effects of disruptions in food supply chains on product availability and food prices in India due to Covid 19. Commonly in the relevant literature, the studies suggest that supply chain disruptions have led to price increases (Meier and Pinto, 2020; Cavallo et al. 2014; Glick and Taylor, 2010; Attinasi et al. 2022; Santacreu and LaBelle, 2022). On the contrary, Greenwood and Hanke (2022) discuss that inflation in the U.S. is not due to problems in the supply chain but the result of the excess monetary growth in the market.

This chapter primarily aims at investigating price instability originating from supply chain disruptions. For this purpose, a group of countries is determined based on the dominance in a focus country's export and import activities. Here the specified focused country is Turkey. For the variable representing the supply chain disruption, Purchasing Managers' Index (PMI) data is preferred, and for the variable as an indicator of inflation, Producer Price Index (PPI) is selected. PMI is one of the most reliable indices and a more precise indicator of the current global business environment. It helps to describe the existing market conditions and provides the signals of the following terms' potential price instabilities. It is based on a survey and consists the variables such as manufacturing, backlogs of work, output and input prices, suppliers' delivery times, stocks of finished goods, and employment. As for PPI data, it has more representative power compared to Consumer Price Index (CPI) because it also considers the costs to the industry. The data covers the period of 2011 - 2022 on a monthly basis. The data source for PMI is S&P Global (2022).

The chapter examines the relationship between these two variables by considering co-movement and association between the countries. The empirical method of the chapter is based on Bayesian Vector Autoregression (BVAR) modeling. BVAR models contribute to detecting the interdependent relationships in the series and consider the effect of their lagged values (see Koop and Korobilis (2010) for the details of Bayesian VAR). In the chapter, in addition to the partial causal relationship analysis, the author tries to answer the following questions: Do the interdependent PMIs lead the countries to experience similar price instability issues? Is there a co-movement or contagion effect between the countries' Purchasing Managers' indices?

Today, The Russia-Ukraine war, which started when the pandemic slowed down, will disrupt the supply chain due to the international trade restrictions. Also, this will again have consequences on price levels. More importantly, the situation will influence inflation expectations as well. Therefore, whatever the primary reason, exploring the price stabilities caused by supply chain disruptions in-depth and being agile in responding to sudden changes have gained importance. For the war case, disruptions may not be widespread and abrupt as is in the pandemic, nevertheless, the phenomenon highlights the need to be prepared for these kinds of developments in supply chain management. It will be essential to develop new policies and alternative strategies that will require measures to remodel supply chain and logistics processes.

The author organizes the sections of this book chapter as follows. The first section provides the theoretical background and the main hypothesis of the study. The following section describes the data and provides details about the BVAR methodology to investigate the relationship between supply chain disruptions and inflation. It is followed by the section involving the estimation results and a discussion of the empirical findings from the models. The last section encapsulates the overall results of the chapter and offers some concluding remarks.

Background

Working on inflation has always been a natural field of interest in macroeconomics. But after the pandemic and now during the war, it has become an essential topic for researchers. In today's prevailing economic environment, many countries have experienced inflation regardless of whether it is developed or developing. Inflation levels of countries are now high and persistent, and according to the recent figures of the OECD, inflation on average in the OECD increased by 9.2 percent in April 2022, compared with April of the previous year: "*Nine OECD countries recorded double-digit inflation rates, with the highest rates experienced in Turkey and Estonia. By contrast, inflation fell in five OECD countries, including Italy, Spain, and the United States.*" (OECD, 2022 June). The supply chain bottleneck is in lead among other drivers of this issue, such as the shift in demand toward goods and away from services or the supply shocks to energy, food, or labor (Agarwal and Kimball, 2022). The book and consequently this chapter discuss this current issue. The chapter focuses on the empirical investigation of the association between inflation and supply chain disruptions.

The empirical literature on the PMI and the PPI association is relatively small, considering the inter-country relationship. Ji-Hong (2017) analyzed the PMI effect for Korean and the United States economies by vector error correction models. Meyer and Habanabakize (2018) also examined the relationship by adding the variable consumer price index, and they found that the consumer price index causes PMI, but PPI causes PMI. Alternatively, Mei-Chih and Chang (2019) used the wavelet theory model to investigate the lead-lag effect between the Chinese and the United States PMI and West Texas Intermediate crude oil prices. Their results indicate that these two countries' PMI affects the oil prices in the different periods, which the reality is a sign of a structural shift. In their models, when they included the PPI data as the control variable, they captured the short-term positive relationship of PPI to the PMI and the crude oil price. In the literature, there is a most recent study of Attinasi et al. (2022) published in ECB economic bulletin. In their paper, they try to measure the supply chain shocks on trade and prices. They used a VAR model having endogenous variables exports, imports, industrial production and CPI, and PPI. Supply chain shock was exogenous in their model. They found that the disruptions have a more significant impact on PPI when compared to CPI.

The present chapter concentrated on a group of countries' data, considering their cross-dependencies of trade: Germany, the United States, and Turkey. Germany is the major trading partner in many countries in the European Union. Germany and the United States are two developed countries that are prominent leaders in international trade. On the other hand, Turkey and the United States are two countries suffering from the inflation issue. In analyzing the inflation issues of these three countries comprehensively, the chapter uses PMI data of the major trading partners of Turkey.

PMI is a kind of general economic performance indicator illustrating whether the condition is stagnant or buoyant. It is a qualified index data based on a survey that gathers feedback from over 40 countries' supply chain leaders. The PMI is a substantially original data and has a considerable amount of representative power over economic activity. This index data is one of the top indicators followed by policymakers, investors, and the business world. Naturally, its benefits and practicality were discussed in the literature. Koenig (2002) and Tsuchiya (2012) illustrated that it is a useful indicator of growth for the manufacturing sector and the overall economy. Koenig (2002) interpreted the effect of the PMI at different levels. A PMI data of a country has a value between 0 and 100. And above the critical level of 50 signalizes an expansion in the economy. However, below 50 implies a contraction in that economy. If the PMI is modeled properly, it provides successful predictions for the PMI (Lindsey and Pavur, 2005). The manufacturing PMI data, which covers new orders, output, employment, suppliers' delivery times, and stocks of purchases, directly reflects the developments in the supply chain. Hence it has a great value in measuring economic activity.

In the model the chapter employs, the PPI data has more representative capacity than the CPI for the price changes. Since, by definition, the PPI reveals the price fluctuations of the output received by the producers in that economy. On the other hand, the CPI's methodology is based on the price changes of specific consumer goods and services over time. Moreover, Attinasi et al. (2022) demonstrated that the supply chain disruptions in their model have a more profound influence on the PPI, which justifies why this chapter uses the PPI as an inflation indicator.

Regarding the method of the chapter, it uses the Bayesian VAR model. A VAR model measures the relationship between multiple time series and their lagged values as they vary over time. It is suitable to work on the endogenous relationship among the variables. Also, the VAR is a productive method allowing for nowcasting, which is a need in developing instantaneous policies during these periods. The chapter estimated the VAR model from a Bayesian perspective. The data sets include many countries, and some indices are collected for the different base years. This reality, in some cases, drives the researchers to study with a shorter period. As is known, the data for a limited time with many variables, Bayesian procedure is more efficient. Therefore, considering data availability and dissimilarity of the base year of the data, the Bayesian estimation method outperforms.

DATA AND METHODS

To analyze the dynamic interrelationships between time series, VAR models suggest a proper way in the empirical investigation. These models have a high potential for developing policy analysis and forecasting dynamic macroeconomic variables (Bernanke, Boivin and Eliasz, 2005; Koop, 2013; Clark, 2011). A VAR, as a multivariate generalization of univariate autoregressive models (Del Negro and Schorfheide, 2011), allow for modeling each time series as a linear function of the lagged values of other time series and an error term. In a VAR model, the interdependent structure is estimated with considering change of its' endogenous variables over time. Following a common notation, one specifies the model accordingly.

Let $y_t=(y_{1t}, y_{2t}, \ldots, y_{nt})'$ represents n endogenous variables observed at time t. For these variables with the autoregressive process of order k, $\beta 1_, \beta 2, \ldots, \beta k$ i_s k×k autocorrelation coefficients matrices, the basic VAR(k) model has the form,

$$y_t = \alpha + \beta_1 y_{t-1} + \ldots + \beta_k y_{t-k} + \varepsilon_t$$

where εt ~ $i.i.d$ $N(0,\Sigma)$ with a k×k covariance matrix, Σ. In matrix notation, the model can be written as,

$$Y = XB' + E$$

Here $B=(B_1, B_2, \ldots, B_k)$ is stated an autoregressive matrix having $n \times nk$ dimensional, where X is $m \times nk$-dimensional, and Y and E matrices are both $m \times n$-dimensional, for $t=1\ldots m$ observations. The total number of elements in the coefficient matrix B is $n+n^2k$, and obviously, the estimation procedure becomes computationally burdensome as the number of endogenous variables increases. However, Bayesian analysis overcomes this issue by introducing informative prior distributions. Since the empirical part of the chapter relies heavily on the idea of application with almost more than a dozen endogenous variables, resolving this issue gains prominence. Under the Bayesian VAR framework, the interdependencies between the countries' PMIs and their lagged values were analyzed. As the general form of VAR model is given above, one can now continue with enlightening on the data.

Data

Countries' monthly PMIs and PPIs data are from 2011/01 to 2022/02, totaling to 134 observations for each. The selected twelve countries, Germany, United States, United Kingdom, Italy, France, Spain, Netherlands, Russia, China, South Korea, Japan and Canada, are Turkey's major trading partner countries. The government of India was officially calculating only a Wholesale Price Index (WPI) until 2017 and was not following PPI procedure. So, the indices of India were discarded and eventually, thirteen countries' indices in total for each variable were considered.

The empirical analysis uses Purchasing Managers' Index and Producer Price Index data. PPI data covers all commodities in the market, and all PPIs are measured with respect to the base year 2010. The data source for PPI is mainly International Financial Statistics (IFS, 2022). There were missing observations for the countries U.S., Korea, and Japan. The countries' own official statistical data tables provide longer but with a different base year data. These observations were rebased and added to the dataset.

PMI data measures supply chain managers' operation levels in the manufacturing sector. The data on PMI is provided by the database of IHS Markit, which is a part of S&P Global. The PMI series are seasonally adjusted.

Table 1 represents descriptive statistics of the countries' PMIs and PPIs. These country-based figures summarize the data for the observed period. For instance, the mean PMI of Germany is interpreted as

Table 1. Descriptive statistics

	Mean	Sd	Median	Geometric Mean	Min.	Max.
Germany PMI	52,86	6,06	52,2	52,51	34,5	66,6
United States PMI	54,02	3,3	53,9	53,91	36,1	63,4
United Kingdom PMI	53,16	4,14	53,25	52,99	32,6	65,6
Turkey PMI	50,61	3,28	50,9	50,5	33,4	58,5
Italy PMI	51,68	5,01	51,9	51,43	31,1	62,8
Netherlands PMI	54,52	5,25	53,5	54,27	40,5	69,4
France PMI	50,69	4,27	50,45	50,5	31,5	59,4
Spain PMI	51,11	4,67	52,2	50,88	30,8	60,4
Russia PMI	50,07	2,76	50,35	49,98	31,3	55,6
China PMI	50,19	1,66	50,25	50,16	40,3	54,9
South Korea PMI	49,68	2,25	49,75	49,63	41,3	55,3
Japan PMI	50,78	2,81	51,3	50,69	38,4	56,6
Canada PMI	52,94	3,36	53,3	52,83	33	58,5
Germany PPI	106,95	4,51	105,65	106,87	102,62	130,13
United States PPI	111,59	6,25	109,14	111,42	101,58	133,11
United Kingdom PPI	110,64	7,09	111,01	110,42	97,15	134,8
Turkey PPI	202,72	112,72	149,13	181,25	105,67	715
Italy PPI	106,69	7,1	105,75	106,49	99,57	149,2
Netherlands PPI	108,57	6,24	109,14	108,4	97,46	144,3
France PPI	106,28	4,57	105,62	106,19	100,38	130,48
Spain PPI	109,98	7,08	108,97	109,78	101,44	147,04
Russia PPI	168,42	39,17	166,32	164,07	110,88	266,6
China PPI	104,4	4,53	105,15	104,3	92,85	113,53
South Korea PPI	104,79	3,35	104,73	104,74	98,43	114,95
Japan PPI	102,98	2,88	102,61	102,94	98,55	114,17
Canada PPI	114,59	8,33	111,79	114,31	103,69	147,2

Source: (The Author's calculations based on IHS Markit - S&P Global data)
Note: Sd: Standard deviation

an average activity level of almost eleven years, which is over 50, meaning that manufacturing is expanding. While the PMI of China has the lowest standard deviation and is the least variational, the PMI of Germany has the highest standard deviation and is the most variational in the last eleven years. As for the mean price changes, the domestic producers in Russia and Turkey are receiving monthly higher prices on average, and in these economies, the prices averagely are rising over the span of eleven years.

During the first wave of the pandemic in 2020, all considered countries experienced the lowest values of their PMIs (see Figure 1). On the other hand, when a similar check is done for their scaled PPIs, it's seen that PPIs started to rise after that period, and still, there is no significant slowdown in this trend for many of them (Figure 1). Notably, the bivariate plots of each country's PPI and PMI reflect their dependent structure, and this is more distinctive when they are at high and low levels.

Estimation of Bayesian VAR Model

The chapter explores its research questions by estimating several BVAR models. Here, the parameters in the Bayesian setting form multiple levels model, which is essentially hierarchical. In deriving the posterior distribution of the model's hyperparameters, conditional distributions are updated using an iterative algorithm. The Bayes' rule is extended with the conditionals as:

$$P(\delta, \theta, y) \propto P(y \setminus \theta, \delta)\, P(\theta \setminus \delta)\, P(\delta)$$

and marginal likelihood as:

$$P(y \setminus \delta) = \int P(y \setminus \theta, \delta)\, P(\theta \setminus \delta)\, d\theta.$$

The term y represents the observations, θ stand for the VAR model's parameters, and δ is a group of unknown prior hyperparameters. When drawing from the distributions, for computational ease, one needs to choose the prior distributions carefully (For the informative prior discussion, see the papers of Koop and Korobilis (2010), Del Negro and Schorfheide (2011), Karlsson (2012)). The preferred hierarchical BVAR model's priors have conjugate prior structure. Following Zellner (1971) and Giannone et al. (2015), the prior specification is done with a natural conjugate Normal – Inverse – Wishart prior (N-IW). Inverse Wishart allows for setting a prior with covariance matrix having no restrictions. Referring to the notation given above, the model's coefficients are defined with B, as vectorize form of $(\alpha, \beta 1, \beta 2, \ldots, \beta k)T$ and the distributions of the parameters are stated as:

$$B \setminus \Sigma \sim N(b, \Sigma \otimes \Omega),\ \Sigma \sim IW(S, v)$$

where b, Ω, S, and v are hyperparameters in δ. Based on this prior parametrization, the chapter adopts Minnesota prior, as proposed in the study of Giannone et al. (2015). The Minnesota prior, which first presented in a working paper of Litterman (1980), assumes that the variables follow a random walk. The Minnesota prior enables less troublesome simulation by setting the variance matrix of the error term fixed. The first two moments of the prior are constituted with three hyperparameters, λ, μ, ψ: λ controls the overall tightness, μ controls the variance of the prior belief, and ψ controls the tightness of the prior implied by artificial observation (Giannone et al., 2015).

The method requires processing the data of indices. After the stationarity check, only PPIs were transformed into their first differencing. The order of the model is specified as "1". Markov Chain Monte Carlo (MCMC) algorithm was run for the BVAR models with 20000 draws of simulations and with 4000 draws as the burn-in. As given above, the assigned hyperparameter in the BVARs is lambda (λ). A standard specification was done by reporting the trace plots and the density plots of this parameter. They indicated that MCMC estimations have converged and the samples were drawn from an efficient chain (see Figure 7). Besides this visual summary, Geweke's statistic was calculated and confirmed the convergence. The computations were implemented using R, BVAR (Kuschnig and Vashold, 2022).

Figure 1. Countries' PMIs (top) and scaled PPIs (bottom)
Source: (The Author's construction)

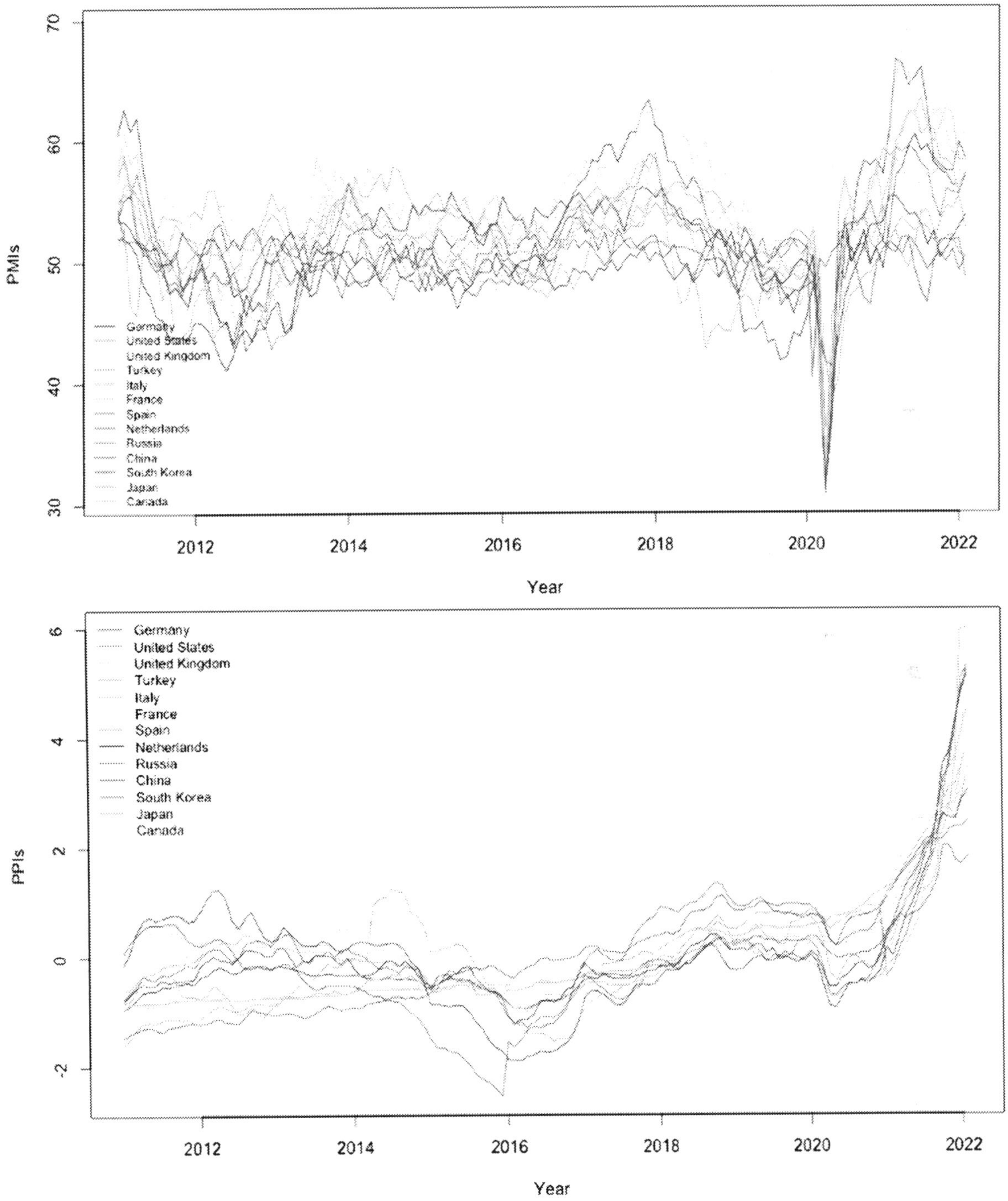

Findings

Table 2. Description of models

Variables	Variable Codes	BVAR1 (PMIs end.)	BVAR2 (PMIs & Germ_ppi end.)	BVAR3 (PMIs & US_ppi end.)	BVAR4 (PMIs & Turk_ ppi end.)
Germany PMI	Germ_pmi	X	X	X	X
United States PMI	US_pmi	X	X	X	X
United Kingdom PMI	UK_pmi	X	X	X	X
Turkey PMI	Turk_pmi	X	X	X	X
Italy PMI	Ita_pmi	X	X	X	X
Netherlands PMI	Neth_pmi	X	X	X	X
France PMI	Fra_pmi	X	X	X	X
Spain PMI	Spa_pmi	X	X	X	X
Russia PMI	Rus_pmi	X	X	X	X
China PMI	Chin_pmi	X	X	X	X
South Korea PMI	Kore_pmi	X	X	X	X
Japan PMI	Jap_pmi	X	X	X	X
Canada PMI	Can_pmi	X	X	X	X
Germany PPI	Germ_ppi		X		X
United States PPI	US_ppi			X	
United Kingdom PPI	UK_ppi				
Turkey PPI	Turk_ppi				X
Italy PPI	Ita_ppi				
Netherlands PPI	Neth_ppi				
France PPI	Fra_ppi				
Spain PPI	Spa_ppi				
Russia PPI	Rus_ppi				
China PPI	Chin_ppi				
South Korea PPI	Kore_ppi				
Japan PPI	Jap_ppi				
Canada PPI	Can_ppi				

Source: (The Author's construction)
Note: end.: endogenous

With different variable settings, four BVAR models are simulated. In the models, all variables are treated as endogenous. This subsection of the chapter reports and interprets the impulse and response functions (IRFs). In addition to IRFs, the forecasts obtained from the models are evaluated. First, Table 2 reports the list of the models covered in the analysis.

Mainly, to make the inferences about the effects of the PMI, impulse response functions are generated. The solid line is the impulse response function, and the shaded areas are basically 95% confidence intervals. All the graphical summaries of IRFs are calculated for 12 months ahead. The impulse response

Figure 2. IRFs of the BVAR1 model

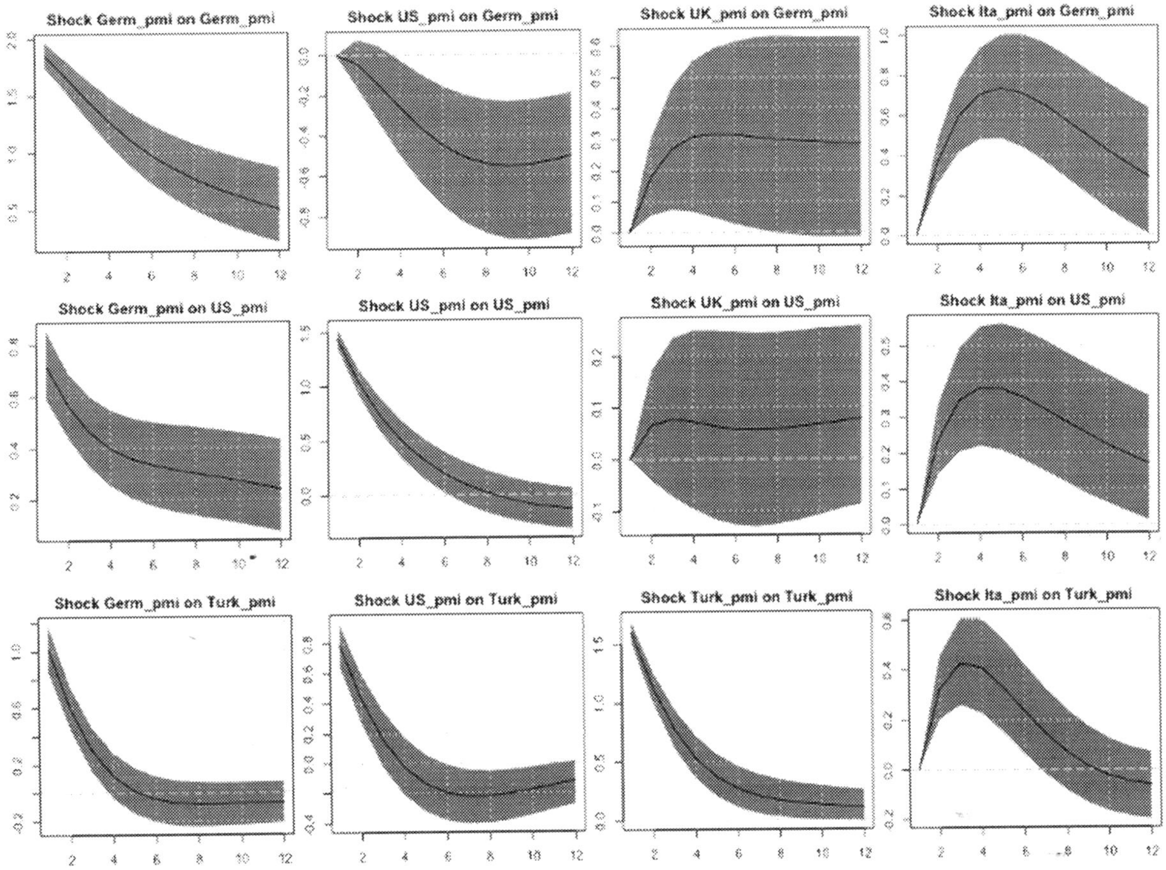

functions in the graphs given in Figure 2 almost always lie within these intervals. If the zero line does not fall into the confidence intervals, it implies that the IRF is statistically different from 0.

The response of countries' PMIs to the shocks of their own PMIs are almost similar for the countries Germany, the United States, and Turkey. Beginning from the first stage, there is an instantaneous shock on each country's own PMI. But then, each of them follows a sharp decline. The response on its own PMIs of the U.S. is positive for the first eight months. With regard to their response on the PMIs of Germany and Turkey, both remain positive for 12 months. The shocks of Germany's PMI on the U.S.' PMI and Turkey's PMI are significant. There are no first-period effects of PMI of Italy on the PMIs of other countries. But for each, it gradually increases until the 5th month, then, after the 6th -7th months, it starts to decline and converges to zero again.

The IRF graph of Italy's PMI shock on Germany's PPI (Figure 3) illustrates that, at the early stages, there is not much response to the PMI shock of Italy, and looks almost stable. It is above the zero line, so positive. Then, between the period of 2nd and 5th month, it moves downwards and it gradually decreases and reaches a steady-state in that month. After that period, it starts to increase. The shock of The U.K.'s PMI drives a similar response on Germany's PPI. But it reaches a steady-state within the 2nd - 4th month and starts to increase by the 3rd month. Germany's PPI response to its own PMI is significant, particularly after the 4th month, the shock is positive and continues to increase through the end of the period.

Figure 3. IRFs of the BVAR2 model

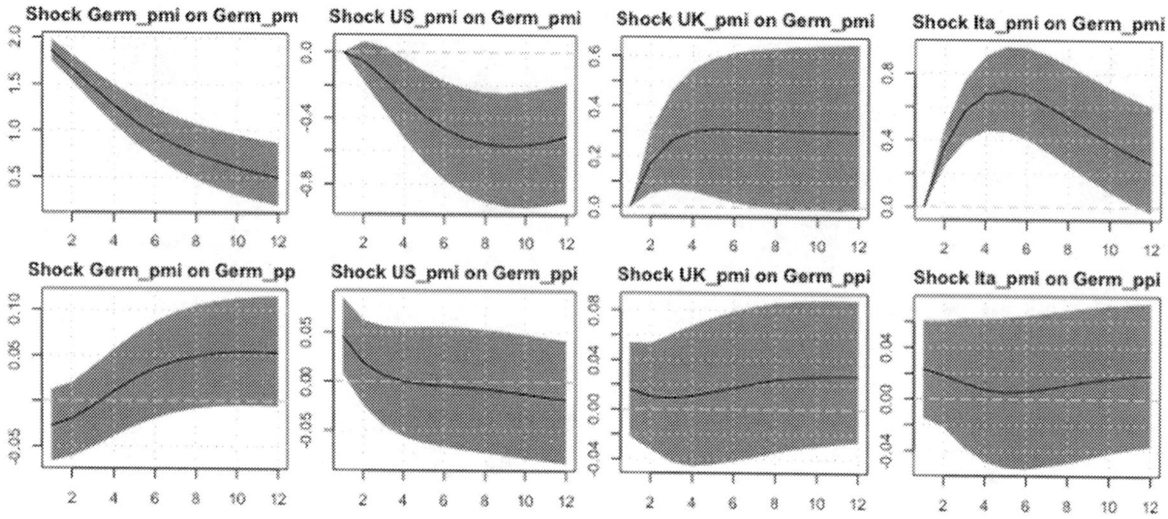

Figure 4 below illustrates the effects of the PMI shocks of four countries on the U.S. PPI. From the last row of the figure, it is obvious that none of the shocks of the countries' PMIs are significant on the U.S.' PPI. In each case, the horizontal zero line lies within the credible intervals. That holds the idea that the PMI shocks of the trading partners to the PPI are simply not the key candidates for explaining the effect on the U.S. inflation. So, it verifies the finding of Greenwood and Hanke's paper (2022) that suggests the inflation issue of the U.S. came from their monetary policies.

Figure 4. IRFs of the BVAR3 model

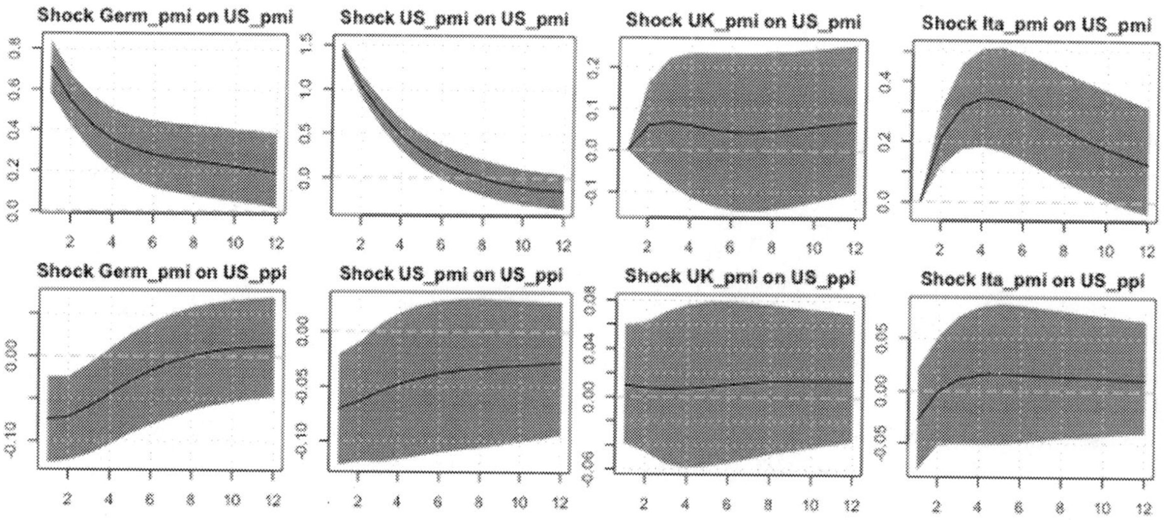

Figure 5 provides the plot of different IRFs showing how Turkey's PPI responses to a given PMI shock change across the countries. The PMI shock of Italy on Turkey's PPI is significant. It begins with

Figure 5. IRFs of the BVAR4 model

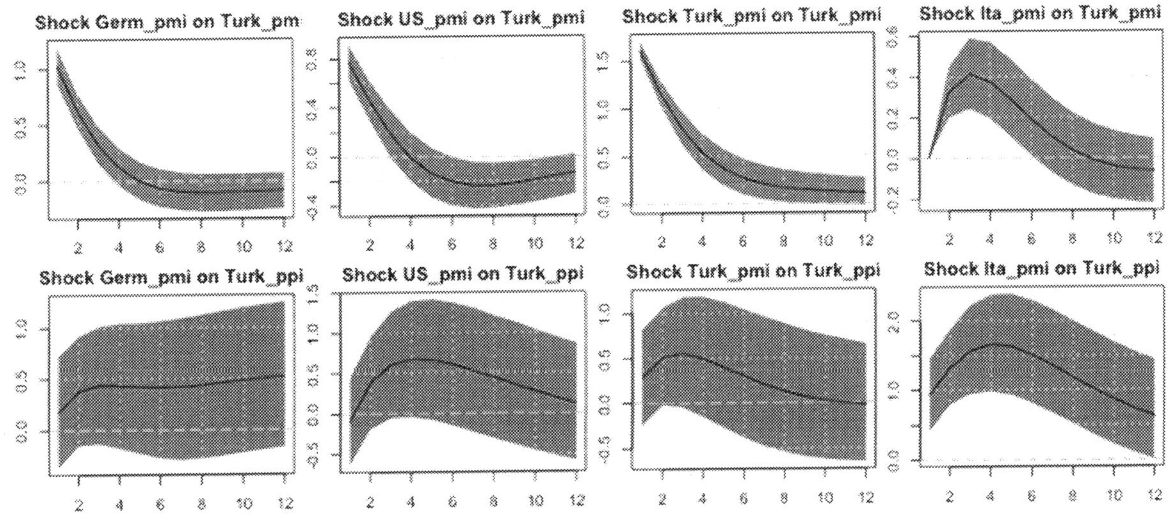

an instantaneous shock on the PPI of Turkey and continues to rise up to the fourth month, then the effect of this shock dies out at the end of 12 months. About the PMI shock of Germany, which is Turkey's one of the major trade partners, there seen a slight uprising effect on the PPI of Turkey, and then keeps going with a minor increase. Both PMI shocks of the U.S. and Turkey are positive, growing up to the fourth month, then dying out.

The PMI shocks on the PPI developments varied somewhat across countries. It is relatively natural to observe the heterogeneous responses to the PMIs. The countries have various economic policies. However, there is an agreement about the PMI shock on the countries' own PPIs. For all cases except the U.S., the PMI shock is not instantaneous, but it is positive, and the PPI moves upward from the beginning. The shocks in PMI lead to a gradual increase in PPI. In Germany's case, this is persistent, though it is not the same for Turkey as time moves on.

Even though this seems a counterintuitive finding, it is consistent with the theoretical expectations (IHS Markit, 2017; Meyer and Habanabakize, 2018; Meyer, 2020; Agarwal and Kimball, 2022). The PMI shocks on the PPIs are predominantly positive. IHS Markit report (2017) expresses this identified influence with a business cycle named the boom-bust cycle. One can start by interpreting the effect of economic expansion. An increase in the economic activity, which can be traced with the increments in the level of the manufacturing PMI, may yield an additional demand for labor in that economy. The wages in the market could increase, and thus, the income could increase. At this stage, the increasing income level in that economy could lead the consumers to grow their demands. Then, to satisfy the market demand, the producers are expected to raise their supply. Again, this growing demand causes a rise in the prices of the products. Which eventually results in inflation in that economy. However, inflation could shrink market demand.

The forecast plots in Figure 6 summarize the forecasts of focused countries' PMIs and PPIs for the following 12 months, with the credible intervals denoted as the gray shaded areas. As the shaded areas become enlarge, it implies that the uncertainty is increasing. The BVAR1 model yielding the predictions of the PMIs, suggests a slight decline in the PMI of Germany for one year ahead while the PMIs of the U.S. and Turkey remain almost unchanged. According to the predictions from the BVAR2 model, the

PPI of Germany will fall in the next twelve months. The forecast of the BVAR3 model illustrates that the PPI of the U.S. will significantly tend to decrease. Finally, from the BVAR4 model, twelve months-ahead PPI forecasts of Turkey display that there will be a decline in the PPI.

DISCUSSION AND IMPLICATION

The results of this chapter will benefit from many aspects. The findings of it would appeal to the audience, from economic policymakers to the chief or ruling supply chain managers. It provides new insights into the decision of which suppliers the country should be connected with most so that they can deal with the potential shortages in the relevant sector. For the policy makers, understanding the dynamics of the possible relationship between countries' PMIs and their price stability may provide intellectual information for shaping a sustainable trade network, seeking new strategic trade agreements, or leading to economic diversifications. Furthermore, the possible supply chain risks are manageable better once the most interdependent trading countries are determined. No doubt, at a micro-level, controlling these risks would create additional efficiency in the overall economy. On the technical side, BVAR modeling gives macroeconomic policymakers a tool for planning and stabilizing the price fluctuations, to an extent. Therefore, especially to control inflation, the economic policymakers should focus on managing supply chain risks reflected by trading partners.

LIMITATIONS AND FUTURE RESEARCH DIRECTIONS

Nonetheless, this chapter has a few limitations and promises of some further research. One is about specifying variables in the model. The chapter could have estimated the model with additional indices such as the Economic resilience index and Fragile State Index (for the U.S.). These indices may contribute to understanding why the PMI's effect on the PPI is distinctive on the country bases. However, these indices are collected yearly. Technically, the estimations may be re-obtained for a Bayesian Structural VAR model. An empirical investigation of this structural model could reveal whether there is a suggestive relationship between them. With progressive modeling, using both Bayesian VAR and Bayesian DFA models could have provided a tactful way to model. Because DFA models contribute to detecting the underlying patterns in the series by considering the effect of unobservable variables. Finally, a more comprehensive examination of all intercountry relationships may shed light on the understanding of the supply chain mechanisms and may provide a basis for strategic management.

CONCLUSION

Economic indicators of global improvements have been deteriorating due to the pandemic and the war. The shortage of the goods such as gas, semiconductors chips, or rubbers was unexpected. These developments led to a rise in price levels and caused cost-push inflation even for most developed countries. Hence, time-oriented, dynamic analysis became prominent more than ever. The inflation issue becomes more persistent and has more widespread effects. Specifically, during the unstable terms, exploring the inflation using the standard models with common variables is less effective. Instead, considering the

Figure 6. Forecast from the BVAR models

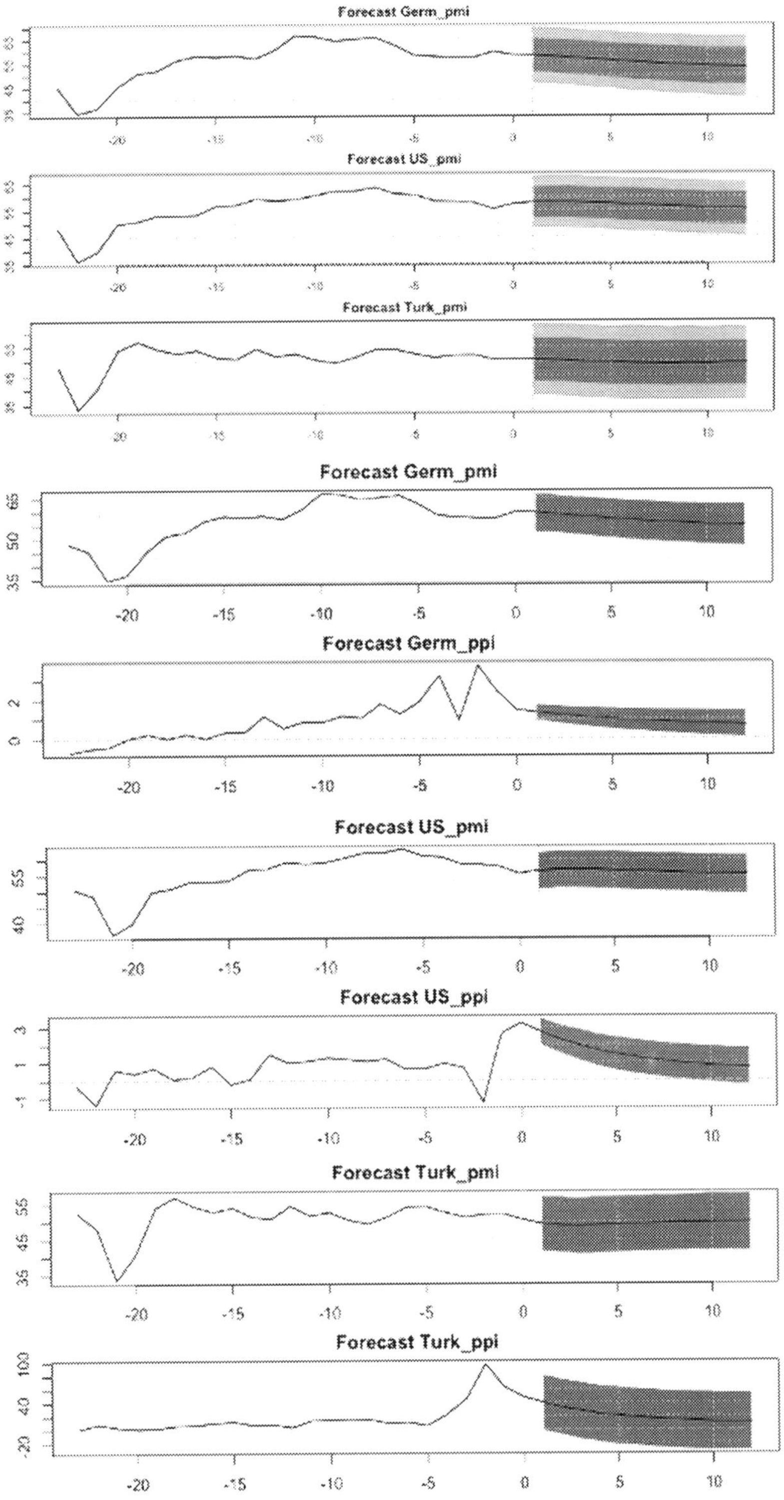

main effects like supply chain disruptions and manufacturing provides more realistic and updated ways. With these motivations, the chapter discussed the association between Purchasing Managers' Index and the Producers Price Index of countries. While PMIs characterize the supply chain disruptions, PPIs characterize the inflation. The chapter focuses on the cases of a group of specific economies and chooses three countries' PPIs: Germany, the United States, and Turkey. The author run Bayesian sampling for four BVAR models and explored the PMI and PPI relationships of countries. Employing the model, PMIs' shocks, their survivals, and responses on PPIs were captured. As a baseline prior, Minnesota prior was specified in all models. The graphical results of Impulse Response Functions indicated that Germany's PPIs response to the shock of PMIs of Germany, the United States, Italy, and the United Kingdom are significantly high. The United States' PPIs response to the shock of PMIs of Germany, the United States, Italy, and the United Kingdom are significant, but not high. Finally, Turkey's PPIs response to the shock of PMIs of Turkey, the United States, and Italy are significantly high. The overall results unfolded that the United States PPIs were explained well only with the United States' PMIs. Unlike the United States and Germany, the PMI shocks of Germany, the United States, and Italy on the PPIs of Turkey are highly informative. This can be interpreted by the different structure of developing countries than the developed countries, which are less foreign-dependent. AS for the United States case, Greenwood and Hanke (2022) discuss that inflation in the U.S. is the result of the excess monetary growth in the market. For this reason, other countries' PMIs do not have many effects on the United States PPI. The IRF outcomes validate the boom-bust business cycle with PMI data proposed by IHS Markit (2017). The results of the forecasts suggested a not decreasing trend for both the PPIs trend of Turkey and Germany. But the PPI trend of the United States will decrease. The PMI forecasts of both Germany and the United States illustrate slight increases, but almost a flat trajectory is seen for the PMI forecasts of Turkey. Policymakers may apply the estimation procedure to nowcasting. Additionally, it can help to manage the supply chain risks both for businesses and country levels. For monetary policy, when managing inflation targeting strategy, it would be efficient to consider the PMI effect.

ACKNOWLEDGMENT

This research received no specific grant from any funding agency in the public, commercial, or not-for-profit sectors.

REFERENCES

Agarwal, R., & Kimball, M. (2022). *Will inflation remain high? IMF Publications, Finance and Development.* Retrieved from: https://www.imf.org/en/Publications/fandd/issues/2022/03/Future-of-inflation-partI-Agarwal-kimball

Attinasi, M. G., Balatti, M., Mancini, M., & Metelli, L. (2022). Supply chain disruptions and the effects on the global economy. *ECB Economic Bulletin Boxes*, *8*(1). Retrieved from: https://www.ecb.europa.eu/pub/economic-bulletin/focus/2022/html/ecb.ebbox202108_01~e8ceebe51f.en. html

Baldwin, R., & Tomiura, E. (Eds.). (2020). *Thinking ahead about the trade impact of Covid-19.* CEPR Press.

Ballantyne, A., & Langcake, S. (2016). Why Has Retail Inflation Been So Low? *RBA Bulletin*, 9-18.

Bernanke, B. S., Boivin, J., & Eliasz, P. (2005). Measuring the Effects of Monetary Policy: A Factor-Augmented Vector Autoregressive (FAVAR) Approach. *The Quarterly Journal of Economics*, *120*(1), 387–422. doi:10.1162/0033553053327452

Cavallo, A., Cavallo, E., & Rigobon, R. (2014). Prices and Supply Disruptions During Natural Disasters. *Review of Income and Wealth*, *60*, 449–471. doi:10.1111/roiw.12141

Clark, T. E. (2011). Real-Time Density Forecasts from Bayesian Vector Autoregressions with Stochastic Volatility. *Journal of Business & Economic Statistics*, *29*(3), 327–341. doi:10.1198/jbes.2010.09248

Datta, P. P., & Christopher, M. G. (2011). Information sharing and coordination mechanisms for managing uncertainty in supply chains: A simulation study. *International Journal of Production Research*, *49*(3), 765–803. doi:10.1080/00207540903460216

Del Negro, M., & Schorfheide, F. (2011). Bayesian Macroeconometrics. In *Handbook of Bayesian Econometrics*. Oxford University Press.

Giannone, D., Lenza, M., & Primiceri, G. E. (2015). Prior Selection for Vector Autoregressions. *The Review of Economics and Statistics*, *97*(2), 436–451. doi:10.1162/REST_a_00483

Glick, R., & Taylor, A. M. (2010). Collateral Damage: Trade Disruption and the Economic Impact of War. *The Review of Economics and Statistics*, *92*(1), 102–127. doi:10.1162/rest.2009.12023

Greenwood, J., & Hanke, S. (2022). On Monetary Growth and Inflation in Leading Economies, 2021-2022: Relative Prices and the Overall Price Level. *Journal of Applied Corporate Finance*, *33*(4), 39–51. doi:10.1111/jacf.12479

HIS Markit. (2017). *Interpreting PMI data*. Retrieved from: https://www.pmi.spglobal.com/Public/Home/ PDF/EN_PMIRecruitment

International Monetary Fund. (2022). *International financial statistics (IFS)*. International Monetary Fund.

Ji-Hong, J. (2017). US Purchasing Managers' Index and its Impact on Korea and US. *Journal of Distribution Science*, *15*(3), 17–25. doi:10.15722/jds.15.3.201703.17

Karlsson, S. (2012). *Forecasting with Bayesian Vector Autoregressions*. Working Papers, 2012:12, Orebro University, Swedish Business School.

Koenig, E. F. (2002). Using the Purchasing Managers' Index to assess the economy's strength and the likely direction of monetary policy. *Economic and Financial Policy Review*, *1*(6).

Koop, G. (2013). Forecasting with Medium and Large Bayesian VARs. *Journal of Applied Econometrics*, *28*(2), 177–203. doi:10.1002/jae.1270

Koop, G., & Korobilis, D. (2010). Bayesian Multivariate Time Series Methods for Empirical Macroeconomics. *Foundations and Trends in Econometrics*, *3*(4), 267–358. doi:10.1561/0800000013

Kuschnig, N., & Vashold, L. (2021). BVAR: Bayesian Vector Autoregressions with Hierarchical Prior Selection in R. *Journal of Statistical Software*, *100*(14), 1–27. doi:10.18637/jss.v100.i14

Kuschnig, N., & Vashold, L. (2022). *BVAR: Hierarchical Prior Selection in R.* R package version 1.0.3. https://CRAN.R-project.org/package=BVAR

Lindsey, M. D., & Pavur, R. (2005). As the PMI Turns: A Tool for Supply Chain Managers. *The Journal of Supply Chain Management, 41*(3), 30–39. doi:10.1111/j.1745-493X.2005.tb00182.x

Litterman, R. (1980). *A Bayesian Procedure for Forecasting with Vector Autoregression*. Working paper, Massachusetts Institute of Technology, Department of Economics.

Mahajan, K., & Tomar, S. (2021). COVID-19 and supply chain disruption: evidence from food markets in India. *American Journal of Agricultural Economics, 103*, 35-52. doi:.12158 doi:10.1111/ajae

Meier, M., & Pinto, E. (2020). *COVID-19 Supply Chain Disruptions*. CRC TR 224, Discussion Paper Series. crctr224_2020_239, University of Bonn and University of Mannheim.

Meyer, D. F. (2020). An Empirical Assessment of the Relationships between the Manufacturing Sector, Economic Growth and Changes in Price Indexes: The Case of Poland. *International Journal of Innovation, Creativity and Change, 12*(7), 186–203.

Meyer, D. F., & Habanabakize, T. (2018). Analysis of Relationships and Causality between Consumer Price Index (CPI), the Producer Price Index (PPI) and Purchasing Manager's Index (PMI) in South Africa. *Journal of Economics and Behavioral Studies, 10*(6), 25–32. doi:10.22610/jebs.v10i6.2590

OECD. (2022). *Consumer Price Indices-Complete database*. Retrieved from: https://www.oecd.org/newsroom/consumer-prices-oecd-updated-2-june-2022.htm

Santacreu, A. M., & LaBelle, J. (2022). Global Supply Chain Disruptions and Inflation During the COVID-19 Pandemic. *Review - Federal Reserve Bank of St. Louis.*

Tsuchiya, Y. (2012). Is the Purchasing Managers' Index useful for assessing the economy's strength? A directional analysis. *Economic Bulletin, 32*(2), 1302–1311.

Van Der Putten, R. (2020). *Germany: Supply Chains After Covid-19*. BNP Paribas EcoFlash No: 20-14.

Zellner, A. (1971). *An Introduction to Bayesian Inference in Econometrics*. Wiley.

KEY TERMS AND DEFINITIONS

Bayesian Analysis: A paradigm that relies on a statistical process updating relevant parameters' probabilities by using prior knowledge.

Economic Crisis: An undesired economic condition in which the country experiences some combinations of several issues such as decreasing trade, productivity and investment levels, unemployment, and price instabilities.

Inflation: A continuing increase in the general level of prices of goods and services in an economy and a decrease in purchasing power of money in that economy for a given period.

Producer Price Index (PPI): An index measuring the weighted average of price changes in the goods and services, based on the price levels received or paid by domestic producers.

Purchasing Managers' Index (PMI): A specific measure reflecting the production performance in an economy, based on periodic data collected from supply chain managers.

Supply Chain Bottlenecks: As a broader definition of supply chain disruptions, represent the constraint of the supply chains' usual capacities.

Vector Autoregression (VAR) Model: A multivariate time series model built to examine dynamic relationships between endogenous variables.

APPENDIX

Figure 7. Convergency Diagnostics: MCMC sampling trajectories and the posterior density of lambda (from the BVAR1(upper left panel), the BVAR2(upper right panel), the BVAR3(bottom left panel) and the BVAR4(bottom right panel))

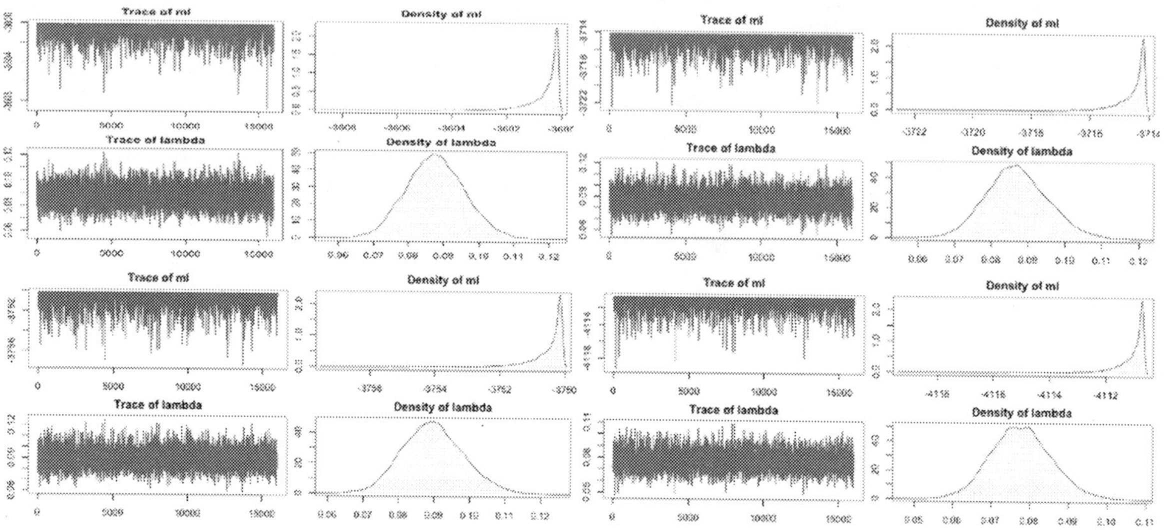

Chapter 10
Sustainability Model for Solid Waste Management to Support the Global Economy

Sami Gören
https://orcid.org/0000-0001-8650-4872
Umm Al-Qura University, Saudi Arabia

ABSTRACT

Extravagancy is the key point of inflation. We consume more than necessary; we generate waste without any responsibility. Expanded consumption and depletion of resources are becoming more serious than ever. As the world population and standard of living are increasing, the amount of solid waste is also increasing. Not only the quantity but also the types of the wastes increase and become difficult to recycle due to composite wastes. With the aim of preserving the environment, this chapter will introduce the sustainability model to support the global economy. Waste management and recycling technologies, which effectively turn waste into resources, will be a great tool, especially in rapidly developing nations. The following should be a Motto in life: "the practice of treasuring and using all things as long as possible." While economies continue to grow, this motto spirit restrained the generation of waste and motivated the development of technology for reuse, recycling, and effective use through heat recovery for energy.

INTRODUCTION

Sustainability can be explained as the ability to meet the needs of humanity without compromising the needs of future generations. It is very important to make our life continue without any interruptions and deficiencies while ensuring the continuity of production and diversity (Tchobanoglous, et.al., 1993). Sustainability is used to leave a world in which economic, ecological, and social conditions can be maintained for future generations.

In 1987, a report had published by United Nations with the title of "Our Common Future" and the word "sustainability" had been used for the first time (UN 2030). Since then, it becomes one of the most attractive subjects that people start to discuss. The content of the report was related with the problems

DOI: 10.4018/978-1-6684-5876-1.ch010

arising from rapid industrialization and population growth and trying to find solutions to these problems. It was a warning about the negative consequences of economic development and globalization on the environment. At that time, the most important subject was the ozone hole caused by human activity over Antarctica (UN 2030).

After the report of "Our Common Future" politicians and social scientists as well as economists impropriate the subject by discussing the environment and development as a single issue (USEPA 2010). The goals of economic and social development must be defined in terms of sustainability in all countries.

After starting the awareness about sustainability, today, it is still widely believed that sustainability can only be achieved by using the resources provided by nature at a speed that allows for spontaneous regeneration, despite the fact that the world's resources and the environment are moving towards the limit of depletion as a result of human activities (EC 2010). After a certain period, we may not have any more oil or some important minerals and ores for a lifestyle as we have now. We may not be able to supply energy as we used to have, or we may not continue manufacturing necessary daily products anymore. In this case, life will be more difficult and more challenging. This period is inevitable, if not for us but sure, for our children. Consequently, we have to preserve our children's future by using the natural resources in a reasonable way, by not polluting the environment and by consuming less. This is what the "sustainability's" real meaning.

When "sustainability" is mentioned, first the environmental meaning comes to mind, however, this concept actually expresses a holistic perspective that includes ecological, social conditions and economic components (EC 2010). Sustainability should not be thought of only in the environmental sense. We should not consume tomorrow's resources from today. Not only the minerals but also biological resources should have been protected.

LITERATURE REVIEW

The rapidly increasing population and changing living standards make it difficult to control and manage both the waste volume and diversifying waste composition (Goren 2005). The increase in the size of the pollution and the potential risks associated with it caused by solid wastes made the waste management more important that before. Deficiency of the natural resources bring the problem of economic, social and environmental problems. For this reason, it is necessary to analyze the elements of integrated solid waste management that include all stages from waste generation to final disposal and their relations with each other (Ozcan, et.al. 2016).

Waste management aims to minimize the effects of the disposal of wastes generated on the environment and economy. The shortest way to achieve this goal is to naturally reduce the amount of waste. The target of having a better and more prosperous life, makes the people face with more problems and challenge. The health is under threat of increasing pollution. There is a huge destruction of natural resources and the fact that every product produced is ultimately turned into waste. Consequently, recycling is the most important starting point for waste management. By recycling the materials are used as a source of raw material. In fact, the word "recycling" is used as a general phrase for such kinds of activities, and it has many sub steps like reduce, reuse and etc (Öztürk, et.al. 2005).

A while ago, the phrase of "3R" was widely used to express these types of activities, that is the acronym of "Reduce, Reuse, Recycle" (Ölander, et.al. 2006). Before using them as a source of raw material for another manufacturing processes, the amount of waste should be reduced by us as conscious consumers.

"Reduce" covers, consuming less and producing less amount of waste. It can be adopted, for example by cooking less and finishing all the cooked food that lets you not to waste your food; also buying less not to make the foods rotten while waiting in the fridge.

"Reuse" is changing the proposed use of a material that we used before. For example, using the jam jars as a pencil holder. Of course, this includes buying durable goods instead of "one-time-use" materials. Many food items are available both in plastic packs and also in glass packages. We have to prefer the glass, paper or steel packages that is not generating waste and will be easy to reuse with another purpose. This will decrease plastic consumption. There is a huge health threat and pollution caused by overused plastic good. It is necessary to decrease plastic use because the recycling process of plastics is problematic. Although glass, aluminium, and steel can be recycled for many times, plastics can only be recycled one or two times and this process is always downcycling. It is almost impossible to manufacture the same or upper quality of plastic material with recycled plastic. Only lower standard material can be manufactured with this process. Consequently, we have to search for new solutions to lower plastic dependency. Durable, long-term containers and bottles should have more share in business life and daily life (Goren 2019). Down payment system for depositation of the containers, bottles can supply autonomous cycle between the customer and the producer. One-time use containers and bottles may harm the environment and economy as well.

The technical term "Recycle" has the meaning of using the wastes as a source of raw material for the same type of manufacturing. Economists think that manufacturing from recycling is expensive. According to them, it is cheaper to throw away any material than using it again. However, this type of thinking may harm the environment by increasing the waste quantity & pollution and economy as well because the resources are limited. As the resources decrease, the costs of production will increase. 6R is a new terminology used instead of 4R. The classical 4R represents the "REDUCE, REUSE, RCYCLE and RECOVER", nowadays new "R's" join to this group as REPRESS and REMOVE to form 6R. Repress has the meaning of prevention of the waste. It is a priority state that comes before "reduce"; because "reduce" means still generating waste (Damiano 2013). However, we have to move on thinking and acting on not generating any waste. The last "R" is REMOVE, stating that after overall waste management and treatment techniques, deal with the side products or remaining like ash, sludge, residue, etc. These remainings should not go to the landfill, new techniques should be developed to reuse or permanently destroy them. This is the main idea in "zero waste" concept. Actually, the "R"s can be increased with "rethink", "repair", "repurpose", etc.

METHODOLOGY

Waste Management is the minimization of household, medical, hazardous and non-hazardous wastes, their separate collection at the source, their intermediate storage, the establishment of transfer stations for wastes when necessary, the transportation of wastes, their recovery, pre-treatment, operation of recovery and disposal facilities. Transfer stations play an important role in solid waste management and make solid waste transportation service efficient and effective. Transfer stations act as a step between the collection of solid wastes and the transportation of wastes to the facilities where they will be disposed of. Domestic solid wastes brought to the stations by collection vehicles are loaded on larger volume vehicles and transported to disposal facilities (Burney 2003). One of the most important reasons for the need for transfer stations is to reduce the cost of transporting wastes to treatment facilities. It is possible to design and operate transfer stations in different ways, but the generally used method involves compacting the wastes and reducing their volume. Thus, the transportation process with the highest cost in solid waste management becomes more economical. In addition, thanks to the transfer stations, this time can be directed to collection processes by saving the time spent on transportation, especially in settlements at long distances. The amount of fuel used, and therefore air emissions, is reduced and weathering effect of the heavy trucks to the highways is prevented. Most importantly, transfer stations contribute to reducing the traffic load in densely populated cities.

Integrated waste management requires to select and apply the correct methods and technologies to all kind of waste by getting the highest efficiency without having impact on the environment. By maintaining the consistence with the local and international laws and regulations (Burney 2003).

The operation is not limited to waste dumping to the landfill site, but also monitoring and performing the maintenance when necessary, after the closure of the landfill site. This is a necessity due to the landfill gas generation. The landfill gas will continue to be produced even after decades from the closure of the landfill site. The organic materials continue to decompose and produce landfill gas even though no fresh organics come to the landfill site. When the landfill site is closed, the power generation unit will continue to operate.

The amount of recycling and recovery is the most important parameter that shows the efficiency of the integrated solid waste system. The rate of recovery of solid wastes depends on the correct setting of the recovery targets and the establishment of a system suitable for these targets. Targets must be determined in a realistic matter in the recovery program while setting the goals.

Whichever system is used, it is inevitable that some remaining waste will go to landfill. Solid waste dumping areas are special storage areas built for the removal of solid wastes from our environment in a way that will not harm the environment and human health. It is the most widely used method in the world due to its economy and ease of operation. However, in the Landfill Directive published by the EU, targets have been set to reduce the amount of biodegradable domestic solid waste sent to landfills. Special wastes like bulky wastes, home appliances or industrial wastes that contain domestic content should be included in the system separately from urban wastes during the collection and subsequent management of wastes. Special wastes should be managed separately from domestic wastes due to both heavy metals and unfavourable elements in their content. The accumulator and battery wastes, which contain a certain amount of mercury, cadmium and lead, need to be handled and stored in a controlled manner. The reason for the separate collection of such wastes from domestic waste is to reduce the amount of heavy metals in landfills and incineration plants.

Medical wastes originating from health and research institutions should be collected, stored, transported and finally disposed of separately without harming public health and the environment. The most important problem of medical waste is that it is an important factor in the spread of infectious diseases. It should be strictly ensured that the medical wastes of hospitals, clinics, research and other health institutions are collected separately in standard bags. Various penal sanctions should be applied to organizations that do not use bags that comply with the standards or that collect their medical wastes together with other wastes.

Hazardous wastes are domestic and industrial wastes that contain substances that are dangerous for human health and the environment and have the potential to be harmful. Since such wastes are toxic, flammable, combustible and explosive, these wastes must be collected and disposed of separately from domestic wastes.

Construction and demolition wastes are the wastes generated as a result of the repair, modification, renewal, demolition of residential bridges, roads and similar structures and natural disasters. Construction and demolition wastes, which constitute a significant percentage of solid wastes and are released as a result of all kinds of construction activities, adversely affect the balance of the ecosystem if not taken under control. As with all wastes, waste management for construction and demolition waste should be managed in a similar hierarchy as resource recovery, waste reduction, reuse, recycling, recovery and final disposal. Most developed world countries have made significant progress in the reduction, reuse and recycling of these wastes. Reducing, reusing and recycling construction and demolition wastes are important steps to reduce the amount of these wastes before they go to final disposal.

Environmental pollution is increasing tremendously due to the increase in population. With the current and potential risks associated with solid waste like the decrease in natural resources, causing pollution of the unattended waste, cost of removing the waste as economic problems and other social reasons, solid waste management is becoming increasingly important and complex (Haldeman, et.al., 2009).

Increasing waste amount necessitates well-planned management. This management contains all types of wastes collection, transportation, and treatment, which is called integrated waste management. Collection and removal away quickly from the daily life of the citizens, is not enough. Appropriately disposing of it is one of the most important chains for waste management. Increasing awareness will be the key solution for sustainability, by consuming less and by throwing in a smart way.

There are different types of waste, such as municipal solid waste (domestic waste), industrial waste, and medical waste (Goren 2019) that the local authorities should handle, for this reason, solid waste management has become a tremendous challenge for local authorities, especially in developing countries.

Managing the solid waste in an optimum way, will sustain high standard of living conditions for the society and also ensure hygiene and a healthy environment by supporting the economy (Alvord, et.al., 2004). This process directly depends on the corporation of the public and private sectors with the local authorities by starting the separation of recyclable materials from their houses and working places. Paper, plastic, metal, glass, etc are accepted as recyclable materials that is possible to use as a raw material or additive for any type of production. With this method, it will become possible to prevent nature and continue manufacturing without disturbing nature. Separating these types of recyclable wastes is called as "source separation" and will be the most important part of the recycling activities. By this method, the wastes will be completely reached to the correct industry and they will not be polluted with food remaining. Dirtying food and drink remaining decrease the quality of the waste and makes them unable to use as raw material for the same type of reproduction. On the other hand, sophisticated packaging by using composite material cause problem with recycling. In that case, it can only go to "refuse-derived fuel (RDF) plant" which has less value compared with the usage as an additive or source of raw material.

Source separation should be continued by effective collection planning. In order to achieve efficiency, the places of the waste containers should be well designed and should be updated and improved by monitoring on the site. Collection and transportation are the biggest shares of the collection cost. As it cannot be automized and exactly depends on manpower, it took time and effort. Due to the fuel consumption and the maintenance cost of the transportation trucks, this process has the highest share. Metropolitan cities should have transfer stations to avoid small trucks rambling over the city. This will supply less fuel consumption for the unit weight of the waste and also reduce the risk of accidents by spending less time in the traffic. On the other hand, will not contribute to traffic jams either.

After transporting to the recycling facilities or treatment plants successfully, new processes will start according to the types of the wastes and according to the purpose. Organic wastes can go to biological treatment facilities such as compost plants, bio methanization plants or bio-drying processes.

Sustainable Development Goals (SDGs) of the United Nations (UN 2030) give a good approach to the methodology that should be taken in general. The details should be decided according to the local situation and condition in order to get success in managing the waste efficiently. The local conditions are related to but not limited to the population, demography, climate, season, cultural background, laws & regulations, waste types, and landforms of the city.

The cost of waste management is an important item for local governments, they should assign a huge budget for waste management activities. In fact, if the waste management can be done in an effective and sustainable method, it will be a great chance for them to decrease the budget, moreover, even get a good income from integrated waste management. Integrated waste management is very important to the achieve Sustainable Development. The integrated waste management methods should be in line with the local and international legislations.

Advanced thermal treatment (ATT) technologies (incineration, gasification, pyrolysis, plasma technology) and biological systems such as composting and biomethanization based on waste decomposition, as well as landfill systems are widely used in the disposal of solid wastes around the world (Ni, et.al., 2006). The most important factor in the selection of the disposal method is the cost and the availability of the common waste type. Of course, common waste type is a parameter for developed countries. Today, although high-cost systems such as gasification and pyrolysis are widely used in developed countries, it is seen that in developing countries mostly the landfilling is used, regardless the type of the waste. There is a question here, whether the landfilling is a sanitary landfilling or uncontrolled open dumping. In fact, this is a great threat to the environment. Landfill sites should be designed and operated as a well-planned engineering project, so that there will be no impact to the environment and protect from soil, water and air pollution. Another factor in the selection of a disposal system is the lack of space. Since the counties like Japan and some of the European countries do not have sufficient areas for landfill, systems that will minimize the volume of waste such as incineration are preferred (Tucker, et.al., 2003).

ANALYSIS

Sustainable waste management is adopted as a priority policy target all over the world, by minimizing the amount of wastes, preventing overusing of natural resources, and ensuring the highest possible recovery of the wastes generated. Policies and targets adopted for this purpose are tried to be controlled by laws, directives and regulations published by national and international authorities. EU waste management policy is also based on the principles of prevention, recovery and safe disposal.

Regardless of the methods used to recover the recyclable components in solid waste, these wastes must be collected regularly and economically. Two basic methods are applied in the collection of recyclable wastes: consumer brings and collect from the consumer. The ‘fetch’ method is a passive method for the collector and relies heavily on consumer activity. People take their waste to collection boxes or sorting/processing centres. Consumers can do this voluntarily, for a very low price, for some conveniences or for exemptions. The efficiency of this method is directly proportional to the environmental awareness of the people. The deposit system is also a kind of ‘fetch’ method. In the deposit system, the person who does not bring back the package is given an indirect penalty equal to the deposit amount. In the method of "taking" or "collecting" from the source, which is an active system for the collector, the separately collected wastes are collected by the local government or authorized institution. The tools used in separate collection are generally uncompressed and multi-compartment tools. Dedicated special vehicles and personnel are required for this job. Separate collection at source is more common than fetching.

The most common application in the world for the collection of packaging waste (recyclables) is source separation and accumulation at the source. The collection of waste can be carried out by the local government or authorized institutions or organizations. In this application, separate deposition at the source is usually done with three containers. There are three containers for recyclable waste; Paper-cardboard type wastes are placed in one of them, one for plastic wastes and other packaging wastes (aluminium, metal, etc.) are placed in the third container. Of course, this three-container type can be applied for a temporary period, because glass, different types of plastics and metals are not covered by this system. Gradually, the number of the waste bins and the types of recyclables can be increased. In this method, the recyclable wastes collected in separate containers are collected periodically with appropriate tools.

Organic wastes are the wastes that constitute the most important percentage in the solid waste content. Separate collection of these wastes at the source plays an important role in the management of biological assets such as compost and biomethanization obtained from these wastes. When we look at the world today, we see that there are countless compost plants. It is a known fact that the product quality produced in the compost facility varies depending on the operating conditions of the facility and the efficiency of the system, as well as the composition of the waste entering to the facility. The fact that the incoming waste contains products such as plastic, glass and metal reduces the quality of the compost. Today, developed countries tend to make compost by separating even organic matcrials. In particular, composting studies continue without mixing kitchen wastes and garden wastes. Separate collection of organic wastes is also important in biomethanization, which is another system used in the evaluation of organic waste. In this system, it is aimed to obtain biogas by providing only organic matter input. In this way, inorganic or inert materials that will prevent the decomposition of organic matter and natural microbial decomposition are not desired.

In order to include solid wastes in an integrated system, it is necessary to examine the current situation first. In current conditions, many parameters such as waste characterization, amount, collection and transportation methods, disposal method, socioeconomic status and development level of the region constitute important milestones for the planning of the system.

By examining the current waste management and analysing its efficiency, it is possible to have idea about where will this system fit in the future. In order to carry a successful and efficient waste management, first of all, waste composition must be known. After the waste characterization, it can be decided how to evaluate waste in terms of economic and sustainable development. The characterization of the waste has direct relationship with the culture, climate and the socioeconomic development of the region where the waste is generated. By conducting waste characterization studies the composition of the waste determined and it will give an idea about how it should be processed.

One of the most important point for the planning of the solid waste management system is the future of the city. A realistic estimation should be done for the future population of the city, accordingly the investment size can be designed successfully. For this purpose, different population estimation scenarios should be taken into consideration and the most appropriate estimation should be preferred, taking into account of the migration capability and development of the city in the future.

One of the biggest cost items for the waste management is the collection process. If the efficiency is high for this collection process, not only the overall cost decrease but also recycling rates will increase.

A successful collection system will bring the success of an integrated solid waste management system. For an ordinary waste management daily garbage are collected and send to the landfill area whether it is an open dumping place or sanitary landfill. The main objective here is to clean the garbage containers and streets immediately without taking into consideration of recycling and cost effectiveness. Even though cleaning is indispensable, the garbage can be converted to have value by small efforts like waste identification and source separation.

EU directives and local directives propose to make waste management efficient and expand the source recovery and reduce the input of organic matter to landfills. In this case, the importance of the efficient collection increases even more.

DISCUSSION AND CONCLUSION

People's awareness about environmental issues and sustainability is increasing with the effect of education at schools and with the help of social media. With this awareness, the effects of climate change, global warming, and increasing plastic pollution have started to be recognized by larger populations. Providing sustainability and nature protection has yet to become the political goal of many determined candidates. Local governments launch activities to fulfil the public's aspirations.

With the help of these types of trends and activities, eating natural and healthy is much more important than before. For this reason, people want to know the source and production processes of their food more than before. This makes the producers be more careful about the sub-suppliers and the processes. As a courtesy to their customers, they begin to provide detailed information about where and how the food is sourced. It's not just buy and sell for the supply chain any more.

The supply chain and logistics industry have become more under pressure compared with the past because of the necessity of supplying more fresh and more natural (without preservatives) food on time as demanded. This gives a boost to the economy through more investment and by creating more jobs. These improvements benefit the producers and farmers as well. People started to ask whether the farmers were completely paid or if the children were used illegally for production. Are any human beings or animals harmed by these production and manufacturing activities? How about the carbon footprint of this product? Consequently, the supply chain has to answer all these questions and meet the demands of the people. This triggers the business life to rise to a more corporate and professional level.

The strategy for collection, transportation, and treatment should be developed according to the local conditions and waste categorization by field strategy.

In order to support the global economy, integrated waste management should be planned to include all materials that constitute the composition of the solid waste and the technologies that turn to account of all types of waste for each region.

The economic values that can be obtained from the solid waste system are the inputs from recyclable materials, compost, and biogas that can be obtained from anaerobic compost plants and landfills. The income to be obtained from these is closely related to the market conditions and the cost of the investment to be made. For this reason, it is necessary to make a very detailed and realistic economic analysis at the planning stage.

An efficient and integrated solid waste management system should have the following features.

The efficiency of the planning is directly related to the amount of waste collected. However, it is a fact that the amount of waste generation depends primarily on the population. You are successful to the extent you collect. The more you collect, the more successful you will be. For this reason, extensive regional planning should be done with particular attention to each region's facts and conditions. Moreover, it should be flexible enough to adapt to various changes in environmental, spatial, and waste characteristics that may occur over time.

The collection of waste accounts for the largest percentage of the cost of the solid waste management system. The success of an integrated solid waste management system is directly proportional to the success of the collection system, because reaching the target of the solid waste management system depends on the regular, continuous, and timely collection of waste from its sources. In addition, since the public first encounters the system with the collection component, they evaluate the system accordingly.

The efficiency of a solid waste system should be evaluated by two components: in terms of financial conditions and the amount of material collected. In financial determination, it is checked how much of the income obtained from the system covers the expenses. It can be said that the higher the percentage of covered cost, the higher the efficiency of the system. The income from the system consists of the sale of recovered, recycled materials and the income from the energy produced.

If the amount of waste coming to the landfill site decreases, it is an indicator that more recyclables are being collected, which results in an increase in the income. If the material recovery and the income from this management reach the highest value together, it means that this is the most optimum system.

The followings are the key principles for implanting and implementing waste management.

1- Increase the awareness of the public about the limited resources and the damage given to the environment during industrial activities and manufacturing processes.
2- As a main strategy for the waste management, reduce the waste and especially prevent food waste.
3- Realize the value of what you own by treasuring them. Reduce the generation of waste by reusing the products for other purposes.
4- Increase the charity and aid organizations for a better world. This can be achieved by starting to donate the unnecessary goods in your house and taking care for the others.
5- Do the shopping as a wholesale and support responsible shopping
6- Prefer ecological and natural products while shopping.
7- Choose the durable containers like glass, steel instead of plastic containers.
8- Support the recycling activities by separating your wastes at your house (source separation).
9- Do not mix the food wastes (organics) with the other waste.
10- Food wastes should be sent to compost or biomethanization plant to get economic value. By this method, landfill sites will not become full quickly.
11- While performing source separation, do not dirty the packaging waste. Dirty recyclables lose their economic value.
12- Source separation should be performed correctly according to the material types. Plastics have many categories and metals should be separated at least as steel and aluminium.
13- Packaging wastes are not garbage, they can be recycled effectively.
14- Store the separated waste safely.
15- "Zero waste" is possible by taking care about our daily life.
16- Energy generation is possible from the wastes.
17- The most effective power transmission line is the local one, for this reason on demand energy system should be set up by using "waste to energy (WTE)" systems.

18- Energy production from the waste will help to have extra income and also prevent from waste treatment costs.
19- Waste collection and street cleaning should be done simultaneously.
20- Transfer stations should be set up at the big cities in order to increase the collection efficiency and also reduce fuel consumption and also accident risk and the traffic jam. This will help to support the economy and reduce the carbon footprint of waste management system.
21- Industrial wastes should not be mixed with domestic wastes.
22- Air pollution should be prevented by advanced flue gas filtering systems.
23- Hazardous wastes should be registered and monitored carefully.
24- Marine pollution at the harbours should be prevented by strict control system for the ships.
25- Mass transportation should be encouraged to reduce carbon oxides and nitrogen oxides.
26- Green technologies and zero waste industrial activities should be supported by the government.
27- Active campaigns for tree planting should be organized by private and government bodies.
28- Open dump sites should be rehabilitated.
29- Sanitary landfill sites should be gradually reduced by diverting all types of wastes to recycle industry or energy recovery.
30- The goals of recovery must be resource protection, environmental protection, energy recovery and space saving.

The recovery and waste reduction programs should be implemented and prepared according to certain policies and targets and successful results are obtained.

The primary objective of any program to be prepared on solid waste control is to encourage all individuals and municipalities to act more responsibly by considering the environmental impacts while removing waste.

If the public is not interested in recovery, it will be very difficult to reach the targeted rates. The most important factor in providing this interest is the education of people. Therefore, the society should be informed and educated at every stage of the solid waste management plan.

The training elements that can be used within the scope of training and implementation policies should be written and visual briefing, local seminar programs and the real application with technical support. Education should start from students and women. Visual documents should be emphasized for education. When the separate collection will start, the public should be notified in advance with the documents to be distributed. In these documents, the importance of separate collection and how it will be done, the responsibility of the public should be explained. Training and reminder notes and logos can be placed on water, natural gas and electricity bills.

All these efforts are for a cleaner world and a sustainable development that is not a burden to the economy.

REFERENCES

Alvord, S. H., Brown, L. D., & Letts, C. W. (2004). Social entrepreneurship and societal transformation: An exploratory study. *The Journal of Applied Behavioral Science*, *40*(3), 260–282. doi:10.1177/0021886304266847

Burney, S. (2003). *The Use of Chemical Composition Data in Waste Management Planning, Waste Management*. Elsevier.

European Commission. (2010). *Being Wise with The Waste: The EU's Approach to Waste Management*. Belgium: European Union. http://ec.europa.eu/environment/waste/pdf/ WASTE%20BROCHURE.pdf

Fiorillo, D. (2013). Household Waste Recycling: National Survey Evidence From Italy. *Journal of Environmental Planning and Management*, *56*(8), 1125–1151. doi:10.1080/09640568.2012.709180

Goren. (n.d.). *Lecture notes of "Recycling Technologies"*. College of Engineering at Al-Lith, Umm Al-Qura University.

Gören, S. (2005). *Sanitary Landfill*. Forart Publications.

Haldeman, T., & Turner, J. W. (2009). Implementing a Community-Based Social Marketing Program to Increase Recycling. *Social Marketing Quarterly*, *15*(3), 115–127.

Ni, M., Leung, D. Y. C., Leung, M. K. H., & Sumathy, K. (2006). An overview of hydrogen production from biomass. *Fuel Processing Technology*, *87*(5), 461–472. doi:10.1016/j.fuproc.2005.11.003

Ölander, F., & Thøgersen, J. (2006). The A-B-C of Recycling. *European Advances in Consumer Research*, *7*, 297–302.

Ozcan, H. K., Guvenc, S. Y., Guvenc, L., & Demir, G. (2016). Municipal Solid Waste Characterization According to Different Income Levels: A Case Study. *Sustainability*, *8*(10), 1044. doi:10.3390u8101044

Öztürk, İ., Demir, İ., Özabalı, A., & Tezer, H. (2005). *İstanbul İçin AB Çevre Mevzuatı İle Uyumlu Entegre Katı Atık Yönetimi Stratejik Planı*. Istac Publications 2005, IBB Istanbul Municipality.

Tchobanoglous, G., Theisen, H., & Vigil, S. (1993). *Integrated Solid Waste Management: Engineering Principles and Management Issues*. McGraw Hill.

Tucker, P., & Speirs, D. (2003). Attitudes and Behavioural Change in Household Waste Management Behaviours. *Journal of Environmental Planning and Management*, *46*(2), 289-307.

United Nations. (2015). *United Nation Sustainable Development Goals (2030)*. UN.

USEPA. (2011). *Municipal Solid Waste Generation, Recycling, and Disposal in the United States: Facts and Figures for 2010; EPA-530-F-14-001*. AM-BRA GmbH.

Chapter 11
Identifying Key Issues to Handle the Inflation Problem in the Healthcare Industry Caused by Energy Prices:
An Evaluation With Decision-Making Models

Serkan Eti
https://orcid.org/0000-0002-4791-4091
İstanbul Medipol University, Turkey

Hasan Dinçer
İstanbul Medipol University, Turkey

Yaşar Gökalp
https://orcid.org/0000-0002-3390-4597
İstanbul Medipol University, Turkey

Serhat Yüksel
İstanbul Medipol University, Turkey

Dilan Kararoğlu
https://orcid.org/0000-0002-8895-9317
İstanbul Medipol University, Turkey

ABSTRACT

This study investigated how energy inflation in the health sector can be controlled. In this context, research has been carried out using both the AHP and the DEMATEL methods. A comprehensive literature review was carried out, and four different criteria were determined. In order to determine which of these criteria is more important, an analysis was carried out using these two different methods. According to the results obtained, it has been determined that the use of renewable energy is the most important factor in eliminating the inflation caused by energy prices in the health sector. Because the best criterion is the same for both the results of AHP and DEMATEL, this situation gives information about the coherency and reliability of the study. Hence, appropriate strategies can be provided based on these results to minimize the inflation problem in the healthcare industry. The findings indicate that it would be appropriate for hospitals to give importance to the use of renewable energy. In this way, hospitals will be able to produce the energy they need themselves.

DOI: 10.4018/978-1-6684-5876-1.ch011

INTRODUCTION

Inflation is accepted as one of the most critical problems for the economies. Because high inflation creates uncertainties, companies will not be willing to make new investments in these markets. Due to this situation, the main causes of the inflation can be found, and necessary actions should be taken to overcome this problem. Inflation caused by energy prices poses a serious threat to the health sector. This is because the energy consumption in hospitals is very high. Some equipment used in hospitals, such as a tomography device, consumes a very high amount of energy. On the other hand, energy consumption is high as hospitals provide services all day long. Therefore, the increase in energy prices has a significant impact on hospitals. Therefore, necessary measures should be taken to eliminate the inflation caused by energy prices in the health sector.

In this study, it was investigated how energy inflation in the health sector can be controlled. In this context, research has been carried out using both the AHP and the DEMATEL method. A comprehensive literature review was carried out and 4 different criteria were determined. Energy efficiency is very important in order to solve the energy-related inflation problem. In this context, healthcare companies need to identify and implement practices that can save energy. In this way, less energy will be used in the field, and this will contribute to less impact of inflation. Another important issue in this process is state support (Haiyun ct al., 2021). The high inflation problem affects the investments of hospitals negatively. Due to the increasing uncertainty, hospitals have difficulties in determining prices (Yuan et al., 2021). This situation both leads to a decrease in investments and reveals customer dissatisfaction. In order to contribute to the solution of this problem, some support can be provided to hospitals by the state. This will help to eliminate the mentioned negative effect (Zhao et al., 2021).

The use of renewable energy allows hospitals to produce their own energy. This situation contributes to the elimination of the energy-related inflation problem. In this framework, if the hospitals are able to supply the amount of energy they need themselves, their dependence on foreign energy will be eliminated (Li et al., 2021). Therefore, rising energy prices will not affect hospitals much in this case. Hospitals that produce their own energy will be able to manage energy-based inflation more easily (Fang et al., 2021). The implementation of strict rules by the states can also be preferred in managing the inflation problem (Liu et al., 2021). In this framework, the government tries to prevent inflation by interfering with prices. However, this method has been severely criticized as it is a harsh intervention in the free market (Zhou et al., 2021).

To determine which of these criteria is more important, an analysis was carried out using these two different methods. While making calculations by using two different methods, a comparative evaluation can be conducted. This situation has a positive contribution to control the validity and coherency of the analysis results. Accordingly, because the best criterion is the same for both the results of AHP and DEMATEL, this situation gives information about the coherency and reliability of the study. Hence, appropriate strategies can be provided based on these results to minimize inflation problem in healthcare industry.

The biggest limitation of this study is that only the health sector is considered in the review process. Therefore, other sectors such as banking and automotive may also be considered in future studies. In this way, the inflation problem will be managed effectively for different sectors. This will contribute to the stability of the country's economy. In this study, AHP and DEMATEL methods were considered. In other studies, these techniques can also be used with fuzzy numbers. Thus, it will be possible to test the reliability of the findings obtained.

Theoretical Background

Risk management is a vital factor for the healthcare industry. Risk refers to the factors that prevent the achievement of a goal. In other words, a person, institution or state has some goals for their own situation. However, achieving this goal is not easy. In this process, some obstacles may be encountered. As an example, let's assume that a business aims to increase its profitability. In the country in which this business operates, the government may increase taxes on certain business activities. As this will increase the costs of the business, there will be a decrease in profitability (Qiu et al., 2020). As can be seen, the business aimed to increase its profitability and an unexpected event such as a tax increase occurred. This situation hindered the company's goal of increasing its profitability. In summary, the tax increase situation, which creates an obstacle to the profitability target of the enterprise, is accepted as the risk of the enterprise (Wang et al., 2021).

This situation is not limited to tax increases only. Countless very different events can occur and slow down or prevent the business from achieving its goals. In this context, individuals or businesses should first determine these factors in detail. In order to achieve this goal, businesses need to perform a very comprehensive analysis (Yüksel, 2017). In this way, it will be possible to classify the risks that affect the activities of the enterprises. After that, the effects and probabilities of the risks mentioned should be determined. Not all risks have the same negative impact on businesses. In parallel with this, the probability of occurrence of every risk is not the same. In this framework, the effects and possibilities of risks should be determined. In this way, it will be possible to identify the risk types that are more important (Kim et al., 2021).

After determining the impact and probabilities of risk types, control steps should be designed to effectively manage these risks. Each control step will be determined specifically for the type of risk. As it can be understood from here, no control step will be created for the risk types that are not determined in the first stage of the risk management process (Dinçer et al., 2017). In other words, it is not possible to create control steps for risk types that could not be detected incorrectly. After the control steps are determined, an important part of the risk management process is established. At the last stage, it should be tested whether the control steps created by performing periodic controls are successful in managing the specified risks (Yang et al., 2021).

Risk management is also important for hospitals. Hospitals are in contact with many different segments such as patients, doctors, patient relatives, health workers. The performance of hospitals may decrease due to the actions taken by any of these groups (Silahtaroğlu et al., 2021). For example, if a doctor fails to fulfill his responsibilities properly, the hospital can suffer a serious loss of image. On the other hand, hospitals are also responsible to the state in terms of tax liability and fulfillment of certain standards. In this context, if hospitals fail to fully fulfill their obligations, they may be subject to high penalties by the legal authority (Varga et al., 2021). Considering the mentioned points, hospitals also need to establish an effective risk management system.

Hospitals also face some financial risks. This situation is especially valid for private hospitals. In financial terms, the type of risk that hospitals should pay the most attention to is liquidity risk. Liquidity risk means that hospitals do not have liquid assets to pay their debts. In this context, hospitals are required to hold liquid assets, taking into account their short-term debts (Dinçer et al., 2020). In addition, business investments should not be made with all liquid assets. This will reduce the liquid assets of hospitals and businesses will not be successful in case of possible debt payment. Therefore, not all assets should be integrated into business investments (Gökalp et al., 2021). This will increase the liquidity power of hospitals.

Another type of risk that hospitals should pay attention to financially is the foreign exchange risk. The interest rates of exchange rates may be low compared to the Turkish lira. In other words, it may make more sense for hospitals to borrow in foreign currency. In this context, some hospitals may prefer to borrow in foreign currency in order to pay less interest. However, this situation creates exchange rate risk. In this context, if the foreign currency appreciates against the Turkish lira, the exchange rate will increase. In this case, the hospital that borrows in foreign currency will become more indebted. However, too high the exchange rate will cause hospitals to suffer too much. Therefore, hospitals that borrow in foreign currency should consider this issue and develop effective strategies to manage this risk.

Accordingly, inflation is accepted as one of the most critical problems for the economies. Because high inflation creates uncertainties, companies will not be willing to make new investments in these markets. Due to this situation, the main causes of the inflation can be found, and necessary actions should be taken to overcome this problem. Inflation caused by energy prices poses a serious threat to the health sector (Benami et al., 2021). This is because the energy consumption in hospitals is very high. Some equipment used in hospitals, such as a tomography device, consumes a very high amount of energy. On the other hand, energy consumption is high as hospitals provide services all day long. Therefore, the increase in energy prices has a significant impact on hospitals. Therefore, necessary measures should be taken to eliminate the inflation caused by energy prices in the health sector.

LITERATURE EVALUATION

Brosemer et al. (2020) discussed the impact of the COVID-19 epidemic on the energy sovereignty crisis in four different ways. The current crises under the name of energy sovereignty are explained. More focus is on North America. The crises discussed in this article are analyzed and two policy recommendations are presented. First, countries can issue enforcement orders to prevent power outages. Second, there may be the application of intrusive finances to better study energy systems. Banerjee et al. (2021) examined the impact of energy poverty on health and education. Poverty and income levels have a significant impact in the health sector. Regression method was used in the study. The results reveal that the limited access to electricity in countries is an important obstacle for economic development. In addition, poverty in energy is very important for us to have knowledge of the health outcomes of these countries.

Castán Broto and Kirshner (2020) explain that energy plays a major role in healthcare, especially during the COVID-19 pandemic. The findings show that sustainable energy has increased at a rapid pace in recent years. It is emphasized that more investments should be made in energy in health services. According to Pan et al. (2021) examined how energy poverty affects public health. GMM was used as a method in the study. As a result, it has been found that energy poverty negatively affects public health. As a suggestion, it was said that the transition to renewable energy should be increased. On the other hand, Khan et al. (2020) examined environmental sustainability in the public, health, and logistics sectors in ASEAN countries. It has been found that logistics operations contribute positively to environmental sustainability. It has been suggested that the use of renewable energy in logistics should be increased for better export opportunities.

Churchill and Smyth (2021) examined whether energy poverty in Australia is related to health problems. As a method, 13 wave representative panel data were used. As a result, as energy poverty increases, general health declines occur. Zhang et al. (2019) examined whether energy poverty in China is related to health problems. Household-level data from the Chinese Family Panel studies are used for analysis. The findings show that energy poverty in China has a negative impact on health. Azam et al. (2019) examined the relationship of economic growth and development in China with energy use. Canonical cointegration regression method was used in the analysis. As a result, the efficient consumption of energy in China has a positive effect on economic growth and foreign direct investment. To increase the economic growth and development in China, it is recommended to use energy effectively and efficiently.

Oliveras et al. (2021) examined the relationship between energy poverty, energy poverty and health in the European Union. Regression models were used in the study. The findings of this study show that energy poverty increased during the economic crisis in the European Union. Another finding is that energy poverty reduces the efficiency of health services. According to Yu et al. (2021) explained how to achieve flexible self-executing health monitoring systems. In hospitals, it has been found that sensors that can work well with low energy can be obtained. Brambilla and Sangiorgio (2020) explained that energy efficiency should be increased to reduce the harmful effects of the construction industry on the environment. As à result, it has been found that asthma symptoms are more common in new buildings with high energy efficiency due to poor ventilation.

Gasparotto and Martinello (2021) have examined the effects of coal, which is an energy source, on human health. The negative effects of the harmful gases emitted by coal when it is burned, on both the environment and human health are mentioned. It has been said that it is necessary to reduce the use of coal for good public health. It is recommended to use coal mining methods that are not harmful to the environment. Another suggestion is to increase the efforts for the implementation of clean energy all over the world. Cheng et al. (2020) examined the application areas of cellulosic materials in energy, environment, and health. In this context, they stated that energy efficiency is very important for the health sector. Yue et al. (2019) examined how progress should be made in linking health management and energy management strategies. In the study, different energy management strategies were designed to increase the use of hybrid electric vehicles. The findings are that the production of hybrid electric vehicles will increase as the use of renewable energy sources increases.

Oum (2019) examined the effects of energy poverty on health and education. Probit, ordinary least square and two-stage least square models were used in the study. The findings are that access to electricity is essential in energy-poor households. Wang et al. (2021) explained that energy efficiency should be increased for the development of green technologies in the future. In this way, it is emphasized that sustainable development will become a long-term goal. Oliveras et al. (2020) examined the relationship between energy poverty and drug consumption. Data were analyzed and compared using Barcelona health survey statistics. It has been concluded that energy poverty is higher in low- and middle-income countries. It has also been found that countries with energy poverty have worse health status, more need for health services, and higher drug use.

Hernandez and Siegel (2019) examined the negative impact of energy insecurity on health. Logistic regression models were used. Some inequalities between energy insecurity and health problems were found to be strongly related. Therefore, it has been suggested that energy insecurity should be investigated more and the measurements found should be improved. Li et al. (2021) examined the application of high-energy and powerful battery systems for battery electric vehicles to have higher power. As a result, it has been found that the application of these systems will bring good results in order to minimize the negative effects of both energy loss and aging cost. Kose (2019) examined the relationship between energy poverty and health problems in Turkey. In the study, a household survey addressing nations was applied. It was concluded that there is a strong relationship between energy use and health problems.

Hu et al. (2019) examined what needs to be done to increase the impact of battery hybrid electric vehicles in energy management economically. It has been determined that correct pricing has a very important role in this process. Nawaz (2021) examined the relationship of energy poverty in Pakistan between climate shocks and health problems. The results found are that energy poverty in Pakistan has a significant impact on climate and health. In addition, it has been determined that climate shocks and energy shortages have negative effects on children's health. In conclusion, for a healthy society, governments need to improve energy services and increase their incentives in this area.

Haseeb et al. (2019) examined the determinants of R&D expenditures and health expenditures in ASEAN countries. They made the review both for the short term and for the long term. ARDL model was used in the study. In the short term, energy consumption did not have a significant impact on R&D expenditures. It has been found that economic growth, environmental pollution, and energy consumption have an impact on health expenditures and R&D expenditures in the long run. Zhang et al. (2021) examined energy efficiency improvements. When energy efficiency is increased, 21% energy savings, 8% reduction in carbon emissions and 13% reduction in air pollution have been observed. As a recommendation, it is said that health, air quality and carbon elements should be combined with energy efficiency to create more opportunities. Rosenthal et al. (2018) examined the furnaces used with LPG and biomass energy in 40 low- and middle-income countries and the effects of the use of these furnaces on health and climate. It has been concluded that the use of clean energy has positive effects on human health.

METHODOLOGY

Analytic Hierarchy Process (AHP)

AHP is a multi-criteria decision-making technique (Eti et al., 2021). The steps of AHP are given below.

Step 1. Expert opinions are generated with a 9-point scale and pairwise comparison matrix (A).

$$A = \begin{bmatrix} 1 & \cdots & a_{1n} \\ \vdots & 1 & \vdots \\ a_{n1} = 1/a_{1n} & \cdots & 1 \end{bmatrix}$$

Here, the values in the diagonals are 1 because it shows the comparison of the criteria with themselves.

Step 2. The matrix A is normalized. For this, it is divided by column totals (Eti et al., 2020).

$$a'_{ij} = \frac{a_{ij}}{\sum_{i=1}^{n} a_{ij}} i, j = 1, 2, \ldots, n$$

Step 3. The priority vector is calculated. For this, row averages are taken.

$$w_i = \frac{1}{n} \sum_{j=1}^{n} a'_{ij}$$

Step 4. Calculate the Consistency Rate. For this, the following equations are used.

$$CI = \frac{\lambda_{max} - n}{n-1}.$$

There,

$$\lambda_{max} = \frac{1}{n} \sum_{i=1}^{n} \frac{\sum_{j=1}^{n} a_{ij} w_j}{w_i}$$

e RI value is determined from the Random Index table. This Consistency Ratio (CR)

$$CR = \frac{CI}{RI}$$

calculated by Eq. If this value is below 0.1, the matrix A is said to be consistent.

The Decision-Making Trial and Evaluation Laboratory (DEMATEL)

DEMATEL method is one of the weighting methods like AHP. The advantage of the DEMATEL method over the AHP method is that it allows the interaction between the criteria to be seen (Kou et al., 2021). The steps of this method are given below (Meng et al., 2021).

Step 1. A direct relationship matrix (A) is created with the arithmetic mean of the expert opinions.

$$A = \begin{bmatrix} 1 & \cdots & a_{1n} \\ \vdots & \ddots & \vdots \\ a_{n1} & \cdots & 1 \end{bmatrix}$$

Step 2. The direct relationship matrix is normalized. The normalized direct relationship matrix (X) is calculated with the following formula (Jun et al., 2021).

$$s = \max\left(\max\sum_{i=1}^{n} a_{ij}, max\sum_{j=1}^{n} a_{ij} \right)$$

$$X = \frac{A}{s}$$

Step 3. The total relationship matrix (T) is created (Ding et al., 2021).

$$T = X(I - X)^{-1}$$

The I matrix in the formula is the unit matrix (Yang et al., 2021).

Step 4. Row and column sum vectors (D, R) are created.

$$D_j = \sum_{i=1}^{n} t_{ij}$$

$$R_i = \sum_{j=1}^{n} t_{ij}$$

Step 5. The weights (W) are calculated.

$$w_i = \frac{D_i + R_i}{\sum_{i=1}^{n} (D_i + R_i)}$$

AN APPLICATION WITH DECISION-MAKING MODEL

In this study, it is aimed to identify key issues to handle inflation problem in healthcare industry caused by energy prices. In the first stage, a detailed literature evaluation is conducted regarding these topics. Table 1 gives information about the selected criteria.

Energy efficiency is very important in order to solve the energy-related inflation problem. In this context, healthcare companies need to identify and implement practices that can save energy. In this way, less energy will be used in the field, and this will contribute to less impact of inflation. Another important issue in this process is state support (Haiyun et al., 2021). The high inflation problem affects

Table 1. Selected Criteria

Criteria	References
Energy Saving	Dong et al. (2022); Kostis et al. (2022); Yu et al. (2019)
Government Supports	Zhang et al. (2022); Bhuiyan et al. (2022); Yüksel et al. (2022a,b)
Renewable Energy	Kou et al. (2022); Yüksel and Dinçer (2022)
Strict Regulations	Mukhtarov et al. (2022); Dinçer et al. (2022)

the investments of hospitals negatively. Due to the increasing uncertainty, hospitals have difficulties in determining prices (Yuan et al., 2021). This situation both leads to a decrease in investments and reveals customer dissatisfaction. In order to contribute to the solution of this problem, some support can be provided to hospitals by the state. This will help to eliminate the mentioned negative effect (Zhao et al., 2021).

The use of renewable energy allows hospitals to produce their own energy. This situation contributes to the elimination of the energy-related inflation problem. In this framework, if the hospitals are able to supply the amount of energy they need themselves, their dependence on foreign energy will be eliminated (Li et al., 2021). Therefore, rising energy prices will not affect hospitals much in this case. Hospitals that produce their own energy will be able to manage energy-based inflation more easily (Fang et al., 2021). The implementation of strict rules by the states can also be preferred in managing the inflation problem (Liu et al., 2021). In this framework, the government tries to prevent inflation by interfering with prices. However, this method has been severely criticized as it is a harsh intervention in the free market (Zhou et al., 2021). For the analysis, opinions of 3 experts in the field were taken. Experts have academic studies both in the field of energy and in the field of health. The AHP decision matrix of the experts is given in Table 2.

Table 2. AHP Decision Matrix

Criteria	Energy Saving	Government Supports	Renewable Energy	Strict Regulations
Energy Saving	1	3,914	0,436	5,646
Government Supports	0,255	1	0,158	3,914
Renewable Energy	2,289	6,31	1	7,958
Strict Regulations	0,177	0,255	0,125	1

Based on Table 1, the weighting of the criteria is given in Table 2. When Table 3 is examined, it is seen that the most important criterion is renewable energy. The AHP weight of the renewable energy criterion is 0.543. Energy saving is the second most important criterion after renewable energy. AHP weight is 0.292. Thirdly, government supports were found. AHP weight is 0.11. Finally, restrictive regulations were found. AHP weight was found to be 0.049. In the study, the lambda value was 4.17, the CI value was 0.05, and the RI value was 0.9. In the light of these values, the consistency ratio for the AHP method was examined and the obtained consistency ratio was calculated as 0.064. Since the said value is less than 0.1, it is concluded that the weights are consistent and usable.

Table 3. Weighting of AHP Criteria

Criteria	Weights	Ranking
Energy Saving	0,292	2
Government Supports	0,114	3
Renewable Energy	0,543	1
Strict Regulations	0,049	4

Table 4. Expert Opinions of DEMATEL

DEMATEL	Energy Saving	Government Supports	Renewable Energy	Strict Regulations
Energy Saving	0	2	0,333333333	2
Government Supports	1	0	1	1
Renewable Energy	3	2,66	0	2,66
Strict Regulations	0,33	0,33	0	0

DEMATEL was used as another weighting method. The expert opinions about the DEMATEL are given in Table 4.

Based on Table 4, DEMATEL steps were applied. The weights taken from DEMATEL are given in Table 4. When Table 5 is examined, it is understood that renewable energy is the most important criterion according to the DEMATEL method. Its weight is 0.297. Unlike AHP, government supports were found as the second and energy saving as the third. Restrictive regulations, on the other hand, were found as the last and fourth criterion, as in the AHP. Its weight is also 0.196.

Table 5. Weighting of DEMATEL Criteria

Criteria	Weights	Ranking
Energy Saving	0,251	3
Government Supports	0,256	2
Renewable Energy	0,297	1
Strict Regulations	0,196	4

Because the best criterion is the same for both the results of AHP and DEMATEL, this situation gives information about the coherency and reliability of the study. Hence, appropriate strategies can be provided based on these results to minimize inflation problem in healthcare industry.

SOLUTIONS AND RECOMMENDATIONS

Inflation caused by energy prices poses a serious threat to the health sector. This is because the energy consumption in hospitals is very high. Some equipment used in hospitals, such as a tomography device, consumes a very high amount of energy. On the other hand, energy consumption is high as hospitals provide services all day long. Therefore, the increase in energy prices has a significant impact on hospitals. Therefore, necessary measures should be taken to eliminate the inflation caused by energy prices in the health sector.

In this study, it was investigated how energy inflation in the health sector can be controlled. In this context, research has been carried out using both the AHP and the DEMATEL method. A comprehensive literature review was carried out and 4 different criteria were determined. In order to determine which of these criteria is more important, an analysis was carried out using these two different methods. According to the results obtained, it has been determined that the use of renewable energy is the most important factor in eliminating the inflation caused by energy prices in the health sector.

Considering these results, it would be appropriate for hospitals to give importance to the use of renewable energy. In this way, hospitals will be able to produce the energy they need themselves. This will reduce the dependence of hospitals on foreign energy. Therefore, in case of an increase in energy prices, the losses of hospitals that have their own energy will decrease to a minimum. In other words, the increase in energy prices in the international market will not be of great importance for hospitals that do not purchase energy from outside.

In this context, it would be appropriate to install solar panels on the roofs of hospitals. In this way, hospitals will be able to meet their energy needs with solar energy. There are some factors that hospitals should pay attention to in this process. First, a detailed cost-benefit analysis should be done during the solar panels' installation process. This will minimize the risk of loss of projects. On the other hand, solar panels with high efficiency should be preferred. This will contribute to the production of more energy. Moreover, a detailed examination should be made about the company that will be supported in this process. In this context, companies that quickly resolve customer complaints should be considered. Otherwise, in case of a possible disruption in the process, electricity supply in hospitals will be difficult. This will also prevent hospitals from providing services.

FUTURE RESEARCH DIRECTIONS

The biggest limitation of this study is that only the health sector is considered in the review process. Therefore, other sectors such as banking and automotive may also be taken into account in future studies. In this way, the inflation problem will be managed effectively for different sectors. This will contribute to the stability of the country's economy. In this study, AHP and DEMATEL methods were considered. In other studies, these techniques can also be used with fuzzy numbers. Thus, it will be possible to test the reliability of the findings obtained.

CONCLUSION

In this study, it is aimed to identify key issues to handle inflation problem in healthcare industry caused by energy prices. In the first stage, a detailed literature evaluation is conducted regarding these topics. Based on this evaluation, four different criteria are selected for this issue. The weights of these items are computed by considering both AHP and DEMATEL approaches. According to the calculations with AHP, it is seen that the most important criterion is renewable energy. Energy saving is the second most important criterion in this framework. On the other hand, with respect to the calculation results of DEMATEL, it is concluded that renewable energy is the most important criterion. However, unlike AHP, government supports were found as the second and energy saving as the third. Because the best criterion is the same for both the results of AHP and DEMATEL, this situation gives information about the coherency and reliability of the study. Hence, appropriate strategies can be provided based on these results to minimize inflation problem in healthcare industry. Considering these results, it would be appropriate for hospitals to give importance to the use of renewable energy. In this way, hospitals will be able to produce the energy they need themselves. This will reduce the dependence of hospitals on foreign energy. Therefore, in case of an increase in energy prices, the losses of hospitals that have their own energy will decrease to a minimum. In other words, the increase in energy prices in the international market will not be of great importance for hospitals that do not purchase energy from outside.

REFERENCES

Azam, M., Khan, A. Q., & Ozturk, I. (2019). The effects of energy on investment, human health, environment and economic growth: Empirical evidence from China. *Environmental Science and Pollution Research International*, *26*(11), 10816–10825. PMID:30778925

Banerjee, R., Mishra, V., & Maruta, A. A. (2021). Energy poverty, health and education outcomes: Evidence from the developing world. *Energy Economics*, *101*, 105447.

Benami, E., Jin, Z., Carter, M. R., Ghosh, A., Hijmans, R. J., Hobbs, A., ... Lobell, D. B. (2021). Uniting remote sensing, crop modelling and economics for agricultural risk management. *Nature Reviews Earth & Environment*, *2*(2), 140–159.

Bhuiyan, M. A., Dinçer, H., Yüksel, S., Mikhaylov, A., Danish, M. S. S., Pinter, G., ... Stepanova, D. (2022). Economic indicators and bioenergy supply in developed economies: QROF-DEMATEL and random forest models. *Energy Reports*, *8*, 561–570.

Brambilla, A., & Sangiorgio, A. (2020). Mould growth in energy efficient buildings: Causes, health implications and strategies to mitigate the risk. *Renewable & Sustainable Energy Reviews*, *132*, 110093.

Brosemer, K., Schelly, C., Gagnon, V., Arola, K. L., Pearce, J. M., Bessette, D., & Olabisi, L. S. (2020). The energy crises revealed by COVID: Intersections of Indigeneity, inequity, and health. *Energy Research & Social Science*, *68*, 101661. PMID:32839694

Castán Broto, V., & Kirshner, J. (2020). Energy access is needed to maintain health during pandemics. *Nature Energy*, *5*(6), 419–421.

Cheng, H., Lijie, L., Wang, B., Feng, X., Mao, Z., Vancso, G. J., & Sui, X. (2020). Multifaceted applications of cellulosic porous materials in environment, energy, and health. *Progress in Polymer Science*, *106*, 101253.

Churchill, S. A., & Smyth, R. (2021). Energy poverty and health: Panel data evidence from Australia. *Energy Economics*, *97*, 105219.

Dinçer, H., Hacıoğlu, Ü., & Yüksel, S. (2017). A strategic approach to global financial crisis in banking sector: A critical appraisal of banking strategies using fuzzy ANP and fuzzy topsis methods. *International Journal of Sustainable Economies Management*, *6*(1), 1–21.

Dinçer, H., Yüksel, S., & Martinez, L. (2020). A comparative analysis of incremental and disruptive innovation policies in the European banking sector with hybrid interval type-2 fuzzy decision-making models. *International Journal of Fuzzy Systems*, *22*(4), 1158–1176.

Dinçer, H., Yüksel, S., & Martínez, L. (2022). Collaboration enhanced hybrid fuzzy decision-making approach to analyze the renewable energy investment projects. *Energy Reports*, *8*, 377–389.

Ding, Z., Yüksel, S., & Dinçer, H. (2021). An Integrated Pythagorean fuzzy soft computing approach to environmental management systems for sustainable energy pricing. *Energy Reports*, *7*, 5575–5588.

Dong, W., Zhao, G., Yüksel, S., Dinçer, H., & Ubay, G. G. (2022). A novel hybrid decision making approach for the strategic selection of wind energy projects. *Renewable Energy*, *185*, 321–337.

Eti, S. (2021). The use of quantitative methods in investment decisions: a literature review. *Research Anthology on Personal Finance and Improving Financial Literacy*, 1-20.

Eti, S., Kalkavan, H., Dinçer, H., & Yüksel, S. (2020). Predicting the role of Islamic banking on sustainable economic development: An analysis for Turkey with ARIMA model. In *Handbook of research on creating sustainable value in the global economy* (pp. 146–164). IGI Global.

Fang, S., Zhou, P., Dinçer, H., & Yüksel, S. (2021). Assessment of safety management system on energy investment risk using house of quality based on hybrid stochastic interval-valued intuitionistic fuzzy decision-making approach. *Safety Science*, *141*, 105333.

Gasparotto, J., & Martinello, K. D. B. (2021). Coal as an energy source and its impacts on human health. *Energy Geoscience*, *2*(2), 113–120.

Gökalp, Y., Dinçer, H., & Eti, S. (2021). The role of health policies for the strategic investment decisions of the international companies. In *Management Strategies to Survive in a Competitive Environment* (pp. 321–333). Springer.

Haiyun, C., Zhixiong, H., Yüksel, S., & Dinçer, H. (2021). Analysis of the innovation strategies for green supply chain management in the energy industry using the QFD-based hybrid interval valued intuitionistic fuzzy decision approach. *Renewable & Sustainable Energy Reviews*, *143*, 110844.

Haseeb, M., Kot, S., Hussain, H. I., & Jermsittiparsert, K. (2019). Impact of economic growth, environmental pollution, and energy consumption on health expenditure and R&D expenditure of ASEAN countries. *Energies*, *12*(19), 3598.

Hernández, D., & Siegel, E. (2019). Energy insecurity and its ill health effects: A community perspective on the energy-health nexus in New York City. *Energy Research & Social Science*, *47*, 78–83. PMID:32280598

Hu, X., Zou, C., Tang, X., Liu, T., & Hu, L. (2019). Cost-optimal energy management of hybrid electric vehicles using fuel cell/battery health-aware predictive control. *IEEE Transactions on Power Electronics, 35*(1), 382-392.

Jun, Q., Dinçer, H., & Yüksel, S. (2021). Stochastic hybrid decision-making based on interval type 2 fuzzy sets for measuring the innovation capacities of financial institutions. *International Journal of Finance & Economics*, *26*(1), 573–593.

Khan, S. A. R., Zhang, Y., Kumar, A., Zavadskas, E., & Streimikiene, D. (2020). Measuring the impact of renewable energy, public health expenditure, logistics, and environmental performance on sustainable economic growth. *Sustainable Development*, *28*(4), 833–843.

Kim, S., Lee, G., & Kang, H. G. (2021). Risk management and corporate social responsibility. *Strategic Management Journal*, *42*(1), 202–230.

Kose, T. (2019). Energy poverty and health: The Turkish case. *Energy Sources. Part B, Economics, Planning, and Policy*, *14*(5), 201–213.

Kostis, P., Dinçer, H., & Yüksel, S. (2022). Knowledge-Based Energy Investments of European Economies and Policy Recommendations for Sustainable Development. *Journal of the Knowledge Economy*, 1–33.

Kou, G., Olgu Akdeniz, Ö., Dinçer, H., & Yüksel, S. (2021). Fintech investments in European banks: A hybrid IT2 fuzzy multidimensional decision-making approach. *Financial Innovation*, *7*(1), 1–28. PMID:35024283

Kou, G., Yüksel, S., & Dinçer, H. (2022). Inventive problem-solving map of innovative carbon emission strategies for solar energy-based transportation investment projects. *Applied Energy*, *311*, 118680.

Li, W., Cui, H., Nemeth, T., Jansen, J., Ünlübayir, C., Wei, Z., ... Sauer, D. U. (2021). Cloud-based health-conscious energy management of hybrid battery systems in electric vehicles with deep reinforcement learning. *Applied Energy*, *293*, 116977.

Li, Y. X., Wu, Z. X., Dinçer, H., Kalkavan, H., & Yüksel, S. (2021). Analyzing TRIZ-based strategic priorities of customer expectations for renewable energy investments with interval type-2 fuzzy modeling. *Energy Reports*, *7*, 95–108.

Liu, Y., Gong, X., Yüksel, S., Dinçer, H., & Aydın, R. (2021). A multidimensional outlook to energy investments for the countries with continental shelf in East Mediterranean region with hybrid decision making model based on IVIF logic. *Energy Reports*, *7*, 158–173.

Meng, Y., Wu, H., Zhao, W., Chen, W., Dinçer, H., & Yüksel, S. (2021). A hybrid heterogeneous Pythagorean fuzzy group decision modelling for crowdfunding development process pathways of fintech-based clean energy investment projects. *Financial Innovation*, *7*(1), 1–34.

Mukhtarov, S., Yüksel, S., & Dinçer, H. (2022). The impact of financial development on renewable energy consumption: Evidence from Turkey. *Renewable Energy*.

Nawaz, S. (2021). Energy poverty, climate shocks, and health deprivations. *Energy Economics, 100*, 105338.

Oliveras, L., Artazcoz, L., Borrell, C., Palència, L., López, M. J., Gotsens, M., & ... Marí-Dell'Olmo, M. (2020). The association of energy poverty with health, health care utilisation and medication use in southern Europe. *SSM - Population Health, 12*, 100665. PMID:33195789

Oliveras, L., Peralta, A., Palència, L., Gotsens, M., López, M. J., Artazcoz, L., & ... Marí-Dell'Olmo, M. (2021). Energy poverty and health: Trends in the European Union before and during the economic crisis, 2007–2016. *Health & Place, 67*, 102294. PMID:33526205

Oum, S. (2019). Energy poverty in the Lao PDR and its impacts on education and health. *Energy Policy, 132*, 247–253.

Pan, L., Biru, A., & Lettu, S. (2021). Energy poverty and public health: Global evidence. *Energy Economics, 101*, 105423.

Qiu, D., Dinçer, H., Yüksel, S., & Ubay, G. G. (2020). Multi-faceted analysis of systematic risk-based wind energy investment decisions in E7 economies using modified hybrid modeling with IT2 fuzzy sets. *Energies, 13*(6), 1423.

Rosenthal, J., Quinn, A., Grieshop, A. P., Pillarisetti, A., & Glass, R. I. (2018). Clean cooking and the SDGs: Integrated analytical approaches to guide energy interventions for health and environment goals. *Energy for Sustainable Development, 42*, 152–159. PMID:29861575

Silahtaroğlu, G., Dinçer, H., & Yüksel, S. (2021). Defining the significant factors of currency exchange rate risk by considering text mining and fuzzy AHP. In *Data Science and Multiple Criteria Decision Making Approaches in Finance* (pp. 145–168). Springer.

Varga, S., Brynielsson, J., & Franke, U. (2021). Cyber-threat perception and risk management in the Swedish financial sector. *Computers & Security, 105*, 102239.

Wang, L., Wu, W. M., Bolan, N. S., Tsang, D. C., Li, Y., Qin, M., & Hou, D. (2021). Environmental fate, toxicity and risk management strategies of nanoplastics in the environment: Current status and future perspectives. *Journal of Hazardous Materials, 401*, 123415. PMID:32763705

Wang, Y., Nie, H., Han, J., An, Y., Zhang, Y. M., & Zhang, S. X. A. (2021). Green revolution in electronic displays expected to ease energy and health crises. *Light, Science & Applications, 10*(1), 1–14. PMID:33550329

Yang, F., Kalkavan, H., Dinçer, H., Yüksel, S., & Eti, S. (2021). Gaussian-based soft computing approach to alternative banking system for sustainable financial sector. *Complexity*.

Yang, J., Xie, H., Yu, G., & Liu, M. (2021). Antecedents and consequences of supply chain risk management capabilities: An investigation in the post-coronavirus crisis. *International Journal of Production Research, 59*(5), 1573–1585.

Yu, H., Li, N., & Zhao, N. (2021). How Far Are We from Achieving Self-Powered Flexible Health Monitoring Systems: An Energy Perspective. *Advanced Energy Materials, 11*(9), 2002646.

Yu, Z., Liu, W., Chen, L., Eti, S., Dinçer, H., & Yüksel, S. (2019). The effects of electricity production on industrial development and sustainable economic growth: A VAR analysis for BRICS countries. *Sustainability*, *11*(21), 5895.

Yuan, G., Xie, F., Dinçer, H., & Yüksel, S. (2021). The theory of inventive problem solving (TRIZ)-based strategic mapping of green nuclear energy investments with spherical fuzzy group decision-making approach. *International Journal of Energy Research*, *45*(8), 12284–12300.

Yue, M., Jemei, S., Gouriveau, R., & Zerhouni, N. (2019). Review on health-conscious energy management strategies for fuel cell hybrid electric vehicles: Degradation models and strategies. *International Journal of Hydrogen Energy*, *44*(13), 6844–6861.

Yüksel, S. (2017). Determinants of the credit risk in developing countries after economic crisis: A case of Turkish banking sector. In *Global financial crisis and its ramifications on capital markets* (pp. 401–415). Springer.

Yüksel, S., & Dinçer, H. (2022). Identifying the strategic priorities of nuclear energy investments using hesitant 2-tuple interval-valued Pythagorean fuzzy DEMATEL. *Progress in Nuclear Energy*, *145*, 104103.

Yüksel, S., Dinçer, H., Çağlayan, Ç., Uluer, G. S., & Lisin, A. (2022b). Bitcoin Mining with Nuclear Energy. In *Multidimensional Strategic Outlook on Global Competitive Energy Economics and Finance*. Emerald Publishing Limited.

Yüksel, S., Dinçer, H., Mikhaylov, A., Adalı, Z., & Eti, S. (2022a). Key Issues for the Improvements of Shallow Geothermal Investments. In *Sustainability in Energy Business and Finance* (pp. 183–194). Springer.

Zhang, D., Li, J., & Han, P. (2019). A multidimensional measure of energy poverty in China and its impacts on health: An empirical study based on the China family panel studies. *Energy Policy*, *131*, 72–81.

Zhang, S., Xie, Y., Sander, R., Yue, H., & Shu, Y. (2021). Potentials of energy efficiency improvement and energy–emission–health nexus in Jing-Jin-Ji's cement industry. *Journal of Cleaner Production*, *278*, 123335.

Zhang, Y., Zhang, Y., Gong, C., Dinçer, H., & Yüksel, S. (2022). An integrated hesitant 2-tuple Pythagorean fuzzy analysis of QFD-based innovation cost and duration for renewable energy projects. *Energy*, 123561.

Zhao, Y., Xu, Y., Yüksel, S., Dinçer, H., & Ubay, G. G. (2021). Hybrid IT2 fuzzy modelling with alpha cuts for hydrogen energy investments. *International Journal of Hydrogen Energy*, *46*(13), 8835–8851.

Zhou, P., Luo, J., Cheng, F., Yüksel, S., & Dinçer, H. (2021). Analysis of risk priorities for renewable energy investment projects using a hybrid IT2 hesitant fuzzy decision-making approach with alpha cuts. *Energy*, *224*, 120184.

KEY TERMS AND DEFINITIONS

AHP: Analytic hierarchy process.

DEMATEL: Decision-making trial and evaluation laboratory.

Chapter 12
Green Transformation in Logistics Within the Scope of the European Green Deal

Mehri Banu Erdem
https://orcid.org/0000-0002-9763-3271
Kahramanmaraş Sütçü İmam University, Turkey

Nuri Özgür Doğan
https://orcid.org/0000-0002-7892-1550
Nevşehir Hacı Bektaş Veli University, Turkey

ABSTRACT

Problems such as global warming, climate change, and depletion of resources have arisen due to the increase in consumption around the world, the use of resources as if they are endless, and the creation of environmental pollution. This put the future of all living things in danger. For this reason, the European Union took action and led the world in this regard by issuing the European Green Deal in December 2019. The European Green Deal directly or indirectly concerns the entire sector. Therefore, businesses should integrate their activities with greening through planning and R&D studies in this regard. At this point, one of the most affected industries is logistics. Sustainable logistics is part of the European Green Deal. In this chapter, the issue of sustainable logistics has been evaluated within the scope of the European Green Deal.

INTRODUCTION

With the increase in population and the change in consumption habits, waste production also increases and the need for new management models arises. Taking the necessary steps by businesses on these issues has revealed the understanding of sustainability. Sustainability is an issue that should be considered in the business as a whole and applied in all business lines and units. For this reason, the recent increase in

DOI: 10.4018/978-1-6684-5876-1.ch012

the logistics activities of enterprises necessitates the evaluation of sustainability among strategic issues in these areas as well.

The most concrete steps in the axis of green theory in international relations have been taken under the leadership of the EU, which has a concrete sense of the effects of environmental pollution and climate change. Standing out with its green new order and green economy policies in the 21st century, the EU has developed the 2020 Strategy and the 2030 Climate and Energy Framework for sustainable and comprehensive growth in the fight against climate change. With these strategies, in order to protect the natural balance of the environment and reduce the speed of climate change, it has set targets that will reduce the greenhouse gas emissions of the member countries, limit the use of fossil fuels and increase energy efficiency compared to the previous data. On a global scale, the EU has also taken a leading role in initiatives based on a total fight against global warming and climate change, such as the Kyoto Protocol and the Paris Climate Agreement, under the leadership of the EU (Kakışım, 2022).

Environmental issues examined within the scope of sustainability approach are seen in direct relation with green understanding. The studies to be done in order to minimize the damages caused by the enterprises to the environment are carried out with a green understanding. Green understanding is a concept that is used for studies that will cause less damage to the environment and are made with environmental protection awareness. This understanding has become synonymous with some important practices. Reducing carbon emissions has an important place in the work of green-minded businesses in connection with their sustainability goals. In addition, it is possible to manage the business with a more environmentally friendly green approach, thanks to the attention to the use of natural resources and the innovations made (Chopra & Meindl, 2017).

The EU has put forward a new strategy that has social, economic, cultural, technological and foreign policy dimensions, which is more advanced, modern, transformative, inclusive and in some areas legally binding for member states. Under the leadership of the European Commission, it has published the European Green Deal, which basically aims to eliminate carbon (greenhouse gas) emissions (creating a carbon neutral climate) in Europe by 2050. The EU is preparing for a green transformation that will transform the ecosystem and production infrastructure of the third countries that trade with the EU, as well as the member states, support climate and environmental security, and in a way enable the European Green Deal (EGD) to have a global impact (Kakışım, 2022)

EUROPEAN GREEN DEAL

The European Union (EU) plays an important role in policies to combat climate change and has been a pioneer in this regard for a long time. It adopted a strategy for climate change in 1992, and in 1996 it set the target to limit global warming to more than 2 degrees Celsius above pre-industrial levels. In 2001, the EU cemented its reputation as an international leader in tackling climate change for the Kyoto Protocol to come into force despite the US withdrawal (Siddi, 2020).

In December 2015, with the Paris Climate Agreement, the EU also took a leading role in initiatives such as emission reduction, renewable energy and energy efficiency, which are based on a total fight against global warming and climate change (Siddi, 2020). However, the inadequacy of both the EU-wide strategies determined by the EU and international initiatives in combating global warming and climate change, and the inability to reduce greenhouse gas emissions and global warming to the desired levels have forced the EU to develop a new strategy (Kakışım, 2022).

Within the scope of combating climate change on a global scale, significant international steps such as the United Nations Framework Convention on Climate Change (1994), the Kyoto Protocol (2005), and the Paris Agreement (2016) aimed to reduce greenhouse gas emissions and global temperatures. The European Commission has brought the European Green Deal (EGD) to the agenda as a continuation of the Paris Agreement, as a solution to the climate change and the problems it causes (Karakuş at al., 2022). By announcing the European Green Deal in 2019, the EU initiated a comprehensive transformation for the transition to a green economy in the fight against the climate crisis. In this context, it has aimed to be the first climate neutral continent in the world by 2050, to ensure the transition to a circular economy, to ensure sustainable development and sustainable finance, to separate economic growth from resource use, and to ensure that no community or region is left behind in all these processes (European Commission, 2019a).

It has presented the European Green Deal as a package of measures to become the world's first zero carbon continent in terms of climate by 2050. These measures range from reducing emissions, investing in technological development and innovation and protecting Europe's natural environment with an initial roadmap of these core policies. The European Commission has presented an ambitious target in its Biodiversity Strategy 2030, Farm to Fork and the European Climate Law, which includes activities such as sustainable soil (Montanarella & Panagos, 2021).

The Farm to Fork Strategy deals with sustainability in terms of EU food systems and is an important element of the European Green Deal. Sustainable food production is to encourage diets to increase consumption of sustainable foods, including fruits, vegetables, nuts, whole grains and seeds, as well as reducing emissions from processing, reducing pollution and its positive health effects (Haines & Scheelbeek, 2020). The Biodiversity Strategy includes the establishment of a Europe-wide network of protected areas on land and at sea. With this strategy, 30% of both land and sea surface will be protected. The strategy also includes plans to ensure implementation, track progress, acquire and improve knowledge, and establish a governance framework for businesses to make better financial decisions (Fetting, 2020).

To achieve climate targets, greenhouse gas emissions must be addressed alongside production-related emissions. The European Green Deal includes the rapid move towards a circular economy based on reuse, remanufacturing, shared use and recycling. It includes making better regulations to avoid further exposure to toxic chemicals that emerge in these processes and minimizing health risks by implementing them (Haines & Scheelbeek, 2020). The green economy is an economic model that aims to develop with low carbon emissions, protects the environmental system while providing resource efficiency, and aims to create welfare for all. EU within the scope of green economy; It has developed policies in energy and infrastructure systems, transportation, industry, agriculture and many more. For example; In its energy policies, it has updated the "Clean Energy for All Europeans" package to strengthen the energy system and protect the environment by ensuring the transition to clean energy (European Commission, 2019b). The circular economy action plan, which is one of the requirements of the green economy and one of the most important elements of the European Green Deal, has been accepted (European Commission, 2020a).

The EU aims to be climate neutral by 2050. In order to transform this politically committing and promoting legal obligation, he proposed a European Climate Law. To achieve this goal, all industry of the EU economy need to take action. For example (European Commission, 2021)

- Giving importance to the environmental friendliness of the technologies used or to be supplied
- Supporting the industrial sector to innovate
- Dissemination of healthier, cheaper and cleaner public and private transport modes

- Decarbonisation of the energy sector
- More energy efficient buildings are designed
- Working with international partners and stakeholders to improve environmental standards globally

Considering the great concerns about global warming and climate change, the EU has seriously expressed its political determination to combat this problem by setting many targets on increasing energy efficiency and reducing carbon emissions through renewable energy sources. These targets highlight the key priorities for the EU that it aims to achieve with the European Green Deal (Hanfer & Raimondi, 2020).

The main purpose of the agreement is to achieve the goals of the Paris Climate Agreement and to initiate a major economic and social transformation (Economic Development Foundation, 2021). The Paris Climate Agreement is the most important legally binding climate action plan created in 2015 to combat global climate change. The Paris Climate Agreement aims to keep the global average temperature increase below 2°C compared to the pre-industrialization period and below 1.5°C (United Nations Framework Convention on Climate Change, 2015). The EU signed the Paris Climate Agreement in 2016 and put it into effect, and paved the way for the Paris Agreement to be accepted globally (Official Journal of European Union, 2016). In line with the targets of the Paris Climate Agreement, the EU has aimed to reduce its greenhouse gas emissions by at least 40% by 2030 compared to the 1990 level (European Commission, 2016). This rate was later updated in the European Climate Law and set as a target of at least 55% emission reduction in 2030 compared to 1990. At the same time, the target of providing 33.1%-33.7% of EU energy from renewable energy and increasing energy efficiency by 32.5% by 2030 has been determined (European Commission, 2020b).

EU Member States are required to meet legally binding targets aimed at gradually reducing greenhouse gas emissions by 2020, 2030 and 2050. Three targets are particularly important in the EU. For 2020, the 20-20-20 targets of the climate and energy package are 20 percent greenhouse gas reductions compared to 1990 values. It includes the goals of the climate and energy framework for 2030, which requires the EU as a whole to reduce greenhouse gas emissions by 40 percent by 2030 compared to 1990 levels. Finally, the European green agreement is a cornerstone of the goals in terms of achieving the EU's long-term strategic vision for reaching 80 percent by 2050, as well as for greenhouse gas reduction (Fleming & Mauger, 2021).

The EU aims to be a global role model in tackling the climate crisis and realizing its sustainable development goals (European Commission, 2019a). In this direction, the Commission has determined some areas of action to achieve the climate targets by 2050 (European Commission, 2019a). These areas are climate law, biodiversity, clean energy, farm-to-fork, sustainable industry, sustainable agriculture, pollution reduction, nature conservation, financing green projects, making buildings energy efficient, ensuring a just transition for all and leading green change globally (Küçük & Dural, 2022).

ELEMENTS OF THE EUROPEAN GREEN DEAL

The main objectives of EGD include zero carbon emissions by 2050 and the reorganization of the activities of all sectors such as industry, energy, transportation and agriculture accordingly (Üstün, 2021). EGD is actually a general policy strategy, not a law. Existing standards and regulations will be revised and implemented in a few years (Fetting, 2020). As seen in Figure 1, EGD has eight key areas. These areas

Figure 1. European Green Deal (European Comission, 2019a)

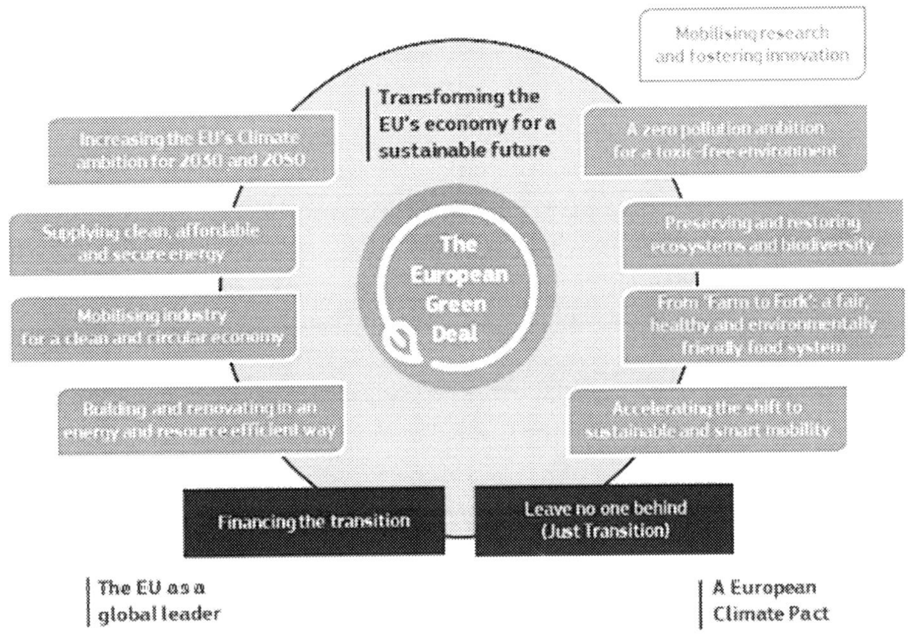

are sustainable industry, renovating and building, secure affordable and clean energy, farm to fork, zero pollution, sustainable mobility, biodiversity and mobilizing industry for a clean and circular economy.

Clean, Affordable and Secure Energy

Aiming to decarbonize the EU's energy system, the clean energy transformation of the EGD focuses on three fundamental principles; ensuring a secure and affordable energy supply, developing a fully integrated, interconnected and digitized energy market, increasing the energy performance of buildings by prioritizing energy efficiency, and development of an energy industry based largely on renewable sources (European Commission, 2019a). Achieving these three goals means energy efficiency and sustainable energy.

The energy used to heat and cool buildings is huge. Reducing this energy use and switching to renewable energy sources are among the main sustainable energy goals. In order to save energy in buildings, natural air conditioning systems are used (Karakuş et al., 2022). In addition, it is planned to launch the national carbon pricing mechanism for certain sectors by the end of the fourth quarter of 2022. However, practices such as emissions trading, carbon tax or transition to new technologies will result in increased costs, especially in power plants and industry using coal and natural gas. The costs incurred will be returned to the consumer as a price difference. There is a risk that green practices will become an instrument of the market economy. Transforming into economic industries and making them only for profit will make these practices even more expensive (Talu, 2015; Üstün, 2021).

Sustainable Industry

In the European Green Deal, it is mentioned that the entire industry should take action in order to achieve the climate neutral and circular economy targets (European Commission, 2019). In general, as in all countries of the world, Turkey has a linear economy and this economy slows down the development of the country's economies, while harming the environment. With the increasing population, production volume and growing economy, environmental effects are also increasing day by day. In order to prevent this, resource use must be decoupled from economic growth. Discretization means the same amount of production with less resources or more production with less resources. In other words, discretization means less damage to the environment while growing economically (Ucal et al., 2017; Karakuş et al., 2022).

The main objectives of the circular economy are resource reduction, reuse and recycling. In this way, while saving energy, the use of raw materials and the amount of waste are reduced. The role of industry is very important at this point. With the prohibitions on single-use packaging put into practice in China, the ban on plastic bags and the taxation system based on the amount of waste, reductions in the rate of waste generated during the production phase can be achieved (Lee et al., 2020). In this way, the industries responsible for waste production can restructure their production policies.

Building and Renovating

It is an undeniable fact that the energy consumption of buildings is high. Initiating a transformation for energy-friendly buildings is also one of the important elements in the European Green Deal. It is an important step for the construction industry to initiate initiatives and necessary R&D studies in this regard in terms of adaptation to green mobility. Among the things to be done in this regard, it can be counted that the energy to be used in the building consists primarily of renewable energies.

In the European Union, buildings account for 40% of the energy consumed. In order to achieve the 55% emission reduction in the 2030 climate target, energy consumption from buildings must be reduced by 14% and greenhouse gas emissions by 60%. The fact that the buildings comply with the new standards in terms of energy will significantly reduce energy consumption. Especially in terms of insulation and energy efficiency, old buildings need to be built in accordance with new standards (Fetting, 2020).

Farm to Fork

The farm to fork strategy aimed to make European food systems environmentally friendly, healthy and fair. Sustainability in food should, inter alia, separate from environmental impact, adapt to and mitigate climate change, reverse biodiversity decline and encourage the public to eat healthy (Fetting, 2020). In this context, it is also planned to prevent imported foods from entering EU markets if they do not comply with EU health and environmental requirements. Food production causes soil, air and water pollution. It leads to biodiversity loss and climate change and excessive natural resources are consumed during food production. Therefore, policies aimed at drastically reducing the use of pesticides, fertilizers and antibiotics in agriculture and fisheries are envisaged as part of the European Green Deal (Üstün, 2021).

Zero Pollution

Environmental pollution basically occurs in nature in the form of air, soil and water pollution and ultimately affects the whole ecosystem, including humans (İbadullayeva et al., 2019). Pollution brings with it problems such as climate changes, global warming, soil becoming unproductive and non-nutritive, scarcity of food and beverage, depletion of water resources, change in world geography, energy shortage, decrease in biological diversity due to extinction of living things. This pollution is caused by motor vehicles and vehicles, solid wastes, radiation caused by some technological devices, industrial wastes and noise pollution, air pollution arising from the fuel and energy used in heating the buildings. Steps must be taken quickly to change this life-threatening situation facing the whole world. Conditions causing pollution and their solutions should be determined, and R&D studies should be carried out in order to accelerate this solution.

Sustainable Mobility

The transport industry in the EU was responsible for a quarter of emissions, including aviation, in 2018. In order to reach the carbon neutral target for 2050, greenhouse gas emissions in the transportation sector must be reduced by 90%. The Commission proposed the Smart Mobility and Sustainability Strategy in December 2020. The Strategy includes three pillars of the European Commission (2020c):

- Making all modes of transport more sustainable
- More widespread use of multimodal transport in transport towards sustainability
- Accelerating the transition to sustainability by providing incentives

With this strategy, it is aimed to increase integration in the transportation industry, to make multimodal transportation more efficient, to shift transportation to railways and inland waterways, to introduce new digital technologies, to put new charging points into use, and to give more priority to sustainable urban mobility. It is expected that the target of the European Green Deal to reduce emissions from the transport industry by 90% will be achieved.

Biodiversity

According to the 2019 Global Assessment Report of the Intergovernmental Science Policy Platform on Biodiversity and Ecosystem Services, the main causes of biodiversity erosion worldwide are climate change, changes in the way sea and land use, wasteful and ignorant use of natural resources. In this direction, the European Union announced the Biodiversity Strategy Plan as of 2020 and expanded the scope of land and sea areas rich in biodiversity in particular. It has decided to take new measures regarding the protection of forests and increasing forest areas and the protection of oceans and seas (Üstün, 2021). The Biodiversity Strategy refers to the establishment of a Europe-wide network of protected areas on land and at sea. In addition, the strategy includes establishing better policies to facilitate management to improve finances, ensure implementation, improve knowledge, monitor progress and enable better decision making (Fetting, 2020).

Mobilizing Industry for a Clean and Circular Economy

In order to comply with the circular economy concept and to implement the zero waste management system effectively, it is seen that the waste management legislation of the European Union (EU) is shaped in accordance with the steps of the waste management hierarchy, as is the case throughout the world (Mısır & Arıkan, 2022).

The Industrial Strategy was published in March 2020. It outlines three key objectives. These are (Fetting, 2020).

- Providing an equal playing field and maintaining global competitiveness
- To be climate neutral with sustainable movement of industry by 2050
- Shaping Europe's digital future in a sustainable way

The strategy includes plans to reduce climate change, decarbonize all industries, and support sustainability with smart mobility industries. It promotes digital transformation towards low carbon in industry. R&D studies and action plans for the elimination of carbon emissions in the economy should be addressed in the entire industries (Fetting, 2020).

GREEN TRANSFORMATION IN LOGISTICS

The concept of sustainability in the global sense came to the fore in the report "Our Common Future", also known as the Brundtland Report, published by the United Nations World Commission on Environment and Development in 1987. In the report, sustainable development was defined as the movement to meet the needs of the present without taking risk the needs of future generations (WCED, 1987). The United Nations Conference on Environment and Development held in Rio de Janeiro in 1992 signed five pacts framing "sustainable development" as the inclusive policy of the 21st century. Many references to "sustainable development" are proposed at this conference, a form of development that integrates economic growth and environmental protection (Basiago, 1998).

One of the industries where important developments and changes are expected is transportation, more specifically logistics activities (Taş & Aylak, 2022). Transport provides the movement of people and goods, increasing economic growth and quality of life. On the other hand, it causes a number of problems with harmful effects on the environment and public health. These issues are the main driver to support innovation that makes transportation greener, safer and more efficient (Tsakalidis et al., 2020). According to The Council of Logistics Management's (CLM) definition, logistics is the process of planning, organizing, executing and supervising the procedures necessary for the effective and efficient transportation and storage of all products and related information, including services, from the point of origin to the destination, in line with the customer's needs. (Mabert & Venkataramanan, 1998).

On the other hand, logistics definitions now need to be revised to include not only a forward but also a reverse flow, suggesting recycling and material substitution. Termination of the forward flow, in a way, it also means that the materials in the current flow expire or are scrapped. In the light of all these mentioned, if it is necessary to make an up-to-date and comprehensive definition, "Logistics is the systematic flow of goods and services, from the point of origin to the end user, from the point of origin to the end user, including the transfer of information between the procurement, handling, transportation, storage and distribution, and inventory control and scrapping activities (Erturgut, 2016).

Businesses operating in the logistics industry should support the management of the climate crisis by adopting the strategies determined by the countries (Jäger-Waldau et al., 2020). Environmental concerns have increased over time and have changed the success criteria of enterprises in logistics activities and the target point in supply chain management. Thus, the concepts of green supply chain, sustainable supply chain, sustainable logistics, reverse logistics and green logistics have gained an important place on the agenda (Taş & Aylak, 2022).

It is the failure of damaged, defective and expired products within the supply chain for the purpose of repair, maintenance, separation or destruction. This type of approach brings with it an understanding called green management in enterprises, which can be explained as the correct use of resources and the development of a recycling culture. This understanding has two effects. First, social and individual responsibility, sensitivity and environmental awareness have increased. The trends towards the use of recyclable products predominate in consumption habits. Secondly, the responsibility of the producers (Manufacturers' responsibilities for environmental awareness and resource use) are increasing. The concept of Extended Producer Responsibility (EPR) is emerging more clearly and is gaining importance. Within the framework of this responsibility, producers are responsible for the recycling of a product that has completed its economic life and/or its technological, or they must also ensure that they are properly disposed of where it is not economically feasible (Erdal et al., 2008).

Along with industrialization, there has been an increase in environmental problems as a result of many activities such as the release of toxic gases into the air, the pollution of soil and water with chemical wastes (Büyüközkan et al., 2008). At this point, the concept of green logistics comes into play. Green logistics is the execution of logistics activities by prioritizing the environment (Thiell et al., 2011). GSCM encompasses the various activities of the business, including the delivery of products and services to consumers, purchasing, manufacturing, raw material sourcing, and green product design (Sarkis, 2003; Taş & Aylak, 2022). Within the scope of the European Green Deal, a number of targets related to logistics activities have been set by the European Union and action plans to be followed in achieving this target have been prepared.

European Green Deal Transport Plan

The European Green Deal sustainable mobility plan is based on three concepts. These are sustainable mobility, smart mobility, resilient mobility. The practices that can be done for sustainable mobility are as follows (European Commission, 2020c):

- Increase the uptake of zero-emissions, low-carbon infrastructure and renewable fuels for vehicles, aircraft and ships – for example, installing public charging points by 2030
- Build ports and airports with zero emissions – for example, promoting sustainable marine and aviation fuels through new initiatives
- Making urban and interurban mobility sustainable and healthy – for example, developing extra bicycle infrastructure and doubling high-speed train traffic within 10 years.
- Going green in freight transport by doubling rail transport in freight traffic by 2050.
- Providing incentives for users and pricing carbon – for example, establishing fair and efficient pricing by taking a comprehensive set of measures across all transport.

Digitalization and innovation will shape how cargo and passengers will move in the future, if the conditions are right according to the current situation. The practices that can be done for smart mobility are as follows (Fetting, 2020):

- Transforming multimodal mobility into automated and connected ones. For example, enabling passengers to purchase tickets for multi-modal journeys and seamlessly switch between these multiple modes.
- Creating smarter mobility with artificial intelligence and innovation and increasing its use. For example, conditioning unmanned aerial vehicles and drones supporting further activities towards establishing a European joint mobility data area.

One of the industries most affected by the COVID-19 pandemic has been transportation. Many actors in the industry are experiencing financial and operational difficulties. The practices that can be done for smart mobility are as follows (European Commission, 2020c):

- Strengthening the single market. For example, to build a better structure in the industry by increasing efforts and investments in the modernization of fleets in all modes, both in the public and private sectors, to complete the Trans-European transport network by 2030.
- Making mobility transparent and fair for all. For example, making all zones affordable and accessible to all travelers, including those with limited mobility. Making the industry more attractive for employees. To improve transportation safety in all modes.

In addition to ensuring sustainability in transportation, it is also necessary to ensure competitiveness and durability. Besides, this development should not leave anyone behind. It is essential that rural and remote areas remain connected, that mobility is accessible and affordable for all, that the sector provides attractive jobs and offers good social conditions (Fetting, 2020).

Sustainable Logistics

Events that take place in the world and that concern large masses indirectly affect all commercial enterprises. When this situation is evaluated in terms of the logistics industry, environmental sustainability and global warming emerge as the most important problems. Unconscious consumption of natural resources, deficiencies in waste management, increases in emission rates and individuals raised without environmental awareness have an important place in the emergence of global warming. Emission values are directly related to the carbon emissions of vehicles used in transportation. Since transportation is one of the most important components of the logistics industry, it can be said that the share of the industry in global warming is large. Considering that 60% of the total oil consumed in the world and 25% of the total energy consumed is consumed by the transportation industry, the importance of the industry in terms of environmental sustainability can be better understood (Rorigue et al., 2020).

Carbon emissions in the logistics industry account for a quarter of the EU's emissions, and their levels are increasing. In 2019, there has been increasing societal pressure on logistics firms to reduce emissions to combat climate change. The European Association of Railway and Infrastructure Companies (CER) and its members stepped in to address these challenges. Railways are ready to find a solution to this climate problem through technology. It plays an significant role in the transition to sustainability in transportation by offering an alternative to long road transportation, especially with high-speed rail, short-haul flights and many exit-destination points. According to a recent European Commission (EC) study, high-speed train offers a lot of benefits in terms of variable infrastructure and external costs. For this reason, it is an investment made in a highly efficient mode of transportation in order to significantly reduce the negative effects of logistics on nature (Kostyrko, 2021).

The concept of sustainability is shaped by the components of society, environment and economy, as seen in Figure 2. These components are the main reasons for the changes to be experienced in the industry in terms of sustainability. Social awareness is increasing day by day, people have started to put cleaner and healthier options ahead of cost. Clean transportation has become more important than cheap transportation for people, and this is a situation that will spread rapidly with the increase of social awareness. In addition, the studies carried out by the state will progress in this direction. Incentives are now provided to companies or vehicles that pollute the environment less. Such factors make these three basic determinants more meaningful (Chopra & Meindl, 2017).

Figure 2. Components of Sustainable Logistics (Altuntaş & Türker, 2012; Çetin & Sain, 2018)

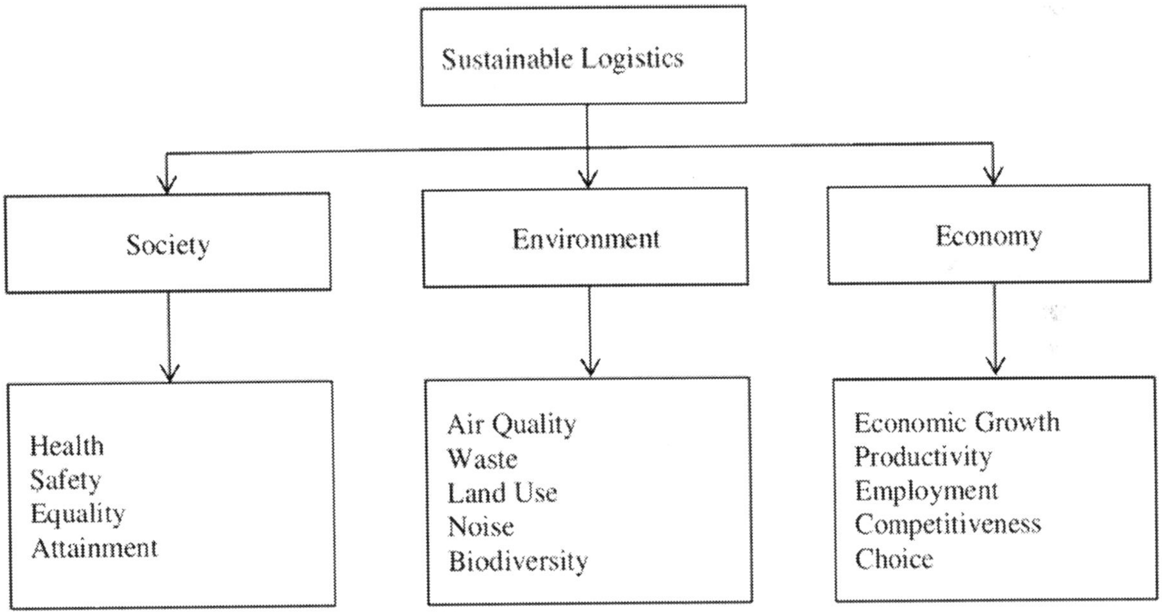

As shown in Figure 2, sustainable logistics has three basic components: society, environment and economy. Community component consist of health, safety, equality and attainment; environmental component consists of air quality, waste, land use, noise and biodiversity; the economy component consists of economic growth, productivity, employment, competitiveness and choice. Being environmentally sustainable means sustainability in issues such as the use of natural resources, preventing the pollution of nature and turning to renewable resources. For this, it focuses on the sustainability of environmental life by focusing on issues such as waste, wastewater, emissions, spills and leaks, biodiversity, atmospheric balance, environmental management, natural resource consumption, water management and ecosystem (Fettahlıoğlu & Birin, 2016).

In economically sustainable logistics, issues such as minimizing costs, maximizing profits, growth, development and progress are on the agenda. In order to reduce carbon emissions and minimize fuel consumption, applications such as the selection of suitable transportation vehicles, regular maintenance and repairs, reducing transportation distances, and reducing the traffic caused around the warehouse or factory are among the things that can be done for sustainable logistics (Erol & Özmen, 2008). There are things that can be done in storage processes for sustainable logistics. For example, reducing stocks will provide improvement in terms of greenhouse gases (Çamlıca & Akar, 2014). Keeping stocks at reasonable levels will reduce finished product stocks, raw material, cooling and heating costs, especially in smaller enterprises (Dey et al., 2011).

Overall, there are significant benefits to be gained from implementing health and environmentally sustainable logistics under the European Green Deal. Taking advantage of them, however, requires careful design and evaluation of policy choices. One of the challenges, for example, is that rising fossil fuel prices increase fuel poverty, with potentially undesirable negative consequences such as increased inequalities. When sustainability is applicable in logistics activities, triple earnings policies that benefit society, the environment and the economy are also implemented (Bell et al., 2019). A fair transition can be achieved by considering the principles of equality and justice in every step taken in line with climate change adaptation and mitigation policies. In other words, just transition can be defined as the process in which a just and egalitarian approach of society is based for a carbon-free life (McCauley & Heffron, 2018).

Accelerating the transition to sustainable transport strategies, as recommended in the European Green Deal, could yield significant health benefits, especially if active travel such as walking and cycling and greater use of public transport are encouraged (Haines & Scheelbeek, 2020). With the European Green Deal (EGD), which entered into force recently, it is necessary to go a long way in renewal in order to make the sector environmentally friendly by focusing on green solutions in the logistics industry (Taş & Aylak, 2022).

Green Logistics

The understanding of sustainability, legal obligations, environmental concerns and social responsibility that has emerged in the logistics industry with the increase in sensitivity on the subject in the recent period pushes businesses to engage in green logistics activities. Considering its importance for businesses, the importance of green logistics is increasing day by day due to factors such as economic factors, the green image becoming an important market label, ensuring customer satisfaction and the government's environment-oriented programs (Acar A.Z., Köseoğlu A.M., 2014).

According to Chang and Qin (2008), green logistics is the planning, organization, execution and supervision of a logistics system aimed at reducing carbon emissions through environmental management and advanced logistics technology. Zhao et al. (2009) also defined the meaning of green logistics as reducing waste and resource consumption, improving resource usage, optimizing resource allocation and using environmental technology and minimizing environmental pollution through rational planning while implementing logistics activities (Qaiser et al., 2017).

Based on promoting the more efficient and effective use of resources (Yangınlar & Sarı, 2014) green logistics is an effort to minimize the use of natural resources and to minimize the effects on the environment through actions such as substitutes. For this reason, green logistics is expressed as minimizing the environmental effects of logistics activities (Rogers & Tibben-Lembke, 2001). With this aspect, green logistics represents a managerial understanding in which product development strategies and environmental awareness strategies are combined and therefore products are produced in a way that does not harm the environment (Gültaş & Yücel, 2015).

Green logistics aims to minimize the damage to the environment, especially in the transportation step of the logistics process. Showing the necessary sensitivity about the use of natural resources and carrying out innovative practices with an environmentalist understanding can be considered within the green approaches of enterprises (Chopra & Meindl, 2017). Environmental management, green procurement, cooperation with stakeholders and economic design are included in the sub-dimensions of green logistics practices (Wang et al., 2013).

On the other hand, one of the tools used to reduce greenhouse gas emissions of countries is the implementation of an effective carbon pricing mechanism. In line with the targets raised in the fight against climate change in the world, an increasing number of countries are implementing national carbon pricing mechanisms. There are 61 national carbon pricing mechanisms, 31 of which are emissions trading systems and 30 of which are carbon taxes, which are currently implemented or planned to be implemented in the world (World Bank, 2020).

The rapid development of green supply chain management (GSCM) has brought green movement in the logistics industry and encouraged integrating environmental management into activities. It has become a necessity for logistics service providers to make more efforts regarding environmental problems in order to offer more environmentally friendly products and services to customers (Murphy & Poist, 2003; Sarkis et al., 2017). For this reason, it is necessary to work more on environmental issues in the logistics industry. According to PricewaterhouseCoopers (PwC), transportation and logistics are among the most fundamental industries to prevent climate change on a global scale after the energy sector. Reducing fuel consumption and CO_2 emissions should be among the priorities of the industry. In particular, strategies to reduce carbon emissions range from the adoption of more alternative energy and hybrid vehicles, the use of lighter vehicles and the development of new service models from strategies to reduce fuel consumption from road vehicles. Minimizing noise pollution is among the other environmental agenda items of the industry (Seroka-Stolka, 2014).

Reverse Logistics

A reverse movement should also be considered in logistics practices for sustainability (Ersoy, 2006). Because it is an extremely incomplete approach to think of logistics activities as only transporting products and services from the place of production to the place of consumption. So the life cycle of products does not end when they reach the consumer (Öz, 2011).

The first definitions of reverse logistics were made by Lambert and Stock (1993), and it was defined as "going in the wrong direction on a one-way road" due to the importance of one-way shipping (from the manufacturer to the consumer, forward logistics). During the 1980s, the concept of reverse logistics was seen as the product movement from the customer to the manufacturer, which is the opposite of the primary flow (Rogers & Tibben-Lembke, 2001). Stock (2001) includes reverse logistics, end-of-life products, product returns and reuse of faulty products with material supply, recycling, waste disposal and incineration(renewal), repair and remanufacturing (known as reproduction).

The rules set by the legislators to protect human and environmental health have enabled companies to give more importance to reverse logistics activities. It has been realized by companies that production inputs cannot be provided economically in the near future if natural resources continue to be consumed unconsciously. For this reason, not only by considering legal obligations and customer perception but also for a sustainable production, companies aim to reduce the negative effects of supply chain activities on the environment. At this point, effective management of reverse logistics activities reduces the carbon footprint caused by production processes. The processes of repairing and reusing the products, identifying the functional parts of the product and using it in other products, remanufacturing the products, and obtaining raw materials by recycling some products all provide less resource use (Fleischmann et al., 2003). Recycling and reuse of product packages stands out as another reverse logistics activity that reduces the carbon footprint. Likewise, the "compression" method of the wastes to be disposed of or the products and parts to be recycled can take up less space in the transport vehicles. As a result, the ability to transport more products at once reduces the amount of carbon released to the environment by reducing the total number of trips required (Bai & Sarkis, 2013).

The circular economy requires the adoption of an economic approach in which, on the one hand, the value of the product is preserved by recycling materials and resources into the product cycle after their use, on the other hand, the amount of waste is kept to a minimum. The widely used production/consumption structure, which is based on the linear economy model that covers the production, use and disposal processes of products, is gradually being replaced by a sustainable and innovation-based circular economy system in the world, where waste is recycled and re-evaluated, resource efficiency is ensured and raw material costs are reduced (Ministry of Trade: Republic of Turkey, 2022). Circular economy principles are listed as follows; rethink, repair, reduce, remanufacture, reuse, repurpose, refurbish and recycle (Yılmaz, 2022). Circular economy principles overlap with reverse logistics activities. Therefore, reverse logistics activities are among the main sectors that play a major role in achieving the targets set within the scope of the European Green Deal.

Multimodal Transportation

Today, transportation is defined as shipping. Transportation in the world can be defined as the services that take the role of moving people and transporting the products produced to the point of consumption. National or international transportation activities indirectly shape the economy through the circulation of products and services. The main purpose of transportation; product, human or information flow is to meet the need. With the effect of the perfect competition market and the global market, production activities in the industrial field have increased significantly. The differentiation of consumer needs also plays an active role in this increase. Transportation and logistics activities are carried out in order to meet the products and services produced with the customers. However, both in production activities and transportation activities, the responsibility towards the environment and future generations is ignored directly or indirectly, causing harm to all humanity as well as the environment. We need to use sustainable systems for a more livable world. The use of sustainable system is of great importance especially for the logistics and transportation industry, which consumes 60% of the total oil and 25% of the energy in the world (Çetin & Sain, 2018). The business model of this system is the intermodal transportation system in the transportation industry (Takcı & Üre, 2021).

Intermodal transport; these are the services performed by using two or more modes of transport, without unloading the products from the transport vehicle on which they are loaded, without any handling. Thanks to the fact that it is a fast, safe, environmentally friendly and low-cost transportation method that is not affected by adverse weather conditions, it is seen that the global competitiveness of the companies using the intermodal transportation system has increased (Takcı & Üre, 2021).

Greening mobility must be the new license for the transport sector to grow. Infrastructures such as greening mobility, high-speed affordable rail network, charging and refueling for vehicles with zero emissions should be based on a developed, interconnected and efficient transportation system in Europe (European Commission, 2020b).

The restrictions that the EU may impose on the transportation sector, which is the backbone of foreign trade, will be reflected in both the transportation and manufacturing industry. Therefore, it is necessary to change the cargoes, which are mostly preferred by road transportation, to transportation types such as railway and intermodal transportation, which are environmentally friendly transportation types. Therefore, this can ensure correct design in logistics centers with modes of transport where freight transfers are simplified. Based on the principle of sustainability, some practices and regulations may be amended (Taş & Aylak, 2022).

CONCLUSION AND EVALUATION

Logistics activities should be handled with an environmentally friendly policy. Using less and environmentally friendly raw materials in packaging and researching alternative transportation methods are typical examples of steps to be taken in this regard. Businesses take various steps to reduce the harmful effects of transportation on the environment. Primarily, fuel use, noise pollution and traffic congestion are discussed. An environmentally friendly business should choose vehicles running on unleaded gasoline when purchasing vehicles, and should resort to rail transportation for long-distance transportation. If road transport is a must, the product should be transported with vehicles equipped with technology that ensures that the fuel used is discharged from the exhaust in a way that does not pollute the environment, and green motor vehicles should be preferred (Eşmen et al., 2015).

According to Chuang (2008), a resource-based understanding dominates the foundation of the economy. This understanding will have to change with the developing world and technology. In this case, companies that are managed on a resource basis need to put technology on their foundation. With technology, it will be easier for companies to reach their sustainability goals (Beken, 2016).

The use of fossil fuels in transportation is very important in terms of greenhouse gas emissions. Greenhouse gas emissions from transportation in urban areas are one of the main triggers of climate change. Fossil fuel use can be reduced by using electric or hybrid vehicles instead of using fossil fuel vehicles (Kammen & Sunter, 2016). The power of hybrid vehicles is lower than gasoline vehicles (Kebriaei et al., 2015), but if the use of hybrid vehicles can be determined well, this situation may cease to be a disadvantage. Hybrid vehicles are more convenient for urban use, unlike roads with high slopes and extra-urban use. For this reason, higher efficiency can be obtained when hybrid vehicle use is preferred considering environmental conditions and intended use (Karakuş et al., 2022).

Sustainable logistics has an important place in the European Green Deal. Reverse logistics and green logistics, which are the two dimensions of sustainable logistics, group the activities to be carried out for this purpose. While reverse logistics focuses on the revaluation of end-of-life products, green logistics focuses on low carbon emissions of equipment, vehicles and vehicles used during forward and reverse logistics activities. Therefore, sustainable logistics is one of the important strategies on the way to the European Green Deal goals.

REFERENCES

Acar, A. Z., & Köseoğlu, A. M. (2014). *Lojistik Yaklaşımıyla Tedarik Zinciri Yönetimi*. Nobel.

Altuntaş, C., & Türker, D. (2012). Sustainable supply chains: A content analysis of sustainability reports. *Dokuz Eylul University The Journal of Graduate School of Social Sciences*, *14*(3), 39–64.

Bai, C., & Sarkis, J. (2013). Green information technology strategic justification and evaluation. *Information Systems Frontiers*, *15*(5), 831–847. doi:10.100710796-013-9425-x

Basiago, A. D. (1998). Economic, social, and environmental sustainability in development theory and urban planning practice. *The Environmentalist*, *19*(2), 145–161. doi:10.1023/A:1006697118620

Beken, H. G. (2016). Sürdürülebilirlik ve rekabet edebilirlik yolu yeşil lojistik mi. *Balkan ve Yakın Doğu Sosyal Bilimler Dergisi*, *2*(01), 78–88.

Bell, R., Khan, M., Romeo-Velilla, M., Stegeman, I., Godfrey, A., Taylor, T., Morris, Staatsen, van der Vliet, Kruize, Anthun, Lillefjell, Espnes, Chiabai, de Jalón, Quiroga, Martinez-Juarez, Máca, Zvěřinová, ... Costongs, C. (2019). Ten lessons for good practice for the INHERIT Triple Win: Health, Equity, and Environmental Sustainability. *International Journal of Environmental Research and Public Health*, *16*(22), 4546. doi:10.3390/ijerph16224546 PMID:31744247

Büyüközkan, G., Feyzioğlu, O., & Nebol, E. (2008). Selection of the strategic alliance partner in logistics value chain. *International Journal of Production Economics*, *113*(1), 148–158. doi:10.1016/j.ijpe.2007.01.016

Çamlıca, Z., & Akar, G. S. (2014). Sustainability practices in the logistics sector. *Gümüshane University Electronic Journal of the Institute of Social Science, 5*(11).

Çetin, Ö. Ü. O., & Sain, A. D. (2018). Sustainability practices in logistics sector. *Iv. Internatıonal Caucasus-Central Asıa Foreıgn Trade And Logıstıcs Congress*.

Chopra, S., & Meindl, P. (2017). Strategy, planning, and operation. *Supply Chain Management*, 13–17.

Chuang, L. (2008). The status and problems of small and middle textile and garment enterprises of Henan province. *2008 International Seminar on Business and Information Management*, *2*, 386-389.

Dey, A., LaGuardia, P., & Srinivasan, M. (2011). Building sustainability in logistics operations: A research agenda. *Management Research Review*, *34*(11), 1237–1259. doi:10.1108/01409171111178774

Economic Development Foundation. (2020). *AB Yeşil Mutabakatı temel unsurları ve yol haritası*. https://www.ikv.org.tr/images/files/AB_Yesil_Mutabakati_Temel_Unsurlari_ve_Yol_Haritasi.pdf

Erdal, M., Görçün, Ö. F., Görçün, Ö., & Saygılı, M. S. (2008). *Entegre lojistik yönetimi*. Beta Yayınları.

Erol, İ., & Özmen, A. (2008). Measuring environmental sustainability performance: An application in the retail industry. Economics. *Business and Finance*, *23*(266), 70–94.

Ersoy, M. Ş. (2006). *Logistics and Turkey's position*. Status Journal. January.

Erturgut, R. (2016). *Lojistik ve tedarik zinciri yönetimi*. Nobel.

Eşmen, O., Bedük, F., & Bedük, A. (2015). *Green Logistics for a Liveable World: Practice Examples both in Turkey and the World.* Academic Press.

European Commission. (2016). *The Road from Paris: assessing the implications of the Paris Agreement and accompanying the proposal for a Council decision on the signing, on behalf of the European Union, of the Paris agreement adopted under the United Nations Framework Convention on Climate Change.* COM (2016) 110 final. https://eur-lex.europa.eu/legalcontent/ EN/TXT/?uri=COM:2016:110:FIN

European Commission. (2019a). *The European green deal. COM (2019) 640 final.* https://eurlex.europa.eu/legalcontent/EN/TXT/?uri=COM%3A2019%3A640%3AFIN

European Commission. (2019b). *Clean energy for all Europeans.* https://op.europa.eu/s/vdHz

European Commission. (2020a). *A new circular economy action plan.* COM (2020) 98 final. https://eur-lex.europa.eu/legal-content/EN/TXT/?uri=COM%3A2020%3A98%3AFIN

European Commission. (2020b). *Communication from the commission to the European parliament, the council, the European economic and social committee and the committee of the regions.* Author.

European Commission. (2020c). *Communication on a Sustainable and Smart Mobility Strategy- putting European transport on track for the future.* https://ec.europa.eu/transport/sites/transport/files/legislation/com20200789.pdf

European Commission. (2021). *A European Green Deal.* European Commission. https://ec.europa.eu/info/strategy/priorities-2019-2024/european-green-deal_en

Fettahlıoğlu, H. S., & Cansu, B. (2016). In terms of sustainability the factors that affect reverse logistic activities and sustainable marketing. *Journal of Kahramanmaraş Sütçü İmam University Faculty of Economics and Administrative Sciences, 6*(2), 89–114.

Fetting, C. (2020). *The European Green Deal.* ESDN Office.

Fleischmann, M., Van Nunen, J. A., & Gräve, B. (2003). Integrating closed-loop supply chains and spare-parts management at IBM. *Interfaces, 33*(6), 44–56. doi:10.1287/inte.33.6.44.25189

Fleming, R. C., & Mauger, R. (2021). Green and just? An update on the 'European Green Deal'. *Journal for European Environmental & Planning Law, 18*(1), 164–180. doi:10.1163/18760104-18010010

Gültaş, P., & Yücel, M. (2015). Green Logistics: Green Local Transportation The Model of Malatya Municipality. *Journal of Academıc Approaches, 6*(2), 70–83.

Hafner, M., & Raimondi, P. P. (2020). Priorities and challenges of the EU energy transition: From the European Green Package to the new Green Deal. *Russian Journal of Economics, 6*(4), 374–389. doi:10.32609/j.ruje.6.55375

Haines, A., & Scheelbeek, P. (2020). European Green Deal: A major opportunity for health improvement. *Lancet, 395*(10233), 1327–1329. doi:10.1016/S0140-6736(20)30109-4 PMID:32394894

İbadullayeva, J., Jumaniyazova, K., Azimzadeh, S., Canıgür, S., & Ferhan, E. (2019). The effects of environmental pollution on human health. *Turkish Medical Students Research Journal, 1*(3), 52–58.

Jäger-Waldau, A., Kougias, I., Taylor, N., & Thiel, C. (2020). How photovoltaics can contribute to GHG emission reductions of 55% in the EU by 2030. *Renewable & Sustainable Energy Reviews*, *126*, 109836. doi:10.1016/j.rser.2020.109836

Kakışım, C. (2022). The European Green Deal: An analysis from perspective of green theory. *Journal of Strategic and Social Researhes*, *6*(1), 1–16.

Kammen, D. M., & Sunter, D. A. (2016). City-integrated renewable energy for urban sustainability. *Science*, *352*(6288), 922–928. doi:10.1126cience.aad9302 PMID:27199413

Karakuş, D. N., Nazan, A. N., Turp, M. T., & Kurnaz, L. (2022). A global view of basic practice approaches within the scope of the EU Green Deal and sustainable development goals. *Dokuz Eylul University The Journal of Graduate School of Social Sciences*, *24*(1), 47–67.

Kebriaei, M., Niasar, A. H., & Asaei, B. (2015, October). Hybrid electric vehicles: An overview. In *2015 International Conference on Connected Vehicles and Expo (ICCVE)* (pp. 299-305). IEEE. 10.1109/ICCVE.2015.84

Kostyrko, R. V. (2021). *Development of logistics in a pandemic*. Academic Press.

Küçük, G., & Dural, B. Y. (2022). The European Green Deal and the transition to a green economy: An evaluation of energy scenarios. *Anadolu University Journal of Social Sciences*, *22*(1), 137–156.

Lambert, D. M., & Stock, J. R. (1993). *Strategic logistics management* (Vol. 69). Irwin.

Lee, R. P., Meyer, B., Huang, Q., & Voss, R. (2020). Sustainable waste management for zero waste cities in China: potential, challenges and opportunities. *Clean Energy*, *4*(3), 169-201.

Mabert, V. A., & Venkataramanan, M. A. (1998). Special research focus on supply chain linkages: Challenges for design and management in the 21st century. *Decision Sciences*, *29*(3), 537–552. doi:10.1111/j.1540-5915.1998.tb01353.x

McCauley, D., & Heffron, R. (2018). Just transition: Integrating climate, energy and environmental justice. *Energy Policy*, *119*, 1–7. doi:10.1016/j.enpol.2018.04.014

Ministry of Trade, Republic of Türkiye. (2022). https://ticaret.gov.tr/

Mısır, A., & Arıkan, O. (2022). Circular economy and zero waste management in European Union (EU) and Turkey. *Journal of Environment. Climate and Sustainability*, *1*(1), 69–78.

Montanarella, L., & Panagos, P. (2021). The relevance of sustainable soil management within the European Green Deal. *Land Use Policy*, *100*, 104950. doi:10.1016/j.landusepol.2020.104950

Murphy, P. R., & Poist, R. F. (2003). Green perspectives and practices: A "comparative logistics" study. *Supply Chain Management*, *8*(2), 121–132. doi:10.1108/13598540310468724

Official Jounal of European Union. (2016). *On The Conclusion, On Behalf Of The European Union, Of The Paris Agreement Adopted Under The United Nations Framework Convention On Climate Change*. https://data.europa.eu/eli/dec/2016/1841/oj

Öz, M. (2011). New Approaches In Logistics. *Journal of Kahramanmaraş Sütçü İmam University Faculty of Economics and Administrative Sciences*, *1*(1), 141–155.

Qaiser, F. H., Ahmed, K., Sykora, M., Choudhary, A., & Simpson, M. (2017). Decision support systems for sustainable logistics: A review and bibliometric analysis. *Industrial Management & Data Systems*.

Rodrigue, J. P. (2020). *The geography of transport systems*. Routledge. doi:10.4324/9780429346323

Rogers, D. S., & Tibben-Lembke, R. (2001). An Examination Of Reverse Logistics Practices. *Journal of Business Logistics*, *22*(2), 129–148. doi:10.1002/j.2158-1592.2001.tb00007.x

Sarkis, J. (2003). A strategic decision framework for green supply chain management. *Journal of Cleaner Production*, *11*(4), 397–409. doi:10.1016/S0959-6526(02)00062-8

Sarkis, J., Meade, L., & Talluri, S. (2017). E-logistics and the natural environment. In *The ecology of the new economy* (pp. 35–51). Routledge. doi:10.4324/9781351282048-3

Seroka-Stolka, O. (2014). The development of green logistics for implementation sustainable development strategy in companies. *Procedia: Social and Behavioral Sciences*, *151*, 302–309. doi:10.1016/j.sbspro.2014.10.028

Siddi, M. (2020). *The European Green Deal: Assessing its current state and future implementation*. Finnish Institute of International Affairs.

Stock, J. R. (2001). Reverse logistics in the supply chain. *Revista Transport & Logistics*, *44*, 44–48.

Takcı, M. B., & Üre, M. S. (2021). Sustainable Business Model Intermodal: Ekol Logistics Example. *On Eurasian Economies 2021*, 272.

Talu, N. (2015). Climate change policy in Turkey. Academic Press.

Thiell, M., Zuluaga, J. P. S., Montañez, J. P. M., & van Hoof, B. (2011). Green logistics: Global practices and their implementation in emerging markets. In *Green finance and sustainability: Environmentally-aware business models and Technologies* (pp. 334–357). IGI Global.

Tsakalidis, A., van Balen, M., Gkoumas, K., & Pekar, F. (2020). Catalyzing sustainable transport innovation through policy support and monitoring: The case of TRIMIS and the European green deal. *Sustainability*, *12*(8), 3171.

Ucal, M., An, N., & Kurnaz, L. (2017). New terms and approaches in economy in the process of climate change. *Dokuz Eylul University Journal of Social Sciences Institute*, *19*(3), 373–402.

United Nations Framework Convention on Climate Change (UNFCCC). (2015). *Paris Agreement*. https://unfccc.int/sites/default/files/english_paris_agreement.pdf

Üstün, K. T. (2021). The beginning of a new era: European Green Deal and its effects on Turkish environmental law and policies. *Homeland Journal of Politics and Management*, *16*(36), 329–366.

Wang, Y. F., Chen, S. P., Lee, Y. C., & Tsai, C. T. S. (2013). Developing green management standards for restaurants: An application of green supply chain management. *International Journal of Hospitality Management*, *34*, 263–273.

WCED. (1987). World commission on environment and development. *Our Common Future, 17*(1), 1-91.

World Bank. (2020). *State and Trends of Carbon Pricing 2020*. https://openknowledge.worldbank.org/bitstream/handle/10986/33809/9781464815867.pdf?sequence=4&isAllowed=y

Yangınlar, G., & Sarı, K. (2014). *Yeşil lojistik uygulamaları ve işletme performansı üzerine bir literatür araştırma. III*. Ulusal Lojistik ve Tedarik Zinciri Kongresi.

Yılmaz, F. (2022). Energy management and Turkey: An assessment in the framework of The European Green Deal. *Academia Journal of Nature and Human Sciences*, *8*(1), 19–37.

Zhao, P., Liu, J., & He, L. (2009, December). Study on the development of modern green logistics in China. In *2009 International Conference on Innovation Management* (pp. 43-46). IEEE.

Chapter 13
COVID-19 Pandemic-Related Supply Chain Disruptions and Impacts on the Global Economy

Yeliz Demirkıran
https://orcid.org/0000-0003-3998-7001
Yaşar University, Turkey

ABSTRACT

Humanity and the business world have had a very challenging period in the last two years due to unprecedented disease outbreaks. In December 2019, a novel infectious respiratory disease was found in Wuhan, Hubei Province, China. This disease affected almost all industries and all countries, regardless of developed or developing. The pandemic caused supply chain disruptions around the globe. In this study, the author presented the supply chain disruptions in detail caused by the COVID-19 pandemic, which is a specific type of disruption factor, and showed their global economic impacts. Country- and industry-specific cases and examples are examined. In addition, the measures that have been taken by the government authorities to alleviate the global economic impact of the pandemic are discussed.

INTRODUCTION

The World Health Organization (WHO, 2021) defines this disease as Covid-19 (Coronavirus) which is caused by the SARS-CoV-2 virus. Since its outbreak for the first time in December 2019, Covid-19 has spread rapidly around the globe. As of June 8, 2022, there are 530,266,292 confirmed cases and 6,299,364 deaths (WHO, 2022). In the first phase of the pandemic, the authorities have taken strict steps to stop the virus from spreading. At regular intervals, the lockdown in which people can only leave home in special circumstances was imposed by many governments (Atayah et al., 2021). International travel was restricted, and most of the cross-borders were closed (Wing et al., 2020). Passenger and freight transportation by air, sea, or highway is prohibited by the regulations.

The manufacturing industry is almost closed worldwide. Hotels and restaurants are closed at the beginning stage of the pandemic and then they worked at 50% of their capacity. The passenger trans-

DOI: 10.4018/978-1-6684-5876-1.ch013

portation is restricted. IATA (2020) reported that in June 2020, international passenger traffic decreased by 96.8% and domestic traffic by 67.6% compared to June 2019. It will take until 2024 for global air passenger volume to return to pre-COVID-19 levels. (Kwon, 2020). Thus, the tourism and travel industry had financial problems. Social events that host large gatherings such as music concerts, sports, and cultural events were closed. Services in restaurants, hairdressers, and taxi usage have been blocked. Employees in many sectors were laid off or their wages were cut (Zou et al., 2020). It has more severe and varied consequences than earlier epidemic outbreaks such as the SARS-2003 and H1N1-2009 outbreaks (Chowdhury et al., 2021). Regardless of industry, various disruptions in supply chain of various products and services have been experienced.

Craighead et al. (2007) defined supply chain disruptions as "*unplanned and unanticipated events that disrupt the normal flow of goods and material in a supply chain and, as a consequence, expose firms to operational and financial risks*". Chowdhury et al. (2021) categorize the factors causing disruptions into four groups: natural, man-made, system failure, and financial. Earthquakes, floods, cyclones, and extreme weather conditions are examples of natural disasters. Strikes, traffic congestion, port congestion, theft, and fire are examples of man-made interruptions. Machine or technological failures, as well as obsolescence are examples of system failures. Exchange rate and bank interest fluctuations, as well as import-export restrictions, are all examples of financial disruptions. These disruptions have several impacts on the particular area in a supply chain such as the demand side, supply side, production, transportation, or the whole supply chain network. These impacts are demand drop, demand surge, reduced productivity, storage and access restrictions, raw material shortage and transportation interruptions. While previous natural disasters generally created demand-side interruptions, covid-19 caused interruptions on both the demand and supply sides (Kwon, 2020).

The covid-19 pandemic affected the consumption behavior of the consumers. While there was a decrease in the demand for certain products and services, especially in airline services, on the other side, panic buying behavior was observed in certain products such as medical supplies and hygiene products. The companies tried to cope up with the increased demand for these kinds of products by a quota limit. For instance, the demand for toilet paper is increased tremendously (Paul and Chowdhury, 2020). As well as fluctuations in demand, production decrease that appears due to the layoffs or decreasing the labor capacity, caused supply chain disruptions. There were also storage and access restrictions to products. Some companies had to close their warehouses after detecting the increase in the number of positive cases. Amazon is one of these firms. They closed the New Jersey warehouse temporarily until 26 December 2020 (Bhalla, 2020). One of the major disruptions is the raw material access problem. China is one of the biggest raw material providers for the manufacturing industry. Companies whose supply chains depend on suppliers in China have experienced significant disruption due to the closure or limited use of shipping terminals in China (Fortune, 2022).

In particular, the coexistence of negative demand shocks and negative supply shocks, which are called twin shocks, causes deterioration in macroeconomic indicators (Pakdemirli et al., 2020). The covid-19 pandemic crisis is a kind of twin shock. In this period of time, firstly supply disruptions existed since the country's home ban enforcement caused production to stop. Even if production continues, products could not be taken out of the borders due to customs barriers. Global trade in goods and services has been disrupted and the global economy has been greatly affected by this crisis. According to UNCTAD (2021b) report, global merchandise trade declined by almost 7.4% and global service trade declined 20% in 2020 compared with 2019. The World Bank stated that goods trade appears to have bottomed out in April 2020, with yearly declines of roughly 20%. COVID-19 has produced a trade contraction that is greater than that experienced during the financial crisis of 2008-2009 (UNCTAD, 2021a). A report published by Fortune Magazine points out 94% of the "Fortune 1000 Companies" consider Covid-19 as a supply chain disruption (Sherman, 2020). It caused disruptions in the global production lines, supply chain, international trade, and the worldwide shipping and aviation network (Kwon, 2020).

Therefore, we presented the supply chain disruptions in detail caused by the covid-19 pandemic which is a specific type of disruption factor in section 3 but before we discussed the difference between supply chain disruptions caused by covid-19 and other disasters in section 2. Within the scope of the study, we always talked about the bad effects of covid-19 on the supply chain and their economic dimension, but in section 4, we explained the opportunities of the covid-19 related disruptions. At last, we presented the global economic impact of the covid-19 based supply chain disruptions with the macroeconomic indicators in section 5.

THE DIFFERENCE BETWEEN COVID-19 AND OTHER SUPPLY CHAIN DISTRIBUTIONS

Moritz (2020) explains the differences in disruptions between covid-19 and other reasons in 7 dimensions. They are geography, scope, demand vs supply, prior planning & experience, financial system, term, and human impact & behavior.

Geography: The disruptions does not valid in the whole geography of the earth. The disruptions caused by a natural disaster generally affect only a region or country, not the entire earth (Xu et al., 2020). Especially, hurricanes or earthquakes damage the region in which they occur. For example, Hurricane Katrina damaged New Orleans, not the whole world but the covid-19 pandemic damaged the economic and social systems of the whole world. Therefore, covid-19-related disruptions differ from the other kind of disruptions in terms of geography. That is why it is called a global pandemic. This is an important distinction because in a regional disruption the other regions or countries may give help to sustain the current systems such as supply chain system or healthcare system etc. (Moritz, 2020).

Scope: The covid-19 disruption differs from the other disruptions in terms of scope. While a hurricane may affect the petrochemical industry, the covid-19 affected almost all industries due to the home bans, and isolation implementations of governments. For example, Hurricane Katrina caused to stop oil and gas production in the Gulf of Mexico (Karp, 2005). Thus, the oil industry is affected by the hurricane disaster. In the covid-19 pandemic era, while the demand is decreased tremendously in the tourism and travel industry (Duro et al., 2021) the demand for some specific products such as toilet paper increased in the manufacturing industry (Paul and Chowdhury, 2020). Therefore, the scope of the disruptions is not similar.

Demand versus Supply: Many supply chain disruptions exist on the supply side. For example, the 2001 fire in Philips Electronics chip plant affected the telephone producers Nokia and Ericsson. They supply the chips for their telephone production but due to the fire in the plant they could not purchase the chips and they had lost a market share (WSJ, 2001). However, the covid-19 pandemic caused both supply and demand disruptions. There were problems in the supply side; on the other hand, problems such as the contraction in demand for flight or hotel reservations, and cancellations came to the fore.

Prior planning & experience: The disruptions differ from each other also in terms of planning and experience. For instance, in earthquake or tornado circumstances the governments and non-governmental organizations have action plans for best and worst scenarios. They have detailed plans for how people will be rescued, which hospitals those people will be taken to, where those people whose homes are damaged or at risk will continue to live, and how to provide food and clothing to people. However, in pandemic circumstances, many issues are unknown or limited known (Moritz, 2020). In a pandemic condition, prevention methods, recovery of infected people, and the medicine and medical equipment which is required are unknown. That is why the disruptions caused by a natural disaster or pandemic are different from each other. Many countries had problems with supplying facemasks, vaccines and ventilators. The factories decided to produce ventilators and face masks but they need time to design and manufacture. Even if they can have the vaccine, the inventory conditions are not ready in many countries. Therefore, supplying these kinds of medical equipment is disrupted.

Financial system: In many disruptions, the financial system is affected. For example, the September 11 events affected the financial system of the U.S. The GDP growth rate decreased and the unemployment rate increased (Roberts, 2009). In contrast, in the covid-19 pandemic, the financial system of the global economy is affected entirely. Many factories had to be closed, and some of them dismissed their workers to decrease their fixed costs. Therefore, many governments explained financial aid packages to the companies, some of them paid the companies for part-time work, or some of them postponed the tax payments (Duran and Acar, 2020). Meanwhile, steps have been taken to facilitate the trade among countries by the governments. In this manner, the global economy and global financial systems are trying to be recovered.

Term: The term refers the time period that covers the disruption. Most of the disasters, such as tsunamis, earthquakes and accidents are generally limited to short periods (Xu et al., 2020). Many disruptions are not long-lasting. For example, in a flood disaster the demand for the emergency products like health services, and accommodation services can be predicted according to the magnitude of the disaster. In an earthquake, the need for emergency products can be forecasted in a short time according to the magnitude and domain of the earthquake and the population of the epicenter of the earthquake. The time that the demand for the emergency products is predictable or at least quantifiable. However, in the covid-19 pandemic era, the demand for the emergency products such as health services, ventilation machines, facial masks, and medicines is not known because the pandemic duration is unknown. It has been hard to forecast the number of infected people and death rates due to the variations of the viruses (Moritz, 2020).

Human impact & behavior: All disasters may affect human psychology and therefore behavior. The fear of the people who are injured physically or physiologically diminishes gradually after the disaster. However, the covid-19 pandemic duration is unknown. Uninfected people are worried more since they do not know what effect it will have when the virus is infected (Choi et al., 2020b) Some of them may need intensive treatment and some of them may have the disease in a very mild form, like the flu. In addition to this uncertainty, the policymakers did not give sufficient information to the public not to worry them. Uncertainty and lack of enough information cause low compliance with lockdown measures of governments (Atkinson-Clement and Pigalle, 2021). Besides that, many people were afraid of losing their jobs as well as being afraid of being infected. This uncertainty and lack of right information created stress, fear, anxiety, and physiological damage (Rozman and Tominc, 2021). According to the Choi et al. (2020b) study, 19 and 14% of the respondents had depression and anxiety relatively during the COVID-19 pandemic in Hong Kong. Some people continue their lives in a very conservative mood. They have paid attention to social distance rules and hygiene rules, they are still using facial masks although the government has lifted the obligation. Some people do not pay attention to these kinds of regulations.

Buying behavior is changed due to the change in human behaviors and online shopping by using e-trade websites became very popular (Ali, 2020). The people met all kinds of their needs from these websites.

TYPES OF DISRUPTIONS RELATED TO COVID-19

Demand Drop

Demand drop is decreasing amount of demand for a product in a time period. Since the restrictions of governments to avoid the spread of the virus, the people had to stay home. They could travel for neither business nor holiday. Only the people who have special permission from the government could travel. Therefore, the airline industry and hospitality industry have experienced demand disruption. According to the International Civil Aviation Organization (ICAO), passenger transportation around the globe fell by 80% in April and May of 2020 compared with the first two months of 2020. IATA (2020) reported that in June 2020, international passenger traffic decreased by 96.8% and domestic traffic by 67.6% compared to June 2019. It will take until 2024 for global air passenger volume to return to pre-COVID-19 levels. (Kwon, 2020). As a result, airline revenues fell from $420 billion to $244 billion. Since most of the countries closed their airports and restricted travel, more than approximately 1,6 billion passengers canceled their flights and this resulted in a revenue loss of approximately 35 billion dollars (Vo and Tran, 2021). A few airlines continue to operate. Qatar is one of them. The Fly Emirates also continued to work by decreasing the number of destinations from 150 to 2 (Xu. et al., 2020). According to WTO (2020), the number of international tourist arrivals decreased by 22% in the first quarter of 2020 compared with the same period in 2019. The annual decline in 2020 compared to 2019 corresponds to almost 80%. Since the industry is labor-intensive, many people experienced unemployment risk. Tourism industry is the most adverse affected industry in covid-19 pandemic (Hilmola et al., 2020).

According to OPEC, the demand for oil decreased by 1.7 million barrels per day (BPD) in the first half of 2020 due to the covid-19 effect on the global economy and so the production level decreased (Övünç, 2020). The demand for textile products decreased due to the fear of spending money (Xu et al., 2020). According to the Mc Kinsey & Company report the revenue of textile and footwear dropped by 30% in 2020 according to the previous year (Berg et. al., 2020).

Demand Surge

Demand surge is an increasing amount of demand for a product in a time period. Hilmola et al. (2020) declared that not all retail sales had been affected adversely in the early phases of the pandemic. For example, grocery sales increased due to lockdowns. People could not go to restaurants to eat. They purchased grocery goods more than they purchased before the pandemic.

Toilet paper is another example of a product whose demand has unexpectedly surged. The toilet paper companies could not meet the demand at the outset of covid-19. They tried to cope with this panic buying behavior by limiting the number of purchasing the product. In many countries, all supplying firms' toilet paper is out of stock, and there is no other product on the market to replace it. This unexpected buying behavior should be managed and strategies should be developed by the companies to overcome the demand surge in the pandemic era. Paul and Chowdhury (2020) proposed four strategies to improve their service level for increased demand for toilet paper: (i) manufacturing resource sharing, (ii) collective emergency sourcing, (iii) manufacturing basic quality products, (iv)minimum size packing. Sometimes demand surges and drops may occur at the same time for the same product. For instance, toilet paper demand increased tremendously due to the people who stay at home for their safety. Therewithal, the demand for commercial toilet paper decreased. The large roll of commercial toilet paper which is used in restaurants, airports, and shopping malls is not consumed anymore due to the restrictions. Thus, this is an example of both drop and surge for the different types of the same product.

Concurrently, there was a tremendous increase in the global demand for medical supplies such as hand sanitizers, facemasks, and test kits (Butt, 2021). Especially, the demand for facemasks and contagious clothing for frontline medical staff was high. After the early stage of the pandemic innovative masks became vital for virus protection and to reduce mask shortages (Ji et al., 2020). The level of demand for these kinds of products had never reached such a level until then. As China is the only supplier of medical equipment to the international market, its production capacity could not be enough for the demand of the whole market. Therefore, the governments required the different manufacturers to produce this kind of equipment to avoid the shortage. Many local producers produced ventilators and facemasks as their capabilities let them. For instance, Tesla motors and Peugeot produced ventilators (Xu et al., 2020). The demand for drugs such as hydroxychloroquine and chloroquined which are used in the treatment of cough, cold medications, or pain relief is also increased (Xu et al., 2020).

The demand for electronic products such as personal computers or tablets increased by 4.6% until December 2020. Consequently, the demand for software products increased by 4% during 2020. Thus, the electronic industry is one of the least affected industries by the pandemic (De Vet et al., 2021).

Reduced Productivity

Reduced productivity means a reduction in output. Reduced productivity can appear due to the lack of workers, lack of equipment, or almost any other situation that reduces a company's output. In the covid-19 pandemic era, the availability of workers decreased because of self-isolation, mobility restrictions, illness, death, and dismissals (Butt, 2021). Thus, the country's production capacity is decreased. In any stage of the supply chain, the production level may decrease for many reasons but in this pandemic era in all stages of the supply chain productivity is reduced due to the reduced number of employees (Xu et al., 2020). Some of them are laid off, and some of them worked part-time. Even if they work full-time or part-time, their productivity performance decreased due to the emotional and physical anxiety triggered by the pandemic. Sysco company which is a leading supplier for restaurants laid off 33% of its employees by the end of March 2020. Decreased number of employees caused decreased production level for the company. The rest of the employees continue to work in their jobs with low morale, fear, anxiety due to the uncertainty of the pandemic, and fear of losing their jobs. Therefore, productivity took another hit (Pulsinelly, 2020). In order to maintain the motivation of employees, Wolor et al., (2020) recommended working from home and working with shifts in their study.

Storage and Access Restrictions

Natural disasters and pandemic outbreaks are the main reasons for the shutdowns of production and storage facilities. At these times, the problem appears about accessing to the products even though they have been produced. For instance, An Amazon Canada warehouse in Brampton, Ont. has been shut down due to the positive cases and the workers are self-isolated for two weeks through the covid-19 outbreak

(CBC News, 2021). Amazon also closed its warehouse in New Jersey due to the Covid-19 outbreak. This shutdown forced supply chain leaders. They had to change their warehouse layouts according to social distancing rules for their workers' safety (Palmer, 2020). Butt (2021) showed the importance of warehousing and inventory management in his study. He interviewed with 36 managers from many companies in various sectors such as production, procurement, and distribution in China. The respondents from the distribution companies implied that they tried to manage the covid-19 disruptions by modifying their inventory policies and plans. Although some of them reduced their inventory levels, some of them reserved safety stock to meet the normal demand, the preventions could not be enough to have an inventory buffer.

The storage stage of supply chain disrupted due to the covid-19 pandemic and many industries have had their share from this pandemic. For instance, meat production has been disrupted due to its requirement for special keeping conditions. The risk of virus infection caused access restrictions. The products are repacked to keep them from the virus. Therefore, the storage buildings needed to be updated according to the new requirements of the pandemic era.

In the food industry, online product availability for vegetables, fruits, and editable oils decreased by 10% in the pandemic era (Mahajan and Tomar, 2021). The decrease in the quantity of the products is caused by the deceleration in daily truck movement due to the implementation of strict border controls. Longer distances between the production locations and retail stores cause much more fall in the quantity of product availability. The authors proposed three strategies to overcome this supply chain disruption. One of them is about warehousing. They emphasized the importance of warehousing in urban and rural centers.

Raw Material Shortage

Supply chain disruption can not be discussed without discussion of China. China is one of the most popular suppliers of raw materials worldwide. A supply shock occurred due to the lockdown in China. Thus, the production in many industries in almost all countries declined. For example, the disruption in China has affected all industries in the USA. To obtain cotton for garments and shoes, microprocessors for laptops, and chemical ingredients for pharmaceutical production became problem for the United States in the pandemic era. Therefore, retailers, technology companies, and health centers have been affected by shortages in China. For example, Apple had trouble in exporting iPhone casings and memory chips from China. They announced a purchase limit of 2 phones per person and also they explained a delay in the release of the new version of the iPhone officially due to the supply chain disruptions (Forbes, 2020).

This chip shortfall affected also the automobile industry. Before the covid-19 pandemic, more than $34 billion of automotive parts are imported from China every year (Ritcher, 2020). However, since China had to close the firms to prevent the spread of the virus, it is getting harder and harder for automobile manufacturers to procure the parts they need. CEO of Daimler, Ola Källenius explained that supply shortages in terms of semiconductors are their main problem in the recent business environment. In addition, the CEO of Volvo, Jim Rowan explained that they do not have enough chipsets (Shead, 2022). Volkswagen closed its automobile factory in China due to the lack of parts (Xu et al., 2020). Many factories in China are now operational again but it seems that the problems in the supply chain will not stop unless the restriction on the transportation of non-vital products between countries are removed.

The medicine industry is also affected by the raw material shortage in the pandemic era. India is the third-largest exporter of medicine raw materials in the world, therefore, plays a critical role as a supplier of medicine. However, 70% of the medicine industry in India depends on the raw material suppliers in China and since the production delays in China the medical industry has been damaged (Xu et al., 2022). The drug production companies in India had struggled to obtain raw materials for antibiotics and vitamins from Chinese companies which are closed for weeks to avoid the spread of the pandemic (Maital and Barzani, 2020).

Factory Closures

According to the survey conducted by the Economist Intelligence Unit, the automotive industry is one of the most affected industries in adverse among the following 6 industries: Footwear & apparel; food & beverage; manufacturing; IT &electronics; healthcare, pharmaceuticals, and biotechnology. The survey was applied to 175 supply chain managers. 51.7% of them from the automotive industry claim that the disruptions in the supply chain are "very important". The main reason for the disruption was chip shortage since they are also used in many industries such as electronics. During the lockdown, the demand for personal computers increased. Therefore, chips which are the main components of the computers were not enough for the automobile manufacturers (Lee, 2021). Thus, many car manufacturer companies had to be closed average of 30 days. For instance, Tesla Motor closed its factories in Shanghai, California, and New York (Xu et al., 2020). In 2020, the automobile industry suffered production losses of 4,024,036 motor vehicles which correspond to 22.3% of the European union's total production in 2020. The demand for automobiles in the EU decreased by almost 29% in September 2020, according to the same period in the previous year (Ritcher, 2020).

Besides the companies in the automotive industry, many companies in the food industry are also closed during the pandemic outbreak. The fooddive team listed the closed companies in the food industry, in USA. Some of that companies are Golden State Foods Corporation (California), Mission Foods Commerce (California), S&S Foods (California), Sauer Brands Mauldin (South Caroline), Flowers Foods Savannah (Georgia), Reser's Fine Foods Topeka (Kansas), El Milagro (Chicago), Cargill Big Lake (Minnesota), Flower Foods Tucker (Georgia), etc. Besides, some of the companies reopened after configuring their facility according to the social distance rules. They are Fosters Farms Fresno (California), pacific Seafood Newport (Oregon), Johnsonville Holton (Kansas), Smithfield Foods Sioux Falls (South Dakota) etc. (Fooddive, 2020).

Transportation Interruptions

The COVID-19 pandemic has caused considerable damage to many industries worldwide. The logistics industry is one of them. The delays, cancellations, and postponements have been experienced in international logistics in terms of maritime, air, and road transportation due to the large-scale travel restrictions and the closing of borders. There are many studies that show the impact of covid-19 on the logistics sector. (Chowdhury, 2021; Pujawan and Pah, 2022). Some of them investigate the impacts, and some of them investigate the strategies that should be taken in the pandemic era. For instance, GS and Swetha (2020) defined 7 pandemic impacts on the logistics industry. They are more demand for products due to shipment delays, shipment difficulties, shortage of labor, transport isolation, angry customers, lack of safety measures, and technology uplift. Yang et al (2021) examined the impacts of the covid-19 pandemic on the express logistics sector. They showed both positive and negative effects on the express industry. To increase express logistics service demand, online shopping demand should be stimulated. In addition, resumption of production decreased the negative effect of the pandemic gradually on the express logistics industry. Chinese logistics firms learned to meet the demands of consumers whose consumption behaviors have changed due to a series of prevention measures such as lockdown, isolation, social distance, wearing masks, and contactless delivery. Chinese firms were ready to assist the firms that need help to fight with the pandemic. For instance, Chinese medical experts went to Italy to help the firms to adopt similar measures such as building hospitals and using masks (World Economic Forum, 2020).

Other industries are affected by the disruptions in transportation. The food industry is one of them. Almost all stages of food production depend on labor. The processes such as seeding and picking are labor-intensive. Due to labor shortages and transportation disruptions, exports of rice from India, the world's largest exporter, have been banned. A scarcity of trucks, missed flights, time-consuming inspections, and quarantine in customs have all slowed the distribution of fresh food (Xu et al., 2020). According to the global report on food crisis (2021), the size and severity of the food crises increased in 2020 when the effects of covid-19 were added to the wars and climate crisis.

Air Transportation

The number of scheduled flights decreased by 28.7% compared to the same period in 2019. Travel restrictions increased the cost of air travel by 30% in April 2020 compared to January 2020 (Vo and Tran, 2021). According to the international transport organization by the end of March 2020, cargo flights had declined by about 21% compared to the same period in last year (Vo and Tran, 2021). 65% of commercial air freight was not transported due to the restricted flights in March and April 2020. Thus, air transport decreased by 19%. In order to compensate for the revenue loss, the airline companies used their passenger capacity to carry air cargo (Vo and Tran, 2021). Almost 55% of the air freights are carried in the belly of the passenger planes (Xu et al., 2020). As seen in Figure 1, the volume of transportation by air decreased from 80 billion dollars in January 2020 to 20 billion dollars in February 2020 and a considerable increase was not observed until May 2020. The Figure also shows the reduction in the volume of transportation by sea and road between January and May 2020. As shown in Figure 1, the only transportation mode which has increased volume of transportation is rail way.

Sea Freight Transportation

Besides the demand and supply fluctuations, container shortages that disrupted the global trade appeared and it was the most important supply chain problem of the pandemic. According to the International Federation of Freight Forwarders Associations (FIATA), the procedures applied to the crew working in container ships caused employee shortages to handle cargo. The containers waited in border areas. Therefore, the shipping costs have increased by %20 in June 2020 compared to January 2020 (Vo and Tran, 2021). Many of the factories stop producing due to the increased number of infected employees. Some of them reopened but some of them were not due to the increased costs. Although the factories continued to produce and the employees continued to work from home, there was a problem to carry the goods globally. Since the empty containers could not be positioned to the necessary points for importing firms, the companies that export and import products internationally could not find a container to carry their products (Toygar et al., 2022). The trade balance of the entire world was disturbed. Since more than 80% of world trade is carried out by sea (Xu et al., 2020) the container crisis has greatly affected world trade. Although the previous supply and demand crisis has affected the trade costs, in none of them, the

Figure 1. International Transportation (Vo and Tran, 2021)

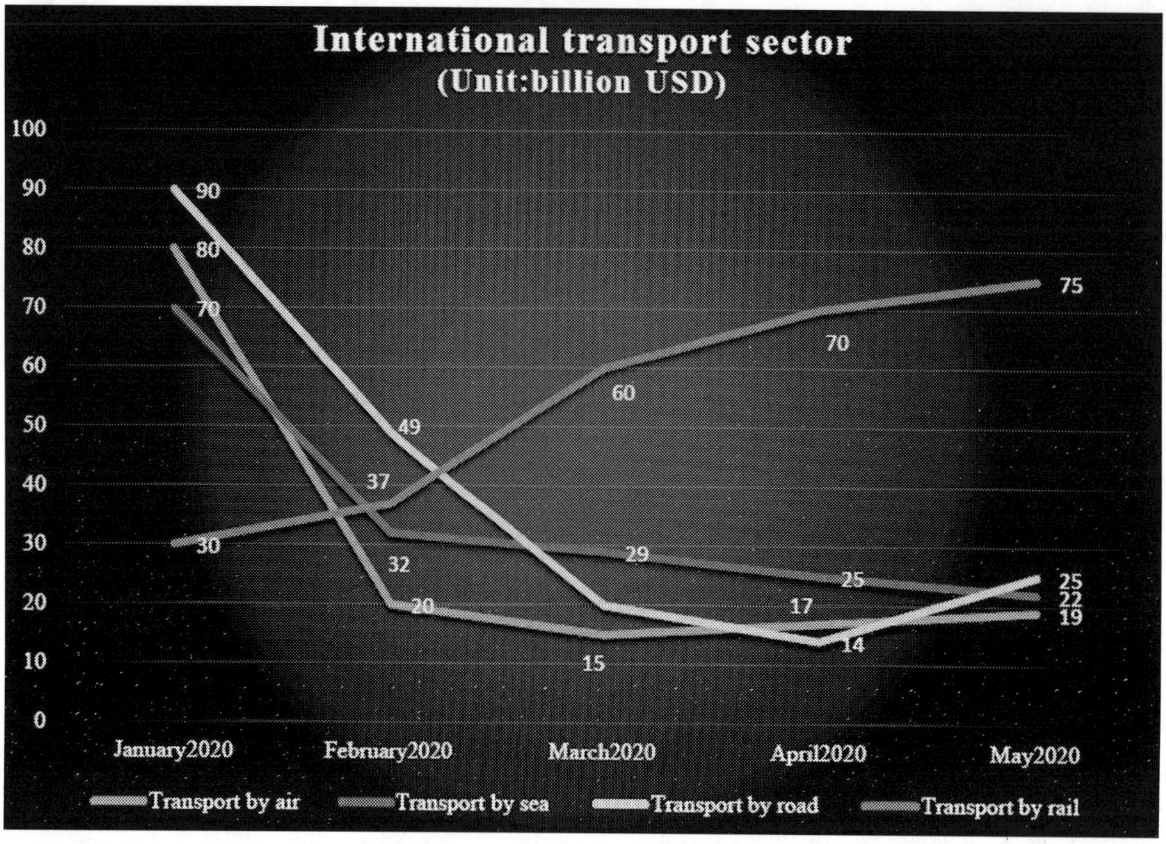

trade costs increase by 50% in a short time like 3 months (Vo and Tran, 2021). Besides that, the lack of truck drivers who pick up the containers and strict rules in customs caused delays in maritime freight.

Road Transportation

Road transportation is affected from the lack of truck drivers. Almost 70% of trucks were out of circulation due to driver shortage. The employee shortage causes 40% increase in transportation costs in April 2020 (Vo and Tran, 2021).

Rail Transportation

Rail transportation is the less affected mode of transport by the covid-19 pandemic. Since rail transportation needs fewer drivers, it was not affected by the isolation and quarantine procedures as much as the other modes of transport. As a result, in May 2020, rail transportation rose by 70% (Vo and Tran, 2021). The aforementioned covid-19 related supply chain disruptions are summarized in the Table 1.

Table 1. Examples of supply chain disruptions in various industries and countries

Disruption type	Industry	Country	Reference
Demand drop	Manufacturing and Logistics	Finland, Estonia, Sweden, and Norway	(Hilmola et al., 2020)
	Logistics (Air transportation)	Global	(Vo and Tran, 2021); (Xu et al., 2020)
	Oil	Global	(Övünç, 2020)
	Textile	Global	(Berg et al., 2020)
	Tourism	Global	(WTO, 2020)
	Automotive	EU	(Ritcher, 2020)
	Logistics (Express logistics)	China	(Yang et al., 2021)
Demand surge	Food (Grocery)	Global	(Hilmola et al., 2020)
	Manufacturing (Toilet paper)	Global	(Paul and Chowdhury, 2020)
	Manufacturing (Medical supplies)	Global	(Butt, 2021); (Ji et al., 2020); (Xu et al., 2020)
	Manufacturing (Electronic products)	Global	(De Vet et al., 2021)
	Logistics (Rail transportation, freight transportation)	Global	(Vo and Tran, 2021)
Reduced productivity	Food	India	(Mahajan and Tomar, 2021); (Butt, 2021)
Raw material shortage	Manufacturing (electronics, textile, pharmaceutical)	USA	(Forbes, 2020); (Shead, 2022); (Xu et al., 2020)
Factory closures	Automotive	Shanghai, California, and New York	(Xu et al., 2020)
	Food	USA	(Fooddive, 2020)
Transportation interruption	Logistics (air transportation, sea freight transportation, road transportation)	Global	(Vo and Tran, 2021); (GS and Swetha, 2020); (Toygar et al., 2022)
	Food	India	(Xu et al., 2020)

OPPORTUNITIES OF SUPPLY CHAIN DISRUPTIONS BASED ON COVID-19 PANDEMIC

A crisis does not mean always a threat. For instance, when the SARS Virus broke out, the Chinese businesses went into lockdown. At that time Alibaba, an online shopping platform appeared (Maital and Barzani, 2020) and the value of its market capital is now 247 billion dollars (Forbes, 2022). Supply chain disruptions are also not always in adverse. They sometimes can be an opportunity for some companies. Especially demand surge can be a good chance to reach more sales amount than if it did not happen before. For instance, household cleaning and beauty care products producer, Church & Dwight, explained an increase in demand in the first and second quarters of 2020. Therefore, they increased their production and warehouse capacity according to the new level of demand.

In some circumstances, supply chain disruptions had a positive impact on revenues. Veselovska (2020) examined the supply chain structures of the companies in Central European countries between 2019 and 2020. The companies operated in the field of grocery, services, production, agriculture, construction, and transport of material. The author also evaluated the company's economic indicators in terms of revenue between 2019 and 2020. One of the interesting findings of the study is the determination of no decrease in revenue of grocery companies during this time period. Half of the grocery companies increased their revenue between 26-50%. The supply chain disruptions caused a transformation in some cases. For example in Canada, pickup and delivery services are required due to the social distancing implementation. Therefore, many grocery companies found out and improved new business models (Gray, 2020). Online grocery delivery is improved (Hobbs, 2020).

The pandemic has also an impact on the environment in terms of global CO_2 emission levels in addition to the economic impacts. In 2020, the global CO_2 emission decreased by 5% which corresponds to 2.6 Gigatons which brings emission levels last seen ten years ago (United Nations Conference on Trade and Development, 2020). At the outset of the covid-19, the number of merchant ships such as container and cargo ships and also tankers decreased and as consequence the amount of pollutant emissions reduced. For instance, level of NOx emissions decreased by 13.3% in 2020 compared to the same period in 2019 (Shi and Weng, 2021).

Although the financial performances of almost whole industries in the global world have been affected in adverse (Choi, 2020a; Queiroz et al., 2020), Atayah et al., (2021) proposed in their study indeed the covid-19 pandemic does not affect the financial performance of the logistics firms negatively. On average, the financial indicators such as earnings per share (EPS) return on assets (ROA), return on equity (ROE), and increased by 21% 123%, and 391% relatively according to the previous ten years.

COVID-19 PANDEMIC IMPACTS ON THE GLOBAL ECONOMY

According to several studies and government reports (Choi, 2020a; Queiroz et al., 2020; Statistica, 2022) almost the economies of all countries have been affected by the covid-19 pandemic. GDP is a common indicator of the economy of the countries. Therefore, the effect of the covid-19 pandemic can be measured by this indicator. As shown in Figure 2 global gross domestic product (GDP) decreased from 87.390 billion US dollars in 2019 to 84.971 billion dollars in 2020 (Statistica, 2022). That means the Worldwide GDP is decreased by 3% in 2020 because of the pandemic (Barman et al., 2021).

The effect rates differ among them according to the prevention and regulations against the outbreak and their development level of them (World Development Report, 2022). The countries are divided into two groups as developed and developing countries by United Nations. The developed countries are self-sufficient in terms of economy and industrialization. However, the developing countries are going through the initial levels of industrial development along with low per capita income. The categorization is done according to the level of human development index (HDI) which means an assessment of average accomplishment in important characteristics of human development: a long and healthy life, being knowledgeable, and having a reasonable standard of living (United Nations, 2022). The standard of living dimension is measured by gross national income (GNI) per capita or gross domestic product (GDP) (United Nations, 2022). In Table 2, the GDP in million dollars and the growth rates in GDP for the years 2019, 2020, and 2021 are shown. This table shows that even the most developed countries in the world have been adversely affected economically by the covid-19 pandemic. For example GDP of Canada, the United Kingdom, and Italy decreased by 6, 4, and 6% respectively in 2020. The situation is worse in developing countries in Table 2. The GDP decreased by 13, 24, 12, and 13% in Argentina, Brazil, Peru, and Russia respectively in 2020. An economic contraction has been experienced in both developed and developing countries in 2020. Although it is not clear from the values in Table 2, ac-

Figure 2. The global growth rate in GDP (Source: Statistica, 2022)

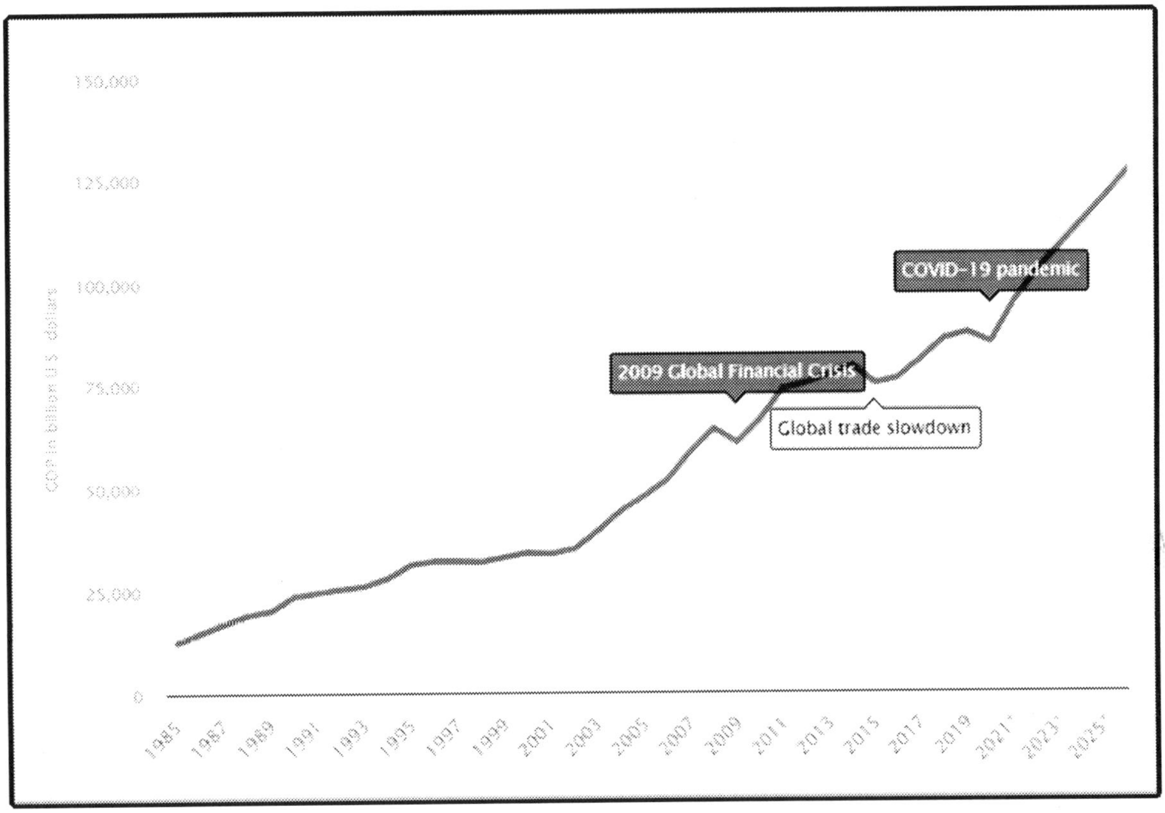

cording to the United Nations Conference on Trade and Development (2020) the developed countries' economies affected more harshly than the developing countries, at -5,8 and -2,1% respectively as well.

The research reports indicate that there is no sector or country that is not affected by either the supply or the demand shock. However, not all of them have been affected by the pandemic equally. For instance, Atayah et al. (2021) compared the financial performances of logistics firms in G20 countries and they showed that while the financial performance of 14 countries improved, only six of them deteriorated (Germany, Korea, Russia, Mexico, Saudi Arabia, and the UK). Because while some of them follow the rules such as mask distance and isolation, these applications have not been made in some countries due to economic concerns.

Although China is the only country with a positive GDP value of 3% in Table 2, Zou et al. (2020) claim that, the GDP of China fell by approximately 7%. The rate of unemployment decreased by 6%. In the early stage of the pandemic, in terms of size, investment, and consumption, China's added value decreased by 13.5, 24.5, and 20.5 percent, respectively (Zou et al., 2020). China is one of the most affected countries due to the pandemic. Factory closures caused lower output and then higher prices. The economists take attention to the stagflation signals (Tan, 2021).

One of the criteria on which macroeconomic stability depends is inflation (Pakdemirli et al., 2020). Inflation is defined as a rise in the price of goods and services over time and it rise as the cost of goods and services rises. As a result, the value of money decrease. Inflation has turned out to be a major problem for almost whole countries in the post-pandemic era. Besides, especially in developing countries,

Table 2. GDP values in developed and developing countries

Developed Countries	GDP-2019 (Billion $)	GDP-2020 (Billion $)	GDP-2021 (Billion $)	Growth rate in GDP between 2019 and 2020	Growth rate in GDP between 2020 and 2021
Belgium	533.157	513.087	578.996	-4%	13%
Canada	1,741.58	1,643.41	1,883.49	-6%	15%
Denmark	350.104	352.243	392.57	1%	11%
France	2,717.20	2,598.91	2,938.27	-4%	13%
Germany	3,861.55	3,803.01	4,319.29	-2%	14%
Italy	2,005.14	1,884.94	2,106.29	-6%	12%
Japan	5,148.78	5,048.69	5,378.14	-2%	7%
Sweden	531.283	537.61	625.948	1%	16%
United Kingdom	2,833.30	2,710.97	3,124.65	-4%	15%
United States	21,433.23	20,932.75	22,675.27	-2%	8%
Developing Countries	**GDP-2019 (Billion $)**	**GDP-2020 (Billion $)**	**GDP-2021 (Billion $)**	**Growth rate in GDP between 2019 and 2020**	**Growth rate in GDP between 2020 and 2021**
Argentina	444.458	388.279	418.15	-13%	8%
Brazil	1,877.11	1,434.08	1,491.77	-24%	4%
Bulgaria	68.563	68.561	77.782	0%	13%
China	14,340.60	14,722.84	16,642.32	3%	13%
India	2,870.50	2,708.77	3,049.70	-6%	13%
Indonesia	1,120.04	1,059.64	1,158.78	-5%	9%
Peru	230.746	203.772	225.918	-12%	11%
Russia	1,689.30	1,473.58	1,710.73	-13%	16%
Thailand	544.152	501.888	538.735	-8%	7%
Turkey	760.94	719.537	794.53	-5%	10%

Source: IMF database, 2021

the exchange rates and energy prices of developing countries are depreciated (Handfield et al., 2020). Recently, the rising prices and supply chain disruptions indicate that the global economy is not getting better. Despite the precautions, the pandemic affected negatively the macroeconomic indicators such as inflation, and unemployment rate (Duran and Acar, 2020). In 2020 and 2021, the global inflation rate amounted to approximately 3.18 and 4.35 percent respectively compared to the previous years (Aaron, 2022).

After the early stage of the pandemic, the government authorities lowered the custom barriers by alleviating tariffs and regulations especially in the countries whose economies depend on import. Therefore, in 2021 the growth rates turned into positive values. As shown the Figure 2, the global GDP is 94.935 billion US dollars in 2021. According to the previous year, it increased 11.7%. Thus, we can interpret the effect of the pandemic as waning and passing after 2020. This happened by the economic precautions that the governments take to sustain the economy worldwide in many countries. Some of them are shown in Table 3.

Table 3. Precautions have taken by governments to fight with the economic effects of covid-19

Type of precautions	Precautions	Implemented country
Monetary policy measures	Forcing banks to take regulatory action and put a suspension on principal and interest payments to COVID-19 debtors.	Ireland, China, Nigeria, Italy
	Liquidity is provided by central banks to financial markets.	USA, China
	Central banks are purchasing rising-value bonds and assets.	Australia, EU, Canada
	Central banks decreased the interest rates.	Turkey, USA, NewZeland, Japan, England, Nigeria, South Korea, Canada
	Loans to banks, SMEs, the public health sector, individuals, and major businesses.	England, USA, Australia, Nigeria
Fiscal policy measures	Approval of a major federal stimulus package for the COVID-19 pandemic-affected sectors and industries.	England, USA, Australia, Nigeria, Turkey
	Payments of social aid to each household	USA, Australia, Turkey
	Financial support for individuals	USA, Australia, Turkey, England, India

Source: Duran and Acar, 2020.

CONCLUSION

As the covid-19 virus appeared in China for the first time, the Chinese Government took urgent strict precautions such as curfew to prevent the spread of the virus. Afterwards the number of cases and deaths are begin to be tracked by the world health organization. Meanwhile the other countries begun to take precautions to prevent the infection by closing or limiting the customs clearance for passengers and goods, by closing the companies to isolate the infected workers and by the implementation of home-ban. These applications caused a change in human behavior and therefore, purchasing behavior. The prior requirements of the people changed. Thus, supply chain interruptions began to appear. Sometimes demand of a product increased tremendously and demand of another product decreased at the same time. For instance while the demand of toilet paper, medical supplies such as hand sanitizers, facemasks, ventilators, test kits, electronic products such as personal computers or tablets are increased, on the other hand, demand of flight and hospitality, textile products are decreased. Another important supply chain disruption is the reduced productivity often due to dismissal, part-time employment or psychological negative effects. Since the production facilities could not produce goods as much as to meet the demand, the supply chain is disrupted. Raw material shortage is also considered as a disruption type in this study. Since China was an important point in the start of the pandemic and the raw material supplier of almost all countries worldwide, there were a big raw material supply problem in pandemic era. Many factories in automobile industry could not provide chip sets for their automobile production and had to close their facilities. In the post-pandemic era the disruption in the automobile industry still continues. Raw material shortage resulted in factory closures, which is another type of supply chain disruption. As can be seen from this example a supply chain disruption cause to another type of disruption. As well as the production facilities, the warehouse facilities are also had to be closed temporarily due to the increased number of infected workers. The layouts of the warehouses are modified according to the social distance rules to save the health of the employees. During the modification of the warehouses, access problems have emerged, which is a different type of disruption. The last type of supply chain disruption which is considered in this study is transportation interruptions.

As mentioned in section 3, at the outset of covid-19 the scheduled flights decreased due to the decreased level of demand and regulations implemented by government. Therefore, the good movement by airline decreased. In the later phase of the pandemic, the regulations are alleviated but the people still do not prefer to fly in a closed environment. Thus, the capacities of the passenger planes are used to carry cargoes instead of people. At the same time, a container crisis, in which the importers could not find empty available container to carry the goods overseas, has appeared and influenced harshly most of the global trade. Lack of truck driver is the main problem of the road transportation. All transportation modes have different effect on supply chain. Rail transport has been the only mode of transport with increasing volume of goods carried in pandemic era since it was not affected by the isolation and quarantine procedures. The negative effects in the transportation modes has influenced the volume of global trade. According to UNCTAD (2021b) report, global merchandise trade declined by almost 7.4% and global service trade declined 20% in 2020 compared with 2019. The exporter and importer countries could not send or receive their products for many different reasons and due to the restrictions and precautions taken by the authorities. The drop in the global trade caused global economic damage for various industries and countries. The worldwide GDP is decreased by 3% in 2020 because of the pandemic (Barman et al., 2021). Despite the precautions, the pandemic affected negatively the macroeconomic indicators such as inflation (Duran and Acar, 2020). In 2020 and 2021, the global inflation rate amounted to approximately 3.18 and 4.35 percent respectively compared to the previous years (Aaron, 2022).

REFERENCES

Aaron, O. (2022). *Global inflation rate from 2016 to 2026*. Retrieved May 20, 2022 from https://www.statista.com/statistics/256598/global-inflation-rate-compared-to-previous-year/

Ali, B. J. (2020). Impact of COVID-19 on consumer buying behavior toward online shopping in Iraq. *Economic Studies Journal, 18*(42), 267–280.

Atayah, O. F., Dhiaf, M. M., Najaf, K., & Frederico, G. F. (2021). Impact of COVID-19 on financial performance of logistics firms: Evidence from G-20 countries. *Journal of Global Operations and Strategic Sourcing., 15*(2), 172–196. doi:10.1108/JGOSS-03-2021-0028

Atkinson-Clement, C., & Pigalle, E. (2021). What can we learn from Covid-19 pandemic's impact on human behaviour? The case of France's lockdown. *Humanities and Social Sciences Communications, 8*(1), 1–12. doi:10.105741599-021-00749-2

Barman, A., Das, R., & De, P. K. (2021). Impact of COVID-19 in food supply chain: Disruptions and recovery strategy. *Current Research in Behavioral Sciences., 2*, 100017. doi:10.1016/j.crbeha.2021.100017

Berg, A., Haug, L., Hedrich, S., & Magnus, K.-H. (2020). *Time for change How to use the crisis to make fashion sourcing more agile and sustainable.* McKinsey & Company. https://www.ilo.org/wcmsp5/groups/public/—ed_dialogue/—sector/documents/briefingnote/wcms_741344.pdf

Bhalla, A. (2020). *Amazon shuts New Jersey facility till Dec.26 on virus spike among workers*. Retrieved March 29, 2022, from https://www.reuters.com/article/us-health-coronavirus-amazon-com-warehou-idUSKBN28V06J

Butt, A. S. (2021). Strategies to mitigate the impact of COVID-19 on supply chain disruptions: A multiple case analysis of buyers and distributors. *International Journal of Logistics Management*.

CBC News. (2021). Retrieved May 11, 2022 from https://www.cbc.ca/news/canada/toronto/amazon-site-closed-brampton-covid19-1.5947898

Choi, E. P. H., Hui, B. P. H., & Wan, E. Y. F. (2020b). Depression and anxiety in Hong Kong during COVID-19. *International Journal of Environmental Research and Public Health*, *17*(10), 3740. doi:10.3390/ijerph17103740 PMID:32466251

Choi, T.-M. (2020a). Innovative 'bring-service-near-your-home' operations under corona-virus (COVID- 19/SARS-CoV-2) outbreak: Can logistics become the messiah? *Transportation Research Part E, Logistics and Transportation Review*, *140*, 101961. doi:10.1016/j.tre.2020.101961 PMID:32346356

Chowdhury, P., Paul, S. K., Kaisar, S., & Moktadir, M. A. (2021). COVID-19 pandemic related supply chain studies: A systematic review. *Transportation Research Part E, Logistics and Transportation Review*, *148*, 102271. doi:10.1016/j.tre.2021.102271 PMID:33613082

Craighead, C. W., Blackhurst, J., Rungtusanatham, M. J., & Handfield, R. B. (2007). The severity of supply chain disruptions: Design characteristics and mitigation capabilities. *Decision Sciences*, *38*(1), 131–156. doi:10.1111/j.1540-5915.2007.00151.x

De Vet, J. M., Nigohosyan, D., Ferrer, J. N., Gross, A. K., Kuehl, S., & Flickenschild, M. (2021). Impacts of the COVID-19 Pandemic on EU Industries. European Parliament.

Duran, M. S., & Acar, M. (2020). Bir virüsün dünyaya ettikleri: Covid-19 pandemisinin makroekonomik etkileri. *International Journal of Social and Economic Sciences*, *10*(1), 54–67.

Duro, J. A., Perez-Laborda, A., Turrion-Prats, J., & Fernández-Fernández, M. (2021). Covid-19 and tourism vulnerability. *Tourism Management Perspectives*, *38*, 100819. doi:10.1016/j.tmp.2021.100819 PMID:34873568

Fooddive. (2020). *Tracking coronavirus closures at food and beverage factories*. Retrieved March 20, 2022, from https://www.fooddive.com/news/tracking-coronavirus-closures-at-food-and-beverage-factories/576559/

Forbes. (2020). *New delay reported for Apple's iphone 12 launch*. Retrieved May 7, 2022, from https://www.forbes.com/sites/gordonkelly/2020/09/24/apple-iphone-12-pro-max-release-date-new-iphone-11-pro-max-upgrade/?sh=502b16ec5b3e

Forbes. (2022). Retrieved May 20, 2022, from https://www.forbes.com/companies/alibaba-group/?sh=49fa6a2219f5

Fortunes. (2022). *China's hard-line covid-zero response to omicron could trigger supply-chain chaos*. Retrieved April 28, 2022, from https://fortune.com/2022/01/13/china-omicron-covid-zero-port-shutdown-lockdown-supply-chain/

Global report on food crisis. (2021). Retrieved April 8, 2022, from https://docs.wfp.org/api/documents/WFP-0000127413/download/?_ga=2.107110212.73355866.1654068456-1668939605.1654068456

Gray, R. S. (2020). Agriculture, transportation, and the COVID-19 crisis. *Canadian Journal of Agricultural Economics/Revue canadienne d'agroeconomie, 68*(2), 239-243.

GS, D. G., & Swetha, M. S. S. (2020). Pandemic impact: Challenges faced by entrepreneurs of logistics industry. *Journal of Contemporary Issues in Business and Government, 26*(2), 516.

Handfield, R. B., Graham, G., & Burns, L. (2020). Corona virus, tariffs, trade wars and supply chain evolutionary design. *International Journal of Operations & Production Management, 40*(10), 2020. doi:10.1108/IJOPM-03-2020-0171

Hilmola, O. P., Lähdeaho, O., Henttu, V., & Hilletofth, P. (2020). COVID-19 pandemic: Early implications for North European manufacturing and logistics. *Sustainability, 12*(20), 8315. doi:10.3390u12208315

Hobbs, J. E. (2020). Food supply chains during the COVID-19 pandemic. *Canadian Journal of Agricultural Economics/Revue canadienne d'agroeconomie, 68*(2), 171-176.

IMF database. (2021). Retrieved May 24, 2022, from https://www.imf.org/en/Publications/WEO/weo-database/2021/April/select-countries?grp=2001&sg=All%20countries

International Air Transport Association [IATA]. (2020). *Recovery Delayed as International Travel Remains Locked Down.* Retrieved April 10, 2022 from https://www.iata.org/en/pressroom/pr/2020-07-28-02/

Ji, D., Fan, L., Li, X., & Ramakrishna, S. (2020). Addressing the worldwide shortages of face masks. *BMC Materials, 2*(1), 1-11.

Karp, R. (2005). *Katrina and oil prices.* https://www.cfr.org/interview/katrina-and-oil-prices

Kwon, O. K. (2020). How is the COVID-19 pandemic affecting global supply chains, logistics, and transportation? *Journal of International Logistics and Trade, 18*(3), 107–111.

Lee, Y. N. (2021). *Survey finds auto industry hit hardest by supply chain disruptions during covid pandemic.* Retrieved April 15, 2022, from https://www.cnbc.com/2021/08/25/auto-industry-supply-chains-hit-hardest-during-covid-pandemic-survey.html

Liu, W., Liang, Y., Bao, X., Qin, J., & Lim, M. K. (2020). China's logistics development trends in the post COVID-19 era. *International Journal of Logistics Research and Applications*, 1-12.

Mahajan, K., & Tomar, S. (2021). COVID-19 and supply chain disruption: Evidence from food markets in India. *American Journal of Agricultural Economics, 103*(1), 35–52.

Maital, S., & Barzani, E. (2020). The global economic impact of COVID-19: A summary of research. *Samuel Neaman Institute for National Policy Research, 2020*, 1–12.

Moritz, B. (2020). Supply chain disruptions and COVID-19. *Supply Chain Management Review, 27*(3).

Övünç, K. (2020). *Covid-19 has adverse impact on oil demand: OPEC.* Retrieved May 25, 2022, from https://www.aa.com.tr/en/energy/international-organization/covid-19-has-adverse-impact-on-oil-demand-opec/28559

Pakdemirli, B., Bayraktar, Z., Ünalmiş, A. N., & Takmaz, S. (2020). *Pandemi Ekseninde Küresel Değişim Ve Yeni Ekonomik Düzen*. Akçağ Yayınları.

Palmer, A. (2020). *Amazon closes New Jersey warehouse after workers test positive for coronavirus*. Retrieved April 20, 2022, from https://www.cnbc.com/2020/12/20/amazon-closes-new-jersey-warehouse-after-covid-19-infections.html

Paul, S. K., & Chowdhury, P. (2020). Strategies for managing the impacts of disruptions during COVID-19: An example of toilet paper. *Global Journal of Flexible Systems Managment*, *21*(3), 283–293.

Pujawan, I. N., & Bah, A. U. (2022). Supply chains under COVID-19 disruptions: Literature review and research agenda. In *Supply Chain Forum. International Journal (Toronto, Ont.)*, *23*(1), 81–95.

Pulsinelly, O. (2020). *Sysco reveals size of workforce cuts due to covid-19*. Retrieved May 26, 2022, from https://www.bizjournals.com/houston/news/2020/05/05/sysco-reveals-size-of-workforce-cuts-due-to-covid.html

Queiroz, M. M., Ivanov, D., Dolgui, A., & Fosso Wamba, S. (2020). Impacts of epidemic outbreaks on supply chains: Mapping a research agenda amid the COVID-19 pandemic through a structured literature review. *Annals of Operations Research*, 1–38.

Ritcher, F. (2020). *U.S. Car indutry most reliant on Chinese parts*. Retrieved May 14, 2022, from https://www.statista.com/chart/20913/chinese-exports-of-motor-vehicle-parts-and-accessories/

Roberts, B. W. (2009). The macroeconomic impacts of the 9/11 attack: Evidence from real-time forecasting. *Peace Economics, Peace. Science & Public Policy*, *15*(2), 341–367.

Rozman, M., & Tominc, P. (2021). The physical, emotional and behavioral symptoms of health problems among employees before and during the COVID-19 epidemic. *Employee Relations: The International Journal*, *44*(7), 19–45.

Shead, S. (2022). *Chip supply issues are still giving some of the world's biggest companies a major headache*. Retrieved April 26, 2022, from https://www.cnbc.com/2022/05/02/chip-shortage-hurts-apple-nokia-daimler-and-volvo.html

Sherman, E. (2020). 94% of the Fortune 1000 are seeing Coronavirus Supply Chain Disruptions: Report. *Fortune*. Retrieved May 20, 2022, from https://fortune.com/2020/02/21/fortune-1000-coronavirus-china-supply-chain-impact/

Shi, K., & Weng, J. (2021). Impacts of the COVID-19 epidemic on merchant ship activity and pollution emissions in Shanghai port waters. *The Science of the Total Environment*, *790*, 148198.

Statistica. (2022). Retrieved May 20, 2022, from https://www.statista.com/statistics/268750/global-gross-domestic-product-gdp/

Tan, W. (2021). *China's economy is showing signs of stagflation, economists warn*. Retrieved May 20, 2022, from https://www.cnbc.com/2021/11/01/china-economy-shows-signs-of-stagflation-price-inflation-economists.html

Toygar, A., Yildirim, U., & İnegöl, G. M. (2022). Investigation of empty container shortage based on SWARA-ARAS methods in the COVID-19 era. *European Transport Research Review*, *14*, 8.

UNCTAD. (2021a). *Covid-19 and maritime transport. Impact and responses*. Retrieved May 28, 2022, from https://unctad.org/system/files/official-document/dtltlb2021d1_en.pdf

UNCTAD. (2021b). *Global merchandise trade exceeds pre-covid-19 level, but services recovery falls short*. Retrieved March 29, 2022, from https://unctad.org/news/global-merchandise-trade-exceeds-pre-covid-19-level-services-recovery-falls-short#:~:text=According%20to%20the%20report%2C%20world,when%20trade%20fell%20by%2022%25

United Nations. (2022). *Human development reports*. Retrieved May 20, 2022, from https://hdr.undp.org/en/content/human-development-index-hdi

United Nations Conference on Trade and Development. (2020). *Impact of the pandemic on trade and development: Transitioning to a new normal*. Author.

Veselovska, L. (2020). Supply chain disruptions in the context of early stages of the global COVID-19 outbreak. *Problems and Perspectives in Management*, *18*(2), 490–500.

Vo, T. D., & Tran, M. D. (2021). The impact of covid-19 pandemic on the global trade. *International Journal of Social Science and Economics Invention*, *7*(1), 1–7.

WHO. (2021). Retrieved March 28, 2022, from https://www.who.int/health-topics/coronavirus#tab=tab_1

WHO. (2022). Retrieved March 28, 2022, from https://covid19.who.int/

Wing Shin, R. T., Stoller, C., & Woon Yew, D. L. (2020). Issues on the logistics challenges in the pandemic period. *Journal of Critical Reviews*, 776-780.

Wolor, C. W., Susita, D., & Martono, S. (2020). How to Maintain Employee Motivation Amid The Covid-19 Virus Pandemic. *International Journal of Economics & Business Administration*, *8*(4), 78–86.

World Development Report. (2022). *Finance for an equitable recovery*. Author.

World Economic Forum. (2020). *China Is Sending Medical Experts and Supplies to Help Italy Fight Coronavirus*. Retrieved April 13, 2022, from, https://www.weforum.org/agenda/2020/03/coronavirus-covid-19-italy-china-supplies/

WSJ. (2001). *A fire in Albuquerque sparks crisis for European cell-phone-giants*. Retrieved May 25, 2022, from https://www.wsj.com/articles/SB980720939804883010

WTO. (2020). *International tourism numbers could fall 60–80% in 2020*. Retrieved May 25, 2022, from https://www.unwto.org/news/covid-19-international-tourist-numbers-could-fall-60-80-in-2020

Xu, Z., Elomri, A., Kerbache, L., & El Omri, A. (2020). Impacts of COVID-19 on global supply chains: Facts and perspectives. *IEEE Engineering Management Review*, *48*(3), 153–166.

Yang, S., Ning, L., Jiang, T., & He, Y. (2021). Dynamic impacts of COVID-19 pandemic on the regional express logistics: Evidence from China. *Transport Policy*, *111*, 111–124.

Yuniarti, D., & Rosadi, D. (2021). Inflation of Indonesia during the COVID-19 pandemic. *Journal of Physics: Conference Series*, *1821*(1), 012039.

Zou, P., Huo, D., & Li, M. (2020). The impact of the COVID-19 pandemic on firms: a survey in Guangdong Province, China. *Global Health Research and Policy, 5*(1), 1-10.

Chapter 14
Can Renewable Energy Investments Be a Solution to the Energy-Sourced High Inflation Problem?

Hasan Dinçer
İstanbul Medipol University, Turkey

Serhat Yüksel
İstanbul Medipol University, Turkey

Çağatay Çağlayan
İstanbul Medipol University, Turkey

Duygu Yavuz
İstanbul Medipol University, Turkey

Dilan Kararoğlu
https://orcid.org/0000-0002-8895-9317
İstanbul Medipol University, Turkey

ABSTRACT

The aim of this study is to examine the relationship between renewable energy and inflation. Within this framework, Turkey is taken into consideration. In this context, the data regarding inflation rate and renewable energy usage for the years between 1990 and 2020 is examined. This data is obtained from the website of the World Bank. Engle Granger cointegration analysis is considered to examine the relationship between these factors. The findings demonstrate that there is a long-term relationship between the variables. In other words, it is understood that renewable energy usage affects inflation for Turkey in the long term. Therefore, it would be appropriate for countries to prioritize renewable energy investments. In this way, countries will be able to produce their own energy, and their dependence on foreign energy will decrease. Thus, they will not be affected much by the increases in energy prices. In this context, investments should be made primarily in renewable energy technologies.

DOI: 10.4018/978-1-6684-5876-1.ch014

INTRODUCTION

Inflation causes the uncertainty in the country's economy to rise. This situation worries investors. The reason for this is that it is difficult to predict the prices of goods in the market for the future because of inflation. This leads to a decrease in investments (Mukhtarov et al., 2022). As a result, the stability of the country's economy deteriorates. Thus, the problem in the country's economy grows even more. In summary, the inflation problem needs to be solved. One of the most important causes of high inflation problem is energy. In other words, due to the increase in energy prices, the prices of other goods in the country also increase (Zhang et al., 2022). The reason for this is that energy, which is one of the most important raw materials, is effective in the formation of the price of each commodity.

Therefore, it is also important for countries to have their own energy resources and to manage the high inflation problem. This situation is even more difficult for countries that do not have energy resources such as oil and natural gas within their borders (Dong et al., 2022). Since these countries are dependent on foreign energy, they cannot interfere with the increase in energy prices. In this context, the use of renewable energy is important for these countries. Since natural resources such as sun and wind are taken into consideration in these types of energy, renewable energies mean the country's own energy (Dinçer et al., 2022). Therefore, renewable energy resources can be increased to effectively combat the high inflation problem.

Turkey is also a country dependent on foreign energy in terms of energy. In parallel, Turkey has been struggling with the problem of high inflation for a long time. In this study, the relationship between renewable energy and inflation is examined. Within this framework, Turkey is taken into consideration. In this context, the data regarding inflation rate and renewable energy usage for the years between 1990 and 2020 is examined. This data is obtained from the website of World Bank. Engle Granger cointegration analysis is considered to examine the relationship between these factors.

Theoretical Background

The energy problem is one of the biggest problems of our age. Various reasons can be mentioned that cause this problem, but the main reason is the increasing energy need in parallel with the increasing world population. After the industrial revolution, global production, consumption, and human population are increasing rapidly (Stearns, 2020). Considering that energy is a basic need for people, the increasing energy demand must be met. Every energy produced in parallel with the increasing energy demand has various costs. In addition to material costs, environmental costs can also be mentioned. One of them is environmental pollution. Most of the global energy demand is provided by fossil fuels. Since fossil fuels are carbon-based fuels, they are one of the main causes of environmental pollution, especially air pollution. Accordingly, energy production, which is increased at the same rate to meet the increasing energy demand, pollutes the environment more if fossil fuels are used. Fossil fuels are natural energy sources containing hydrocarbons and high levels of carbon. Natural gas, oil and coal are prime examples of fossil fuels (Kalair, et al., 2021). Fossil fuels, which are widely used by industrial environments, are basically formed by the dissolution of dying living organisms in an oxygen-free environment for millions of years. The process of generating electricity in power plants that produce energy using fossil fuels is simply based on the combustion process. The steam released by the combustion of fossil fuels is used to turn turbines. Electricity is generated by the rotation of the turbines.

Various technological developments in the centuries we live in have increased the demand for fossil fuels. For example, gasoline derived from petroleum is one of the determinants of global trade. There are various advantages in the use of fossil fuels in energy production, but when the disadvantages of fossil fuels are considered, the search for solutions in response to the increasing energy demand on a global scale should turn to energy sources that are alternative to fossil fuels (Yuksel, et al., 2022). An example of these advantages is low cost. Access to reserves of fossil fuel resources is usually not very complicated. Therefore, operating costs remain at low levels. In addition, fossil fuels are easy to transport and store. Therefore, transportation and storage costs are relatively low. As a result, it can be said that although fossil fuels are not beneficial in the long run, they are still powerful and cheap energies. When fossil fuels are examined in detail, it will be seen that they have disadvantages in various areas such as environment, health, and economy. The first among the disadvantages of fossil fuels is the environmental effects of these fuels. Carbon emissions are among the main causes of environmental pollution. Carbon emission, together with air and water pollution, directly affects human health negatively (Hanif, 2018). Accordingly, it should be said that an increase in respiratory tract diseases is observed in cities and countries where carbon emissions are intense (Kostis et al., 2022). Therefore, long-term diseases in countries where fossil fuels are used intensively increase health expenditures, cause loss of workforce, directly affect the happiness of individuals negatively, and experience economic fragility (Dinçer, et al., 2021).

One of the biggest global threats caused by carbon emissions is global warming. There are many social and economic problems caused by global warming. The temperature figures around the world are increasing every year. Increasing temperatures seriously threaten the life of living things by causing drought. Agricultural activities, which decrease with drought, cause a significant decrease in the number of products produced and create an imbalance in supply and demand for products (Bai, et al., 2020). As the demand for the products is higher than the supply, the inflation problem will occur. Thus, many people will experience difficulties in accessing food (Adalı et al., 2022). All this shows that the main cause of global warming and many other problems is based on the intense use of fossil fuels (Kou et al., 2022). Therefore, although fossil fuels provide small advantages in the short run, they cause serious problems in the long run. Considering this situation, investments in nuclear energy and renewable energies should increase and energy production should be shifted to these types of energy (Johnsson, et al., 2019).

Nuclear energy and renewable energies are among the energy sources offered as alternatives to fossil fuels. Nuclear energy is one of the most controversial types of energy. One of the most basic components of a nuclear reactor is its core. The core contains fissionable fuel. Thus, uranium, the element with the most protons and neutrons, is used in nuclear power plants. With the fission reaction, uranium is split, releasing a large amount of heat. The high temperature formed after the fission reaction evaporates the water and enables the turbines to rotate. Thus, the motion energy required for energy production is realized. The amount of heat released in nuclear power plants is quite high. Therefore, in nuclear reactors, it is very important to control the rate of fission, or in other words, the flow of neutrons, which takes place in the form of a chain reaction. The chain reaction control process is carried out with control rods. These rods contain neutron-holder material. This material may be cadmium, hafnium, or boron. Thanks to the control rods, the neutron density in the environment can be reduced, thus enabling the power level to be controlled. A high amount of heat is obtained through fission reactions that take place in nuclear power plants. So, a nuclear reactor going out of control will have devastating effects (Yüksel, et al., 2021). Considering the advantages and disadvantages of nuclear energy, it is clearly understood why this type of energy is the most discussed energy and why there are indecisions in the applied nuclear energy policies.

One of the biggest advantages of nuclear energy is that the energy produced has zero carbon characteristics. Almost no harmful gases are released into the atmosphere. Considering the problems of global warming and carbon-based environmental pollution, nuclear energy is one of the most effective methods in solving these problems (Dinçer, et al., 2020). Another most important advantage of nuclear energy is that it promises uninterrupted energy for 24 hours. The energy produced does not change due to weather conditions or seasonal reasons. Another important feature that makes nuclear energy stand out among its alternatives is the high uranium reserves. With all these advantages, although nuclear power plants meet the energy needs of a country in a significant amount, they have various disadvantages (Yüksel, et al., 2021).

When talking about the disadvantages of nuclear energy, the first thing that comes to mind is usually the explosion risk of nuclear power plants. Nuclear power plants are equipped with extremely strict safety measures, but accidents can happen. In this case, accidents that may occur may cause high loss of life and property and genetic defects of future generations (Yüksel and Çağlayan, 2020). The nuclear power plants in Fukushima and Chernobyl are the most obvious examples for these accidents. Nuclear power is a good option to avoid pollution from carbon-based fuels, but nuclear power plants also produce certain amounts of radioactive waste. Therefore, one of the disadvantages of nuclear energy is the waste management problem. Uncontrolled processes or mistakes in waste management negatively affect human health in the long run. There are problems in the public acceptance of nuclear energy, as both waste storage and nuclear power plants are damaged by factors such as natural disasters and terrorist attacks, which will cause great destruction. Therefore, the possibility that nuclear energy investments will not be supported by the local people is among the disadvantages of nuclear energy (Xie, et al., 2020). Finally, one of the major disadvantages of nuclear energy is the high cost of installation. Nuclear energy investors face financial difficulties due to high costs. Although all these disadvantages of nuclear energy led investors to alternative energy sources such as renewable energies, it would be correct to say that nuclear power plants have been made quite safe with developing technologies. Minimizing the disadvantages of the said energy together with the developing technology helps nuclear energy to keep its quality as an energy source with high potential. For example, using thorium as a fuel in nuclear power plants, the explosion risk of nuclear energy and the waste management problem can be minimized, but more studies need to be done on this method (Jones, 2013).

Renewable energy is the type of energy that has emerged as an alternative to nuclear energy and fossil fuels and remains popular. The concept of renewable energy is explained as the energy source that can be available the next day of the energy consumed in the natural cycle (Bhuiyan et al., 2022). Renewable energy sources are generally listed as solar, wind, biomass, geothermal, hydraulic, hydrogen and wave energy. They have an important position in terms of sustainability, since there is no decrease in their reserves after the consumption of these energy resources (Ray, 2019) The reason why renewable energy sources are so popular is that they give confidence due to their various advantages (Li et al., 2021). When the advantages of renewable energies are mentioned, the first thing that comes to mind is minimizing carbon emissions. No carbon-based or other harmful gases are produced during the electricity generation from renewable energy sources (Wan et al., 2022). Therefore, the energy produced has the status of green energy and does not harm the environment. It can be said that renewable energies have an important contribution to the fight against global warming by minimizing carbon emissions. In addition, maintenance costs are low as no flammable fuel is used in renewable energies (Xie et al., 2021). This situation increases the interest of renewable energy investors in renewable energies (Fang et al., 2021). Renewable energies are already being used to generate hot water or electricity in some rural areas or metropolitan areas (Bayrakcı and Kocar, 2012). Therefore, renewable energy investments are energy investments with high public acceptance.

Considering the advantages and potential of renewable energies, the relationship between renewable energies and inflation is questioned. Inflation can be defined as the process of continuous price increase or the continuous depreciation of money (Berry, 2019). Although inflation is mostly seen as an economic problem, it is a phenomenon that also affects sociological dynamics (Serezli et al., 2021). High inflation reduces the purchasing power of individuals, leading to livelihoods and lower quality of life. The uncertainty created by high inflation creates a chain of negativities that affect each other in the decision-making process and future expectations of individuals and companies, in the investment process, in the credit and labour market, and in foreign markets.

The relationship between inflation and energy became stronger after the industrial revolution. After the industrial revolution, the importance of energy in the production process and therefore the dependence of economies on energy has increased, as production shifts from muscle power and relies more on machines (Haiyun et al., 2021). Although energy is not the only input that leads to economic growth, it is considered an extremely important input for economic growth. In other words, energy use and economic growth are interrelated. Many studies have shown that there is a positive relationship between energy consumption and economic growth (Shahbaz, et al., 2020). As the amount of energy used increases, the level of welfare also increases. Therefore, changes in energy prices affect all other economic processes and cause inflation rates to increase or decrease. For example, any increase in the price of natural gas will mean increased electricity costs for households or industries. This situation will negatively affect the welfare of the society by causing inflation. Therefore, it is essential to develop policies to reduce foreign dependency in energy in terms of ensuring and consolidating economic stability. In this study, the contribution of renewable energies to energy-based inflation in the countries where they are located by reducing foreign dependency in energy is examined.

LITERATURE EVALUATION

Human life would be impossible if it lacked energy. Reliable, inexpensive, and easily accessible energy is essential to modern life. It is projected that global energy consumption will continue to rise in the future. In 2005, 40% of the world's power came from coal, 20% from gas, 16% from nuclear, 16% from hydro, 7% from oil, and 2% from small hydro, geothermal, and other renewable sources (Muneer, et al., 2005). Renewable, nuclear, and fossil fuels are the three primary forms of power production technologies now in use. It's been a long time since crude fossil fuels such as coal and oil have been widely used. Due to a variety of reasons, many nations in the globe are unable to use nuclear energy. Renewable energy sources are readily available all around the world for the benefit of humankind. Renewable energy sources include the sun, wind, and water. For the first time in history, the world's energy demands are being met by renewable sources. Currently, the renewable energy industry is growing at a faster rate than the entire energy market. Renewable energy sources might eventually make up a larger share of the world's overall energy consumption in certain long-term scenarios (solar, wind, geothermal, modern biomass, and more traditional resource). These possibilities suggest that by the middle of the twenty-first century, renewable energy sources might provide 50% of the country's energy demands (Akella, et al., 2009).

There were numerous things that sprang to mind during the economic crisis of 2007-2009. Many theories have been put out as to why the global economy collapsed during an oil crisis. Subprime mortgage crisis originated from Great Depression and worldwide recession, leading to the most catastrophic financial disaster in history. This financial crisis has been exacerbated by high energy costs (Kaufmann, et al., 2011). Belke et al. (2011) looked at the long-term link between energy use and real GDP, including energy costs, for 25 OECD nations between 1981 and 2007. Whether or not it has an impact on the economics of energy conservation initiatives has been a highly debated topic. The so-called relationship between energy consumption and economic development has been thoroughly studied, but no agreement has yet been achieved (Apergis & Payne, 2009). Belke (2011) claim that in addition to energy use, capital, and labor as production inputs, the growth hypothesis also plays a crucial role in growth. In other words, when energy use declines, so does real GDP. Real GDP suffers because of the economy's dependence on energy. The effective use of energy and the reduction of greenhouse gas emissions via the use of alternative energy sources are two of the most important goals of energy policy. Not only should national considerations like energy supply infrastructure, efficiency, and institutional limits be considered in the future.

According to the findings of one research, consumers' inflation predictions are closely tied to the price of gasoline (Binder, 2018). Gas prices are very volatile, and their appeal means that the sensitivity of inflation expectations to gas prices is critical to determining the best monetary policy to combat price volatility. Housing is a long-term hedge against consumer price inflation. Residential real estate's long-term hedge against energy inflation is unknown. Protecting residential property against inflation in the short term is often based on inflation expectations and inflation surprises, although they are seldom decisive (Yeap & Lean, 2017). As energy costs rise, they may lead to a tightening of monetary policy that reduces liquidity and consequently reduces domestic demand, notwithstanding the official inflation rate. There is a correlation between changes in the world economy and the price dynamics of commodities and housing, for example, when there is an increase in global liquidity and commodity prices rise significantly (Batten et al., 2010; Belke et al., 2010; 2014; Hammoudeh and Yuan, 2008; Ratti and Vespignani, 2013; Ratti and Vespignani, 2015). Breitenfellner, et al., (2014)'s research showed a clear link between energy and property values. According to this research, which included 18 OECD nations and spanned 37 years, energy price inflation has a significant effect in home price modifications. He concluded that energy price inflation plays a critical role in both addressing issues of price stability and ensuring the financial market's long-term viability. Energy prices have both direct and indirect impacts on building expenses in terms of equipment manufacturing and operation, as well as raw material consumption, which in turn affects the volume and cost of housing. As a result, rising energy costs push up the cost of a home (Agnello, et al., 2016). Rising energy costs may have a significant influence on housing prices, but this is especially true in the OECD nations because the housing sector accounts for a significant share of overall energy usage (Swan & Ugursal, 2009).

In both rich and developing nations, changes in energy supply may have a significant influence on economic development, according to others (Stern and Cleveland, 2004). A society must decide on an optimal energy mix and stress the presence of both better and lower quality kinds of energy when energy services vary. Scaling up better quality energy services might result in incremental profits. The shift from low-quality energy services to high-quality energy services may be accelerated rather than stifled by policies to control energy consumption. Energy regulators should thus adopt a method (such as a tax or a price limit) that maintains energy service costs consistent while simultaneously decreasing the price of energy made possible by technological progress if their objective is to divorce economic development from consumption (Bentzen, 2004).

In some studies, it has been stated that the inflation rate increases with the increase in oil prices. (Salisu et al., 2017). In addition, Clark and Terry (2010) explained in their study that energy prices increased due to increasing price pressures due to the increase in oil prices. In addition, some studies have stated that all rising energy prices increase product prices, thus increasing inflation. (He, et al., 2016). Parallel to this, Sek (2017) explained in his study that the sectors that use oil intensively show more vulnerability in oil prices. Therefore, it was said that the 10% increase in global oil inflation increased the domestic inflation rate by 0.4%. (Choi, et al., 2018). For this reason, Breitenfellner (2015) explained in his study that the transition to financial markets is easier to understand due to the increase in oil prices. Especially, some studies have emphasized that the monetary policy implemented in that country is effective as one of the reasons for the increase in inflation and energy prices. (Bachmeier and Cha, 2011; Yellen, 2017). In another study, it was stated that the use of renewable energy sources has a negative effect on the exchange rate in the long run. At the same time, it was stated that the exchange rate gained value with the increase in the use of renewable energy. (Deka, et al., 2022). It is stated that if the use of renewable energy, which is known to be the target of the United Nations, is encouraged, the currencies of the countries will increase in value and lead to zero carbon. (Deka and Dube, 2021). In addition, Baghestani (2014) stated in his study that oil trading countries should determine long-term strategies to protect themselves from unpredictable fluctuations in crude oil prices. Some studies show that energy storage systems have the power to hedge cash flows. (Krömer and Gatzert, 2018). Thus, it has been stated in some studies that institutional reforms will strengthen the government system and increase foreign dependency. (Su et al., 2020). It is stated in the literature that energy prices are also effective in determining food prices. (Irz et al., 2013). It is said that non-energy goods and services may also affect energy inflation. (Castro et al., 2017).

AN APPLICATION ON TURKEY

Data Set and Variables

In this study, it is aimed to identify the long-term relationship between renewable energy usage and inflation. For this purpose, Turkey is taken into consideration. In this framework, the data regarding inflation rate and renewable energy usage for the years between 1990 and 2020 is examined. This data is obtained from the website of World Bank.

Engle Granger Cointegration Analysis

Engle Granger cointegration analysis is preferred to identify long-term relationship among the factors. In other words, it is aimed to understand whether there is a strong relationship between the variables. For this purpose, firstly, the variables are considered for stationary analysis (Yüksel and Kavak, 2019). In this process, it is evaluated if the variables have a unit root or not. According to the rules of Engle Granger methodology, all variables should be stationary in the same difference. Otherwise, it is concluded that the variables are not appropriate for the cointegration analysis (Dinçer et al., 2021).

After the unit root test, a regression analysis is performed between the variables. In this regression analysis, the way of the relationship (positive or negative) is identified. In the following step, the residuals of the regression analysis results are provided (Yüksel et al., 2020). In the final step, these residuals are also subject to stationary analysis. If the residual set has a unit root, it means that there is no long-term relationship between the determinants. However, if the residual set is stationary, this situation gives information that a long-term relationship is found between the variables (Yuksel and Zengin, 2016).

ANALYSIS RESULTS

The first stage in the analysis process is directly related to stationary analysis. For this purpose, Augmented Dickey Fuller (ADF) test is taken into consideration. Table 1 gives information about the unit root test result for the variable of inflation regarding the level value.

Because the probability value is 0.2772 (lower than 0.50), it is identified that the variable has a unit root. Therefore, another analysis is performed for the first difference of this variable. The details of the analysis results are given in Table 2.

It is seen that the probability value of the first difference is 0.0333. Because this value is lower than the critical value (0.05), it is determined that inflation variable is stationary in its first difference. This process is performed for the variable of renewable energy. Table 3 gives information about the unit root test result for the variable of renewable energy regarding the level value.

Since the probability value (0.3001) is greater than 0.05, it is identified that renewable energy variable has a unit root. Because of this situation, the unit root test is also performed for the first difference of this variable. Table 4 includes the results the unit root test with respect to the first difference of the renewable energy variable.

Because the probability value (0.0000) is lower than 0.05, it is understood that the first difference of the renewable energy variable does not have a unit root. As a result, it is seen that both the variables of inflation and renewable energy investments are stationary on their first differences. Therefore, it is concluded that this situation satisfies the requirement. In other words, these two variables can be considered for Engle Granger cointegration analysis.

In the following step, a regression analysis is conducted for these variables. Because in this study it is aimed to evaluate the impact on renewable energy on the inflation, the renewable energy variable is selected as independent variable whereas inflation is considered for dependent variable. Table 5 explains the results of regression analysis.

It is understood that renewable energy usage has a negative impact on the inflation because coefficient value of renewable energy variable is negative (-2.600794). In the next step, the residuals are obtained from this regression analysis. In the final part of this analysis, unit root test is conducted for the dataset of residuals. Table 6 demonstrates the stationary analysis results of the residual set.

The probability value of the stationary analysis result is 0.0000. It is seen that there is a long-term relationship between the variables because this value is lower than 0.05. Therefore, it is concluded that renewable energy usage affects the inflation for Turkey in the long term.

SOLUTIONS AND RECOMMENDATIONS

In this study, it has been understood that renewable energy is effective in reducing inflation. Therefore, it would be appropriate for countries to prioritize renewable energy investments. In this way, countries will be able to produce their own energy and their dependence on foreign energy will decrease (Zhou

Table 1. Unit Root Test Results of Inflation Variable (Level Value)

Null Hypothesis: INF has a unit root			
Exogenous: Constant, Linear Trend			
Lag Length: 4 (Automatic - based on SIC, maxlag=7)			
		t-Statistic	Prob.*
Augmented Dickey-Fuller test statistic		-2.614556	0.2772
Test critical values:	1% level	-4.356068	
	5% level	-3.595026	
	10% level	-3.233456	
*MacKinnon (1996) one-sided p-values.			
Augmented Dickey-Fuller Test Equation			
Dependent Variable: D(INF)			
Method: Least Squares			
Date: 03/08/22 ...... Time: 15:15			
Sample (adjusted): 1995 2020			
Included observations: 26 after adjustments			

Variable	Coefficient	Std. Error	t-Statistic	Prob.
INF(-1)	-0.210403	0.080474	-2.614556	0.0170
D(INF(-1))	0.019039	0.106305	0.179103	0.8598
D(INF(-2))	-0.013372	0.107709	-0.124150	0.9025
D(INF(-3))	0.249028	0.102623	2.426634	0.0254
D(INF(-4))	0.351715	0.105989	3.318398	0.0036
C	8.449384	8.645164	0.977354	0.3407
@TREND("1990")	-0.229321	0.331851	-0.691036	0.4979

R-squared	0.623714	Mean dependent var	-3.574463
Adjusted R-squared	0.504887	S.D. dependent var	7.530887
S.E. of regression	5.299054	Akaike info criterion	6.397738
Sum squared resid	533.5194	Schwarz criterion	6.736456
Log likelihood	-76.17059	Hannan-Quinn criter.	6.495276
F-statistic	5.248920	Durbin-Watson stat	1.273327
Prob(F-statistic)	0.002442		

et al., 2021). Thus, they will not be affected much by the increases in energy prices. In this context, investments should be made primarily in renewable energy technologies. In this way, it will be possible to reduce costs (Meng et al., 2021). Investors will also attach more importance to renewable energy projects, as they have a cost advantage. In addition, state support is also very important in this process.

It would be appropriate to offer cost advantages to renewable energy investments, thanks to incentives such as tax exemptions to be provided by the states (Yüksel and Ubay, 2021).

Table 2. Unit Root Test Results of Inflation Variable (First Difference)

Null Hypothesis: D(INF) has a unit root				
Exogenous: Constant, Linear Trend				
Lag Length: 1 (Automatic - based on SIC, maxlag=7)				
		t-Statistic	Prob.*	
Augmented Dickey-Fuller test statistic		-3.776681	0.0333	
Test critical values:	1% level	-4.323979		
	5% level	-3.580623		
	10% level	-3.225334		
*MacKinnon (1996) one-sided p-values.				
Augmented Dickey-Fuller Test Equation				
Dependent Variable: D(INF,2)				
Method: Least Squares				
Date: 03/08/22 ...... Time: 15:21				
Sample (adjusted): 1993 2020				
Included observations: 28 after adjustments				
Variable	Coefficient	Std. Error	t-Statistic	Prob.
D(INF(-1))	-1.081331	0.286318	-3.776681	0.0009
D(INF(-1),2)	0.049855	0.200217	0.249007	0.8055
C	-4.145369	4.970518	-0.833991	0.4125
@TREND("1990")	0.117926	0.268140	0.439795	0.6640
R-squared	0.520728	Mean dependent var	-0.249836	
Adjusted R-squared	0.460819	S.D. dependent var	15.58184	
S.E. of regression	11.44159	Akaike info criterion	7.843950	
Sum squared resid	3141.838	Schwarz criterion	8.034265	
Log likelihood	-105.8153	Hannan-Quinn criter.	7.902131	
F-statistic	8.691968	Durbin-Watson stat	1.974347	
Prob(F-statistic)	0.000442			

Table 3. Unit Root Test Results of Renewable Energy Variable (Level Value)

Null Hypothesis: RE has a unit root				
Exogenous: Constant, Linear Trend				
Lag Length: 0 (Automatic - based on SIC, maxlag=7)				
			t-Statistic	Prob.*
Augmented Dickey-Fuller test statistic			-2.558777	0.3001
Test critical values:	1% level		-4.296729	
	5% level		-3.568379	
	10% level		-3.218382	
*MacKinnon (1996) one-sided p-values.				
Augmented Dickey-Fuller Test Equation				
Dependent Variable: D(RE)				
Method: Least Squares				
Date: 03/08/22 ...... Time: 15:24				
Sample (adjusted): 1991 2020				
Included observations: 30 after adjustments				
Variable	Coefficient	Std. Error	t-Statistic	Prob.
RE(-1)	-0.389783	0.152332	-2.558777	0.0164
C	9.119664	3.800299	2.399723	0.0236
@TREND("1990")	-0.198184	0.081590	-2.429018	0.0221
R-squared	0.195274	Mean dependent var		-0.520142
Adjusted R-squared	0.135665	S.D. dependent var		1.208821
S.E. of regression	1.123837	Akaike info criterion		3.166013
Sum squared resid	34.10123	Schwarz criterion		3.306133
Log likelihood	-44.49020	Hannan-Quinn criter.		3.210839
F-statistic	3.275893	Durbin-Watson stat		2.160589
Prob(F-statistic)	0.053241			

FUTURE RESEARCH DIRECTIONS

In future research, more specific evaluations can be conducted. For instance, the effects of solar energy or wind energy on the inflation can be evaluated. Thus, more specific and appropriate strategies can be presented for the countries to struggle high inflation problem. Additionally, different country or country groups can be taken into consideration. This situation provides an opportunity to make a comparative evaluation.

Table 4. Unit Root Test Results of Renewable Energy Variable (First Difference)

Null Hypothesis: D(RE) has a unit root			
Exogenous: Constant, Linear Trend			
Lag Length: 0 (Automatic - based on SIC, maxlag=7)			
		t-Statistic	Prob.*
Augmented Dickey-Fuller test statistic		-6.962293	0.0000
Test critical values:	1% level	-4.309824	
	5% level	-3.574244	
	10% level	-3.221728	
*MacKinnon (1996) one-sided p-values.			

Augmented Dickey-Fuller Test Equation				
Dependent Variable: D(RE,2)				
Method: Least Squares				
Date: 03/08/22 ...... Time: 15:26				
Sample (adjusted): 1992 2020				
Included observations: 29 after adjustments				
Variable	Coefficient	Std. Error	t-Statistic	Prob.
D(RE(-1))	-1.301135	0.186883	-6.962293	0.0000
C	-0.742576	0.498108	-1.490795	0.1480
@TREND("1990")	0.003690	0.027001	0.136679	0.8923

R-squared	0.650897	Mean dependent var	-0.006411
Adjusted R-squared	0.624043	S.D. dependent var	1.983954
S.E. of regression	1.216468	Akaike info criterion	3.327478
Sum squared resid	38.47467	Schwarz criterion	3.468922
Log likelihood	-45.24843	Hannan-Quinn criter.	3.371777
F-statistic	24.23828	Durbin-Watson stat	2.139040
Prob(F-statistic)	0.000001		

CONCLUSION

In this study, the relationship between renewable energy and inflation is examined. Within this framework, Turkey is taken into consideration. In this context, the data regarding inflation rate and renewable energy usage for the years between 1990 and 2020 is examined. This data is obtained from the website of World Bank. Engle Granger cointegration analysis is considered to examine the relationship between these factors. The findings demonstrate that there is a long-term relationship between the variables. In other words, it is understood that renewable energy usage affects the inflation for Turkey in the long term.

Table 5. Regression Analysis Results

Dependent Variable: D(INF)				
Method: Least Squares				
Date: 03/08/22 …… Time: 15:34				
Sample (adjusted): 1991 2020				
Included observations: 30 after adjustments				
Variable	Coefficient	Std. Error	t-Statistic	Prob.
D(RE)	-2.600794	1.585269	1.640602	0.0121
C	-0.248049	2.056630	-0.120609	0.9049
R-squared	0.087697	Mean dependent var		-1.600830
Adjusted R-squared	0.055115	S.D. dependent var		10.61633
S.E. of regression	10.31962	Akaike info criterion		7.570312
Sum squared resid	2981.849	Schwarz criterion		7.663725
Log likelihood	-111.5547	Hannan-Quinn criter.		7.600196
F-statistic	2.691574	Durbin-Watson stat		1.975859
Prob(F-statistic)	0.112068			

Table 6. Unit Root Test Results of Residual Variable

Null Hypothesis: D(RESID01) has a unit root			
Exogenous: Constant, Linear Trend			
Lag Length: 0 (Automatic - based on SIC, maxlag=7)			
		t-Statistic	Prob.*
Augmented Dickey-Fuller test statistic		-8.380989	0.0000
Test critical values:	1% level	-4.323979	
	5% level	-3.580623	
	10% level	-3.225334	
*MacKinnon (1996) one-sided p-values.			
Augmented Dickey-Fuller Test Equation			
Dependent Variable: D(RESID01,2)			
Method: Least Squares			
Date: 03/08/22 ...... Time: 15:39			
Sample (adjusted): 1993 2020			
Included observations: 28 after adjustments			

Variable	Coefficient	Std. Error	t-Statistic	Prob.
D(RESID01(-1))	-1.479671	0.176551	-8.380989	0.0000
C	-1.430178	5.800374	-0.246567	0.8073
@TREND("1990")	0.073281	0.315799	0.232049	0.8184

R-squared	0.737642	Mean dependent var	-0.152615
Adjusted R-squared	0.716653	S.D. dependent var	25.32144
S.E. of regression	13.47869	Akaike info criterion	8.141054
Sum squared resid	4541.877	Schwarz criterion	8.283790
Log likelihood	-110.9748	Hannan-Quinn criter.	8.184690
F-statistic	35.14478	Durbin-Watson stat	2.453953
Prob(F-statistic)	0.000000		

REFERENCES

Adalı, Z., Dinçer, H., Eti, S., Mikhaylov, A., & Yüksel, S. (2022). Identifying New Perspectives on Geothermal Energy Investments. In *Multidimensional Strategic Outlook on Global Competitive Energy Economics and Finance*. Emerald Publishing Limited. doi:10.1108/978-1-80117-898-320221002

Agnello, L., Castro, V., Hammoudeh, S., & Sousa, R. M. (2017). Spillovers from the oil sector to the housing market cycle. *Energy Economics*, *61*, 209–220. doi:10.1016/j.eneco.2016.11.004

Akella, A. K., Saini, R. P., & Sharma, M. P. (2009). Social, economical and environmental impacts of renewable energy systems. *Renewable Energy*, *34*(2), 390–396. doi:10.1016/j.renene.2008.05.002

Apergis, N., & Payne, J. E. (2009). Energy consumption and economic growth: Evidence from the Commonwealth of Independent States. *Energy Economics*, *31*(5), 641–647. doi:10.1016/j.eneco.2009.01.011

Bachmeier, L. J., & Cha, I. (2011). Why don't oil shocks cause inflation? Evidence from disaggregate inflation data. *Journal of Money, Credit and Banking*, *43*(6), 1165–1183. doi:10.1111/j.1538-4616.2011.00421.x

Baghestani, H. (2014). Inflation expectations and energy price forecasting. *OPEC Energy Review*, *38*(1), 21–35. doi:10.1111/opec.12016

Bai, X., Shen, W., Wu, X., & Wang, P. (2020). Applicability of long-term satellite-based precipitation products for drought indices considering global warming. *Journal of Environmental Management*, *255*, 109846. doi:10.1016/j.jenvman.2019.109846 PMID:31747628

Batten, J. A., Ciner, C., & Lucey, B. M. (2010). The macroeconomic determinants of volatility in precious metals markets. *Resources Policy*, *35*(2), 65–71. doi:10.1016/j.resourpol.2009.12.002

Bayrakcı, A. G., & Kocar, G. (2012). Utilization of renewable energies in Turkey's agriculture. *Renewable & Sustainable Energy Reviews*, *16*(1), 618–633. doi:10.1016/j.rser.2011.08.027

Belke, A., Dobnik, F., & Dreger, C. (2011). Energy consumption and economic growth: New insights into the cointegration relationship. *Energy Economics*, *33*(5), 782–789. doi:10.1016/j.eneco.2011.02.005

Belke, A. H., Bordon, I. G., & Hendricks, T. W. (2014). Monetary policy, global liquidity and commodity price dynamics. *The North American Journal of Economics and Finance*, *28*, 1–16. doi:10.1016/j.najef.2013.12.003

Bentzen, J. (2004). Estimating the rebound effect in US manufacturing energy consumption. *Energy Economics*, *26*(1), 123–134. doi:10.1016/S0140-9883(03)00047-1

Berry, R. A. (2019). The Effects of Inflation on Income Distribution in Colombia: Some Hypotheses and a Framework for Analysis. In *Economic Policy and Income Distribution in Colombia* (pp. 113–131). Routledge. doi:10.4324/9780429051357

Bhuiyan, M. A., Dinçer, H., Yüksel, S., Mikhaylov, A., Danish, M. S. S., Pinter, G., Uyeh, D. D., & Stepanova, D. (2022). Economic indicators and bioenergy supply in developed economies: QROF-DEMATEL and random forest models. *Energy Reports*, *8*, 561–570. doi:10.1016/j.egyr.2021.11.278

Binder, C. C. (2018). Inflation expectations and the price at the pump. *Journal of Macroeconomics*, *58*, 1–18. doi:10.1016/j.jmacro.2018.08.006

Breitenfellner, A., Cuaresma, J. C., & Mayer, P. (2015). Energy inflation and house price corrections. *Energy Economics*, *48*, 109–116. doi:10.1016/j.eneco.2014.08.023

Castro, C., Jiménez-Rodríguez, R., Poncela, P., & Senra, E. (2017). A new look at oil price pass-through into inflation: Evidence from disaggregated European data. *Economics and Politics*, *34*(1), 55–82. doi:10.100740888-016-0048-9

Choi, S., Furceri, D., Loungani, P., Mishra, S., & Poplawski-Ribeiro, M. (2018). Oil prices and inflation dynamics: Evidence from advanced and developing economies. *Journal of International Money and Finance, 82*, 71–96. doi:10.1016/j.jimonfin.2017.12.004

Clark, T. E., & Terry, S. J. (2010). Time variation in the inflation passthrough of energy prices. *Journal of Money, Credit and Banking, 42*(7), 1419–1433. doi:10.1111/j.1538-4616.2010.00347.x

Deka, A., Cavusoglu, B., & Dube, S. (2021). Does renewable energy use enhance exchange rate appreciation and stable rate of inflation? *Environmental Science and Pollution Research International*, 1–10. PMID:34601688

Deka, A., & Dube, S. (2021). Analyzing the causal relationship between exchange rate, renewable energy and inflation of Mexico (1990–2019) with ARDL bounds test approach. *Renewable Energy Focus, 37*, 78–83. doi:10.1016/j.ref.2021.04.001

Dinçer, H., Lisin, A., Ubay, G. G., & Çağlayan, Ç. (2021). Identifying the Best Financing Sources for Renewable Energy Companies in Latin American Countries. In *Strategic Approaches to Energy Management* (pp. 1–12). Springer. doi:10.1007/978-3-030-76783-9_1

Dinçer, H., Yüksel, S., Çağlayan, Ç., & Uluer, G. S. (2020). The contribution of nuclear energy investment on sustainable financial and economic development. *Journal of Financial Economics and Banking, 1*(1), 39–51.

Dinçer, H., Yüksel, S., & Martínez, L. (2022). Collaboration enhanced hybrid fuzzy decision-making approach to analyze the renewable energy investment projects. *Energy Reports, 8*, 377–389. doi:10.1016/j.egyr.2021.12.006

Dinçer, H., Yüksel, S., & Uluer, G. S. (2021). Understanding the impact of trade war between the US and China on oil price volatility. In *Global Tariff War: Economic, Political and Social Implications*. Emerald Publishing Limited. doi:10.1108/978-1-80071-314-720211013

Dong, W., Zhao, G., Yüksel, S., Dinçer, H., & Ubay, G. G. (2022). A novel hybrid decision making approach for the strategic selection of wind energy projects. *Renewable Energy, 185*, 321–337. doi:10.1016/j.renene.2021.12.077

Fang, S., Zhou, P., Dinçer, H., & Yüksel, S. (2021). Assessment of safety management system on energy investment risk using house of quality based on hybrid stochastic interval-valued intuitionistic fuzzy decision-making approach. *Safety Science, 141*, 105333. doi:10.1016/j.ssci.2021.105333

Haiyun, C., Zhixiong, H., Yüksel, S., & Dinçer, H. (2021). Analysis of the innovation strategies for green supply chain management in the energy industry using the QFD-based hybrid interval valued intuitionistic fuzzy decision approach. *Renewable & Sustainable Energy Reviews, 143*, 110844. doi:10.1016/j.rser.2021.110844

Hammoudeh, S., & Yuan, Y. (2008). Metal volatility in presence of oil and interest rate shocks. *Energy Economics, 30*(2), 606–620. doi:10.1016/j.eneco.2007.09.004

Hanif, I. (2018). Energy consumption habits and human health nexus in Sub-Saharan Africa. *Environmental Science and Pollution Research International, 25*(22), 21701–21712. doi:10.100711356-018-2336-0 PMID:29790046

He, L., Ding, Z., Yin, F., & Wu, M. (2016). The impact of relative energy prices on industrial energy consumption in China: A consideration of inflation costs. *SpringerPlus, 5*(1), 1–21. doi:10.118640064-016-2661-z PMID:27398277

Irz, X., Niemi, J., & Liu, X. (2013). Determinants of food price inflation in Finland—The role of energy. *Energy Policy, 63*, 656–663. doi:10.1016/j.enpol.2013.09.023

Johnsson, F., Kjärstad, J., & Rootzén, J. (2019). The threat to climate change mitigation posed by the abundance of fossil fuels. *Climate Policy, 19*(2), 258–274. doi:10.1080/14693062.2018.1483885

Jones, K. (2013). *Richard Martin: SuperFuel (Thorium, the Green Energy Source for the Future)*. Academic Press.

Kalair, A., Abas, N., Saleem, M. S., Kalair, A. R., & Khan, N. (2021). Role of energy storage systems in energy transition from fossil fuels to renewables. *Energy Storage, 3*(1), e135. doi:10.1002/est2.135

Kaufmann, R. K., Gonzalez, N., Nickerson, T. A., & Nesbit, T. S. (2011). Do household energy expenditures affect mortgage delinquency rates? *Energy Economics, 33*(2), 188–194. doi:10.1016/j.eneco.2010.07.007

Kostis, P., Dinçer, H., & Yüksel, S. (2022). Knowledge-Based Energy Investments of European Economies and Policy Recommendations for Sustainable Development. *Journal of the Knowledge Economy*, 1–33. doi:10.100713132-022-00972-5

Kou, G., Yüksel, S., & Dinçer, H. (2022). Inventive problem-solving map of innovative carbon emission strategies for solar energy-based transportation investment projects. *Applied Energy, 311*, 118680. doi:10.1016/j.apenergy.2022.118680

Krömer, S., & Gatzert, N. (2018). Renewable energy investments with storage: a risk-return analysis. *International Journal of Energy Sector Management.*

Li, Y. X., Wu, Z. X., Dinçer, H., Kalkavan, H., & Yüksel, S. (2021). Analyzing TRIZ-based strategic priorities of customer expectations for renewable energy investments with interval type-2 fuzzy modeling. *Energy Reports, 7*, 95–108. doi:10.1016/j.egyr.2020.11.167

Meng, Y., Zhou, R., Dinçer, H., Yüksel, S., & Wang, C. (2021). Analysis of inventive problem-solving capacities for renewable energy storage investments. *Energy Reports, 7*, 4779–4791. doi:10.1016/j.egyr.2021.06.086

Mukhtarov, S., Yüksel, S., & Dinçer, H. (2022). The impact of financial development on renewable energy consumption: Evidence from Turkey. *Renewable Energy, 187*, 169–176. doi:10.1016/j.renene.2022.01.061

Ratti, R. A., & Vespignani, J. L. (2013). Why crude oil prices are high when global activity is weak? *Economics Letters, 121*(1), 133–136. doi:10.1016/j.econlet.2013.07.002

Ray, P. (2019). Renewable energy and sustainability. *Clean Technologies and Environmental Policy, 21*(8), 1517–1533. doi:10.100710098-019-01739-4

Salisu, A. A., Isah, K. O., Oyewole, O. J., & Akanni, L. O. (2017). Modelling oil price-inflation nexus: The role of asymmetries. *Energy*, *125*, 97–106. doi:10.1016/j.energy.2017.02.128

Sek, S. K. (2017). Impact of oil price changes on domestic price inflation at disaggregated levels: Evidence from linear and nonlinear ARDL modeling. *Energy*, *130*, 204–217. doi:10.1016/j.energy.2017.03.152

Serezli, E., Yüksel, S., Tamer, İ., & Dinçer, H. (2021). The Role of Innovative Renewable Energy Investment Strategies on Macroeconomic Stability. In *Financial Strategies in Competitive Markets* (pp. 165–178). Springer. doi:10.1007/978-3-030-68612-3_12

Shahbaz, M., Raghutla, C., Chittedi, K. R., Jiao, Z., & Vo, X. V. (2020). The effect of renewable energy consumption on economic growth: Evidence from the renewable energy country attractive index. *Energy*, *207*, 118162. doi:10.1016/j.energy.2020.118162

Stearns, P. N. (2020). *The industrial revolution in world history*. Routledge. doi:10.4324/9781003050186

Stern, D. I., & Cleveland, C. J. (2004). *Energy and Economic Growth*. Rensselaer Polytechnic Institute.

Su, C. W., Khan, K., Tao, R., & Umar, M. (2020). A review of resource curse burden on inflation in Venezuela. *Energy*, *204*, 117925.

Swan, L. G., & Ugursal, V. I. (2009). Modeling of end-use energy consumption in the residential sector: A review of modeling techniques. *Renewable & Sustainable Energy Reviews*, *13*(8), 1819–1835. doi:10.1016/j.rser.2008.09.033

Wan, Q., Zhao, X., Liu, H., Dinçer, H., & Yüksel, S. (2022). Assessing the New Product Development Process for the Industrial Decarbonization of Sustainable Economies. *SAGE Open*, *12*(1). doi:10.1177/21582440211067231

Xie, Y., Peng, Y., Yüksel, S., Dınçer, H., Uluer, G. S., Çağlayan, Ç., & Li, Y. (2020). Consensus-based public acceptance and mapping of nuclear energy investments using spherical and pythagorean fuzzy group decision making approaches. *IEEE Access: Practical Innovations, Open Solutions*, *8*, 206248–206263. doi:10.1109/ACCESS.2020.3037344

Xie, Y., Zhou, Y., Peng, Y., Dinçer, H., Yüksel, S., & an Xiang, P. (2021). An extended pythagorean fuzzy approach to group decision-making with incomplete preferences for analyzing balanced scorecard-based renewable energy investments. *IEEE Access: Practical Innovations, Open Solutions*, *9*, 43020–43035. doi:10.1109/ACCESS.2021.3065294

Yeap, G. P., & Lean, H. H. (2017). Asymmetric inflation hedge properties of housing in Malaysia: New evidence from nonlinear ARDL approach. *Habitat International*, *62*, 11–21. doi:10.1016/j.habitatint.2017.02.006

Yellen, J. L. (2017). Inflation, uncertainty, and monetary policy. *Business Economics (Cleveland, Ohio)*, *52*(4), 194–207. doi:10.105711369-017-0057-x

Yüksel, S., & Çağlayan, Ç. (2020). The factors affecting the investors' decisions: A study on nuclear energy investments. *Economics Literature*, *2*(2), 177–185. doi:10.22440/elit.2.2.5

Yüksel, S., Dinçer, H., Çağlayan, Ç., & Uluer, G. S. (2021). Determining the Optimal Financial Strategies for Nuclear Energy Companies. In *Financial Strategies in Competitive Markets* (pp. 1–16). Springer. doi:10.1007/978-3-030-68612-3_1

Yüksel, S., Dinçer, H., Çağlayan, Ç., & Uluer, G. S. (2021). Strategy development to improve the business performance of nuclear energy companies. In *Management Strategies to Survive in a Competitive Environment* (pp. 33–46). Springer. doi:10.1007/978-3-030-72288-3_3

Yüksel, S., Dinçer, H., Çağlayan, Ç., Uluer, G. S., & Lisin, A. (2022). Bitcoin Mining with Nuclear Energy. In *Multidimensional Strategic Outlook on Global Competitive Energy Economics and Finance*. Emerald Publishing Limited. doi:10.1108/978-1-80117-898-320221019

Yüksel, S., Dinçer, H., & Karakuş, H. (2020). Determination of Income and Expense Items That Have a High Impact on The Profitability of Turkish Banks. *Journal of Financial Economics and Banking*, *1*(1), 1–9.

Yüksel, S., & Kavak, P. T. (2019). Do financial investment decisions affect economic development?: An analysis on mortgage loans in Turkey. In *Handbook of research on global issues in financial communication and investment decision making* (pp. 168–191). IGI Global. doi:10.4018/978-1-5225-9265-5.ch009

Yüksel, S., & Ubay, G. G. (2021). Determination of optimal financial government incentives in wind energy investments. In *Strategic outlook in business and finance innovation: Multidimensional policies for emerging economies*. Emerald Publishing Limited. doi:10.1108/978-1-80043-444-820211003

Yuksel, S., & Zengin, S. (2016). Causality relationship between import, export and growth rate in developing countries. *International Journal of Commerce and Finance*, 2(1), 147–156.

Zhang, Y., Zhang, Y., Gong, C., Dinçer, H., & Yüksel, S. (2022). An integrated hesitant 2-tuple Pythagorean fuzzy analysis of QFD-based innovation cost and duration for renewable energy projects. *Energy*, *248*, 123561. doi:10.1016/j.energy.2022.123561

Zhou, P., Luo, J., Cheng, F., Yüksel, S., & Dinçer, H. (2021). Analysis of risk priorities for renewable energy investment projects using a hybrid IT2 hesitant fuzzy decision-making approach with alpha cuts. *Energy*, *224*, 120184. doi:10.1016/j.energy.2021.120184

Chapter 15
Breaking Supply Chains and Inflationist Impact in the COVID-19 Process:
The Example of Turkey

Meltem Duğru
Trakya Üniversitesi Uzunköprü Uygulamali Bilimler Yüksekokulu, Turkey

ABSTRACT

The COVID-19 pandemic started as a process full of uncertainties, and the first case was detected in Turkey in March 2020. The panic process that started after that date has had negative effects on the economy in the following periods. While the effects have reflections on foreign trade due to the fact that it is a global process, the change in consumption and demand patterns in the country has changed all the balances. Thus, it is important to address the changes in almost every aspect of our lives and to examine them during the crisis period. Breaking the supply chains in the changing balances and to understand the importance of the supply chains accordingly are the subjects of this study. This study investigated how Turkey spent the COVID-19 process due to its economic structure and geopolitical location and, in addition, how it managed its supply chains. As a result of the research, it was concluded that if the deficits in the supply chains can be evaluated, the crisis process can be turned into an opportunity.

INTRODUCTION

Due to the systematic structure brought about by globalization, supply chains have become quite complex. Due to this tangle of relations, it seems unlikely that countries can act independently of each other. The Covid-19 disease, which emerged in 2019 and was declared a pandemic, has been the most real indicator of how interconnected the countries of supply chains.

Although there is no economic reason for the outbreak of the epidemic, when it is evaluated in terms of its consequences, it is seen that it has turned into an economic crisis that affects the whole world. This disease, which broke out in the Asian Region but spread rapidly to other countries in the world, is

DOI: 10.4018/978-1-6684-5876-1.ch015

destabilizes global economies. The world, which is both a producer and a consumer, is difficulties in both aspects. The fact that production came to a standstill in the face of an unexpected shock has caused and continues to cause order and stock problems for many sectors.

In order to produce a good, not all inputs are provided from the sources within the country. In order to produce a good, not all inputs are provided from the sources within the country. Purchasing these inputs from countries where they are cheaper creates an advantage when evaluated in terms of efficiency. In other words, the existence of cheap alternatives necessitates the trade of intermediate goods or raw materials with other countries. From this point of view, it is seen that almost all of the world's countries make both production and distribution through their supply chains. However, the fact that this trade flow encounters problems affects developing countries such as Turkey and Argentina, which have a fragile structure, even more. When the pandemic period is evaluated, it is seen that not only the financial fragility but also the vaccination rates and the quality of the health system are among the reasons that disrupt the flow of trade.

In countries where vaccination is slow or the health system is inadequate, workers cannot be employed due to the prolonged closing time. The closure of workplaces, factories, institutions or ports causes the duration of the trade relationship with other countries to prolong. Moreover, to be inadequate of labor force during the transportation of goods from one place to another causes difficulties in transportation. In addition to all these, problems occur in production and distribution when the workforce dies due to illness or does not want to work anymore in the sectors that provide the relevant supplies. For example, the chip crisis in the automotive industry has been one of the most important indicators of the rupture in supply chains. The slowdown of production due to various reasons in chip producing companies, or even coming to a standstill, has caused disruptions in orders. Because the supply chain includes a process that starts from the manufacturer, reaches the distributor, retailer and finally the consumer. Incorrectly to be planning of this process or to be encountering an unexpected situation has affected all links of the chain. As a result of this reduction in supply, prices in the automotive market increased extraordinarily compared to the previous period. In fact, consumers have increased their demands with the expectation that prices will rise even more. At this point, a production planning problem was encountered and it is seen that this problem still continues.

Constrictions in energy supply have also led to price increases in sectors where energy is used, just like in the automotive sector. In particular, the economies of countries that are heavily dependent on energy imports, such as Turkey, have been severely affected by these fluctuations. The agricultural sector, where energy dependency is high and basic foodstuffs are produced, is closely followed in Turkey as well as in all countries of the world. When the share of the agricultural sector in Turkey from past to present is examined, it can be said that every positive or negative development related to the agricultural sector is important for Turkey, since it is an indispensable field. When evaluated in this sense, it is seen that the increase in fuel and electricity costs also seriously affects the agricultural sector. When look at the pandemic period, both the rupture in the supply chains and the increase in the energy costs, which are imported to a large extent, are reflected in the agricultural inputs and increase the production costs. There are reflections of these cost increases have reflections on the economy. Moreover, the increase in fertilizer, seed and drug prices has become so important that it creates a food crisis for countries that import these inputs and produce agricultural products.

In addition to the evaluation made mainly on the basis of supply so far, it is necessary to mention demand or consumption. The reason for this is the decrease in total consumption expenditures as a result of the rise in the general level of prices stemming from production declines. As a result of the decrease in consumption expenditures, the national product of many countries has also decreased. At the same time, the contraction in demand caused a relative contraction in supply. Although consumption increased in an environment of panic and uncertainty when the closures started in the early days of the epidemic, after this time the tendency to save started. There was no change in the demand for basic consumer goods, but luxury consumption was postponed. Although the idea of saving predominated for a while, it was observed that the demand increased afterwards in order to protect against inflation, which was in a constantly increasing trend. The producer sector, which was not ready for the changing consumer spending patterns, could not adapt to this and the supply was insufficient to meet the demand.

The depreciation of the domestic currencies of developing countries against the dollar also put companies that borrowed in foreign currency into difficulties in this process. Investments have decreased, have followed by income declines with employment. Uncertainty in the purchasing decisions of consumers whose incomes decreased has did another reason that affected new investments or made them come to life with a delay. On the other hand, the increase in imported input costs significantly have affected the price policies of companies. Since the increase in the exchange rate caused cost pressure, the sales of the companies that had to reflect this on their prices have decreased.

As a result, in this economic system, it is seen that supply and demand progress in an intertwined cycle and supply chains have a very complex structure. It is possible that every crisis experienced in the world, where the reality of globalization exists, can have a global impact. It is clear that it will take time to adapt to the new world order after the crisis and its delayed effects may affect macroeconomic balances over time. For this reason, if a serious break occurs in the supply chains of all world economies, including Turkey, it is possible that they will encounter higher inflation rates. If such a situation occurs, a process in which cost inflation cannot be stopped will be inevitable. For these reasons, the issue of how supply chains affect the global economy and Turkey during the Covid-19 process is important. Based on all of these, in this study, the extent to which Turkey, which is a developing economy, was affected by this process, the effects of the break in supply chains and the phenomenon of inflation on the economy were investigated.

BACKGROUND

Inflation

There are many definitions in the literature for the phenomenon of inflation, both narrowly and broadly. However, it is generally accepted as a continuous increase in the general level of prices. Therefore, first of all, it is necessary to define price stability. Price stability is achieved when economic agents no longer care about possible changes in the general price level when making economic decisions (Greenspan, 1996). Therefore, paying attention to price changes and being felt most in daily life shows that there is no price stability. If price stability is in the form of an upward deterioration in developing countries such as Turkey, it can lead to serious inflation problems. Thus, the meltdown in the disposable income of households and companies may cause them to buy less or give up some of them.

The upward trend in prices is a common situation in developing countries such as Turkey. When the reasons for price increases are examined, it is seen that they are generally caused by costs. Due to the fragility of the economy and financial structure, it shows itself in a short time by reflecting on the costs. For this reason, when the economic history from past to present is examined, it can be said that the times

Figure 1. Inflation Rates in the 2000s
Data Source: (TÜİK, 2022a)

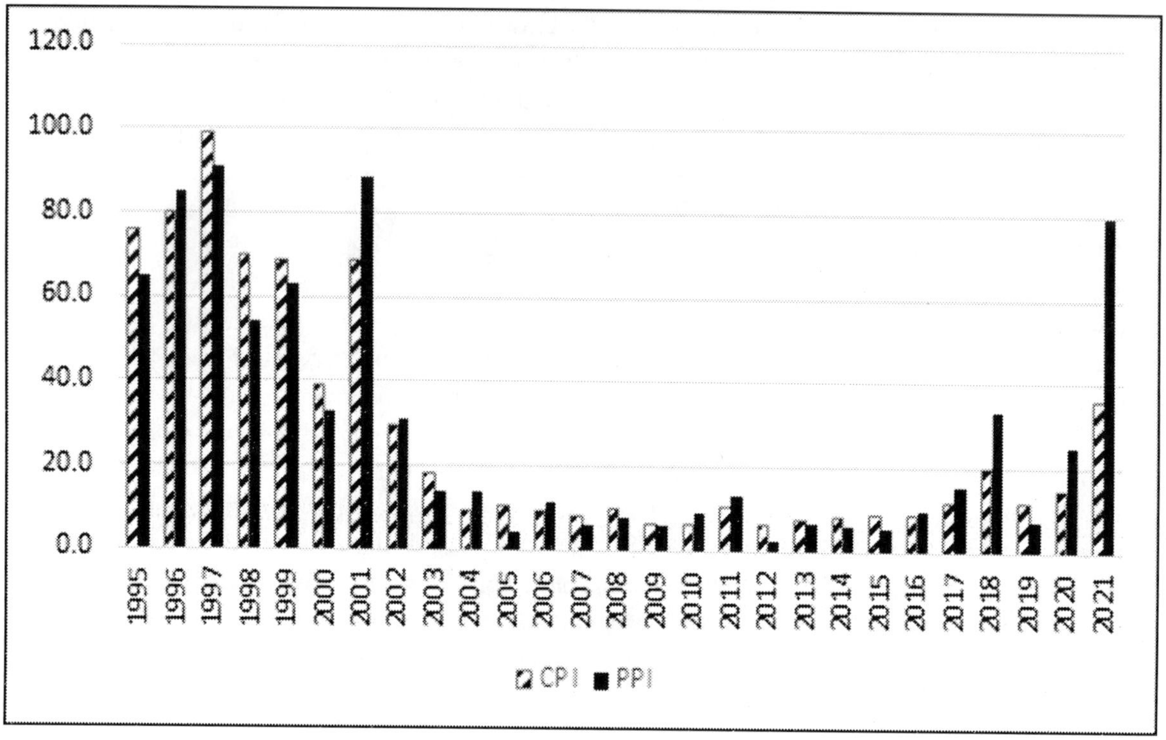

when inflation was the main actor were in the majority. The fact that the inflation phenomenon means a lot for Turkey makes it necessary to analyze it from a historical perspective.

With the legacy inherited from the Ottoman Empire, Turkey was left alone with debts in the first years of the Republic. At the same time, various efforts were made to keep the macroeconomic indicators, including inflation, positive. The economic crises experienced from time to time affected the implemented programs and created problems in reaching the targets. Considering today's modern societies, as a result of the complex system brought about by globalization, the globalization of crises has also occurred. The most recent example of this situation has been experienced with the Covid-19 crisis. The Covid-19 pandemic, which emerged suddenly and unexpectedly for the world, has confirmed how complex the process is. Countries that have direct trade relations with each other have been more affected by this, and countries outside this trade relationship have also suffered indirectly. Again, issues such as the development level of countries and vaccination rates were also influential in this process due to the fact that there was a fast spreading virus. When the whole process is taken into account, it has been observed that Turkey, which has aimed for price stability for many years, faced the highest inflation rates in the 2000s after the 2001 crisis. These ratios are presented with the help of Figure 1.

As can be seen from the graph, significant increases occurred in both PPI and CPI during the 2000-2001 crisis years. The reason for the increase in inflation rates in these years is not entirely related to the internal dynamics of the Turkish economy. The negativities that emerged in Russia just before the crisis and the subsequent Marmara earthquake caused permanent damage to the economy. Again, the economic crisis that emerged in Argentina at the beginning of the 2000s created problems in the current account balance through international capital movements. In addition, as a result of problems with the financial system in the country, inflation reached 70 percent. Afterwards although the economic programs implemented and the change of the inflation targeting strategy ended this rise somewhat, it has reminded itself again in recent years with the Covid-19 epidemic.

In some studies based on inflation during the epidemic period, some findings were obtained regarding the differences between developed and developing countries. In this period, while the phenomenon of deflation emerged for developed countries, it was observed that the phenomenon of inflation predominated in developing countries. Especially at the beginning of the epidemic period, the decrease in oil prices has led to thoughts that it will reduce the inflationary pressure in Turkey. However, the fact that oil prices were not the only factor causing inflation enabled the research to be deepened (Banerjee et al., 2020). In addition to the inflationary pressure, the tension experienced with the contraction in both the demand and supply sides revealed the danger of stagflation. The concept of inflation, which most of the developing countries are used to, has begun to make itself felt by disrupting the economic balances in developed countries. Exactly at this point, inflation, which has emerged as a major problem, combined with a recession in the economy to become a major problem stands as a possibility in front of the world.

Stagflation is a concept that was first introduced in the 1970s. In these years, the end of the Bretton Woods system and the oil crisis have brought together many economic problems. This process, which broke out with the increase in oil prices by the Petroleum Exporting Countries (OPEC), led to stagnation in production and in the world economy. The decrease in production capacity as a result of the negative supply shock has led to an increase in unemployment. Although the rise in unemployment rates slightly decreased inflation, it became high and continuous as a result of the continued increase in oil prices. When this rise combined with the stagnation in other macroeconomic indicators, the crisis has emerged (Mankiw, 2017). It was the economist Milton Friedman who expressed this concept. In his 1968 study, Friedman suggested that inflation and unemployment can coexist (Friedman, 1968). In the Covid-19 process, it was observed that macro variables followed a fluctuating course. In particular, the fact that the measurements to be made on the employment side could not be made in a healthy way due to reasons such as closures and business process changes, caused no clear results to be obtained. In addition, it was observed that there were changes in the driving forces of inflation. Because the collapse of economic activity, the sudden decrease in oil prices and the depreciation of the exchange rates of developing countries made it difficult for economists to forecast inflation (Banerjee et al., 2020).

The slowdown in production as a result of the disruptions in the supply chains during the epidemic and the increase in unemployment caused the supply-demand balance to deteriorate. The addition of high price increases to these problems reminded the economies of the 1970s. Despite the stagflation experienced in those years, measures such as increasing interest rates and reducing expenditures brought inflation under control on the one hand, and slowed the growth rate on the other. Countries that have increased interest rates and the FED which is expected to increase more than once in 2022, are looking for ways to get out of this cycle. Compared to the 1970s, this process we are in, seems to be advantageous because there are more tools and economic policies. For these reasons, the estimated inflation rates are more moderate. Graph 2 shows OECD inflation forecasts for some countries and regions.

As can be seen from the chart, when the first quarter of 2022 is evaluated, it is seen that a consistent expectation has been established for China and OECD countries. However, the same cannot be said for the Euro Zone and the USA. Because it is seen that the actual inflation rates are at least 1 point higher than expected. If evaluated for the USA, it has been declared that it is the highest inflation rate since 1982 by the economy administration. The monetary expansion carried out by the USA in the early stages

Figure 2. OECD Inflation Forecasts for China, Euro Area, OECD Countries (%)
Data Source: (OECD, 2022)

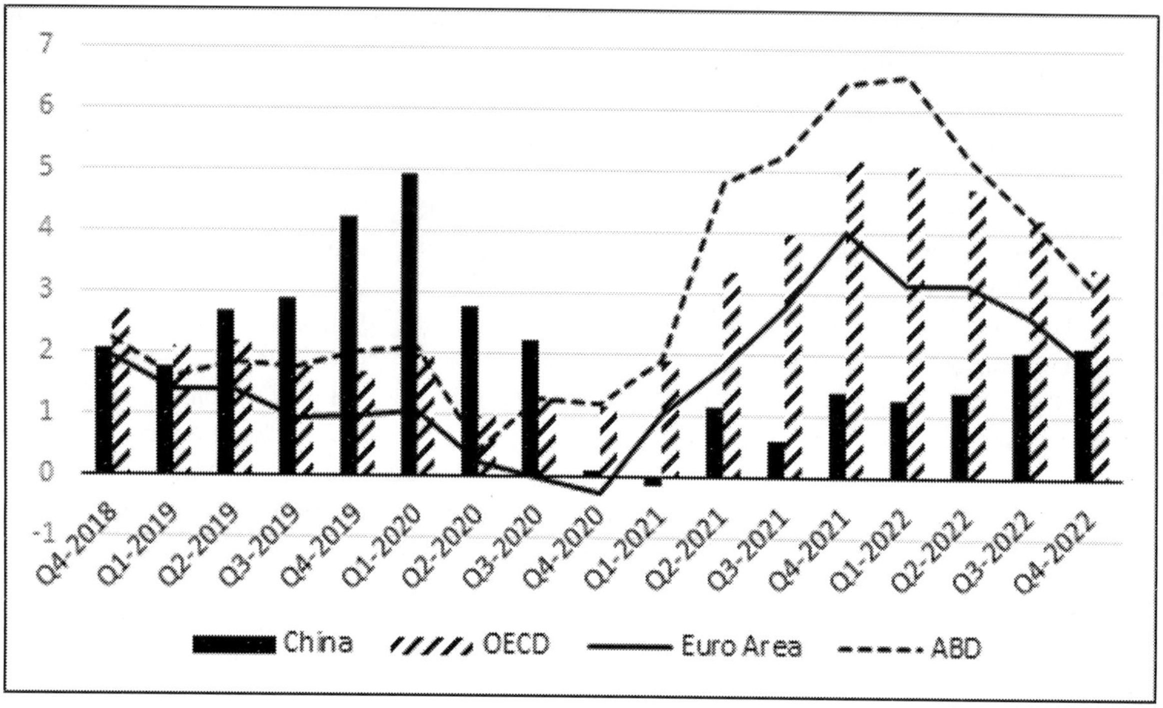

of the epidemic caused an increase in demand. In the same period, disruptions in supply chains brought along price increases along with monetary expansion. The Russia-Ukraine war that followed, fueling food and energy prices, and caused increased inflation. Especially for European countries, which have a high energy dependence on Russia, the realization of the war upset all the balances. The Euro Zone trying to get out of the Covid process with the least damage has made a statement that interest rate interventions will be made at an earlier date for price increases that exceed expectations. As a result, the rise in food and energy prices, as in the whole world, has shaken the USA and European countries economically and continues to dominate.

The deterioration in supply chains which more understood the importance of during the crisis periods, has become one of the important reasons for the increase in inflation especially during the epidemic period. The reason for this is, the markets which faced with an unfamiliar situation cannot adequately measure and predict the situation they are in. It is very worrying that the regions affected by the epidemic are important regions in terms of supply. For this reason, it is necessary to examine the supply chains in detail.

Supply chain

Supply is a common goal of almost every function in the chain and is strategically important because of its impact on costs and market share. The management of this chain, works like a balancing mechanism and offers a different perspective to stocks. At the same time, it provides integration by bringing a new approach to a classically functioning system (Houlihan, 1988). If we look at the scope of the supply chain, it starts with the source of supply and ends at the point of consumption. There are activities related to the planning, coordination and control of materials, parts, finished and piece products from the supplier to the customer. In addition to these transportation and distribution works, supplier management, material management, purchasing, facility planning, production management, customer service and information flow also complete the process. In fact, the purpose of managing this chain is to ensure that in order to provide a high level of customer service, customer needs operate in harmony with the material flow to be obtained from the supplier (Stevens, 1989).

Supply chain management, on the other hand, is a process that companies engage in to gain competitive advantage. Thanks to the convenience created by technology and communication, developments such as the increase in product diversity, developments in information technology, the inclusion of enterprises in the global system, the increasing use of outsourcing and the short product life cycle make the management of supply chains complicated. In particular, the existence of the internet contributes to both the ever-increasing and diversifying needs and the situations that can be considered as opportunities for the business by providing instant access. Thus, businesses can respond to new product and service demands in a shorter time. In other words, companies must manage the process well in order not to face situations that drive their supply chains out of control, such as over stock, increased costs, decreased profits and customer service that should not be. Therefore, the right supply chain strategies should be combined with the right demand and supply (Lee, 2002). It is necessary to make updates in the supply chains in order to accurately predict expectations regarding certain factors such as the changing social structure, going out of the ordinary in consumption patterns, and changes in shopping methods. It is clear that countries and sectors that can respond quickly to these changes can overcome the crisis with less damage than others.

The biggest example of the changing social structure is the consumer habits that started to change during the epidemic and are no longer the same as before. While the demand for some products and services has increased, for others it has decreased. Particularly, there has been a serious decrease in energy consumption compared to the global financial crisis in 2008. The measures taken by countries due to the contagiousness of the epidemic and than the ensuing recession caused a decrease of approximately 8.8 percent in oil demand in 2020 (IEA, 2021). In addition, people started to work from home and their old lifestyles were replaced by a new one. Before, when people went to their workplaces for the purchase of a need, they now use the online ordering method over the internet. E-commerce has become frequently used in ready-made clothing along with the food sector. In fact, businesses have started to sell by promoting and marketing over the internet, sometimes from home and sometimes by renting a place with cheaper rent. There has also been an increase in the demand for larger and more roomed houses by individuals who have turned part of their homes into offices. As a result, it is seen that this changing demand and marketing understanding has also changed the habits in the supply chains. For this reason, it is important that the supply chain infrastructure is designed according to the new order, not according to the old methods. This new order entered into a restructuring after the Covid-19 epidemic, thus caused to emerge some problems in the supply chains. Thus, the advantageous situation of the Asian region, whose importance in both supply chains and production was high until the crisis period, was opened to discussion with the crisis period.

The Covid-19 Process and the Breaking of Supply Chains

Covid-19, which was announced to have first appeared in the Wuhan region of the People's Republic of China, has spread to other countries of the world with an unexpected speed. As a result of the seriousness of the epidemic and its effectiveness in a short time, it was declared as a pandemic which means a global epidemic by the World Health Organization (WHO) at the beginning of 2020. Due to the fact that the epidemic is contagious and an unusual situation, countries have started to seek various remedies. Thus, they prepared package of measures within the framework of their own dynamics and put them into practice together with the other measures they took. Within the scope of the measures, especially the restrictions at the border crossings and the quarantine practices made at certain periods caused the current system to be disrupted. As a result of the disruptions experienced, the sectoral activities based on labor force showed itself as slowing down or coming to a standstill. This contraction in supply also affected employment by narrowing the demand for labor. On the other hand, as a result of the decrease in the productivity of employment and the uncertainty formed, consumers have reduced their demands and the threat of recession has emerged.

The process described above was not limited to just one country or sector, affected all world economies. Considering the integration levels of the countries, it was seen that the epidemic created serious problems in terms of international trade and investment activities. In addition, it also reminded the importance of supply chains in the face of an unexpected and sudden shock. In fact, the Covid-19 process has given the world some signals about supply chains. Although this situation was noticed by many countries before the epidemic, it was ignored due to cost advantages. However, with the epidemic, starting to the closure of the factories and the serious decrease in the production capacities of the facilities have brought this fact to light.

Facility closures or supply shortages across an expanded supply network have created a domino effect and disrupted these chains. There has been a process in which more than 200 of the Fortune Global 500 companies and their close suppliers are directly affected under the assumption that they are located in and around Wuhan. At the same time, in addition to the fact that Wuhan, which is the transportation center of many industries, is the largest port of the People's Republic of China has a developed infrastructure in air, land and sea transportation, has had an impact both directly and indirectly (Kilpatrick & Barter, 2020). Due to its many advantages, the People's Republic of China gained quite well in this monopolistic structure until the epidemic and increased its per capita national product to $ 9,770 in 2018 (Worldbank, 2022b). However, the increase in the costs of the supply chains rather than the increase in the production cost experienced with the crisis made the countries of the world look for alternatives. Because the fact that the supply chains are largely in the same region carries a risk, just as seen during the epidemic period, except during a normal times.

There are main reasons why supply chains have serious problems during the epidemic period. These reasons (Ercin, 2020):

- As a result of the pandemic, the production of raw materials decreased and this caused fluctuations in prices. At the same time, the service provided by the logistics sector faced problems. As a result of all these, the trade of companies importing raw materials was adversely affected.
- Another problem for companies was their sales forecasts. Because supply chain programs are based on sales decisions. Since the predictability was limited during the epidemic period, it was very difficult to make instant decisions and then to plan the supply chain.

- Finally, in addition to the difficulty of managing the stages from the beginning to the end of the business process, there were problems in delivery and payment to the customer. At the same time, the fluctuating market balance caused delays in the delivery times of the demanded products or services.

As can be seen, due to the critical importance of supply chains concerning all markets, they can affect the whole world in the face of sudden shocks. A disruption in these chains can make it hard a sector in itself or many sectors as seen during the pandemic process. In other words, it seems that it is more difficult to predict where the economic dimensions of the epidemic may reach, apart from estimating how serious the epidemic may reach (BOMA, 2007).

For this reason, there are some measures to be taken in the short term regarding supply chains. These; ensuring the safety of employees and customers, enabling companies to improve their crisis management and taking action plans as well as taking measures to improve continuity in their supply chains. At the same time, it is another short-term measure for companies to adjust their working capital by regulating their cash flows and liquidity management. In the medium and long term, other recommendations are to make technological infrastructure investments, to make risk analyzes of supplier companies and to create micro supply chains (Ercin, 2020).

When the structure of supply chains is evaluated today, it is seen that the process from production to sales is in the form of an a nested system. This system has a complex structure and is carried out in a planned manner. In a globalized structure, the extent of the countries' participation or which angle to in this system entirely shaped by their own decisions. Because countries can buy any raw material and intermediate goods that they cannot produce themselves or produced at a higher cost from other countries, thanks to this network. Thus, there is a structure that both the public and the private sector are in or prefer to be in on the basis of sectors.

Global Trade and Turkey's Foreign Trade Process

Considering the last two decades, China has become very important for the global economy. This increasing importance of China is not just about being an exporter or producing consumer goods. It is also about being the main supplier of intermediate inputs to manufacturing companies abroad. China, which realized 4 percent of the global trade in the manufacture of intermediate goods in 2002, has expanded its trade volume by 20 percent today. Especially since it produces automotive, precision instruments, machinery and communication tools, any interruption in the supply of these products has become very important for the rest of the world. The blocking of the supply of critical parts by Chinese manufacturers or the Chinese government causes serious problems for other suppliers in the production capacity and, in the export processes of these products after the production stage. For example, in some European countries, the fact that automobile manufacturers cannot reach the critical parts necessary for their production has affected their activities. Again, it has been difficult for some companies in Japan to obtain the necessary parts to assemble digital-capable cameras. For this reason, stock management became difficult and there were problems in order and delivery times. Thus, the supply cuts in China adversely affected the general exports of the world countries (UNCTAD, 2020). Considering the trade relationship of the epidemic region, it is seen that the largest share belongs to the USA. However, it should be noted that Germany, France, England and Spain also have significant activities (Dun &Bradstreet, 2020). The export and import data of China, which has foreign trade relations with many countries in the world and ranks first in world exports and second in imports, with some countries during the Covid-19 process should be carefully examined. According to these data, the USA ranks first among the countries that export the most from China in 2019 and 2020. Despite the long-standing trade wars between the two countries, it is seen that the trade relationship continues increasingly. Following the USA, countries such as Hong Kong, Japan and Vietnam maintain their trade in a stable manner, although their export volumes are less. While Turkey took its place in the lower ranks, its exports from China amounted to 17,321,763 dollars in 2019 and increased to 20,356,568 dollars by 2020. Thus, the export volume gained an upward momentum compared to the previous period. On the import side, similar figures could not be achieved. The volume of imports made by China from Turkey was at very low levels. However, it can be said that its imports with countries such as Taiwan, Japan, South Korea and the USA are highly developed and much more voluminous than Turkey (ITC, 2022a).

Similar to the previous years, the expansion in China's foreign trade volume continued in 2021 as well. In fact, the volume in 2021 has reached the level that will break its own record. At the same time, it exceeded expectations by showing a growth performance of 4.8 percent in the first quarter of 2022 compared to the previous period. However, the continuation of the Covid-19 process and the fact that the Chinese government continues to trade under these conditions arouses great curiosity for the statistics for the rest of the year.

When we look at Turkey's foreign trade partners, as explained in Table 1, China comes first among the importing countries. Considering the years 2019, 2020 and 2021, it is seen that China has come to a more advantageous position than Russia and Germany. While the import volume with Turkey was 19,128,160 dollars in 2019, it increased to 32,329,157 dollars in 2021. Although there was no rapid increase when Covid-19 was first detected, it made a serious attack in 2021 when the epidemic began to lose its effect. If Turkey's foreign trade balance is evaluated in terms of exports, Germany takes the lead as a good partner. Although Germany narrowed its export volume with Turkey in 2020, it compensated for this contraction in 2021 and reached more export volume. In Table 1, the import and export figures of the top ten countries with which Turkey has foreign trade are presented in detail.

Among the products imported from China, which ranks first in terms of imports, voice recorders, telephone sets for cellular networks and other wireless networks, electric motors and generators and telephone devices, all kinds of parts including electrical machinery and equipment, necessary parts and accessories for the iron and steel industry, various chemical products, furniture, and parts that appeal to many sectors such as glass are coming. Products such as iron and steel, mineral fuels, grain, animal feed, fertilizer, paper and cardboard goods are purchased from Russia, which has lost its import leadership to China in recent years. Products such as parts and accessories of vehicles other than railway or tramway wagons, parts of machinery and boilers, iron and steel goods, textiles, edible fruits, nuts, citrus fruits, aircraft parts, weapons and ammunition, glassware are sold to Germany and the USA where the most exports are made (ITC, 2022b).

When we look at the countries most affected by the epidemic period, there are countries with which Turkey has foreign trade with high volumes. The virus, which first appeared in the Asian region, spread to the world in a short time, and in the following process, it caused Europe to become the center of the epidemic. Thus, the problems experienced in the production process have largely stopped economic activities due to the deterioration in international trade. As a result of the negative developments experienced in 2019 reflected on the growth figures in 2020, there was a contraction in the global economy. With the contraction experienced, the global growth rate was announced as -3.3 percent in 2020, but Turkey

Table 1. Top 10 countries to which Turkey imports and exports

Export (Thousand dollars)				Import (Thousand dollars)			
Country	**2019**	**2020**	**2021**	**Country**	**2019**	**2020**	**2021**
Germany	16.617.244	15.978.698	19.316.249	China	19.128.160	23.041.354	32.239.157
ABD	8.970.658	10.182.966	14.721.715	Russia	23.115.236	17.829.309	28.959.361
United Kingdom	11.278.615	11.235.582	13.704.975	Germany	19.280.399	21.732.759	21.726.150
Italy	9.753.018	8.082.560	11.474.359	ABD	11.847.373	11.524.951	13.148.129
Iraq	10.223.292	9.142.047	11.129.720	Italy	9.349.593	9.199.617	11.561.815
Spain	8.138.744	6.683.488	9.615.257	India	6.635.217	4.830.115	7.936.138
France	7.945.607	7.195.168	9.111.756	France	6.760.064	6.988.074	7.931.527
Netherlands	5.761.921	5.195.120	6.768.687	South Korea	5.777.022	5.734.268	7.597.084
Israel	4.463.820	4.704.088	6.355.997	Spain	4.446.113	5.039.428	6.311.611
Russia	4.152.137	4.506.681	5.774.963	Belgium	3.229.280	3.716.088	5.628.382

Data Source: (TÜİK, 2022b)

became one of the few countries that differentiated positively. Between the years 2019-2021, Turkey's foreign trade balance and growth rates are presented with the help of Table 2.

Table 2. Foreign Trade Balance and Growth Rates in Turkey Between 2019-2021

Year	Turkey's foreign trade balance (billion dollars)	Turkey growth (%)
2019	-29,476,049	0.9
2020	-49,856,433	1.8
2021	-46,133,088	11.0

Data Source: (ITC, 2022c; TÜİK, 2022c).

When Turkey's foreign trade figures for 2019 are evaluated, the total export volume was approximately 181 billion dollars, while its total imports were at the level of 210 billion dollars. Based on these figures, the foreign trade volume reached 391 billion dollars in total and the foreign trade deficit was 29.5 billion dollars. On the other hand, the growth rate of the economy was realized as 0.9 percent, above the forecasts. Looking at the foreign trade figures for 2020, exports decreased a little more and amounted to approximately 170 billion dollars. On the contrary, there was an increase in imports and a volume of approximately 219.5 billion dollars was achieved. There was no major change in the foreign trade volume, however, due to the widening of the gap between imports and exports, the foreign trade deficit increased and reached the level of 49.85 billion dollars. The Turkish economy, which was experiencing an intense epidemic period, recorded a growth of 1.8 percent in 2020. Looking at the overall year 2021, there has been a significant increase in exports compared to the previous two periods, reaching a volume of approximately 225 billion dollars. Imports also kept pace with this increase and figures reaching 271.5 billion dollars were seen. For this reason, the total foreign trade volume increased and approached 496.5 billion dollars in total. Despite a significant increase in volume, the foreign trade deficit of 2021 remained at the level of 46 billion dollars. Economic growth, on the other hand, was at higher rates compared to G-20, EU and OECD countries (ITC, 2022c; TÜİK, 2022c; Worldbank, 2022a).

Considering these years, including the Covid-19 epidemic, foreign trade partners are important. During these periods, the most exported countries were Germany, USA, England and Italy, respectively. Imports were made from China, Russia, Germany, USA and Italy. The products subject to foreign trade are composed of raw materials, consumption and investment goods. It is very important that there is no problem in the supply chain of intermediate goods, consumption and investment goods to be imported, especially for Turkey, which is trying to carry out an export-based foreign trade with a high level of imported inputs. Otherwise, there will be a possibility of serious problems in the functioning of an export-based economy model.

In global trade, when 2021 is evaluated, the figures of the trade of goods and services before the Covid-19 epidemic have been reached. The global trade value realized in 2021 reached its highest level ever with $28.5 trillion. This increase was 13 percent compared to 2019 and 25 percent compared to 2020. However, the same cannot be said for the global trade volume in 2022. The reason for this is the ongoing Ukraine-Russia War. The continuation of the war in the following processes remains uncertain for the estimation of the 2022 world trade volume (UNCTAD, 2022).

Like all the countries of the world, Turkey has tried to produce economic policies depending on the developments both in the country and abroad. In particular, the uncertainties created by the Covid-19 outbreak have left businesses and households in a difficult situation, along with some sectors. For this reason, the negative effects of the epidemic on the Turkish economy and the results of the breaks in the supply chains are discussed in the next section. Especially automobile and white goods companies had to stop their production because they could not supply the intermediate goods and raw materials they needed. In case of limited production, working periods are shortened or permit processes are initiated.

Developments in Turkey in the Covid-19 Process

The Covid-19 epidemic has affected the supply chains in the world and the Turkish economy has also taken its share from it. The first emergence of the corona virus in China has been seen as an opportunity for our country for supply chains that are likely to be disrupted. However, its spread in Turkey in a very short time destroyed these expectations, and on the contrary, it caused panic in industries producing with imported inputs. Especially automobile and white goods companies had to stop their production because they could not supply the intermediate goods and raw materials they needed. In case of limited production, working periods are shortened or permit processes are initiated.In some countries such as Turkey, incentives were given under the name of short-time working allowance and measures were taken to prevent workers from being fired.

The measures taken in Turkey after the first case was detected on March 10 caused the production to be interrupted and even to a standstill. The slowdown of the production wheels with together the world has also slowed down the economic life, too. As a result of both in order to get out of this slowdown and to be difficult and uncertainties of the process, manufacturers have sought different ways. For this reason, instead of producing products that have problems in supply, products aimed at meeting the urgent needs of the day were preferred. Masks, plastic gloves, disinfectants and protectors, which are the most widely used in the treatment and prevention of the spread of the disease, and respiratory devices used for intubated patients have begun to be produced. Those whose capacity and means of production were suitable for these productions wanted to benefit from the conditions of the period. At the same time, the fact that it cannot be produced in every country of the world and that it creates a demand for sudden needs has caused it to be mutually accepted.

When it was announced that the contagiousness of the virus is at a high level and that hands should be washed constantly, the demand for cleaning and hygiene products increased along with it. Hand soaps, bleach, toilet paper and disinfectant products, especially cologne, entered a rapid sales process. It has not been easy to meet this rapid demand for cleaning and hygiene products. The stocking of some products by consumers has emerged as another reason for the deterioration of supply chains. Thus, both the purchase of the necessary products and the vacant shelves as a result of uncertain supply caused the supply chains to go through difficult processes. However, these disruptions were managed well with great effort by those in charge and the shelves were refilled. In addition, the thought that most of these products should be disposable or need to be bought again when they are exhausted has increased the sales of cleaning and hygiene products.

Another sector with increasing sales and demand was the food sector. Due to the possibility of supply constraints, people have turned to mass shopping and stocking from the markets. Although the restrictions applied in Turkey are sometimes long, certain time intervals have been determined in order to go to the markets in the same neighborhood. The fact that people's freedoms are subject to time constraints on the one hand creates uneasiness, on the other hand, not being able to find what they are looking for on the market shelves at the specified hours has caused concern. However, when the process in Turkey is evaluated in terms of the retail and food sector, it has been revealed that there are no serious problems in supply chains and consumption. Only as a result of the measures taken, businesses such as restaurants and cafes were in a difficult situation, and some of them had to close their workplaces.

When analyzed on a sectoral basis, it is seen that the developments in Turkey are in parallel with the developments in the world. During the crisis, positive developments were experienced in the health, pharmaceutical, food, retail and technological sectors, as well as in the personal care and hygiene-based products market and in the field of e-commerce. This situation is easily understood from the credit card and debit card statistics made during the epidemic period. According to these statistics, it can be determined that the most positively affected sectors are the food and retail sector. However, as a result of the contraction in the supply and demand side, the opposite is true especially for the service sector. Especially considering the changing consumption habits, it is seen that the tourism sector is greatly affected. The tourism sector is one of the most influential sectors in terms of making a positive contribution to Turkey's current account balance. In addition, it can be said that the transportation sector has contracted due to the closure of borders and the necessity of travel restrictions. Thus, serious disruptions have occurred in the supply chains and foreign trade activities have narrowed considerably. In addition to these, sectors such as automotive, real estate and construction, manufacturing, textile, energy, agriculture and finance are among those that were adversely affected in a short time (TÜRMOB, 2020).

It is not only consumers who were affected by the crisis created by the epidemic. Manufacturers have also experienced positive or negative developments according to the conditions of the period they are in, and they continue to do so. It is clear that they have difficulties in terms of production structures and supply stages with the experiences they have gained in the face of this sudden situation.

After the start of the epidemic process, a survey was conducted for Turkey with 314 participating enterprises in May 2020. In this survey, it was aimed to measure the performance of companies on the impact of the epidemic on the supply chain and it was determined that the companies had the most difficulty in demand forecasting. On the other hand, it has been observed that the difficulties in demand forecasting are mostly experienced in terms of industrial products or production, pharmaceuticals, health

Table 3. Literature review-1

Author	Conclusion
Banerjee et al., 2020	Panel quantile regression results were interpreted in the study conducted with a total of 43 countries, 12 of which were developed and 31 of which were developing. For developed countries, it is predicted that the collapse associated with the Covid-19 crisis will cause a downward movement in inflation in the short term, while it is stated that it will move inflation upwards for some developing countries.
Erdoğan et al., 2020	In the research conducted with the spatial panel data method for 28 EU members and member countries, it has been revealed that the changes in the exchange rate and money supply are the main reasons for the increase in inflation. Again, the fact that countries are neighbor to each other has also been effective in increasing the contagiousness of inflation.
Cavallo, 2020	In the research conducted for 16 countries, the effect of Covid-19 on the CPI was investigated. It has been observed that the inflation rate caused by the Covid-19 process is higher than the official CPI data announced in the USA, and there are similar results with the Covid baskets in 10 countries.
Apergis & Apergis, 2021	As a result of the examination on the US inflation of Covid-19 using daily data and the GARCHX model, it was revealed that the course of inflation expectations and the volatility in these expectations were positively affected by the pandemic process.

services and products, as well as covering all sectors. Since the devastating effect of the epidemic on the sectors is difficult to predict, it is thought that the use of remote working method negatively affects the performance of the supply chains team. For this reason, studies on structuring the operation parts for the post-epidemic period have been prioritized (Deloitte, 2020).

Turkey continues to take some precautions in terms of supply chains as well as trying to overcome the epidemic process in the best way possible. When these measures are spread over time, they are of a nature to help economic units that trade. The measures announced by the Ministry of Commerce under the name of 'Covid-19 Trade Measures' have been differentiated within themselves. It has been announced on its page by making separate arrangements for export, import, customs, domestic trade, consumer and artisan-craftsman cooperatives (TB, 2022). Thus, it is aimed to minimize the negative effects of the crisis within the scope of some regulations and activities.

In the literature, there are many studies on the break in supply chains and the inflationary process experienced during the Covid-19 process. Some of these studies are presented with the help of Table 3.

In the study published in the BIS bulletin, based on the phenomenon of inflation in the Covid-19 process for 43 countries' economies, developed and developing countries were discussed separately. While it has been determined that the crisis process has an increasing effect downside risks on inflation in the short term for developed countries, it is stated that for some developing countries, it will lead to a significant increase in the upside risks to inflation in connection with the exchange rate (Banerjee et al., 2020). In a study conducted for US inflation, it was determined that the volatility in inflation expectations and expectations was positive with the Covid-19 process by using swap rates (Apergis & Apergis, 2021). For the European Union member and candidate countries, the increase in the exchange rate and the expansion of the money supply by the countries were determined as the primary reasons for the increase in inflation (Erdoğan et al., 2020). Again, in a study conducted on 16 countries including the USA, it was concluded that the inflation created by Covid-19 was higher than the CPI rates announced in the USA and that it caused food prices to rise more due to social distance rules (Cavallo, 2020).

Table 4. Literature review-2

Author	Conclusion
Erdem, 2021	It has been discussed whether Covid-19 has any effect on imports and exports during the periods specified in the research conducted for Turkey. Structural change analysis was performed after the break period was determined by Bai and Perron tests. In February 2020, a break was detected and it was concluded that foreign trade was affected.
Ay, 2021	In the research conducted on the effects of the Covid-19 epidemic on Turkey's exports, it was determined that it had a serious contractionary effect in the second quarter of 2020.
Barua, 2021	In the study, it was stated that the global economy could be dragged into stagflation as a result of being seriously affected by the pandemic period.
Han et al., 2022	Based on the case situation during the Covid-19 epidemic process, the effect of the Turkish economy on the basic economic indicators has been examined. As a result of the analysis, it was seen that there was a significant difference between travel incomes and Covid-19 case results. Other variables with significant differences were determined as Euro, dollar, foreign exchange reserves, total loans, total payments, expenditure amount, consumer loans, unemployment, number of vehicles and imports. On the other hand, no significant difference was found between house sales, growth, inflation and exports.

The problems experienced during the Covid-19 process not only created inflation, but also disrupted the foreign trade balances of the countries. Especially the large share of foreign trade in the economy of countries such as Turkey makes the destruction caused by crises such as Covid-19 important. In a study covering the epidemic period, a break was determined for export and import indicators in February 2020. Although it was observed that the slopes of the import and export curves changed for a short time, it was observed that they quickly became old. Based on these indicators, it was stated that disruptions in supply chains could be an opportunity due to our proximity to the European continent (Erdem, 2021). In another study, which made a similar determination, it was determined that the contraction in exports at the beginning of 2020 deepened in the second quarter of the year. It has been revealed that the economy recovered in June, however, there was fluctuation in foreign trade due to the restriction measures taken afterwards (Ay, 2021). The effect on the basic economic indicators was examined with the t test and the Mann-Whitney U test, and it was determined that the epidemic process was effective on these indicators (Han et al., 2022). Barua, on the other hand, argued that due to the global impact scale of the COVID-19 outbreak will push many of the world's economies into recession and depression. He even stated that the large-scale effects of the continuation of the pandemic may cause stagflation (Barua, 2021).

Table 5. Literature review-3

Author	Conclusion
Siche, 2020	It has been stated that the Covid-19 crisis affects food safety and supply chains. At the same time, it has been determined that these negativities are more effective on the vulnerable population.
Hobbs, 2021	In the study conducted for Canada and the USA, performance in agri-food supply chains is discussed. It has also been stated that global investments lead to permanent changes.
Kerr, 2021	Based on the case situation during the Covid-19 epidemic process, the effect of the Turkish economy on the basic economic indicators has been examined. As a result of the analysis, it was seen that there was a significant difference between travel incomes and Covid-19 case results. Other variables with significant differences were determined as Euro, dollar, foreign exchange reserves, total loans, total payments, expenditure amount, consumer loans, unemployment, number of vehicles and imports. On the other hand, no significant difference was found between house sales, growth, inflation and exports.

In another study conducted for Canada and the USA, the change in agri-food supply chains was discussed. It has been stated that these chains have performed quite well during the pandemic, but when evaluated globally, the investments made have driven food retailing to permanent changes (Hobbs, 2021). In another study conducted for Canada, it was determined that although there were short-term interruptions for certain products during the epidemic process, market shelves were not left empty as a result of directing the supply chains. It has been stated that international trade in agricultural food products is minimally affected and there are no major problems in food imports (Kerr, 2021). Another study investigating the impact of the epidemic on food and agricultural supply chains found that food security was affected by the crisis and had a greater impact on the most vulnerable population (Siche, 2020).

CONCLUSION

The processes in which quarantines were experienced in the middle of 2020 caused very difficult times for the world. This period, when globalization reached its peak, showed once again how important international cooperation is. The Covid-19 crisis, which stunned everyone, emphasized that unity is necessary in all areas due to the level of integration of the world.

Despite the fact that Covid-19 is a crisis that has shaken the whole world socially and economically, what it left behind will continue to be discussed when it is completely over. Because a familiar world order is being reconstructed. Supply chains are also at the forefront of this structuring, with the task of being one of the most important building blocks. It is thought that planning will be made with more rational and more sustainable moves at the stage of supply chains. The reason for this is that problems are encountered above expectations during the crisis period.

An important issue that has been realized regarding supply chains during the crisis is that suppliers or their chains are predominantly located in the same regions. For this reason, it has come to the fore to keep it in more strategic locations rather than just being collected in one place. It is clear that it would be an opportunity for some world countries to want to expand the concentration of supply chains in one region due to both the financing cost and the production cost. At this point, considering both its geographical location and capacity, Turkey is thought to be one of the best alternatives in terms of supply chains. Thus, it will be a big step in achieving the economic stability it needs. In addition, it may bring positive results such as the revival of some idle areas in the manufacturing sector or the sector's desire to make productions that they had given up before. The difficulties in the sectors as a result of the disruptions in the supply chains may justify these efforts for the future, and may also inspire some sub-sectors to turn this crisis into an opportunity.

When all these are evaluated, no matter how negative and unmanageable the process is, it will bring opportunities for some countries and sectors. Capturing the technology contained in new supply chains will gain importance today and in the future. Supply chain technologies including digitalization make it necessary to include artificial intelligence, the use of robotics and 5G technologies. For this reason, it is thought that even though there are renewal or structuring in many areas, the countries that attach importance to digitalization will be in the part that provides the greatest advantage.

REFERENCES

Apergis, E., & Apergis, N. (2021). Inflation expectations, volatility and Covid-19: Evidence from the US inflation swap rates. *Applied Economics Letters, 28*(15), 1327–1331. doi:10.1080/13504851.2020.1813245

Ay, İ. C. (2021). COVID-19 Pandemisinin Türkiye'nin İhracatı Üzerine Etkileri İçin Bir Analiz. *JOEEP: Journal of Emerging Economies and Policy*, *6*(1), 41–60.

Banerjee, R. N., Mehrotra, A., & Zampolli, F. (2020). Inflation at risk from Covid-19. Bank for International Settlements, 28.

Barua, S. (2020). Understanding Coronanomics: The economic implications of the coronavirus (COVID-19) pandemic. *Journal of Developing Areas, 55*(3), 435–450. doi:10.1353/jda.2021.0073

Boma. (2007). Planning Guide for Commercial Buildings Influenza Pandemic. *Building Owners and Managers Association of Canada*, 4-95.

Cavallo, A. (2020). Inflation with Covid consumption baskets (No. w27352). National Bureau of Economic Research.

Deloitte. (2020). *COVID-19 Sonrası Tedarik Zincirlerinde Kazananlar ve Kaybedenler*. https://www2.deloitte.com/content/dam/Deloitte/tr/Documents/consumer-business/Covid19sonrasitedarikzinciri.pdf

Dun & Bradstreet. (2020). *Business Impact of the Coronavirus: Business and Supply Chain Analysis Due to the Coronavirus Outbreak, Special Brifing Dun & Bradstreet*. https://www.dnb.com/marketing/media/supplier-report-coronavirus.html

Ercin, S. (2020). Covid-19 döneminde etkili tedarik zinciri yönetimi. *KPMG*, 1-39.

Erdem, A. (2021). Covid-19 Salgınının Türkiye'nin Dış Ticaretine Etkisi: Bir Yapısal Kırılma Analizi. *İzmir İktisat Dergisi, 36*(3), 617-627.

Erdoğan, S., Yıldırım, D. Ç., & Gedikli, A. (2020). Dynamics and determinants of inflation during the COVID-19 pandemic period in European countries: A spatial panel data analysis. *Duzce Medical Journal, 22*(Special Issue), 61–67. doi:10.18678/dtfd.794107

Friedman, M. (1968). The role of monetary policy. *Essential Readings in Economics, 58*(1), 215–231.

Greenspan, A. (1996). Achieving price stability: A summary of the Bank's 1996 symposium. *Economic Review-Federal Reserve Bank of Kansas City, 81*, 1–5.

Han, A., Pehlivan, C., & Konat, G. (2022). COVİD-19 pandemi sürecinin türkiye ekonomisine etkilerinin ampirik analizi. *Sağlık ve Sosyal Refah Araştırmaları Dergisi, 4*(1), 32–49.

Hobbs, J. E. (2021). Food supply chain resilience and the COVID-19 pandemic: What have we learned? *Canadian Journal of Agricultural Economics/Revue canadienne d'agroeconomie, 69*(2), 189-196.

Houlihan, J. B. (1988). International supply chains: A new approach. *Management Decision, 26*(3), 13–19. doi:10.1108/eb001493

IEA. (2021). *Global Energy Review 2021. International Energy Agency 'Assessing the effects of economic recoveries on global energy demand and CO2 emissions in 2021'*. IEA.

ITC. (2022a). *China's foreign trade data*. Retrieved April 19, 2022, from http://jbr.org/articles.html www.trademap.org

ITC. (2022b). *Goods Imported and Exported by Turkey*. Retrieved April 20, 2022, from www.trademap.org

ITC. (2022c). *Turkey's foreign trade balance*. Retrieved April 19, 2022, from www.trademap.org

Kerr, W. A. (2021). Agriculture after a year with COVID-19: Any long-term implications for international trade policy? *Canadian Journal of Agricultural Economics/Revue canadienne d'agroeconomie, 69*(2), 261-267.

Kilpatrick, J., & Barter, L. (2020). *COVID-19: managing supply chain risk and disruption*. Deloitte.

Lee, H. L. (2002). Aligning supply chain strategies with product uncertainties. *California Management Review, 44*(3), 105–119. doi:10.2307/41166135

Mankiw, N. G. (2017). *Makroekonomi* (Ö. F. Çolak, Ed.). Efil Publishing House. doi:10.34156/9783791037844

OECD. (2022). *Inflation forecast*. Retrieved May 02, 2022, from https://data.oecd.org

Siche, R. (2020). What is the impact of COVID-19 disease on agriculture? *Scientia Agropecuaria, 11*(1), 3–6. doi:10.17268ci.agropecu.2020.01.00

Stevens, G. C. (1989). Integrating the supply chain. *International Journal of Physical Distribution & Materials Management, 19*(8), 1-8.

TB. (2022). *Türkiye Cumhuriyeti Ticaret Bakanlığı Covid-19 Ticaret Önlemleri*. Retrieved April 25, 2022, from https://covid19.ticaret.gov.tr/

TÜİK. (2022a). *Inflation Rates in Turkey*. Retrieved April 23, 2022, from https://data.tuik.gov.tr/

TÜİK. (2022b). *Turkey Imports and Exports*. Retrieved April 22, 2022, from https://data.tuik.gov.tr/

TÜİK. (2022c). *Foreign Trade Balance and Growth Rates in Turkey*. Retrieved April 22, 2022, from https://data.tuik.gov.tr/

TÜRMOB. (2020). Korona Salgınının Türkiye Ekonomisine Etkisi Değerlendirmeler ve Öneriler Raporu. *TÜRMOB Yayınları, 503*, 1–101.

UNCTAD. (2020). *Global Trade Impact of the Coronavirus (COVID-19) Epidemic*. United Nations Conference on Trade and Development.

UNCTAD. (2022). Global Trade. *United Nations Conference on Trade and Development*, 1-7.

World Bank. (2022a). *Foreign Trade Balance and Growth Rates in Turkey*. Retrieved May 10, 2022, from https://databank.worldbank.org/

World Bank. (2022b). *GDP per capita (current US$) – China*. Retrieved April 10, 2022, from https://data.worldbank.org/indicator/NY.GDP.PCAP.CD?end=2020&locations=CN&start=2000

Chapter 16
Will BRENT Reach the $300 Mark?

Ulas Akkucuk
https://orcid.org/0000-0001-6731-0634
Usak University, Turkey

ABSTRACT

Petrol crises have crippled the economies of the developed nations may times in modern history. Still, fossil fuels are an important source of transportation, and price changes deeply affect the social and economic wellbeing of the citizens. While research on alternative fuels is on the rise and there are many incentives, the reliance on fossil fuels is not diminished. Lately, as a result of the conflict in Ukraine, petrol prices went up again. This chapter will shed light on the past crises and will try to examine how much further petrol prices can go. Also, the relationship between energy prices and subjective wellbeing will be illustrated with examples from the literature. The chapter will also offer some suggestions for a sustainable green world.

INTRODUCTION

Petroleum prices have always been a cause of great concern for governments in the West especially when it comes to being reelected for office and when opinion polls are showing decline in popularity. Petroleum prices are generally referenced by the Brent Petrol prices although there are many different petroleum markets around the world. West Texas Intermediate or WTI is also another petrol price index that is widely used around the world. While green energy movements are gaining speed around the world, still petroleum is the main source of passenger vehicles fuel and increases in the prices hurt the household economy the most. Popular culture also fuels this and motivates politicians to find a way to reduce the prices. For this reason, it is important to study the trends in petrol prices and risks of petrol prices reaching certain critical threshold levels. When we look at the last five year movement of the oil prices we see a relative area of stability followed by a dip because of the Covid pandemic then a rise following the increase in production and consumption around the world. Figure 1 provides the time series chart of the Brent oil prices in the last five years. We can observe here interesting extreme lows

DOI: 10.4018/978-1-6684-5876-1.ch016

Figure 1. Last five years Brent prices
Source: Dynamic chart generated by bloomberght.com/emtia/brent-petrol

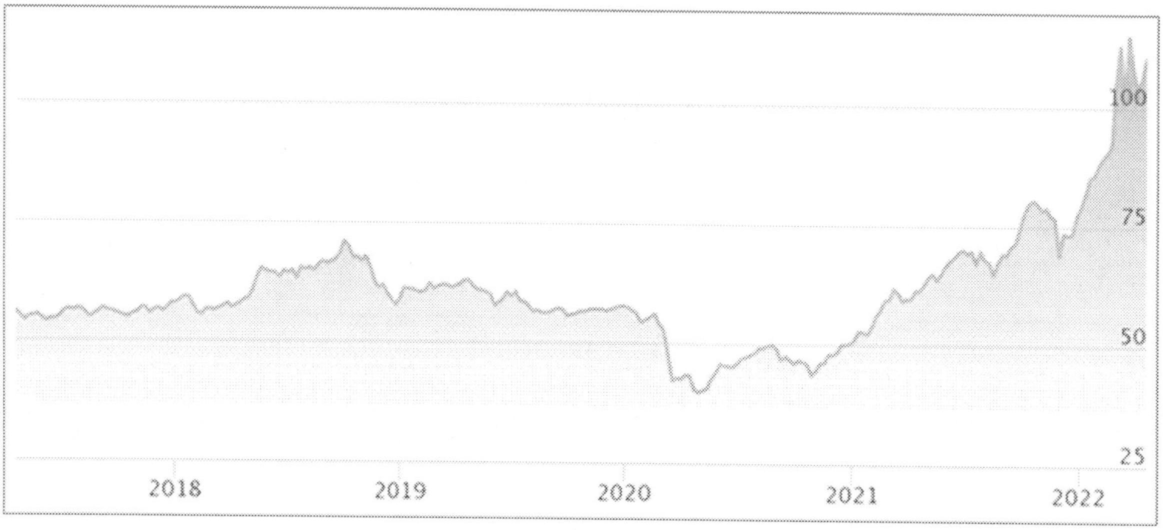

and highs in a time period of less than two years. For example the lowest value was recorded on April 21 2020 of $9.12 per barrel due to the lockdowns occurring as a result of the global pandemic which affected the industrialized parts of the world and slowed the consumption of energy. We also observe a high on March 8 2022 of $133.18 per barrel which is obviously a result of the military conflict between Russia and Ukraine which started on February 24. There is relative stability between 2017 and the 2020 pandemic with prices around $50 a barrel.

Factors that may be effective in the increase of petrol prices may be due to manufacturing sector demand or supply side shortages. Supply side shortages may be due to conflicts such as wars or refinery problems. Supply side shortages may also be intentional as in the OPEC countries restricting the flow of oil to increase prices and in response to political decision by the USA. Also as it happened after the Covid pandemic the increase in production suddenly after a long period of dormancy may stimulate the increase in petrol prices. With the exception of countries that are net exporters of crude oil, rising prices mean that prices of staples such as food also increase. Therefore the increase in petrol prices will definitely affect the economic well-being of the developing countries the most. In the developed world also this increase may particularly hurt because of the use of passenger cars and no viable alternative being present for individual transportation. This paper will proceed as follows: First the literature concerning the relationship between petrol price and economic well-being will be discussed. Following that the econometric studies about the past rises and falls of the petrol prices will be presented. Finally the outlook for the rest of the 20's will be forecasted using numerical techniques. The chapter will then end with a conclusion emphasizing the investment into non fossil fuel alternatives for a green future.

RELATIONSHIPS BETWEEN ECONOMIC WELL-BEING AND PETROL PRICES

One of the determinants of the economic well-being of a country can be stated as the rate of inflation. Another very important measure is the rate of unemployment. Perhaps these two measures could define if a country is in dire trouble or is doing very well economically. Actually the misery index calculated by the economic intelligence unit of the economist calculates the misery level by summing the inflation rate and the unemployment rate. Petrol prices obviously determine the transportation costs as most of the transportation of necessary goods and commodities rely on fossil fuels. As the transportation costs increase the cost of bringing vegetables and other food items from the growing centers to the major cities becomes a major problem and prices obviously increase. Increasing prices then are reflected on consumer price indices.

The relationship between petrol prices and inflation has been covered extensively by different authors from a number of countries. One study in Australia by Rangasamy (2017) outlined two major conclusions about the relationship between inflation and petrol prices. The first and major conclusion was that the contribution of increases in petrol prices to headline inflation has increased since the mid-1970s. The other conclusion was that the share of petrol prices exceeded their weight in the consumer price basket in terms of the effects on inflation changes.

Subjective well-being (SWB) is also another area of research used by some economists to measure economic well-being as compared to traditional measures such as inflation and unemployment. These types of measures rely on some form of questions asking the respondents how satisfied they are with their lives. Petrol prices have also been found to adversely affect the SWB scores of Australians in a study published in 2020 analyzing data from 2001 to 2017 (Prakash, Churchill & Smyth, 2020). The effect on the SWB can be caused by the difficulty in participating in leisure activities such as travel and sports induced by the petrol prices or simply due to the negative economic atmosphere caused by the economic hardships caused by inflation. Qian and Yan (2021) also confirm the same result in a study in China.

The increases in petrol prices are also known to affect travel behavior. A study conducted in Australia has examined the possible effects of an increase of petrol prices to 10 per liter (Hensher & Stanley, 2009). In this article the authors explore the likely effects of the increase on "car use, modal share, greenhouse gas emissions, and public transport revenue". Zhang et al. (2021) have conducted a study in China and have found that energy poverty significantly lowers well-being of children. In another study the link between energy poverty and obesity has been explored, the findings indicate that energy poor are more likely to be obese (Prakash & Munyanyi, 2021).

RISES AND FALLS IN PETROL PRICES

1973 Energy Crisis

The energy crisis of 1973 has had a profound impact on the globe. Many studies have been conducted on the causes and results of the crisis (Donatos et al., 1989; Carlisle et al., 2007; Bridge, 2010; McGowan, 2011). In the US, as of 1973 the cars had a very high gas consumption rate which is about 13 miles per gallon (or about 5.5 kilometers per liter, in today's fuel efficient cars you can travel about 20 kilometers per liter and even better) but this was not seen as a problem since the gasoline prices were very cheap. The petrol crises was mainly as result of the US support for Israel in the Arab Israel conflict and as OPEC restricted flow of petrol gas prices rose. The response from the petrol stations was even to the extreme that the opening hours were restricted and even 10 gallon limits were imposed for buying petrol. This crisis profoundly impacted the American society. In times of petrol crises, the expectation about the future prices of gasoline and other durable goods must be calculated by the consumers in order to make their purchasing decisions and it has been observed that the customers make rational decision in this regard when compared to the actual historical series of prices (Daly & Mayor, 1983). As a result of the crises many auto makers turned to producing fuel efficient models and the Japanese makers gained considerable market share.

1979 Energy Crisis

The second energy crises or oil shock was mainly due to the Iran revolution that took place in 1979. The reduction in the global oil supply was not so severe but the reaction from the market almost doubled the oil prices to nearly 40 dollars a barrel. We should also consider that 1 dollar in 1980 is about 3 dollars now so the prices at that time in today's terms were about 120 dollars a barrel. Again at the end of this crises fuel efficient cars were the preferred alternatives by the consumers. Even US President Carter installed energy generating solar panels on top of the roof of the White House in DC. Several researchers have looked into the 1979 energy crises in different aspects. Hartgen et al. (1980) have examined the travel preference changes in response to the 1979 energy crises, and noted that intercity rail traffic rose by 30%. There are also some studies about the public opinion with regard to who caused the oil shortages. In one study Richman (1979) states that majority of the public viewed the main cause of the crises as oil companies who wanted to increase the prices.

2000s Energy Crisis

The period from 1980 until 2003 was relatively stable. Then the prices began to shoot up again. Actually a high of around 147 dollars a barrel was reached in 2008. The increase this time seems more dramatic than the increase during the crises of the 70s but we must also consider inflation in this case. So the increase in petrol prices when inflation is taken into consideration was almost equivalent to the 70s. During this period some research studies were conducted on the effects of the increased prices. One study in Australia looked at the extent of cycling as an alternative mode of transportation and concluded that "In response to high petrol prices we find significant substitution into cycling as a mode of transport in the inner city, wealthy neighborhoods and in the city overall, particularly during the peak commuting periods" (Smith & Kauerman, 2011). Tagkiris (2022) has explored the connection between the energy crises of the 2000s and the global financial crises of the 2008 2009 era. Some authors have focused on studies related to rate meters in response to the energy crises (Gergen et al., 2003). The crises not only influenced Europe and US but also could be felt as far away as Brazil (Jardini et al., 2002).

FUTURE OUTLOOK FOR THE 2020'S

The outlook for the end of the 20s looks even grimmer than the current state of the world economy. Food price increases and food shortages will only increase in the coming years. Such doomsday forecasts are made by a number of prestigious institutions and research centers. Of course it is in the interest of all of humanity to decrease dependence on fossil fuels and reduce climate change. Behavioral changes in consumption patterns will also improve the current situation. From the analysis of the current situation and the growing world population needs it seems likely that the fuel prices will continue to go up. Petrol prices reaching $300 a barrel was the threat issued by the Russian foreign minister after sanctions were placed on Russian exports. Indeed some experts claim that a complete ban on Russian oil could even increase the price of oil to $500 per barrel. Several different methods are available for forecasting the Brent petrol prices. Forecasting methods include decomposition of trend, seasonality and cyclical components as well as the random movements. Abdollahi and Ebrahimi (2020) have proposed a hybrid model for forecasting crude oil prices. Here the authors use ANFIS, ARFIMA, and Markov-switching genetic algorithms, with results showing that the latter produces the best results. Some forecasting models for crude oil try to estimate the one day ahead prices while some others may be longer term. Indeed Lee and Huh (2017) have estimated the 2040 prices to be $169 per barrel using Bayesian Model with informative priors. In 2017 when this work was written the price was around $60. So we can see how quickly the prices have gone up and even way before 2040 the prices have peaked at around $133 during March of 2022. In this article we used the Brent prices collected daily between 23/4/2012 to 8/4/2022 (April to April). The data set contains 2538 data points corresponding to 10 years. The beginning price is $116.66 and ending price is $101.26. The last year has seen the biggest increase with Brent rising from $60 to $100. There are various techniques that can capture the trend in the data. These techniques are classified under exponential smoothing methods. Variations of exponential smoothing that can include a trend in the data are Holt's exponential smoothing and Brown's linear trend. While different parameter selections may yield much different forecast values statistical software packages can optimize the parameters for forecast. In this manner thc forccast for 2040 using Holt's methods is found to be about $230 per barrel. Using Brown's trend option the forecasts are much inflated and exceed $2000 per barrel. On the other hand inflation rate of 8% alone can spike the rates to $500 in 12 years' time. By considering these results and using subjective evaluations as well a price of $300 per barrel as per the title of the paper by 2040 or earlier is very likely.

RECOMMENDATIONS AND DISCUSSION

The fact that petrol prices affect well-being measures for the economy either in subjective measures or objective instruments such as inflation and umeployment, warrants special attention by policy makers in non oil producing countries to this matter. Our article tried to shed light into this very important phenomenon as the war in Ukraine and other crises yet waiting to happen threaten to increase the barrel price of oil to well beyond 200 dollars a barrel into the proximity of 300 dollars a barrel. Being able to forecast the cost of petrol is very important for petrol importing countries as well as petrol exporting countries which rely heavily on the revenues for supporting their government services. New studies on forecasting the oil prices both in the short term and the long term are therefore necessary. Also studies on millennials (the very young generation) such as Akkucuk & Turan (2016) may be needed to understand the concerns of the future decision makers.

Sustainability is a multidisciplinary area and concerns all disciplines. This relatively new concept has been under continuous investigation by different academics for a long time. Sustainability in transportation is also a growing area of interest. Logistics, Supply Chain and Recycling are noticeably among the areas most often studied by sustainability and related areas researchers (Akkucuk, 2016; Gencer, 2016; Gencer & Akkucuk, 2016). Akkucuk and Sekercioglu (2016) demonstrate a case where an NGO is working to foster sustainable ecotourism in Turkey, this type of ecologically sensitive tourism may also reduce the amount of petrol spent in travel and affect the economy positively. Studies in different business fields can also be taken advantage of in order to increase the awareness about environmental issues (Akkucuk & Kucukkancabas, 2007; Akkucuk, 2014; Akkucuk, 2017; Akkucuk & Teuman, 2016; Akkucuk, 2009).

As possible solutions to the problem of increasing petrol prices on society some subsidies may be considered. Ozgur et al. (2021) explore the impact of a subsidy system to reduce the negative impacts of rising fuel prices in Turkey. Subsidies are already used for petrol products intended for airplanes and boats. This however leads to possible tax evasion and is under strict control of the tax authorities. The effect of fuel subsidies are also under consideration in different countries such as Malaysia (Li & Su, 2017; Ramli et al., 2021; Kasipillai & Chan, 2008; Johari et al., 2015; Davis, 2014; Solarin, 2022; Ying & Harun, 2019; Benes et al., 2015; Kadooni et al., 2015; Narayanan et al., 2007). Fuel subsidies may need to be financed by taxes which in turn could affect overall happiness (Sasmaz & Sakar, 2020).

Reducing the dependence on fossil fuels is the most important goals of governments in Europe and in the US. The Ukraine Russia conflict has shown once more that the reliance on fossil fuels from a single source, as in natural gas from Russia, creates significant problems. Rather than diversifying the sources of fossil fuels and finding and drilling new resources the switch to renewable sources should be the number one priority of the governments.

Alternative transportation methods especially mass transit alternatives are also considered as a major solution to the growing problem of fossil fuel consumption. Actually as it has been said before in this paper the 1979 energy crises has cause a rapid increase in rail transit use in the US. If we switch to rail transit as the major alternative for short distance intercity travel the dependence on fossil fuels will be further reduced. Alternative fuels such as hydrogen could also be considered (Manieniyan et al., 2009). Many studies have been conducted that explore the positive effects of renewable energy (Sasmaz et al., 2020; 2021).

REFERENCES

Abdollahi, H., & Ebrahimi, S. B. (2020). A new hybrid model for forecasting Brent crude oil price. *Energy*, *200*, 117520. doi:10.1016/j.energy.2020.117520

Akküçük, U. (2009). İş etiğinde Sarbanes-Oxley (SOX) Yasası'nın etkisi ve toplam kalite yönetimi uygulamalarında yansımaları. *İş Ahlakı Dergisi*, *2*(3), 7-17.

Akkucuk, U. (2014). Application of lean six sigma methodology in design and improvement of financial services. In *Globalization of Financial Institutions* (pp. 151–164). Springer. doi:10.1007/978-3-319-01125-7_11

Akkucuk, U. (2016). SCOR Model and the Green Supply Chain. In U. Akkucuk (Ed.), *Handbook of Research on Waste Management Techniques for Sustainability* (pp. 108–124). IGI Global. doi:10.4018/978-1-4666-9723-2.ch006

Akkucuk, U. (Ed.). (2017). *Ethics and Sustainability in Global Supply Chain Management*. IGI Global. doi:10.4018/978-1-5225-2036-8

Akkucuk, U., & Kucukkancabas, S. (2007). Analyzing the Perceptions of Turkish Universities Using Multidimensional Scaling (MDS) Analysis. *Bogazici Journal of Economics and Administrative Sciences*, *21*, 125–141.

Akkucuk, U., & Sekercioglu, C. H. (2016). NGOs for Environmental Sustainability: The Case of Kuzeydoga Foundation. *Fresenius Environmental Bulletin*, *25*(12), 6038–6044.

Akkucuk, U., & Teuman, B. (2016). Assessing service quality in online banking services. *Problems and Perspectives in Management*, *14*(2), 183–191. doi:10.21511/ppm.14(2-1).2016.07

Akkucuk, U., & Turan, C. (2016). Mobile use and online preferences of the millenials: A study in Yalova. *Journal of Internet Banking and Commerce*, *21*(1), 142.

Benes, K., Cheon, A., Urpelainen, J., & Yang, J. (2015). *Low oil prices: An opportunity for fuel subsidy reform*. Columbia University.

Bridge, G. (2010). Past peak oil: political economy of energy crises. In *Global political ecology* (pp. 321–338). Routledge.

Carlisle, J. E., Feezell, J. T., Smith, E. R., & Michaud, K. E. (2017). *The politics of energy crises*. Oxford University Press.

Daly, G. G., & Mayor, T. H. (1983). Reason and rationality during energy crises. *Journal of Political Economy*, *91*(1), 168–181. doi:10.1086/261134

Davis, L. W. (2014). The economic cost of global fuel subsidies. *The American Economic Review*, *104*(5), 581–585. doi:10.1257/aer.104.5.581

Donatos, G. S., & Mergos, G. J. (1989). Energy demand in Greece: The impact of the two energy crises. *Energy Economics*, *11*(2), 147–152. doi:10.1016/0140-9883(89)90008-X

Gencer, Y. G. (2016). Mystery of Recycling: Glass and Aluminum Examples. In U. Akkucuk (Ed.), *Handbook of Research on Waste Management Techniques for Sustainability* (pp. 172–191). IGI Global. doi:10.4018/978-1-4666-9723-2.ch009

Gencer, Y. G., & Akkucuk, U. (2016). Reverse Logistics: Automobile Recalls and Other Conditions. In U. Akkucuk (Ed.), *Handbook of Research on Waste Management Techniques for Sustainability* (pp. 125–154). IGI Global. doi:10.4018/978-1-4666-9723-2.ch007

Gergen, M. J., Cannon, G. D. Jr, & Tewksbury, D. G. (2003). Market-Based Ratemaking and the Western Energy Crisis of 2000 and 2001. *Energy LJ*, *24*, 321.

Hartgen, D. T., Neveu, A. J., Brunso, J. M., Banas, J. S., & Miller, J. W. (1979). *Changes in Travel in response to the 1979 Energy Crisis*. https://trid.trb.org/view/145170

Hensher, D. A., & Stanley, J. K. (2009). What if petrol increased to $10 per litre in Melbourne?: Implications for travel behaviour and public transport demand. *Road & Transport Research: A Journal of Australian and New Zealand Research and Practice, 18*(3), 61-68.

Jardini, J. A., Ramos, D. S., Martini, J. S. C., Reis, L. B. D., & Tahan, C. M. A. (2002). Brazilian energy crisis. *IEEE Power Engineering Review*, *22*(4), 21–24. doi:10.1109/MPER.2002.994845

Johari, A., Nyakuma, B. B., Nor, S. H. M., Mat, R., Hashim, H., Ahmad, A., ... Abdullah, T. A. T. (2015). The challenges and prospects of palm oil based biodiesel in Malaysia. *Energy*, *81*, 255–261. doi:10.1016/j.energy.2014.12.037

Kardooni, R., Yusoff, S. B., & Kari, F. B. (2015). Barriers to renewable energy development: Five fuel policy in Malaysia. *Energy & Environment, 26*(8), 1353–1361. doi:10.1260/0958-305X.26.8.1353

Kasipillai, J., & Chan, P. (2008). Travel demand management: Lessons for Malaysia. *Journal of Public Transportation, 11*(3), 3. doi:10.5038/2375-0901.11.3.3

Lee, C.-Y., & Huh, S.-Y. (2017). Forecasting Long-Term Crude Oil Prices Using a Bayesian Model with Informative Priors. *Sustainability, 9*(2), 190. doi:10.3390/su9020190

Li, Y., Shi, X., & Su, B. (2017). Economic, social and environmental impacts of fuel subsidies: A revisit of Malaysia. *Energy Policy, 110*, 51–61. doi:10.1016/j.enpol.2017.08.015

Manieniyan, V., Thambidurai, M., & Selvakumar, R. (2009). Study on energy crisis and the future of fossil fuels. *Proceedings of SHEE, 10*, 2234–3689.

McGowan, F. (2011). Putting energy insecurity into historical context: European responses to the energy crises of the 1970s and 2000s. *Geopolitics, 16*(3), 486–511. doi:10.1080/14650045.2011.520857

Narayanan, S., Sua, T. Y., Raman, S. R., Alavi, K., Yee, C. L., Abdullah, N., & Husin, A. (2007). The challenges of raising revenues and restructuring subsidies in Malaysia. *Kajian Malaysia, 25*(2), 1–28. doi:10.21315/km2016.34.2.1

Ozgur, O., Aydin, L., Karagol, E. T., & Ozbugday, F. C. (2021). The fuel price pass-through in Turkey: The case study of motor fuel price subsidy system. *Energy, 226*, 120399. doi:10.1016/j.energy.2021.120399

Prakash, K., Churchill, S. A., & Smyth, R. (2020). Petrol prices and subjective wellbeing. *Energy Economics, 90*, 104867. doi:10.1016/j.eneco.2020.104867

Prakash, K., & Munyanyi, M. E. (2021). Energy poverty and obesity. *Energy Economics, 101*, 105428. doi:10.1016/j.eneco.2021.105428

Qian, Y., & Yan, L. (2021). Petrol Prices and Subjective Well-Being: Longitudinal Data Evidence From China. *Energy Research Letters, 2*(4), 28125. doi:10.46557/001c.28125

Ramli, A. R., Kadir, J. M. A., Ismail, N., Othman, A. A., & Melo, P. C. (2021). Fuel Subsidies, Fuel Consumption, and Road Transport Emissions: A systematic review. *Environment-Behaviour Proceedings Journal, 6*(16), 275–281. doi:10.21834/ebpj.v6i16.2721

Rangasamy, L. (2017). The impact of petrol price movements on South African inflation. *Journal of Energy in Southern Africa, 28*(1), 120–132. doi:10.17159/2413-3051/2017/v28i1a1597

Richman, A. (1979). The polls: Public attitudes toward the energy crisis. *Public Opinion Quarterly, 43*(4), 576–585. doi:10.1086/268557

Sasmaz, M. U., Karamıklı, A., & Akkucuk, U. (2021). The relationship between renewable energy use and health expenditures in EU countries. *The European Journal of Health Economics, 22*(7), 1129–1139. doi:10.100710198-021-01312-1 PMID:33954841

Şaşmaz, M. Ü., & Şakar, E. (2020). *The effect of taxes and public expenditures on happiness: Empirical evidence from OECD countries*. doi:10.21833/ijaas.2020.08.014

Sasmaz, M. U., Sakar, E., Yayla, Y. E., & Akkucuk, U. (2020). The relationship between renewable energy and human development in OECD countries: A panel data analysis. *Sustainability, 12*(18), 7450. doi:10.3390u12187450

Smith, M. S., & Kauermann, G. (2011). Bicycle commuting in Melbourne during the 2000s energy crisis: A semiparametric analysis of intraday volumes. *Transportation Research Part B: Methodological, 45*(10), 1846–1862. doi:10.1016/j.trb.2011.07.003

Solarin, S. A. (2022). Modelling two dimensions of poverty in selected developing countries: The impact of fossil fuel subsidies. *Social Indicators Research, 160*(1), 357–379. doi:10.100711205-021-02815-3

Tagkiris, D. (2022). *The interconnection between 2000s energy crisis and the global financial crisis. The role of NOCs and IOCs as part of the global recession* (Master's thesis). Πανεπιστήμιο Πειραιώς.

Ying, L. S., & Harun, M. (2019). The impact of removing fuel subsidies on domestic outputs in Malaysia. *International Journal of Academic Research in Business & Social Sciences, 9*(3), 641–653. doi:10.6007/IJARBSS/v9-i3/5732

Zhang, Q., Appau, S., & Kodom, P. L. (2021). Energy poverty, children's wellbeing and the mediating role of academic performance: Evidence from China. *Energy Economics, 97*, 105206. doi:10.1016/j.cncco.2021.105206

ADDITIONAL READING

Adelabu, N. S. (2012). The political economy of oil deregulation in Nigeria's fourth republic: Prospects and challenges. *Journal of Emerging Trends in Educational Research and Policy Studies, 3*(3), 193–198.

Baka, J. E. (2017). Political-industrial ecologies of energy. In *Handbook on the Geographies of Energy*. Edward Elgar Publishing. doi:10.4337/9781785365621.00047

Bridge, G. (2010). Past peak oil: political economy of energy crises. In *Global political ecology* (pp. 321–338). Routledge.

Bridge, G. (2010). Geographies of peak oil: The other carbon problem. *Geoforum, 41*(4), 523–530. doi:10.1016/j.geoforum.2010.06.002

Ezeoha, A. E., & Uche, C. U. (2017). State legitimacy and the unending crisis of petrol subsidy reforms in Nigeria. *Society & Natural Resources, 30*(10), 1181–1196. doi:10.1080/08941920.2017.1290180

Guyer, J. I., & Denzer, L. (2013). Prebendalism and the people: the price of petrol at the pump. In Democracy and Prebendalism in Nigeria (pp. 53-77). Palgrave Macmillan. doi:10.1057/9781137280770_3

Hensher, D. A., & Stanley, J. K. (2009). What if petrol increased to $10 per litre in Melbourne?: Implications for travel behaviour and public transport demand. *Road & Transport Research: A Journal of Australian and New Zealand Research and Practice, 18*(3), 61-68.

Hoogvelt, A. (2010). Globalisation, crisis and the political economy of the international monetary (dis) order. *Globalizations, 7*(1-2), 51–66. doi:10.1080/14747731003593133

Huber, M. T. (2013). *Lifeblood: Oil, freedom, and the forces of capital*. U of Minnesota Press. doi:10.5749/minnesota/9780816677849.001.0001

Hunter, C. (2002). Sustainable tourism and the touristic ecological footprint. *Environment, Development and Sustainability*, *4*(1), 7–20. doi:10.1023/A:1016336125627

Lane, B. (1994). Sustainable rural tourism strategies: A tool for development and conservation. *Journal of Sustainable Tourism*, *2*(1-2), 102–111. doi:10.1080/09669589409510687

Lempinen, H. (2019). The Politics of Energy and Sustainability. In *Arctic Energy and Social Sustainability* (pp. 17–42). Palgrave Pivot. doi:10.1007/978-3-030-02269-3_2

Liu, Z. (2003). Sustainable tourism development: A critique. *Journal of Sustainable Tourism*, *11*(6), 459–475. doi:10.1080/09669580308667216

McIntyre, G. (1993). *Sustainable tourism development: guide for local planners*. World Tourism Organization (WTO).

Newman, J. I., & Giardina, M. D. (2011). Part I NASCAR Nation As/In Petrol Empire. In Sport, Spectacle, and NASCAR Nation (pp. 151-161). Palgrave Macmillan.

Richards, G., & Hall, D. (Eds.). (2003). *Tourism and sustainable community development* (Vol. 7). Psychology Press.

Savitzky, S., & Urry, J. (2015). Oil on the Move. In *Cargomobilities* (pp. 180–198). Routledge. doi:10.4324/9781315866673-11

Sharpley, R. (2000). Tourism and sustainable development: Exploring the theoretical divide. *Journal of Sustainable Tourism*, *8*(1), 1–19. doi:10.1080/09669580008667346

Simpson, A., & Smits, M. (2016). Transitions to energy and climate security in Thailand: Adam Simpson and Mattijs Smits. In *Handbook of Transitions to Energy and Climate Security* (pp. 296–311). Routledge. doi:10.4324/9781315723617-20

Sims, R. (2009). Food, place and authenticity: Local food and the sustainable tourism experience. *Journal of Sustainable Tourism*, *17*(3), 321–336. doi:10.1080/09669580802359293

Tosun, C. (2001). Challenges of sustainable tourism development in the developing world: The case of Turkey. *Tourism Management*, *22*(3), 289–303. doi:10.1016/S0261-5177(00)00060-1

Tynkkynen, V. P. (2019). *The energy of Russia: hydrocarbon culture and climate change*. Edward Elgar Publishing. doi:10.4337/9781788978606

Wroe, D. (2012). Donors, dependency, and political crisis in Malawi. *African Affairs*, *111*(442), 135–144. doi:10.1093/afraf/adr076

KEY TERMS AND DEFINITIONS

Brent Petrol: A certain type of crude oil that is drilled in the North Sea and sets the standard for petrol prices around the world.

Core Inflation: Inflation measure excluding cost of food and energy. The underlying logic is that these are very volatile and price changes will cause variation in the inflation measures.

CPI: A measure of the price level of the country called the consumer price index, changes in CPI are used to measure the rate of inflation.

Headline Inflation: Raw inflation reported by statistical agencies around the world, this measure considers a fixed basket of goods and bases the CPI on that.

Inflation: A rise in the general price level of the country.

Inflation Basket: Is the collection of goods and services that will be used to measure and report inflation. It is a matter of discretion how this bucket should be updated, and weights do naturally change as the prices increase disproportionately.

Solar Power: Energy derived directly from sunlight by means of panels.

Sustainable Transportation: Practicing transportation in a way that preserves the natural resources and lowers emissions.

WPI: A measure of inflation faced by the manufacturing industry, generally there is a lag between the WPI and CPI levels as the manufacturers hold on to prices as much as possible to smooth the production and deplete inventories.

Chapter 17
Automotive Industry Challenges:
Crises, Disruptions, and Taxes

Ulas Akkucuk
https://orcid.org/0000-0001-6731-0634
Usak University, Turkey

ABSTRACT

The automotive sector is one of the important sectors in both the developed world and the developing countries. For developing countries, this industry is a course of income coming from export models. For the developed nations, the automotive sector can create quality jobs and offer after-sales and service job opportunities as well. The automotive industry was challenged during the COVID-19 pandemic as shortages for some parts halted production in different parts of the world. Also, sales of automobiles increased in some parts due to commuters avoiding mass transit in fear of the pandemic. Tax collection is also another issue associated with this industry. In some countries, heavy taxes are levied on the vehicles with some possible drawbacks. This chapter will talk about the causes and remedies for the disruptions in the supply chain. The issue of taxation will also be discussed offering some possible solutions. Green energy and public transportation will be offered as remedies to the problems of the industry and the more general problem of global warming.

INTRODUCTION

The automotive sector is considered as the most important sector in developed countries and drives a major supplier industry as well. Automotive supplies range from tires to stereo equipment and automotive companies are major customers for many different types of industries. Direct automotive manufacture provides high quality jobs for a skilled labor force. On the other hand the sales and after sales services create jobs for many, regardless of whether the cars are manufactured domestically or imported. Also even imported cars may be using some parts purchased from the host country. Automotive industry was born in Europe but also flourished in the US and Japan later on. Turkey started importing automobiles

DOI: 10.4018/978-1-6684-5876-1.ch017

Figure 1. Number of motor vehicles in Turkey from 1936 until 2021
Source: Dynamic chart generated by drdatastats.com using TUIK data.

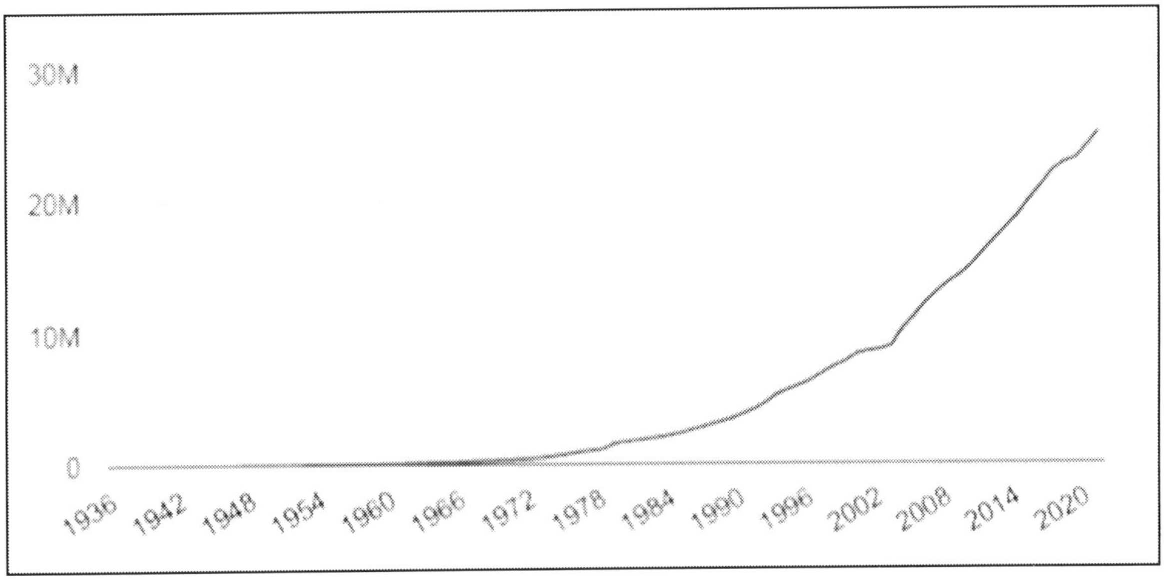

but later on during the 60s decided to manufacture its own brands. Figure 1 provides the time series chart of the number of motor vehicles registered in Turkey starting with 1936. Here we can see the dramatic increase in the number of vehicles from 7536 in 1936 to 25 million and above in 2021. Naturally most people associate the level of welfare of a country with the number of motor vehicles registered but especially passenger cars are more important as in developed countries the ownership rates are very high. Figure 2 provides the number of registered passenger cars in Turkey from 1936 to 2021. We can also see here a sharp increase from 3815 vehicles in 1936 to over 13.5 million vehicles in 2021. There is still a long way to go as the ownership rate per capita is lagging behind many developed countries. The other types of vehicles registered range from buses, motorcycles, trucks to tractors. We can immediately see that about half of the registered vehicles are passenger vehicles and the rest are commercial or special duty vehicles. Motorcycles are showing a dramatic increase and the numbers are close to four million now. This is due to the high fuel efficiency of the motorcycles and the low purchase costs. As the number of passenger vehicles per capita is concerned Turkey has leveled of around 15 vehicles per 100 people and this number does not seem to increase lately. As for the total motor vehicles this ratio corresponds to roughly 25 vehicles. It seems that there is still a long way to go for Turkey to reach the levels of car ownership that is seen in the developed world.

Taking the above into consideration, factors that may be effective in the increase of car ownership may be manifold. Prices may be driven up by supply side shortages. Also as is the case with Turkey the government simply sees passenger cars as an easy way to generate revenue and this is clearly not sustainable. This paper will proceed as follows: First the literature concerning the disruptions in the automotive supply chain will be discussed. Following that a brief review of past crises and the effects on the automotive sector will be presented. Finally the relationship between special car taxes and car sales will be explored, especially with a focus on Turkey. The chapter will then end with a conclusion

Figure 2. Number of passenger vehicles in Turkey from 1936 until 2021
Source: Dynamic chart generated by drdatastats.com using TUIK data.

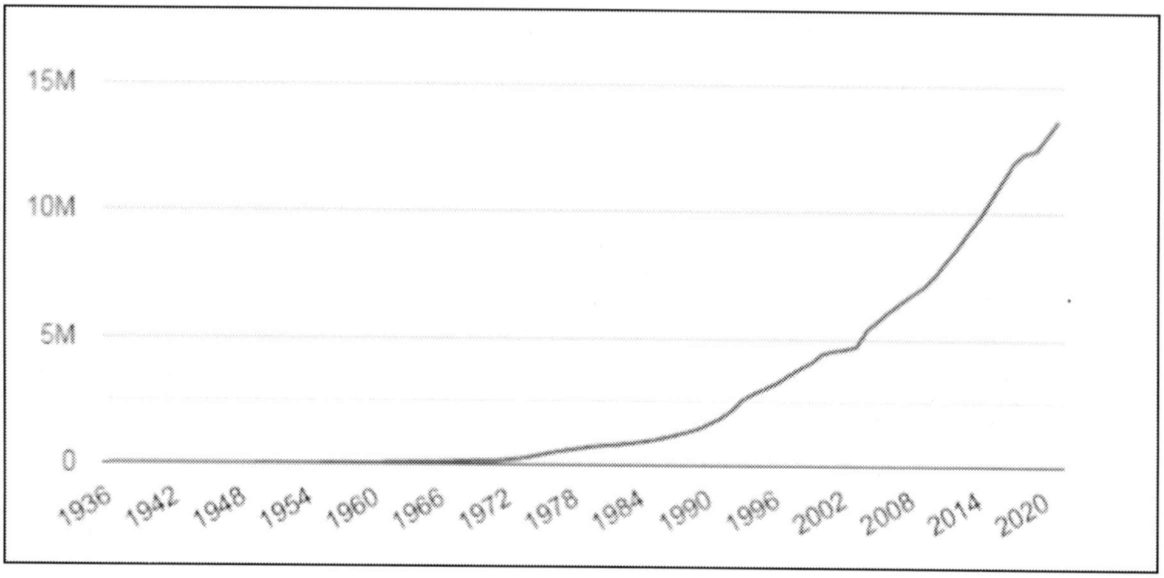

emphasizing the investment into car technologies using non fossil fuel alternatives for a greener future for the whole world.

DISRUPTIONS IN THE SUPPLY CHAIN

Automotive producers rely heavily on parts and supplies produced in diverse parts of the world. As a result of the geographic diversity of the parts, a conflict in one part of the world such as the war in Ukraine might influence the production of one part and therefore halt production in the assembly line where the main assembly is taking place. The type of disruptions could range from wars, diseases and natural events such as earthquakes. The earthquake in Kobe Japan that took place in 1995 for example halted the assembly line of the Toyota plant due to a part that could not be made in Kobe. We know that due the spread of the Covid-19 virus many plats needed to be shut down due to the spread of the infection. Similar disruptions happened recently with the Ukraine Russia war.

The disruptions in automotive supply chains have been studied widely in the literature. There are different approaches taken by the academic studies in terms of how risks can be mitigated due to disruptions. Approaches to reducing the risk of disruptions could range from choosing local suppliers to designing the products with fewer parts. Kamalahmadi et al. (2022) discuss the various effects of flexibility and redundancy on supply chain disruptions. Craighead et al. (2007) also define the supply chain characteristics that are critical in determining supply chain resilience; these are listed as "density, complexity, and node criticality". Some academic studies have looked into major disasters such as earthquakes and tsunamis (Leckcivilize, 2012; Lim & Tan, 2018). Some studies have focused on particular companies and display their best tactics in dealing with the disruptions as a result of the Pandemic (Sudan & Taggar, 2022). Numerical simulations can also be used to study the effects of potential supply chain disruptions and design a resilient supply chain (Korniejczuk, 2019). The disruptions in the manufacturing sectors also are known to affect inflation adversely, in fact a study by La Belle and Santacreu (2022) has found that the PPI (Producer price index) inflation in the US would be lower by up to 20% in 2021 had it not been for the disruptions as a result of the Covid 19 pandemic. Disruptions have also been studies in terms of different sectors such as automotive, PC and home furniture (Ishida, 2020).

Regardless of which industry a firm is operating firms must be careful to reduce the risk of supply chain disruptions. Management of safety stocks and inventories plays a key role in reducing the risk of stopping production for multiple plant multiple supplier manufacturing systems. Management of the inventories and risk pooling are also effective strategies. For the automotive industry the lack of computer chips has also motivated the producers to design simpler models not using so much complicated technologies.

EFFECT OF CRISES ON AUTOMOTIVE SALES

1970s Energy Crisis

The 1973 and 1979 oil crises have had profound effects on global politics and especially on the automotive industry. The oil crisis increases the cost of inputs (oil in this case) that are critical for transporting the raw materials. Also the cost of oil that is needed to run the automobiles increase hence making it difficult to drive them. Both of these facts make it difficult for people to purchase new vehicles. Lee and Ni (2002) suggest that the oil price shocks affect the economy mainly by delaying the purchase of durable goods. In some countries the governments had to step in and introduce legislation that will protect the local producers against the competition in times of hardship. Ramirez Perez (2020) looks at the era between 1973 and 1985 and explains how European Union governments introduced legislation that will protect the European automotive manufacturers.

2008-2009 Financial Crises

The 2009 crises had an effect that even superseded the effects of the oil shocks. Automotive sales in the US dropped from near 20 million to 10 million actually such a dramatic fall that it could be comparable to auto sales in 1981 (20 years earlier). Ashton (2009) gives a very detailed account of the crises. To summarize the global financial crisis of the 2008-2009 period we could mention the following points.

- The main reason was the subprime mortgage market and the bubble in housing prices that later collapsed.
- The irresponsible loans given out by many financial institutions required government bailout at the end.
- The automotive manufacturers also came to near bankruptcy and were bailed out by the government.
- To solve the problem a Federal act called the American Recovering and Reinvestment Act of 2009 came to being.

The 2009 crises have been the most dramatic crises in the automotive history. Some countries that rely on exports to saturated markets in the west were mainly affected as well. Pavlinek (2015) investigates the industries in Slovakia and Czechia that experienced plant closure as a result of the crises. A number of studies have also been made detailing the effect of crises on the automotive sector especially in developing countries (Sturgeon & Van Biesebroek, 2010; Acemoglu, 2009; Wad, 2009; Weber, 2009; Rosenfeld, 2009).

TAXES AND THE AUTOMOTIVE MARKET

The taxes on vehicles may be levied on new car purchase and also a yearly fee may be charged based on certain parameters. In some countries sales tax is also applied to second hand purchases. Taxes in Turkey have been blamed as the main reason why per capita ownership is still low and the car pool is very old. Taxes related to motor vehicles in Turkey may be listed as follows:

- ÖTV new car purchase (Excise Tax)
- KDV new car purchase (VAT)
- KDV and ÖTV from fuel
- MTV each year from motor vehicle (motor vehicles tax)

The governments levying automotive taxes face a dilemma. The higher the tax rates the lower the total tax collection may become. So as a result setting the tax rates too high might actually diminish government tax revenue. Taxes are an important part of a government's job definition and taxes have been known to affect key variables such as happiness (Sasmaz & Sakar, 2020). In some cases governments may choose to impose taxes to reduce consumption of unhealthy foods or beverages (Chaloupka et al., 2019). The phenomenon of tax revenue dropping as a result of increased taxes has been studied under the name "Laffer Curve" (Trabandt & Uhlig, 2011; Laffer, 2004; Buchanan & Lee, 1982; Wanniski, 1978; Blinder, 1981; Malcomson, 1986; Mirowski, 1982; Agell & Persson, 2001; Feige & McGee, 1983; Lin & Jia, 2019; Megersa, 2015; Tatu, 2014). Taxes in Turkey for automotive products have always been blamed for the old age of the fleet and the lower equipment that is offered on most vehicles.

When we analyze the Turkish car sales between the period 2002 to 2020 we see that the sales are mostly stagnant at an average value of 750,000 per year. There are some up and downs but the critical value of 1 million car sales has not been exceeded. During this period the population of Turkey has increased by 25%. During this time the value of the Turkish currency was not very stable as well, USD TL exchange rate went from 1.49 to 6.92 almost 5 fold increase. The government tax collection seemed to work very well until the year 2015 but then we se a great decline in terms of the real taxes collected from motor vehicles and petroleum products. Calculating taxes collected in nominal TL shows and increase except the final year of analysis 2020, but when we correct taxes for population, USD, and even for US inflation we see a different picture. Some graphs explain the situation very well. First we present in Figure 3 the yearly sales in the Turkish market as of the year of analysis in this paper the Turkish market is number 18 in the world with a sales number of 770,000.

Next in Figure 4 we look at the tax collected from different sources related to motor vehicles. The sources of tax are separated into three groups namely the petroleum related taxes (top line), the special consumption taxes from sales of new motor vehicles (called ÖTV – middle line) and finally the bottom line gives the recurring motor vehicles taxes (MTV) collected from all vehicles new and old with different rates. We see here a steady increase in all areas until 2017 but later even in nominal terms some

Figure 3. Number of passenger vehicles sold in Turkey from 2002 until 2020
Source: Dynamic chart generated by drdatastats.com using TUIK data.

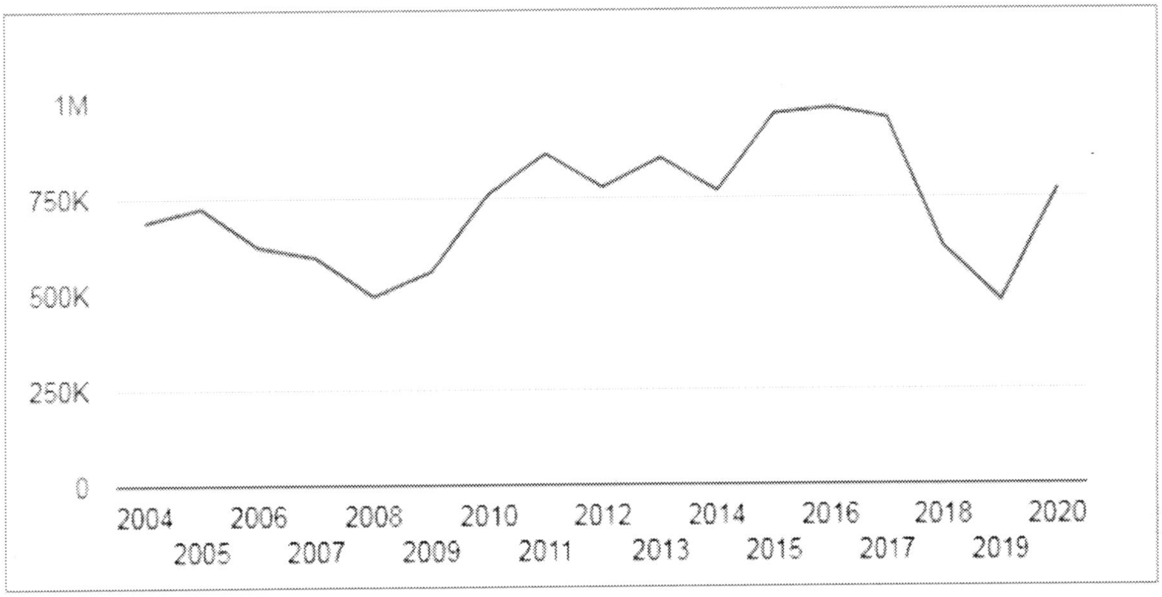

of the tax revenues fall. The reason for this is that due to the fluctuations in USD TL exchange rates the car prices become very expensive so some consumers had to delay purchases. Also due to the pandemic government relaxed taxing on petroleum so the top line fell dramatically after 2019. The MTV collected from all cars new and old seems to be very stable as this is not collected at a very high rate ad is applied to the whole motor vehicle pool which stays stable from year to year. To explain this chart better we need to convert the figures to USD and even take into account the US inflation. Figure 5 provides the two lines showing the taxes adjusted for the USD TL exchange rate and the US inflation of 2% per year.

This chart tells a much critical story. The real tax collection from motor vehicle related sources is actually way below the start of the analysis year of 2002. The peak year of 2013 2014 were the golden years in terms of government budget and tax collection. In the recent years the government has had a recurring budget deficit and this keeps increasing.

There are also other problems and issues with the current taxation system which are listed below:

- High taxes store value so some are recaptured when cars are sold as second hand. So this may not be a bad thing.
- Some safety options may be sacrificed due to high taxes such as emergency brake assist.
- Break even selection decision of fuel efficient hybrid vs. traditional models brings us a different picture because of the effect of taxes.
- Given two models Hybrid and regular, it will take 1 million kilometers for first model to break even!
- Turkey pays USD for oil imports and hence high taxes do not favor more efficient models indeed older cars are even favored as MTV drops to very low values as the cars age

Figure 4. Taxes from three sources collected in Turkey from 2002 until 2020 (in TL)
Source: Author.

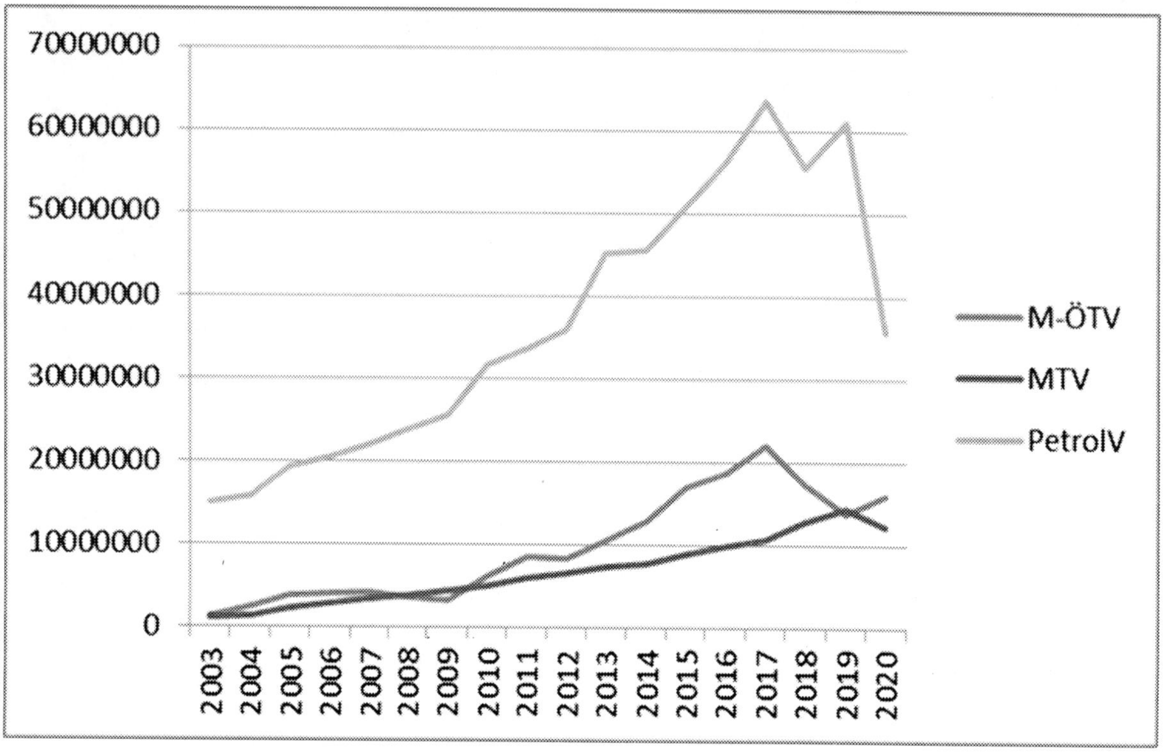

RECOMMENDATIONS AND DISCUSSION

The fact that automotive industry is about to undergo major changes from the competition of electric cars and the sharing mobility solutions leaves governments in doubt as to how they should rely on one of their greatest sources of tax revenue. Our article tried to shed light into this very important phenomenon of changing the tax structures. In the future taxation methods should be based on emission rather than simply engine size. Electric cars and sharing mobility should also be emphasized. Also new studies on millennials such as Akkucuk & Turan (2016) may be needed to understand the concerns of the future decision makers with respect to taxes levied on automotive products. Different business fields such as marketing and quality can also be consulted in order to improve the issues automotive industry is facing (Akkucuk & Kucukkancabas, 2007; Akkucuk, 2014; Akkucuk, 2017; Akkucuk & Teuman, 2016; Akkucuk, 2009).

The concept of "Sustainability" as it related to many disciplines has been under examination by academics from diverse disciplines for an extensive period of time. Sustainability in transportation and logistics is similarly an emergent area of interest by the scholarly community. Logistics, Supply Chain Management, Reverse Logistics and Recycling are among some of the areas most commonly focused on by researchers interested in sustainability field (Akkucuk, 2016; Gencer, 2016; Gencer & Akkucuk, 2016). Akkucuk and Sekercioglu (2016) exhibit a case where a small NGO in Turkey is operational in nurturing sustainable ecotourism. This type of ecologically sensitive tourism may also reduce the amount of petrol spent in travel and affect the economy positively.

Figure 5. Taxes from three sources collected in Turkey from 2002 until 2020 (in USD and real USD adjusted for 2% inflation)
Source: Author.

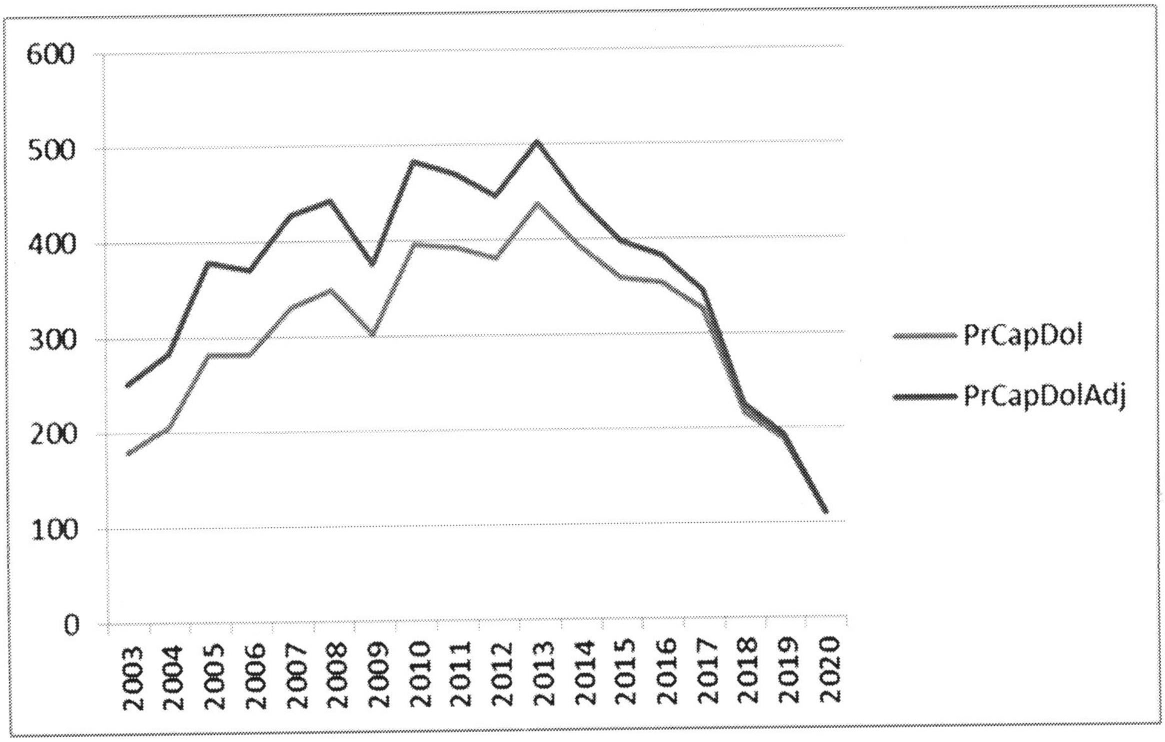

Mobility concept took on a new meaning with developments such as shared ride services. Electric cars are also fast replacing the traditional combustion engines. The electric cars do not produce gases and if the electricity generation is green enough the impact on the environment is low. For disruptions in the supply chain the cars need to be simpler with fewer locally sourced parts. Also the taxes levied by the government should reflect mostly the impact on the environment and taxes should not be used to the extreme.

REFERENCES

Acemoglu, D. (2009). The crisis of 2008: structural lessons for and from economics. *Globalization and Growth*, 37.

Agell, J., & Persson, M. (2001). On the analytics of the dynamic Laffer curve. *Journal of Monetary Economics*, *48*(2), 397–414. doi:10.1016/S0304-3932(01)00074-5

Akküçük, U. (2009). İş etiğinde Sarbanes-Oxley (SOX) Yasası'nın etkisi ve toplam kalite yönetimi uygulamalarında yansımaları. *İş Ahlakı Dergisi*, *2*(3), 7-17.

Akkucuk, U. (2014). Application of lean six sigma methodology in design and improvement of financial services. In *Globalization of Financial Institutions* (pp. 151–164). Springer. doi:10.1007/978-3-319-01125-7_11

Akkucuk, U. (2016). SCOR Model and the Green Supply Chain. In U. Akkucuk (Ed.), *Handbook of Research on Waste Management Techniques for Sustainability* (pp. 108–124). IGI Global. doi:10.4018/978-1-4666-9723-2.ch006

Akkucuk, U. (Ed.). (2017). *Ethics and Sustainability in Global Supply Chain Management*. IGI Global. doi:10.4018/978-1-5225-2036-8

Akkucuk, U., & Kucukkancabas, S. (2007). Analyzing the Perceptions of Turkish Universities Using Multidimensional Scaling (MDS) Analysis. *Bogazici Journal of Economics and Administrative Sciences*, *21*, 125–141.

Akkucuk, U., & Sekercioglu, C. H. (2016). NGOs for Environmental Sustainability: The Case of Kuzeydoga Foundation. *Fresenius Environmental Bulletin*, *25*(12), 6038–6044.

Akkucuk, U., & Teuman, B. (2016). Assessing service quality in online banking services. *Problems and Perspectives in Management*, *14*(2), 183–191. doi:10.21511/ppm.14(2-1).2016.07

Akkucuk, U., & Turan, C. (2016). Mobile use and online preferences of the millenials: A study in Yalova. *Journal of Internet Banking and Commerce*, *21*(1), 142.

Ashton, P. (2009). An appetite for yield: The anatomy of the subprime mortgage crisis. *Environment & Planning A*, *41*(6), 1420–1441. doi:10.1068/a40328

Blinder, A. S. (1981). Thoughts on the Laffer curve. In *The supply-side effects of economic policy* (pp. 81–92). Springer. doi:10.1007/978-94-009-8174-4_3

Buchanan, J. M., & Lee, D. R. (1982). Politics, time, and the Laffer curve. *Journal of Political Economy*, *90*(4), 816–819. doi:10.1086/261091

Chaloupka, F. J., Powell, L. M., & Warner, K. E. (2019). The use of excise taxes to reduce tobacco, alcohol, and sugary beverage consumption. *Annual Review of Public Health*, *40*(1), 187–201. doi:10.1146/annurev-publhealth-040218-043816 PMID:30601721

Craighead, C. W., Blackhurst, J., Rungtusanatham, M. J., & Handfield, R. B. (2007). The severity of supply chain disruptions: Design characteristics and mitigation capabilities. *Decision Sciences*, *38*(1), 131–156. doi:10.1111/j.1540-5915.2007.00151.x

Feige, E. L., & McGee, R. T. (1983). Sweden's Laffer curve: Taxation and the unobserved economy. *The Scandinavian Journal of Economics*, *85*(4), 499–519. doi:10.2307/3439948

Gencer, Y. G. (2016). Mystery of Recycling: Glass and Aluminum Examples. In U. Akkucuk (Ed.), *Handbook of Research on Waste Management Techniques for Sustainability* (pp. 172–191). IGI Global. doi:10.4018/978-1-4666-9723-2.ch009

Gencer, Y. G., & Akkucuk, U. (2016). Reverse Logistics: Automobile Recalls and Other Conditions. In U. Akkucuk (Ed.), *Handbook of Research on Waste Management Techniques for Sustainability* (pp. 125–154). IGI Global. doi:10.4018/978-1-4666-9723-2.ch007

Ishida, S. (2020). Perspectives on supply chain management in a pandemic and the post-COVID-19 era. *IEEE Engineering Management Review*, *48*(3), 146–152. doi:10.1109/EMR.2020.3016350

Kamalahmadi, M., Shekarian, M., & Mellat Parast, M. (2022). The impact of flexibility and redundancy on improving supply chain resilience to disruptions. *International Journal of Production Research*, *60*(6), 1992–2020. doi:10.1080/00207543.2021.1883759

Korniejczuk, K. (2019). *Simulating severe supply chain disruptions with multiple suppliers and firms* (Doctoral dissertation). Iowa State University.

LaBelle, J., & Santacreu, A. M. (2022). Global supply chain disruptions and inflation during the COVID-19 pandemic. *Review - Federal Reserve Bank of St. Louis*.

Laffer, A. B. (2004). The Laffer curve: Past, present, and future. *Backgrounder (Washington, D.C.)*, *1765*(1), 1–16.

Leckcivilize, A. (2012). *The Impact of Supply Chain Disruptions: Evidence from the Japanese Tsunami*. London School or Economics and Political Science.

Lee, K., & Ni, S. (2002). On the dynamic effects of oil price shocks: A study using industry level data. *Journal of Monetary Economics*, *49*(4), 823–852. doi:10.1016/S0304-3932(02)00114-9

Lim, A. H. Y., & Tan, C. L. (2018). JIT and supply chain disruptions following a major disaster: A case study from the auto industry. *Global Business and Organizational Excellence*, *37*(6), 51–58. doi:10.1002/joe.21887

Lin, B., & Jia, Z. (2019). Tax rate, government revenue and economic performance: A perspective of Laffer curve. *China Economic Review*, *56*, 101307. doi:10.1016/j.chieco.2019.101307

Malcomson, J. M. (1986). Some analytics of the Laffer curve. *Journal of Public Economics*, *29*(3), 263–279. doi:10.1016/0047-2727(86)90029-0

Megersa, K. A. (2015). The laffer curve and the debt-growth link in low-income Sub-Saharan African economies. *Journal of Economic Studies (Glasgow, Scotland)*, *42*(5), 878–892. doi:10.1108/JES-06-2014-0095

Mirowski, P. (1982). What's wrong with the Laffer Curve? *Journal of Economic Issues, 16*(3), 815-828.

Pavlínek, P. (2015). The impact of the 2008–2009 crisis on the automotive industry: Global trends and firm-level effects in Central Europe. *European Urban and Regional Studies*, *22*(1), 20–40. doi:10.1177/0969776412460534

Ramírez Pérez, S. M. (2020). Embedding the market during times of crisis: The European automobile cartel during a decade of crisis (1973–1985). *Business History*, *62*(5), 815–836. doi:10.1080/00076791.2019.1575037

Rosenfeld, H. (2009). The North American auto industry in crisis. *Monthly Review (New York, N.Y.), 61*(2), 18–36. doi:10.14452/MR-061-02-2009-06_2

Şaşmaz, M. Ü., & Şakar, E. (2020). *The effect of taxes and public expenditures on happiness: Empirical evidence from OECD countries*. doi:10.21833/ijaas.2020.08.014

Sturgeon, T., & Van Biesebroeck, J. (2010). *Effects of the crisis on the automotive industry in developing countries: a global value chain perspective.* World Bank Policy Research Working Paper, (5330).

Sudan, T., & Taggar, R. (2022). COVID-19 Induced Supply Chain Disruptions and Automotive Industry: A Case Study of Maruti Suzuki India Limited and Mitigation Strategies. *Global Economics Science*, 35-52.

Tatu, Ş. (2014). An application of debt Laffer curve: Empirical evidence for Romania's case. *Romanian Journal of Fiscal Policy, 5*(1), 29–38.

Trabandt, M., & Uhlig, H. (2011). The Laffer curve revisited. *Journal of Monetary Economics, 58*(4), 305–327. doi:10.1016/j.jmoneco.2011.07.003

Wad, P. (2009). The automobile industry of Southeast Asia: Malaysia and Thailand. *Journal of the Asia Pacific Economy, 14*(2), 172–193. doi:10.1080/13547860902786029

Wanniski, J. (1978). Taxes, revenues, and the Laffer curve. *The Public Interest, 50*, 3.

Weber, J. (2009). *Automotive development processes: Processes for successful customer oriented vehicle development.* Springer Science & Business Media. doi:10.1007/978-3-642-01253-2

ADDITIONAL READING

Aswicahyono, H., Anas, T., & Damuri, Y. R. (1999). The development of the Indonesian automotive industry (No. WPE051). Centre for Strategic and International Studies.

Bilas, V., Franc, S., & Arbanas, B. (2013). The impact of current economic crisis on the automotive industry. *Economic Thought and Practice, 22*(1), 299–320.

Brandenburg, M. (2016). Supply chain efficiency, value creation and the economic crisis–An empirical assessment of the European automotive industry 2002–2010. *International Journal of Production Economics, 171*, 321–335. doi:10.1016/j.ijpe.2015.07.039

Catalan Vidal, J. (2017). The stagflation crisis and the European automotive industry, 1973–85. *Business History, 59*(1), 4–34. doi:10.1080/00076791.2016.1237505

Domański, B., Guzik, R., Gwosdz, K., & Dej, M. (2013). The crisis and beyond: the dynamics and restructuring of automotive industry in Poland. *International Journal of Automotive Technology and Management, 13*(2), 151-166.

Hoeft, F. (2021). The case of sales in the automotive industry during the COVID-19 pandemic. *Strategic Change, 30*(2), 117–125. doi:10.1002/jsc.2395

Jeong, S. I. (2004). *Crisis and restructuring in East Asia: The case of the Korean Chaebol and the automotive industry*. Springer. doi:10.1057/9780230510982

Marati, N., Gupta, R. G., & Vaithilingam, B. (2020, January). Multilayer ceramic capacitors crisis management in automotive industry. In *2020 IEEE International Conference on Power Electronics, Smart Grid and Renewable Energy (PESGRE2020)* (pp. 1-6). IEEE. 10.1109/PESGRE45664.2020.9070770

Oh, S. Y. (2014). Shifting gears: Industrial policy and automotive industry after the 2008 financial crisis. *Business and Politics*, *16*(4), 641–665. doi:10.1515/bap-2014-0015

Olegovna, S. N., Zakharovna, T. A., & Andreevna, U. E. (2015). Situation in Russian automotive industry and automotive market in crisis. *European Journal of Economics and Management Sciences*, (2), 103-107.

Pardi, T. (2017). Industrial policy and the British automotive industry under Margaret Thatcher. *Business History*, *59*(1), 75–100. doi:10.1080/00076791.2016.1223049

Pavelková, D., Homolka, L., Knápková, A., Kolman, K., & Pham, H. (2018). EVA and key performance indicators: The case of automotive sector in pre-crisis, crisis and post-crisis periods. *Economia e Sociologia*, *11*(3), 78–95. doi:10.14254/2071-789X.2018/11-3/5

Pavlínek, P. (2015). The impact of the 2008–2009 crisis on the automotive industry: Global trends and firm-level effects in Central Europe. *European Urban and Regional Studies*, *22*(1), 20–40. doi:10.1177/0969776412460534

Pavlínek, P., Aláez-Aller, R., Gil-Canaleta, C., & Ullibarri-Arce, M. (2017). *Foreign Direct Investment and the development of the automotive industry in Eastern and Southern Europe*. ETUI Research Paper-Working Paper.

Pavlínek, P., & Ženka, J. (2010). The 2008–2009 automotive industry crisis and regional unemployment in Central Europe. *Cambridge Journal of Regions, Economy and Society*, *3*(3), 349–365. doi:10.1093/cjres/rsq026

Sabbagha, O., Ab Rahman, M. N., Ismail, W. R., & Hussain, W. M. H. W. (2016). Impact of quality management systems and after-sales key performance indicators on automotive industry: A literature review. *Procedia: Social and Behavioral Sciences*, *224*, 68–75. doi:10.1016/j.sbspro.2016.05.401

Sturgeon, T., & Florida, R. (2000). *Globalization and jobs in the automotive industry. Final report to the Alfred P. Sloan Foundation. International Motor Vehicle Program*. Center for Technology, Policy, and Industrial Development, Massachusetts Institute of Technology.

Sturgeon, T., & Van Biesebroeck, J. (2010). *Effects of the crisis on the automotive industry in developing countries: a global value chain perspective*. World Bank Policy Research Working Paper, (5330).

Sturgeon, T. J., & Van Biesebroeck, J. (2009). Crisis and protection in the automotive industry: a global value chain perspective. *Effective crisis response and openness: Implications for the trading system*, 285-305.

Sturgeon, T. J., & Van Biesebroeck, J. (2011). Global value chains in the automotive industry: An enhanced role for developing countries? *International Journal of Technological Learning. Innovation and Development*, *4*(1-3), 181–205.

Wu, X., Zhang, C., & Du, W. (2021, July). An analysis on the crisis of "chips shortage" in automobile industry——Based on the double influence of COVID-19 and trade friction. *Journal of Physics: Conference Series, 1971*(1), 012100. doi:10.1088/1742-6596/1971/1/012100

KEY TERMS AND DEFINITIONS

Automotive Taxes: Taxes that are levied on automobiles only apart from VAT which is levied on all products.

Cylinder Volume: A measure of the size of the engine which is a basis for taxation in some countries.

Emissions Rating: A measure of the carbon dioxide emissions from the gasoline or diesel motor are. Different countries have various rating systems.

MTV: A form of tax that recurs every year and is paid in two installments in Turkey.

ÖTV: A special form of tax levied on motor vehicle in Turkey and may result in a significant markup of the vehicle price.

PPI: Producer price index, a measure of inflation sometimes referred to as WPI (wholesale price index).

Sustainable Transportation: Practicing transportation in a way that preserves the natural resources and lowers emissions.

VAT: Value added tax, KDV in Turkey.

Chapter 18

Internal Audit, Internal Control Systems in Finance Industry in the Changing Business Environment, Evidence From Turkey as an Emerging Economy:

Banking Applications, Internal Systems

Fatih Kayhan
Kırklareli University, Turkey

ABSTRACT

The purpose of this chapter is to review internal audit and internal control functions in the banking industry by taking into account the international COSO framework. The financial industry is regarded as one of the key elements of a stable economy. It is a well-known fact that financial institutions in general—banks in particular (public or private, foreign or local)—need to have a sound internal system to implement the high principle of 'maker-checker-supervisor-auditor'. The study examines the application of internal systems in the Turkish banking industry primarily and covers not only the theory, application, and legislative sides, but also organizational structure and development of audit and control activity in the banking sector.

INTRODUCTION

The origins of the profession of internal audit date back to the beginning of 1900. Looking at the evolution of internal audit, it is observed that there exist 4 basic audit approaches historically: Control-based audit, process-based audit, risk-based audit and risk-management-based audit. The process from tradi-

DOI: 10.4018/978-1-6684-5876-1.ch018

tional internal audit to risk management-based internal audit has been affected by the changing needs of businesses, the effects of the globalization process on businesses, the technology-based changes experienced, and the changing internal and external environment and accounting-economy-based crises (Pehlivanlı, 2020:13).

Last 20 years witnessed the rise of off-site-audit and remote-audit (e-audit). Before internet and financial technologies became widespread, only onsite audits and control were applicable. However, rise in information technologies made great changes in business models and in return in internal audit / control functions.

The scope of this study is limited to internal audit and internal control activities in banks (and partly other financial institutions) in Turkey. Therefore, independent audit activities are out of scope of this study. Independent auditor examines the sectoral characteristics and sectoral regulations in which the client is operating; besides, he/she examines business accounting policies, business risks, and business internal control structure (Pehlivanlı, 2020:40).

The motivation of this study is attributable to two important factors: Firstly, it is important to note that internal systems of financial institutions have changed considerably after the year 2000 in line with the improvements in financial technologies and change in the style of business and operations in the World and Turkey. Secondly, it is significant to observe the very fact that these changes in the way of doing business and internal audit culture have repercussions on the effectiveness and efficiency of the financial (in particular, the banks) and non-financial industry.

The rest of the chapter is organized as follows: The first part covers general framework pertaining to internal control, internal audit and related literature. Application in banking industy is examined in the second part. The third part briefly analyses regulatory framework for banking particularly. The last part concludes the chapter.

1. GENERAL REMARKS ON INTERNAL AUDIT AND INTERNAL CONTROL AND LITERATURE

Internal Audit

The Institute of Internal Auditors-IIA[1] defines the concept of internal audit as 'an independent and objective assurance and consulting activity designed to add value and improve an organization's operations'. IIA specifies standards on its official website as follows: International Standards for the Professional Practice of Internal Auditing (Standards) are principle-focused and provide a framework for performing and promoting internal auditing. The *Standards* are compulsory requirements, they are made up of: 1. Statements of basic requirements for the professional practice of internal auditing and for evaluating the effectiveness of its performance. 2. Interpretations (They clarify terms or concepts within the statements.) 3. Glossary terms.

It is important to take into account both the statements and their interpretations to comprehend and apply the *Standards* in an accurate way. The *Standards* utilize terms that have been referred to specific meanings as noted in the Glossary, which is also part of the *Standards* (https://www.theiia.org/en/standards/what-are-the-standards/).

Internal Control and COSO Framework: International Approaches

One of the main functions of management is control. Various models and reports on Internal Control have been published, and the most accepted control model in the world is the COSO Internal Control Framework developed by COSO in 1992 (Pehlivanlı, 2010, 31).

COSO Internal Control Framework: Generally speaking, internal control is a management activity that increases the probability of achieving the organization's objectives. The main features of Internal Control are as follows; Internal Control is a process, it is carried out by employees, it provides reasonable assurance, it is a means to achieve objectives (Pehlivanlı, 2010: 32).

Internal Control Framework Horizental Components: Control environment, risk assessment, control activities, information and communication, follow-up. On the other hand, vertical components are made up of objectives of the internal control system: Operations (activities), financial reporting and compliance (Pehlivanlı, 2010, 37-38).

Risk Management and its relationship with Independent Audit: The Internal Control system basically constitutes the first step of risk management. There is an inverse relationship between the internal control system and audit risk; as the effectiveness of the internal control system increases, the audit risk decreases, and as the effectiveness of the internal control decreases, the audit risk increases. (Pehlivanlı, 2010, 38-39)

Mashina et al. (2016) argues that implementation of an adequate internal audit, is an evidence through the examination stages as COSO Framework. Some of the components of the implementation of the examination conducted by COSO method approach has been appropriate control environment, risk activities control, information and communication, and monitoring part of the internal control system. Another study underlines the internal control function: Kim et al. (2011) study internal control weakness (ICW) and bank loan contacting, they use a sample of borrowing firms that disclosed internal control weaknesses (ICW) under Section 404 of the Sarbanes-Oxley Act, this study compares various features of loan contracts between firms with ICW and those without ICW. Based on the findings, they argue that banks increase loan rates charged to ICW firms after their disclosure of internal control problems and that banks reduce loan rates after firms remediate previously reported ICW.

A Brief Review of Risk Management and Compliance Functions

Risk Management divisions of the banks in Turkey is one of the departments that have developed after the restructuring of Turkish Banking System. Risk Management consists of three main branches, namely, Credit Risk, Market Risk and Operational Risk. Risk management line of business developed parallel to Basel norms. 'Business Continuity' is the key element of operational risk, this term refers to the following funtions: Measuring, mitigating, monitoring and reporting related risk related to operational resilience; determination of business continuity strategy, risk appetite, classification of risks and operational resilience framework by identifying non-financial risks that will affect business continuity.

From another point of view, banks are dedicated to define and then take precaution against the following risk points:

- Reputation Risk,
- Environmental and Social risk
- Operational Risk

- Market Risk
- Interet Rate, FX (Foreign Currency) Risk
- Liquidity Risk
- Credit Risk
- Counterparty Risk
- Country (Credit) Risk
- Concentration Risk
- Other Risks

When it comes to Compliance Function, it can be asserted that banks and other financial institutions attribute great significance to compliance department. Basel Committee on Banking Supervision defines the basic definitions about the compliance function in its report on 'Compliance and the compliance function in banks (2005)' as follows:

'1. As part of its ongoing efforts to address bank supervisory issues and enhance sound practices in banking organizations, the Basel Committee on Banking Supervision (the Committee) is issuing this high level paper on compliance risk and the compliance function in banks. Banking supervisors must be satisfied that effective compliance policies and procedures are followed and that management takes appropriate corrective action when compliance failures are identified.

2. Compliance starts at the top. It will be most effective in a corporate culture that emphasises standards of honesty and integrity and in which the board of directors and senior management lead by example. It concerns everyone within the bank and should be viewed as an integral part of the bank's business activities. A bank should hold itself to high standards when carrying on business, and at all times strive to observe the spirit as well as the letter of the law. Failure to consider the impact of its actions on its shareholders, customers, employees and the markets may result in significant adverse publicity and reputational damage, even if no law has been broken.
3. The expression "compliance risk" is defined as the risk of legal or regulatory sanctions, material financial loss, or loss to reputation a bank may suffer as a result of its failure to comply with laws, regulations, rules, related self-regulatory organisation standards, and codes of conduct applicable to its banking activities (together, "compliance laws, rules and standards").
4. Compliance laws, rules and standards generally cover matters such as observing proper standards of market conduct, managing conflicts of interest, treating customers fairly, and ensuring the suitability of customer advice. They typically include specific areas such as the prevention of money laundering and terrorist financing, and may extend to tax laws that are relevant to the structuring of banking products or customer advice. A bank that knowingly participates in transactions intended to be used by customers to avoid regulatory or financial reporting requirements, evade tax liabilities or facilitate illegal conduct will be exposing itself to significant compliance risk.
5. Compliance laws, rules and standards have various sources, including primary legislation, rules and standards issued by legislators and supervisors, market conventions, codes of practice promoted by industry associations, and internal codes of conduct applicable to the staff

members of the bank. For the reasons mentioned above, these are likely to go beyond what is legally binding and embrace broader standards of integrity and ethical conduct.'

Literature Review

This section covers some of the previous studies in regard to the internal control and internal audit.

Simpson and Gleason (1999) examine the link between the ownership and structure of the board of directors and internal control system. The impact of board structure and ownership on the probability of financial distress is analyzed with a sample of 300 banks. Findings show that when one person is both a CEO and chairman of the board, there is lower likelihood of financial stress. They also find that other factors do not have a significant effect.

Spira and Page (2003) study risk management, internal control and the changing role of internal audit in UK and argue that developments in corporate governance reporting requirements offer opportunities for the appropriation of risk and management of risk by groups that want to promote their interests.

Başpınar (2004) reviews the audit standards in Turkey and World and maintains that since auditing is a question of accuracy, relevance and rationality, it is a necessity to question the audit activity itself. Ensuring quality and reliability in auditing is available if audit activities comply with the predetermined criteria. Auditing standards are the set of criteria related to the quality of the work done in a place; they cover the auditor in terms of his/her personal characteristics, and audit process itself.

British Treasury defines internal audit in its document 'Public Internal Audit Standarts' as follows: '*Internal auditing is an organization's independent and impartial evaluation service*' (Korkmaz, 2007:4).

Aslan (2010) evaluate the concept of internal audit as a management function and maintains that Iinternal audit, which is one of the five basic functions of management, has become a basic element that organizations need in order to remain strong and to exhibit sustainable success in today's world where competition is intensified and risks are constantly increasing. Since it assumes a function that strengthens the success, reliability and accountability of the top management in institutions, its importance is increasing. In many countries, both in the private sector and in the public administration, internal audit has a legal infrastructure.

Opromolla and Maccarini (2010) analyze the application of the rules about the control system in the banking system in Italy in regard to a legislative decree. They argue that Italian banks abide by legislative requirements presented on prevention of corporate crimes and companies liability.

Okur (2010) in his study reviewing the concepts of auditor ('*Teftiş*') and Internal Audit argues that while comparing and discussing these terms, it is important to pay attention to their contribution to the audit function and also take into account cumulative audit experiences plus new developments in this profession.

Regarding the relation between internal control and internal audit, Kızılboga and Ozsahin (2013) study the impact of effective internal control system on the activity of internal audit and internal auditor: They argue that effective internal control systems are conducive to internal auditor in that its existence ensures sustainability in achieving corporate goals and allows internal auditors to focus on consultancy services that support the functions of adding value and improving the institution.

Yüksel et al. (2016) evaluate the perception of internal audit (commonly called as 'board of auditors' in the case of Turkish banking sector) by bank personnel throgh a questionnaire conducted in Turkish banking industry with 174 personnel that work in different line of business other than audit function. Based on the findings of analysis, they contend that personnel with the title of sub-manager have more positive opinions (trust) about the board compared to managers. Besides, those who work in branches have relatively more positive opinions about the board when compared to those who work in head office.

Bozkurt (2016:30) reviews tne concepts of risk, corporate risk management and internal audit and argues that in order to ensure an effective corporate risk management, internal audit has roles and responsibilities. Internal audit can be defined as the catalyst for the process of corporate risk management, therefore it must be adopted by all parties in the corporations.

Utami et al. (2020) examine the effect of information technology (IT) governance, internal control, and organizational culture of early prevention of fraud based on the bank personnel's perception in Indonesia and maintain that internal control and organizational culture have a significant positive impact on early warning for fraud. In addition they find that IT governance has a positive but not statistically significant affect on early warning for fraud.

A recent and important study (carried out with quantitave approach) is the paper by Koutoupis and Malisiovas (2020): They investigate whether and how the internal control system influences the credit risk, profitability, and compliance of the banking industry in U.S. Based on the COSO Framework, Basel Committee Frameworks, and the literature, the components of the internal controls are quantified. They find that Risk Assessment, Control Activities, and Information and Communication components remarkably influence credit risk. The first (Control Environment) and last (Monitoring) components have a significant impact on credit risk. Furthermore, internal controls significantly affect the profitability and compliance of U.S. banks, except for the Risk Assessment component in the first case and the Control Environment component in the second case, respectively. Finally they maintain that 'control activities component' and 'the information and communication component' have a significant and positive relationship with the profitability of the banks (on the other hand, these two components are significantly and negatively correlated with the banks' compliance).

Kaban (2020:199) reviews internal audit according to the purpose in banks with a case study and maintain that basic distinctions among the ordinary audit, inspection and investigation works are as follows: Unlike ordinary audits and inspections that are conducted for non-criminal actions, the subject of the investigation is criminal activities; besides, ordinary audit activities are carried out with a plan (regular activity), but investigations are –by their very nature- irregular activities (i.e., not planned before); investigations are conducted in a much more comprehensive manner when compared to regular audit activities.

Kartal and Kızıl (2020) study Reporting and Resolution of Internal Audit and Internal Control Findings in Banks and examine the Context of Regulation on Banks' Information Systems and Electronic Banking Services. They argue that the audit findings that are output of the assurance activities carried out by the internal control and internal audit should be reported on a consolidated basis by way of a monitoring system, should be observed by the top management of the bank, and these activities should be continued for all audit findings, not only for the information system findings.

2. BANKING APPLICATIONS

The Turkish banking sector has experienced major reforms after the financial crisis in 2001 that took place in Turkey. The important components of these reforms included measures for strong regulation and supervision as well as restructuring and recapitalization of banks. After these were carried out with success, the Turkish banking sector was somehow protected against the adverse effects of the global crisis in 2008. The global financial crisis is considered to have a relatively limited adverse effect on the Turkish banking sector, even though Turkish economy was severely affected by this crisis (US, 2015: 10)

As of December 2021, according to recent data by BRSA, there are 55 banks that operate in Turkish Banking Sector as 34 deposit banks (also known as commercial/conventional banks), 15 development and investment banks and 6 participation banks (non-interest banking) with totally 11.098 branches and 202.000 personnel. Total assets increased to approximately TL 9.213 billion as of December 2021 (https://www.bddk.org.tr/Veri/EkGetir/17?ekId=77).

In Turkish Banking Organizational Structure (Head Office Organization), those departments (units) directly report to Board of Directors: Board of Auditors *(Teftiş Kurulu)*, Internal Control (*İç Kontrol*), Compliance *(Uyum)* and Risk Management Units (*Risk Yönetimi).* Althogh these report to the very same Board Member, Risk Management division differs from other three units in that risk management has also to do with executive functions. All in all, it can be said that although General Manager of the banks is the top executive of all units, these 4 departments report directly to Board Member in an effort to ensure the principle of check and balance, separation of powers, *maker-checker-supervisor-auditor* principle. The rationale behind this is simple; executive and auditing functions should be separated in order to ensure efficiency and sustainable corporate structure of the banks, which are the key financial institutions of the economy as a whole.

In practice, internal audit department (Board of Auditors = '*Teftiş Kurulu*') in Turkish banking industry carries out audit and investigation activities in head office departments, branches and subsidiary companies (insurance, brokerage companies, factoring, leasing, portfolio management company as well as non-financial subsidiaries). Branches (especially in commercial banks and participation banks) are of three types: Retail Branches (individual banking, SME banking), Commercial Branches and Corporate Branches (that performs banking activities for only large-scale companies). Apart from these three branches, some of the deposit banks (commercial banks) may have specially designed branches like free-zone branches. On the other hand, internal control departments carry out only control activities and field reports. The key factor that differentiates internal audit from internal control is that internal audit department also reviews the activities of internal control department so that internal control activities are conducted in line with bank's internal policies.

Internal audit activities in the branches cover those audit fields: Retail Loans, Operations (all operations in the branches) and Commercial/Corporate Loans. Retail loans are composed of cash and non-cash loans for individuals and SME (Small and Medium Enterprises). For all loans/credits (retail / commercial / corporate), the following audit points are reviewed:

- The accuracy of loan allocation (whether or not allocation of a loan is in line with the loan/credit allocation policy of the bank),
- Documentation (whether or not necessary documents for a loan allocation/utilization are received from the customer)
- Collateral (This has to do with whether the pre-determined collaterals are obtained from customers before loan utilization. These collaterals are defined in 'credit appoval form' ('*kredi tebliğ mektubu*'). The audit/control covers not only the quantity of the collaterals but also their quality.
- Investigation about the customer (This control is whether the customer are checked with respect to the credibility; the customers previous loan repayments are to be closely followed up).

- Loan repayments of the existing disbursements (Whether or not failure to repay principal or interest amounts and/or installments are processed in accordance with banking law, regulation and internal policies of the bank).

Internal audit and internal control functions are partly alike in that the above mentioned controls are performed by both departments during regular internal audits/controls. However, these two departments differ in that internal audit activities are more comprehensive, that is, internal audit units also review whether internal control activies are carried out in conformity with rules and regulations. In case of wrongdoing/wrongful conduct/ corruption in branches, it is internal audit that deals with the issues.

As far as internal audit activities in Head Office Units are concerned, those departments are especially subject to internal audit: Loans operations, foreign trade operations, branch operations, treasury operations and other operational units. Apart from operation departments, accounting units are subject to internal audit. These are the departments that are commonly covered for internal audit. Loan allocation department (*'Kredi Tahsis ve İzleme'*), budget department, risk management and other departments can also be audited when deemed necessary by the Board and top management. Internal control departmens may also regularly carry out control activities for these departments, but the scope and purpose of internal audit is different from that of internal control. The scope of internal audit is rather comprehensive.

These audit and control activities –in head office divisions or branches- can be performed via on-site and off-site reviews with the help of developing reporting tools, that enable early warning reporting. Recent improvements in financial technology made it available to review activities of the audited units promptly and effectively.

Control mechanisms are categorized in 3 *lines of defense* especially in foreign banks (those private banks are owned by foreign banking groups with respect to shareholder structure). *The first line defense* is regarded as operational units that are controlling documents of clients. *The second line of defense* is considered as 'internal control' that reviews the first line defense controls; it should be underlined that some divisions other than internal control departments may also be regarded as part of the second line of defense (For example, legal department or central operational functions as well as 'loan allocation department'). In the final analysis, internal audit is the only *third line of defense*.

A Brief Review of Non-Banking Financial Institutions in Regard To Internal Audit and Internal Control

Insurance companies have internal audit, internal control, risk management and compliance departments. The following departments are subject to internal audit and internal control activities: Technical-Operation departments (especially those that create accounting entries), finance-accounting departments, fund operations departments, collection department, procurement and administrative affairs, compensation department, information technologies, line of business (sales), technical units.

Brokerage Firms (*'Aracı Kurumlar'*) and Portfolio Management Companies have their own internal control departments with respect to all capital market activities conducted by operational, financial units of these firms so that all activities of these firms are done in conformity with the law and regulations of capital market law as well as secondary legislatin by Capital Market Board (*Sermaye Piyasası Kurulu*). When these two types of non-banking financial instiutions are subsidiary of the banks, their activities are reviewed by internal audit department of the bank.

Factoring and leasing companies have internal control divisions that closely review all the transactions performed in operational and executive divisions (domestic and international factoring operations, mid-offices, finance-accounting, administrative units). In accordance with the related law and regulations, internal control of these non-banking financial institutions (they provide funding for clients, in this way their activities partly resemble banks with respect to fund utilization) are in place so that all factoring / financial lease activities are in line with international and domestic rules and regulations as well as company internal policies. If these two types of non-banking financial institutions are subsidiary of the banks (in the event of a financial supermarket), their activities are reviewed by internal audit of the bank ('*parent company supervision*').

3. GOVERNING LEGISLATION RELATED TO INTERNAL SYSTEMS IN TURKISH BANKING SECTOR AND INTERNATIONAL FRAMEWORK

In the case of Turkey, the regulation by Banking Regulation and Supervisory Agency (regulatory body for the banks) regarding internal systems is numbered 29057, dated 11 July 2014. The regulation is title as '*Regulation on Internal Systems of Banks and Internal Capital Adequacy Evaluation Process*' (*Bankaların İç Sistemleri ve İçsel Sermaye Yeterliliği Değerlendirme Süreci Hakkında Yönetmelik*). This regulation was issued upon the related articles and provisions of the Turkish Banking Law (No. 5411) in force and became effective at the very same date and became binding for all banks operating in Turkey. The second part of this legal document specifies establishment of internal systems and responsibilities of senior management of the banks: According to Article 4, banks are obliged to set up and operate adequate and effective internal systems, covering their branches, partnerships, within the framework of the procedures and principles set forth in the regulation, in order to monitor and control the risks they are exposed to, within the scope and structure of their activities compatible with changing conditions. Units within the scope of internal systems are established within the organizational structure of the bank, depending on the board of directors.

Legislative chronology for internal auditing in the world and in Turkey:

- Sarbanes Oxley Act, 2002
- Public Financial Management and Control Law, 2003
- Banking Law, 2005
- Corporate Governance Principles, 2003 and 2005

Sarbanes Oxley Act is a corporate governance act that required heavy reponsibilities for top management of listed-companies (publicly held companies). This act is based on accounting. Corruptions taking place in companies and resulting in financial crises caused governments to take action and in return this act was adopted in USA. Main topics of this act (2002) are as follows:

- Public companies accounting oversight board,
- Independence of Auditors,
- Corporate Responsibility
- Financial Statements
- Analyst conflicts of interest

- Commission's resources and authority
- Works and Reports
- Responsibility of the institution and the criminal in fraud
- Increasing penalties for white-collar crimes
- Corporate Tax Return
- Corporate Corruption and Responsibility

Developments and crises in the field of Internal Audit and Corporate Governance are parallel. Emerging crises both cause the system to be questioned and result in taking measures to make the system work more effectively (Pehlivanlı, 2020: 20)

When considering internal audit regarding capital market activities, Capital Market Board of Turkey (*SPK-Sermaye Piyasası Kurulu*) and regulations of this regulatory and supervisory institution are of vital significance. The Board issues secondary legislation in line with Capital Markets Law (Numbered 6362) in order to ensure that all capital market acitivities are in line with rules and regulations in force. The rationale/motivation behind the law and the secondary legislations (regulation and others) is that rights of the clients of the capital markets must be protected.

CONCLUSION

From 2020 to today's world, it is seen that internal audit and internal control has changed considerably in line with changing business environment in regard to financial technologies, cybersecurity, pandemic disease, changing business styles, regulatory envioronment in general. Banking industry and non-banking financial industries have also been influenced by those changes to a great extent. Therefore, financial insitutions improved their internal systems in an effort to be in harmony with new business conditions.

To this end, for the new era of business in general and for the year of 2022, The IIA defined top 12 risks that are likely to influence firms. It can be asserted that these can also be applied to financial institutions. Those 12 risks are defined as follows: Cybersecurity, Talent Management, Organizational Governance, Data Privacy, Culture, Economic and Political Volatility, Change in Regulatory Environment, Supplier and Vendor Management, Distruptive Innovation, Social Sustainability, Supply Chain Disruption,Environmental Sustainability.

This study concludes that internal audit and internal control systems (in financial world and in Turkish financial system) are changing in harmony with improvements and developments in the world. A key recommendation for the regulators of today's world can be as follows: The new rules and regulations shaping the auditing and control activities in financial institutions should take into account the impact of these rules on changing business environment. This is significant in that for smootly functioning financial organizations, lines of business, operations and internal systems (audit and control) should operate in coordination and cooperation.

REFERENCES

Aslan, B. (2010). Bir Yönetim Fonksiyonu Olarak İç Denetim. *Sayıştay Dergisi*, (77), 63-86. Retrieved from https://dergipark.org.tr/en/pub/sayistay/issue/61532/919029

Banking Regulation and Supervision Agency of Turkey. (2021). *Turkish Banking Sector Main Indicators Report*. https://www.bddk.org.tr/Veri/EkGetir/17?ekId=90

Basel Committee on Banking Supervision - Bank for International Settlements. (2005, April). Retrieved July 21, 2022, from https://www.bis.org/publ/bcbs113.pdf

Başpınar, A. (2004). Türkiye'de ve Dünyada Denetim Standartlarının Oluşumuna Genel Bir Bakış. *Maliye Dergisi*, 146.

BDDK. (n.d.). Retrieved July 21, 2022, from https://www.bddk.org.tr/

Bozkurt, C. (2016). Risk, Kurumsal Risk Yönetimi ve İç Denetim. *Denetişim*, (4), 17-30. Retrieved from https://dergipark.org.tr/tr/pub/denetisim/issue/22481/240477

Duyurular. (n.d.). Retrieved July 21, 2022, from https://www.tbb.org.tr/tr

Home: The Institute of Internal Auditors: The IIA. (n.d.). Retrieved July 21, 2022, from https://www.theiia.org/

Kaban, İ. (2020). Bankalarda Amacına Göre İç Denetim: Türkiye Bankacılık Sektörü Özelinde Örnek Denetim Vakaları. *Optimum Ekonomi ve Yönetim Bilimleri Dergisi*, *7*(1), 181–200. doi:10.17541/optimum.570629

Kartal, M. T., & Kizil, C. (2020). Bankalarda İç Denetim ve İç Kontrol Bulgularının Raporlanması ile Çözümlenmesi: Bankaların Bilgi Sistemleri ve Elektronik Bankacılık Hizmetleri Hakkında Yönetmelik Kapsamında Bir İnceleme [Reporting and Resolution of Internal Audit and Internal Control Findings in Banks: An Examination within the Context of Regulation on Banks' Information Systems and Electronic Banking Services]. *Turkish Studies - Economics, Finance, Politics Journal*, *15*(3), 1485–1500.

Kim, J. B., Song, B. Y., & Zhang, L. (2011). Internal Control Weakness and Bank Loan Contracting: Evidence from SOX Section 404 Disclosures. *The Accounting Review*, *86*(4), 1157–1188. doi:10.2308/accr-10036

Kızılboğa, R., & Özşahin, F. (2013). Etkin Bir İç Kontrol Sisteminin İç Denetim Faaliyetine ve İç Denetçilere Katkısı. *Niğde Üniversitesi İktisadi ve İdari Bilimler Fakültesi Dergisi*, *6*(2), 220–236.

Korkmaz, U. (2007). Kamuda İç Denetim. *Bütçe Dünyası*, *2*(25), 4–15.

Koutoupis, A. G., & Malisiovas, T. (2021). The effects of the internal control system on the risk, profitability, and compliance of the U.S. banking sector: A quantitative approach. *International Journal of Finance & Economics*, 1–15. doi:10.1002/ijfe.2498

Mahsina, M., Poniwati, A., & Hidayati, K. (2016). Coso Framework: An Internal Audit & Effectiveness Analysis of Banking Internal Control on Credit Investment Aspect. *International Conference on Education for Economics, Business, and Finance (ICEEBF)*.

Okur, Y. (2010). Türkiye'de Teftiş ve İç Denetim: Kavramlar, Beklentiler ve Hayatla Yüzleşme. *Maliye Dergisi* 158.

Opromolla, G., & Maccarini, M. (2010). The control system in the Italian banking sector: Recent changes in the application of Legislative Decree No. 231 of June 8, 2001. *Journal of Investment Compliance, 11*(2), 16–22. doi:10.1108/15285811011056330

Pehlivanlı, D. (2020). *Modern İç Denetim, Güncel İç Denetim Uygulamaları*. Beta Yayınevi.

Simpson, W. G., & Gleason, A. E. (1999). Board structure, ownership, and financial distress in banking firms. *International Review of Economics & Finance, 8*(3), 281–292. doi:10.1016/S1059-0560(99)00026-X

Spira, L. F., & Page, M. (2003). Risk management: The reinvention of internal control and the changing role of internal audit. *Accounting, Auditing & Accountability Journal, 16*(4), 640–661. doi:10.1108/09513570310492335

US. (2015). Do Banks Respond Asymmetrically to the Global Crisis? Evidence From Turkey. *Journal of BRSA Banking and Financial Markets. Banking Regulation and Supervision Agency, 9*(2), 9–44.

Utami, W., Nugroho, L., Mappanyuki, R., & Yelvionita, V. (2020). Early Warning Fraud Determinants in Banking Industries. *Asian Economic and Financial Review, 10*(6), 604–627. doi:10.18488/journal.aefr.2020.106.604.627

Yüksel, S., Zengin, S., & Kartal, M. T. (2016). Banka Personelinin Teftiş Kuruluna Bakış Açısının Değerlendirilmesi. *Finans Politik ve Ekonomik Yorumlar*, (622) 101-115. Retrieved from https://dergipark.org.tr/en/pub/fpeyd/issue/48023/607332

ENDNOTE

[1] Established in 1941, The Institute of Internal Auditors (IIA) is an international professional association with global headquarters in USA. https://www.theiia.org/en/about-us/

Chapter 19

Blockchain in International Trade Documents Management Using NAHP Technique:

Case of Kapikule and Istanbul Border Customs

Kenan Güler
ATEZ Software Technologies, Turkey

Esengul Salihoglu
https://orcid.org/0000-0002-2005-1986
Sivas Cumhuriyet University, Turkey

Emre Ozturk
https://orcid.org/0000-0002-6327-4549
ATEZ Software Technologies, Turkey

Osman Pala
Karamanoglu Mehmetbey University, Turkey

ABSTRACT

This study aims to explore the potential of blockchain technology in digitalization of documents used in foreign trade processes and to embody the advantages it can bring to customs clearance processes. The work is in two stages. In the first stage, the authors examined the document flow between the parties in customs clearance processes through three different digitalization scenarios using blockchain technology. They have come to the conclusion that rapid adaptation to innovations based on blockchain technology in the field of document management in international trade customs clearance processes is advantageous. In the second stage, they analyzed the priorities of the rational decision-making process with the NAHP method. The main challenges facing the transition to new technology are the need to train staff for new systems, the need to develop and improve new internal processes, the time spent reaching agreements with trading partners in the transition period, and the alignment of technological developments with legislation.

DOI: 10.4018/978-1-6684-5876-1.ch019

1. INTRODUCTION

Differences between countries, especially in the level of technological sophistication, the richness of natural resources and the commodity prices have increased the need for foreign trade. In 2019 world economy, the total foreign trade volume reached 25 trillion US$, 19.4 trillion US$ of which consisted of trade in goods and 6.1 trillion US$ portion of trade in services in 2019 (UNCTAD, 2021). The WTO reports that world trade volume has grown by nearly 300 times over the half-century from 1950 to 2020. Even though there is a significant growth in foreign trade volume, business processes are still very traditional and complex. In a typical international trade finance transaction in the traditional form, dozens of documents circulate between approximately 20 parties many times and a total of more than a hundred pages of paper documents are used for a single transaction (Law Commission, 2022).

Blockchain is one of the most important digitalization technology and has many features to bring innovations to traditional foreign trade systems. These features can be listed as decentralization, anonymity, auditability and immutability (Zheng et al., 2017). Thanks to Blockchain applications based on distributed ledger technology, it is possible to create original electronic documents that cannot be copied peer-to-peer (P2P), whose data source can be guaranteed without the need for a trusted third party (Mihajlov et al., 2019). Thanks to these features, blockchain technology have the potential to offer many advantages such as transparency, reliability and time and cost savings needed in the traditional form of foreign trade ecosystem. International institutions, especially the World Trade Organisation (WTO), World Customs Organisation (WCO), United Nations Conference on Trade and Development (UNCTAD), Organisation for Economic Co-operation and Development (OECD) and International Chamber of Commerce (ICC) expect blockchain technology to have serious effects in the fields of trade and logistics and are actively working in these fields. One of these initiatives, the Intelligent Technology and Trade Initiative (ITTI) was organized in 2017 by the World Trade Organization (WTO). ITTI, where academics, negotiators and business leaders came together, agreed that both blockchain and augmented intelligence (AI) have the potential to increase commercial exchange (WTO, 2017). It is predicted that using blockchain and AI technologies will decrease intermediaries in foreign trade and increase confidence (ICC Brasil, 2018). Particular attention is paid to the idea of transitioning to electronic documents under the revised Kyoto Convention and through the Recent Framework Agreement on Facilitating Cross-Border Paperless Trade in Asia and the Pacific (Shope, 2022).

The main purpose of this article is to investigate the potential cost and time-saving effects of the use of blockchain technology in digitalization processes in international trade. For this purpose, the possible advantages in practice were tried to be embodied by estimating the application of blockchain technology in the field of international trade through scenarios and it was aimed to contribute to the field in this respect. Three different scenarios (partial digitalization, intermediate digitalization and full digitalization) were created regarding the digitalization of foreign trade documents using blockchain technology and the change was measured in comparison to the current situation. The reason for examining digitalization in three different scenarios is the possibility of involving foreign trade stakeholders in digitalization processes at different levels. In the literature, the innovations that blockchain technology will bring are mostly discussed in the theoretical dimension. The most important contribution of this study to the literature is the implementation of digitalization scenarios at different levels over real customs clearance procedures and the concrete presentation of the advantages that can be provided.

The remainder of the article is organized as follows. In section two, the need for digitalization and examples of blockchain technology application in foreign trade processes were given. The digitalization scenarios created were included in section three. Section four presents methodology and case study. NAHP analysis is presented in section five. Section six presents the conclusion of this study. Finaly, the conclusions of this study and outlines of the future research directions are discussed in section seven.

2. BLOCKCHAIN TECHNOLOGY IN TERMS OF INTERNATIONAL TRADE

It is important to take steps towards standardizing documents and processes in all participating countries in international trade. With the development of technology, the integration of the internet of things, big data analysis, cloud computing systems, distributed ledger and blockchain applications in all countries will provide a great convenience in foreign trade processes. Blockchain technology can provide a high level of security during the implementation of automated processes (Szewczyk, 2019). Storing data on foreign trade transactions on a private blockchain can ensure that activities in international trade processes are completely transparent. Thus, the actors involved in the process can access the transaction data in real time.

DLT (Distributed Ledger Technology) offers the possibility to produce electronic documents valid in shipping, trade and finance, which can mimic the characteristics of paper documents. DLT-based documents are transferable, do not require a central authority, and can be recorded and tracked in a ledger in an unalterable way. Control of electronic information rests with the person holding the private key. It offers the ability to protect sensitive business information that is not publicly visible. Unlike DLT, it operates as a centrally managed registry system based on multilateral private agreements (Law Commission, 2022).

While blockchain technology has great potential for building the digital future, it faces several technical challenges. First, scalability is a big concern. Larger blocks require larger storage space. Storing larger data means slower dissemination of information on the network. If it is desired to maintain such a large blockchain with fewer users on the network, there will be a gradual transformation to a centralized structure. Therefore, the trade-off between block size and security can force parties to choose (Zheng et al., 2017). Second, miners can claim larger revenues as the block size and number grow (Eyal and Sirer, 2014). Also, existing consensus algorithms such as proof of work or proof of stake face some serious problems. For example, the phenomenon that the rich get richer while proof of work consumes a lot of electrical energy can occur in the process of proof of work (Zheng et al., 2017). At this point, it is important to decide when blockchain technology is needed for industries and companies. The decision tree in the report prepared by the World Economic Forum (WEF) on this subject is a guide for the necessity of using blockchain in 11 questions (WEF, 2018).

Since it is commerce, not only the use of blockchain technology but also which blockchain technology is used is also important. Data privacy and protection of trade secrets in commerce are mandated by law. At the same time, because the data is shared transparently with the stakeholders in the blockchain network, it is necessary to know the parties with which the data is shared. For this reason, unlike cryptocurrency transactions, private and permissioned blockchain networks come to the fore in commercial platforms. In private and permissioned networks, stakeholders do not remain anonymous; their identities are clear and all stakeholders know and accept transactions that each other can make on the blockchain network. In this way, on one hand, data confidentiality is ensured, on the other hand, an agreement is reached by the stakeholders and transparency is realized. Stakeholders can digitalize their business processes by utilizing blockchain technology, with the trust provided by private and permissioned networks.

According to the PwC (2019) report, the main applications of Blockchain technology in transportation and logistics are automation of transportation processes, product authentication, payment automation, tracking of goods flow, digitalization and automation of information flow (Gonczol et al., 2020; PwC, 2019). Commercial applications developed based on blockchain technology continue to increase both in number and volume. Some examples are summarized below:

Ambrosus is a permissioned blockchain-based ecosystem for supply chains, optimized for interconnectivity with IoT devices, sensors, and ERP systems. It builds on the Ethereum Blockchain but uses a Proof-of-Authority consensus protocol.

CargoX Blockchain Document Transfer (BDT) is a smart & cost-effective solution for the transportation industry. Built on the public Ethereum Blockchain, Recipients can **validate the source** and **prove ownership** of their documents.

ePhyto certificate in the Port of Antwerp was set up for a specific apple trade between New Zealand (Port of Napier) and the Port of Antwerp. It lowered costs for exporters by eliminating high document delivery costs, increased efficiency for importers by reducing time loss and simplified administrative processes by providing an electronic archive.

Insurwave is the world's first blockchain platform for marine insurance. They take insurers, clients, brokers, and third parties and connect them to distributed common ledgers that capture data about identities, exposures and risks, integrating this information with insurance contracts.

Trace aims at trusted data exchanges in fragmented supply chains and has projects focusing on Standards & Certifications, trust in manufacturing, food traceability, fashion and apparel traceability, enterprise data interoperability, industrial data marketplace, rail travel safety, sustainable agriculture and financial flows.

Peer Ledger owns the USPTO patent for blockchain identity translator and has two apps. The first one focuses on trusted, immutable records of transactions, documents and metrics across an entire supply chain. The second one records and communicates COVID-19 tests and vaccines in real-time.

The transition from paper to electronic documents is facilitated by technological advancements. Electronic papers used in international commerce operations must be globally compatible. Studies on the national and international legal requirements for electronic documents are being conducted in this regard. The Model Law on Electronic Transferable Records (MLETR) created by the United Nations Commission on International Trade Law is one of the main projects. Another is the United Nations Convention on Contracts for the Carriage of Goods Wholly or Partly by Sea 2008 (UNCLOS). MLTER establishes a legal parity between ownership of a transferable paper document and control of an electronic transferable record (like a bill of exchange). As a result, its goal is to make electronic records transferrable (Law Commission, 2022). Under the revised Kyoto Convention, special attention is paid to the idea of establishing a possible roadmap forward through the Framework Agreement on Facilitating Cross-Border Paperless Trade in Asia and the Pacific (Shope, 2022).

Table 1. Digitalization Scenarios

DIGITALIZATION STEPS	PROCESS SAVINGS	COST SAVINGS	TIME SAVINGS	DOCUMENT SAVINGS
Scenario - 1 / Partial Digitalization	22%	1%	2%	26%
Scenario - 2 / Intermediate Digitalization	41%	25%	13%	67%
Scenario - 3 / Full Digitalization	61%	67%	33%	100%

3. USE CASES: SCENARIOS OF DIGITALIZATION OF LAND EXPORT USING BLOCKCHAIN TECHNOLOGY

In this study, we examined land export customs clearance processes in European countries, Turkey's largest trade partner. The research was conducted to answer a single fundamental question; could the documents used in the customs clearance process be arranged using blockchain technology to provide cost and time advantages? The scenarios based on this question are presented below.

We aim to determine and concretely reveal the expected gains of the use of Blockchain technology in documentation, cost, and time in the export process with the use of the formerly known Blockchain Trade Platform (BTP), now a Global Single Window (aGSW) developed by ATEZ Software Technologies Inc.

BTP is leveraging smart contracts to automate processes and establishing an environment of trust between stakeholders through consensus mechanisms and digitalizing operating processes. The use of blockchain technology provides significant gains in different aspects for stakeholders who take an active role in the export process.

We investigated the currently existing land export processes, listed under 4 main headings: Export preparation, TCGB registration (Customs Declaration Registration), Transit Registration and Border Crossing, and 41 subheadings. The study covers the process from the signing of the sales contract between the exporter and the importer until the goods leave the Kapıkule Border Customs to Bulgaria. We examined the procedures by which the exporter initiates the export process step by step. These steps include presenting information and documents to all relevant stakeholders (Export preparation), transactions carried out by the Customs Broker in the export process and the declaration registration (TCGB registration), preparation of the necessary documents for transit for the Transporter/Agency, transactions in the customs area and movement to the border customs (Transit Registration) and transactions that the vehicle and documents are subject to at the border customs (Border Gate crossing).

The export processes of the exporters, served by DCS Digital Customs Services Inc. (DCS) for each subheading procedures in the current workflow, were monitored from start to finish. The data from the UND (International Transporters Association) 2019-2022 strategy plan, the export data from DCS for the last 5 years, and the data obtained from the Turkish Ministry of Trade GET-APP are used for the duration of times spent, document costs and expenses incurred during the current workflow.

Digitalization processes with the use of blockchain technology are examined in three different scenarios based upon the data obtained from the current workflow analysis: partial, intermediate and full digitalization.

When we examine these scenarios;

Scenario 1 (Partial Digitalization): Within the scope of said scenario, only the export-related operations and transactions between the private sector stakeholders are integrated. The data exchange between these stakeholders is completely transferred to the electronic environment and eliminates the processes of copying documents and/or data that would be deemed redundant. Except for the aforementioned stakeholders, no integration was made with semi-public (TİM (Turkish Exporters Assembly), TOBB (Association of Chambers of Trade and Industry of Turkey)) etc.) and public institutions and organizations, and the data and document exchange continued in line with the current order.

Only the physical documents belonging to the private sector have been digitalized, automating some procedures (such as sharing the e-invoice separately with the relevant stakeholders, checking the e-invoice information and reporting the consignor information to the customs consultant) with smart contracts, and achieving time savings due to the digitalization of these manual processes.

Table 2. Scenario 1 – Time Gains Due to Digitalization of Manual Procedures

PROCESS TITLE	PROCESS SAVINGS	COST SAVINGS	TIME SAVINGS	DOCUMENT SAVINGS
Export Preparation Improvement Rate	42%	0%	18%	33%
Customs Declaration Registration Improvement Rate	22%	2%	0%	50%
Transit Declaration Registration Improvement Rate	22%	0%	4%	20%
Border Crossing Improvement Rate	0%	0%	0%	0%
Total Improvement Rate	22%	1%	2%	26%

Scenario 2 (Intermediate Digitalization): In this scenario, a significant digitalization has been achieved in foreign trade procedures with the integrations between the private sector and semi-public institutions (TIM, TOBB, etc.). The procedures of public institutions and the use cases of the documents allocated/registered by these institutions are left the same as they currently are. Significant document time and cost savings are achieved in this scenario based on the digitalization of the documents allocated by the stakeholders, which are private and semi-public institutions, after assuming that these documents are accepted by the public institutions.

If blockchain technology is adopted by semi-public institutions and organizations (such as TIM, TOBB) in addition to the private sector companies, the control and approval mechanisms carried out by these organizations during the export process, the physical supply of free circulation and origin documents, information and document sharing between these institutions will be digitalized. In total, improvements are expected to be 13% in time, 25% in costs and 67% in documentation.

Scenario 3 (Full Digitalization): Full integration is achieved between all stakeholders of foreign trade, namely the private sector, the semi-public and the public institutions and a fully digital ecosystem is created. Documents are created electronically by the original owner of the data and the data on

Table 3. Scenario 2 – Time Gains Due to Intermediate Digitalization

PROCESS TITLE	PROCESS SAVINGS	COST SAVINGS	TIME SAVINGS	DOCUMENT SAVINGS
Export Preparation Improvement Rate	75%	65%	53%	76%
Customs Declaration Registration Improvement Rate	33%	49%	31%	100%
Transit Declaration Registration Improvement Rate	11%	0%	36%	40%
Border Crossing Improvement Rate	36%	0%	4%	45%
Total Improvement Rate	41%	25%	13%	67%

these documents are shared electronically to the authorized parties over a reliable platform, document and data duplication is prevented and procedures operating in paper media and documents in paper media are completely eliminated.

Table 4. Scenario 3 – Time Gains Due to Full Digitalization

PROCESS TITLE	PROCESS SAVINGS	COST SAVINGS	TIME SAVINGS	DOCUMENT SAVINGS
Export Preparation Improvement Rate	92%	100%	70%	100%
Customs Declaration Registration Improvement Rate	67%	61%	74%	100%
Transit Declaration Registration Improvement Rate	22%	52%	81%	100%
Border Crossing Improvement Rate	55%	81%	18%	100%
Total Improvement Rate	61%	67%	33%	100%

With full digitalization, we are talking about an export process where ministries are now included in the blockchain ecosystem and the legislation is updated in accordance with the use of blockchain technology. In addition, all risk inspections and controls, tax payments, physical documents required in customs and transportation processes and all other operational processes made by the ministries due to lack of trust will be improved, resulting in 67% improvement in cost, 33% in time, and 100% in physical documentation[1].

Above, three different scenarios have been created to examine the time and cost advantages that the trade flow in Kapıkule Border Customs, one of the most important and largest customs office in Turkey, can provide at different levels of digitalization. The scenarios created were evaluated in comparison to the current situation. Thus, it is aimed to fill the gap in the literature by making an application about the benefits of blockchain technology.

Table 5. Benefit Criteria

Benefit Criteria	Definition	ID
Time	Thanks to technology, since paper documents will be prepared in the form of smart contracts using blockchain technology, the time spent on their arrangement and circulation in paper form between the parties will be reduced.	BC1
Documents	It will be possible to reduce or even eliminate the number of issued paper documents.	BC2
Cost	A significant reduction will be achieved in the costs spent for the printing, approval and circulation of documents between foreign trade parties.	BC3
Transactions	Costs are expected to decrease substantially, as the need for labor, materials and equipment for the preparation of documents will decrease. Since business processes will become simpler, transaction benefits will be provided. Confirmation/approval of the authenticity of the documents will eliminate the circulation of documents representing the goods and services subject to trade in complex processes and the processes will be simplified.	BC4

4. METHODOLOGY AND CASE STUDY

In the previous section, the time and cost advantages of using electronic documents in business processes at different levels of digitalization were examined. In this section, besides the benefits of the transition to electronic documents, the obstacles (costs) to be overcome are evaluated. Considering the benefit and cost criteria, an answer was sought to the question of which decision is the most appropriate. At this stage of the study, the benefit and cost criteria were determined by taking the opinions of experts in technology, logistics and foreign trade process management. A solution to the current problem was sought with the Multi-Criteria Decision Making method based on the determined criteria. As a Multi-Criteria Decision Making Method, Neutrosophic AHP Method was preferred, with the thought that it could better represent the evaluations made according to subjective expert opinions.

4.1. Potential Effects Of Digitalization Of Business Documents

Thanks to the digitalization reform of commercial documents, it is expected that operational costs and time wasted will be reduced, efficiency, transparency and security will increase. In this context, reducing paper consumption is a positive development for a sustainable environment. However, there will be costs to change. The need to train staff on new systems, the need to develop and improve new internal processes, the time spent negotiating with trading partners during the transition period, and the harmonization of legal arrangements are the first to come to mind. It is also important to carefully consider the environmental impacts of using DLT (Law Commission, 2022).

4.2. Determination of Cost-Benefit Criteria

In line with expert opinions, four benefit-oriented criteria were determined. The criteria are listed below:

Cost-oriented criteria are listed under the following five headings:

In the multiple decision criteria (MCDM) problem, where the best strategy to be applied in digitalization in customs procedures is tried to be determined, four alternatives are defined as follows:

After defining the digitalization scenarios, the literature was scanned. A very limited number of publications examining the use of blockchain technology in foreign trade processes with Analytic Hierarchy

Table 6. Cost Criteria

Cost Criteria	Definition	ID
Regulatory Compliance	In order for blockchain technology to be used in processes, legal issues regarding smart contracts should be examined within the framework of current regulations. Smart contracts are different from electronic contracts. Because, smart contracts are designed to be self-contained, self-managed, accurate and transparent as a computer program. Smart contracts should also be included in legal regulations. Legal arrangements are based on the physical holding of commercial documents such as bills of lading, bills of lading and warehouse receipts, or the idea of "actual property (possession)". Current laws do not allow property to be secured via electronic documents. Only property rights are granted on tangible assets. In this context, parties such as banks and logistics companies that operate on commercial documents cannot fully transition to paperless processes without making necessary changes in legal regulations (Law Commission, 2022). The risk of failure to fulfill administrative commitments in connection with legal regulations, and the lagging behind of the legislation and legal regulations in technological developments are also evaluated under this heading. Another point is that electronic documents approved by electronic signature have the same legal consequences as handwritten documents. However, contracts prepared with smart contracts have not yet been fully accepted.	CC1
Software Development Costs	In order to use blockchain technology by converting foreign trade documents into smart contracts, high investments must be made first. Since economies of scale with blockchain and DLT have not yet occurred, the specialist workforce and technology required for software development are very costly. In this context, investments are expected to be made by developed countries rather than underdeveloped and developing countries.	CC2
Development and Implementation Times	The involvement of the countries that are party to international trade in the digitalization processes at different levels will complicate the functioning of the system.	CC3
Support and Update Costs	The scarcity of trained specialist workforce and the lack of widespread use of technology increase support and update costs.	CC4
Security Layer and Privacy Levels	The parts of the privacy risks, whether the information will be shared by all parties or whether the parties will be restricted from accessing the information in their jurisdictions, are not completely clear. Multilateral contract frameworks in international trade should be seen by different parties and the stages of signing them should be regulated. The digitization of private multilateral agreements will be of great benefit. However, when electronic documents are processed, complexity may increase and uncertainties may arise in courts. Because electronic contracts only bind the parties to the agreement (Law Commission, 2022). Because smart contracts are coded as a computer program, they happen automatically. For this reason, when the privacy risk is taken into account, the control and supervision of smart contracts in matters such as the fight against fraud and money laundering becomes important. It is important for security that smart contracts can be audited by competent authorities in regulating their privacy levels.	CC5

Process (AHP) and Neutrosophic Analytic Hierarchy Process (NAHP) could be found in the literature. Some of the publications that can be accessed from the literature are reported below.

Vafadarnikjoo et al. (2021), using the NAHP in their study, analyzed the barriers to the adoption of blockchain technology in manufacturing supply chains. They proposed an action plan for the transition

Table 7. Senarios

ID	Senario Type	Definition
A1	The Current Situation	
A2	Senario 1	partial digitization
A3	Senario 2	medium level of digitization
A4	Senario 3	full digitization

to blockchain technology in an emerging economy. According to the findings, it was concluded that the most critical obstacle in the adoption of blockchain technology is "transaction-level uncertainties". Other barriers to the adoption of blockchain technology are listed as "informal economy", "managerial commitments", "difficulties in scalability" and "privacy risks".

Tadesse et al. (2021) investigated the logistics applications that companies in low-income countries can easily adopt in digitalization. They identified key criteria for digitized logistics applications and applied them to an expert survey to determine criteria weights using the analytical hierarchy process (AHP). As a result of the survey, economic benefit, infrastructure and affordability criteria were the criteria given the highest weight by the experts. Experts participating in the survey suggested that the use of cutting-edge technologies such as the internet of things (IoT), blockchain and big data analytics (BDA) would be beneficial. They concluded that identifying appropriate practices, taking into account local conditions in low-income countries, can help policymakers and logistics professionals adopt enabling technologies.

Yoon et al. (2020) sought to find the appropriate factors for the adoption of the use of blockchain in the maritime and port logistics industry in Korea to improve the implementation and implementation strategy of blockchain technology for maritime logistics. According to the results of the analysis made with the AHP method, consultants and academics think that the blockchain has not reached technological maturity. Logistics companies, on the other hand, gave mixed answers about the benefits of blockchain and adopting new technology. They conclude that the adoption of blockchain technology in seaport logistics is highly influenced by economic factors, mostly related to financial and time-related issues.

Chang et al. (2019) examined the potential paradigm shift that blockchain technology can create in all processes of international trade, from logistics to trade finance, by including application examples. According to the researchers, technology-intensive structuring of financial processes of international trade is possible through the implementation of blockchain and smart contract-based platforms.

5. NEUTROSOPHIC ANALYTIC HIERARCHY PROCESS

The Analytic Hierarchy Process (AHP) was developed by Saaty (1977) as an MCDM method and has become one of the most useful tools for decision-making practitioners through the years. However some papers such as Radwan et al. (2016) and Kahraman et al. (2020) criticized the AHP about not covering properly the perspective of human ideas. They both suggested using neutrosophic sets and logic to encapsulate the imprecisions of decision-makers about the MCDM problem.

Smarandache (1998) introduced the neutrosophic sets which can capture inconsistency and indeterminacy of information with truth (t), indeterminacy (i), and falsity (f) membership functions as an extension of fuzzy sets.

Suppose $O = (t_1, i_1, f_1)$ and $P = (t_2, i_2, f_2)$ are two single-valued neutrosophic numbers. Smarandache (2016) defined some mathematical operations for single valued neutrosophic sets as follows;

$$O \oplus P = (t_1 + t_2 - t_1 t_2, i_1 i_2, f_1 f_2) \tag{1}$$

$$O \otimes P = (t_1 t_2, i_1 + i_2 - i_1 i_2, f_1 + f_2 - f_1 f_2) \tag{2}$$

$$kO = (1-(1-t_1)^k, i_1^k, f_1^k)\ k\hat{I}R \text{ and } k>0 \tag{3}$$

Radwan et al. (2016) defined the Neutrosophic Analytic Hierarchy Process (NAHP) as follows;

First, the hierarchy of the decision problem must be structured and leveled as criteria, sub criteria and alternatives. The pairwise comparison of the elements of each level is made with respect to the element of the next level through the bottom to the top. To convert crisp AHP pairwise comparison matrix into neutrosophic numbers, a scale was employed in Table 1. After neutrosophic transformation, the consistency of these neutrosophic decision matrix have to be calculated. Rather than using the proposal of Radwan et al (2016) for consistency measurement, we directly used the equations that Xu and Liao (2013) proposed. Since the evualation of consistency by Radwan et al. (2016) which was also adapted from Xu and Liao (2013) leads to inconsistency even in decision matrix that has less than five dimensions. If the dimension of decision matrix increases, Radwan et al. (2016) method's compatibility would diminish rapidly due to using product of only 4 elements of the matrix. Xu and Liao (2013) defined consistency of fuzzy decision matrix which can also be used for neutrosophic decision matrix as follows,

Step 1: For $k>x+1$ let $O_{xk} = \left(t'_{xk}, i'_{xk}, f'_{xk}\right)$ where

$$t'_{xk} = \frac{\sqrt[k-x-1]{\prod_{d=x+1}^{k-1} t_{xd}t_{dk}}}{\sqrt[k-x-1]{\prod_{d=x+1}^{k-1} t_{xd}t_{dk}} + \sqrt[k-x-1]{\prod_{d=x+1}^{k-1} (1-t_{xd})(1-t_{dk})}} \tag{4}$$

$$i'_{xk} = \frac{\sqrt[k-x-1]{\prod_{d=x+1}^{k-1} i_{xd}i_{dk}}}{\sqrt[k-x-1]{\prod_{d=x+1}^{k-1} i_{xd}i_{dk}} + \sqrt[k-x-1]{\prod_{d=x+1}^{k-1} (1-i_{xd})(1-i_{dk})}} \tag{5}$$

$$f'_{xk} = \frac{\sqrt[k-x-1]{\prod_{d=x+1}^{k-1} f_{xd}f_{dk}}}{\sqrt[k-x-1]{\prod_{d=x+1}^{k-1} f_{xd}f_{dk}} + \sqrt[k-x-1]{\prod_{d=x+1}^{k-1} (1-f_{xd})(1-f_{dk})}} \tag{6}$$

Step 2: For $k=x+1$ let

$$O_{xk} = (t_{xk}, i_{xk}, f_{xk}) \tag{7}$$

Step 3: For $k<x$ let let

Table 8. AHP and NAHP scales

AHP scale	NAHP scale	NAHP reciprocals
Equally (1)	(0.50, 0.50, 0.50)	(0.50, 0.50, 0.50)
2	(0.55, 0.40, 0.45)	(0.45, 0.60, 0.55)
Moderately (3)	(0.60, 0.35, 0.40)	(0.40, 0.65, 0.60)
4	(0.65, 0.30, 0.35)	(0.35, 0.70, 0.65)
Essentially (5)	(0.70, 0.30, 0.30)	(0.30, 0.70, 0.70)
6	(0.75,0.25, 0.25)	(0.25,0.75, 0.75)
Very Strongly (7)	(0.80, 0.25, 0.20)	(0.20, 0.75, 0.80)
8	(0.85,0.20, 0.15)	(0.15,0.80, 0.85)
Extremely (9)	(0.90, 0.10, 0.10)	(0.10, 0.90, 0.90)

Resource: Saaty (1977) and Radwan et al. (2016)

$$O_{xk} = \left(f'_{xk}, 1 - i'_{xk}, t'_{xk}\right) \tag{8}$$

Then, Consistency Ratio

$$(CR) = \frac{1}{2(n-1)(n-2)} \sum_{x=1}^{n} \sum_{k=1}^{n} \left(\left| t'_{xk} - t_{xk} \right| + \left| i'_{xk} - i_{xk} \right| + \left| f'_{xk} - f_{xk} \right| \right) \tag{9}$$

can be calculated as above and must be less than 0.1.

If the consistency is achieved, the neutrosophic preferences are calculated with averaging its rows, otherwise the pairwise comparison has to be done again until the inconsistency is resolved.

After obtaining the prefences of all decision matrix. The overall sub criteria preferences are calculated by multiplying main criteria and sub criteria preferences using Eq. (2).

If the alternatives have quantitative scores for sub criteria, then the overall alternative scores of each sub criteria are calculated by multiplying the overall sub criteria preferences and alternative scores using Eq. (3), otherwise it can be evaluated by using Eq. (2).

The mean of the overall alternative scores are obtained for each alternative by simply dividing the sum of the overall alternative scores by the number of sub criteria.

The last process is the deneutrosophication step and we proposed an innovation to not hamper the magnitude differences between the overall alternative scores, and also it guarantees that the outcomes would be positive values.

Let $A_{[m*3]}$ is the matrix that includes all the m alternatives in rows and (*t, i, f*) values of them in columns. Then the crisp outputs as $S(A)_{[m*1]}$ follows;

$$S(A)_{[m*1]} = \frac{\left(-\min\left(A_{[:,t]} - \left(2 + \min(A_{[:,:]})\right) A_{[:,i]} - A_{[:,f]}\right) + A_{[:,t]} - 2A_{[:,i]} - A_{[:,f]}\right)}{4} \tag{10}$$

Figure 1. Benefits and Costs in Blockchain Integration

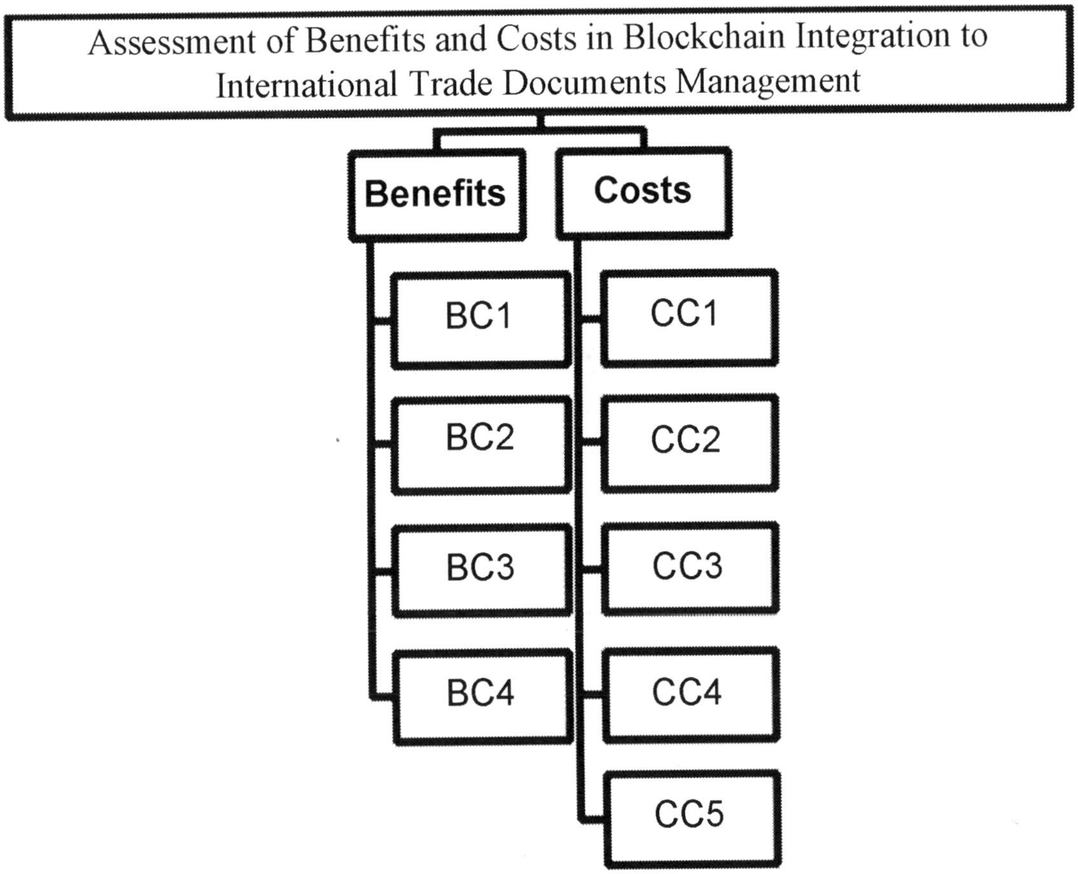

6. EXPERIMENTAL RESULTS

In this study, the problem of Assessment of Benefits and Costs in Blockchain Integration to International Trade Documents was examined by using NAHP.

The pairwise comparison and calculated weights for the benefit and cost main criteria with respect to goal is presented in Table 9.

Table 9. The pairwise comparison for main criteria transformed into NAHP

	Benefit	Cost	Importance
Benefit	(0.5,0.5,0.5)	(0.85,0.2,0.15)	(0.675,0.35,0.325)
Cost	(0.15,0.8,0.85)	(0.5,0.5,0.5)	(0.325,0.65,0.675)

To check consistency of pairwise comparison for sub criteria with respect to benefit and cost main criteria, we employed both original AHP, NAHP by Radwan et al. (2016) and our proposed consistency measurements and obtained CR values for the benefit 0.031, 0.107, and 0.058, respectively, and for the cost 0.057, 0.1240, and 0.0782, respectively. So, with using Radwan et al. (2016) consistency measurement it is likely very difficult to achieve consistency, where as our proposed consistency calculation has results in line with the original AHP. Meanwhile, all CR were obtained below the critical point of 0.1 with both AHP and our proposed NAHP in our problem.

In Table 10, the overall importance of main and sub criteria are presented. The overall weights were calculated by using Eq. (2).

Table 10. The overall weights of criteria

Main Criteria	Weight	Sub Criteria	Weight	Overall Weight
Benefit	(0.675,0.35,0.325)	BC1	(0.5625,0.4125,0.4375)	(0.3797,0.6181,0.6203)
		BC2	(0.4,0.6375,0.6)	(0.27,0.7644,0.73)
		BC3	(0.475,0.5375,0.525)	(0.3206,0.6994,0.6794)
		BC4	(0.5625,0.4125,0.4375)	(0.3797,0.6181,0.6203)
Cost	(0.325,0.65,0.675)	CC1	(0.66,0.33,0.34)	(0.2145,0.7655,0.7855)
		CC2	(0.49,0.52,0.51)	(0.1593,0.832,0.8407)
		CC3	(0.49,0.5,0.51)	(0.1593,0.825,0.8407)
		CC4	(0.33,0.68,0.67)	(0.1073,0.888,0.8928)
		CC5	(0.53,0.47,0.47)	(0.1723,0.8145,0.8277)

While the alternatives of the problem were scored for all beneficial oriented sub criteria by the experts, for the cost oriented sub criteria the pairwise comparison were made by the decision makers. So we used Eq. (3) for obtaining alternatives' score respect to beneficial oriented sub criteria, and employed Eq. (2) for the cost oriented ones. Later, the average of them were calculated for each alternative and Table 11 presented the overall scores of each alternative and their deneutrosophied or crisp values with our proposed NAHP by using Eq. (10).

Table 11. The overall scores of alternatives with respect to goal

Alternative	Neutrosophic Values	Crisp values	Rank
A1	(0.0482,0.9254,0.9308)	0.0675	4
A2	(0.0507,0.9155,0.9209)	0.1163	3
A3	(0.0794,0.8857,0.8883)	0.2994	2
A4	(0.1139,0.8505,0.8496)	0.5168	1

According to results, presented in Table 11 the A4 is the best alternative for the problem. We also obtained the final scores of alternatives A1, A2, A3, and A4 by utilizing AHP as 0.0657, 0.138, 0.3016, 0.4947 and NAHP by Radwan et al. (2016) as 0.1722, 0.193, 0.2711, and 0.3638, respectively. Although the ranking for each method has not changed, in terms of magnitudes between scores of alternatives, it is seen that our proposed method reflects the original AHP better than Radwan et al. (2016).

7. CONCLUSION AND POLICY RECOMMENDATIONS

Foreign trade, which is of great importance in the world economy, includes quite traditional and complex processes. It is seen that digitalization in the foreign trade sector has accelerating effects thanks to new technologies. Blockchain is one of the new technologies that have emerged recently. Blockchain technology based on distributed ledger technology displays a groundbreaking and multidisciplinary image. Blockchain technology offers the potential to provide significant improvements in international trade, logistics and procurement processes.

This article is designed in two stages. The first stage is aimed to understand the advantages of the transition from traditional paper documents to digital documents in foreign trade processes. In line with the determined target, the benefits of the transition to digital documents with blockchain technology were estimated by using the export data of DCS Digital Customs Services Inc. for the last 5 years and the data received from the Ministry of Commerce GET-APP. The probabilities obtained in line with the estimations are reported by dividing them into three groups, from low-level digitalization to medium and full digitalization. With the estimations, it is aimed to make the benefits of blockchain technology to foreign trade processors more visible and understandable. In line with the estimations, it has been concluded that as digitalization increases, time loss in processes and operational costs decrease. In the first stage of this study, the importance and advantages of rapid adaptation to innovations based on blockchain technology in the field of document management in international trade customs clearance processes at three different levels of digitalization are highlighted.

In the second stage of the study, a solution was sought for the problem of which decision would be appropriate considering the cost criteria as well as the benefits of the transition to electronic documents. The Neutrophic AHP method, which is a Multi-Criteria Decision Making Method (MCDM), was used to solve the problem. The main problems are the need to train personnel on new systems, the need to develop and improve new internal processes, the time spent in reaching an agreement with trading partners in the transition period and the harmonization of legal regulations.

According to the results of the Neutrophic AHP analysis, the effect of the benefit-oriented criteria on decision making was higher than the cost-oriented criteria. In the MCDM problem, where the best strategy for digitalization in customs procedures is tried to be determined, Scenario 3, which has the greatest costs and includes full digitalization, has emerged as the best solution option with NAHP and the high benefits it provides have been decisive here. It was followed by Scenarios 2 and 1, respectively, which included medium and partial digitization. According to these results, it is seen that any level of digitalization to be implemented will be better than the current situation.

Although full digitalization is the best option, the hurdles to overcome are difficult, making progressive digitalization more feasible in the short run. In this context, it may be more appropriate to continue working with the option of using both smart contracts and documents in traditional form. The important point here is to ensure that transactions can be made with electronic documents and smart contracts without affecting the validity or functioning of contract systems. Regulations and developments regarding contracts currently concluded in the electronic environment will guide on how to apply legal regulations to smart contracts. Foreign trade documents, whether paper or electronic, should be subject to the same laws and regulations. To ensure equivalence between paper and electronic foreign trade documents, it is necessary to simply arrange the regulation and legal characterization of both.

The rapid change from paper documents to electronic documents and smart contracts continues. In this context, we foresee that smart contracts and therefore Blockchain technology will find a place in all areas of the economy in the global universe of the future because of their functionality. In the light of developments toward digitalization, it is important to incorporate Blockchain technology into existing processes, considering its advantages and costs. In this context, it should create roadmaps for the use of blockchain technology for industry stakeholders. We believe that it is important for institutions regulating and supervising foreign trade processes to encourage stakeholders conducting foreign trade processes to adapt to digital technologies and to create legal and technological infrastructures suitable for developments in the world.

As a result, with this study, we made an exemplary evaluation that can illuminate the future potential applications of blockchain technology. From now on, it is important to continue to investigate the effects of technological developments on markets, especially in customs procedures, banking, insurance and logistics sectors, to establish a comprehensive environment of trust and facilitate trade automation.

REFERENCES

Chang, S. E., Chen, Y. C., & Wu, T. C. (2019). Exploring blockchain technology in international trade: Business process re-engineering for letter of credit. *Industrial Management & Data Systems.Customs, 119*(8), 1712-1733. doi:10.1108/IMDS-12-2018-0568

Eyal, I., & Sirer, E. G. (2014). Majority is not enough: Bitcoin mining is vulnerable. In *International conference on financial cryptography and data security* (pp. 436–454). Springer., . doi:10.1007/978-3-662-45472-5_28

Gonczol, P., Katsikouli, P., Herskind, L., & Dragoni, N. (2020). Blockchain Implementations and Use Cases for Supply Chains - A Survey. *IEEE Access: Practical Innovations, Open Solutions, 8*, 11856–11871. doi:10.1109/ACCESS.2020.2964880

ICC Brasil. (2018). *International Chamber of Commerce*. ITTI Discussion Paper. https://unctad.org/system/files/non-official-document/dtl_eWeek2018c04-ICCBrasil_en.pdf

Kahraman, C., Oztaysi, B., & Cevik Onar, S. (2020). Single & interval-valued neutrosophic AHP methods: Performance analysis of outsourcing law firms. *Journal of Intelligent & Fuzzy Systems, 38*(1), 749–759. doi:10.3233/JIFS-179446

Law Commission. (2022). Reforming the Law. *Electronic trade documents, Summary*. https://www.lawcom.gov.uk/project/electronic-trade-documents/#related

Mihajlov, M., Toshevska-Trpchevska, K., & Kikerkova, I. (2019). Towards the application of blockchain technology for improving trade facilitation in CEFTA 2006. *Ekonomska Misao i Praksa*, (1), 209–222.

PwC. (2019). *CEE Transport&Logistics Trend Book 2019*. Available online: https://www.pwc.com/hu/hu/kiadvanyok/assets/pdf/transport-logistics-trendbook-2019-en.pdf

Radwan, N. M., Senousy, M. B., & Alaa El Din, M. R. (2016). *Neutrosophic AHP multi criteria decision making method applied on the selection of learning management system*. Infinite Study.

Republic of Turkey Ministry of Trade. (2018). *Workshop Final Report on Reducing Documents and Costs Related to Foreign Trade Transactions and Increasing Awareness on This Subject, Ankara, 2018*. https://ticaret.gov.tr/data

Saaty, T. L. (1977). A scaling method for priorities in hierarchical structures. *Journal of Mathematical Psychology*, *15*(3), 234–281. doi:10.1016/0022-2496(77)90033-5

Shope, M. (2022). Distributed Ledger Technology in International Trade: Rethinking the Role and Necessity of the Customs Declaration. *Stanford Journal of Blockchain Law & Policy*, *5*(114). https://heinonline.org/HOL/LandingPage?handle=hein.journals/sjblp5&div=7&id=&page

Smarandache, F. (1998). *A unifying field in logics neutrosophy: Neutrosophic probability, set and logic*. American Research Press.

Smarandache, F. (2016). Subtraction and division of neutrosophic numbers. *Critical Review*, 13(13) 103–110.

Szewczyk, P. (2019). Application of blockchain technology in supply chain management. Silesian University of Technology Publishing House, Scientific Papers of Silesian University of Technology 2019, Organization and Management Series No.136. http://dx.doi.org/10.29119/1641-3466.2019.136.45

Tadesse, M. D., Gebresenbet, G., Tavasszy, L., & Ljungberg, D. (2021). Assessment of Digitalized Logistics for Implementation in Low-Income Countries. *Future Transportation*, *1*(2), 227–247. doi:10.3390/futuretransp1020014

UNCTAD. (2021). *United Nations Conference on Trade and Development*. Available online: https://unctad.org/system/files/official-document/ditctab2020d4_en.pdf

Vafadarnikjoo, A., Badri Ahmadi, H., Liou, J. J., Botelho, T., & Chalvatzis, K. (2021). Analyzing blockchain adoption barriers in manufacturing supply chains by the neutrosophic analytic hierarchy process. *Annals of Operations Research*, 1–28. doi:10.100710479-021-04048-6

WEF. (2018). *Blockchain Beyond the Hype A Practical Framework for Business Leaders*. Available online: http://www3.weforum.org/docs/48423_Whether_ Blockchain_WP.pdf

World Trade Organization. (2017). *Principles of the trading system*. https://www.wto.org/ english/thewto_e/whatis_e/tif_e/fact2_e.htm

Xu, Z., & Liao, H. (2013). Intuitionistic fuzzy analytic hierarchy process. *IEEE Transactions on Fuzzy Systems*, *22*(4), 749–761. doi:10.1109/TFUZZ.2013.2272585

Yoon, J. H., Kim, J. S., & Park, H. G. (2020). A study on the priorities of blockchain adoption for port logistics in Korea using AHP: Focused on Busan and Incheon ports. *Muyeog Yeon'gu*, *16*(1), 1–24.

Zheng, Z., Xie, S., Dai, H., Chen, X., & Wang, H. (2017, June). An overview of blockchain technology: Architecture, consensus, and future trends. In 2017 IEEE international congress on big data (BigData congress). IEEE.

ENDNOTES

1 Some points taken into account in the calculations are listed below.

* The voyages between Muratbey-Kapıkule Customs Administrations were taken into account in the calculations.

** All time calculations in customs procedures are taken from the GET-APP program. (GET APP data of DCS declarations in the January-November 2019 range are used).

*** In the scenarios, it is assumed that institutions are integrated by transacting on a common platform.

**** Costs are calculated over the averages of the official invoices paid by the institutions. (Document costs are taken from the attached Ministry of Commerce document).

***** In the calculations, transactions with standard processes that do not require special permission and are carried out during working hours are exemplified.

****** Regarding the number and duration of transportation and transportation, DCS NCTS data and UND 2019-2022 strategic plan in the link were used.

******* Calculations are based on the Republic of Turkey Ministry of Trade (2018)'s Workshop Final Report on Reducing Documents and Costs Related to Foreign Trade Transactions and Raising Awareness on this Subject.

Compilation of References

Aaron, O. (2022). *Global inflation rate from 2016 to 2026.* Retrieved May 20, 2022 from https://www.statista.com/statistics/256598/global-inflation-rate-compared-to-previous-year/

Abdal, A., & Ferreira, D. M. (2021). Deglobalization, Globalization, and the Pandemic: Current Impasses of the Capitalist World-Economy. *Journal of World-systems Research, 27*(1), 202–230. doi:10.5195/jwsr.2021.1028

Abdollahi, H., & Ebrahimi, S. B. (2020). A new hybrid model for forecasting Brent crude oil price. *Energy, 200*, 117520. doi:10.1016/j.energy.2020.117520

Acar, A. Z., & Köseoğlu, A. M. (2014). *Lojistik Yaklaşımıyla Tedarik Zinciri Yönetimi.* Nobel.

Acemoglu, D. (2009). The crisis of 2008: structural lessons for and from economics. *Globalization and Growth*, 37.

Adalı, Z., Dinçer, H., Eti, S., Mikhaylov, A., & Yüksel, S. (2022). Identifying New Perspectives on Geothermal Energy Investments. In *Multidimensional Strategic Outlook on Global Competitive Energy Economics and Finance*. Emerald Publishing Limited. doi:10.1108/978-1-80117-898-320221002

Agarwal, R., & Kimball, M. (2022). *Will inflation remain high? IMF Publications, Finance and Development.* Retrieved from: https://www.imf.org/en/Publications/fandd/issues/2022/03/Future-of-inflation-partI-Agarwal-kimball

Agell, J., & Persson, M. (2001). On the analytics of the dynamic Laffer curve. *Journal of Monetary Economics, 48*(2), 397–414. doi:10.1016/S0304-3932(01)00074-5

Agnello, L., Castro, V., Hammoudeh, S., & Sousa, R. M. (2017). Spillovers from the oil sector to the housing market cycle. *Energy Economics, 61*, 209–220. doi:10.1016/j.eneco.2016.11.004

Akan, D., Yıldırım, İ., & Yalçın, S. (2014). Okul Müdürleri Liderlik Stili Ölçeğinin Geliştirilmesi (OMLSÖ). *Electronic Journal of Social Sciences, 13*(51).

Akella, A. K., Saini, R. P., & Sharma, M. P. (2009). Social, economical and environmental impacts of renewable energy systems. *Renewable Energy, 34*(2), 390–396. doi:10.1016/j.renene.2008.05.002

Akküçük, U. (2009). İş etiğinde Sarbanes-Oxley (SOX) Yasası'nın etkisi ve toplam kalite yönetimi uygulamalarında yansımaları. *İş Ahlakı Dergisi, 2*(3), 7-17.

Akkucuk, U. (2014). Application of lean six sigma methodology in design and improvement of financial services. In *Globalization of Financial Institutions* (pp. 151–164). Springer. doi:10.1007/978-3-319-01125-7_11

Akkucuk, U. (2016). SCOR Model and the Green Supply Chain. In U. Akkucuk (Ed.), *Handbook of Research on Waste Management Techniques for Sustainability* (pp. 108–124). IGI Global. doi:10.4018/978-1-4666-9723-2.ch006

Akkucuk, U. (Ed.). (2017). *Ethics and Sustainability in Global Supply Chain Management*. IGI Global. doi:10.4018/978-1-5225-2036-8

Akkucuk, U., & Gencer, Y. G. (2017, April). EFQM Model and Sustainability of Organizations. *International Conference on Advances in Management Engineering and Information Technology*.

Akkucuk, U., & Kucukkancabas, S. (2007). Analyzing the Perceptions of Turkish Universities Using Multidimensional Scaling (MDS) Analysis. *Bogazici Journal of Economics and Administrative Sciences*, *21*, 125–141.

Akkucuk, U., & Sekercioglu, C. H. (2016). NGOs for Environmental Sustainability: The Case of Kuzeydoga Foundation. *Fresenius Environmental Bulletin*, *25*(12), 6038–6044.

Akkucuk, U., & Teuman, B. (2016). Assessing service quality in online banking services. *Problems and Perspectives in Management*, *14*(2), 183–191. doi:10.21511/ppm.14(2-1).2016.07

Akkucuk, U., & Turan, C. (2016). Mobile use and online preferences of the millenials: A study in Yalova. *Journal of Internet Banking and Commerce*, *21*(1), 142.

Akşit, H. (2008). *Yönetim ve Yöneticilik*. Kum Saati Yayınları.

Akter, S. (2020). The impact of COVID-19 related 'stay-at-home' restrictions on food prices in Europe:findings from a preliminary analysis. *Food Security*, *12*(4), 719–725. doi:10.100712571-020-01082-3 PMID:32837638

Al Salaimeh, S., Saraireh, Z., Hammad, J., & Rawashdeh, A. (2015). Design a Model of Language Identification Tool. *International Journal of Information & Computation Technology*, *5*(1), 11–18.

Al-Atwi, J. (2010). *The Impact of Complexity of Work Procedures on Institutional Performance An Empirical Study on Employees of the Ministry of Justice in Tabuk Region in the Kingdom of Saudi Arabia* [Master Thesis]. Mu'tah University, Jordan.

Al-Enezi, F. (2010). *The Impact of Human Resource Management Functions on Achieving Organizational Excellence in Saudi Customs* [Master Thesis]. Yarmouk University.

Al-Hiasat, K. M. (2005). *The Efficiency and Effectiveness of the Strategy of Human Resources Management and Institutional Performance in Jordanian Press Institutions* [Ph.D. Thesis]. Amman Arab University.

Ali, B. J. (2020). Impact of COVID-19 on consumer buying behavior toward online shopping in Iraq. *Economic Studies Journal*, *18*(42), 267–280.

Al-Karkhi, M. (2009). *Strategic Planning, an applied theoretical presentation*. Dar Al-Manahij for Publishing and Distribution, Jordan.

Al-Khashali, S. J. (2009). Knowledge Management and its Impact on Organizational Performance: A Field Study in Jordanian Industrial Companies. *Arab Journal of Management*, *29*(1), 84–109.

Allen, F., & Carletti, E. (2010). An overview of the crisis: Causes, consequences, and solutions. *International Review of Finance*, *10*(1), 1–26. doi:10.1111/j.1468-2443.2009.01103.x

Alpkan, L. (2006). Stratejik Planlama Süreci Bileşenlerinin Firma Performansına Etkileri. *Kocaeli Üniversitesi Sosyal Bilimler Enstitüsü Dergisi*, 21-47.

Al-Rashidi, K. M. (2009). *The Effect of Effective Application of Human Resources Management Functions on Institutional Performance from the Viewpoint of Employees in Saudi Ministries in the Riyadh Region* [Master Thesis]. Mutah University, Karak.

Al-Safou, R. D. A. (2009). *Elements of Operations Strategy and Their Impact on the Balanced Scorecard* [Master Thesis]. University of Mosul, Iraq.

Altan, M. (2013). *Uluslararası Ekonomi Politik.* Anadolu Üniversitesi Yayınları.

Altomonte, C., di Mauro, F., Ottaviano, G., Rungi, A., & Vicard, V. (2012). *Global value chains during the great trade collapse: a bullwhip effect?* ECB Working Paper, No. 1412. European Central Bank (ECB).

Altuntaş, C., & Türker, D. (2012). Sustainable supply chains: A content analysis of sustainability reports. *Dokuz Eylul University The Journal of Graduate School of Social Sciences, 14*(3), 39–64.

Alvord, S. H., Brown, L. D., & Letts, C. W. (2004). Social entrepreneurship and societal transformation: An exploratory study. *The Journal of Applied Behavioral Science, 40*(3), 260–282. doi:10.1177/0021886304266847

Al-Zoubi, M. A. (2009). *The Impact of Participatory Leadership on Improving the Performance of Human Resources in Kuwaiti Industry Companies.* University of Jordan.

American Trucking Associations. (2021, Oct. 25). *Driver Shortage Update 2021.* https://www.trucking.org/sites/default/files/2021-10/ATA%20Driver%20Shortage%20Report%202021%20Executive%20Summary.FINAL_.pdf

Apergis, E., & Apergis, N. (2021). Inflation expectations, volatility and Covid-19: Evidence from the US inflation swap rates. *Applied Economics Letters, 28*(15), 1327–1331. doi:10.1080/13504851.2020.1813245

Apergis, N., & Payne, J. E. (2009). Energy consumption and economic growth: Evidence from the Commonwealth of Independent States. *Energy Economics, 31*(5), 641–647. doi:10.1016/j.eneco.2009.01.011

Armantier, O., Kos¸ar, G., Pomerantz, R., Skandalis, D., Smith, K.T., Topa, G., & Van der Klaauw, W. (2020). *How Economic Crises Affect Inflation Beliefs: Evidence From the COVID-19 Pandemic.* Federal Reserve Bank of New York Staff Report 949.

Ashton, P. (2009). An appetite for yield: The anatomy of the subprime mortgage crisis. *Environment & Planning A, 41*(6), 1420–1441. doi:10.1068/a40328

Aslan, B. (2010). Bir Yönetim Fonksiyonu Olarak İç Denetim. *Sayıştay Dergisi,* (77), 63-86. Retrieved from https://dergipark.org.tr/en/pub/sayistay/issue/61532/919029

Atayah, O. F., Dhiaf, M. M., Najaf, K., & Frederico, G. F. (2021). Impact of COVID-19 on financial performance of logistics firms: Evidence from G-20 countries. *Journal of Global Operations and Strategic Sourcing., 15*(2), 172–196. doi:10.1108/JGOSS-03-2021-0028

Atkinson-Clement, C., & Pigalle, E. (2021). What can we learn from Covid-19 pandemic's impact on human behaviour? The case of France's lockdown. *Humanities and Social Sciences Communications, 8*(1), 1–12. doi:10.105741599-021-00749-2

Attinasi, M. G., Balatti, M., Mancini, M., & Metelli, L. (2022). Supply chain disruptions and the effects on the global economy. *ECB Economic Bulletin Boxes, 8*(1). Retrieved from: https://www.ecb.europa.eu/pub/economic-bulletin/focus/2022/html/ecb.ebbox202108_01~e8ceebe51f.en. html

Aydın, Ö. (2020). *Liderlik Kuramları Açısından PKK Terör Örgütünde Liderlik ve Abdullah Öcalan.* Gazi Üniversitesi Sosyal Bilimler Enstitüsü Siyaset Bilimi Ve Kamu Yönetimi Anabilim Dalı, Yayınlanmamış Doktora Tezi.

Ay, F.A., & Keleş, K. (2017). Etkileşimci ve Dönüşümcü Liderlik Tarzlarının İşten Ayrılma Niyeti Ve İş Performansı Üzerinde Etkisi. *Gümüşhane Üniversitesi Sağlık Bilimleri Dergisi, 6*(4), 193–203.

Ay, İ. C. (2021). COVID-19 Pandemisinin Türkiye'nin İhracatı Üzerine Etkileri İçin Bir Analiz. *JOEEP: Journal of Emerging Economies and Policy*, *6*(1), 41–60.

Aykanat, Z., & Yıldırım, A. (2012). Etik Liderlik Ve Örgütsel Adalet İlişkisi: Teorik Ve Uygulamalı Bir Araştırma. *Fırat Üniversitesi Sosyal Bilimler Dergisi*, 260-274.

Aytürk, N. (2007). *Yönetim Sanatı. 5*. Baskı, Nobel Yayınları.

Azam, M., Khan, A. Q., & Ozturk, I. (2019). The effects of energy on investment, human health, environment and economic growth: Empirical evidence from China. *Environmental Science and Pollution Research International*, *26*(11), 10816–10825. PMID:30778925

Bachmeier, L. J., & Cha, I. (2011). Why don't oil shocks cause inflation? Evidence from disaggregate inflation data. *Journal of Money, Credit and Banking*, *43*(6), 1165–1183. doi:10.1111/j.1538-4616.2011.00421.x

Baghestani, H. (2014). Inflation expectations and energy price forecasting. *OPEC Energy Review*, *38*(1), 21–35. doi:10.1111/opec.12016

Bagliano, F. C., & Morana, C. (2012). The Great Recession: US dynamics and spillovers to the world economy. *Journal of Banking & Finance*, *36*(1), 1–13. doi:10.1016/j.jbankfin.2011.06.002

Bai, C., & Sarkis, J. (2013). Green information technology strategic justification and evaluation. *Information Systems Frontiers*, *15*(5), 831–847. doi:10.100710796-013-9425-x

Bai, X., Shen, W., Wu, X., & Wang, P. (2020). Applicability of long-term satellite-based precipitation products for drought indices considering global warming. *Journal of Environmental Management*, *255*, 109846. doi:10.1016/j.jenvman.2019.109846 PMID:31747628

Bakan, İ., & Büyükbeşe, T. (2010). Liderlik "Türleri" ve "Güç Kaynaklarına "İlişkin Mevcut- Gelecek Durum Karşılaştırması. *Karamanoğlu Mehmetbey Üniversitesi Sosyal ve Ekonomik Araştırmalar Dergisi*, *2010*(2), 73–84.

Baker, S. R., Farrokhnia, R., Meyer, S., Pagel, M., & Yannelis, C. (2020). *How does household spending respond to an epidemic? Consumption during the 2020 COVID-19 pandemic*. NBER Working Papers 26949. National Bureau of Economic Research.

Baldwin, R., & di Mauro, B. W. (Eds.). (2020). *Economics in the time of COVID-19*. CEPR Press.

Baldwin, R., & Tomiura, E. (Eds.). (2020). *Thinking ahead about the trade impact of Covid-19*. CEPR Press.

Ballantyne, A., & Langcake, S. (2016). Why Has Retail Inflation Been So Low? *RBA Bulletin*, 9-18.

Banerjee, R. N., Mehrotra, A., & Zampolli, F. (2020). Inflation at risk from Covid-19. Bank for International Settlements, 28.

Banerjee, R., Mishra, V., & Maruta, A. A. (2021). Energy poverty, health and education outcomes: Evidence from the developing world. *Energy Economics*, *101*, 105447.

Banker, R. D., Chang, H. H., & Majundar, S. K. (2009). Framework for Analyzing Changes in Strategic Performance. *Strategic Management Journal*, *17*(9), 23–36.

Banker, R. D., Chang, H., & Pizzini, M. J. (2004). The Balanced Scorecard: Judgemental Effects of Performance Measures Linked to Strategy. *The Accounting Review*, *79*(1), 1–23. doi:10.2308/accr.2004.79.1.1

Banking Regulation and Supervision Agency of Turkey. (2021). *Turkish Banking Sector Main Indicators Report*. https://www.bddk.org.tr/Veri/EkGetir/17?ekId=90

Bardt, H., Ezell, S., Flores, T., González, N., Hattingh, C., Randolph, S., & Bandini, C. (2021). *Global Value Chains After the COVID-19 Crisis*. Global Trade and Innovation Policy Alliance.

Barichello, R. (2020). *The COVID-19 Pandemic: Anticipating its Effects on Canada's Agricultural Trade. Canadian Journal of Agricultural Economics/Revue CanadienneD'agroeconomie*. doi:10.1111/cjag.12244

Barman, A., Das, R., & De, P. K. (2021). Impact of COVID-19 in food supply chain: Disruptions and recovery strategy. *Current Research in Behavioral Sciences.*, *2*, 100017. doi:10.1016/j.crbeha.2021.100017

Barua, S. (2020). Understanding Coronanomics: The economic implications of the coronavirus (COVID-19) pandemic. *Journal of Developing Areas*, *55*(3), 435–450. doi:10.1353/jda.2021.0073

Barykin, S. E., Kapustina, I. V., Korchagina, E. V., Sergeev, S. M., Yadykin, V. K., Abdimomynova, A., & Stepanova, D. (2021). Digital Logistics Platforms in the BRICS Countries: Comparative Analysis and Development Prospects. *Sustainability*, *13*(20), 11228. doi:10.3390u132011228

Basel Committee on Banking Supervision - Bank for International Settlements. (2005, April). Retrieved July 21, 2022, from https://www.bis.org/publ/bcbs113.pdf

Basiago, A. D. (1998). Economic, social, and environmental sustainability in development theory and urban planning practice. *The Environmentalist*, *19*(2), 145–161. doi:10.1023/A:1006697118620

Başpınar, A. (2004). Türkiye'de ve Dünyada Denetim Standartlarının Oluşumuna Genel Bir Bakış. *Maliye Dergisi*, 146.

Bass, B. M. (1990). *Bass & Stogdill's Handbook of Leadership, Theory, Research, and Managerial Applications, 3*. The Free Press.

Bass, B. M. (1990). From transactional to transformational leadership: Learning to share the vision. *Organizational Dynamics*, *18*(3), 19–31. doi:10.1016/0090-2616(90)90061-S

Bass, B. M., & Steidlmeier, P. (1999). Ethics, Character And Authentic Transformational Leadership Behavior. *The Leadership Quarterly*, *10*(2), 181–217. doi:10.1016/S1048-9843(99)00016-8

Batırlık, S. N., & Gencer, Y. G. (2021). Sanal Takımlar Üzerine Literatür Taraması. *Social Sciences Studies Journal*, *80*(7), 1156–1163. doi:10.26449ssj.3128

Batırlık, S. N., Gencer, Y. G., & Akkucuk, U. (2022). Global Virtual Team Leadership Scale (GVTLS) Development in Multinational Companies. *Sustainability*, *14*(2), 1038. doi:10.3390u14021038

Batten, J. A., Ciner, C., & Lucey, B. M. (2010). The macroeconomic determinants of volatility in precious metals markets. *Resources Policy*, *35*(2), 65–71. doi:10.1016/j.resourpol.2009.12.002

Bayrakcı, A. G., & Kocar, G. (2012). Utilization of renewable energies in Turkey's agriculture. *Renewable & Sustainable Energy Reviews*, *16*(1), 618–633. doi:10.1016/j.rser.2011.08.027

Bayram, E. (2015). Çok Uluslu İşletmelerde Örgütsel Yapıya Dair Farklılıklar ve Çok Uluslu İşletmelerin Türkiye'deki Yönetim Yapıları. Yüksek Lisans Tezi, Eskişehir: Anadolu Üniversitesi Sosyal Bilimler Enstitüsü.

BDDK. (n.d.). Retrieved July 21, 2022, from https://www.bddk.org.tr/

Beken, H. G. (2016). Sürdürülebilirlik ve rekabet edebilirlik yolu yeşil lojistik mi. *Balkan ve Yakın Doğu Sosyal Bilimler Dergisi*, *2*(01), 78–88.

Belke, A. H., Bordon, I. G., & Hendricks, T. W. (2014). Monetary policy, global liquidity and commodity price dynamics. *The North American Journal of Economics and Finance*, *28*, 1–16. doi:10.1016/j.najef.2013.12.003

Belke, A., Dobnik, F., & Dreger, C. (2011). Energy consumption and economic growth: New insights into the cointegration relationship. *Energy Economics*, *33*(5), 782–789. doi:10.1016/j.eneco.2011.02.005

Bello, W. (2013). *Capitalism's Last Stand? Deglobalization in the Age of Austerity*. Zed Books. doi:10.5040/9781350218895

Bell, R., Khan, M., Romeo-Velilla, M., Stegeman, I., Godfrey, A., Taylor, T., Morris, Staatsen, van der Vliet, Kruize, Anthun, Lillefjell, Espnes, Chiabai, de Jalón, Quiroga, Martinez-Juarez, Máca, Zvěřinová, ... Costongs, C. (2019). Ten lessons for good practice for the INHERIT Triple Win: Health, Equity, and Environmental Sustainability. *International Journal of Environmental Research and Public Health*, *16*(22), 4546. doi:10.3390/ijerph16224546 PMID:31744247

Benami, E., Jin, Z., Carter, M. R., Ghosh, A., Hijmans, R. J., Hobbs, A., ... Lobell, D. B. (2021). Uniting remote sensing, crop modelling and economics for agricultural risk management. *Nature Reviews Earth & Environment*, *2*(2), 140–159.

Benes, K., Cheon, A., Urpelainen, J., & Yang, J. (2015). *Low oil prices: An opportunity for fuel subsidy reform*. Columbia University.

Bentolila, S., Jansen, M., & Jiménez, G. (2018). When credit dries up: Job losses in the great recession. *Journal of the European Economic Association*, *16*(3), 650–695. doi:10.1093/jeea/jvx021

Bentzen, J. (2004). Estimating the rebound effect in US manufacturing energy consumption. *Energy Economics*, *26*(1), 123–134. doi:10.1016/S0140-9883(03)00047-1

Berg, A., Haug, L., Hedrich, S., & Magnus, K.-H. (2020). *Time for change How to use the crisis to make fashion sourcing more agile and sustainable*. McKinsey & Company. https://www.ilo.org/wcmsp5/groups/public/—ed_dialogue/—sector/documents/briefingnote/wcms_741344.pdf

Bernanke, B. S., Boivin, J., & Eliasz, P. (2005). Measuring the Effects of Monetary Policy: A Factor-Augmented Vector Autoregressive (FAVAR) Approach. *The Quarterly Journal of Economics*, *120*(1), 387–422. doi:10.1162/0033553053327452

Berry, R. A. (2019). The Effects of Inflation on Income Distribution in Colombia: Some Hypotheses and a Framework for Analysis. In *Economic Policy and Income Distribution in Colombia* (pp. 113–131). Routledge. doi:10.4324/9780429051357

Bezemer, D. J. (2011). The credit crisis and recession as a paradigm test. *Journal of Economic Issues*, *45*(1), 1–18. doi:10.2753/JEI0021-3624450101

Bhagat, D., & Dhar, U. R. (2011). Agriculture Supply Chain Management: A Review. *IUP Journal of Supply Chain Management*, *8*(3), 7–25.

Bhalla, A. (2020). *Amazon shuts New Jersey facility till Dec.26 on virus spike among workers*. Retrieved March 29, 2022, from https://www.reuters.com/article/us-health-coronavirus-amazon-com-warehou-idUSKBN28V06J

Bhuiyan, M. A., Dinçer, H., Yüksel, S., Mikhaylov, A., Danish, M. S. S., Pinter, G., ... Stepanova, D. (2022). Economic indicators and bioenergy supply in developed economies: QROF-DEMATEL and random forest models. *Energy Reports*, *8*, 561–570.

Binder, C. C. (2018). Inflation expectations and the price at the pump. *Journal of Macroeconomics*, *58*, 1–18. doi:10.1016/j.jmacro.2018.08.006

Blake, R., & Mouton, J. (1964). The Managerial Grid: The Key To Leadership Excellence. Gulf Publishing Co.

Blinder, A. S. (1981). Thoughts on the Laffer curve. In *The supply-side effects of economic policy* (pp. 81–92). Springer. doi:10.1007/978-94-009-8174-4_3

Board of Governors of the Federal Reserve System. (2022, May 1). *Economic Research*. Federal Bank of St. Louis. https://research.stlouisfed.org/

Boating, A.A.A. (2007). *The Role of Human Resource Information Systems (HRIS) in Strategic Human Resource Management (SHRM)* [Master's thesis]. Swedish School of Economics and Business Administration.

Bobdey, S., & Ray, S. (2020). Going viral–Covid-19 Impact Assessment: A Perspective beyond Clinical Practice. *Journal of Marine Medical Society, 22*(1), 9–12. doi:10.4103/jmms.jmms_12_20

Boiral, O., Brotherton, M.-C., Rivaud, L., & Guillaumie, L. (2021). Organizations' Management of the COVID-19 Pandemic: A Scoping Review of Business Articles. *Sustainability, 2021*(13), 3993. doi:10.3390u13073993

Bolat, T., & Ve Seymen, O. A. (2003). Örgütlerde İş Etiği Ve Kariyer Yönetimi İlişkisi: Normatif Etik Boyutuyla Bir Değerlendirme. *Yönetim Dergisi: İstanbul Üniversitesi İşletme Fakültesi İşletme İktisadı Enstitüsü, 14*(45), 3-19.

Boma. (2007). Planning Guide for Commercial Buildings Influenza Pandemic. *Building Owners and Managers Association of Canada*, 4-95.

Boz, D., Aktı, Ü., Duran, C., & Behdioğlu, S. (2020). Vicdani Liderlik Ölçeği. *Dumlupinar University Journal Of Social Science/Dumlupinar Üniversitesi Soysyal Bilimler Dergisi*, (66).

Bozkurt, C. (2016). Risk, Kurumsal Risk Yönetimi ve İç Denetim. *Denetişim*, (4), 17-30. Retrieved from https://dergipark.org.tr/tr/pub/denetisim/issue/22481/240477

Brambilla, A., & Sangiorgio, A. (2020). Mould growth in energy efficient buildings: Causes, health implications and strategies to mitigate the risk. *Renewable & Sustainable Energy Reviews, 132*, 110093.

Brandon-Jones, E., Brian, S. C., Autry, W., & Kenneth, P. J. (2014). A Contingent Resource-Based Perspective Of Supply Chain Resilience And Robustness. *The Journal of Supply Chain Management*, 54–75.

Brandon-Jones, E., Squire, B., & Van Rossenberg, Y. G. T. (2014). The impact of supply base complexity on disruptions and performance: The moderating effects of slack and visibility. *International Journal of Production Research, 53*(22), 6903–6918. doi:10.1080/00207543.2014.986296

Breitenfellner, A., Cuaresma, J. C., & Mayer, P. (2015). Energy inflation and house price corrections. *Energy Economics, 48*, 109–116. doi:10.1016/j.eneco.2014.08.023

Bridge, G. (2010). Past peak oil: political economy of energy crises. In *Global political ecology* (pp. 321–338). Routledge.

Bristol. (2020). *The government threw us under the bus': How Bristol food businesses are working to survive coronavirus.* Bristol Cable Media.

Broadberry, S., & Harrison, M. (2005). *The economics of World War I.* Cambridge University Press. doi:10.1017/CBO9780511497339

Brosemer, K., Schelly, C., Gagnon, V., Arola, K. L., Pearce, J. M., Bessette, D., & Olabisi, L. S. (2020). The energy crises revealed by COVID: Intersections of Indigeneity, inequity, and health. *Energy Research & Social Science, 68*, 101661. PMID:32839694

Buchanan, J. M., & Lee, D. R. (1982). Politics, time, and the Laffer curve. *Journal of Political Economy, 90*(4), 816–819. doi:10.1086/261091

Buluş, A., & Kabaklarlı, E. (2010). 1929 Ekonomik Buhranı İle Son Dönem Global Krizin Karşılaştırılması. *Sosyal Ekonomik Araştırmalar Dergisi, 10*(19), 1–22.

Bulut, H., & Meydan, C. H. (2018). Liderlik Tarzlarının Çalışanların Ses Verme Davranışına Etkisi: Kamuda Bir Araştırma. *Ankara Üniversitesi Sbf Dergisi*, 223-244.

Burney, S. (2003). *The Use of Chemical Composition Data in Waste Management Planning, Waste Management*. Elsevier.

Butt, A. S. (2021). Strategies to mitigate the impact of COVID-19 on supply chain disruptions: A multiple case analysis of buyers and distributors. *International Journal of Logistics Management.*

Büyüközkan, G., Feyzioğlu, O., & Nebol, E. (2008). Selection of the strategic alliance partner in logistics value chain. *International Journal of Production Economics, 113*(1), 148–158. doi:10.1016/j.ijpe.2007.01.016

Çam, E. (2011). Çok Uluslu Şirketler ve Gelişen Ülkeler. *İstanbul Üniversitesi İktisat Fakültesi Mecmuası, 45*(1-4).

Çamlıca, Z., & Akar, G. S. (2014). Sustainability practices in the logistics sector. *Gümüshane University Electronic Journal of the Institute of Social Science, 5*(11).

Can, H. Y., Azizoğlu, Ö. A., & Aydın, E. M. (2011). *Organizasyon ve Yönetim*. Siyasal Kitabevi.

Canöz, K., & Öndoğan, A. (2015). Kriz yönetiminde dönüşümcü liderin rolü. *Gümüşhane Üniversitesi İletişim Fakültesi Elektronik Dergisi, 3*(1), 36–61.

Carlisle, J. E., Feezell, J. T., Smith, E. R., & Michaud, K. E. (2017). *The politics of energy crises*. Oxford University Press.

Carvalho, V.M., Hansen, S., Ortiz, A., Ramon Garcıa, J., Rodrigo, T., Rodriguez Mora, S. & Ruiz, J. (2020). *Tracking the COVID-19 Crisis with High-Resolution Transaction Data (DP14642)*. CEPR Discussion Papers.

Castán Broto, V., & Kirshner, J. (2020). Energy access is needed to maintain health during pandemics. *Nature Energy, 5*(6), 419–421.

Castro, C., Jiménez-Rodríguez, R., Poncela, P., & Senra, E. (2017). A new look at oil price pass-through into inflation: Evidence from disaggregated European data. *Economics and Politics, 34*(1), 55–82. doi:10.100740888-016-0048-9

Cavallo, A. (2020). Inflation with Covid consumption baskets (No. w27352). National Bureau of Economic Research.

Cavallo, A., Cavallo, E., & Rigobon, R. (2014). Prices and Supply Disruptions During Natural Disasters. *Review of Income and Wealth, 60*, 449–471. doi:10.1111/roiw.12141

CBC News. (2021). Retrieved May 11, 2022 from https://www.cbc.ca/news/canada/toronto/amazon-site-closed-brampton-covid19-1.5947898

Çelik, H. (2016). *Demokratik liderlik ve örgütsel güven ilişkisi: Balıkesir merkez ilçeleri örneği*. Academic Press.

Çelik, V. (1997). Eğitim yönetiminde vizyoner liderlik. *Kuram ve Uygulamada Eğitim Yönetimi, 12*(12), 465–474.

Çetin, Ö. Ü. O., & Sain, A. D. (2018). Sustainability practices in logistics sector. *Iv. Internatıonal Caucasus-Central Asıa Foreıgn Trade And Logıstıcs Congress.*

Chaloupka, F. J., Powell, L. M., & Warner, K. E. (2019). The use of excise taxes to reduce tobacco, alcohol, and sugary beverage consumption. *Annual Review of Public Health, 40*(1), 187–201. doi:10.1146/annurev-publhealth-040218-043816 PMID:30601721

Chandrasekaran, N., & Raghuram, G. (2014). *Agribusiness Supply Chain Management*. CRC Press.

Chang, S. E., Chen, Y. C., & Wu, T. C. (2019). Exploring blockchain technology in international trade: Business process re-engineering for letter of credit. *Industrial Management & Data Systems.Customs, 119*(8), 1712-1733. doi:10.1108/IMDS-12-2018-0568

Chen, N., Zhou, M., Dong, X., Qu J., Gong, F., & Han, Y. (2020). Epidemiological and Clinical Characteristics of 99 Cases of 2019 Novel Coronavirus Pneumonia in Wuhan, China: A Descriptive Study. *Lancet.*

Cheng, H., Lijie, L., Wang, B., Feng, X., Mao, Z., Vancso, G. J., & Sui, X. (2020). Multifaceted applications of cellulosic porous materials in environment, energy, and health. *Progress in Polymer Science, 106*, 101253.

Choi, T. M. (2020). Innovative "Bring-Service-Near-Your-Home Operations Under Corona-Virus (COVID-19/SARS-CoV-2) Outbreak: Can Logistics Become the Messiah?" *Transportation Research Part E: Logistics and Transportation Review*.

Choi, E. P. H., Hui, B. P. H., & Wan, E. Y. F. (2020b). Depression and anxiety in Hong Kong during COVID-19. *International Journal of Environmental Research and Public Health, 17*(10), 3740. doi:10.3390/ijerph17103740 PMID:32466251

Choi, S., Furceri, D., Loungani, P., Mishra, S., & Poplawski-Ribeiro, M. (2018). Oil prices and inflation dynamics: Evidence from advanced and developing economies. *Journal of International Money and Finance, 82*, 71–96. doi:10.1016/j.jimonfin.2017.12.004

Choi, T. Y., & Krause, D. R. (2006). The supply base and its complexity:Implications for transaction costs, risks, responsiveness, and innovation. *Journal of Operations Management, 24*(5), 637–652. doi:10.1016/j.jom.2005.07.002

Choi, T.-M. (2020a). Innovative 'bring-service-near-your-home' operations under corona-virus (COVID- 19/SARS-CoV-2) outbreak: Can logistics become the messiah? *Transportation Research Part E, Logistics and Transportation Review, 140*, 101961. doi:10.1016/j.tre.2020.101961 PMID:32346356

Chopra, S., & Meindl, P. (2017). Strategy, planning, and operation. *Supply Chain Management*, 13–17.

Chowdhury, P., Paul, S. K., Kaisar, S., & Moktadir, M. A. (2021). COVID-19 pandemic related supply chain studies: A systematic review. *Transportation Research Part E, Logistics and Transportation Review, 148*, 102271. doi:10.1016/j.tre.2021.102271 PMID:33613082

Chowdhury, R. (2017). The rana plaza disaster and the complicit behavior of elite NGOs. *Organization, 24*(6), 938–949. doi:10.1177/1350508417699023

Chuang, L. (2008). The status and problems of small and middle textile and garment enterprises of Henan province. *2008 International Seminar on Business and Information Management*, 2, 386-389.

Churchill, S. A., & Smyth, R. (2021). Energy poverty and health: Panel data evidence from Australia. *Energy Economics, 97*, 105219.

Cicala, S. (2020). *Early economic impacts of COVID-19 in Europe: a view from the grid.* Working Paper, University of Chicago.

Clark, T. E. (2011). Real-Time Density Forecasts from Bayesian Vector Autoregressions with Stochastic Volatility. *Journal of Business & Economic Statistics, 29*(3), 327–341. doi:10.1198/jbes.2010.09248

Clark, T. E., & Terry, S. J. (2010). Time variation in the inflation passthrough of energy prices. *Journal of Money, Credit and Banking, 42*(7), 1419–1433. doi:10.1111/j.1538-4616.2010.00347.x

CNN. (2022, Jan. 13). *Here's why grocery stores are struggling to stock their empty shelves.* https://edition.cnn.com/2022/01/11/business-food/grocery-store-shelves-empty/index.html

Craighead, C. W., Blackhurst, J., Rungtusanatham, M. J., & Handfield, R. B. (2007). The severity of supply chain disruptions: Design characteristics and mitigation capabilities. *Decision Sciences, 38*(1), 131–156. doi:10.1111/j.1540-5915.2007.00151.x

Daly, G. G., & Mayor, T. H. (1983). Reason and rationality during energy crises. *Journal of Political Economy, 91*(1), 168–181. doi:10.1086/261134

Datta, P. P., & Christopher, M. G. (2011). Information sharing and coordination mechanisms for managing uncertainty in supply chains: A simulation study. *International Journal of Production Research, 49*(3), 765–803. doi:10.1080/00207540903460216

Davis, L. W. (2014). The economic cost of global fuel subsidies. *The American Economic Review, 104*(5), 581–585. doi:10.1257/aer.104.5.581

De Vet, J. M., Nigohosyan, D., Ferrer, J. N., Gross, A. K., Kuehl, S., & Flickenschild, M. (2021). Impacts of the COVID-19 Pandemic on EU Industries. European Parliament.

de Wit, E., van Doremalen, N., Falzarano, D., & Munster, V. J. (2016). SARS and MERS: Recent insights into emerging coronaviruses. *Nature Reviews. Microbiology, 14*(8), 523–534. doi:10.1038/nrmicro.2016.81 PMID:27344959

Deaton & Deaton. (2020). Food Security and Canada's Agricultural System Challenged by COVID-19. *Canadian Journal of Agricultural Economics/Revue canadienned'agroeconomie, 68*(2), 143–149. doi:10.1111/cjag.v68.2

Deka, A., Cavusoglu, B., & Dube, S. (2021). Does renewable energy use enhance exchange rate appreciation and stable rate of inflation? *Environmental Science and Pollution Research International*, 1–10. PMID:34601688

Deka, A., & Dube, S. (2021). Analyzing the causal relationship between exchange rate, renewable energy and inflation of Mexico (1990–2019) with ARDL bounds test approach. *Renewable Energy Focus, 37*, 78–83. doi:10.1016/j.ref.2021.04.001

Del Negro, M., & Schorfheide, F. (2011). Bayesian Macroeconometrics. In *Handbook of Bayesian Econometrics*. Oxford University Press.

Deloitte. (2020). *COVID-19 Sonrası Tedarik Zincirlerinde Kazananlar ve Kaybedenler*. https://www2.deloitte.com/content/dam/Deloitte/tr/Documents/consumer-business/Covid19sonrasitedarikzinciri.pdf

Derevyankina, E. S., & Yankovskaya, D. G. (2020). The impact of Covid-19 on supply chain management and global economy development. *International Journal of Supply Chain Management, 9*(4), 765–774.

Dey, A., LaGuardia, P., & Srinivasan, M. (2011). Building sustainability in logistics operations: A research agenda. *Management Research Review, 34*(11), 1237–1259. doi:10.1108/01409171111178774

Didea, L., & Ilie, D. M (2020). The State of Emergency and the Economic Repercussions. A New "Avalanche" of Insolvencies. *J.L. & Admin. Sci., 89*(13).

Diewert, W. E., & Fox, K. J. (2020). *Measuring real consumption and CPI bias under lockdown conditions*. NBER Working Papers 27144, National Bureau of Economic Research.

Dinçer, H., Hacıoğlu, Ü., & Yüksel, S. (2017). A strategic approach to global financial crisis in banking sector: A critical appraisal of banking strategies using fuzzy ANP and fuzzy topsis methods. *International Journal of Sustainable Economies Management, 6*(1), 1–21.

Dinçer, H., Lisin, A., Ubay, G. G., & Çağlayan, Ç. (2021). Identifying the Best Financing Sources for Renewable Energy Companies in Latin American Countries. In *Strategic Approaches to Energy Management* (pp. 1–12). Springer. doi:10.1007/978-3-030-76783-9_1

Dinçer, H., Yüksel, S., Çağlayan, Ç., & Uluer, G. S. (2020). The contribution of nuclear energy investment on sustainable financial and economic development. *Journal of Financial Economics and Banking, 1*(1), 39–51.

Dinçer, H., Yüksel, S., & Martinez, L. (2020). A comparative analysis of incremental and disruptive innovation policies in the European banking sector with hybrid interval type-2 fuzzy decision-making models. *International Journal of Fuzzy Systems, 22*(4), 1158–1176.

Dinçer, H., Yüksel, S., & Martínez, L. (2022). Collaboration enhanced hybrid fuzzy decision-making approach to analyze the renewable energy investment projects. *Energy Reports*, *8*, 377–389.

Dinçer, H., Yüksel, S., & Uluer, G. S. (2021). Understanding the impact of trade war between the US and China on oil price volatility. In *Global Tariff War: Economic, Political and Social Implications*. Emerald Publishing Limited. doi:10.1108/978-1-80071-314-720211013

Ding, Z., Yüksel, S., & Dinçer, H. (2021). An Integrated Pythagorean fuzzy soft computing approach to environmental management systems for sustainable energy pricing. *Energy Reports*, *7*, 5575–5588.

Djukic, G. & Ilic, B. (2020). Sustainable development, social protection and responsibility. *Sürdürülebilir kalkınma, sosyal koruma ve sorumluluk*, *2*(1), 83-91.

Doh, J., Budhwar, P., & Wood, G. (2021). Long-term energy transitions and international business: Concepts, theory, methods, and a research agenda. *Journal of International Business Studies*, *52*(5), 951–970. doi:10.105741267-021-00405-6 PMID:33716348

Donatos, G. S., & Mergos, G. J. (1989). Energy demand in Greece: The impact of the two energy crises. *Energy Economics*, *11*(2), 147–152. doi:10.1016/0140-9883(89)90008-X

Dong, W., Zhao, G., Yüksel, S., Dinçer, H., & Ubay, G. G. (2022). A novel hybrid decision making approach for the strategic selection of wind energy projects. *Renewable Energy*, *185*, 321–337.

Dun & Bradstreet. (2020). *Business Impact of the Coronavirus: Business and Supply Chain Analysis Due to the Coronavirus Outbreak, Special Brifing Dun & Bradstreet*. https://www.dnb.com/marketing/media/supplier-report-coronavirus.html

Duran, M. S., & Acar, M. (2020). Bir virüsün dünyaya ettikleri: Covid-19 pandemisinin makroekonomik etkileri. *International Journal of Social and Economic Sciences*, *10*(1), 54–67.

Duro, J. A., Perez-Laborda, A., Turrion-Prats, J., & Fernández-Fernández, M. (2021). Covid-19 and tourism vulnerability. *Tourism Management Perspectives*, *38*, 100819. doi:10.1016/j.tmp.2021.100819 PMID:34873568

Duyurular. (n.d.). Retrieved July 21, 2022, from https://www.tbb.org.tr/tr

Ebrahimy, E., Igan, D., & Peria, S. M. (2020). *The Impact of COVID-19 on Inflation: Potential Drivers and Dynamics*. International Monetary Fund.

Economic Development Foundation. (2020). *AB Yeşil Mutabakatı temel unsurları ve yol haritası*. https://www.ikv.org.tr/images/files/AB_Yesil_Mutabakati_Temel_Unsurlari_ve_Yol_Haritasi.pdf

Edwards, M. R. (1992). Symbiotic leadership: A creative partnership for managing organizational effectiveness. *Business Horizons*, *35*(3), 28–34. doi:10.1016/0007-6813(92)90066-I

El-Erian, M. (2020). *The Coming Coronavirus Recession and the Uncharted Territory Beyond*. Foreign Affairs, Media Report. Available at: https://www.foreignaffairs.com/articles/2020-03-17/coming-coronavirus-recession

Ellyat, H. (2021). *Supply chain chaos is already hitting global growth. And it's about to get worse*. CNBC.

Erçetin, Ş. (2000). *Lider Sarmalında Vizyon, 2*. Baskı, Nobel Yayın Dağıtım.

Ercin, S. (2020). Covid-19 döneminde etkili tedarik zinciri yönetimi. *KPMG*, 1-39.

Erdal, M., Görçün, Ö. F., Görçün, Ö., & Saygılı, M. S. (2008). *Entegre lojistik yönetimi*. Beta Yayınları.

Erdem, A. (2021). Covid-19 Salgınının Türkiye'nin Dış Ticaretine Etkisi: Bir Yapısal Kırılma Analizi. *İzmir İktisat Dergisi, 36*(3), 617-627.

Erdoğan, İ. (2002). *Eğitimde Değişim Yönetimi*. Pegem Yayıncılık.

Erdoğan, S., Yıldırım, D. Ç., & Gedikli, A. (2020). Dynamics and determinants of inflation during the COVID-19 pandemic period in European countries: A spatial panel data analysis. *Duzce Medical Journal*, *22*(Special Issue), 61–67. doi:10.18678/dtfd.794107

Erol, İ., & Özmen, A. (2008). Measuring environmental sustainability performance: An application in the retail industry. Economics. *Business and Finance*, *23*(266), 70–94.

Ersan, E. (2020). Vizyoner Liderlik Özellikleriyle Mustafa Necati Bey. *Uluslararası Liderlik Çalışmaları Dergisi: Kuram ve Uygulama, 3*(1), 58-64.

Ersoy, M. Ş. (2006). *Logistics and Turkey's position.* Status Journal. January.

Erturgut, R. (2016). *Lojistik ve tedarik zinciri yönetimi*. Nobel.

Eşmen, O., Bedük, F., & Bedük, A. (2015). *Green Logistics for a Liveable World: Practice Examples both in Turkey and the World*. Academic Press.

Eti, S. (2021). The use of quantitative methods in investment decisions: a literature review. *Research Anthology on Personal Finance and Improving Financial Literacy*, 1-20.

Eti, S., Kalkavan, H., Dinçer, H., & Yüksel, S. (2020). Predicting the role of Islamic banking on sustainable economic development: An analysis for Turkey with ARIMA model. In *Handbook of research on creating sustainable value in the global economy* (pp. 146–164). IGI Global.

European Commission (2019). *Performance of freight transport (tkm): Statistical pocketbook 2019*. Directorate General for Mobility and Transport (DG MOVE).

European Commission. (2010). *Being Wise with The Waste: The EU's Approach to Waste Management*. Belgium: European Union. http://ec.europa.eu/environment/waste/pdf/ WASTE%20BROCHURE.pdf

European Commission. (2016). *The Road from Paris: assessing the implications of the Paris Agreement and accompanying the proposal for a Council decision on the signing, on behalf of the European Union, of the Paris agreement adopted under the United Nations Framework Convention on Climate Change*. COM (2016) 110 final. https://eur-lex.europa.eu/legalcontent/ EN/TXT/?uri=COM:2016:110:FIN

European Commission. (2019a). *The European green deal. COM (2019) 640 final*. https://eurlex.europa.eu/legalcontent/EN/TXT/?uri=COM%3A2019%3A640%3AFIN

European Commission. (2019b). *Clean energy for all Europeans*. https://op.europa.eu/s/vdHz

European Commission. (2020a). *A new circular economy action plan*. COM (2020) 98 final. https://eur-lex.europa.eu/legal-content/EN/TXT/?uri=COM%3A2020%3A98%3AFIN

European Commission. (2020b). *Communication from the commission to the European parliament, the council, the European economic and social committee and the committee of the regions*. Author.

European Commission. (2020c). *Communication on a Sustainable and Smart Mobility Strategy- putting European transport on track for the future*. https://ec.europa.eu/transport/sites/transport/files/legislation/com20200789.pdf

European Commission. (2021). *A European Green Deal*. European Commission. https://ec.europa.eu/info/strategy/priorities-2019-2024/european-green-deal_en

Eyal, I., & Sirer, E. G. (2014). Majority is not enough: Bitcoin mining is vulnerable. In *International conference on financial cryptography and data security* (pp. 436–454). Springer., . doi:10.1007/978-3-662-45472-5_28

Fang, S., Zhou, P., Dinçer, H., & Yüksel, S. (2021). Assessment of safety management system on energy investment risk using house of quality based on hybrid stochastic interval-valued intuitionistic fuzzy decision-making approach. *Safety Science*, *141*, 105333.

FAO. (2021). *The impact of disasters and crises on agriculture and food security*. Food and Agriculture Organization of United Nations.

Feige, E. L., & McGee, R. T. (1983). Sweden's Laffer curve: Taxation and the unobserved economy. *The Scandinavian Journal of Economics*, *85*(4), 499–519. doi:10.2307/3439948

Fettahlıoğlu, H. S., & Cansu, B. (2016). In terms of sustainability the factors that affect reverse logistic activities and sustainable marketing. *Journal of Kahramanmaraş Sütçü İmam University Faculty of Economics and Administrative Sciences*, *6*(2), 89–114.

Fetting, C. (2020). *The European Green Deal*. ESDN Office.

Financial Times. (2020). *Global recession already here, say top economists*. Available at: https://www.ft.com/content/be732afe-6526-11ea-a6cd-df28cc3c6a68

Findlay, R., & O'Rourke, K. (2008). *Power and Plenty: Trade, War, and the World Economy in the Second Millennium*. Princeton University Press.

Fiorillo, D. (2013). Household Waste Recycling: National Survey Evidence From Italy. *Journal of Environmental Planning and Management*, *56*(8), 1125–1151. doi:10.1080/09640568.2012.709180

Fleischmann, M., Van Nunen, J. A., & Gräve, B. (2003). Integrating closed-loop supply chains and spare-parts management at IBM. *Interfaces*, *33*(6), 44–56. doi:10.1287/inte.33.6.44.25189

Fleming, R. C., & Mauger, R. (2021). Green and just? An update on the 'European Green Deal'. *Journal for European Environmental & Planning Law*, *18*(1), 164–180. doi:10.1163/18760104-18010010

Flemming, P. L. (2017). Building a Climate of Change with a link through Transformational Leadership and Corporate Culture: A Management key to a Global Environment. *International Journal of Business and Social Research*, *7*(1), 44–55.

Fooddive. (2020). *Tracking coronavirus closures at food and beverage factories*. Retrieved March 20, 2022, from https://www.fooddive.com/news/tracking-coronavirus-closures-at-food-and-beverage-factories/576559/

Forbes. (2020). *New delay reported for Apple's iphone 12 launch*. Retrieved May 7, 2022, from https://www.forbes.com/sites/gordonkelly/2020/09/24/apple-iphone-12-pro-max-release-date-new-iphone-11-pro-max-upgrade/?sh=502b16ec5b3e

Forbes. (2022). Retrieved May 20, 2022, from https://www.forbes.com/companies/alibaba-group/?sh=49fa6a2219f5

Fortunes. (2022). *China's hard-line covid-zero response to omicron could trigger supply-chain chaos*. Retrieved April 28, 2022, from https://fortune.com/2022/01/13/china-omicron-covid-zero-port-shutdown-lockdown-supply-chain/

Friedman, M. (1968). The role of monetary policy. *Essential Readings in Economics*, *58*(1), 215–231.

Gaillard, N. (2020). *Country Risk. Subtitle The Bane of Foreign Investors*. Springer., doi:10.1007/978-3-030-45788-4

Gaiotti, E. (2013). Credit availability and investment: Lessons from the great recession. *European Economic Review*, *59*, 212–227. doi:10.1016/j.euroecorev.2012.12.007

Gasparotto, J., & Martinello, K. D. B. (2021). Coal as an energy source and its impacts on human health. *Energy Geoscience, 2*(2), 113–120.

Gençer, Y. G. (2018). Measuring value along the supply chain: A study on white goods sector. *Elektronik Sosyal Bilimler Dergisi, 17*(66), 688–703.

Gençer, Y. G., & Akküçük, U. (2018). The Preference of Turkish Consumers on Converged Products: The Smartphone Example. *İstanbul Gelişim Üniversitesi Sosyal Bilimler Dergisi, 5*(1), 221-230.

Gencer, Y. G. (2016). Mystery of recycling: Glass and aluminum examples. In *Handbook of research on waste management techniques for sustainability* (pp. 172–191). IGI Global. doi:10.4018/978-1-4666-9723-2.ch009

Gencer, Y. G. (2017). Structural Design of an E-Commerce Business: Yemeksepeti.com Example From Turkey. *The China Business Review, 16*(7), 327–336.

Gencer, Y. G. (2019). The Necessity of Sustainability in Operations Management in Terms of Various Sectors. In *Ethical and Sustainable Supply Chain Management in a Global Context* (pp. 77–85). IGI Global. doi:10.4018/978-1-5225-8970-9.ch005

Gencer, Y. G., & Akkucuk, U. (2016). Reverse logistics: Automobile recalls and other conditions. In *Handbook of research on waste management techniques for sustainability* (pp. 125–154). IGI Global. doi:10.4018/978-1-4666-9723-2.ch007

Gencer, Y. G., & Akkucuk, U. (2017). Measuring quality in automobile aftersales: AutoSERVQUAL Scale. *Amfiteatru Economic, 19*(44), 110.

Georgieva, K. (2020). *IMF Managing Director Kristalina Georgieva's Statement Following a G20 Ministerial Call on the Coronavirus Emergency*. IMF Press statement. Available at: https://www.imf.org/en/News/Articles/2020/03/23/pr2098-imf-managing-director-statement-following-a-g20-ministerial-call-on-the-coronavirus-emergency

Gergen, M. J., Cannon, G. D. Jr, & Tewksbury, D. G. (2003). Market-Based Ratemaking and the Western Energy Crisis of 2000 and 2001. *Energy LJ, 24*, 321.

Giannone, D., Lenza, M., & Primiceri, G. E. (2015). Prior Selection for Vector Autoregressions. *The Review of Economics and Statistics, 97*(2), 436–451. doi:10.1162/REST_a_00483

Glick, R., & Taylor, A. M. (2010). Collateral Damage: Trade Disruption and the Economic Impact of War. *The Review of Economics and Statistics, 92*(1), 102–127. doi:10.1162/rest.2009.12023

Global report on food crisis. (2021). Retrieved April 8, 2022, from https://docs.wfp.org/api/documents/WFP-0000127413/download/?_ga=2.107110212.73355866.1654068456-1668939605.1654068456

Glowacz, M., & Rees, D. (2016). Using Jasmonates and Salicylates to Reduce Losses Within the Fruit Supply Chain. *European Food Research and Technology, 242*(2), 143–156. doi:10.100700217-015-2527-6

Goffman, E. (2020). In the wake of COVID-19, is glocalization our sustainability future? *Sustainability: Science, Practice, and Policy, 16*(1), 48–52.

Gökalp, Y., Dinçer, H., & Eti, S. (2021). The role of health policies for the strategic investment decisions of the international companies. In *Management Strategies to Survive in a Competitive Environment* (pp. 321–333). Springer.

Goleman, D. (1998). *Working with emotional intelligence*. Bantam.

Gonczol, P., Katsikouli, P., Herskind, L., & Dragoni, N. (2020). Blockchain Implementations and Use Cases for Supply Chains - A Survey. *IEEE Access: Practical Innovations, Open Solutions, 8*, 11856–11871. doi:10.1109/ACCESS.2020.2964880

Goren. (n.d.). *Lecture notes of "Recycling Technologies"*. College of Engineering at Al-Lith, Umm Al-Qura University.

Gören, S. (2005). *Sanitary Landfill*. Forart Publications.

Govindan, K., Mina, H., & Alavi, B. (2020). A Decision Support System for Demand Management in Healthcare Supply Chains Considering the Epidemic Outbreaks: A Case Study of Coronavirus Disease 2019 (COVID-19). *Transportation Research Part E, Logistics and Transportation Review*, *138*, 101967. doi:10.1016/j.tre.2020.101967 PMID:32382249

Gray, R. S. (2020). Agriculture, transportation, and the COVID-19 crisis. *Canadian Journal of Agricultural Economics/ Revue canadienne d'agroeconomie*, *68*(2), 239-243.

Gray, R. S. (2020). *Agriculture, Transportation, and the COVID-19 Crisis*. Canadian Journal of Agricultural Economics/ Revue CanadienneD'agroeconomie. doi:10.1111/cjag.12235

Greenspan, A. (1996). Achieving price stability: A summary of the Bank's 1996 symposium. *Economic Review-Federal Reserve Bank of Kansas City*, *81*, 1–5.

Greenwood, J., & Hanke, S. (2022). On Monetary Growth and Inflation in Leading Economies, 2021-2022: Relative Prices and the Overall Price Level. *Journal of Applied Corporate Finance*, *33*(4), 39–51. doi:10.1111/jacf.12479

Groshen, E. L. (2020). COVID-19's impact on the U.S. labor market as of September 2020. *Business Economics (Cleveland, Ohio)*, *55*(4), 213–228. doi:10.105711369-020-00193-1 PMID:33204039

Grunwald, J., & Flamm, K. (1985). *The global factory: Foreign assembly in international trade*. Brookings Institution.

GS, D. G., & Swetha, M. S. S. (2020). Pandemic impact: Challenges faced by entrepreneurs of logistics industry. *Journal of Contemporary Issues in Business and Government*, *26*(2), 516.

Güler, S. (2007). *Fiedler'in Lpc Ölçeği İle Lise Yöneticilerinin Liderlik Tiplerinin Belirlenmesi*. Yayınlanmış Yüksek Lisans Tezi, Yeditepe Üniversitesi Sosyal Bilimler Enstitüsü.

Gül, H., & Çöl, G. (2003). Atıf Teorisinde Belirtilen Karizmatik Lider Özelliklerinin Üçlü Örgütsel Bağlılık Modeliyle İlişkileri Üzerine Bir Araştırma. *Atatürk Üniversitesi İktisadi Ve İdari Bilimler Fakültesi Dergisi*, *3*, 4.

Gültaş, P., & Yücel, M. (2015). Green Logistics: Green Local Transportation The Model of Malatya Municipality. *Journal of Academıc Approaches*, *6*(2), 70–83.

Güney, S. (1999). *Davranış Bilimleri Açısından Atatürk'ün Liderliği*. Ocak Yayınları.

Güven, S. (2016). Postmodern Dönemde Siyasal Alanın Yapısal Dönüşümü ve Postmodern Siyasi Liderlik. *Akdeniz Üniversitesi İletişim Fakültesi Dergisi*, (25), 294–318.

Hafner, M., & Raimondi, P. P. (2020). Priorities and challenges of the EU energy transition: From the European Green Package to the new Green Deal. *Russian Journal of Economics*, *6*(4), 374–389. doi:10.32609/j.ruje.6.55375

Hailu, G. (2020). Economic Thoughts on COVID-19 for Canadian Food Processors. *Canadian Journal of Agricultural Economics/Revue canadienned'agroeconomie*, *68*(2), 163–169.

Haines, A., & Scheelbeek, P. (2020). European Green Deal: A major opportunity for health improvement. *Lancet*, *395*(10233), 1327–1329. doi:10.1016/S0140-6736(20)30109-4 PMID:32394894

Hair, J. F. Jr., Black, W.C., Babin, B.J., Anderson, R.E., & Tatham, R.L. (2005). Multivariate Data Analysis (6th ed.). Pearson

Haiyun, C., Zhixiong, H., Yüksel, S., & Dinçer, H. (2021). Analysis of the innovation strategies for green supply chain management in the energy industry using the QFD-based hybrid interval valued intuitionistic fuzzy decision approach. *Renewable & Sustainable Energy Reviews*, *143*, 110844.

Haldeman, T., & Turner, J. W. (2009). Implementing a Community-Based Social Marketing Program to Increase Recycling. *Social Marketing Quarterly*, *15*(3), 115–127.

Hammoudeh, S., & Yuan, Y. (2008). Metal volatility in presence of oil and interest rate shocks. *Energy Economics*, *30*(2), 606–620. doi:10.1016/j.eneco.2007.09.004

Han, A., Pehlivan, C., & Konat, G. (2022). COVİD-19 pandemi sürecinin türkiye ekonomisine etkilerinin ampirik analizi. *Sağlık ve Sosyal Refah Araştırmaları Dergisi*, *4*(1), 32–49.

Handfield, R. B., Graham, G., & Burns, L. (2020). Corona virus, tariffs, trade wars and supply chain evolutionary design. *International Journal of Operations & Production Management*, *40*(10), 2020. doi:10.1108/IJOPM-03-2020-0171

Hanif, I. (2018). Energy consumption habits and human health nexus in Sub-Saharan Africa. *Environmental Science and Pollution Research International*, *25*(22), 21701–21712. doi:10.100711356-018-2336-0 PMID:29790046

Hartgen, D. T., Neveu, A. J., Brunso, J. M., Banas, J. S., & Miller, J. W. (1979). *Changes in Travel in response to the 1979 Energy Crisis*. https://trid.trb.org/view/145170

Hartog, D. N., & Koopman, P. L. (2009). Örgütlerde Liderlik. *Endüstri, İş ve Örgüt Psikolojisi*, *2*, 195–219.

Haseeb, M., Kot, S., Hussain, H. I., & Jermsittiparsert, K. (2019). Impact of economic growth, environmental pollution, and energy consumption on health expenditure and R&D expenditure of ASEAN countries. *Energies*, *12*(19), 3598.

He, L., Ding, Z., Yin, F., & Wu, M. (2016). The impact of relative energy prices on industrial energy consumption in China: A consideration of inflation costs. *SpringerPlus*, *5*(1), 1–21. doi:10.118640064-016-2661-z PMID:27398277

Hensher, D. A., & Stanley, J. K. (2009). What if petrol increased to $10 per litre in Melbourne?: Implications for travel behaviour and public transport demand. *Road & Transport Research: A Journal of Australian and New Zealand Research and Practice, 18*(3), 61-68.

Hernández, D., & Siegel, E. (2019). Energy insecurity and its ill health effects: A community perspective on the energy-health nexus in New York City. *Energy Research & Social Science*, *47*, 78 83. PMID:32280598

Hey, J. (2020). Coronavirus: Measuring the Market Impact. *Fruitnet*. www.fruitnet.com/asiafruit/article/181021/coronavirus-measuring-the-market-impact

Hilmola, O. P., Lähdeaho, O., Henttu, V., & Hilletofth, P. (2020). COVID-19 pandemic: Early implications for North European manufacturing and logistics. *Sustainability*, *12*(20), 8315. doi:10.3390u12208315

HIS Markit. (2017). *Interpreting PMI data*. Retrieved from: https://www.pmi.spglobal.com/Public/Home/ PDF/EN_PMIRecruitment

Hobbs, J. E. (2020). Food supply chains during the COVID-19 pandemic. *Canadian Journal of Agricultural Economics/Revue canadienne d'agroeconomie, 68*(2), 171-176.

Hobbs, J. E. (2021). Food supply chain resilience and the COVID-19 pandemic: What have we learned? *Canadian Journal of Agricultural Economics/Revue canadienne d'agroeconomie, 69*(2), 189-196.

Home: The Institute of Internal Auditors: The IIA. (n.d.). Retrieved July 21, 2022, from https://www.theiia.org/

Hörisch, J., Wulfsberg, I., & Schaltegger, S. (2019). The inñuence of feedback and awareness of consequences on the development of corporate sustainability action over time. *Business Strategy and the Environment, 29*(2), 638–650. doi:10.1002/bse.2394

Horowit, J. (2020). *The global coronavirus recession is beginning.* CNN. Media Report. Available at: https://edition.cnn.com/2020/03/16/economy/global-recession-coronavirus/index.html

Houlihan, J. B. (1988). International supply chains: A new approach. *Management Decision, 26*(3), 13–19. doi:10.1108/eb001493

Hu, X., Zou, C., Tang, X., Liu, T., & Hu, L. (2019). Cost-optimal energy management of hybrid electric vehicles using fuel cell/battery health-aware predictive control. *IEEE Transactions on Power Electronics, 35*(1), 382-392.

Huang, C., Wang, Y., Li, X., Ren, L., Zhao, J., & Hu, Y. (2020). *Clinical Features of Patients Infected with 2019 Novel Coronavirus in Wuhan.* Lancet. doi:10.1016/S0140-6736(20)30183-5

Hummel, P., & Hörisch, J. (2020). The hidden power of language: How 'value creation accounting' inñuences decisions on expenditures, cost reductions and staff costs, *Sustainability Accounting. Management and Policy Journal, 11*(1), 187–206. doi:10.1108/SAMPJ-04-2018-0111

IATA. (2020). *Potential for revenue losses of $113bn due to COVID-19 crisis.* IATA.

İbadullayeva, J., Jumaniyazova, K., Azimzadeh, S., Canıgür, S., & Ferhan, E. (2019). The effects of environmental pollution on human health. *Turkish Medical Students Research Journal, 1*(3), 52–58.

Ibn-Mohammed, T., Mustapha, K. B., Godsell, J., Adamu, Z., Babatunde, K. A., Akintade, D. D., Acquaye, A., Fujii, H., Ndiaye, M. M., Yamoah, F. A., & Koh, S. C. L. (2021). *A critical analysis of the impacts of COVID-19 on the global economy and ecosystems and opportunities for circular economy strategies.* https://www.sciencedirect.com/science/article/pii/S0921344920304869 doi:10.1016/j.resconrec.2020.105169

ICC Brasil. (2018). *International Chamber of Commerce.* ITTI Discussion Paper. https://unctad.org/system/files/non-official-document/dtl_eWeek2018c04-ICCBrasil_en.pdf

IEA. (2021). *Global Energy Review 2021. International Energy Agency 'Assessing the effects of economic recoveries on global energy demand and CO2 emissions in 2021'.* IEA.

Ilic, B., Djukic, G., & Nikolic, M. (2022). Rural tourism of Eastern Serbia: Human resources management and motivation. *Economy of Agriculture, 69*(1), 241-255. doi:10.5937/ekoPolj2201241I

Ilic, B. S., & Salaimeh, S. A. (2022). Management of telecommunication operator services in Serbia–Case study Eastern Serbia. *WSEAS Transactions on Business and Economics, 19*(1), 977–984.

IMCO. (2020). *Deglobalization. Implications for investors.* Oxford Economics.

IMF database. (2021). Retrieved May 24, 2022, from https://www.imf.org/en/Publications/WEO/weo-database/2021/April/select-countries?grp=2001&sg=All%20countries

International Air Transport Association [IATA]. (2020). *Recovery Delayed as International Travel Remains Locked Down.* Retrieved April 10, 2022 from https://www.iata.org/en/pressroom/pr/2020-07-28-02/

International Monetary Fund. (2022). *International financial statistics (IFS).* International Monetary Fund.

Irwin, D. A. (2020). *The pandemic adds momentum to the deglobalization trend.* Peterson Institute for International Economics.

Irz, X., Niemi, J., & Liu, X. (2013). Determinants of food price inflation in Finland—The role of energy. *Energy Policy, 63*, 656–663. doi:10.1016/j.enpol.2013.09.023

İşcan. (2010). *Ömer Faruk, ve Ufuk Sayın.* Örgütsel Adalet, İş Tatmini ve Örgütsel Güven Arasındaki İlişki. Atatürk Üniversitesi İktisadi Ve İdari Bilimler Dergisi.

Ishida, S. (2020). Perspectives on supply chain management in a pandemic and the post-COVID-19 era. *IEEE Engineering Management Review, 48*(3), 146–152. doi:10.1109/EMR.2020.3016350

ITC. (2022a). *China's foreign trade data.* Retrieved April 19, 2022, from http://jbr.org/articles.html www.trademap.org

ITC. (2022b). *Goods Imported and Exported by Turkey.* Retrieved April 20, 2022, from www.trademap.org

ITC. (2022c). *Turkey's foreign trade balance.* Retrieved April 19, 2022, from www.trademap.org

Ivanov, D.Implications for STEM education. (2020). Predicting the Impacts of Epidemic Outbreaks on Global Supply Chains: A Simulation-Based Analysis on the Coronavirus Outbreak (COVID-19/SARS-CoV-2) Case. *Transportation Research Part E, Logistics and Transportation Review, 136*, 101922. doi:10.1016/j.tre.2020.101922 PMID:32288597

Jagannathan, R., Kapoor, M., & Schaumburg, E. (2013). Causes of the great recession of 2007–2009: The financial crisis was the symptom not the disease. *Journal of Financial Intermediation, 22*(1), 4–29. doi:10.1016/j.jfi.2012.06.002

Jäger-Waldau, A., Kougias, I., Taylor, N., & Thiel, C. (2020). How photovoltaics can contribute to GHG emission reductions of 55% in the EU by 2030. *Renewable & Sustainable Energy Reviews, 126*, 109836. doi:10.1016/j.rser.2020.109836

James, H. (2018). Deglobalization: The Rise of Disembedded Unilateralism. *Annual Review of Financial Economics, 10*(1), 219–237. doi:10.1146/annurev-financial-110217-022625

Jaques, E., & Clement, S.D (1994). Executive Leadership: A Practical Guide to Managing Complexity. Carson-Hall & Co. Publishers.

Jaravel, X., & O'Connell, M. (2020). *Inflation Spike and Falling Product Variety during the Great Lockdown.* CEPR Discussion Papers No. 14880.

Jardini, J. A., Ramos, D. S., Martini, J. S. C., Reis, L. B. D., & Tahan, C. M. A. (2002). Brazilian energy crisis. *IEEE Power Engineering Review, 22*(4), 21–24. doi:10.1109/MPER.2002.994845

Javorcik, B. (2020). Coronavirus will Change the Way the World Does Business for Good Businesses will be Forced to Rethink their Global Value Chains. *Financial Times.*

Jaworski, K. (2021). Measuring food inflation during the COVID-19 pandemic in real time using online data: A case study of Poland. *British Food Journal, 123*(13), 260–280. doi:10.1108/BFJ-06-2020-0532

Ji, D., Fan, L., Li, X., & Ramakrishna, S. (2020). Addressing the worldwide shortages of face masks. *BMC Materials, 2*(1), 1-11.

Ji-Hong, J. (2017). US Purchasing Managers' Index and its Impact on Korea and US. *Journal of Distribution Science, 15*(3), 17–25. doi:10.15722/jds.15.3.201703.17

Johari, A., Nyakuma, B. B., Nor, S. H. M., Mat, R., Hashim, H., Ahmad, A., ... Abdullah, T. A. T. (2015). The challenges and prospects of palm oil based biodiesel in Malaysia. *Energy, 81*, 255–261. doi:10.1016/j.energy.2014.12.037

Johnsson, F., Kjärstad, J., & Rootzén, J. (2019). The threat to climate change mitigation posed by the abundance of fossil fuels. *Climate Policy, 19*(2), 258–274. doi:10.1080/14693062.2018.1483885

Jones, K. (2013). *Richard Martin: SuperFuel (Thorium, the Green Energy Source for the Future).* Academic Press.

Jun, Q., Dinçer, H., & Yüksel, S. (2021). Stochastic hybrid decision-making based on interval type 2 fuzzy sets for measuring the innovation capacities of financial institutions. *International Journal of Finance & Economics, 26*(1), 573–593.

Kaban, İ. (2020). Bankalarda Amacına Göre İç Denetim: Türkiye Bankacılık Sektörü Özelinde Örnek Denetim Vakaları. *Optimum Ekonomi ve Yönetim Bilimleri Dergisi, 7*(1), 181–200. doi:10.17541/optimum.570629

Kahraman, C., Oztaysi, B., & Cevik Onar, S. (2020). Single & interval-valued neutrosophic AHP methods: Performance analysis of outsourcing law firms. *Journal of Intelligent & Fuzzy Systems, 38*(1), 749–759. doi:10.3233/JIFS-179446

Kakışım, C. (2022). The European Green Deal: An analysis from perspective of green theory. *Journal of Strategic and Social Researhes, 6*(1), 1–16.

Kalair, A., Abas, N., Saleem, M. S., Kalair, A. R., & Khan, N. (2021). Role of energy storage systems in energy transition from fossil fuels to renewables. *Energy Storage, 3*(1), e135. doi:10.1002/est2.135

Kamalahmadi, M., Shekarian, M., & Mellat Parast, M. (2022). The impact of flexibility and redundancy on improving supply chain resilience to disruptions. *International Journal of Production Research, 60*(6), 1992–2020. doi:10.1080/00207543.2021.1883759

Kammen, D. M., & Sunter, D. A. (2016). City-integrated renewable energy for urban sustainability. *Science, 352*(6288), 922–928. doi:10.1126cience.aad9302 PMID:27199413

Kano, L., Tsang, E. W. K., & Yeung, H. (2020). Wc. (2020). Global value chains: A review of the multi-disciplinary literature. *Journal of International Business Studies, 51*(4), 577–622. doi:10.105741267-020-00304-2

Karakuş, D. N., Nazan, A. N., Turp, M. T., & Kurnaz, L. (2022). A global view of basic practice approaches within the scope of the EU Green Deal and sustainable development goals. *Dokuz Eylul University The Journal of Graduate School of Social Sciences, 24*(1), 47–67.

Kardooni, R., Yusoff, S. B., & Kari, F. B. (2015). Barriers to renewable energy development: Five fuel policy in Malaysia. *Energy & Environment, 26*(8), 1353–1361. doi:10.1260/0958-305X.26.8.1353

Karlsson, S. (2012). *Forecasting with Bayesian Vector Autoregressions*. Working Papers, 2012:12, Orebro University, Swedish Business School.

Karp, R. (2005). *Katrina and oil prices*. https://www.cfr.org/interview/katrina-and-oil-prices

Kartal, M. T., & Kizil, C. (2020). Bankalarda İç Denetim ve İç Kontrol Bulgularının Raporlanması ile Çözümlenmesi: Bankaların Bilgi Sistemleri ve Elektronik Bankacılık Hizmetleri Hakkında Yönetmelik Kapsamında Bir İnceleme [Reporting and Resolution of Internal Audit and Internal Control Findings in Banks: An Examination within the Context of Regulation on Banks' Information Systems and Electronic Banking Services]. *Turkish Studies - Economics, Finance, Politics Journal, 15*(3), 1485–1500.

Kasipillai, J., & Chan, P. (2008). Travel demand management: Lessons for Malaysia. *Journal of Public Transportation, 11*(3), 3. doi:10.5038/2375-0901.11.3.3

Kaufmann, R. K., Gonzalez, N., Nickerson, T. A., & Nesbit, T. S. (2011). Do household energy expenditures affect mortgage delinquency rates? *Energy Economics, 33*(2), 188–194. doi:10.1016/j.eneco.2010.07.007

Kaya, M., & Cahit, A. (2011). Küreselleşmenin Tarihsel Gelişimi. *Dicle Üniversitesi İktisadi ve İdari Bilimler Fakültesi Dergisi*, 14-36.

Kayıran, M., & Saygın, S. (2019). İzmir İktisat Kongresi. *Eskişehir Osmangazi Üniversitesi Türk Dünyası Uygulama ve Araştırma Merkezi Yakın Tarih Dergisi*, 27-70.

Kaymakçı, O. (2013). Küresel Ekonomide Çok Uluslu Şirketler Ve Türkiye'deki Yansımaları. *Manisa Celal Bayar Üniversitesi Sosyal Bilimler Dergisi*, 224-249.

Kebriaei, M., Niasar, A. H., & Asaei, B. (2015, October). Hybrid electric vehicles: An overview. In *2015 International Conference on Connected Vehicles and Expo (ICCVE)* (pp. 299-305). IEEE. 10.1109/ICCVE.2015.84

Kefi, H., & Kalika, M. (2005). Survey of Strategic Alignment Impacts on Organizational Performancein International European Companies. *Proceeding of the 38th Hawaii International Conference on System Sciences*, 1-10.

Kemp, P. S., Froese, R., & Pauly, D. (2020). COVID-19 provides an opportunity to advance a sustainable UK ðsheries policy in a post-Brexit brave new world. *Marine Policy*, *120*, 104–114. doi:10.1016/j.marpol.2020.104114 PMID:32834407

Ker, N. (2020). Experience Versus Expectation: Farmers' Perceptions of Smart Farming Technologies for Cropping Systems Across Europe. *Precision Agriculture*, *21*(1), 34–50. doi:10.100711119-019-09651-z

Kerr, W. A. (2021). Agriculture after a year with COVID-19: Any long-term implications for international trade policy? *Canadian Journal of Agricultural Economics/Revue canadienne d'agroeconomie, 69*(2), 261-267.

Khan, S. A. R., Zhang, Y., Kumar, A., Zavadskas, E., & Streimikiene, D. (2020). Measuring the impact of renewable energy, public health expenditure, logistics, and environmental performance on sustainable economic growth. *Sustainable Development*, *28*(4), 833–843.

Kilpatrick, J., & Barter, L. (2020). *COVID-19: managing supply chain risk and disruption*. Deloitte.

KimI. K. (2022, February 26) Consumers' Preference for Downsizing Over the Package Price Increase. doi:10.2139/ssrn.4044401

Kim, J. B., Song, B. Y., & Zhang, L. (2011). Internal Control Weakness and Bank Loan Contracting: Evidence from SOX Section 404 Disclosures. *The Accounting Review*, *86*(4), 1157–1188. doi:10.2308/accr-10036

Kim, S., Lee, G., & Kang, H. G. (2021). Risk management and corporate social responsibility. *Strategic Management Journal*, *42*(1), 202–230.

Kızılboğa, R., & Özşahin, F. (2013). Etkin Bir İç Kontrol Sisteminin İç Denetim Faaliyetine ve İç Denetçilere Katkısı. *Niğde Üniversitesi İktisadi ve İdari Bilimler Fakültesi Dergisi*, *6*(2), 220–236.

Koenig, E. F. (2002). Using the Purchasing Managers' Index to assess the economy's strength and the likely direction of monetary policy. *Economic and Financial Policy Review*, *1*(6).

Köksal, O. (2011). *Organizasyonel Etkinliği Sağlamanın Yeni Yolu: Simbiyotik Liderlik*. Academic Press.

Koop, G. (2013). Forecasting with Medium and Large Bayesian VARs. *Journal of Applied Econometrics*, *28*(2), 177–203. doi:10.1002/jae.1270

Koop, G., & Korobilis, D. (2010). Bayesian Multivariate Time Series Methods for Empirical Macroeconomics. *Foundations and Trends in Econometrics*, *3*(4), 267–358. doi:10.1561/0800000013

Korkmaz, U. (2007). Kamuda İç Denetim. *Bütçe Dünyası*, *2*(25), 4–15.

Korniejczuk, K. (2019). *Simulating severe supply chain disruptions with multiple suppliers and firms* (Doctoral dissertation). Iowa State University.

Kose, T. (2019). Energy poverty and health: The Turkish case. *Energy Sources. Part B, Economics, Planning, and Policy*, *14*(5), 201–213.

Kostis, P., Dinçer, H., & Yüksel, S. (2022). Knowledge-Based Energy Investments of European Economies and Policy Recommendations for Sustainable Development. *Journal of the Knowledge Economy*, 1–33.

Kostyrko, R. V. (2021). *Development of logistics in a pandemic*. Academic Press.

Kotler, P. (2000). *Marketing Management*. Prentice Hall.

Kou, G., Olgu Akdeniz, Ö., Dinçer, H., & Yüksel, S. (2021). Fintech investments in European banks: A hybrid IT2 fuzzy multidimensional decision-making approach. *Financial Innovation*, *7*(1), 1–28. PMID:35024283

Kou, G., Yüksel, S., & Dinçer, H. (2022). Inventive problem-solving map of innovative carbon emission strategies for solar energy-based transportation investment projects. *Applied Energy*, *311*, 118680.

Koutoupis, A. G., & Malisiovas, T. (2021). The effects of the internal control system on the risk, profitability, and compliance of the U.S. banking sector: A quantitative approach. *International Journal of Finance & Economics*, 1–15. doi:10.1002/ijfe.2498

Krömer, S., & Gatzert, N. (2018). Renewable energy investments with storage: a risk-return analysis. *International Journal of Energy Sector Management*.

Kuchler, T., Russel, D., & Stroebel, J. (2020). *The geographic spread of COVID-19 correlates with structure of social networks as measured by Facebook*. NBER Working Papers 26990, National Bureau of Economic Research.

Küçük, G., & Dural, B. Y. (2022). The European Green Deal and the transition to a green economy: An evaluation of energy scenarios. *Anadolu University Journal of Social Sciences*, *22*(1), 137–156.

Kumar, S., Afrouzi, H., Coibion, O., & Gorodnichenko, Y. (2015). Inflation targeting does not anchor inflation expectations: Evidence from firms in New Zealand. *Management*, *24*(5), 637–652.

Kuschnig, N., & Vashold, L. (2022). *BVAR: Hierarchical Prior Selection in R*. R package version 1.0.3. https://CRAN.R-project.org/package=BVAR

Kuschnig, N., & Vashold, L. (2021). BVAR: Bayesian Vector Autoregressions with Hierarchical Prior Selection in R. *Journal of Statistical Software*, *100*(14), 1–27. doi:10.18637/jss.v100.i14

Kuscu, M., & Arslan, H. (2016). Virtual Leadership At Distance Education Teams. *Turkish Online Journal of Distance Education, 17*(3).

Kwan, S. H., & Mertens, T. M. (2020). Market assessment of COVID–19. *FRBSF Economic Lett.*, *2020*(14), 1–5.

Kwon, O. K. (2020). How is the COVID-19 pandemic affecting global supply chains, logistics, and transportation? *Journal of International Logistics and Trade*, *18*(3), 107–111.

LaBelle, J., & Santacreu, A. M. (2022). Global supply chain disruptions and inflation during the COVID-19 pandemic. *Review - Federal Reserve Bank of St. Louis*.

Laffer, A. B. (2004). The Laffer curve: Past, present, and future. *Backgrounder (Washington, D.C.)*, *1765*(1), 1–16.

Lambert, D. M., & Stock, J. R. (1993). *Strategic logistics management* (Vol. 69). Irwin.

Larry Elliot, L. (2020). Prepare for the coronavirus global recession. *The Guardian*. Available at: https://www.theguardian.com/business/2020/mar/15/prepare-for-the-coronavirus-global-recession

Law Commission. (2022). Reforming the Law. *Electronic trade documents, Summary*. https://www.lawcom.gov.uk/project/electronic-trade-documents/#related

Leal Filho, W., Brandli, L. L., Lange Salvia, A., Rayman-Bacchus, L., & Platje, J. (2020). COVID-19 and the UN sustainable development goals: Threat to solidarity or an opportunity? *Sustainability, 12*(13), 5343. doi:10.3390u12135343

Leckcivilize, A. (2012). *The Impact of Supply Chain Disruptions: Evidence from the Japanese Tsunami.* London School or Economics and Political Science.

Lee, C.-Y., & Huh, S.-Y. (2017). Forecasting Long-Term Crude Oil Prices Using a Bayesian Model with Informative Priors. *Sustainability, 9*(2), 190. doi:10.3390/su9020190

Lee, R. P., Meyer, B., Huang, Q., & Voss, R. (2020). Sustainable waste management for zero waste cities in China: potential, challenges and opportunities. *Clean Energy, 4*(3), 169-201.

Lee, Y. N. (2021). *Survey finds auto industry hit hardest by supply chain disruptions during covid pandemic.* Retrieved April 15, 2022, from https://www.cnbc.com/2021/08/25/auto-industry-supply-chains-hit-hardest-during-covid-pandemic-survey.html

Lee, H. L. (2002). Aligning supply chain strategies with product uncertainties. *California Management Review, 44*(3), 105–119. doi:10.2307/41166135

Lee, K., & Ni, S. (2002). On the dynamic effects of oil price shocks: A study using industry level data. *Journal of Monetary Economics, 49*(4), 823–852. doi:10.1016/S0304-3932(02)00114-9

Likert, R., & Likert, J. G. (1976). *New Ways of Managing Conflict.* McGraw-Hill.

Lim, A. H. Y., & Tan, C. L. (2018). JIT and supply chain disruptions following a major disaster: A case study from the auto industry. *Global Business and Organizational Excellence, 37*(6), 51–58. doi:10.1002/joe.21887

Lin, B., & Jia, Z. (2019). Tax rate, government revenue and economic performance: A perspective of Laffer curve. *China Economic Review, 56*, 101307. doi:10.1016/j.chieco.2019.101307

Lindsey, M. D., & Pavur, R. (2005). As the PMI Turns: A Tool for Supply Chain Managers. *The Journal of Supply Chain Management, 41*(3), 30–39. doi:10.1111/j.1745-493X.2005.tb00182.x

Litterman, R. (1980). *A Bayesian Procedure for Forecasting with Vector Autoregression.* Working paper, Massachusetts Institute of Technology, Department of Economics.

Liu, W., Liang, Y., Bao, X., Qin, J., & Lim, M. K. (2020). China's logistics development trends in the post COVID-19 era. *International Journal of Logistics Research and Applications*, 1-12.

Liu, W., Dunford, M., & Gao, B. A. (2018). Discursive construction of the Belt and Road Initiative: From neo-liberal to inclusive globalization. *Journal of Geographical Sciences, 28*(9), 1199–1214. doi:10.100711442-018-1520-y

Liu, Y., Gong, X., Yüksel, S., Dinçer, H., & Aydın, R. (2021). A multidimensional outlook to energy investments for the countries with continental shelf in East Mediterranean region with hybrid decision making model based on IVIF logic. *Energy Reports, 7*, 158–173.

Li, W., Cui, H., Nemeth, T., Jansen, J., Ünlübayir, C., Wei, Z., ... Sauer, D. U. (2021). Cloud-based health-conscious energy management of hybrid battery systems in electric vehicles with deep reinforcement learning. *Applied Energy, 293*, 116977.

Li, Y. X., Wu, Z. X., Dinçer, H., Kalkavan, H., & Yüksel, S. (2021). Analyzing TRIZ-based strategic priorities of customer expectations for renewable energy investments with interval type-2 fuzzy modeling. *Energy Reports, 7*, 95–108.

Li, Y., Shi, X., & Su, B. (2017). Economic, social and environmental impacts of fuel subsidies: A revisit of Malaysia. *Energy Policy, 110*, 51–61. doi:10.1016/j.enpol.2017.08.015

Mabert, V. A., & Venkataramanan, M. A. (1998). Special research focus on supply chain linkages: Challenges for design and management in the 21st century. *Decision Sciences*, *29*(3), 537–552. doi:10.1111/j.1540-5915.1998.tb01353.x

Maffioli, E. M. (2020). How is the World Responding to the 2019 Coronavirus Disease Compared with the 2014 West African Ebola Epidemic? The Importance of China as A Player in the Global Economy. *The American Journal of Tropical Medicine and Hygiene*, *102*(5), 924–925. doi:10.4269/ajtmh.20-0135 PMID:32162604

Mahajan, Caleb, Singh, Watkins, & Geyer. (2014). Post-harvest Treatments of Fresh Produce. *Philosophical Transactions of the Royal Society A: Mathematical, Physical and Engineering Sciences*, *372*.

Mahajan, K., & Tomar, S. (2021). COVID-19 and supply chain disruption: evidence from food markets in India. *American Journal of Agricultural Economics*, *103*, 35-52. doi:.12158 doi:10.1111/ajae

Mahajan, K., & Tomar, S. (2021). COVID-19 and supply chain disruption: Evidence from food markets in India. *American Journal of Agricultural Economics*, *103*(1), 35–52.

Mahsina, M., Poniwati, A., & Hidayati, K. (2016). Coso Framework: An Internal Audit & Effectiveness Analysis of Banking Internal Control on Credit Investment Aspect. *International Conference on Education for Economics, Business, and Finance (ICEEBF)*.

Mail, D. (2022, Jan. 11). *'It's like a Soviet store during 1981': Grocery stores across the US have empty shelves as supply chain crisis and COVID combine to make basics like milk, bread, meat, canned soups and cleaning products hard to find.* https://www.dailymail.co.uk/news/article-10392001/Empty-shelves-grocery-stores-US.html

Maital, S., & Barzani, E. (2020). The global economic impact of COVID-19: A summary of research. *Samuel Neaman Institute for National Policy Research*, *2020*, 1–12.

Malcomson, J. M. (1986). Some analytics of the Laffer curve. *Journal of Public Economics*, *29*(3), 263–279. doi:10.1016/0047-2727(86)90029-0

Manieniyan, V., Thambidurai, M., & Selvakumar, R. (2009). Study on energy crisis and the future of fossil fuels. *Proceedings of SHEE*, *10*, 2234–3689.

Mankiw, N. G. (2017). *Makroekonomi* (Ö. F. Çolak, Ed.). Efil Publishing House. doi:10.34156/9783791037844

Mańkowska, M., Pluciński, M., Kotowska, I., & Filina-Dawidowicz, L. (2021). Seaports during the COVID-19 Pandemic: The Terminal Operators' Tactical Responses to Disruptions in Maritime Supply Chains. *Energies*, *14*(14), 4339–4360. doi:10.3390/en14144339

Marcén, M., & Morales, M. (2021). The intensity of COVID-19 non-pharmaceutical interventions and labor market outcomes in the public sector. *Journal of Regional Science*, *61*(4), 775–798. doi:10.1111/jors.12535 PMID:34230691

Markard, J., & Rosenbloom, D. (2020). A tale of two crises: COVID-19 and climate. *Sustainability: Science, Practice, and Policy*, *16*(1), 53–60.

McCauley, D., & Heffron, R. (2018). Just transition: Integrating climate, energy and environmental justice. *Energy Policy*, *119*, 1–7. doi:10.1016/j.enpol.2018.04.014

McGowan, F. (2011). Putting energy insecurity into historical context: European responses to the energy crises of the 1970s and 2000s. *Geopolitics*, *16*(3), 486–511. doi:10.1080/14650045.2011.520857

McKibbin, W. J., & Fernando, R. (2020). The global Macroeconomic Impacts of COVID-19: Seven Scenarios [Working Papers]. Canberra, AU: CAMA, The Australian National University.

Megersa, K. A. (2015). The laffer curve and the debt-growth link in low-income Sub-Saharan African economies. *Journal of Economic Studies (Glasgow, Scotland)*, *42*(5), 878–892. doi:10.1108/JES-06-2014-0095

Meier, M., & Pinto, E. (2020). *COVID-19 Supply Chain Disruptions*. CRC TR 224, Discussion Paper Series. crc-tr224_2020_239, University of Bonn and University of Mannheim.

Meng, Y., Wu, H., Zhao, W., Chen, W., Dinçer, H., & Yüksel, S. (2021). A hybrid heterogeneous Pythagorean fuzzy group decision modelling for crowdfunding development process pathways of fintech-based clean energy investment projects. *Financial Innovation*, *7*(1), 1–34.

Meng, Y., Zhou, R., Dinçer, H., Yüksel, S., & Wang, C. (2021). Analysis of inventive problem-solving capacities for renewable energy storage investments. *Energy Reports*, *7*, 4779–4791. doi:10.1016/j.egyr.2021.06.086

Meyer, D. F. (2020). An Empirical Assessment of the Relationships between the Manufacturing Sector, Economic Growth and Changes in Price Indexes: The Case of Poland. *International Journal of Innovation, Creativity and Change*, *12*(7), 186–203.

Meyer, D. F., & Habanabakize, T. (2018). Analysis of Relationships and Causality between Consumer Price Index (CPI), the Producer Price Index (PPI) and Purchasing Manager's Index (PMI) in South Africa. *Journal of Economics and Behavioral Studies*, *10*(6), 25–32. doi:10.22610/jebs.v10i6.2590

Meyer, K., & Peng, M. (2016). Theoretical foundations of emerging economy business research. *Journal of International Business Studies*, *47*(1), 3–22. doi:10.1057/jibs.2015.34

Mian, A., & Sufi, A. (2010). The great recession: Lessons from microeconomic data. *The American Economic Review*, *100*(2), 51–56. doi:10.1257/aer.100.2.51

Mihajlov, M., Toshevska-Trpchevska, K., & Kikerkova, I. (2019). Towards the application of blockchain technology for improving trade facilitation in CEFTA 2006. *Ekonomska Misao i Praksa*, (1), 209–222.

Ministry of Trade, Republic of Türkiye. (2022). https://ticaret.gov.tr/

Mirowski, P. (1982). What's wrong with the Laffer Curve? *Journal of Economic Issues, 16*(3), 815-828.

Mirza, M. M. Q. (2003). Climate change and extreme weather events: Can developing countries adapt? *Climate Policy*, *3*(3), 233–248. doi:10.3763/cpol.2003.0330

Mısır, A., & Arıkan, O. (2022). Circular economy and zero waste management in European Union (EU) and Turkey. *Journal of Environment. Climate and Sustainability*, *1*(1), 69–78.

Montanarella, L., & Panagos, P. (2021). The relevance of sustainable soil management within the European Green Deal. *Land Use Policy*, *100*, 104950. doi:10.1016/j.landusepol.2020.104950

Moritz, B. (2020). Supply chain disruptions and COVID-19. *Supply Chain Management Review*, *27*(3).

Mukhtarov, S., Yüksel, S., & Dinçer, H. (2022). The impact of financial development on renewable energy consumption: Evidence from Turkey. *Renewable Energy*.

Murphy, P. R., & Poist, R. F. (2003). Green perspectives and practices: A "comparative logistics" study. *Supply Chain Management*, *8*(2), 121–132. doi:10.1108/13598540310468724

Mvumi, B., Matsikira, L. T., & Mutambara, J. (2016). The Banana Post-Harvest Value Chain Analysis in Zimbabwe. *British Food Journal*, *118*(2), 272–285. doi:10.1108/BFJ-08-2014-0293

Naidoo, R., & Fisher, B. (2020). Reset sustainable development goals for a pandemic world. *Nature*, *583*(7815), 198–201. doi:10.1038/d41586-020-01999-x PMID:32632244

Naktiyok, A. (2006). *E-Liderlik: E-Liderlik Özelliklerinin İncelenmesine Yönelik Bir Araştırma*. Academic Press.

Nandi, S., Sarkis, J., Hervani, A. A., & Helms, M. M. (2021). Redesigning Supply Chains using Blockchain-Enabled Circular Economy and COVID-19 Experiences. *Sustainable Production and Consumption*. https://www.sciencedirect.com/science/article/pii/S2352550920313592 doi:10.1016/j.spc.2020.10.019

Napolitano, G. (2011, April). The two ways of global governance after the financial crisis: Multilateralism versus co-operation among governments. *International Journal of Constitutional Law*, *9*(2), 310–339. doi:10.1093/icon/mor038

Narayanan, S., Sua, T. Y., Raman, S. R., Alavi, K., Yee, C. L., Abdullah, N., & Husin, A. (2007). The challenges of raising revenues and restructuring subsidies in Malaysia. *Kajian Malaysia*, *25*(2), 1–28. doi:10.21315/km2016.34.2.1

Nawaz, S. (2021). Energy poverty, climate shocks, and health deprivations. *Energy Economics*, *100*, 105338.

NHS Press Conference. (2020, Feb. 4). *National Health Commission (NHC) of the People's Republic of China*. http://www.nhc.gov.cn/xcs/xwbd/202002/235990d202056cfcb202043f202004a202070d202007f209703b202113c202000.shtml

Ni, M., Leung, D. Y. C., Leung, M. K. H., & Sumathy, K. (2006). An overview of hydrogen production from biomass. *Fuel Processing Technology*, *87*(5), 461–472. doi:10.1016/j.fuproc.2005.11.003

Notteboom, T., Pallis, T., & Rodrigue, J. P. (2021). Disruptions and resilience in global container shipping and ports: The COVID-19 pandemic versus the 2008–2009 financial crisis. *Maritime Economics & Logistics*, *23*(2), 179–210. doi:10.105741278-020-00180-5

OECD. (2022). *Consumer Price Indices-Complete database*. Retrieved from: https://www.oecd.org/newsroom/consumer-prices-oecd-updated-2-june-2022.htm

OECD. (2022). *Inflation forecast*. Retrieved May 02, 2022, from https://data.oecd.org

Official Journal of European Union. (2016). *On The Conclusion, On Behalf Of The European Union, Of The Paris Agreement Adopted Under The United Nations Framework Convention On Climate Change*. https://data.europa.eu/eli/dec/2016/1841/oj

Okur, Y. (2010). Türkiye'de Teftiş ve İç Denetim: Kavramlar, Beklentiler ve Hayatla Yüzleşme. *Maliye Dergisi* 158.

Ölander, F., & Thøgersen, J. (2006). The A-B-C of Recycling. *European Advances in Consumer Research*, *7*, 297–302.

Oliveras, L., Artazcoz, L., Borrell, C., Palència, L., López, M. J., Gotsens, M., & ... Marí-Dell'Olmo, M. (2020). The association of energy poverty with health, health care utilisation and medication use in southern Europe. *SSM - Population Health*, *12*, 100665. PMID:33195789

Oliveras, L., Peralta, A., Palència, L., Gotsens, M., López, M. J., Artazcoz, L., & ... Marí-Dell'Olmo, M. (2021). Energy poverty and health: Trends in the European Union before and during the economic crisis, 2007–2016. *Health & Place*, *67*, 102294. PMID:33526205

Opromolla, G., & Maccarini, M. (2010). The control system in the Italian banking sector: Recent changes in the application of Legislative Decree No. 231 of June 8, 2001. *Journal of Investment Compliance*, *11*(2), 16–22. doi:10.1108/15285811011056330

Oum, S. (2019). Energy poverty in the Lao PDR and its impacts on education and health. *Energy Policy*, *132*, 247–253.

Övünç, K. (2020). *Covid-19 has adverse impact on oil demand: OPEC*. Retrieved May 25, 2022, from https://www.aa.com.tr/en/energy/international-organization/covid-19-has-adverse-impact-on-oil-demand-opec/28559

Özalp, İ. (1984). *Çok Uluslu İşletmelerin Yönetimi*. Anadolu Üniversitesi Basımevi.

Ozcan, H. K., Guvenc, S. Y., Guvenc, L., & Demir, G. (2016). Municipal Solid Waste Characterization According to Different Income Levels: A Case Study. *Sustainability*, *8*(10), 1044. doi:10.3390u8101044

Özgür, R. Ö., & Zanbak, M. (2019). Dış Ticarette Uzmanlaşma: Türkiye'de Endüstrilere Yönelik Bazı Tespitler. *İnsan E Toplum Bilim Araştırmaları Dergisi,* 1411-1436.

Ozgur, O., Aydin, L., Karagol, E. T., & Ozbugday, F. C. (2021). The fuel price pass-through in Turkey: The case study of motor fuel price subsidy system. *Energy*, *226*, 120399. doi:10.1016/j.energy.2021.120399

Ozili, P. (2020b). COVID-19 in Africa: Socio-economic impact, policy response and opportunities. *The International Journal of Sociology and Social Policy*. Advance online publication. doi:10.1108/IJSSP-05-2020-0171

OziliP. K. (2020a). 100 Quotes from the Global Financial Crisis: Lessons for the future. *Available at* SSRN 3500921. doi:10.1108/978-1-80043-095-220201014

Öz, M. (2011). New Approaches In Logistics. *Journal of Kahramanmaraş Sütçü İmam University Faculty of Economics and Administrative Sciences*, *1*(1), 141–155.

Öztürk, İ., Demir, İ., Özabalı, A., & Tezer, H. (2005). *İstanbul İçin AB Çevre Mevzuatı İle Uyumlu Entegre Katı Atık Yönetimi Stratejik Planı*. Istac Publications 2005, IBB Istanbul Municipality.

Öztürk, Ş., Nas, F., & İçöz, E. (2008). 24th January Decisions Neo-Liberal Policies and Agriculture Of Turkey. *Pau J Soc Sci Ins, 1*(2), 15-32.

Pakdemirli, B., Bayraktar, Z., Ünalmiş, A. N., & Takmaz, S. (2020). *Pandemi Ekseninde Küresel Değişim Ve Yeni Ekonomik Düzen*. Akçağ Yayınları.

Palmer, A. (2020). *Amazon closes New Jersey warehouse after workers test positive for coronavirus*. Retrieved April 20, 2022, from https://www.cnbc.com/2020/12/20/amazon-closes-new-jersey-warehouse-after-covid-19-infections.html

Palomares, G. (2006). *Relaciones internacionales en el siglo XXI*. Tecnos.

Pan, L., Biru, A., & Lettu, S. (2021). Energy poverty and public health: Global evidence. *Energy Economics*, *101*, 105423.

Paul, J., & Dhir, S. (Eds.). (2021). *Globalization, Deglobalization, and New Paradigms in Business*. Palgrave Macmillan. doi:10.1007/978-3-030-81584-4

Paul, S. K., & Chowdhury, P. (2020). Strategies for managing the impacts of disruptions during COVID-19: An example of toilet paper. *Global Journal of Flexible Systems Managment*, *21*(3), 283–293.

Pavlínek, P. (2015). The impact of the 2008–2009 crisis on the automotive industry: Global trends and firm-level effects in Central Europe. *European Urban and Regional Studies*, *22*(1), 20–40. doi:10.1177/0969776412460534

Pehlivanlı, D. (2020). *Modern İç Denetim, Güncel İç Denetim Uygulamaları*. Beta Yayınevi.

Petrini, C. (2001). *Slow food, the case for taste*. Columbia University Press.

Platje, J., Harvey, J., & Rayman-Bacchus, L. (2020). COVID-19 – reñections on the surprise of both an expected and unexpected event. *The Central European Review of Economics and Management*, *4*(1), 149–162. doi:10.29015/cerem.874

Portland Press Herald. (2022, May 15). *Fewer nuggets, smaller salads: Shrinkflation hits U.S. restaurants*. https://www.pressherald.com/2022/05/15/fewer-nuggets-smaller-salads-shrinkflation-hits-u-s-restaurants/

Prakash, K., Churchill, S. A., & Smyth, R. (2020). Petrol prices and subjective wellbeing. *Energy Economics*, *90*, 104867. doi:10.1016/j.eneco.2020.104867

Prakash, K., & Munyanyi, M. E. (2021). Energy poverty and obesity. *Energy Economics*, *101*, 105428. doi:10.1016/j.eneco.2021.105428

Pujawan, I. N., & Bah, A. U. (2022). Supply chains under COVID-19 disruptions: Literature review and research agenda. In *Supply Chain Forum. International Journal (Toronto, Ont.)*, *23*(1), 81–95.

Pulsinelly, O. (2020). *Sysco reveals size of workforce cuts due to covid-19.* Retrieved May 26, 2022, from https://www.bizjournals.com/houston/news/2020/05/05/sysco-reveals-size-of-workforce-cuts-due-to-covid.html

PwC. (2019). *CEE Transport&Logistics Trend Book 2019*. Available online: https://www.pwc.com/hu/hu/kiadvanyok/assets/pdf/transport-logistics-trendbook-2019-en.pdf

Qaiser, F. H., Ahmed, K., Sykora, M., Choudhary, A., & Simpson, M. (2017). Decision support systems for sustainable logistics: A review and bibliometric analysis. *Industrial Management & Data Systems*.

Qian, Y., & Yan, L. (2021). Petrol Prices and Subjective Well-Being: Longitudinal Data Evidence From China. *Energy Research Letters*, *2*(4), 28125. doi:10.46557/001c.28125

Qin, J. Y. (2020). *WTO Reform: Multilateral Control over Unilateral Retaliation – Lessons from the US-China Trade War*. Wayne State University Law School Research Paper No. 2020-73. doi:10.2139/ssrn.3654510

Qiu, D., Dinçer, H., Yüksel, S., & Ubay, G. G. (2020). Multi-faceted analysis of systematic risk-based wind energy investment decisions in E7 economies using modified hybrid modeling with IT2 fuzzy sets. *Energies*, *13*(6), 1423.

Queiroz, M. M., Ivanov, D., Dolgui, A., & Fosso Wamba, S. (2020). Impacts of epidemic outbreaks on supply chains: Mapping a research agenda amid the COVID-19 pandemic through a structured literature review. *Annals of Operations Research*, 1–38.

Radelet, S., & Sachs, J. (1998). *The onset of the East Asian financial crisis (No. w6680)*. National Bureau of Economic Research. doi:10.3386/w6680

Radwan, N. M., Senousy, M. B., & Alaa El Din, M. R. (2016). *Neutrosophic AHP multi criteria decision making method applied on the selection of learning management system*. Infinite Study.

Rady, D. A. M. (2012). Greece debt crisis: Causes, implications and policy options. *Academy of Accounting and Financial Studies Journal*, *16*, 87.

Ramírez Pérez, S. M. (2020). Embedding the market during times of crisis: The European automobile cartel during a decade of crisis (1973–1985). *Business History*, *62*(5), 815–836. doi:10.1080/00076791.2019.1575037

Ramli, A. R., Kadir, J. M. A., Ismail, N., Othman, A. A., & Melo, P. C. (2021). Fuel Subsidies, Fuel Consumption, and Road Transport Emissions: A systematic review. *Environment-Behaviour Proceedings Journal*, *6*(16), 275–281. doi:10.21834/ebpj.v6i16.2721

Rangasamy, L. (2017). The impact of petrol price movements on South African inflation. *Journal of Energy in Southern Africa*, *28*(1), 120–132. doi:10.17159/2413-3051/2017/v28i1a1597

Rasiah, R., Gammeltoft, P., & Jiang, Y. (2010). Home government policies for outward FDI from emerging economies: Lessons from Asia. *International Journal of Emerging Markets*, *5*(3/4), 333–357. doi:10.1108/17468801011058415

Ratti, R. A., & Vespignani, J. L. (2013). Why crude oil prices are high when global activity is weak? *Economics Letters*, *121*(1), 133–136. doi:10.1016/j.econlet.2013.07.002

Rauch, C. F., & Behling, O. (1984). Functionalism: Basis for an Alternate Approach to the Study of Leadership. In J. G. Hunt, D. Hosking, C. Schriesheim, & R. Stewart (Eds.), *Leaders and Managers: International Perspectives on Managerial Behavior and Leadership* (pp. 45–62). Pergamon. doi:10.1016/B978-0-08-030943-9.50012-7

Ray, P. (2019). Renewable energy and sustainability. *Clean Technologies and Environmental Policy*, *21*(8), 1517–1533. doi:10.100710098-019-01739-4

Ray, S., & Ray, I. A. (2011). An insight into the vision of charismatic leadership: Evidence from recent administrative change in West Bengal province of India. *European Journal of Business and Management*, *3*(9), 55–67.

Reiche, B. S., Lee, Y. T., & Allen, D. G. (2019). Actors, structure, and processes: A review and conceptualization of global work integrating IB and HRM research. *Journal of Management*, *45*(2), 359–38.

Reinalda, B. (2009). *Routledge History of International Organizations: From 1815 to the Present Day*. Routledge. doi:10.4324/9780203876572

Republic of Turkey Ministry of Trade. (2018). *Workshop Final Report on Reducing Documents and Costs Related to Foreign Trade Transactions and Increasing Awareness on This Subject, Ankara, 2018*. https://ticaret.gov.tr/data

Reuters. (2020). *Coronavirus, oil collapse erase $5 trillion from U.S. stocks*. Author.

Richman, A. (1979). The polls: Public attitudes toward the energy crisis. *Public Opinion Quarterly*, *43*(4), 576–585. doi:10.1086/268557

Ritcher, F. (2020). *U.S. Car indutry most reliant on Chinese parts*. Retrieved May 14, 2022, from https://www.statista.com/chart/20913/chinese-exports-of-motor-vehicle-parts-and-accessories/

Robbins, S. P., & Judge, T. A. (2013). Örgütsel Davranış. Ankara: Nobel.

Roberts, B. W. (2009). The macroeconomic impacts of the 9/11 attack: Evidence from real-time forecasting. *Peace Economics, Peace. Science & Public Policy*, *15*(2), 341–367.

Rodrigue, J. P. (2020). *The geography of transport systems*. Routledge. doi:10.4324/9780429346323

Rodrik, D. (2000). How far will international economic integration go? *Journal of Economic Perspective*, *14*(1), 177-186.

Rodrik, D. (2007). *One Economics Many Recipes, Globalization, Institutions and Economic Growth*. Princeton University Press. doi:10.1515/9781400829354

Rogers, D. S., & Tibben-Lembke, R. (2001). An Examination Of Reverse Logistics Practices. *Journal of Business Logistics*, *22*(2), 129–148. doi:10.1002/j.2158-1592.2001.tb00007.x

Rosenfeld, H. (2009). The North American auto industry in crisis. *Monthly Review (New York, N.Y.)*, *61*(2), 18–36. doi:10.14452/MR-061-02-2009-06_2

Rosenthal, J., Quinn, A., Grieshop, A. P., Pillarisetti, A., & Glass, R. I. (2018). Clean cooking and the SDGs: Integrated analytical approaches to guide energy interventions for health and environment goals. *Energy for Sustainable Development*, *42*, 152–159. PMID:29861575

Rozman, M., & Tominc, P. (2021). The physical, emotional and behavioral symptoms of health problems among employees before and during the COVID-19 epidemic. *Employee Relations: The International Journal*, *44*(7), 19–45.

Saaty, T. L. (1977). A scaling method for priorities in hierarchical structures. *Journal of Mathematical Psychology*, *15*(3), 234–281. doi:10.1016/0022-2496(77)90033-5

Safwan, A.S. (2007). The Optimal Management of Informational Servicing Logistic Systems. *Leonardo Journal of Sciences*, *10*(1).

Safwan, A. S., & Mohammad, B. Y. (2014). Functional structure of special computerized information system. *Journal of Environmental Science, Computer Science and Engineering & Technology*, *4*(1), 1–12.

Safwan, A. S., Zafer, M., Avramenko, V. P., & Shtangee, S. V. (2012). Optimal Resource Allocation Under Bad Compatibility of Functional Limitations. *International Journal of Computer Science and Technology*, *3*(1).

Saleh, R. M., Ramzani, S. R., & Phung, S. P. (2018). Shrinkflation from consumer's perspective: An exploratory study using crystal products in Egypt. *Eurasian Journal of Analytical Chemistry*, *13*(6).

Salisu, A. A., Isah, K. O., Oyewole, O. J., & Akanni, L. O. (2017). Modelling oil price-inflation nexus: The role of asymmetries. *Energy*, *125*, 97–106. doi:10.1016/j.energy.2017.02.128

Santacreu, A. M., & LaBelle, J. (2022). Global Supply Chain Disruptions and Inflation During the COVID-19 Pandemic. *Review - Federal Reserve Bank of St. Louis*.

Sapir, J. (2016). Jacques Sapir: Donald Trump, président de la démondialisation? *Le Figaro*. https://www.lefigaro.fr/vox/monde/2016/11/10/31002-20161110ARTFIG00233-jacques-sapir-donald-trump-president-de-la-demondialisation.php

Sapir, J. (2011). *La demondialisation*. Seuil.

Sarkis, J. (2003). A strategic decision framework for green supply chain management. *Journal of Cleaner Production*, *11*(4), 397–409. doi:10.1016/S0959-6526(02)00062-8

Sarkis, J., Meade, L., & Talluri, S. (2017). E-logistics and the natural environment. In *The ecology of the new economy* (pp. 35–51). Routledge. doi:10.4324/9781351282048-3

Şaşmaz, M. Ü., & Şakar, E. (2020). *The effect of taxes and public expenditures on happiness: Empirical evidence from OECD countries*. doi:10.21833/ijaas.2020.08.014

Sasmaz, M. U., Karamıklı, A., & Akkucuk, U. (2021). The relationship between renewable energy use and health expenditures in EU countries. *The European Journal of Health Economics*, *22*(7), 1129–1139. doi:10.100710198-021-01312-1 PMID:33954841

Sasmaz, M. U., Sakar, E., Yayla, Y. E., & Akkucuk, U. (2020). The relationship between renewable energy and human development in OECD countries: A panel data analysis. *Sustainability*, *12*(18), 7450. doi:10.3390u12187450

Sek, S. K. (2017). Impact of oil price changes on domestic price inflation at disaggregated levels: Evidence from linear and nonlinear ARDL modeling. *Energy*, *130*, 204–217. doi:10.1016/j.energy.2017.03.152

Sels, L., Winne, S., Maes, J., Delmotte, J., Faems, D., & Forrier, A. (2002). *How HRM affects corporate financial performance: Evidence from Belgian SMEs*. Katholieke Universiteit Leuven.

Sendjaya, S., Sarros, J. C., & Santora, J. C. (2008). Defining and measuring servant leadership behaviour in organizations. *Journal of Management Studies*, *45*(2), 402–424. doi:10.1111/j.1467-6486.2007.00761.x

Serezli, E., Yüksel, S., Tamer, İ., & Dinçer, H. (2021). The Role of Innovative Renewable Energy Investment Strategies on Macroeconomic Stability. In *Financial Strategies in Competitive Markets* (pp. 165–178). Springer. doi:10.1007/978-3-030-68612-3_12

Seroka-Stolka, O. (2014). The development of green logistics for implementation sustainable development strategy in companies. *Procedia: Social and Behavioral Sciences*, *151*, 302–309. doi:10.1016/j.sbspro.2014.10.028

Sgarbossa, F., & Russo, I. (2017). A Proactive Model in Sustainable Food Supply Chain: Insight From a Case Study. *International Journal of Production Economics*, *183*, 596–606. doi:10.1016/j.ijpe.2016.07.022

Shahbaz, M., Raghutla, C., Chittedi, K. R., Jiao, Z., & Vo, X. V. (2020). The effect of renewable energy consumption on economic growth: Evidence from the renewable energy country attractive index. *Energy*, *207*, 118162. doi:10.1016/j.energy.2020.118162

Sharifi, H., Ismail, H. S., & Reid, I. (2006). Achieving agility in supply chain through simultaneous 'design of' and 'design for' supply chain. *Journal of Manufacturing Technology Management*, *17*(8), 1078–1098. doi:10.1108/17410380610707393

Sharma, R., Shishodia, A., Kamble, S., Gunasekaran, A., & Belhadi, A. (2020). Agriculture supply chain risks and COVID-19: Mitigation strategies and implications for the practitioners. *International Journal of logistics Research and Application*, 1-27. doi:10.1080/13675567.2020.1830049

Shavshukov, V. M., & Zhuravleva, N. A. (2020). Global Economy: New Risks and Leadership Problems. *Int. J. Financial Stud.*, *8*(1), 7. doi:10.3390/ijfs8010007

Shawabkah, A. M., Kadir, M. R. B. A., Nori, W., & Hassan, H. B. (2022). Validating the Framework of the Accounting Information Systems Components and Firm Performance: A Conceptual Study. *Wseas Transactions On Business And Economics*, *19*, 985–999.

Shead, S. (2022). *Chip supply issues are still giving some of the world's biggest companies a major headache.* Retrieved April 26, 2022, from https://www.cnbc.com/2022/05/02/chip-shortage-hurts-apple-nokia-daimler-and-volvo.html

Sherman, E. (2020). 94% of the Fortune 1000 are seeing Coronavirus Supply Chain Disruptions: Report. *Fortune*. Retrieved May 20, 2022, from https://fortune.com/2020/02/21/fortune-1000-coronavirus-china-supply-chain-impact/

Shih, W. C. (2020). Global supply chain in a post-pandemic world. *Harvard Business Review*, (September-October), 2020.

Shi, K., & Weng, J. (2021). Impacts of the COVID-19 epidemic on merchant ship activity and pollution emissions in Shanghai port waters. *The Science of the Total Environment*, *790*, 148198.

Shope, M. (2022). Distributed Ledger Technology in International Trade: Rethinking the Role and Necessity of the Customs Declaration. *Stanford Journal of Blockchain Law & Policy*, *5*(114). https://heinonline.org/HOL/LandingPage?handle=hein.journals/sjblp5&div=7&id=&page

Siche, R. (2020). What is the Impact of COVID-19 Disease on Agriculture? *Scientia Agropecuaria*, *11*(1), 3–6. doi:10.17268ci.agropecu.2020.01.00

Siddi, M. (2020). *The European Green Deal: Assessing its current state and future implementation.* Finnish Institute of International Affairs.

Silahtaroğlu, G., Dinçer, H., & Yüksel, S. (2021). Defining the significant factors of currency exchange rate risk by considering text mining and fuzzy AHP. In *Data Science and Multiple Criteria Decision Making Approaches in Finance* (pp. 145–168). Springer.

Simpson, W. G., & Gleason, A. E. (1999). Board structure, ownership, and financial distress in banking firms. *International Review of Economics & Finance*, *8*(3), 281–292. doi:10.1016/S1059-0560(99)00026-X

Sintema, E. J. (2020). *Effect of COVID-19 on the performance of grade 12 students.* Academic Press.

Smarandache, F. (1998). *A unifying field in logics neutrosophy: Neutrosophic probability, set and logic*. American Research Press.

Smarandache, F. (2016). Subtraction and division of neutrosophic numbers. *Critical Review*, 13(13) 103–110.

Smith, M. S., & Kauermann, G. (2011). Bicycle commuting in Melbourne during the 2000s energy crisis: A semiparametric analysis of intraday volumes. *Transportation Research Part B: Methodological*, *45*(10), 1846–1862. doi:10.1016/j.trb.2011.07.003

Sohrabi, C., Alsafi, Z., & O'Neill, N. (2020). World Health Organization Declares Global Emergency: A Review of the 2019 Novel Coronavirus (COVID19). *International Journal of Surgery*, *76*, 71–76. doi:10.1016/j.ijsu.2020.02.034

Solarin, S. A. (2022). Modelling two dimensions of poverty in selected developing countries: The impact of fossil fuel subsidies. *Social Indicators Research*, *160*(1), 357–379. doi:10.100711205-021-02815-3

Soltani, E., Meer, R., & Williams, T. M. (2009). A Contrast of HRM and TQM Approaches to Performance Management: Some Evidence. *British Journal of Management*, *16*(3), 48–59.

Soltani, E., Van der Meer, R., Gennard, J., & Williams, T. (2003). A TQM Approach to HR Performance Evaluation Criteria. *European Management Journal*, *21*, 323–337. doi:10.1016/S0263-2373(03)00052-5

Spears, L. C. (2010). Character and servant leadership: Ten characteristics of effective, caring leaders. *The Journal of Virtues & Leadership*, *1*(1), 25–30.

Spero, J. E., & Hart, J. A. (1997). *The Politics of International Economic Relations*. Routledge. doi:10.4324/9781315006154

Spira, L. F., & Page, M. (2003). Risk management: The reinvention of internal control and the changing role of internal audit. *Accounting, Auditing & Accountability Journal*, *16*(4), 640–661. doi:10.1108/09513570310492335

Statistica. (2022). Retrieved May 20, 2022, from https://www.statista.com/statistics/268750/global-gross-domestic-product-gdp/

Stearns, P. N. (2020). *The industrial revolution in world history*. Routledge. doi:10.4324/9781003050186

Steinberg, F. (2005). *Cooperación y Conflicto en el Sistema Comercial Multilateral: La Organización Mundial de Comercio como Institución de Gobernanza Económica Global* (Tesis Doctoral). Departamento de Análisis Económico: Teoría Económica e Historia Económica de la Facultada de Ciencias Económicas y Empresariales de la Universidad Autónoma de Madrid, España.

Stern, D. I., & Cleveland, C. J. (2004). *Energy and Economic Growth*. Rensselaer Polytechnic Institute.

Stevens, G. C. (1989). Integrating the supply chain. *International Journal of Physical Distribution & Materials Management*, *19*(8), 1-8.

Stiglitz, J. E. (2010). *Interpreting the Causes of the Great Recession of 2008. Financial system and macroeconomic resilience: revisited*. Bank for International Settlements.

Stock, J. R. (2001). Reverse logistics in the supply chain. *Revista Transport & Logistics*, *44*, 44–48.

Stogdill, R. M., & Shartle, C. L. (1948). Methods for determining patterns of leadership behavior in relation to organization structure and objectives. *The Journal of Applied Psychology*, *32*(3), 286–291. doi:10.1037/h0057264 PMID:18867065

Stone, C. M. (2003). *A study of the relationship between principals' leadership behaviors and the school culture as perceived by the teachers*. The University of Mississippi.

Stott, P. (2016). How climate change affects extreme weather events. *Science*, *352*(6293), 1517–1518. doi:10.1126cience.aaf7271 PMID:27339968

Sturgeon, T., & Van Biesebroeck, J. (2010). *Effects of the crisis on the automotive industry in developing countries: a global value chain perspective.* World Bank Policy Research Working Paper, (5330).

Su, C. W., Khan, K., Tao, R., & Umar, M. (2020). A review of resource curse burden on inflation in Venezuela. *Energy*, *204*, 117925.

Sudan, T., & Taggar, R. (2022). COVID-19 Induced Supply Chain Disruptions and Automotive Industry: A Case Study of Maruti Suzuki India Limited and Mitigation Strategies. *Global Economics Science*, 35-52.

Swan, L. G., & Ugursal, V. I. (2009). Modeling of end-use energy consumption in the residential sector: A review of modeling techniques. *Renewable & Sustainable Energy Reviews*, *13*(8), 1819–1835. doi:10.1016/j.rser.2008.09.033

Szewczyk, P. (2019). Application of blockchain technology in supply chain management. Silesian University of Technology Publishing House, Scientific Papers of Silesian University of Technology 2019, Organization and Management Series No.136. http://dx.doi.org/10.29119/1641-3466.2019.136.45

Tadesse, M. D., Gebresenbet, G., Tavasszy, L., & Ljungberg, D. (2021). Assessment of Digitalized Logistics for Implementation in Low-Income Countries. *Future Transportation*, *1*(2), 227–247. doi:10.3390/futuretransp1020014

Tagkiris, D. (2022). *The interconnection between 2000s energy crisis and the global financial crisis. The role of NOCs and IOCs as part of the global recession* (Master's thesis). Πανεπιστήμιο Πειραιώς.

Takcı, M. B., & Üre, M. S. (2021). Sustainable Business Model Intermodal: Ekol Logistics Example. *On Eurasian Economies 2021*, 272.

Talu, N. (2015). Climate change policy in Turkey. Academic Press.

Tan, W. (2021). *China's economy is showing signs of stagflation, economists warn.* Retrieved May 20, 2022, from https://www.cnbc.com/2021/11/01/china-economy-shows-signs-of-stagflation-price-inflation-economists.html

Taş, A., & Çetiner, A. (2011). Ortaöğretim Okulu Müdürlerinin Dönüşümcü Liderlik Davranışlarını Gerçekleştirme Durumlarına İlişkin Öğretmen Görüşleri. *Journal of Turkish Educational Sciences*, *9*(2), 369,392.

Taşçıer, A. M. (2018). Neoliberalizmde Merkezileşme- Yerelleşme Gerilimi: İl Özel İdareleri, Yikob Örnekleri ve Yerelde Merkezileşme. *Gazi Üniversitesi Sosyal Bilimler Dergisi*, 650-662.

Taslak, S. (2008). Göreve İlişkin Çalışmalarda Etkileşimci ve Dönüşümcü Liderlik Üzerine Etiksel Bir Değerlendirme. *Erciyes Üniversitesi İ.İ.B.F. Dergisi*, 121-144.

Tatu, Ş. (2014). An application of debt Laffer curve: Empirical evidence for Romania's case. *Romanian Journal of Fiscal Policy*, *5*(1), 29–38.

Tayfur, M., Beytekin, O. F., & Yalçınkaya, M. (2013). İlköğretim Okul Yöneticilerinin Etik Liderlik Özellikleri İle Okullardaki Örgütsel Güven Düzeyinin İncelenmesi (İzmir İl Örneği). *Dicle Üniversitesi Ziya Gökalp Eğitim Fakültesi Dergisi*, 84-106.

TB. (2022). *Türkiye Cumhuriyeti Ticaret Bakanlığı Covid-19 Ticaret Önlemleri*. Retrieved April 25, 2022, from https://covid19.ticaret.gov.tr/

Tchobanoglous, G., Theisen, H., & Vigil, S. (1993). *Integrated Solid Waste Management: Engineering Principles and Management Issues*. McGraw Hill.

Thiell, M., Zuluaga, J. P. S., Montañez, J. P. M., & van Hoof, B. (2011). Green logistics: Global practices and their implementation in emerging markets. In *Green finance and sustainability: Environmentally-aware business models and Technologies* (pp. 334–357). IGI Global.

Tokmak, M. (2020). Dönüştürücü ve Etkileşimci Liderlik Tarzı İle Negatif İnovasyon Algısı Arasındaki İlişkiye Yönelik Bir Araştırma. *Kahramanmaraş Sütçü İmam Üniversitesi Sosyal Bilimler Dergisi*, 441-464.

Tokol, A. (2001). Çok Uluslu Şirketler ve Endüstri ilişkilerine Etkileri. *Endsütri İlişkileri ve İnsan Kaynakları Dergisi, 3*(2).

Tosun, K. (1987). *İşletme Yönetimi: Genel Esaslar*. İstanbul: İ. Ü. İşletme Fakültesi Yayınları, no:186.

Toygar, A., Yildirim, U., & İnegöl, G. M. (2022). Investigation of empty container shortage based on SWARA-ARAS methods in the COVID-19 era. *European Transport Research Review*, *14*, 8.

Trabandt, M., & Uhlig, H. (2011). The Laffer curve revisited. *Journal of Monetary Economics*, *58*(4), 305–327. doi:10.1016/j.jmoneco.2011.07.003

Tsakalidis, A., van Balen, M., Gkoumas, K., & Pekar, F. (2020). Catalyzing sustainable transport innovation through policy support and monitoring: The case of TRIMIS and the European green deal. *Sustainability*, *12*(8), 3171.

Tsolakis, N. K., Keramydas, C. A., Toka, A. K., Aidonis, D. A., & Iakovou, E. T. (2014). Agrifood Supply Chain Management: A Comprehensive Hierarchical Decision making Framework and a Critical Taxonomy. *Biosystems Engineering*, *120*, 47–64. doi:10.1016/j.biosystemseng.2013.10.014

Tsuchiya, Y. (2012). Is the Purchasing Managers' Index useful for assessing the economy's strength? A directional analysis. *Economic Bulletin*, *32*(2), 1302–1311.

Tucker, P., & Speirs, D. (2003). Attitudes and Behavioural Change in Household Waste Management Behaviours. *Journal of Environmental Planning and Management*, *46*(2), 289-307.

TÜİK. (2022a). *Inflation Rates in Turkey*. Retrieved April 23, 2022, from https://data.tuik.gov.tr/

TÜİK. (2022b). *Turkey Imports and Exports*. Retrieved April 22, 2022, from https://data.tuik.gov.tr/

TÜİK. (2022c). *Foreign Trade Balance and Growth Rates in Turkey*. Retrieved April 22, 2022, from https://data.tuik.gov.tr/

Tuna, I. (2015). Verilişinin 70.Yılında Demokratikleşme Belgesi Olarak Türk Siyasal Hayatında Dörtlü Takrir. *Çağdaş Türkiye Tarihi Araştırmaları Dergisi*, 203-219.

Tuna, M., Bircan, H., & Yeşiltaş, M. (2012). Etik Liderlik Ölçeğinin Geçerlilik ve Güvenilirlik Çalışması: Antalya Örneği. *Atatürk Üniversitesi İktisadi Ve İdari Bilimler Dergisi*, 143-155.

TÜRMOB. (2020). Korona Salgınının Türkiye Ekonomisine Etkisi Değerlendirmeler ve Öneriler Raporu. *TÜRMOB Yayınları*, *503*, 1–101.

U.S. Bureau of Labor Statistics. (2022, June 3). *The Employment Situation - February 2022*. https://www.bls.gov/news.release/pdf/empsit.pdf

Ucal, M., An, N., & Kurnaz, L. (2017). New terms and approaches in economy in the process of climate change. *Dokuz Eylul University Journal of Social Sciences Institute*, *19*(3), 373–402.

UNCTAD. (2020). *Global Trade Impact of the Coronavirus (COVID-19) Epidemic*. United Nations Conference on Trade and Development.

UNCTAD. (2021). *United Nations Conference on Trade and Development*. Available online: https://unctad.org/system/files/official-document/ditctab2020d4_en.pdf

UNCTAD. (2021a). *Covid-19 and maritime transport. Impact and responses*. Retrieved May 28, 2022, from https://unctad.org/system/files/official-document/dtltlb2021d1_en.pdf

UNCTAD. (2021b). *Global merchandise trade exceeds pre-covid-19 level, but services recovery falls short*. Retrieved March 29, 2022, from https://unctad.org/news/global-merchandise-trade-exceeds-pre-covid-19-level-services-recovery-falls-short#:~:text=According%20to%20the%20report%2C%20world,when%20trade%20fell%20by%2022%25

UNCTAD. (2022). Global Trade. *United Nations Conference on Trade and Development*, 1-7.

United Nations Conference on Trade and Development. (2020). *Impact of the pandemic on trade and development: Transitioning to a new normal*. Author.

United Nations Framework Convention on Climate Change (UNFCCC). (2015). *Paris Agreement*. https://unfccc.int/sites/default/files/english_paris_agreement.pdf

United Nations. (2015). *United Nation Sustainable Development Goals (2030)*. UN.

United Nations. (2022). *Human development reports*. Retrieved May 20, 2022, from https://hdr.undp.org/en/content/human-development-index-hdi

US. (2015). Do Banks Respond Asymmetrically to the Global Crisis? Evidence From Turkey. *Journal of BRSA Banking and Financial Markets. Banking Regulation and Supervision Agency*, *9*(2), 9–44.

USEPA. (2011). *Municipal Solid Waste Generation, Recycling, and Disposal in the United States: Facts and Figures for 2010; EPA-530-F-14-001*. AM-BRA GmbH.

Üstün, K. T. (2021). The beginning of a new era: European Green Deal and its effects on Turkish environmental law and policies. *Homeland Journal of Politics and Management*, *16*(36), 329–366.

Utami, W., Nugroho, L., Mappanyuki, R., & Yelvionita, V. (2020). Early Warning Fraud Determinants in Banking Industries. *Asian Economic and Financial Review*, *10*(6), 604–627. doi:10.18488/journal.aefr.2020.106.604.627

Vafadarnikjoo, A., Badri Ahmadi, H., Liou, J. J., Botelho, T., & Chalvatzis, K. (2021). Analyzing blockchain adoption barriers in manufacturing supply chains by the neutrosophic analytic hierarchy process. *Annals of Operations Research*, 1–28. doi:10.100710479-021-04048-6

Valmohammadi, C., & Ahmadi, M. (2015). The impact of knowledge management practices on organizational performance: A balanced scorecard approach. *Journal of Enterprise Information Management*, *28*(1), 131–159.

van Dam, Y. K., & Webbink, J. F. (2020). Reñecting on reñections on COVID-19. *The Central European Review of Economics and Management*, *4*(2), 7–19. doi:10.29015/cerem.876

Van Der Putten, R. (2020). *Germany: Supply Chains After Covid-19*. BNP Paribas EcoFlash No: 20-14.

van der Vorst, J. G., Beulens, A. J., & van Beek, P. (2000). Modelling and Simulating Multi-Echelon Food Systems. *European Journal of Operational Research*, *122*(2), 354–366. doi:10.1016/S0377-2217(99)00238-6

Vanham, P. (2019). *A brief history of globalization*. World Economic Forum.

Varga, S., Brynielsson, J., & Franke, U. (2021). Cyber-threat perception and risk management in the Swedish financial sector. *Computers & Security*, *105*, 102239.

Veselovska, L. (2020). Supply chain disruptions in the context of early stages of the global COVID-19 outbreak. *Problems and Perspectives in Management*, *18*(2), 490–500.

Vointece, S. K. (2008). *Learning Embedded in Organization's Culture Influences Organizational Performance*. University of New Mexico.

Vo, T. D., & Tran, M. D. (2021). The impact of covid-19 pandemic on the global trade. *International Journal of Social Science and Economics Invention*, *7*(1), 1–7.

Wad, P. (2009). The automobile industry of Southeast Asia: Malaysia and Thailand. *Journal of the Asia Pacific Economy*, *14*(2), 172–193. doi:10.1080/13547860902786029

Wallace, M. J., & Szilagyi, A. D. (1982). *Managing behavior in organizations*. Pearson Scott Foresman.

Wang, L., Wu, W. M., Bolan, N. S., Tsang, D. C., Li, Y., Qin, M., & Hou, D. (2021). Environmental fate, toxicity and risk management strategies of nanoplastics in the environment: Current status and future perspectives. *Journal of Hazardous Materials*, *401*, 123415. PMID:32763705

Wang, Y. F., Chen, S. P., Lee, Y. C., & Tsai, C. T. S. (2013). Developing green management standards for restaurants: An application of green supply chain management. *International Journal of Hospitality Management*, *34*, 263–273.

Wang, Y., Nie, H., Han, J., An, Y., Zhang, Y. M., & Zhang, S. X. A. (2021). Green revolution in electronic displays expected to ease energy and health crises. *Light, Science & Applications*, *10*(1), 1–14. PMID:33550329

Wanniski, J. (1978). Taxes, revenues, and the Laffer curve. *The Public Interest*, *50*, 3.

Wan, Q., Zhao, X., Liu, H., Dinçer, H., & Yüksel, S. (2022). Assessing the New Product Development Process for the Industrial Decarbonization of Sustainable Economies. *SAGE Open*, *12*(1). doi:10.1177/21582440211067231

Washington Post. (2022, Jan. 19). *Why Are U.S. Grocery Shelves Out of Everything Again?* https://www.washingtonpost.com/business/why-are-us-grocery-shelves-out-of-everything-again/2022/01/18/1afc0028-784b-11ec-9dce-7313579de434_story.html

Way, S. A., Tracey, J. B., Fay, C. H., Wright, P. M., Snell, S. A., Chang, S., & Gong, Y. (2015). Validation of a multidimensional HR flexibility measure. *Journal of Management*, *41*(4), 1098–1131.

WCED. (1987). World commission on environment and development. *Our Common Future*, *17*(1), 1-91.

Weber, J. (2009). *Automotive development processes: Processes for successful customer oriented vehicle development*. Springer Science & Business Media. doi:10.1007/978-3-642-01253-2

WEF. (2018). *Blockchain Beyond the Hype A Practical Framework for Business Leaders*. Available online: http://www3.weforum.org/docs/48423_Whether_ Blockchain_WP.pdf

WHO. (2021). Retrieved March 28, 2022, from https://www.who.int/health-topics/coronavirus#tab=tab_1

WHO. (2022). Retrieved March 28, 2022, from https://covid19.who.int/

Wing Shin, R. T., Stoller, C., & Woon Yew, D. L. (2020). Issues on the logistics challenges in the pandemic period. *Journal of Critical Reviews*, 776-780.

Wirtz, J., Heracleous, L., & Pangarkar, N. (2008). Managing human resources for service excellence and cost effectiveness at Singapore Airlines. *Managing Service Quality*, *18*(1), 4–19.

Witt, M. A. (2019). De-globalization: Theories, predictions, and opportunities for international business research. *Journal of International Business Studies*, *50*(7), 1053–1077. doi:10.105741267-019-00219-7

Wolor, C. W., Susita, D., & Martono, S. (2020). How to Maintain Employee Motivation Amid The Covid-19 Virus Pandemic. *International Journal of Economics & Business Administration*, *8*(4), 78–86.

World Bank. (2016). *World Bank Data.* http://data.worldbank.org/?display=default

World Bank. (2020). *State and Trends of Carbon Pricing 2020.* https://openknowledge.worldbank.org/bitstream/handle/10986/33809/9781464815867.pdf?sequence=4&isAllowed=y

World Bank. (2022a). *Foreign Trade Balance and Growth Rates in Turkey.* Retrieved May 10, 2022, from https://databank.worldbank.org/

World Bank. (2022b). *GDP per capita (current US$) – China.* Retrieved April 10, 2022, from https://data.worldbank.org/indicator/NY.GDP.PCAP.CD?end=2020&locations=CN&start=2000

World Development Report. (2022). *Finance for an equitable recovery.* Author.

World Economic Forum. (2020). *China Is Sending Medical Experts and Supplies to Help Italy Fight Coronavirus.* Retrieved April 13, 2022, from, https://www.weforum.org/agenda/2020/03/coronavirus-covid-19-italy-china-supplies/

World Health Organization. (2020). *WHO: Coronavirus disease 2019 (COVID-19) situation report – 23.* https://www.who.int/docs/default-source/coronaviruse/situation-reports/20200212-sitrep-20200223-ncov.pdf?sfvrsn=20200241e20200219fb20200278_20200212

World Trade Organization. (2017). *Principles of the trading system.* https://www.wto.org/ english/thewto_e/whatis_e/tif_e/fact2_e.htm

WSJ. (2001). *A fire in Albuquerque sparks crisis for European cell-phone-giants.* Retrieved May 25, 2022, from https://www.wsj.com/articles/SB980720939804883010

WTO. (2020). *International tourism numbers could fall 60–80% in 2020.* Retrieved May 25, 2022, from https://www.unwto.org/news/covid-19-international-tourist-numbers-could-fall-60-80-in-2020

WTO. (2021). *World trade report 2021. Economic resilience and trade.* World Trade Organization.

Xie, Y., Peng, Y., Yüksel, S., Dınçer, H., Uluer, G. S., Çağlayan, Ç., & Li, Y. (2020). Consensus-based public acceptance and mapping of nuclear energy investments using spherical and pythagorean fuzzy group decision making approaches. *IEEE Access: Practical Innovations, Open Solutions, 8*, 206248–206263. doi:10.1109/ACCESS.2020.3037344

Xie, Y., Zhou, Y., Peng, Y., Dinçer, H., Yüksel, S., & an Xiang, P. (2021). An extended pythagorean fuzzy approach to group decision-making with incomplete preferences for analyzing balanced scorecard-based renewable energy investments. *IEEE Access: Practical Innovations, Open Solutions, 9*, 43020–43035. doi:10.1109/ACCESS.2021.3065294

Xinhuanet News Report. (2020). http://www.xinhuanet.com/english/2020-01/09/c_138690570.htm

Xu, Z., Elomri, A., Kerbache, L., & El Omri, A. (2020). Impacts of COVID-19 on global supply chains: Facts and perspectives. *IEEE Engineering Management Review, 48*(3), 153–166.

Xu, Z., & Liao, H. (2013). Intuitionistic fuzzy analytic hierarchy process. *IEEE Transactions on Fuzzy Systems, 22*(4), 749–761. doi:10.1109/TFUZZ.2013.2272585

Yahşi, F. (2007). *Küreselleşme ve İstihdam.* Yüksek Lisans Tezi, Çukurova Üniversitesi Sosyal Bilimler Enstitüsü.

Yaman, S., Demir, B., Batırlık, S. N., & Zeren, F. (2021). Lojistik Sektörü ve Ekonomik Büyüme Arasındaki İlişkinin İncelemesi: G20 Ülkeleri Üzerine Bir Araştırma. *The Journal of International Scientific Researches, 6*(1), 1–9.

Yang, B., & Yang, Y. (2010). Postponement in supply chain risk management: A complexity Perspective. *International Journal of Production Research, 8*(7), 1901–1912. doi:10.1080/00207540902791850

Yang, F., Kalkavan, H., Dinçer, H., Yüksel, S., & Eti, S. (2021). Gaussian-based soft computing approach to alternative banking system for sustainable financial sector. *Complexity*.

Yangınlar, G., & Sarı, K. (2014). *Yeşil lojistik uygulamaları ve işletme performansı üzerine bir literatür araştırma. III.* Ulusal Lojistik ve Tedarik Zinciri Kongresi.

Yang, J., Xie, H., Yu, G., & Liu, M. (2021). Antecedents and consequences of supply chain risk management capabilities: An investigation in the post-coronavirus crisis. *International Journal of Production Research*, *59*(5), 1573–1585.

Yang, S., Ning, L., Jiang, T., & He, Y. (2021). Dynamic impacts of COVID-19 pandemic on the regional express logistics: Evidence from China. *Transport Policy*, *111*, 111–124.

Yavuz, C., & Sivrif, D. (2009). Küreselleşmenin aktörlerinden çokuluslu şirketler ve yönetişim. Küresel Diyalog Konferansı Uluslararası Davraz Kongresi. Isparta, 1217-1236.

Yeap, G. P., & Lean, H. H. (2017). Asymmetric inflation hedge properties of housing in Malaysia: New evidence from nonlinear ARDL approach. *Habitat International*, *62*, 11–21. doi:10.1016/j.habitatint.2017.02.006

Yellen, J. L. (2017). Inflation, uncertainty, and monetary policy. *Business Economics (Cleveland, Ohio)*, *52*(4), 194–207. doi:10.105711369-017-0057-x

Yeloğlu, H. O. (2008). Örgütlerde Yapısal-Stratejik Konfigürasyonlar: Koşulbağımlılık Kuramı, Konfigürasyon Yaklaşımı Bağlamında Örgüt Yapıları Üzerine Önermeler. *Eskişehir Osmangazi Üniversitesi İibf Dergisi*, 155-170.

Yeşiltaş, M., Çeken, H., & Sormaz, Ü. (2012). Etik Liderlik Ve Örgütsel Adaletin Örgütsel Sapma Davranışları Üzerindeki Etkisi. *Muğla Üniversitesi Sosyal Bilimler Enstitüsü Dergisi*, 18-39.

Yılmaz, E. (2005). *'Etik Liderlik' Öğretmenin Dünyası. Odunpazarı Belediyesi Yayınları Eğitim Dizisi-3*. Mikro Yayıncılık.

Yılmaz, F. (2022). Energy management and Turkey: An assessment in the framework of The European Green Deal. *Academia Journal of Nature and Human Sciences*, *8*(1), 19–37.

Ying, L. S., & Harun, M. (2019). The impact of removing fuel subsidies on domestic outputs in Malaysia. *International Journal of Academic Research in Business & Social Sciences*, *9*(3), 641–653. doi:10.6007/IJARBSS/v9-i3/5732

Yin, Y., & Wonderlink, R. G. (2019). MERS, SARS and other coronaviruses as causes of pneumonia. *Respiratory*, *23*, 130–137. PMID:29052924

Yoon, J. H., Kim, J. S., & Park, H. G. (2020). A study on the priorities of blockchain adoption for port logistics in Korea using AHP: Focused on Busan and Incheon ports. *Muyeog Yeon'gu*, *16*(1), 1–24.

Yuan, G., Xie, F., Dinçer, H., & Yüksel, S. (2021). The theory of inventive problem solving (TRIZ)-based strategic mapping of green nuclear energy investments with spherical fuzzy group decision-making approach. *International Journal of Energy Research*, *45*(8), 12284–12300.

Yue, M., Jemei, S., Gouriveau, R., & Zerhouni, N. (2019). Review on health-conscious energy management strategies for fuel cell hybrid electric vehicles: Degradation models and strategies. *International Journal of Hydrogen Energy*, *44*(13), 6844–6861.

Yu, H., Li, N., & Zhao, N. (2021). How Far Are We from Achieving Self-Powered Flexible Health Monitoring Systems: An Energy Perspective. *Advanced Energy Materials*, *11*(9), 2002646.

Yüksel, S., Zengin, S., & Kartal, M. T. (2016). Banka Personelinin Teftiş Kuruluna Bakış Açısının Değerlendirilmesi. *Finans Politik ve Ekonomik Yorumlar*, (622) 101-115. Retrieved from https://dergipark.org.tr/en/pub/fpeyd/issue/48023/607332

Yüksel, S. (2017). Determinants of the credit risk in developing countries after economic crisis: A case of Turkish banking sector. In *Global financial crisis and its ramifications on capital markets* (pp. 401–415). Springer.

Yüksel, S., & Çağlayan, Ç. (2020). The factors affecting the investors' decisions: A study on nuclear energy investments. *Economics Literature*, *2*(2), 177–185. doi:10.22440/elit.2.2.5

Yüksel, S., & Dinçer, H. (2022). Identifying the strategic priorities of nuclear energy investments using hesitant 2-tuple interval-valued Pythagorean fuzzy DEMATEL. *Progress in Nuclear Energy*, *145*, 104103.

Yüksel, S., Dinçer, H., Çağlayan, Ç., & Uluer, G. S. (2021). Determining the Optimal Financial Strategies for Nuclear Energy Companies. In *Financial Strategies in Competitive Markets* (pp. 1–16). Springer. doi:10.1007/978-3-030-68612-3_1

Yüksel, S., Dinçer, H., Çağlayan, Ç., & Uluer, G. S. (2021). Strategy development to improve the business performance of nuclear energy companies. In *Management Strategies to Survive in a Competitive Environment* (pp. 33–46). Springer. doi:10.1007/978-3-030-72288-3_3

Yüksel, S., Dinçer, H., Çağlayan, Ç., Uluer, G. S., & Lisin, A. (2022b). Bitcoin Mining with Nuclear Energy. In *Multidimensional Strategic Outlook on Global Competitive Energy Economics and Finance*. Emerald Publishing Limited.

Yüksel, S., Dinçer, H., & Karakuş, H. (2020). Determination of Income and Expense Items That Have a High Impact on The Profitability of Turkish Banks. *Journal of Financial Economics and Banking*, *1*(1), 1–9.

Yüksel, S., Dinçer, H., Mikhaylov, A., Adalı, Z., & Eti, S. (2022a). Key Issues for the Improvements of Shallow Geothermal Investments. In *Sustainability in Energy Business and Finance* (pp. 183–194). Springer.

Yüksel, S., & Kavak, P. T. (2019). Do financial investment decisions affect economic development?: An analysis on mortgage loans in Turkey. In *Handbook of research on global issues in financial communication and investment decision making* (pp. 168–191). IGI Global. doi:10.4018/978-1-5225-9265-5.ch009

Yüksel, S., & Ubay, G. G. (2021). Determination of optimal financial government incentives in wind energy investments. In *Strategic outlook in business and finance innovation: Multidimensional policies for emerging economies*. Emerald Publishing Limited. doi:10.1108/978-1-80043-444-820211003

Yuksel, S., & Zengin, S. (2016). Causality relationship between import, export and growth rate in developing countries. *International Journal of Commerce and Finance*, *2*(1), 147–156.

Yuniarti, D., & Rosadi, D. (2021). Inflation of Indonesia during the COVID-19 pandemic. *Journal of Physics: Conference Series*, *1821*(1), 012039.

Yurtkoru, E. S. (2001). *The role of leadership in the organizational change process*. Yayımlanmamış Doktora Tezi. Marmara Üniversitesi Sosyal Bilimler Enstitüsü. İstanbul Yüksek Lisans Tezi, Balıkesir Üniversitesi Sosyal Bilimler Enstitüsü.

Yu, Z., Liu, W., Chen, L., Eti, S., Dinçer, H., & Yüksel, S. (2019). The effects of electricity production on industrial development and sustainable economic growth: A VAR analysis for BRICS countries. *Sustainability*, *11*(21), 5895.

Zaleznik, A. (1992). Managers and Leaders: Are Thet Different? *Harvard Business Review*, (March-April), 126–135.

Zellner, A. (1971). *An Introduction to Bayesian Inference in Econometrics*. Wiley.

Zel, U. (2001). *Kişilik ve Liderlik*. Seçkin Yayıncılık.

Zhang, D., Li, J., & Han, P. (2019). A multidimensional measure of energy poverty in China and its impacts on health: An empirical study based on the China family panel studies. *Energy Policy*, *131*, 72–81.

Zhang, Q., Appau, S., & Kodom, P. L. (2021). Energy poverty, children's wellbeing and the mediating role of academic performance: Evidence from China. *Energy Economics*, *97*, 105206. doi:10.1016/j.eneco.2021.105206

Zhang, S., Xie, Y., Sander, R., Yue, H., & Shu, Y. (2021). Potentials of energy efficiency improvement and energy–emission–health nexus in Jing-Jin-Ji's cement industry. *Journal of Cleaner Production*, *278*, 123335.

Zhang, Y., Zhang, Y., Gong, C., Dinçer, H., & Yüksel, S. (2022). An integrated hesitant 2-tuple Pythagorean fuzzy analysis of QFD-based innovation cost and duration for renewable energy projects. *Energy*, 123561.

Zhao, P., Liu, J., & He, L. (2009, December). Study on the development of modern green logistics in China. In *2009 International Conference on Innovation Management* (pp. 43-46). IEEE.

Zhao, Y., Xu, Y., Yüksel, S., Dinçer, H., & Ubay, G. G. (2021). Hybrid IT2 fuzzy modelling with alpha cuts for hydrogen energy investments. *International Journal of Hydrogen Energy*, *46*(13), 8835–8851.

Zheng, Z., Xie, S., Dai, H., Chen, X., & Wang, H. (2017, June). An overview of blockchain technology: Architecture, consensus, and future trends. In 2017 IEEE international congress on big data (BigData congress). IEEE.

Zhou, P., Luo, J., Cheng, F., Yüksel, S., & Dinçer, H. (2021). Analysis of risk priorities for renewable energy investment projects using a hybrid IT2 hesitant fuzzy decision-making approach with alpha cuts. *Energy*, *224*, 120184.

Zhu, G., Chou, M. C., & Tsai, C. W. (2020). Lessons Learned from the COVID-19 Pandemic Exposing the Shortcomings of Current Supply Chain Operations: A Long-Term Prescriptive Offering. *Sustainability*, *2020*(12), 5858. doi:10.3390u12145858

Zou, P., Huo, D., & Li, M. (2020). The impact of the COVID-19 pandemic on firms: a survey in Guangdong Province, China. *Global Health Research and Policy*, *5*(1), 1-10.

Zumla, A., Chan, J. F., Azhar, E. I., Hui, D. S., & Yuen, K. Y. (2016). Coronaviruses–Drug Discovery and Therapeutic Options. *NationalReviews Drug Discovery*, *15*(5), 327–347. doi:10.1038/nrd.2015.37 PMID:26868298

About the Contributors

Ulas Akkucuk is Professor of Quantitative Methods at Usak University Department of Management, Istanbul, Turkey. Dr. Akkucuk has a BS in Industrial Engineering from Bilkent University (1997), an MBA from Bogazici University (2000), and a PhD in Management Science and Information Systems from Rutgers University (2004). He has edited 9 books with IGI Global. He is the editor in chief of International Journal of Environmental Sustainability and Green Technologies and OPTIMUM journals. He has extensive editing and peer review experience.

* * *

Slavica Andjelic was born in Kruševac. She graduated in 2000, received her master's degree in 2007, and PhD in 2009 at Megatrend University - Faculty of Management on topics in the field of economics (master's thesis - "Working capital in small and medium companies ", doctoral thesis" Competitiveness of the rubber industry of Serbia in the world "). Since graduating from high school, she has been engaged in scientific and professional work in practice. Since June 2008, she has been employed at Megatrend University, Faculty of Business studies. From the In 2018, she was employed as the director of the Business School of Vocational Studies "Prof. dr Radomir Bojković" in Kruševac. Since 2021, she has been working as an assistant professor at the School of Modern Business, an academic institution in Belgrade. She is the author and co-author of many scientific articles, published in scientific journals.

Sema Batirlik, after completing her primary and secondary education in the same place, completed her high school education in Afyonkarahisar. In 2014, she enrolled in Yalova University, Department of International Trade and Finance. After completing her undergraduate education in 2019, the same year she started her master's degree in International Trade and Finance at the University of Yalova, International Trade and Finance and graduated in 2021.

Çağatay Çağlayan is currently pursuing undergraduate degree in economics and finance with Istanbul Medipol University, where he is also student with the Health Management Department. His research interests include sustainable energy economics, renewable energy, and nuclear energy. He has some articles and international book chapters related to these topics and one of them is indexed in SSCI.

Yeliz Demirkıran is an Assistant Professor in the Department of Management and Organization, Logistics Program at Yasar University, Izmir, Turkey. She completed her undergraduate degree at the Department of Industrial Engineering in Yaşar University. She then completed her master and doctoral studies in Business Administration at Yaşar University. She teaches courses about Business Administration, Logistics Terminology and Warehousing. Her research interests are Warehousing and Distribution Center Design, Facility location selection.

Hasan Dinçer is a Professor of finance at Istanbul Medipol University, Faculty of Economics and Administrative Sciences, Istanbul-Turkey. Dr. Dinçer has BAs in Financial Markets and Investment Management at Marmara University. He received PhD in Finance and Banking with his thesis entitled "The Effect of Changes on the Competitive Strategies of New Service Development in the Banking Sector". He has work experience in finance sector as portfolio specialist and his major academic studies focusing on financial instruments, performance evaluation, and economics. He is the executive editor of the International Journal of Finance and Banking Studies (IJFBS) and the founder member of the Society for the Study of Business and Finance (SSBF).

Gordana Djukic graduated from the University of Belgrade, Faculty of Economics, Serbia, 2006. She defended her master thesis in 2010 at the same faculty. She defended her doctoral dissertation in 2016 and received her PhD in economics from John Naisbitt University, Faculty of Management in Zajecar. She has acquired the scientific research title of Research Associate in 2017 at the Institute of Economic Sciences in Belgrade.

Meltem Duğru works as a lecturer at Trakya University Uzunköprü School of Applied Sciences, Banking and Insurance Department. She completed her undergraduate education at Uludağ University, Faculty of Economics and Administrative Sciences, Department of Economics. She completed her master's degree in Trakya University, Department of Banking, and her doctorate process continues in the Department of Economics. 'Banking', 'money', 'economy', 'finance' and 'credit' are among the subjects of study. In this context, she has articles published in national and international scientific journals, book chapters and papers presented at conferences. The author has approximately twelve years of banking experience prior to her academic career. After working as a portfolio manager for two years at Garanti Pension A.Ş., she worked as individual portfolio and regional manager at Türkiye Vakıflar Bankası T.A.O. for more than ten years. She is married and has a child.

Oya Ekici holds a BS in Economics from the Faculty of Economics at Istanbul University and an MS and Ph.D. in Econometrics. For postdoctoral research, she's been in the Statistical Science Department of Duke University. She's been working as Assistant Professor in the Quantitative Methods of Business Administration Department in the Faculty of Political Science of Istanbul University since 2013. Ekici teaches undergraduate and graduate courses on Statistics, Advance Statistics, Mathematics, Modeling in Supply Chain, and Decision Theory. She is the author of "MCMC ve Temel Uygulamalari". Ekici's main research interests include Decision making, Bayesian statistics-Time series, MCMC methods, and Macroeconomic applications.

Yasin Galip Gencer is currently working in Yalova University Department of International Trade and Finance as an Associated Professor. He graduated from Bogazici University, Management Department and also has an MBA degree from Bogazici University. He has many studies in the areas of International Trade and Finance, Quantitative Methods and Operations Management as well. Furthermore, he also has a Leadership Communication certificate from Harvard Business School and has engaged in many business ventures in a family run company specializing in automotive and household appliance sales. Besides extensive business experience, he has also studied in Universiteit de Maastricht within the scope of an Erasmus exchange program. He has participated in a number of international conferences and published in proceedings volumes. His research interests are in forecasting automotive demand, determination of productivity and quality in the automotive sales and service sector.

Yaşar Gökalp is a Research Assistant at Istanbul Medipol University. Mr. Gökalp has a BA in Health Management from Sivas Cumhuriyet University. Then, in 2018, he received his master's degree from Istanbul University with the thesis "Reimbursement systems in health institutions: comparison of surgical costs with SUT prices". He continues his doctoral program at Istanbul Medipol University during the thesis period. His research interests are energy, health economics, health finance and multi-criteria decision making techniques.

Sami Goren is an Associate Professor, from Umm-Al Qura University Department of Environmental Engineering, Makkah-KSA. Dr. Goren was graduated from Technical University of Istanbul as a Civil Engineer. He has an MS from Kanazawa University – Japan (1993) and a PhD from Graduate School of Natural Science and Technology in Kanazawa University – Japan (1998). He has worked as faculty in different universities. He has worked as main investigator of a project for waste-water treatment technologies under the fund of TUBITAK (Scientific Board of Turkey) with a number of 109G095, Ankara / Turkey. He has conducted MARMARAY Project. He has taught courses like solid waste management, project management, soil mechanics, etc. at both graduate and undergraduate level. He is a member of Japanese Society of Civil Engineers, Saudi Arabian Water Environment Association and Gulf Engineering Forum. He is doing editorial job in the journals such as CLEAN (Soil, Air, Water), J. of the Air & Waste Management Ass, etc.

Kenan Guler born in 1967, has been engaged in the customs brokerage and consultancy profession since 1987. Dr Guler was granted his Assistant Customs Consultant license in 1988 and A Level Customs Consultant license in 1993. Dr. Guler graduated with a bachelor's degree from Eskisehir University and a master's and PhD from the Department of International Trade at Istanbul Commerce University. He worked in various companies, that provide customs and logistics services in many European countries between 1996 and 1999. Dr Guler established his own company in 1999 and is currently the Chairman of DCS Digital Customs Services Inc., PLH Logistics Services Inc. and Atez Software Technologies Inc. Dr Guler is also the founding partner of Chain & Chain Technologies Ltd. in London.

Elad Harison is the former Head of the Industrial Engineering and Management Department at the Shenkar College of Engineering and Design (Israel) and an affiliated researcher at the United Nations University-MERIT (The Netherlands). He holds a PhD in Economics from the Maastricht University (The Netherlands). His research interests are in the areas of innovation, services, supply chain management and ICT. He has written a book on the economics and policy of software intellectual property rights and has published in international journals including: Research Policy, the International Journal of Information Management, Economics of Innovation and New Technology and the Journal of Air Transport Management. He has been a policy expert on Israeli innovation and on the patentability of computer implemented inventions in EC projects and a member of the EC's Expert Group on Intellectual Property Rights in Internet Collaborations.

Biljana Stojan Ilic, PhD of Management and business, was born on 10/01/1970, in Zajecar, Serbia. She graduated on Business Higher School of Belgrade University, in 1996. She continued further education on the Faculty of Management Zajecar, Megatrend University of Belgrade, in 2007. She Graduated on the Faculty of Management in Zajecar, in 2009. She received the degree of Master of Academic Studies in Management on the same faculty, defended master thesis, and acquired the title of master manager. She defended her doctoral thesis titled "Strategic directions of regional economic and environmental development of the tourist potential of Gamzigrad Spa", 2016. At first PhD Bijana Stojan Ilic was elected assistant professor at her home Faculty of Management Zajecar, during which time (2016-2021) she taught Natural Resources Management at the Basic Academic Studies of Management, at the Basic Academic Studies of Economics, as well as at Doctoral studies in Natural Resources Management. At the Basic Academic Studies of Management and Business she teaches Intercultural Management and Management, and she is entrusted with teaching the subjects Entrepreneurship, Business Organization, Business Decision Making in Master's Studies and Natural Resources Management in Doctoral Studies. At the same time, in the period of 2019, she was engaged at the Faculty of Law, Megatrend University, Belgrade, additionally as an assistant professor.

Cenk C. Karahan, PhD, is an Assistant Professor of Finance at Boğaziçi University Department of Management in Istanbul, Turkey. Dr. Karahan has received his B.S. degree in Industrial and Systems Engineering with minor degrees in Cinema-Television and Business Administration at University of Southern California (2004). He subsequently earned his Master's degree in Engineering Management (2006) and doctoral degree in Industrial and Systems Engineering department (2011) of the same university with a research focused on Financial Engineering. Dr. Karahan's research and teaching interests include quantitative finance, risk management, derivatives, asset pricing and entertainment economics.

Dilan Kararoğlu is studying at Istanbul Medipol University, Department of Health Management. She is working on the Department of Economics and Finance, where she has a double major. The subjects she worked on renewable energy, sustainable energy, nuclear energy.

Han N. Özsöylev, PhD, is an Assistant Professor of Finance at Özyeğin University Faculty of Business in Istanbul, Turkey and Lecturer in Finance at Queen Mary University of London. Dr. Özsöylev has received his B.S. degree in Mathematics at Bilkent University (1999). He subsequently earned his doctoral degree in Economics at University of Minnesota (2004). He had taught at University of Oxford and Koç University in the past. Dr. Özsöylev's research and teaching interests include financial economics, asset pricing, market microstructure and applied economic theory.

Emre Ozturk graduated from department of Mechanical Engineering of Istanbul Technical University, 2016. Completed Post-graduate program of MSc. Management at Warwick Business School, 2017. Working as Business and Product Development Specialist for 4 years at ATEZ Software Technologies.

Osman Pala currently works at the Department of International Trade and Business, Karamanoğlu Mehmetbey University in Turkey. Osman conducts research in the field of Multi Criteria Decision Making, Heuristic Algorithms, Optimization and Data Mining.

Esengul Salihoglu is Assistant Professor of banking in Sivas Cumhuriyet University. Since 2013, she has been a lecturer in the Department of Finance, Banking, and Insurance at Sivas Cumhuriyet University. She was an assistant manager in the international banking division at the Anadolubank Head Office in Istanbul, Turkey, prior to this appointment. She previously spent 11 years working in numerous banks in the area. Uludag University awarded Dr. Salihoglu a bachelor's degree in 1996. In 2002, she earned a master's degree from Marmara University's Department of Banking. In 2018, she received a PhD. Her areas of interest in research are banking, sustainability, digitalization, and finance.

José G. Vargas-Hernández, M.B.A., Ph.D., Member of the National System of Researchers of Mexico and a research professor at Tecnológico Mario Molina Unidad Zapopan formerly at University Center for Economic and Managerial Sciences, University of Guadalajara. Professor Vargas-Hernández has a Ph. D. in Public Administration and a Ph.D. in Organizational Economics. He has undertaken studies in Organisational Behaviour and has a Master of Business Administration, published four books and more than 200 papers in international journals and reviews (some translated to English, French, German, Portuguese, Farsi, Chinese, etc.) and more than 300 essays in national journals and reviews. He has obtained several international Awards and recognition.

Duygu Yavuz is studying at Istanbul Medipol University, Department of Health Management. She is working on the Department of Economics and Finance, where she has a double major. The subjects she worked on; renewable energy, sustainable energy, nuclear energy.

Serhat Yüksel is Associate Professor of finance in İstanbul Medipol University. Before this position, he worked as a senior internal auditor for seven years in Finansbank, Istanbul-Turkey and 1 year in Konya Food and Agriculture University as an assistant professor. Dr. Yüksel has a BS in Business Administration (in English) from Yeditepe University (2006) with full scholarship. He got his master degree from the economics in Boğaziçi University (2008). He also has a PhD in Banking from Marmara University (2015). His research interests lie in banking, finance, and financial crisis. He has more than 70 publications (books, book chapters, scientific articles, etc.).

Index

6R 151, 153

A

Agricultural supply chain 10, 13-15
agro-economy 10, 14
AHP 162-163, 167-168, 170-173, 176, 178, 300-309
Alternative Fuels 257, 262, 268
analysis 18, 21-22, 31, 33, 38-39, 43, 56, 60, 62-63, 75-77, 81, 87, 89, 91-97, 111, 120, 132, 134-136, 140, 144, 148, 156, 158, 162-164, 166, 170, 172, 174, 176-177, 194, 196-197, 215, 220-221, 226-227, 231-232, 234-236, 238, 255, 260, 262, 265, 272-273, 276, 280, 285, 288, 291, 295, 297, 302, 307-308
automotive 69, 73, 163, 172, 205-206, 240, 247, 251, 268-272, 274, 277-280
Automotive Taxes 272, 280

B

balanced scorecard 81-88, 90, 92-103
banking 38-39, 42, 47, 54, 60, 163, 172, 174, 176-177, 234-235, 238, 263, 276, 281-292, 308
Bayesian Analysis 136, 148
Bayesian var analysis 132
Behavioral Finance 24
Beta (Risk) Anomaly 39
beta anomaly 24-25, 29, 31, 33, 36-37
Brent 257-258, 261-262, 267
Brent Petrol 257, 261, 267
business 9, 11, 14-18, 20, 45, 48, 56-58, 61-63, 72, 77-79, 81-83, 85-86, 88, 90, 98-104, 108-109, 113-114, 118-122, 125-127, 132-133, 135, 143, 146-147, 153, 158, 164-165, 177, 179-180, 187, 192-194, 197, 199, 203, 205, 210, 216, 218, 237-238, 243, 245, 247, 255, 261, 265, 274, 277-279, 281-285, 288, 290-291, 294-295, 300, 308-309

C

Capital Asset Pricing Model (CAPM) 27, 39
central banks 41, 51-52, 58
China and Wuhan 239
Compatibility 81, 102, 303
Core Inflation 267
COVID-19 1-2, 4-25, 41-51, 54-58, 61, 70, 76-79, 106, 108, 118, 127, 146, 148, 165, 188, 199-210, 213-219, 239, 241-243, 245-246, 248, 250, 252-256, 268, 270, 277-278, 280, 296
CPI 6, 20, 27, 30, 32, 40, 133, 135, 148, 242, 252, 267
crises 18, 21, 69, 77, 104-105, 108, 118, 129, 165, 173, 176, 207, 242, 253, 257, 259-265, 268-269, 271-272, 282, 289-290
Cylinder Volume 280

D

Deglobalization 62-64, 66-67, 69-78, 80
Delta variant 42
Deltacron 42
DEMATEL 162-163, 168, 171-173, 177-178
disruption 10-12, 17-18, 43, 68, 70-71, 79, 133, 147-148, 172, 199-203, 205-206, 213-214, 216, 247, 256, 268, 290
disruptions 1-2, 4-10, 14-16, 19, 29, 50, 132-135, 146-149, 199-203, 205-210, 212, 214-218, 240, 243-244, 246, 251, 253-254, 268-271, 275-278

E

economic crisis 41, 128, 132, 148, 166, 176-177, 224, 239, 242, 278
Economic Issues 60, 179, 277
Economic Stimulus 1
electric cars 268, 274-275
Emerging Markets 24, 78, 197
emissions 154, 167, 180-191, 193, 210, 217, 222-223,

225, 256, 259, 264, 267-268, 280
Emissions Rating 280
energy 24, 41, 46, 58-59, 77, 134, 151-152, 159-160, 162-163, 165-167, 169-177, 180-185, 188, 191-192, 195-196, 198, 212, 216, 220-231, 233-238, 240, 244-245, 251, 256-260, 262-268, 271, 279, 295
energy investment 162, 174-177, 220, 235, 237-238
environmental impact 151, 184
environmental issues 158, 179-180, 191, 262
equilibrium 1-2, 5, 8, 10, 17, 37-39
equity risk premium 28-29, 37, 39
European Union 135, 161, 166, 176, 179-180, 182, 184-187, 195-196, 206, 252, 271
export 14, 47, 63, 67, 133, 165, 207, 238-239, 247-249, 252-253, 268, 297-299, 307

F

Finance Industry 281
financial crisis 7, 9, 29, 36, 41-42, 61, 65, 69, 78, 174, 177, 201, 225, 245, 265, 271, 279, 286-287
financial performance 90, 92-97, 99, 102-103, 210-211, 214
food supply chain 10, 13, 16, 22, 79, 214, 255

G

GDP growth 12, 58, 202
global climate change 151, 182
global economy 1-2, 4, 6, 10, 12, 16, 20-21, 41-42, 59, 62, 65, 68-71, 77-78, 146, 151, 158, 174, 199-200, 202-203, 210, 212, 224, 241, 247-248
global recession 7, 41-42, 51, 59-61, 265
Global Supply Chain 12, 47, 62, 69, 71, 78-80, 148, 262, 276-277
global supply chains 2, 8, 21, 33, 42, 62, 68-74, 216, 218
globalization 62-76, 78-80, 104, 106, 112, 118, 123-124, 127, 129, 152, 239, 241-242, 254, 262, 275-276, 279, 282
green supply chain management 174, 179, 191, 197, 235

H

Headline Inflation 259, 267
healthcare industry 162-164, 169, 171, 173
human resources 81-87, 90, 92-96, 98-103
human resources management 82, 84-87, 93-96, 99, 101, 103

I

import 14, 80, 125-126, 128, 133, 207, 212, 238-240, 247-248, 252-253
industry 11-12, 14-15, 17-18, 40, 42-43, 45, 48-50, 55, 68-69, 73, 80, 101, 128, 133, 155, 158, 160, 162-164, 166, 169, 171, 173-174, 177, 181-194, 199-201, 203-207, 213, 216, 224, 235, 240, 248, 267-268, 271, 274, 277-282, 284-287, 290, 296, 298, 302, 308
inflation 1, 6-7, 10, 12-16, 18, 20-21, 24-29, 31-33, 35-41, 58-59, 89, 92, 103, 128, 132-135, 142-144, 146-148, 151, 162-163, 165, 169-173, 211-212, 214, 219-222, 224-231, 234-237, 239, 241-244, 252-253, 255-261, 264, 267, 271-273, 275, 277, 280
Inflation Basket 267
integrated solid waste management 151-152, 158-159, 161
intermodal transportation 192-193
internal audit 281-283, 285-292
internal control 281-283, 285-292
international trade 41, 47, 62, 66, 69, 72, 77, 123, 134-135, 201, 246, 248, 254, 256, 293-296, 302, 305, 307-309

L

leadership 65, 67, 78, 83, 101, 104-122, 127, 130, 180, 248
Leadership Scale 119, 130
Leadership Theory 104, 106, 108

M

management 7-8, 10, 14-23, 37, 48, 71, 77, 79, 81-87, 89-90, 93-104, 107, 109, 111-112, 116-118, 120-121, 125, 127, 130-131, 134, 144, 148, 151-161, 164, 166-167, 173-177, 179, 185-192, 194-198, 205, 215-216, 218, 223, 234-236, 238, 244-245, 247, 255-256, 262-264, 266, 271, 274, 276-279, 283-290, 292-293, 300, 307-309
management functions 81, 84-85, 87, 89-90, 93-97, 99-101
Management Innovation 103
MTV 272-273, 280
Multi National Companies 123

N

NAHP Technique 293

nominal return 30, 39

O

oil 13, 42, 46-47, 61, 134, 152, 188, 192, 201, 203, 216, 221, 224, 226, 233-237, 243, 245, 257-258, 260-267, 271, 273, 277
omicron 42, 215
organizational structure 111, 123, 125-126, 130, 281, 287, 289
ÖTV 272, 280

P

pandemic 1, 4-5, 8-22, 24-26, 29, 31, 33, 35, 37, 41-43, 45-48, 50-52, 57-58, 60, 62, 65-66, 68, 70-71, 74, 76-77, 79, 104-105, 118, 132-134, 137, 144, 148, 165, 188, 196, 199-219, 239-240, 242, 246-247, 253-255, 257-258, 268, 270-271, 273, 277-278, 290
petrol 42, 46, 257-267, 274
pharmaceutical supply chain 49
pollution 152-153, 155-156, 158, 160, 167, 173-174, 179-185, 187, 189-191, 193, 195, 217, 221-223, 235-236
post pandemic 17, 104, 118
PPI 133-136, 138, 141-144, 146, 148, 242, 271, 280
price stability 132-133, 144, 225, 241-242, 255
Producer Price Index (PPI) 133, 148
Production Chain 69, 80
production chains 62, 68-70, 72-73
protectionism 62-67, 71, 76, 80
protectionist policies 62-63, 68-69, 76, 130
Public Joint-Stock Company 103
Purchasing Managers' Index (PMI) 56, 133, 149

Q

quantitative easing 1-2, 5, 7-8

R

rational inattention 24-27, 37, 39
Real return 30, 39
recycle 151-153, 160, 192
relocation of production 62-63, 67, 70, 73-74, 80
renewable energy investment 162, 174, 177, 235, 237-238
renewable energy projects 177, 220, 228, 238

S

Security Market Line (SML) 25, 27-28, 34-36, 39
Sharpe Ratio 29, 39
social distancing 4-5, 7, 11-12, 41-42, 45, 48, 54-59, 205, 210
Social Issues 179
solar 172, 175, 223-224, 230, 236, 257, 260, 267
Solar Power 267
solid waste 151-161
Stepwise Multiple Regression 89, 94-97, 103
stock market 24-27, 29-31, 33, 35-39, 41, 47, 56-57
supply chain 1-2, 4-5, 7-20, 22-23, 47, 49, 62, 69-71, 75, 77-80, 120, 125, 130, 132-136, 144, 146, 148-149, 158, 174, 176, 179, 187, 191-192, 194, 196-197, 199-201, 204-210, 212-218, 235, 240, 244-246, 250-251, 254-256, 261-262, 268-271, 274-278, 290, 296, 309
Supply Chain Bottlenecks 132, 149
supply chain disruptions 1-2, 4-5, 7, 16, 132-135, 146, 148-149, 199-201, 205, 208-210, 212, 215-218, 270-271, 276-278
supply chains 1-2, 4-5, 7-9, 13-17, 20-21, 33, 42, 62, 68-74, 78, 132-133, 147-149, 194-195, 200, 216-218, 239-241, 243-247, 250-255, 270, 296, 301, 308-309
Sustainability 13, 20-21, 64, 71, 76-77, 79, 102-103, 118-120, 130-131, 151-152, 155, 158, 161, 165, 177, 179-181, 184-186, 188-191, 193-197, 216, 223, 236, 261-266, 274, 276-277, 285, 290
Sustainable Transportation 257, 267, 280

T

taxes 164, 191, 262, 264, 268-269, 272-276, 278, 280
Trade Balance 207, 239, 248-249, 256
Turkey 24-25, 27, 29-33, 35-37, 40, 104, 110, 120, 123, 127-137, 141-144, 146, 162, 167, 174-175, 179, 184, 192, 194-199, 220-221, 226-227, 231, 234, 236, 238-243, 247-254, 256-257, 261-262, 264, 266, 268-270, 272-275, 280-283, 285-286, 289-293, 297-299, 309-310
Turkey Economy 239

U

unemployment 2, 41, 48, 50, 58-59, 64, 74, 148, 202-203, 211-212, 243, 258-259, 279

V

value chains 8, 62-63, 68-73, 76-77, 79-80, 279
Variance Inflation Factor (VIF) 103
VAT 272, 280
Vector Autoregression (VAR) Model 149
virtual teams 104

W

WPI 136, 267, 280
WTI 257

Printed in the United States
by Baker & Taylor Publisher Services